FAMILY LAW AND PRACTICE

FAMILY LAW AND PRACTICE

Nancy Duffield BA (Hons), Solicitor

Jacqueline Kempton BA (Hons), Solicitor

Christa Sabine BA (Hons), Solicitor

Published by

College of Law Publishing,
Braboeuf Manor, Portsmouth Road, St Catherines, Guildford GU3 1HA

British Library Cataloguing-in-Publication Data

A catalogue record for this book is available from the British Library.

ISBN 978 1 905391 46 2

Typeset by Style Photosetting Ltd, Mayfield, East Sussex

Printed in Great Britain by Ashford Colour Press Ltd, Gosport, Hampshire

Preface

Family law is a dynamic subject, constantly changing, and a challenge to everyone involved with it. We have taken on the challenge in preparing this book. Our main aim has been to prepare a book which provides the legal background for students on the Legal Practice Course. It will be the springboard for students to use to practise the skills learned during the Legal Practice Course. We hope it will also be of use to trainees and newly qualified solicitors who are using these skills for the first time in the real world.

Throughout the book, for uniformity, we have generally referred to the client and the solicitor as 'he'. In reality, it is usually the woman who initiates proceedings on the breakdown of the relationship, and in some places, for example domestic abuse, we have changed the sex of the client to reflect the more usual situation.

In the book the terms 'husband and wife' or 'spouses' should be taken to include civil partners unless the text states otherwise. Similarly 'matrimonial home' includes a civil partnership home.

We would like to acknowledge with thanks the contribution made to this book in the past by Jo Theobald. Our thanks also go to our colleagues at The College of Law who have helped us with this book, and to our long-suffering families and friends who have endured its rebirth.

Unless otherwise mentioned, the law is stated as at 1 September 2007.

NANCY DUFFIELD
JACQUELINE KEMPTON
CHRISTA SABINE
The College of Law

Contents

Table of Cases

A

B

C

M

N

O

P

R

S

T

W

X

Z

Table of Statutes

Table of Statutory Instruments and Codes of Practice

Table of Abbreviations

AJA 1999	Access to Justice Act 1999
CA 1989	Children Act 1989
CAA 1984	Child Abduction Act 1984
CACA 1985	Child Abduction and Custody Act 1985
CAFCASS	Children and Family Court Advisory and Support Service
CGT	capital gains tax
C-MEC	Child Maintenance and Enforcement Commission
CPA 2004	Civil Partnership Act 2004
CPR 1998	Civil Procedure Rules 1998
CSA 1991	Child Support Act 1991
CS(MCSC) Regs 2000	Child Support (Maintenance Calculations and Special Cases) Regulations 2000
CSPSSA 2000	Child Support, Pensions and Social Security Act 2000
DPMCA 1978	Domestic Proceedings and Magistrates' Courts Act 1978
DWP	Department for Work and Pensions
FDR	Financial Dispute Resolution
FLA 1996	Family Law Act 1996
FLBA	Family Law Bar Association
FPR 1991	Family Proceedings Rules 1991
HRA 1998	Human Rights Act 1998
I(PFD)A 1975	Inheritance (Provision for Family and Dependants) Act 1975
MCA 1973	Matrimonial Causes Act 1973
MWPA 1882	Married Women's Property Act 1882
PHA 1997	Protection from Harassment Act 1997
PPO	periodical payments order
SSCSAT	Social Security and Child Support Appeals Tribunal
TLATA	Trusts of Land and Appointment of Trustees Act 1996
WRPA 1999	Welfare Reform and Pensions Act 1999

Chapter 1

Introduction: The Family Practice

1.1 The family client

There is a wide range of reasons why a client would wish to discuss family problems with a solicitor. The most common reason is that a relationship has permanently broken down. Some clients, however, may seek advice because they are encountering temporary difficulties and have no wish to terminate the relationship formally. Yet others may have some domestic problem which they need to resolve but are undecided and unclear as to the future of the relationship.

Whether or not a client has made a firm decision about the relationship, he will usually be reasonably clear about his more immediate problems which prompted him to seek legal advice. The three most common problem areas concern money and property (see **Chapters 4** to **11**), children (see **Chapters 13** and **14**) and protection from domestic abuse (see **Chapter 15**). How these problems are to be dealt with depends in the first place on whether the couple are married (or, in the case of a same-sex couple, whether they have registered a civil partnership) or living together. The problems and concerns of cohabiting couples are virtually indistinguishable from those of married couples or civil partners; the legal remedies, however, are by no means the same and are more limited for cohabitees. A large part of this book is devoted to married couples as these will form the vast majority of the clients for most family solicitors. However, the cohabiting family is considered in detail in **Chapter 16**, and comparisons between the positions of cohabitees, civil partners and spouses are made throughout this book.

In the case of married couples, there is a broad range of solutions to the key problems. The skill of the family lawyer is to match the appropriate solution to the needs of the individual client. Which measures are to be taken will depend on whether the client has made the decision to end the marriage, or whether a more temporary solution is favoured. The marriage may be terminated formally by divorce (or nullity), or the couple may separate formally by judicial separation (these options are considered in **Chapter 3**). Alternatively, the client may not wish to make any final decision about the relationship itself but merely wish to seek advice on a particular problem: for example, a wife may be anxious about her position in the matrimonial home, or a father may be being denied contact with his children.

It is worthwhile pausing to consider some of the likely issues and concerns facing a family client. Whilst there is no such thing as a 'typical' family client (and it would be a mistake to assume that there was), there are certain concerns which are common to many families.

Example

Beverley is a mother with two young children. She has been married to Colin for the last 10 years, but is seeking a divorce because Colin has recently begun to be violent towards her and on one occasion to her son. Beverley does not work and has no savings. She has fled the family home and her main worry is to be able to return to the home in safety.

One of the first issues for the solicitor to consider is how the client will pay for the legal advice. This will also be high on the client's list of concerns. The question of costs, including public funding, is considered in context throughout this book and in **Chapter 2**. A private client should be advised about the costs policy of the firm and will usually be asked to make a payment on account. As with most contentious work, it is difficult to give an accurate prediction of costs in the initial interview as so much depends on the attitude of the other party, and indeed of the client himself. In this example, Beverley is likely to be eligible for public funding.

Beverley's primary need is to seek protection from the violence and to be able to return home. It will be necessary, therefore, to take instructions to prepare for proceedings for a non-molestation and occupation order under the Family Law Act 1996 (FLA 1996) (see **Chapter 15**). As Beverley wishes to obtain a divorce, the solicitor will also need to obtain the information and prepare the documentation required to institute divorce proceedings (see **Chapter 3**). Since the order under FLA 1996 will provide only a temporary solution to Beverley and the children's housing needs, the solicitor must also discuss the future arrangements in relation to the former matrimonial home (see **Chapter 9**). Although it will be some time before this can be dealt with, the solicitor needs to think ahead and obtain public funding in good time to commence ancillary proceedings. The solicitor should also be aware of the need to protect his client's interest in the matrimonial home. He will, therefore, need to establish how the property is held between the parties and make any necessary registrations against the title. In addition, Beverley should be advised to make (or alter) a will. Further, there may be a problem regarding the mortgage, as Colin may stop paying the mortgage if he is ordered to leave the home (although, if an occupation order is made, provision can be included instructing Colin to continue to pay the mortgage). It will probably be necessary, therefore, to advise Beverley regarding maintenance, and possibly to write to the lender to explain any short-term difficulties which there may be in relation to the mortgage. The procedure for obtaining financial orders is considered in **Chapter 10**, and their enforcement and variation is considered in **Chapter 11**.

As it will be some time before any application for maintenance for Beverley can be considered in detail, she should be advised of her entitlements to welfare benefits (see **Chapter 6**) and for maintenance for the children under the Child Support Act 1991 (see **Chapter 7**).

The other important consideration is, of course, the children (see **Chapters 13** and **14**). At an early stage, it is likely to be necessary to raise the question of the children's contact with their father. As with the other issues, this may be agreed upon between the parties (after negotiation), but in Beverley's case, in view of her husband's violence towards her son, she may well object to any contact. If Colin wished to pursue this, it would involve further proceedings (and an extension of any Legal Representation certificate).

It will not always be appropriate to discuss all of these issues at the initial interview but the solicitor will need to be aware of the wider picture from the outset. He will need to raise the various issues at an appropriate stage and encourage his client to confront the future and make informed decisions. The topics covered in this book deal with all of the problems faced by Beverley in the example above. Of necessity, the book takes each issue in turn, but it is important to appreciate from the beginning that all the issues are strongly interrelated and that several disputes and difficulties can occur concurrently.

1.2 The family practitioner

1.2.1 Professional conduct

Family solicitors owe the same duties towards their clients as those of any other solicitor. The solicitor may not act for both parties no matter how amicable their separation. Confidentiality towards clients' affairs must also be observed, for example a client's address cannot be disclosed without his consent. There are, however, particular professional conduct issues which may arise in the context of a family law case. The solicitor may, for example, have previously acted for the husband and wife jointly in a property or business matter during the marriage. On the breakdown of the marriage the husband may ask the solicitor to act for him in the divorce. The solicitor will need to consider whether he has relevant confidential information about the wife which will require the solicitor to decline to act for the husband.

A solicitor acting in a children case may be given information by his client which the client does not wish to be disclosed, and yet which causes the solicitor to believe that the mental or physical safety of a child is at risk. The solicitor will need to consider whether the matter is sufficiently serious to make it an exceptional situation which would justify the solicitor breaching client confidentiality in order to protect the child.

1.2.2 Adviser – not decision-maker

There are certain special considerations to be borne in mind when dealing with a family matter. Family clients are likely to be more vulnerable than other clients. They may have only recently (or are even yet to) come to terms with the breakdown of their relationship and the consequent breakup of their home and family. They will invariably face many problems, be presented with a bewildering array of options, and be called upon to make many important decisions. It is hardly surprising, therefore, that such clients may be tempted to pass the responsibility to make these decisions on to their solicitor. However, it is important that the family solicitor is able to distinguish between advising the client of his choices and influencing the client's decisions, or even assuming certain choices on the client's behalf. However much a client's marriage appears to the solicitor to be irredeemably lost, the solicitor must be careful to advise the client fully of all the options and not to push the client prematurely down the route to divorce. If the solicitor is in any doubt as to what the client really wants to do about his relationship, he should pause to allow the client time to make a free and firm decision. Many clients will find the initial interview an emotional and stressful experience and, bearing in mind that many important and complex matters will have been discussed in the interview, it is sensible to confirm advice given and to set out the options in a letter following the interview. This enables the client to absorb the advice and reflect upon it before embarking upon a particular course of action.

1.2.3 Objectives

A further important consideration for the family solicitor is to keep sight of the client's overall long-term objectives. If a relationship has finally broken down, it is fair to assume that a family client's ultimate objective is to be able to unravel the legal ties of that relationship and to begin life afresh with the minimum of pain and bitterness. This will apply particularly where children are involved. There will be times when a client may be so involved in the detail of a particular dispute that he loses sight of this wider aim. It is here that the good family practitioner can make a positive contribution; by maintaining a sufficiently detached viewpoint the professional may enable a client to refocus on his goal and to regard matters in the round.

In pursuing these long-term objectives the good family solicitor has a very positive role to play. The approach taken by the solicitor can significantly influence a client's response. If a solicitor takes an aggressive stance, advising in terms of 'winning' and 'losing' and 'fighting' and 'giving in', then this is likely to serve to stir up bitterness and lead a client to set his face against compromise. Conversely, the solicitor who attempts to defuse tensions, concentrating on important issues rather than petty matters, and who talks in terms of arriving at fair solutions and compromise is likely to find that his client is more willing to follow this lead. It is important to address the advantages of a negotiated settlement whilst at the same time assuring the client that, where appropriate, a firm stance will be taken to protect his interests. The people most likely to come through the trauma of a divorce or separation successfully are those who have been involved in reaching agreement about important issues. A party is also much more likely to abide by such an agreement than by an arrangement imposed by the court. Most important of all is the benefit of reducing the impact of the disputes on any children who are at risk of being caught in the cross-fire. The Resolution (formerly the Solicitors Family Law Association) Code of Practice (set out in **Appendix 2**) advocates a constructive and non-confrontational approach in family matters. Resolution has a membership of approximately 5,000 family law solicitors and other legal justice professionals. Its Code of Practice is endorsed by The Law Society and supported by many senior members of the judiciary (see, for example, *Dutfield v Gilbert H Stephens & Sons* [1988] Fam Law 473). The Resolution Code of Practice should be read in conjunction with the Law Society's Family Law Protocol, which sets out guidelines for all solicitors for the conduct of proceedings which are designed to promote a constructive and conciliatory approach in family cases.

In order to achieve these objectives, the family practitioner must acquire negotiating skills; he must know when and how to achieve a settlement (see *Skills for Lawyers*). Having successfully negotiated a settlement, the family solicitor must use his drafting skills to draw up a clear and enforceable agreement (see *Skills for Lawyers*). This document may take the form of a consent order (see **Chapter 9**), or a separation agreement (see **Chapter 11**).

If a negotiated settlement cannot be achieved, the matter must be determined in court. Since most proceedings will be dealt with in chambers in the county court the family solicitor will have rights of audience. This will call for the use of advocacy skills (see *Skills for Lawyers*).

If the solicitor's approach to family work is a conciliatory one then this is likely to encourage clients to take advantage of mediation services offered by other agencies (see **1.3**). Conversely, if the solicitor takes a more antagonistic approach and, in particular, is openly cynical about mediation then this will hardly encourage the client to take advantage of this option.

1.2.4 Interviewing skills

The success of the solicitor–client relationship in family cases is to a large extent dependent upon the impression created in the first interview. The practitioner may be in the privileged position of being the first person with whom the client has discussed his relationship difficulties. The client will be sensitive to the atmosphere in that interview, and it is of crucial importance that the solicitor attempts to create the right environment and to adopt an appropriate tone for the interview.

Preparation for the interview is vital. Thought should be given to the length of the interview and its venue, as well as to the information which should be obtained from, and given to, the client. In family matters the interview could also be complicated by the fact that the client may bring his children with him, or have chosen to bring a friend for support. This field of interviewing is a hugely important subject in itself which cannot be considered in detail here, but reference should be made to the section on interviewing in *Skills for Lawyers*). Use of a checklist or instruction sheet will ensure that the information required is obtained. However, care must be taken when using such aids to explain their use to the client and to ensure that the interview does not become too formal or narrow.

1.2.5 Awareness and balance

When a relationship is in crisis, each party may experience a wide range of feelings. These will inevitably vary between individuals, but may variously include disappointment, anger and blame, hurt, sadness, self-doubt, loss, guilt, uncertainty and anxiety. For some time, there may be a sense of relief that an unhappy situation is being addressed. Sometimes, there may be worry and concern for the other partner. It is not uncommon for people in this crisis situation to move inconsistently from one feeling to another. There is no standard reaction to relationship breakdown, and family solicitors need to be aware of the sensitivity of the situation in which they are intervening.

Most clients need, and are entitled to have, solicitors who will advise and support them in these difficult times. Their solicitors may have to act as their champions, protecting their rights and position. However, while maintaining awareness of these legitimate expectations, the family solicitor also needs to be aware that supporting the client can sometimes mean helping him to understand and come to terms with unpalatable consequences, or seeking compromises which the client may prefer not to make. Parents may be able to keep their children's best interests in mind, but in that situation those interests may sometimes blur with the client's own preferences, antagonisms or strength of feeling; and here again the solicitor may have a role in helping the client to be aware of the children's needs and interests as well as the client's.

The family solicitor accordingly has to maintain a balance between the supportive, partisan role and the need to confront the client's perceptions where appropriate. As previously stated, an objective view, sympathetically but not patronisingly expressed, may be necessary to help the client make necessary shifts. The solicitor must also appreciate the extent to which his actions and approach can have an effect, whether helping or damaging, on the client and on the relationship between the parties and their children. Communications with the other side can always be courteous and sensitive, even where tough positions are being stated. Opportunities for dialogue can be established early on and maintained even when confrontation is indicated. This is all consistent with having a sympathetic and effective relationship with the client. Resolution encourages the development of these skills in a number of ways, for example by issuing guides to good practice in various areas of family law - service of correspondence, disclosure, acting for children, and domestic abuse and working with the Bar in family cases - and by holding seminars and workshops on understanding the emotional aspects of family life and of the personal consequences which may follow any change, and increasing members' self-awareness, as well as training in 'black letter' family law.

1.3 Other processes

There are other processes available to complement the work of the family practitioner. The family solicitor should be aware of them and recommend them as appropriate. However, it is important to be able to recognise the boundaries of the practitioners' role and the limitations of their skills. Although the practitioner should consider the possibility of reconciliation for his client, he cannot himself undertake this role. Similarly, the solicitor will wish to facilitate compromise but cannot act as mediator between the parties. Instead, the family practitioner will be familiar with the local agencies and services which are more suitable and capable of performing these roles.

1.3.1 Counselling

Counselling takes different forms and may have different aims. It may involve working with an individual, the couple, members of the family or the whole family together. It may be relatively short term, or may involve longer-term marital or family therapy; and there are different theoretical perspectives.

One of the aims of counselling may be to try to save the relationship where it is under stress, or to establish a reconciliation where it has already broken down. Another may be to explore whether there is any basis for continuing with the relationship and, if so, what has to happen to make this possible. Not uncommonly, a couple may disagree about the future of the relationship, one wishing to end it and the other to continue with it. Counselling may assist them to come to their own conclusion, whether this proves to be preserving the relationship or bringing it to an end. Counselling may therefore help a couple to accept the ending of their relationship if that is appropriate.

1.3.2 Mediation

In family mediation the couple engage the assistance of one or two impartial mediators, who have no authority to make any decisions for them but who use certain skills to help them to resolve their issues by negotiated agreement without adjudication.

The mediator (or co-mediators) will usually meet the parties together (although, in some circumstances, may see them separately) and will try to help them to clarify and resolve their issues on a basis which they find mutually acceptable. Depending on the issues, this may involve obtaining all relevant facts, including, where appropriate, financial data, exploring alternative settlement options and their acceptability and viability, and generally helping the couple to communicate and make decisions. The mediator may give information, but will not advise the couple what terms they should agree, this being a matter for them; and may help them to examine different solutions but will not try to press the one which the mediator may prefer.

Mediation does not aim to save the relationship but to help parties deal by agreement, rather than through the courts, with the consequences of its breakdown.

There are a number of facilitation, communication and management skills which mediators should have and which generally necessitate special training. Mediators should also work to a Code of Conduct which regulates the ethical and practical approach which they adopt. Many solicitors have undergone training as mediators and may belong to the British Association of Lawyer Mediators. Family mediators are also drawn from other ranks, including social workers, probation officers, children and family reporters, psychotherapists, counsellors and mental health professionals.

A solicitor cannot act as a mediator for his own client and would need to refer to an outside organisation or individual mediator. The solicitor should take the earliest opportunity to assess the suitability of mediation as a means of attempting to resolve the client's case. If relevant, information should be given to the client about the availability of mediation and the nature of the process.

1.3.3 Collaborative law

In England and Wales collaborative law is in its infancy, but is growing in importance as family solicitors begin to be trained as collaborative lawyers. Collaborative law operates as a series of meetings aimed at enabling the parties to resolve the issues resulting from the breakdown of a relationship. The process requires the parties and their solicitors to sign up to an agreement promising to try to reach an amicable consensus on all issues without recourse to court proceedings. If it transpires that a settlement cannot be reached then the parties cannot continue to instruct their collaborative lawyers and must instruct other solicitors to represent them in subsequent court proceedings. Therefore both the parties and their solicitors have an interest in making the process work.

Collaborative law views the breakdown of a relationship in the round and enables the parties to explore the issues and find solutions outside the constraints of court proceedings. Mainstream legal issues such as the financial consequences of the ending of the relationship are explored and, if possible, agreed upon; but collaborative law also recognises that the concerns which a client has when a relationship ends may not be of a 'legal' nature and yet those concerns must be addressed if the parties are to be able to make sensible decisions about the future. Collaborative law also allows these issues to be looked at through the use of outside experts, as necessary.

1.4 The family courts

The family practitioner must not only be able to identify the client's needs and determine the correct approach to meet these, but must also decide in which court the remedies will be sought and, if a choice of venue exists, which will be the most appropriate. Often proceedings can be brought in either the county court, or the High Court or the family proceedings court. The jurisdiction of the courts to make orders under the Children Act 1989 (CA 1989) is more complicated and is outlined in **Chapters 13** and **14**.

1.4.1 County court

All proceedings under the Matrimonial Causes Act 1973 (MCA 1973) (ie for divorce, judicial separation or nullity) begin in a divorce county court. This is a county court which has jurisdiction to deal with matrimonial causes (conferred by the Matrimonial and Family Proceedings Act 1984, s 33). In London, the Principal Registry acts also as a divorce county court. Most work is carried out by the district judge from whom appeal may be made to a county court judge. A judge is required to try most defended cases.

1.4.2 The High Court

Generally, proceedings are dealt with in the Family Division of the High Court only if the nature of the issues involves facts or arguments which are complex, difficult or grave. Cases may be transferred down to the county court, or referred up by the latter to the High Court. If, for example, a financial dispute involved substantial sums of money invested in complex assets, perhaps coupled with allegations of non-disclosure or misappropriation, the county court might prefer to decline jurisdiction and transfer the case to the High Court. Certain applications in relation to children (eg wardship) must be brought in the High Court, as must cases seeking a declaration of incompatibility under s 4 of the Human Rights Act 1998 (HRA 1998) (or where an issue in any case may lead to the court considering making such a declaration).

1.4.3 The family proceedings court

Magistrates, when dealing with domestic matters, sit as a family proceedings court. The magistrates (including at least one man and one woman) are selected from the family panel and receive special training to deal with family matters. The hearing is entirely different from criminal proceedings in magistrates' courts and there are restrictions on those who may be present.

Magistrates have no jurisdiction to deal with divorce, nullity or judicial separation proceedings. They can deal with orders for periodical payments and lump sums for married applicants during the marriage; they can also deal with protection orders and children orders.

1.4.4 A family court?

For many years now there have been calls to rationalise family litigation through a single, comprehensive family court. There can be no doubt that a unified family court would end the confusing disparity in procedure, terminology, law and personnel which currently exists in the plethora of family courts. Some steps towards this can be seen in the unified approach adopted in the CA 1989, which requires the same orders and principles to be applied in all courts dealing with applications under that Act. A similar approach has also been adopted under the FLA 1996 in relation to domestic abuse.

In March 2007 the President of the Family Division announced 'A framework for a family court'. This project, aimed at exploring the practicalities of managing a unified family court system, is expected to be piloted in some areas during 2008.

1.5 Human Rights Act 1998

The HRA 1998 incorporated the European Convention for the Protection of Human Rights and Fundamental Freedoms into the law of England and Wales with effect from 2 October 2000. It provides a scheme whereby domestic legislation must be read and given effect so as to be compatible with the rights and freedoms guaranteed by the Convention as far as is possible. If a Convention right is infringed then an application for judicial review, or proceedings against the appropriate public body for failure to act compatibly with the Convention, may be appropriate. The most relevant of the Convention rights for the purposes of family law is Article 8 (right to respect for family and private life), which provides:

1.   Everyone has the right to respect for his private and family life, his home and his correspondence.

2.   There shall be no interference by a public authority with the exercise of this right except such as is in accordance with the law and is necessary in a democratic society in the interests of national security, public safety or the economic well-being of the country, for the prevention of disorder or crime, for the protection of health or morals, or for the protection of the rights and freedoms of others.

Public law relating to children (see **Chapter 14**) is an obvious example of an area of UK law where this Article will need to be taken into account.

If interference with this right is established, the State must show that the interference is justified. There are four underlying principles which justify such interference:

(a)   It must be in accordance with the domestic law.

(b)   It must serve a legitimate aim.

(c)   It must be necessary (ie correspond to a social need and be proportionate to the aim pursued).

(d)   It must not be discriminatory.

Other Convention rights which could give rise to litigation and, potentially, changes in UK law are Article 3 (prohibiting inhuman or degrading treatment); Article 5 (the right to liberty and security of person); Article 6 (right to a fair hearing); and Article 14 (prohibiting discrimination on any ground, including sex, birth or other status). The significance of these Articles will be considered in more detail in the relevant chapters of this book.

A case seeking a declaration of incompatability under s 4 of the HRA 1998 must be brought in the High Court, as must any case which raises an issue which may lead to the court considering making such a declaration (*Practice Direction (Human Rights Act 1998)* (24 July 2000) [2000] Fam Law 670).

1.6 Conclusion

The problems facing a family client are as diverse as families themselves. The challenge facing the family practitioner is to steer a client through those problems on to a new life. This requires the practitioner to fit the appropriate solution from a diverse range of remedies to meet the specific needs of each individual client. To succeed in this, the family solicitor must acquire a firm grasp of a broad range of law and develop a variety of legal skills. A healthy measure of common sense and a sense of humour are also invaluable. Thus equipped, the family practitioner can look forward to a highly interesting and rewarding career.

1.7 Chapter summary

(1)   The family client will usually want advice on money and property, children and protection from violence.

(2)   The family practitioner will need to consider professional conduct, the need to advise but not take decisions for a client, and the need to keep in mind long-term objectives.

(3)   Outside agencies can also help a client, for example counselling and mediation services.

(4)   The courts that generally deal with family matters are the county court (all divorces start here), the High Court (which deals with complex matters) and the family proceedings court (which has no divorce jurisdiction but which deals with finance within marriage and other family matters).

Chapter 2
Funding

2.1 Introduction

At the first interview, one of the client's major concerns may be how he is going to pay for legal advice. A solicitor cannot enter a conditional fee agreement with a client in relation to family proceedings. However, where the client is of modest means, public funding may be available. The Access to Justice Act 1999 (AJA 1999) radically reformed public funding for legal services. The 1999 Act established the Legal Services Commission to oversee and coordinate the provision of legal services. As part of that work the Legal Services Commission administers funding in civil cases (including family cases) through the Community Legal Service. Section 8 of the AJA 1999 established the Funding Code, which sets down criteria for the funding of individual cases.

At the time of writing, the provision of public funding is undergoing a major review. The Legal Services Commission has formulated proposals which, if implemented, will result in the most wide-ranging changes that the scheme has seen for many years. The exact timetable for the introduction of those changes is as yet uncertain and, indeed, is still the subject of consultation with the profession. Nevertheless, it is anticipated that October 2007 will see the introduction of the first part of a radical new funding scheme. Further elements are set to be phased in during 2008.

Under the new scheme, the current system, whereby solicitors are paid an hourly charging rate for the work they undertake, will be replaced in most family cases by a system of fixed fees. The solicitor will therefore receive a set payment for conducting a case. The level of the fee will depend on the type of case, the stage which the case reaches and, in public law children cases, the identity of the client(s). There will, however, be provision for very complex or difficult cases to bypass the scheme and be charged for on an hourly rate instead.

This chapter provides an outline of public funding in relation to family work. The AJA 1999, regulations made under it and the Funding Code (plus guidance on the Code) should be consulted if more detail is needed.

The chapter concludes with a brief look at some other methods a family client may use to pay for legal advice.

2.2   Contracting

A family law solicitor may undertake publicly-funded work only if his firm has a contract with the Legal Services Commission specific to family law. To obtain a contract, a firm must satisfy practice management standards set by the Commission.

Part of the Legal Services Commission's function is to ensure that the clients have access to legal services of a high standard. This is achieved through a scheme of Quality Marks awarded to organisations that are able to demonstrate such standards. To obtain a Quality Mark, a firm of solicitors must be able to show that cases are handled in accordance with quality assurance criteria set by the Commission. Having a Quality Mark is also a condition of a firm maintaining its contract with the Commission.

2.3   Levels of service

The Funding Code sets down various 'levels of service'. Those which are relevant to the family practitioner are Legal Help, General Family Help, Help with Mediation and Legal Representation.

2.4   Legal Help

This enables people who satisfy the means and merits test to obtain advice from a solicitor. It can cover advice on any question of English law or procedure and can, therefore, include correspondence, negotiating or drafting documents for a client. It cannot cover any step in court proceedings (with the exception of undefended divorce (see **3.9.1**)) and, therefore, if litigation follows, Legal Representation (or General Family Help) will have to be obtained.

2.4.1   Financial eligibility

A client must come within the financial limits for both capital and income. The capital limit is at present £8,000. If the client is in receipt of income support, income-based jobseeker's allowance or guaranteed state pension credit, he will automatically qualify; otherwise the solicitor will need to calculate his disposable income and capital. If the client is eligible, he will not have to pay a contribution, but the statutory charge (see **2.9**) may apply.

2.4.2   Sufficient benefit test

Legal Help may be provided only where there is sufficient benefit to the client, having regard to the circumstances, to justify work being carried out. The question to ask is: 'Would a reasonable privately paying client of moderate means pay for this as legal advice?'. Thus Legal Help will not be provided if the claim is clearly hopeless, vexatious or would be an abuse of the process, or if the client is seeking advice on non-legal matters.

2.4.3   Procedure for obtaining advice under Legal Help

Legal Help is carried out under the firm's contract and does not require separate applications to be made to the Legal Services Commission at the outset of each case. Instead, under the terms of its contract, each firm is given a maximum number of new cases (or 'new matter starts') to be undertaken during the period of the contract.

The solicitor will need to ensure that the client is both financially eligible (**2.4.1**) and satisfies the sufficient benefit test (**2.4.2**). The former can be done by completing the Controlled Work 1 Form. Appropriate warning must be given of the impact of the statutory charge (see **2.9**).

2.4.4 Initial financial limit

Once a Controlled Work 1 Form has been completed and signed, the solicitor can carry out work up to a level of costs fixed by the Legal Services Commission.

2.4.5 Limit to number of Controlled Work 1 Forms

The rule in divorce proceedings is that all matters arising from or connected with the divorce must be treated as the same matter, so that only one Controlled Work 1 Form is available for all the proceedings. Thus, if a client fills in a Controlled Work 1 Form initially for his undefended divorce, the original form must be used for any subsequent advice given to him relating to ancillary financial matters, non-molestation and occupation orders, or orders relating to the children. General Family Help or Legal Representation are available for matters other than the undefended divorce, so, in these cases, the Controlled Work 1 Form will be needed only for the initial advice and the time spent making the application for General Family Help or Legal Representation. A solicitor cannot generally provide Legal Help where the client has already received Legal Help in the same matter from another solicitor within the previous six months (unless, for example, the client has reasonable cause to be dissatisfied with the service provided by the first solicitor).

2.4.6 Payment

When the work is completed, the bill on the Controlled Work 1 Form must be completed by the firm and kept on file for audit purposes. The firm will receive a regular monthly payment from the Legal Services Commission, the amount depending on the number of new matter starts specified in the contract.

2.4.7 New funding scheme

Under the current proposals, Legal Help will continue to be a part of the new scheme. The solicitor will receive a fixed fee for the work undertaken on the client's behalf. It is intended that there will be different fixed fees according to whether the solicitor is giving general initial advice, advising the petitioner in a divorce case or giving initial advice in a public law children case. This is likely to be the first part of the new scheme to be introduced in October 2007.

2.5 Mediation

2.5.1 Introduction

In private law children cases and proceedings for financial provision (apart from under the Matrimonial Causes Act 1973, s 37 (see **9.6.2**)), General Family Help or Legal Representation will be refused unless the case is first referred to a mediator, who determines whether mediation is suitable in the circumstances for the dispute and the parties.

Certain cases are exempt from this requirement:

(a)   urgent cases;

(b)   where no recognised mediator is available;

(c)   where the client is the grandparent or other extended family member in private law children proceedings;

(d)   where proceedings are already in existence and the client is the respondent who has been given a court hearing date within the next three months;

(e)   where the applicant has a reasonable fear of violence or significant harm from his or her partner or former partner.

Funding is available for mediation of a family dispute for couples who qualify financially. In such cases, Family Mediation (a further level of service) will pay the mediator's costs.

2.5.2   Help with Mediation

This covers legal advice given to support Family Mediation, for example, drawing up a financial agreement reached by way of mediation and confirming it as a court order.

2.5.2.1   Financial eligibility

If the client receives funding for Family Mediation, he will automatically qualify for Help with Mediation in respect of the same mediation. Similarly, if the client is in receipt of income support or income-based jobseeker's allowance, he will automatically qualify. In other cases, both capital and income must come within the current financial limits. No contribution is payable and the statutory charge (see **2.9**) will not apply.

2.5.2.2   Sufficient benefit test

Help with Mediation may be provided only where there is sufficient benefit to the client to justify the work being carried out. This is the same test as applies in relation to Legal Help (see **2.4.2**). Thus, an agreement should be confirmed in a court order only in circumstances where a privately paying client would be advised to do so.

2.5.2.3   Procedure for obtaining Help with Mediation

The solicitor determines the client's eligibility for Help with Mediation. If the solicitor decides that the client is financially eligible and satisfies the sufficient benefit test, he will grant Help with Mediation immediately. The solicitor will complete form CLSAPP4. The form will be signed by the client and sent to the regional office of the Legal Services Commission.

2.5.2.4   Financial limit

The solicitor can do up to £150 worth of work where mediation relates to children-only issues, up to £250 worth of work where mediation relates to financial-only issues, and up to £350 worth of work for all-issues mediation. These limits can be extended where necessary, provided the authority of the Legal Services Commission is obtained in advance of exceeding the limit.

2.6   General Family Help

This covers helping people to negotiate in a family dispute where no mediation is in progress. It also includes initiating proceedings when this is necessary to secure the early resolution of a family dispute, eg in order to secure disclosure of information. It includes services covered by Legal Help, for example, giving advice or drafting documents. It also covers obtaining a consent order following settlement and related conveyancing work.

2.6.1 Financial eligibility

If the client is in receipt of income support, income-based jobseeker's allowance or guaranteed state pension credit, he will qualify automatically on financial grounds without having to pay a contribution. In other cases, both his capital and income must come within the current financial limits. A contribution may be payable from capital or income depending on resources. It is essential that the solicitor explains to the client the effect of the statutory charge (see **2.9**).

2.6.2 Cost benefit test

General Family Help may be provided only where the benefits to be gained for the client justify the likely cost, such that a reasonable private paying client would be prepared to proceed and instruct solicitors using his own funds. The likely cost of achieving the benefit must be proportionate to the benefit sought. So, for example, where the solicitor receives an offer of settlement from the other party, he must carefully consider whether the additional costs of further negotiation to improve on that offer would be proportionate to any improvement likely to be gained.

2.6.3 Procedure for obtaining General Family Help

General Family Help requires an application to be made to or registered with the Legal Services Commission in every case. The Legal Services Commission will assess whether the client is eligible for funding. The solicitor will complete form CLSAPP3. He will also need to ask the client to complete the relevant means form. This should then be sent to the regional office of the Legal Services Commission. The regional office will assess whether the client qualifies financially and whether the application passes the merits test.

If a certificate is to be granted and the client has a contribution to pay, an offer of funding is sent out direct to the client, with a copy to the solicitor. The client accepts by signing the offer and sending the required contribution to the regional office of the Legal Services Commission. The contribution may be from capital, or income or both. A contribution from capital must normally be paid in full immediately. A contribution from income is normally payable by instalments. If no contribution is payable, the certificate is sent out immediately.

2.6.4 Financial limit

The standard costs limitation is £1,500 worth of work. It is possible to extend this by application to the Legal Services Commission; but if there is little immediate prospect of resolution of the issues, it may be more appropriate to apply for Legal Representation instead (see **2.7**).

2.6.5 New funding scheme

The Legal Services Commission plans to replace General Family Help with a new Family Help scheme. The solicitor will receive a fixed fee for the work undertaken. There will be different levels of Family Help according to how far the case progresses towards litigation. There are also likely to be regional variations in the fees paid to solicitors.

2.7 Legal Representation

This covers representation in court. An application for Legal Representation will be refused unless the case has first been referred to a mediator (see **2.5.1**) and it can be shown that a genuine attempt has been made to resolve the dispute without recourse to contested proceedings and this attempt has failed. This rule does not apply in public law children cases or cases of domestic abuse. Often, therefore, negotiations will initially have been carried out under General Family Help (see **2.6**). When it becomes clear that there is no reasonable prospect of settlement, it will be appropriate to apply for Legal Representation. This can be done by applying to amend the General Family Help certificate to cover Legal Representation. It is not essential, however, for negotiations to have been carried out under General Family Help. It may be the case that this test can be satisfied by negotiations carried out using Legal Help (see **2.4**). In such a case, there will be no need to apply for General Family Help and the solicitor can instead immediately apply for Legal Representation.

In ancillary relief cases the Legal Services Commission has the discretion to refuse Legal Representation if it appears reasonable for the proceedings to be funded privately. Legal Representation will be refused if the client could raise the money to pay his legal fees by selling assets or taking out a loan.

2.7.1 Financial eligibility

This is the same as for General Family Help (see **2.6.1**). Special rules apply to public law children proceedings, where funding is available without reference to means for certain people (see **14.11.4**).

2.7.2 Sufficient benefit test

The test will differ depending on the type of case involved.

2.7.2.1 Private children proceedings and financial proceedings

Legal Representation will be refused unless the likely benefits to be gained from the proceedings for the client justify the likely costs, such that a reasonable privately paying client would be prepared to take or defend the proceedings in all the circumstances.

In addition, in cases for financial provision, Legal Representation will be refused if the prospects of success are:

(a)   borderline (ie where it is not possible to say that prospects of success are better than 50%), unless the case has overwhelming importance to the client or a significant wider public interest; or

(b)   poor (less than 50%).

In private children cases, Legal Representation will be refused if the prospects of success are poor.

2.7.2.2 Public law children proceedings

Legal Representation for children, parents and those with parental responsibility will generally be granted without reference to prospects of success or reasonableness.

2.7.2.3 Domestic abuse proceedings

Legal Representation will be refused unless the likely benefits to be gained from the proceedings for the client justify the likely costs, having regard to the prospects of obtaining the order sought and all other circumstances.

In addition, Legal Representation will be refused if the prospects of success are poor.

2.7.3 Procedure for obtaining Legal Representation

The procedure is the same as for General Family Help (see **2.6.3**).

2.7.4 Financial limit

The standard financial limit for Legal Representation is £2,500, but again this can be extended by application to the Legal Services Commission.

2.7.5 Emergency representation

Emergency applications can be made for Legal Representation in appropriate cases, for example, in cases of domestic abuse.

2.8 Effect of public funding

2.8.1 Duty to notify the court and other parties

Immediately upon receipt of the certificate, or if proceedings have not yet commenced, when they do, the solicitor must file the original public funding certificate at court and must inform all other parties of the fact that the client is publicly funded by serving upon them a notice of issue of funding.

2.8.2 Relationship between solicitor and client

The solicitor will continue to owe the normal solicitor–client duties to a publicly funded client. In addition, the solicitor will owe duties to the Legal Services Commission. If the client acts unreasonably (eg refuses a reasonable offer of settlement), the solicitor must report this to the Legal Services Commission. This duty to the Legal Services Commission overrides the solicitor's usual duty of confidentiality to his client.

2.8.3 Costs

If a publicly funded party loses, it is possible for him to be ordered to pay the winning party's costs. Section 11 of the AJA 1999 provides that such an order for costs is limited in that an unsuccessful publicly funded party cannot be ordered to pay an amount which exceeds the amount (if any) which is a reasonable one for him to pay having regard to all the circumstances, including the means of the parties and their conduct in relation to the dispute. However, the limitation on costs orders contained in s 11 of the AJA 1999 does not apply to most family proceedings (including those under MCA 1973 and CA 1989, Pts I and II). This was a change introduced in 2005 with the intention of ensuring that funded litigants are subject to the same costs risks as privately paying litigants. If the winner is the respondent, he has no choice but to defend the proceedings. In this situation, the court has power under reg 5 of the Community Legal Service (Cost Protection) Regulations 2000 (SI 2000/824) to order that the respondent's costs be paid from the Community Legal Service Fund. Again, with effect from July 2005, this power will no longer apply to most family proceedings.

2.8.4 Payment of solicitor's costs

Once the client is in receipt of public funding, the solicitor will receive payment of his costs from the Legal Services Commission. Just as with a private client, it is possible for the solicitor to receive payment on account of costs and disbursements from the Legal Services Commission.

2.8.5 New funding scheme

Legal Representation is set to remain a feature of the new scheme. It will certainly remain available in domestic abuse cases as these will not be subject to the fixed fee scheme at all. However, the extent to which it will continue to be available for other types of cases is as yet uncertain.

2.9 The statutory charge

The statutory charge is relevant to all types of public funding except Help with Mediation (see **2.5.2.1**).

The solicitor is obliged to explain the effect of the statutory charge when his client applies for public funding. It is vital that the client fully understands the charge, and he should be reminded of it throughout the proceedings. Clients should also be advised periodically as to the approximate costs accumulated.

Once a certificate has been issued, the Legal Services Commission will be responsible for paying the assisted party's legal costs. Those costs will be subject to detailed assessment by the court, or, generally if the costs total less than £2,500, by the Legal Services Commission. The Commission will attempt to recoup these costs where possible. In order to do so, it first claims any money paid pursuant to an order for costs made in favour of the assisted party. Secondly, if a shortfall remains, it will retain any contribution paid by the assisted party under the terms of the offer of public funding. Any surplus will be returned to the assisted party. Thirdly, if there is still a deficit to the fund, the statutory charge will apply (AJA 1999, s 10(7)). The effect of this is that any property (including money) 'recovered or preserved in the proceedings' may be applied to make up the shortfall.

When is property 'recovered or preserved in the proceedings'? It was said in the case of *Hanlon v Law Society* [1980] 2 All ER 199:

> ... property has been recovered or preserved if it has been in issue in the proceedings: recovered by the claimant if it has been the subject of a successful claim, preserved by the respondent if the claim fails ...

The Legal Services Commission will determine from the statements of case, correspondence and order what the issues of the case were.

The statutory charge may even apply where the ownership of the property has not been in dispute but proceedings were brought to determine what should happen to the property, ie whether it is to be sold, transferred or retained (see *Curling v Law Society* [1985] 1 All ER 705 and, similarly, *Parks v Legal Aid Board* [1997] 1 FLR 77).

The charge applies to the costs incurred in all proceedings, meaning the entire cause or matter and not just the ancillary proceedings. Typically, it will include the Legal Help costs of the divorce suit and any costs incurred in a dispute over the children.

The costs are not limited to property obtained as a result of contested proceedings. Whilst a settlement will reduce the overall costs of the case, s 10(7) of the AJA 1999 ensures that a settlement will not avoid the effect of the statutory charge. The charge also applies to compromises arrived at to avoid bringing or continuing the proceedings. Indeed, where there has been a compromise, the property itself does not need to have been in issue for the statutory charge to apply, provided that it has been recovered or preserved in substitution for property which was in issue. For example, if the parties were arguing over the matrimonial home and a compromise was reached which instead transferred a holiday home (which had not been in issue) from the husband's sole name to the wife, the statutory charge can apply to the holiday home (see *Morgan and Others v Legal Aid Board* [2000] 3 All ER 974).

Some property recovered or preserved will be exempt from the charge (reg 44 of the Community Legal Service (Financial) Regulations 2000 (SI 2000/516)). The following are not subject to the statutory charge:

(a)   periodical payments;

(b)   payments on or after the making of an occupation order under Pt IV of the FLA 1996;

(c)   lump sums or property adjustment orders made after divorce in substitution for spousal maintenance under s 31(7A) or (7B) of the MCA 1973; and

(d)   pension attachments or pension sharing orders (other than lump sum pension attachments) under ss 23, 24 and 24B of the MCA 1973.

To facilitate collection of the charge, the assisted party's solicitor is required to pass any money payable to the assisted party under an agreement or court order to the Legal Services Commission. In addition, the solicitor must notify the regional office of the Legal Services Commission of any property recovered or preserved by his client. The solicitor will usually send a copy of the court order or agreement to the regional office of the Legal Services Commission. If a party receives a lump sum well in excess of the anticipated statutory charge, the solicitor may apply to the regional office of the Legal Services Commission for authority to release some of the money to the client provided sufficient sums are retained to cover the firm's costs. In all cases, once the solicitor's costs have been finally determined and the statutory charge has been satisfied, any balance is sent to the assisted party.

There is no discretion to waive the statutory charge, but the Legal Services Commission can agree to postpone enforcement of the charge where it is charged on either:

(a)   property which is expressly stated (in the order or agreement) to be used as a home by the assisted person or his dependants; or

(b)   a lump sum which is agreed or ordered with the express purpose of it being used to purchase a home (the purchase to be made within one year).

In both cases, before agreeing to postponement, the Commission will need to be satisfied that the property represents adequate security for the charge. Historically, provided these conditions were met, the postponement of the statutory charge was virtually automatic. However, following a review of public funding in 2005, the Legal Services Commission emphasised the discretionary nature of its power to postpone. Postponement will therefore not be allowed if, for example, the client could pay the statutory charge immediately by increasing the mortgage on the property. Even where the Legal Services Commission has initially exercised its discretion to allow the statutory charge to be postponed, that postponement will be kept under review and repayment sought immediately in the event of an improvement in the client's financial circumstances.

The charge will be protected by registration against the title of the property and simple interest will accrue. The interest rate is currently 8%. This may influence a client's decision to pay or postpone the charge. In most cases, the charge and interest will be enforced when the home is sold. However, it is possible for the charge to be transferred to a substitute property, provided, first, that the consent of the regional office of the Legal Services Commission is obtained before the charged property is sold and, secondly, that the substitute property represents adequate security.

Where an assisted party recovers both a lump sum and property, the Legal Services Commission will look to take its charge from the money first, attaching the charge to property only as a last resort.

2.10 Human rights

The Legal Services Commission is a public body, and therefore it cannot act in a way that is incompatible with Convention rights under the HRA 1998.

Article 6 of the European Convention on Human Rights provides that 'everyone is entitled to a fair and public hearing within a reasonable time by an independent and impartial tribunal established by law'.

One of the Article 6 rights is thus for effective access to the courts. In *Airey v Ireland* (1979) 2 EHRR 305, a wife wanted to bring proceedings for judicial separation. She could not afford legal representation and her application was complex but she was refused public funding. The European Court held that Article 6 might sometimes compel the State to provide legal assistance if such assistance was indispensable for effective access to court. The court said that complexity of procedure, complicated points of law, the need to call expert witnesses or the emotional involvement of the parties might all result in a requirement that legal assistance be provided. In *Airey*, for access to be effective, the wife required legal representation which, in her case, meant granting public funding.

The European Commission on Human Rights has attempted to confine the application of the *Airey* principles. It recognised that, due to limited resources, States might legitimately restrict the grant of public funding, provided the decision whether or not to grant such funding was not taken arbitrarily.

Under HRA 1998, the Legal Services Commission may be liable to challenge if it fails to grant public funding in circumstances that result in a litigant being unable to have effective access to the court. The Funding Code specifically states that legal assistance must be provided in accordance with Article 6. Yet the Funding Code also restricts public funding in most family cases until after the parties have been referred to mediation. This in itself may be open to challenge.

Arguments for public funding will be stronger when a Convention right is in issue. So, family cases dealing with, for example, Article 8 rights will arguably have a greater call on State resources than cases involving breach of contract. Equally, cases which raise Article 3 issues, such as those concerning child abuse or serious domestic abuse, will need serious consideration and have greater entitlement to legal assistance.

2.11 Other methods of funding

It may be that a client is not eligible for public funding and yet does not have sufficient resources to continue to pay his solicitor's fees on a privately paying basis. It has already been noted that a solicitor cannot enter a conditional fee agreement with a client in relation to family proceedings (see **2.1**). In appropriate cases there are other possible ways in which this problem can be resolved.

2.11.1   A 'Sears Tooth agreement'

This type of agreement is named after the case of *Sears Tooth (A Firm) v Payne Hicks Beach (A Firm) and Others* [1997] 2 FLR 116, where its validity was discussed. In this case, Sears Tooth acted for a wife in ancillary relief proceedings. She agreed to assign any award for financial relief (other than for maintenance) or costs to them as far as was necessary to pay their fees. The court stated that this device was a valid contract to assign a future chose in action and was not contrary to public policy.

2.11.2   Maintenance pending suit

In *A v A (Maintenance Pending Suit; Provision of Legal Fees)* [2001] 1 FLR 377, the judge awarded a sum of maintenance pending suit at such a level as to include money for the wife to pay her solicitor's fees on the basis that she had a pressing need for legal representation.

The ability to include an element for legal fees within an award of maintenance pending suit was endorsed in a number of subsequent cases. The most notable being *Currey v Currey* [2006] EWCA 1338 where the Court of Appeal said that such an award would be appropriate in cases where the applicant was able to demonstrate that he could not reasonably obtain legal advice by any other means. However, the test is stringent since the 'other means' of funding which must be considered first include borrowing money, charging assets, public funding and '*Sears Tooth* agreements'.

2.11.3   Lump sum orders

In *Minwala v Minwala* [2005] 1 FLR 771, in making a lump sum order in favour of the wife, Singer J ordered a further £500,000 as a separate and additional instalment of the lump sum to provide the wife with a fund from which she would be able to pay her legal fees in future anticipated litigation between the parties. The use of such orders will, however, be limited given the restrictions placed on the court's ability to make lump sum orders (see **4.4.1**), but they could be appropriate if, say, at the conclusion of the ancillary relief case, further proceedings were anticipated in relation to the children.

2.11.4   Bank loans

In some instances the only practical solution may be for the client to borrow money in order to meet his legal fees. It is becomingly increasingly common for banks to lend money to fund matrimonial litigation. Across the leading banks the conditions attached to such loans differ. Some banks, for example, will only lend where the client can offer security for the borrowing, other banks require a favourable opinion from counsel on the outcome of the proposed litigation. Whilst perhaps something of a last resort, such loans may be appropriate for some clients. However, the family solicitor must be careful not to infringe any rules of professional conduct when informing a client of the availability of such loans.

2.12   Chapter summary

(1)   Where a client is of modest means, public funding may be available to enable that client to pay for legal advice and representation.

(2)   Family law solicitors can undertake publicly funded work only if their firm has a specialist contract with the Legal Services Commission.

(3)   There are various 'levels of service' which may need to be provided by the family law solicitor:

    (a)   Legal Help;

    (b)   Help with Mediation;

    (c)   General Family Help;

    (d)   Legal Representation.

(4)   Except in public law children cases, the client will need to satisfy both means and merits tests to be eligible for public funding.

(5)   Public funding is not 'free' and will need to be repaid from any property 'recovered or preserved' (with some exceptions) – the statutory charge.

(6)   Where public funding is not available, other methods of paying for legal fees could be considered:

    (a)   a *Sears Tooth* agreement;

    (b)   maintenance pending suit;

    (c)   lump sum orders;

    (d)   bank loans.

Chapter 3

Divorce Law and Procedure

3.1 Introduction

3.1.1 General

Over 140,000 couples divorce each year in England and Wales. This is the highest divorce rate in Europe. By comparison, relatively few proceedings for judicial separation and nullity are brought. This chapter, therefore, deals in detail with the law relating to divorce and contains an outline of the law relating to judicial separation and nullity. The same procedures are available to civil partners, although termed 'dissolution', 'separation' and 'nullity'.

The chapter also deals with the procedure for divorce. Since less than 1% of all divorces are defended, only the undefended procedure is dealt with in detail. A checklist summarising the undefended divorce procedure is given at **3.12.2**.

3.1.2 Human rights

Article 12 of the European Convention on Human Rights gives 'men and women of marriageable age the right to marry and found a family according to the national laws governing the exercise of that right'. Marriage is the only relationship that is given special treatment under the Convention. The protections of Article 12 are limited to unions between members of the opposite sex and Article 12 has no application to same-sex relationships.

By way of contrast, there is no similar right to divorce, whether this is to re-marry or for any other reason (*Johnston v Ireland* (1987) 9 EHRR 203).

3.2 One-year rule

A petition for divorce cannot be presented to the court before the end of a period of one year from the date of the marriage (MCA 1973, s 3). The reason for this restriction is to discourage over-hasty decisions to end such short marriages.

The rule cannot be waived in any circumstances. However, provided that grounds for divorce can be satisfied, a petition may be presented after one year based on matters which occurred during this time; for example, the respondent's adultery or other unreasonable behaviour during the first year of marriage can form the basis of a petition as soon as the year has expired. A solicitor should also bear in mind the alternative solutions which exist to protect a client with matrimonial problems, even during the first year. A decree of nullity or judicial separation is not affected by the one-year rule (see **3.6** and **3.7**). Maintenance can be applied for in the divorce county court (MCA 1973, s 27), or in the family proceedings court (Domestic Proceedings and Magistrates' Courts Act 1978 (DPMCA 1978), s 2). A spouse could be protected from violence by using Pt IV of the FLA 1996 (see **Chapter 15**).

3.3 Jurisdiction of the English courts to hear suits for divorce

3.3.1 General

The English courts do not have the right to deal with a person's matrimonial affairs merely because that person is a British citizen or is present in this country. The position is governed by s 5 of the Domicile and Matrimonial Proceedings Act 1973, which itself incorporates Council Regulation (EC) No 2201/2003 known as Brussels II Revised. The English courts have jurisdiction to hear a divorce suit only where:

(a)   both parties are habitually resident in England and Wales; or

(b)   both parties were last habitually resident in England and Wales, and one of them still resides there; or

(c)   the respondent is habitually resident in England and Wales; or

(d)   the petitioner is habitually resident in England and Wales and has lived there for at least a year immediately before the petition is filed; or

(e)   the petitioner is domiciled in England and Wales and has been residing in England and Wales for at least six months immediately before the petition is filed; or

(f)   both parties are domiciled in England and Wales; or

(g)   if none of (a)–(f) above applies and no court of another EU State has jurisdiction, either of the parties is domiciled in England and Wales on the date when the proceedings are begun.

These various bases of jurisdiction are not ranked in any order of precedence. More than one basis may apply on the individual facts of the case, but only one needs to be satisfied. In practice the easiest approach is for the family solicitor to work down the list and to rely upon the first basis that is applicable to the client's case.

Example

Sophie, who is French, marries Tim, who is English. The couple make their married home in England for 10 years. The marriage breaks down and Sophie returns home to France; Tim remains in England. Six months later Tim decides to seek a divorce through the English courts. On the facts, Tim has been habitually resident and domiciled in England throughout. Sophie has been habitually resident and in England during the marriage, but she is now both habitually resident and domiciled in France. The English courts have jurisdiction to deal with Tim's divorce on the basis of (b), (d) or (e) above. Tim needs to satisfy only one basis, and in practice the simplest approach is rely on the first, ie (b).

3.3.2 Habitual residence

The term 'habitual residence' is not defined in the MCA 1973. In *R v Barnet LB, ex p Shah* [1983] 2 AC 309, it was held that this expression meant the same as ordinary residence, ie voluntary residence with a degree of settled purpose. There must be a regular physical presence which must last for some time. Temporary absences (eg on holiday) will not prevent someone from establishing habitual residence. For the purpose of divorce jurisdiction, a person may also be habitually resident in a country even if his presence there is illegal (*Mark v Mark* [2005] 2 FLR 1193). Habitual residence is a question of fact to be decided on the circumstances of each case. The case of *Ikimi v Ikimi* [2001] EWCA Civ 873, [2001] 2 FLR 1288 makes it clear that a person can have two habitual or ordinary residences existing at the same time.

3.3.3 Domicile

No simple definition of 'domicile' is possible and, if issues arise in this respect, reference should be made to textbooks on private international law.

Broadly, a person is said to be domiciled in a territory having a single legal system if he has his permanent home there.

Everyone has a domicile and can only have one operative domicile at any one time. However, a person's domicile may alter as his circumstances change throughout his life. A person may acquire, and lose, any of three types of domicile. Each is described in outline below.

3.3.3.1 Domicile of origin

A person acquires domicile of origin at birth. In the case of a child whose parents are married, it is the father's domicile. In the case of a child whose parents are not married, it is the mother's domicile. It is therefore irrelevant where the child was born.

A domicile of origin is never lost, and even though it may not be operative for any period during which the person acquires a domicile of choice, it will revive if the domicile of choice is lost until another domicile of choice is acquired.

Example

Maria's domicile of origin is Italy. She marries an Englishman, Nigel, and moves to London, intending that England will be her permanent home. Maria acquires a domicile of choice of England. The marriage breaks down and Maria permanently leaves England to take up temporary residence in Paris whilst she contemplates her future. Maria has lost her English domicile of choice. Her Italian domicile of origin is therefore revived until such time as she acquires a new domicile of choice.

3.3.3.2 Domicile of choice

Every person aged 16 or over may acquire a domicile of choice. This requires, first, residence in a country other than the domicile of origin and, secondly, an intention to remain there permanently or indefinitely. This intention may be shown by becoming a citizen of that country, by the purchase of a home or by the length of time spent in that country. No single factor will be decisive. As with habitual residence, the fact that a person's presence in a particular country is illegal does not prevent his acquiring a domicile of choice in that country.

3.3.3.3 Domicile of dependence

A child can acquire an independent domicile only at 16 years of age, or on marriage under that age. If he is under 16 years old and unmarried, his domicile will follow his father's domicile if his parents are married, or his mother's if his parents are not married. If married parents separate, the child will acquire the domicile of the parent with whom he lives.

Example

Assume that Maria and Nigel, in the example at **3.3.3.1**, had a daughter, Olivia, who lives with Maria after the marriage breaks down. At birth Olivia acquired her domicile of dependence from Nigel, ie England. After the separation, Olivia's domicile follows that of her mother as a domicile of dependence. Olivia therefore has an Italian domicile of dependence.

3.3.4 Choice of forum

In many cases, it will be clear that the divorce will take place in England and Wales. In other cases, for example where one of the couple has been habitually resident in England for the past year but the other has not, it may be possible to choose whether to start proceedings in England and Wales or elsewhere. Such a choice will be governed by a number of factors, such as convenience and the law of the other jurisdiction(s) involved. Where the other jurisdiction is within the EU (apart from Denmark) then the situation will be governed by Brussels II Revised. This states that where a party commences proceedings for divorce, nullity or judicial separation in a jurisdiction of one of the Member States covered by Brussels II Revised, the court of the State which is first seized of the matter shall have exclusive jurisdiction. Any proceedings for divorce, etc subsequently commenced in another Member State must be stayed once the jurisdiction of the first State has been established. Where choice of forum is an issue, the solicitor must contact a lawyer in the other jurisdiction as soon as possible for advice on the legal position should a divorce be started there. Speed will normally be of the essence, since usually proceedings will continue in the jurisdiction where they were first started, any which commence later in an alternative jurisdiction being stayed (and if the other jurisdiction is an EU country covered by Brussels II Revised, this will *always* be the case).

3.3.5 Recognition of foreign decrees by the English courts

A relevant factor when dealing with foreign marriages is to check that the English courts recognise a foreign decree, for example, of divorce. If the English courts recognise the foreign decree then the parties are free to remarry in England and Wales, and no English divorce is necessary or, indeed, possible. However, in these circumstances, the English courts can make ancillary financial orders. If, on the other hand, the foreign decree is not recognised, the parties are still married and they will have to petition for a divorce through the English courts, in which case ancillary orders can be made in the normal way. The law is set out in the FLA 1986 and reference should be made to this, and to relevant textbooks, should an international aspect arise.

3.4 The ground for divorce

3.4.1 General

There is only one ground on which a petition for divorce may be presented to the court by either party to the marriage; that is, that the marriage has broken down irretrievably (MCA 1973, s 1(1)) (see **3.4.2** to **3.4.6** below). However, the court cannot hold that the marriage has broken down unless the petitioner satisfies the court of one or more of the five facts specified in s 1(2) of the MCA 1973. There is no need for there to be a causal relationship between the fact and the breakdown. Therefore, it is no defence to a divorce suit that, for example, the respondent committed adultery after having left the petitioner because the marriage had broken down; the fact does not have to precede and cause the breakdown, but can follow and merely evidence it.

If the court is satisfied that a fact is proved, it must grant the decree nisi unless it is satisfied that the marriage has not broken down (MCA 1973, s 1(4)). This could occur if the parties began living together again before the divorce was granted.

The equivalent process to end a civil partnership is dissolution. The statutory provisions are to be found in the Civil Partnership Act 2004, although they effectively mirror those of the MCA 1973.

3.4.2   Fact A: adultery and intolerability

    (a)   That the respondent has committed adultery *and* the petitioner finds it intolerable to live with the respondent. (MCA 1973, s 1(2)(a), emphasis added)

There are two elements to this fact, which must both be proved to the court:

(a)   adultery; and

(b)   intolerability.

It should be noted that this fact is not available as the basis for a petition to dissolve a civil partnership.

3.4.2.1   Adultery

Case law defines adultery as voluntary sexual intercourse between two persons of the opposite sex, one or both of whom is or are married, but not to each other.

Adultery may be proved or inferred from the following:

(a)   A confession of adultery by the respondent. This is the method often used in undefended divorces. Proof can either be by way of a separate confession statement signed by the respondent, or by the respondent answering 'yes' to a question in the Acknowledgement of Service form which is served on the respondent with the petition. If this method is to be used, the Acknowledgement must be returned to court signed by the respondent personally.

(b)   Birth of a child to the wife on proof that the husband was not the father.

(c)   Circumstantial evidence showing both guilty purpose and the opportunity to gratify it, for example, an enquiry agent's report which shows that the respondent and a member of the opposite sex are cohabiting.

(d)   A finding of paternity against the respondent in Children Act proceedings (Civil Evidence Act 1968, s 12).

(e)   Conviction of the respondent in a criminal court of an offence entailing sexual intercourse, for example, rape (Civil Evidence Act 1968, s 11). Although by definition the act of sexual intercourse is not voluntary on the part of the victim, a conviction for rape will be sufficient to satisfy the definition of adultery as against the perpetrator.

(f)   A finding of adultery against the respondent in an earlier case in the High Court or county court (Civil Evidence Act 1968, s 12). If the petitioner had already been granted a decree of judicial separation on the grounds of adultery, the court can treat the judicial separation decree as sufficient proof of the adultery (MCA 1973, s 4(2)).

3.4.2.2   Intolerability

Intolerability must be proved as well as the adultery, but this element rarely causes any problem. In the first place, the petitioner does not have to show that it was in consequence of the adultery that he found it intolerable to live with the respondent. He could say, for example, that he found it intolerable to live with her because of her treatment of the children, or because of some behaviour of the respondent other than the adultery. Secondly, the test of intolerability is subjective. The petitioner has merely to convince the court that he finds it intolerable to live with the respondent.

The intolerability can be proved by an assertion of intolerability in an affidavit sent to the court as part of the divorce proceedings. In practice, in undefended cases, courts do not even require the petitioner to state the reason why he finds it intolerable to live with the respondent.

3.4.2.3   The co-respondent

The person with whom the respondent committed adultery can be made a party to the divorce proceedings and is called the co-respondent. However, even if the co-respondent is made a party, it is not necessary to obtain an admission of adultery from the co-respondent if the respondent admits the adultery, because the fact requires only evidence that the respondent has committed adultery.

The Family Proceedings Rules 1991 (FPR 1991) (SI 1991/1247) enable a petitioner, if he wishes, not to name the co-respondent in the petition, in which case it will not be necessary to make the co-respondent a party to the divorce. This is an important point to bear in mind, as it could persuade a respondent who is reluctant to involve the co-respondent to admit the adultery and enable the divorce to be undefended. It is wise to make a co-respondent a party in a defended divorce as this could make proving adultery easier.

The Resolution Code of Practice (see **Appendix 2**) recommends that solicitors should discourage a petitioner from naming a co-respondent unless there is a compelling reason to do so. It would therefore seem that, unless a divorce is defended, a solicitor taking a conciliatory approach when drafting the petition should not include the name of the co-respondent or make him a party. Doing this will help to reduce animosity between the parties, and will not prejudice the petitioner in an undefended divorce.

3.4.2.4   Effect of cohabitation

Adultery

The petitioner is not entitled to rely on adultery committed by the respondent if the parties cohabit for a period, or periods together, exceeding six months after the petitioner has discovered the adultery (MCA 1973, s 2(1)).

The purpose behind this provision is to allow the parties a reasonable length of time in which to achieve a reconciliation without prejudicing their ground for divorce.

The time begins to run when the petitioner discovers the adultery. It is not relevant how long ago the adultery was actually committed. The six months can be made up of a number of periods of cohabitation, they need not constitute a continuous period. If the respondent has committed adultery on several occasions, time will not begin to run until after the petitioner learns of the last act of adultery.

Intolerability

Where the parties have lived together for a period or periods not exceeding six months in total after the petitioner knew of the adultery, the court must disregard the cohabitation when considering whether the petitioner finds it intolerable to live with the respondent (MCA 1973, s 2(2)).

This is another attempt to encourage the parties to attempt reconciliation. Without it, any cohabitation after discovery of the adultery could be used by the respondent as evidence that the petitioner did not in fact find it intolerable to live with the respondent.

Example

Abigail and Brian marry in 1991. In 1993 Brian has an affair which ends after one month. In December 2007 a friend tells Abigail about Brian's affair. Initially the couple stay together and try to make the marriage work. However, in February 2008, Abigail decides that she cannot forgive Brian for the affair and she decides to start divorce proceedings. The lengthy cohabitation since the affair took place is irrelevant. Time begins to run only when Abigail knew of the affair, ie December 2007. As less than six months have elapsed since that date, Abigail's petition can proceed based on the adultery in 1993.

3.4.3 Fact B: behaviour

(b)   That the respondent has behaved in such a way that the petitioner cannot reasonably be expected to live with the respondent. (MCA 1973, s 1(2)(b))

3.4.3.1 The respondent's behaviour

The phrase 'cannot reasonably be expected to live with the respondent' lays down an objective test. The court must make a value judgement about the respondent's behaviour and its effect on the petitioner. In contrast to the test for intolerability (see **3.4.2.2**), the petitioner's word alone is not enough. However, the court must have regard to the history of the marriage as well as to the personalities of the individual spouses. In the case of *O'Neill v O'Neill* [1975] 1 WLR 1118, the respondent, after retiring, bought a flat for himself, his wife and teenage daughter. He then personally began extensive renovation, involving mixing cement in the living room and leaving the toilet without a door for eight months, embarrassing his wife and daughter. After two years of the upheaval the wife left, and was entitled to a decree using this fact.

In the case of *Birch v Birch* [1992] 1 FLR 564, the wife's main complaint against the husband was that he was dogmatic and dictatorial, with nationalistic, male chauvinistic characteristics which she had resented for many years. The court granted the divorce and acknowledged that the wife's sensitive nature made it unreasonable for her to go on living with him.

It is a question of fact in each case whether the behaviour is such as to entitle the petitioner to a decree; it does not have to be grave and weighty behaviour. There is also no need to prove that the respondent had any intention to inflict misery on the petitioner.

In practice, again, each case depends on its facts, but typically, in an undefended divorce the court will look for three to six examples of behaviour. A further guide to follow in drafting a behaviour petition is 'first, worst and last'. This will ensure that the length of time that the behaviour has been suffered will be established, the major incidents included and when the latest example occurred.

The sort of conduct that can be included will always depend on the particular circumstances of the case, but relevant matters include physical violence, verbal abuse (which could include insults, threats, nagging), demanding sexual intercourse too often or not agreeing to intercourse at all, intimate relationships with people of the same or opposite sex (even if they fall short of sexual acts), cruelty, and failure to provide money or food as well as failure to provide affection or attention. However, the mere fact that the petitioner has become bored with the marriage, or that the parties are simply incompatible, will not be sufficient.

3.4.3.2   Effect of cohabitation on behaviour

The fact that the petitioner and respondent have lived with each other for a period or periods not exceeding six months in total after the last incident of behaviour relied on must be disregarded in deciding whether the petitioner can reasonably be expected to live with the respondent (MCA 1973, s 2(3)). This is to encourage the parties to consider reconciliation as cohabitation will not immediately prevent a divorce.

If the parties have lived together for longer than six months, this will not be an absolute bar to a petition being granted. However, the court will take the length of the cohabitation into account in determining whether the petitioner can reasonably be expected to live with the respondent. The longer the cohabitation, the less likely it will be that the court will grant the petition. It would always be open to the petitioner to show a good reason why the cohabitation continued. In *Bradley v Bradley* [1973] 1 WLR 1291, the wife had continued to cohabit, but proved to the court that she had no choice but to do so as she had seven children, nowhere else to go and was frightened that unless she went on sleeping with the husband and looking after the house he would seriously injure her.

3.4.4   Fact C: desertion

(c)   That the respondent has deserted the petitioner for a continuous period of at least two years immediately preceding the presentation of the petition. (MCA 1973, s 1(2)(c))

3.4.4.1   What constitutes desertion?

The elements needed to constitute the fact of desertion are as follows:

(a)   There must be a separation. In calculating the period of separation, the date of separation will not be included. In most cases the parties are living apart, but people who are living under the same roof can be separated in law if the common home and the common life have ceased altogether. The petitioner must establish that there are, in fact, two separate households under the same roof (see *Hopes v Hopes* [1948] 2 All ER 920). The court will examine the extent to which the parties share domestic life; whether they cook for each other, eat together and sleep together will all be relevant considerations.

(b)   There must be an intention to desert, ie to bring the matrimonial union permanently to an end.

(c)   The petitioner must not consent or agree to the separation.

(d)   The respondent must not have a just cause for leaving. This could apply if the respondent were away on business, or if his leaving was because of the wife's adultery.

(e)   The desertion must be continuous. Normally, several periods of separation cannot be added together to form the two-year period.

(f)   The desertion must immediately precede the presentation of the petition, ie the date when it is filed.

In practice, desertion is rarely cited in a petition because it is so technical and because other facts can usually be cited where the parties are living separately.

3.4.4.2   Effect of cohabitation on desertion

In considering whether a period of desertion has been continuous, no account is to be taken of a period or periods not exceeding six months in total during which the parties cohabited (MCA 1973, s 2(5)). However, any period of cohabitation cannot be counted as part of the period of desertion.

Example

Lisa deserted Martin on 31 January 2006. They make an attempt at reconciliation and live together for two months in 2007. The cohabitation will not prevent Martin from petitioning on the basis of desertion, but he cannot file the petition until a period of two years and two months has expired since Lisa first deserted. Martin will therefore be able to start divorce proceedings on 1 April 2008.

3.4.5   Fact D: two years' separation and consent

(d)   That the parties to the marriage have lived apart for a continuous period of at least two years immediately preceding the presentation of the petition ... *and* the respondent consents to a decree being granted. (MCA 1973, s 1(2)(d), emphasis added)

The elements which are necessary for this fact are, first, separation and, secondly, the respondent must consent to the decree.

3.4.5.1   Separation

Two years' separation is necessary. The spouses are treated as living apart unless they are living with each other in the same household (MCA 1973, s 2(6)). The test is similar to the test of separation in desertion cases (see **3.4.4.1**); accordingly, people can be living apart even though living under the same roof if they are living completely separate lives. The actual date of separation will not be included when calculating the period of separation.

A physical separation does not of itself constitute living apart. There must also be a mental element, ie one of the spouses must regard the marriage as a mere shell, never intending to live with the other spouse again (*Santos v Santos* [1975] 2 All ER 246). This intention does not necessarily have to be communicated to the other spouse and the petitioner could, in theory, rely on the respondent's intention. However, in practice, it is almost always the petitioner's intention that is relied on, and the standard-form divorce documents are drafted on this basis.

3.4.5.2   Consent

The respondent must consent to the divorce. This consent can be given at the hearing (if any) or before it. If the respondent wishes to indicate his consent before the hearing, he must do so by giving the district judge notice to that effect signed personally by him (FPR 1991, r 2.10). In practice, in an undefended divorce, this is given in the Acknowledgement of Service form returned by the respondent to the court following service of the petition on him. All a respondent has to do is answer 'yes' to one of the standard questions and sign the form personally.

The respondent may give notice to the court at any time before decree nisi that he does not consent, or that he withdraws consent already given. No reason for this is needed (FPR 1991, r 2.10).

Even after the decree nisi has been granted, the court has discretion to rescind the decree nisi on the respondent's application if satisfied that the petitioner misled the respondent (whether intentionally or unintentionally) about any matter which he took into account in deciding to give his consent (MCA 1973, s 10(1)).

This could apply in a situation where the respondent was misled about a financial or property matter, but could also apply where the respondent was misled about the petitioner's intention to remarry. However, in many cases the court will use its discretion to grant the decree absolute even though the respondent has been misled by the petitioner, so long as this does not have serious consequences.

3.4.5.3 Effect of cohabitation on separation

Section 2(5) of the MCA 1973 applies to the continuity of separation in the same way as it does to desertion (see **3.4.4.2**). Therefore, in deciding whether the living apart has been continuous, a period not exceeding, or periods together not exceeding, six months will be ignored. However, they must be added to the total period of separation so that the time that the parties have actually lived apart is at least two years.

3.4.5.4 Financial position of the respondent (MCA 1973, s 10(2))

If the only fact found is Fact D (or Fact E, see **3.4.6**) the respondent may apply to the court for a consideration of his financial position following the divorce (MCA 1973, s 10(2)).

If such an application is made, the court must consider all the circumstances and will not make the decree absolute unless satisfied that:

(a)   the petitioner should not be required to make any financial provision for the respondent; or

(b)   the financial provision made is fair and reasonable, or the best that can be made in the circumstances (MCA 1973, s 10(3)).

The court may proceed without observing the above requirements if it is satisfied that the circumstances make it desirable that the decree should be made absolute without delay *and* that the court has obtained a satisfactory undertaking from the petitioner that he will make such financial provision for the respondent as the court may approve (MCA 1973, s 10(4)).

In practice, s 10 is rarely used, but it can sometimes be of use to a respondent if the petitioner is anxious to obtain the divorce and the threat of a s 10 application will persuade him to agree to a more favourable financial settlement. It is not a defence to the divorce but, in such circumstances, a useful negotiating mechanism. The court has no power under this section actually to make financial orders, so it will generally insist that a court order is obtained in ancillary proceedings under MCA 1973 before the decree absolute is granted.

If the court exercised its discretion under s 10(4) to enable the decree absolute to be granted without satisfactory provision being made (it might do so, eg, if the petitioner's new partner was about to have his child and he urgently wanted to marry her), it would still insist on detailed provisions being included in any undertaking given by the petitioner.

3.4.6 Fact E: five years' separation

(e)   That the parties to the marriage have lived apart for a continuous period of at least five years immediately preceding the petition. (MCA 1973, s 1(2)(e))

After five years' separation, there is no need for the petitioner to obtain the respondent's consent to the divorce and either party can petition. Living apart has the same meaning as in Fact D (see **3.4.5.1**).

There is no defence to a Fact E petition except to deny the separation, or to prove grave hardship under s 5 of the MCA 1973 (see **3.4.6.1**).

The decree may also be delayed by the respondent asking for his financial position to be considered under s 10(2) of the MCA 1973 (see **3.4.5.4**).

3.4.6.1 Grave hardship

It is a defence to proceedings for divorce, where the only fact found is Fact E, that the dissolution of the marriage would result in grave financial or other hardship to the respondent *and* in all the circumstances it would be wrong to dissolve the marriage (MCA 1973, s 5(1)).

In deciding whether s 5 applies, the court must take account of all the circumstances, including the parties' conduct, the interests of the parties, and the interests of any children or other persons concerned (MCA 1973, s 5(2)).

In *Talbot v Talbot* (1971) 115 SJ 870, the husband left his wife for another woman and ceased maintaining his wife and children. He obtained a divorce under Fact E. The court held that the s 5 defence did not apply as his wife's hardship arose from the breakdown of the marriage and not from the prospective divorce. Accordingly, granting the decree would not add to it. The court may also grant the decree even though grave hardship does result, provided it is satisfied that it is not wrong to grant it. In *Brickell v Brickell* [1973] 3 All ER 508, the Court of Appeal looked at the surrounding circumstances, including the conduct of the parties, and concluded that the husband was entitled to a decree, even though the wife would suffer grave financial hardship, because the wife had behaved so badly during the marriage.

The grave hardship most commonly pleaded is financial; this will include the loss of the chance of acquiring any benefit which the respondent might acquire if the marriage were not dissolved (MCA 1973, s 5(3)). If, for example, the husband was contributing to an occupational pension scheme, his wife could be faced with grave financial hardship if he obtained a divorce because she would then cease to be entitled to a widow's pension under his pension scheme (*Julian v Julian* (1973) 116 SJ 763). However, the defence would not succeed if the petitioner could show that the hardship was not grave because, for example, the wife was entitled to her own occupational pension, or the husband could compensate her for the loss with, say, a deferred annuity, or by 'earmarking' the pension or 'splitting' it (see **4.7**). In practice, this defence is usually used by the respondent to persuade the petitioner to make satisfactory financial provision.

Grave hardship may take other forms and may necessitate examination of hardship caused by religious censure or social ostracism. In practice, it is very difficult to establish that such other hardships are grave enough to warrant refusing a decree.

3.4.6.2 Distinction between MCA 1973, s 5 and s 10(2) of the MCA 1973

Section 5 is a complete defence, therefore, if the defence succeeds, the couple remain married. Section 10(2) merely delays the decree absolute. Section 5 requires the respondent to establish 'grave' financial or other hardship, whereas under s 10(2) the respondent must merely show that the provision is not fair and reasonable. It is easier to establish that s 10(2) applies, but its effect is less drastic.

3.4.6.3 Effect of cohabitation on separation

The effect of cohabitation on Fact E is the same as on Fact D (see **3.4.5.3**).

3.5   Protection of children: Matrimonial Causes Act 1973, s 41

Although children are not parties to the divorce, it is accepted that they suffer most on a breakdown of marriage. Therefore, the welfare of the children must be considered before a divorce is finalised.

3.5.1   Child of the family

The MCA 1973 requires the court to consider the welfare of any child who is a 'child of the family'. A child of the family is a child who is either:

(a)   a child of both parties to the marriage; or

(b)   any other child (not having been placed with the parties as foster parents by the local authority or voluntary organisation) who has been treated by both parties as a child of the family (MCA 1973, s 52(1)).

The definition therefore applies to all natural children of both parties, but can apply to a wide variety of more distantly related or unrelated children, for example, step-children or adopted children.

3.5.2   Protection of children on divorce under MCA 1973, s 41

In any proceedings for a decree of divorce or judicial separation the court must consider:

(a)   whether there are any children of the family to whom s 41 applies. The section will apply to any child of the family who, at the date when the court considers the case, is under 16, or any other child of the family of 16 and over to whom the court directs that s 41 shall apply. This could cover a child still in full-time education or who is suffering from a disability; and

(b)   where there are any such children, whether in the light of the arrangements which have been, or are proposed to be, made for their upbringing or welfare it should exercise any of its powers under CA 1989 with respect to any of them (eg that the child resides with a particular parent, or that the child has contact with a parent).

By r 2.39 of the FPR 1991, if no application for a CA 1989 order is pending, this function will normally be carried out by the district judge. He will usually decide on the papers alone without any hearing. In such a case, the court is unlikely to wish to exercise any of its powers under the CA 1989 (for the detailed procedure, see **3.9.12**).

3.5.3   Power to delay decree absolute

The court is given the power to delay the grant of the decree absolute if:

(a)   the circumstances of the case require it, or are likely to require it, to exercise any of its powers under the CA 1989 with respect to any such child; and

(b)   it is not in a position to exercise that power without giving further consideration to the case; and

(c)   there are exceptional circumstances which make it desirable in the interests of the child that the court should give a direction under s 41.

In reality, this power is rarely exercised. However, it could apply, for example, where the court considers that there is a problem with the arrangements for the children, it asks the parents to attend court to explain the circumstances but the parents fail to co-operate and do not attend the appointment. By delaying the decree the court might force the parents to address themselves to the problems and to work out satisfactory arrangements.

3.6 Nullity

This section gives an outline of the decree of nullity which can, in certain circumstances, be sought as an alternative to a decree of divorce. In comparison with divorce, relatively few decrees of nullity are sought.

3.6.1 General

A decree of nullity may declare that a marriage is either void from the outset, in which case it is treated as never having existed at all, or voidable, in which case it will be treated as being valid and subsisting until the decree is obtained.

3.6.2 Void marriages

A marriage will be void in situations which include the following:

(a)   where the parties are too closely related to each other; or

(b)   either party was under 16 years of age at the time of the ceremony; or

(c)   either party was already lawfully married (MCA 1973, s 11).

If a marriage is void, it never existed. Therefore, a decree is not needed to end it. However, since a decree is needed if ancillary financial orders are required, a decree is usually obtained.

3.6.3 Voidable marriages

A marriage will be voidable in situations which include the following:

(a)   non-consummation, either due to incapacity of one party or wilful refusal (non-consummation does not give rise to a voidable civil partnership as, in contrast to marriage, there is no requirement that the relationship between civil partners be of a sexual nature); or

(b)   lack of consent, for example, due to duress; or

(c)   one party was suffering from a mental disorder such as to make them unfit for marriage; or

(d)   an interim gender recognition certificate was issued to the respondent after the marriage.

A voidable marriage exists until such time as a decree of nullity is obtained. A bar to obtaining a decree can exist if the respondent satisfies the court, first, that the petitioner, knowing that the marriage could be ended, behaved in such a way as to lead the respondent reasonably to believe that he would not seek to end it and, secondly, that it would be unjust to the respondent to grant the decree (MCA 1973, s 13(1)).

Generally, the petitioner must apply for the decree within three years of the date of the marriage. This does not apply to non-consummation cases nor to cases based on an interim gender recognition certificate, and, in any event, the court also has a discretion to extend the time limit (MCA 1973, s 13(4)).

3.6.4 Consequences of a decree of nullity

3.6.4.1 Ancillary orders

The parties to a suit for nullity are entitled to apply for all those orders in relation to children, property and finance as are available on divorce.

3.6.4.2 Children

Children born to parents who subsequently obtain a decree of nullity are automatically legitimate if the parents' marriage is voidable, because the marriage existed up to the time of the decree. If the marriage is void, the children will be legitimate if, at the time of conception (or the celebration of the marriage if this is later), both or either of the parents reasonably believed the marriage was valid and the father was domiciled in England and Wales at the time of the birth, or, if he died before the birth, was so domiciled immediately before his death (Legitimacy Act 1976, s 1).

3.6.4.3 Wills

A voidable marriage revokes a previous will, whereas a void marriage, as it never existed, does not have this effect.

When a decree of nullity is granted, whether in respect of a void or voidable marriage, it will have the same effect on a will as a decree of divorce. This means that the former spouse is to be treated as having died on the date of the decree.

Neither spouse will be able to claim in the event of the other's intestacy.

3.6.5 Divorce or nullity?

In some cases, there can be grounds for both divorce and nullity. It is generally better for clients to apply for divorce in these circumstances, as only in divorce is there a procedure known as the 'Special Procedure' available for undefended suits which is cheap and simple. There is no equivalent for nullity cases and every case must be held in open court which adds to the cost and publicity. However, Legal Representation is available, subject to financial eligibility and merits (eg Legal Representation will not be granted if divorce would be a reasonable alternative), even for undefended nullity proceedings. As nullity can be obtained in the first year of marriage, and as there can be religious reasons for wanting to have the marriage declared non-existent rather than dissolved, nullity is sometimes preferred.

3.7 Judicial separation

An alternative to a decree of divorce is a decree of judicial separation (or separation order for civil partners). It does not dissolve the marriage but can be used, for example, if religious beliefs forbid divorce.

3.7.1 Grounds for judicial separation

The grounds on which a decree of judicial separation can be obtained are the same as the facts that need to be proved to obtain a divorce (MCA 1973, s 1(2)) (see **3.4.2** to **3.4.6**). This means that s 2 of the MCA 1973 will apply regarding periods of reconciliation and cohabitation, and s 41 will apply in relation to any children of the family. However, the parties do not need to show irretrievable breakdown (MCA 1973, s 17(2)). The Special Procedure available in undefended divorces applies to undefended petitions for judicial separation although, in contrast to divorce, there is only one stage to the decree. The public funding position on judicial separation is the same as for divorce.

3.7.2 Effect of decree of judicial separation

When a decree of judicial separation has been obtained, the parties are still married as the decree does not dissolve the marriage but only releases the parties from the duty to live together.

3.7.3 Reasons for seeking judicial separation

Reasons for seeking judicial separation include the following:

(a) Judicial separation can be sought at any time after the marriage, so this could assist a spouse who separates within the first year who cannot start divorce proceedings.

(b) The same financial and other ancillary orders can be obtained on judicial separation as on divorce.

(c) Some clients have religious or moral objections to divorce and so this decree offers an alternative.

(d) The fact used in the judicial separation proceedings can subsequently be used as proof of a fact in later divorce proceedings (MCA 1973, s 4(1)).

Note that judicial separation does not affect existing wills and advice should be given to clients recommending that they review their wills in the light of their separation. If, subsequently, a spouse dies intestate, his or her property will devolve as if the other spouse was already dead, so the surviving spouse will not benefit.

3.8 Presumption of death and dissolution of marriage

If the respondent has disappeared in circumstances where it is reasonable to suppose he is dead, the petitioner can apply under s 19 of the MCA 1973 for a presumption of death and dissolution of marriage. There is a presumption that, after seven years' continuous absence, during which time the petitioner has had no reason to believe that the respondent was alive, the respondent is dead.

3.9 Divorce procedure

3.9.1 Legal Help and Legal Representation

On marriage breakdown, it is usual for both spouses to seek legal advice. A solicitor must be able to assess whether a client is eligible for public funding towards his legal costs and advise him accordingly.

An outline of public funding is provided in **Chapter 2**. This section highlights some points of particular relevance to the divorce suit itself.

Legal Representation is not available for undefended divorces save in exceptional circumstances (see **3.9.1.2**). Legal Help is intended to cover the whole of the divorce, including the drafting of the divorce documents. If a client is eligible, Legal Help enables up to £500 worth of work to be undertaken at a fixed rate.

3.9.1.1 Solicitor not acting

Where a solicitor advises under Legal Help, he is not treated by the court as 'acting' for the client and so the solicitor's name will not appear on the court record. The client is a litigant in person, which means that all procedural documents in the divorce must be signed by the client personally.

If Legal Representation is subsequently obtained (eg for an ancillary financial claim), the solicitor must place his name on the court record for that matter by filing a Notice of Acting with the court and serving any other party with a copy. However, so long as the divorce remains undefended, the client will remain a litigant in person in the divorce.

3.9.1.2 Legal Representation

Legal Representation is available for defended divorces but will rarely be granted.

It is possible for Legal Representation to be obtained in an undefended suit, but only where the matter is transferred to open court, for example, for a jurisdictional point to be resolved, or where, by reason of physical or mental incapacity, it is impracticable for the applicant to proceed without representation.

3.9.2 The first interview

The first interview is of crucial importance. It is the first meeting with the client and gives the opportunity for the solicitor to obtain information needed from the client as well as to give advice and plan what is to be done (for general advice on interviewing, see **1.2.4**).

When a client seeks advice on his marriage, it is important to discover what the client wants. Does he want a divorce, or are the parties hoping for a reconciliation?

Assuming that the client wants to obtain a divorce, the following areas will need to be covered in the interview. Appropriate use of a checklist or instruction sheet will help to obtain the information. For example:

(a)   general advice on divorce and alternatives, for example, grounds, timing, mediation;

(b)   information sufficient to complete the divorce petition and the supporting documents;

(c)   general advice on costs, as well as completing the Controlled Work 1 Form if appropriate;

(d)   financial matters, for example, property and maintenance principles and orders that could be made;

(e)   children, for example, advice on general principles and orders available;

(f)   welfare benefits if client has no income;

(g)   public funding: statutory charge. If the client is eligible for public funding for ancillary matters, advice must be given on the effect that the statutory charge will have on any order obtained (for a more detailed explanation, see **2.9**);

(h)   injunction law and procedure. If the client has problems with domestic abuse, appropriate advice should be given (see **Chapter 14**).

A file note of the interview should be made as soon as possible after the interview. A letter should be written to the client reminding him of what happened at the interview and what advice was given, as well as reminding the client of any action he has asked for. Any advice given on costs, especially public funding, should be repeated.

3.9.3 The petition

3.9.3.1 The prescribed information

The FPR 1991 provide that every divorce must be begun by petition. The Rules also set out a list of the information to be contained in a petition. In practice, standard form petitions are available from law stationers or via computer software packages, which are specifically drafted (see **Appendix 3(A)**) to enable the solicitor to insert the prescribed information. This is as follows:

(a)   Names of the parties and date and place of the marriage. This information should be copied exactly from the marriage certificate.

(b)   The last address where the parties lived as husband and wife.

(c)   The ground on which it is alleged that the court has jurisdiction.

(d)   Present occupations and residences of the parties. There are provisions enabling the petitioner's address to be concealed if this is necessary for the protection of the petitioner, for example, where there is a fear of violence from the respondent.

(e)   Information about the children of the family. The full names and dates of birth of all children of the family under 18 years must be given; and where there are children of the family of over 18 years, their names should be given together with the words 'over 18 years'. If any child is over 16 the petition must include details of any further education or training being undertaken.

(f)   Information about any other living child born to the wife during marriage. This will cover any children born to the wife who are not children of the family, for example, children from an extramarital relationship. Details of their full names and dates of birth must be given as above.

(g)   Information about any other court proceedings relating to the marriage or to any children of the family, or between the parties regarding any property of either or both. If there have been any earlier proceedings, full details must be given, including any order made and, if the proceedings related to the marriage, whether the parties have lived together since any order was made.

(h)   Information about whether any action has been taken through the Child Support Agency relating to any children of the family. If an application has been made, details must be given, including the amount awarded.

(i)   Information about any continuing proceedings outside England and Wales relating to the marriage. It is important for the court to be aware of any foreign proceedings relating to the marriage. In some circumstances, the court can adjourn the divorce proceedings until the outcome of the foreign proceedings is known.

(j)   Whether or not any agreement between the parties has been made or is proposed for the support of any party or any child of the family. This statement is needed only if the petition is based on five years' separation (Fact E). It is required in these cases because of the grave financial hardship defence (see 3.4.6.1). The court therefore needs to know about any existing arrangements or proposals.

(k)   Statement that the marriage has irretrievably broken down.

(l)   Statement of the Fact under s 1(2) of the MCA 1973 relied upon, together with particulars of the incidents relied on, but not the evidence by which these will be proved.

The wording used to describe the particulars of the incidents relied upon is a drafting matter for the solicitor. However, examples of how the particulars may appear in the petition are as follows:

Fact A – 'In or about November 2007 in Barchester, Wessex the Respondent committed adultery with a person whom the Petitioner does not wish to name'

Fact D – 'The parties separated on 17 February 2006 and have not lived together since that time'

(m)   The petition must end with a prayer for the following:

(i)   dissolution of the marriage;

(ii)   any claim for ancillary financial relief which is required. It is important that the petitioner makes an application for all forms of ancillary relief which might be needed in the petition. If this is not done, leave of the court will be required for a later application. The petitioner could also be prejudiced as orders for periodical payments can only be backdated to the date of application, which will be the date of the petition unless leave of the court is needed for a later application when it will be the date of actual application. If the petitioner remarries, she will be prevented from making a claim for a lump sum or property adjustment order. If she had applied in the prayer, ie before remarriage, a hearing could take place after remarriage. There is provision on the standard form to claim ancillary relief for any children of the family. If a CSA application is to be made, the court will not usually have jurisdiction to grant periodical payments. However, other forms of ancillary relief, for example a lump sum order, could be applied for;

(iii)   a claim for costs if required. In a divorce under Legal Help, costs will only be those of a litigant in person and, therefore, it is not usual to ask for costs, especially as there is a risk that if costs are sought the respondent might be sufficiently annoyed to defend the petition. When the petition is drafted, it is not certain whether the proceedings will be defended or not, therefore practitioners often draft the prayer for costs in such a way as to ask for costs only if the petition is defended. Where the petitioner is paying privately, costs may be claimed in relation to fault-based divorces. The costs being sought in the prayer will only cover costs incurred in dissolving the marriage. Costs for ancillary matters, for example financial orders, will be sought separately during the ancillary proceedings.

The petition will be signed by the petitioner personally if advice is being obtained under Legal Help, because the petitioner is treated as a litigant in person. If the petitioner is not obtaining advice under Legal Help, the petition may be signed by the solicitor either in his own name, or in the firm's name or, if, unusually, counsel drafted the petition, by counsel.

The remainder of the petition lists the names and addresses of persons to be served with the petition and the petitioner's address for service. Here, although the petitioner receiving advice under Legal Help should strictly add his personal address, a concession enables the name of his solicitors to appear provided the address is stated to be 'care of' the solicitors. This ensures that court documents are sent direct to the solicitors rather than to the petitioner. If there is a co-respondent in a Fact A petition, the co-respondent must be served with the petition, and his address must be added.

3.9.3.2   Amendments

If an error or omission is discovered in a petition – for example, the prayer does not include an application for ancillary financial relief, or the petitioner's domicile is stated incorrectly – it will have to be amended. The petition can be amended without leave of the court before directions for trial are made, unless an answer has been filed in which case leave is required. After directions for trial, leave of the court will generally be needed for amendments (FPR 1991, r 2.11(1)).

Leave can be given without notice if the respondent agrees to the amendment. If the respondent does not agree, an on notice application to the district judge will have to be made. Whenever a petition is amended after service, the amended petition will have to be served on the respondent (and co-respondent).

In practice, very minor amendments – for example, an incorrect date of birth of a child, or incorrect occupation of a party – can be corrected by referring to the error in the petitioner's affidavit (Form M7). The district judge can then give leave for the petition to stand as corrected without the need for re-service.

3.9.4   The supporting documents

The following additional documents must be prepared and filed with the petition.

3.9.4.1   Statement relating to the proposed arrangements for any children of the family (Form M4)

Form M4 is a standard form which gives details of the children of the family. It provides the court with the information it needs in order to consider the arrangements for the children under s 41 of the MCA 1973. (See **Appendix 3(B)**.)

Form M4 covers accommodation, education, child-care arrangements, health, maintenance and arrangements which have been made or which are proposed for contact with the parent with whom the child does not live full time. If the child is disabled or has a medical problem, Form M4 will have to give details of this and, where necessary, be supported by a medical report or doctor's letter giving details of the problem and its likely effect on the child. The petitioner must always sign this form personally even if paying privately.

If practicable, Form M4 should be agreed with the respondent (FPR 1991, r 2.2). This should be attempted by sending the completed and signed Form to the respondent before filing the petition. The Form enables the respondent to add his agreement and signature before returning it to the petitioner. If the respondent's agreement has not been, or cannot be, obtained then the petitioner can still file the petition. In these circumstances, it would be sensible to file with Form M4 a letter explaining the situation to the court.

3.9.4.2   Marriage certificate

If the client cannot produce the original marriage certificate, a certified copy can be obtained on payment of a small fee either from the Superintendent Registrar of Marriages for the district where the marriage took place, or from the General Register Office. If the marriage certificate is in a foreign language, an authenticated translation must also be obtained and filed with the divorce documents.

3.9.4.3   Certificate relating to reconciliation (Form M3)

Where a solicitor is acting for a client, there is an obligation to file a certificate in Form M3 which states whether or not the solicitor has discussed with the petitioner the possibility of a reconciliation and given him details of agencies which are qualified to help effect a reconciliation (FPR 1991, r 2.6(3)).

There is no duty on a solicitor to discuss reconciliation in every case in which he acts. This is left to his discretion and, if he decides not to discuss this matter, he will inform the court of this on Form M3.

The obligation to file this form does not arise if a client is receiving advice under Legal Help as the client is then acting in person. However, this does not prevent a solicitor from advising a client who is receiving advice under Legal Help on reconciliation if appropriate.

3.9.4.4   Service copies of the petition and Form M4

It is necessary to file the original petition plus one copy for each party who is to be served. One copy will be sufficient unless a co-respondent is involved in a Fact A petition, in which case two service copies will be needed.

Form M4 is served on the respondent even if he has already signed the form and agreed to the arrangements; therefore, the original plus one copy of this form should be filed. It is never served on a co-respondent.

3.9.4.5   Fee or application for exemption from fees

A fee is payable on filing the petition. If the client is receiving advice under Legal Help, or is receiving income support or family credit, he is exempt from the fee. However, a form applying for exemption must be completed and filed at court.

3.9.5   Filing

The petition and the appropriate additional documents and fee can be filed at any divorce county court (or the Divorce Registry in London).

3.9.6   Service of the petition

The petition and other appropriate documents must be served on the respondent and any co-respondent (FPR 1991, rr 2.9(1) and 2.24).

3.9.6.1   Usual method of service

The court will usually serve the petition by sending it by first-class post to the address given in the petition.

The court attaches the following to each service copy of the petition:

(a)   A Notice of Proceedings (Form M5). This is a general explanation to the respondent of the divorce procedure with detailed instructions on completing and returning the Acknowledgement of Service.

(b)   An Acknowledgement of Service (Form M6). This is an important procedural document which could furnish proof of service of the petition or of the fact relied on as well as other useful information, for example, whether the respondent intends to defend (see **3.9.7**).

(c)   A copy of the statement as to the arrangements for the children (Form M4). This is attached only to the respondent's copy of the petition. The respondent may have already seen and signed this document because a copy will have already been sent to him by the petitioner.

If the respondent then completes and returns the Acknowledgement of Service to the court, this is proof of service (FPR 1991, r 2.9(5)). When the court receives the Acknowledgement from the respondent, it will send a copy to the petitioner's solicitors.

3.9.6.2   Alternative methods of service

If postal service by the court is unsuccessful or inappropriate, alternative methods of service are available, and proof of service will depend on which method is used.

Personal service

(a)   *By court bailiff.* The petitioner can request bailiff service by lodging the appropriate form. A fee is payable unless the petitioner has filed an exemption form. A description of the respondent, normally a photograph, must also be lodged in order to enable the bailiff to identify the respondent. The bailiff will then serve the documents personally and file a certificate of service. If the Acknowledgement of Service is then returned by the respondent, this will be proof of service; if not, the bailiff's certificate will be used.

(b)   *Service through the petitioner.* The petitioner can request that service is carried out through him under r 2.9(2)(b) of the FPR 1991. A process server will be instructed, or the petitioner's solicitors will themselves serve the documents. The Rules prohibit the petitioner himself from serving the documents on the respondent (FPR 1991, r 2.9(3)). Proof of service in these cases will be by affidavit of service by whoever served the documents.

Deemed service

If the respondent does not return the Acknowledgement of Service to the court, the petitioner can apply for deemed service if he can satisfy the court that the respondent has in fact received the petition (FPR 1991, r 2.9(6)).

An application without notice should be made to the district judge supported by an affidavit showing why the petitioner is of the view that the respondent has received the petition. This can be done by using evidence from a third party, or, for example, even from the petitioner himself that the respondent read the petition and then threw it away, or an open letter from solicitors instructed by the respondent to act for him referring to the petition.

Substituted service

Substituted service will be relevant when all the petitioner's efforts to serve by post and personal service have failed and there is insufficient evidence to apply for deemed service.

An application without notice should be made to the district judge supported by an affidavit setting out the grounds on which the application is made (FPR 1991, r 2.9(9)).

If the order is granted, it will specify the alternative method to be used. This could be by advertisement if there is a reasonable likelihood that it will come to the respondent's notice, for example, by placing it in a newspaper which he is known to read regularly. Another method that could be specified is service on another person, for example, a relative whom he visits regularly, or a person with whom he lives or works.

Dispensing with service

Dispensing with service is used only as a last resort where all other methods have failed and the district judge is of the opinion that it is impracticable to serve the petition, or for other reasons it is necessary or expedient to dispense with service (FPR 1991, r 2.9(11)). It is treated by the court very seriously as, by granting the order, the respondent can find that he is divorced without knowing that a divorce petition had been filed and having had no opportunity to defend. An application without notice should be made to the court supported by an affidavit setting out the grounds for the application (ie why there is a problem and what has been done to trace the respondent). The district judge can require the petitioner to attend to give evidence. Service will be dispensed with only where the petitioner can show that every effort has been made to trace the respondent.

3.9.6.3   Other problems with service

Finding the respondent

If the petitioner does not know the whereabouts of the respondent, enquiries must be made so that postal or personal service can be used. If particular difficulty is encountered, reference should be made to the *Practice Direction (Family Division: Disclosure of Addresses by Government Departments)* [1989] 1 All ER 765. This enables the court to request a search for the respondent's address in the records of the DWP or the Passport Service. If the respondent is in the Armed Services, the relevant service department can be asked for the respondent's address.

Serving on the co-respondent

The petition must also be served on any co-respondent. The co-respondent is not served with a copy of the statement of arrangements for the children. The same methods of service are available as for the respondent.

Service of the petition must also be proved, and this will normally be done by the co-respondent returning the completed Acknowledgement of Service to the court. If this is not done, an alternative method of proving service will have to be used, for example, an affidavit of service following bailiff service or personal service. Otherwise an order for deemed service, substituted service or, as a last resort, an order dispensing with service will have to be obtained.

Service outside England and Wales

Rule 10.6 of the FPR 1991 allows the divorce petition to be served outside England and Wales by post, personally or by substituted service without leave. Alternatively, the standard methods for such service in the High Court or county court can be used (see CPR 1998, Pt 6).

Service on a party under a disability

The court cannot serve the petition if the respondent is a minor (under 18 years of age) or a mental patient. Special rules apply and reference should be made to r 9.2 and r 9.3 of the FPR 1991.

3.9.7   Return of the Acknowledgement of Service

The respondent is required to complete and return the Acknowledgement of Service to the court within seven days of service of the petition (FPR 1991, r 10.8(2)(a)).

The respondent is given guidance as to how to complete this form in the Notice of Proceedings (Form M5). He may also have instructed his own solicitors. When the court sends a copy of the Acknowledgement of Service to the petitioner, the replies to the straightforward questions it contains may reveal the following information:

(a)   Proof of service (see **3.9.6**).

(b)   Whether the respondent intends to defend the petition. Since the reply is not binding on the respondent, he can later change his mind.

(c)   Whether the respondent is satisfied with the proposed arrangements for the children set out in Form M4. Again, he is not bound by his reply and can commence an application under CA 1989 even if he has not indicated this in his reply.

(d)   Whether the respondent has admitted adultery or consented to the decree. If the petition is based on Fact A, the respondent can admit the adultery and, provided he has signed the form personally, this will be sufficient proof of his adultery. If the petition is based on Fact D and the respondent has given his consent in this form, this will be proof of his consent, provided he has signed the form personally.

3.9.8 Requesting directions for trial

Provided the respondent has not given notice of intention to defend and a period of seven days after service of the petition has expired, the next step is for the petitioner's solicitors to lodge a request for directions, which asks for the cause to be put on the Special Procedure list (for undefended divorces), together with an affidavit containing proof of the fact relied on and other essential matters. If the respondent has given a notice of intention to defend, the petitioner must wait 28 days from service of the petition to file a request for directions.

3.9.9 Petitioner's affidavit in support of the petition

The petitioner's affidavit in support of the petition is filed with the request for directions. The Rules provide standard form affidavits to suit each Fact (see FPR 1991, Appendix 1, Form M7(a) to (e)). The affidavit is in question and answer form. The main matters which are dealt with are as follows:

(a)   The petitioner must confirm that the contents of his petition are true and that no amendments or alterations are required.

(b)   If the parties have cohabited since the date of the incidents relied on, the affidavit requires the petitioner to give details of the periods of cohabitation to ensure that the fact is not barred by s 2 of the MCA 1973.

(c)   Any corroborative evidence (FPR 1991, r 2.24(3)), for example, a medical report to confirm the injuries alleged in a Fact B petition. The Acknowledgement of Service will need to be exhibited if the petitioner is relying on it as proof of service, or if it has been signed by the respondent to admit adultery (Fact A), or to consent to the divorce (Fact D).

(d)   The petitioner must confirm that the contents of the Statement of Arrangements (Form M4) are still correct and identify the signature of the respondent on that form.

3.9.10 Directions for trial

Before the district judge can give directions, he has to check the following:

(a)   that the petition has been served. The district judge will check that proof of service is evident from the documents lodged. If the petitioner is relying on return of the Acknowledgement and it is a case where this has been signed personally by the respondent, he will check that the petitioner's affidavit identifies the respondent's signature;

(b)   that the case is undefended. The case will be undefended if:

(i)   the respondent has told the court that he does not intend to defend (usually in the Acknowledgement of Service), or

(ii)   no notice of intention has been given and seven days have elapsed since service of the petition, or

(iii) the respondent has filed a notice of intention to defend but the time limit for filing the answer has expired. Rules 2.12(1) and 2.24(1) of the FPR 1991 provide that this time limit is 28 days from the date of service of the petition;

(c)   if the petition relies on Fact D, that the respondent's consent has been given. Consent can be given either in the Acknowledgement of Service, or in a separate document (FPR 1991, r 2.24(3)).

If all the above matters are satisfied, the district judge will direct that the case be set down in the Special Procedure list (see **3.9.11**).

3.9.11 Special Procedure

Special Procedure is the standard procedure for all undefended divorces.

As soon as practicable after the case has been set down in the Special Procedure list, the district judge will consider the evidence of the petitioner. He will study the court file and in particular the petition, Form M4, the Acknowledgement of Service, the petitioner's affidavit and any exhibits (FPR 1991, r 2.36).

If the district judge is satisfied that the petitioner has proved his case, he will do the following:

(a)   complete and file a certificate to this effect;

(b)   fix a day for the decree nisi to be read out in open court by a judge or district judge;

(c)   if there is a prayer for costs in the petition, make an order for costs if he considers that the petitioner is entitled to them. If he considers that he cannot make an order for costs without further information, he can require the respondent to file a written statement of his reasons for objecting to paying the costs, or refer the matter of costs to the judge or district judge who pronounces the decree nisi. In this case, he will notify the respondent that he must attend court on the date that the decree nisi is to be pronounced to argue his case. If he fails to attend that hearing an order for costs in favour of the petitioner will almost certainly be made;

(d)   consider any children to whom s 41 of the MCA 1973 applies (see **3.9.12**).

The court will then send a copy of the district judge's certificate and the notice of the date on which the decree nisi will be granted to both parties (FPR 1991, r 2.36(2)).

If the district judge is not satisfied that the petitioner has proved his case, he can:

(a)   ask the petitioner to supply further evidence. This could clarify, for example, an uncertainty revealed in the petition relating to domicile or habitual residence, or an ambiguity in the petitioner's affidavit relating to any period during which the petitioner cohabited with the respondent;

(b)   remove the case from the Special Procedure list.

If there is a problem which cannot be resolved by supplying further information, for example, a question of whether there was sufficient behaviour to amount to grounds for a Fact B divorce or a complex jurisdictional issue, there will be a hearing in front of the judge in open court to resolve the problem. If the problem is resolved and the ground for divorce is proved, the decree nisi will be made at the hearing. If not, the petition will be dismissed. Legal Representation is available for this hearing, so the necessary application must be made.

3.9.12 Section 41 certificate

When the district judge grants a certificate that the petitioner has proved his case, he will consider the question of the arrangements for children to whom s 41 of the MCA 1973 applies (see **3.5**).

3.9.12.1 Where there is no pending application for an order under the Children Act 1989

If there has been no application under the CA 1989 made by either party, there being no dispute between the parties as to arrangements for the children, the district judge will examine Form M4 and check that the arrangements proposed are acceptable. When he has done this, he can certify that either:

(a) there are no children of the family to whom s 41 applies; or

(b) there are such children, but that the court need not exercise its powers under the CA 1989.

If, having considered Form M4, he is not satisfied that the arrangements are satisfactory, he can give one of the following directions:

(a) that the parties file further evidence as to the arrangements for the children (eg a medical report);

(b) that a welfare report be prepared;

(c) that either party, or both parties, attend before him.

The evidence so obtained might satisfy the district judge that in fact the arrangements are satisfactory, in which case he can issue a certificate that there is no need for the court to exercise its powers under the CA 1989.

If, on his initial consideration, or having made directions and further investigations the district judge considers that:

(a) the exercise of his powers is, or is likely to be, necessary but the court is not in a position to exercise them without further consideration; and

(b) there are exceptional circumstances which make it desirable in the interests of the child to do so,

then he may direct that the decree nisi of divorce is not made absolute until the court directs.

This power will be used very rarely, and only if delaying the decree will actually be in the interests of the child. This might apply where both parents were happy to proceed with the divorce but had not attempted to make arrangements for the children; withholding the decree absolute could persuade them of the seriousness of their behaviour.

3.9.12.2 Where there are pending proceedings under the Children Act 1989

Where an application has already been made under the CA 1989, it is open to the district judge either to grant a certificate under s 41 of the MCA 1973 enabling the divorce to go ahead, or to delay the grant of the decree absolute by making a direction that there are exceptional circumstances making it desirable to delay the grant of the decree absolute.

3.9.13 Decree nisi

The decree nisi (or conditional order for civil partners) will be read out on the appointed day by the judge or district judge in open court. However, unless there is any dispute as to costs, neither party need attend. A copy of the decree nisi is sent to the parties. This decree does not dissolve the marriage.

3.9.14 Decree absolute

The final step in the undefended divorce procedure is to obtain the decree absolute (or dissolution order for civil partners) which will end the marriage.

3.9.14.1 Petitioner's application

Once six weeks have elapsed since the grant of the decree nisi, the petitioner can apply for the decree absolute by lodging Form M8 together with the prescribed fee (FPR 1991, r 2.49(1)). In extremely rare cases, the court does have the power to reduce this six-week period (*Practice Direction (Divorce: Decree Absolute: Application to Expedite)* [1977] 2 All ER 714). However, when urgency is anticipated it is better to speed up the earlier part of the divorce proceedings rather than relying on this power.

If the petitioner is receiving advice under Legal Help, he will be exempt from the fee.

The district judge will grant the decree absolute provided that the matters set out in r 2.49(2) of the FPR 1991 are satisfied:

(a)   that there is no appeal or re-hearing relating to the decree nisi;

(b)   that the provisions enabling the respondent's financial position to be considered under s 10(2)–(4) of the MCA 1973 do not apply or have been complied with;

(c)   that the court has complied with s 41 of the MCA 1973 and there is no direction to delay the decree absolute;

(d)   that no intervention by the Queen's Proctor or any other person is pending;

(e)   that any order under s 10A of the MCA 1973 has been complied with (see **3.9.14.3**).

The decree absolute certificate (Form M9) is sent to the petitioner and the respondent. The marriage is now dissolved.

It is important not to apply for the decree absolute automatically after the six-week period as there could be good reasons to delay. For example, it might be important to preserve the petitioner's right of occupation under the FLA 1996 (see **9.6.2.1**), or even at this late stage the petitioner might be considering a reconciliation.

If the petitioner delays applying for the decree absolute for more than 12 months after the decree nisi, the application must be accompanied by a written explanation for the delay. This is to ensure that there has not been an attempted reconciliation which may have prejudiced the grounds, and that no child has been born who should be considered under s 41 of the MCA 1973.

3.9.14.2 Respondent's application

The petitioner may choose not to apply to make the decree absolute for the reasons mentioned above, or perhaps where the petitioner knows that the respondent is anxious to remarry and wishes to use the delay as a negotiating weapon in the financial proceedings. In this situation, the respondent can apply for the decree absolute once a period of some four and a half months has elapsed from the date of the decree nisi (ie three months after the earliest date (ie six weeks after decree nisi) on which the petitioner could have obtained the decree absolute) (MCA 1973, s 9(2)). The petitioner must be served with notice of the application (FPR 1991, r 2.50(2)). The court will then consider the respondent's application and any objections that the petitioner has made. The court can then decide to make the decree absolute, require further investigations or, if necessary, rescind the decree nisi.

3.9.14.3 Religious marriages

Historically, some family clients have found themselves in the difficult position of being divorced in law and yet their marriage remains intact according to their own religious rules and customs, usually because the other party refuses to co-operate in ending the marriage according to religious practices. The Divorce (Religious Marriages) Act 2002 inserted provisions into the MCA 1973 designed to overcome this problem. Section 10A applies where the parties have been married according to particular religious usages and must co-operate if the marriage is to be dissolved according to those usages. The court may, on application by either party, order that the decree nisi is not to be made absolute until such time as the parties produce a declaration to the court confirming that they have taken such steps as are necessary to dissolve the marriage according to the appropriate religious usages.

3.10 Defended divorces

As defended divorces are so rare, the detail of defended procedure is outside the scope of this book and reference should be made to specialist textbooks. Certain points should, however, be borne in mind.

3.10.1 Legal Representation

It is extremely rare for Legal Representation to be granted for defending divorces.

If, however, Legal Representation is granted, detailed explanation and advice must be given to a client contemplating a defended divorce of the effects of the statutory charge (see **2.9**).

3.10.2 Notice of intention to defend

If the respondent intends to defend, he will normally return the Acknowledgement of Service stating that he intends to defend the petition. He must give this notice within seven days from service of the petition (FPR 1991, r 10.8(2)(a)).

If he does not file this notice, he can still file an answer. If he does give notice, he is under no obligation to file an answer if he changes his mind.

3.10.3 Filing an answer

The answer is the defence to the petition and must be filed within 28 days of service of the petition (FPR 1991, r 2.12(2)). Problems are often encountered with this time limit, sometimes because the respondent decides to defend only after it has expired; delay in obtaining Legal Representation can also mean that the time limit is exceeded. In these circumstances, reference should be made to r 2.14 of the FPR 1991.

When the case becomes defended, the district judge can transfer the case to the High Court. He will do this only if he considers that, owing to its complexity, difficulty or gravity, it is more appropriate to deal with it in the High Court.

3.10.4 Subsequent procedure

Further statements of case can be filed. Directions for trial will be given. Eventually, usually after a long delay, there will be a hearing in open court.

3.11 Costs

On an application for costs, the decision is always in the discretion of the court, but the general principle is that an order for costs will be made in favour of the successful party. Sometimes such applications are not made, or are expressed as to be pursued only if the divorce is defended. This is particularly common where the divorce is not fault-based and it is thought that to pursue costs would introduce animosity into the proceedings, or where the petitioner is a litigant in person and it may be uneconomic to pursue costs of only a small amount.

3.12 Chapter summary

3.12.1 Divorce law

(1)   No divorce proceedings can begin until one year after the marriage. Decrees of nullity and judicial separation can be sought at any time after the marriage.

(2)   The English courts will have jurisdiction to hear a divorce only if one of the grounds in s 5 of the Domicile and Matrimonial Proceedings Act 1973 is satisfied (these relate to the parties' habitual residence or domicile).

(3)   The only ground for divorce is that the marriage has broken down irretrievably.

(4)   One or more of 'the five facts' must be proved

Fact A: Adultery and Intolerability (not applicable to civil partners)

Fact B: Behaviour

Fact C: Desertion

Fact D: Two Years' Separation and Consent

Fact E: Five Years' Separation.

(5)   Section 10(2) of the MCA 1973 enables a respondent in a Fact D or Fact E divorce to ask the court to consider his financial position after the divorce.

(6)   Section 5(1) of the MCA 1973 is a defence to a Fact E divorce. The respondent must prove that the divorce would result in grave financial or other hardship and it would be wrong to dissolve the marriage.

(7)   Section 41 of the MCA 1973 imposes a duty in divorce proceedings to consider the welfare of any 'child of the family'.

(8)   A decree of nullity can declare that a marriage either never existed at all (a void marriage), or that it did exist but, due to certain circumstances, it has been ended (a voidable marriage).

(9)   A decree of judicial separation can be obtained by proving one of the five facts.

3.12.2 Divorce procedure

UNDEFENDED DIVORCE: SPECIAL PROCEDURE CHECKLIST

PETITIONER

RESPONDENT

(1) Files at court:
- (a) Marriage certificate;
- (b) Petition + copy(ies);
- (c) Form M4 + copy (this should be sent to respondent for signature before filing);
- (d) Form M3 (reconciliation) (only if solicitor on court record);
- (e) Fee or application for exemption.

(2) Receives from court notification of case number allocated.

(3) Receives from court:
- (a) Copy petition;
- (b) Copy Form M4;
- (c) Notice of Proceedings;
- (d) Acknowledgement of Service (Form M6).

(4) Returns completed Form M6 to court.

(5) Receives from court photocopy of completed Form M6.

(6) Files at court:
- (a) Request for Directions;
- (b) Affidavit of Evidence + exhibits.

(7) *Both* parties receive from court: a copy of the district judge's certificate, a copy of s 41 certificate and notice of the date fixed for pronouncement of decree nisi in open court by judge/ district judge.

(8) Decree nisi pronounced – parties need not attend unless directed.

(9) *Both* parties would be notified of any directions made by court if district judge not satisfied with arrangements for children, eg further information or appointment at court.

(10) *Both* parties receive from court copy of decree nisi.

(11) Petitioner files notice of application for decree nisi to be made absolute (after 6 weeks from grant of decree nisi) and the fee (if appropriate).

(12) *Both* parties receive from court copy decree absolute.

Chapter 4

Ancillary Finance: The Law

4.1 Introduction

This chapter deals with the law relating to financial provision on marriage breakdown. It covers the range of financial orders available to spouses under the MCA 1973 and to civil partners under the CPA 2004, and the principles applied by the court when making those orders. This chapter also deals with the wide range of orders available for children under the MCA 1973. However, in the majority of cases, maintenance for children is now governed by the Child Support Act 1991 (CSA 1991) (as amended by the Child Support Pensions and Social Security Act 2000) to the exclusion of the MCA 1973. The CSA 1991 will be considered in **Chapter 7**. However, as financial provision between spouses is closely linked with provision for any children, it is important to appreciate the impact of the CSA 1991 on orders made by the court under the MCA 1973.

A significant minority of maintenance applications for children will continue to be dealt with by the court, and the court also retains sole jurisdiction to make lump sum and property adjustment orders in favour of children.

It should also be borne in mind that the nature of the civil partnership family is such that it may not fall under the provisions of the CSA 1991, for example because the potential payer is not the child's natural parent. Therefore it is more likely to prove necessary for a civil partner to turn to the court for financial orders for children than is the case for a spouse.

4.2 The powers of the court

4.2.1 Orders available

The powers of the court to make financial orders are found in ss 22 to 24B of the MCA 1973 (see **Appendix 1(A)**). The orders fall into two main categories: income orders and capital orders. The *income orders* are:

(a) maintenance pending suit;

(b) periodical payments;

(c) secured periodical payments.

The *capital orders* are more diverse and include:

(a) lump sum orders;

(b)   property adjustment orders (for property to be transferred or held on trust);

(c)   orders for sale;

(d)   pension sharing orders.

4.2.2   When available

Spouses may apply for any of these orders, or indeed all of them, on or after the filing of the divorce petition. However, with the exception of maintenance pending suit (MPS), the application cannot be heard until decree nisi and no order will take effect until decree absolute. By contrast, most applications for provision for children may be made and heard at any time, and such orders take immediate effect.

AVAILABILITY OF FINANCIAL ORDERS

Petition	*Decree nisi*	*Decree absolute*
Application for financial provision can be made	Order for financial provision for spouse can be made	Order for financial provision can come into effect ⟶
		(Periodical payments can be back-dated to the date of the application)
Order for MPS for spouse can be made and take effect ⟶		MPS ends
Order for financial provision for child(ren) can be made and take effect ⟶		

In most cases, the arrangements for financial provision for a spouse are finalised after the divorce itself has gone through. However, parties should take care to apply for financial provision before remarrying, because after they have remarried they are no longer entitled to apply (see MCA 1973, s 28(3) in **Appendix 1(A)** and **10.5.2**).

4.3   Income orders

4.3.1   Maintenance pending suit

An order for periodical payments for a spouse cannot take effect until decree absolute. However, the divorce client may be in urgent need of money before then. Such clients may wish to apply for MPS under s 22 of the the MCA 1973 (the equivalent for civil partners is maintenance pending the outcome of dissolution proceedings). As the name suggests, MPS is an order for regular payments designed to tide a spouse over until the divorce is determined. At that time, an order for full periodical payments may take effect. In practice, however, the court will often not hear an ancillary relief application until some time after decree absolute is declared. If this would cause hardship to the applicant, an application for an interim periodical payments order could be made.

The application for MPS may be made, heard and take effect at any time after the petition has been filed. Any order will terminate on the grant or dismissal of the divorce. MPS is not available for a child; neither is it necessary, because periodical payments may be obtained for a child of the family (if appropriate) as soon as the petition is filed, or alternatively an application may be made to the Child Support Agency for a maintenance assessment.

Such MPS applications are not frequently pursued, as potential applicants often prefer to rely on welfare benefits. There are a number of reasons for this:

(a)   Most applicants will require Legal Representation in order to make an application. This inevitably causes delay, so that, in any event, the applicant has to resort to welfare benefits in the interim.

(b)   In practice, the court generally orders only modest sums to be paid, because the purpose of MPS is to provide adequate temporary provision during the proceedings. However, in *TL v ML and Others* [2006] 1 FLR 465 it was stressed that 'reasonableness' (which the judge equated with fairness) was the approach to be adopted when quantifying MPS and that the marital standard of living was an important factor in achieving 'reasonableness'.

(c)   If the maintenance is so small that it has to be supplemented by income support or jobseeker's allowance, there is no advantage to the applicant as her benefit will be reduced by the maintenance pound for pound (see **Chapter 6**).

(d)   There may be enforcement problems, especially in the early stages of the divorce, if a reluctant respondent or an aggrieved petitioner is still struggling to come to terms with the divorce or his responsibility to maintain the other party (or both).

(e)   There may be a risk that an application for MPS might jeopardise the prospects of an uncontested divorce, or negotiations over the final settlement.

Despite its drawbacks, MPS may be worth pursuing, particularly if a party with ample means leaves another with onerous responsibilities and no ability to meet them.

4.3.2   Periodical payments

Periodical payments usually take the form of weekly or monthly sums. Periodical payments may be paid to a spouse (MCA 1973, s 23(1)(a)), or, in exceptional cases, to a child of the family (see CSA 1991, s 8(3), discussed at **7.4**) or to the spouse caring for the child on that child's behalf (MCA 1973, s 23(1)(d)). Periodical payments may be ordered for children even if the divorce petition is dismissed, either at the time of dismissal or within a reasonable period after the dismissal.

All periodical payments to a party terminate on the death or remarriage of the recipient. Unsecured periodical payments terminate on the death of the paying spouse (MCA 1973, s 28). A periodical payments order (PPO) is unaffected by the remarriage of the payer, save that remarriage could prompt an application to discharge (or reduce) the order if the payer would then be supporting his new spouse.

The court may limit the term of the PPO to years or months if it considers that a party should be able to become independent after a period of adjustment, for example, to allow a wife to retrain and obtain employment. The court is under a duty to consider whether such a limitation on maintenance is feasible (see MCA 1973, s 25A(2) and **4.6.2.1**).

In the few cases where the court has jurisdiction to make a PPO in favour of a child, it will terminate on the child's 17th birthday unless it is in the child's interest for it to continue until he is 18 (see MCA 1973, s 29, in **Appendix 1(A)**). The usual reason for such an extension is that the child will be continuing with full-time education.

The maintenance may continue beyond a child's 18th birthday only if the circumstances in s 29(3) apply, ie:

(a)   the child is (or intends to be) in further education, academic or vocational; or

(b)   there are special circumstances, for example, the child has a mental disability.

4.3.3   Secured periodical payments (MCA 1973, s 23(1)(b) and (e))

A party may be ordered to secure periodical payments which are payable to the other party or a child of the family. This is a device to ensure that the recipient will continue to receive the periodical payments even if the payer's income fluctuates, or if problems of enforcement are anticipated. Secured PPOs work by charging an asset with a sum fixed by the court from which the periodical payments can be met. Typically, that asset will be income producing, for example, shares or rented property. The income yielded by the charged asset will be paid to the recipient up to the amount specified in the PPO. Alternatively, a non-income producing asset such as a valuable painting, could be secured. If the periodical payments were not made from other sources, the asset would be liable to be sold and the proceeds used to pay the sum secured.

Secured PPOs terminate in the same circumstances as unsecured PPOs, save for one exception: unlike ordinary PPOs, secured PPOs do not terminate on the death of the payer. However, his death would be taken into account on any application by his estate to vary or discharge the order.

4.4   Capital orders

The purpose of capital orders is to settle once and for all any disputes in respect of the couple's capital. For most couples the matrimonial home represents the main, if not the only, family capital. This is considered in detail in **Chapter 9**. Some couples will, of course, have considerable assets in addition to the home, including savings, securities, etc which may be the subject of a lump sum order, a property adjustment order, an order for sale or, in the case of pensions, a pension sharing order.

4.4.1   Lump sum orders

Under s 23(1)(c) and (e) of the MCA 1973, the court can order a party to pay to the other, or to a child of the family, a cash lump sum. There are two main reasons for making such an order:

(a)   to adjust the final division of the parties' assets. The order is frequently used in conjunction with an order dealing with the matrimonial home;

(b)   to recompense the applicant for expenses incurred prior to the application as a result of inadequate support from the respondent for the applicant or a child of the family.

A spouse is entitled to apply for one lump sum order only (although see **11.8.1**, which deals with the court's power to make a second lump sum or property adjustment order on an application for variation or discharge of a periodical payments or a secured periodical payments order). The lump sum order may specify payment by several instalments. In common with the other capital orders, a lump sum order cannot be varied. However, there is jurisdiction to deal with an application to vary, suspend and even to discharge instalments of a lump sum. Where the court orders payment of the lump sum to be by instalments or to be deferred, for example to allow the payer time to raise the money, it may order interest to be paid at a specified rate. There is also power to secure payment of the instalments in the same way as for periodical payments.

It is sometimes the case that although there may be no funds immediately available for the payment of a lump sum, it is anticipated that money will be forthcoming. Examples include an expected dissolution of a partnership, or maturity of an assurance policy releasing capital. In such a case, the court may adjourn an application, although it will do so only where there is a real likelihood of a change of circumstances within a relatively short period. The court has said that an application should not be adjourned for longer than about five years (see *Roberts v Roberts* [1986] 2 FLR 152). It has also refused applications for adjournment based on a party's hopes of inheritance on the grounds that it was too uncertain whether and when the inheritance would occur (see *Michael v Michael* [1986] 2 FLR 389 and **4.5.1.2**).

Lump sum orders are also available for children. Whilst they are not common, they may be appropriate in high income families or if a child has a special need, for example he is disabled or has special educational needs. Unlike for spouses, more than one lump sum order can be made for a child, so several orders could be made over a period of time. The Child Support Agency has no jurisdiction to make capital awards for children.

4.4.2 Property adjustment orders

Under s 24 of the MCA 1973, the court has wide powers to redistribute family property between the parties and the children of the family. It may do so by ordering that property be transferred, for example, from one party to the other, or held on trust. Such orders are intended to be final. Consequently, no application may be made (not even for a child) for further property adjustment, neither is it possible to vary these orders (but, again, see **11.8.1** on the court's powers to make a property adjustment order on a variation of a periodical payments order).

4.4.3 Orders for sale

The court has power under s 24A of the MCA 1973 to order a sale of any property in which either party is beneficially entitled. The court can make this order only once it has also made one of the following orders:

(a)   a secured periodical payments order;

(b)   a lump sum order;

(c)   a property adjustment order.

The order for sale may be made at the same time as the above orders or later. The order cannot take effect until decree absolute. The court has power to order that the sale shall not take place until a specified event has taken place or period has expired. For example, it may order that the property in question is not to be sold until essential works on it have been completed. Alternatively, the court may defer the sale to enable a party wishing to avoid the sale and remain in the property (or keep the car/shares, etc) to raise a lump sum to 'buy out' the other party's interest.

Orders for sale may also be used as a method of enforcement by ordering the sale of an asset if the owner has defaulted on a lump sum order (see **Chapter 11**).

The order for sale may contain consequential and supplementary provisions, directing, for example, how the sale price is to be fixed, or who should have the conduct of the sale.

If a party owns property jointly with another person, for example where a husband and his new partner are co-owners of a flat, the court must give the third party, here the partner, the opportunity to make representations on the matter before it decides whether to order the sale of the property. Alternatively, it may be, say, that the partner is living in a property but has no interest in it. In such a case, the s 24A order may include a consequential direction that she is to be given first refusal on the property before it is placed on the open market.

Although ss 24 and 24A apply to all types of property, for most families the matrimonial home is the most significant asset and, therefore, the issue on which feelings often run high. There are various ways of resolving disputes over the home and these are considered in detail in **Chapter 9**.

4.5   Deciding what orders to make

The court has a great deal of discretion and flexibility when deciding on the appropriate division of matrimonial assets on divorce.

When the court is considering provision, whether for the parties to the marriage or for a child of the family, it must begin by considering the statutory criteria laid down in s 25 of the MCA 1973 (in **Appendix 1(A)**).

Section 25(1) states:

> It shall be the duty of the court in deciding whether to exercise its powers under sections 23, 24 or 24A above and, if so, in what manner, to have regard to all the circumstances of the case, first consideration being given to the welfare while a minor of any child of the family who has not attained the age of eighteen.

The section goes on to list factors applicable to provision for spouses (s 25(2)), children of the family (s 25(3)) and further factors for children of the family who are not natural children of both parties (s 25(4)). Those factors are examined below.

Section 25 does not represent an exhaustive list of factors. Indeed, s 25(1) makes it plain that the court must take into account 'all the circumstances of the case'. Thus, the interests of third parties, for example a party's new partner and children, will also be taken into account. A separation agreement or pre-nuptial agreement previously entered into by the parties (see *G v G (Financial Provision: Separation Agreement)* [2000] 2 FLR 18 and *K v K (Ancillary Relief: Prenuptial Agreement)* [2003] 1 FLR 120 and **12.3**) would also be considered as part of 'all the circumstances'.

Any significant feature of the case not covered elsewhere can be considered. For example, the case of *A v T (Ancillary Relief: Cultural Factors)* [2004] 1 FLR 977 was unusual on its facts. An Iranian national living in England married an Iranian woman under a marriage contract entered into in Iran. The marriage ended after seven weeks and divorce proceedings were brought in England. In deciding the ancillary relief application the court found the cultural background of the parties to be a dominant factor, justifying the court taking into account (and indeed largely following) the way in which the courts of Iran would have dealt with such a case.

4.5.1 Provision for a spouse

Section 25(2) of the MCA 1973 lists the following eight factors to be considered by the court when dealing with ancillary relief for a spouse:

(a) the income, earning capacity, property and other financial resources which each of the parties to the marriage has or is likely to have in the foreseeable future [but see s 25B and **4.7.2.1**], including in the case of earning capacity any increase in that capacity which it would be in the opinion of the court reasonable to expect a party to the marriage to take steps to acquire;

(b) the financial needs, obligations and responsibilities which each of the parties to the marriage has or is likely to have in the foreseeable future;

(c) the standard of living enjoyed by the family before the breakdown of the marriage;

(d) the age of each party to the marriage and the duration of the marriage;

(e) any physical or mental disability of either of the parties to the marriage;

(f) the contributions which each of the parties has made or is likely in the foreseeable future to make to the welfare of the family, including any contribution by looking after the home or caring for the family;

(g) the conduct of each of the parties, if that conduct is such that it would in the opinion of the court be inequitable to disregard it;

(h) in the case of proceedings for divorce or nullity of marriage any benefit which, by reason of the dissolution or annulment of the marriage, that party will lose the chance of acquiring.

4.5.1.1 The courts' approach

In recent years there has been something of a re-evaluation of the approach taken by the courts when exercising their powers under s 25. That process began in the landmark case of *White v White* [2000] 2 FLR 981. Until that point, in very broad terms, the courts' approach had been that on marriage breakdown the entitlement of the financially weaker party (usually the wife) was to have her reasonable needs or requirements met, and nothing further. That approach was abandoned in *White*, where the House of Lords said that the courts should not focus exclusively on one factor in this way. Lord Nichols of Birkenhead stated, 'the objective must be to achieve a fair outcome'. All the s 25 factors are ranked equally at the outset and just gain or lose importance in each case, according to the relevant facts of that particular case and what seems to be fair between the parties.

In *White*, the husband and wife had farmed together throughout their 33 years of marriage. Their children were grown up. Their combined matrimonial assets totalled £4.6 million. Mrs White claimed a lump sum of £2.2 million to enable her to continue farming on her own. The trial judge declined to break up the farming enterprise. Having assessed the cost of buying a new home for her and of capitalising her income needs, he awarded her about 20% of the total assets to meet her 'reasonable requirements'. Mrs White appealed. Both the Court of Appeal and the House of Lords agreed that the judge had misdirected himself in treating Mrs White's reasonable requirements as the determining factor and failing to give sufficient weight to the other s 25 factors, especially Mrs White's contribution to the marriage.

Nevertheless, the House of Lords rejected the idea of a presumption, or starting point, of equal division, preferring to leave it to the judge in each particular case to go through the exercise of weighing up all the s 25 factors. Significantly, though, Lord Nichols did go on to say:

Before reaching a firm conclusion and making an order along these lines, a judge would always be well advised to check his tentative views against the yardstick of equality of division. As a general rule, equality should be departed from only if, and to the extent that, there is a good reason for doing so.

There may not be a presumption of equality, but it is clear that it should play an important part in the court's thinking.

Mrs White was eventually awarded approximately 40% of the total net assets. The 'good reason' to depart from the yardstick of equality in her case was that Mr White's father had loaned the couple some money when they started out, without which they would not have been able to buy the first farm.

The House of Lords expanded on this approach in *Miller v Miller; McFarlane v McFarlane* [2006] UKHL 24. The House of Lords said that the general principles to be applied when making financial awards were 'needs, compensation and sharing'. It was recognised that in many cases, of necessity, achieving fairness did not go beyond the stage of dividing the assets so as to try to meet the parties' housing and financial needs, and that often those assets were insufficient to provide adequately for the needs of two homes. However, in appropriate cases fairness demanded that the court should exercise its discretion so as to compensate one party and redress the economic disparity between the parties arising from the way in which they had conducted their marriage. The House of Lords went on to state that there was additionally an 'equal sharing' principle deriving from the basic concept of equality which underlies modern marriages. Echoing his words in *White*, Lord Nichols said that 'when their partnership ends each is entitled to receive an equal share of the assets of the partnership unless there is a good reason to the contrary'.

By the time the case came before the House of Lords the only issue remaining between Mr and Mrs McFarlane was the amount and duration of the periodical payments for Mrs McFarlane. The House of Lords confirmed the earlier award of £250,000 per annum, but extended the duration of the order for Mrs McFarlane's lifetime. The House of Lords said that fairness dictated that Mrs McFarlane should receive this amount far in excess of her reasonable needs in order to compensate her for the abandonment of her career as a successful solicitor at the outset of the marriage in favour of becoming a housewife and mother.

White and *Miller and McFarlane* were 'big money' cases where resources exceeded the parties' needs. However, the principles expressed in these cases are of universal application. The reality in many cases, though, will be that most of the resources are required to meet the parties' basic needs (eg, to house the children and the spouse primarily caring for them) and this will provide good reason to depart from the 'yardstick of equality'.

4.5.1.2   Resources

Although the statute does not list the factors in any specific order of importance, it is clear that generally the determining factor will be the parties' resources, income and capital. This is as much the case for PPOs as for lump sums and property adjustment orders. Whilst it is convenient to consider the various orders for financial provision separately, in reality the orders interrelate. For example, a husband with a high income may be able to transfer the home to his wife because he is able to raise a mortgage to purchase a new home for himself, but this would be a sensible solution only if the wife has enough income to finance the costs of running her home.

The court will take into account the parties' income from all sources. Earnings are the starting point. Fringe benefits, such as a company car, free petrol, paid telephone bills, etc, will also be taken into account.

As well as looking at actual earnings, the court will also consider potential earnings. When assessing a party's earning capacity the court will take a realistic approach. If a wife has qualifications which are in demand and has recent work experience, the court will bear in mind her ability to earn a living taking into account her commitments to the children. Before deciding on a party's earning capacity, the court will carefully consider the person's skills, age and time out of work, the possibility and cost of retraining and the job market. If the court is of the view that a party is perversely refusing to work in order to frustrate a financial application against him, it could make an order by attributing a notional earning capacity to him.

Earning capacity may be significant in determining the duration of periodical payments or a party's occupation of the matrimonial home. If the court considers that a party could reasonably be expected to take steps to increase his earning capacity by, say, undertaking further training, this could prompt the court to limit the period for which maintenance is payable (see **4.6**). It might also result in a reduction of a party's share on sale of the home if a return to work or significant promotion is anticipated with reasonable certainty.

As a general rule, means-tested welfare benefits will not be regarded as a resource since the supporting spouse cannot free himself of his responsibilities to maintain his family by casting that burden onto the taxpayer (*Barnes v Barnes* [1972] 3 All ER 872). However, there will frequently be cases where there are insufficient resources to maintain two households. In such cases, it would be an affront to common sense to ignore the availability of state benefits. The non-means tested child benefit will always be treated as a resource of the party caring for the child. If both parties are claiming benefit, it would be rare for the court to make any order because, as a general principle, the court would not make an order reducing the payer's income below subsistence level.

The court will give a wide interpretation to 'property' and 'financial resources'. The court is not limited to considering assets acquired jointly or during the marriage, or even existing assets. As with income, the court may take into account a party's future prospects, for example, a terminal gratuity, or an interest under a settlement or inheritance (but generally only if the donor has already died). If it is uncertain whether or when a party might acquire the anticipated property, or how much that property will be worth, it might be appropriate for the court to adjourn the application. In such a case, no final decision will be made, leaving the parties to wait and see whether (and to what extent) the anticipated property materialises during the period of the adjournment. In the case of *Michael v Michael* [1986] 2 FLR 389, Nourse LJ said it would be wrong to take into account the possibility of a wife's inheritance from her mother who was in her sixties and suffered from high blood pressure, saying the world was full of women in their eighties who had high blood pressure in their sixties.

Following certain comments made by the House of Lords in *Miller and McFarlane*, there were a number of cases in which it was argued that some assets should be categorised as 'non-matrimonial' and therefore unavailable for the court to distribute on divorce. Such assets might include those which were inherited or owned by one party before the marriage or which have been acquired by one party after separation. In some cases such arguments have enjoyed a measure of success – see, for example, *H v H* [2007] EWHC 459 where the husband's post-separation bonus payments were omitted from the capital assets divided by the court. However, s 25(2)(a) is not confined to assets accumulated during the marriage and it is clear that the courts have the power to deal with the parties' resources whenever and however acquired. How inherited assets or those acquired pre-marriage or post-separation are dealt with depends on the facts of the case. The nature and source of the assets will be taken into account when determining the requirements of fairness. The court will have regard to the circumstances of the acquisition of the assets and may conclude that such assets should be kept by the spouse who acquired or inherited them. However, this depends on the effect of the other s 25 factors, and a claim to keep such property will carry little weight if the other spouse's needs could not be satisfied without it or if the marriage is of long duration.

Income from other members of the household, such as 'board' paid by a working child or lodger, will be taken into account as a resource. More problematic is the extent to which the means of a party's new partner are taken into account. The court cannot redistribute a third party's assets and, therefore, it cannot, for example, order a new wife to pay maintenance to the former wife. However, if a second wife was earning and contributing to the household expenses, it would be wrong if the court was unable to take that fact into account. The practice which has emerged, therefore, is that the court will assess the extent to which contributions made by the new partner reduce the party's outgoings, thereby increasing the money available for maintenance payments (see *Slater v Slater and Another* [1982] 3 FLR 364). The paying spouse would still be expected to share the living costs with his new partner and, therefore, even if that partner was very wealthy and meeting all the expenses, this would not result in the payer being liable to pay his entire income to his first family. If the applicant has a new partner the same principles apply: to the extent that he is supporting the applicant her needs will be reduced. Clearly, the court will have regard to the stability of that relationship and may decide to preserve the party's option to apply to vary an order should the relationship break down. If the recipient remarries, she will lose her entitlement to maintenance altogether.

If a party has not remarried, the court will not speculate on that party's prospects of improving his financial circumstances by finding a partner. Nevertheless, if a party does have a firm intention to remarry or cohabit at the time an order for provision is being sought (including an order by consent), this will amount to a material fact which should be disclosed to the other party and to the court. This information may affect the outcome of proceedings or negotiations, for example as periodical payments terminate on remarriage they may be more appropriate than a lump sum or property adjustment order if a party is soon to be amply supported and housed by his new spouse. If remarriage plans are not disclosed then any order made is liable to be set aside (see *Livesey (formerly Jenkins) v Jenkins* [1985] AC 424 and **11.7**).

4.5.1.3 Needs

Section 25(2)(b) of the MCA 1973 directs the court to consider the parties' needs, obligations and responsibilities: for most couples the primary task will be to assess each party's essential needs. The most basic of these needs is the provision of accommodation for both parties and any children. Also important will be the expenses connected with the accommodation and the costs of food and clothing.

These costs will vary from case to case, depending on the size of the home, the number of people living in it and the general cost of living in the particular locality. In addition to considering these basic needs, the court must also consider the parties' existing obligations, for example, hire-purchase, bank loans, school fees, insurance premiums and television rental, etc. The courts have tended to construe s 25(2)(b) as confining them to have regard only to such requirements as are reasonable – as Ward J stated in *Delaney v Delaney* [1990] 2 FLR 457:

> In all life, for those who are divorced as well as for those who are not divorced, indulging one's whims or even one's reasonable desires must be held in check by the constraints imposed by limited resources and compelling obligations.

However, there will usually be little to gain in increasing the legal costs burden by challenging a party's existing outgoings unless he is being excessively extravagant. If a party is already committed to make certain payments, the courts will be reluctant to disregard the impact of those liabilities on that party's disposable income.

One of the most controversial obligations is that of the respondent who has 'indulged' himself by forming a new relationship (and possibly by having further children). It was noted (at **4.5.1.2**) that the resources of a party's new partner would be borne in mind when assessing that party's disposable income. It is, therefore, only reasonable that if the new partner is financially dependent upon the party, this fact will be taken into account. The court will consider the extent to which the financially dominant party can meet the needs of the other party and the children of the family, bearing in mind his additional responsibilities towards his new partner (and family). The result may be that a substantially reduced order is made, in some cases leaving the applicant to look to the State to meet her needs. The point was made graphically in the case of *Delaney* (above):

> Whilst this court deprecates any notion that a former husband and extant father may slough off the tight skin of familial responsibility and may slither into and lose himself in the greener grass on the other side, nonetheless this court has proclaimed and will proclaim that it looks to the realities of the real world in which we live, and that among the realities of life is that there is a life after divorce. The respondent husband is entitled to order his life in such a way as will hold in reasonable balance the responsibilities to his existing family which he carries into his new life, as well as his proper aspirations for that new future.

In *S v S (Financial Provision: Departing from Equality)* [2001] 2 FLR 246, the good reason for the (in this case, small) departure from equality was that the husband needed more to meet his responsibilities towards his new family.

Similarly, if a respondent has obligations to wives and children of former marriages, these will also be taken into account when considering the application of any subsequent spouse.

Where the parties are well off, the court will look beyond their basic needs, and the other s 25 factors are likely to play a more significant role in determining the outcome.

4.5.1.4   Standard of living

In applying s 25(2)(c), the court will not attempt the impossible by seeking to preserve both parties' standard of living at the level prior to the breakdown of the marriage. On separation, there will be the increased costs of running two households, usually without any increase in either party's income. Instead, the court will endeavour to ensure that the inevitable reduction in the parties' standard of living is borne by them evenly.

Where a couple have lived frugally and enjoyed only a modest standard of living, perhaps preferring to invest their resources in their business or to save for their retirement, the court will look at the wider picture. An applicant would not be penalised for having lived carefully during the marriage by an order for humble provision. On the contrary, the order should reflect the contributions made by the thrifty housekeeper towards the family's prosperity.

4.5.1.5   Ages of the parties and the duration of the marriage

Taken in isolation, the importance of s 25(2)(d) is not immediately obvious. However, taken in conjunction with the other factors, its significance is more apparent: a young wife without children ending a short marriage is likely to have an earning and borrowing capacity, and therefore a package of orders to enable a couple to achieve financial independence (known as a clean break: see **4.6**) may be appropriate. On the other hand, an older spouse leaving a long marriage may have little or no earning capacity, but is likely to have made a greater contribution to the marriage, and there are usually more family assets to distribute. A middle-aged or elderly couple may not necessarily have enjoyed a long marriage. However, if a mature couple have had only a short marriage, the court will bear in mind the consequences of that marriage on the parties. In particular, it will have regard to any loss of prospects resulting from the marriage, for example, jobs or promotion sacrificed or tenancies surrendered on entering into the marriage (see *S v S* [1977] 1 All ER 56). A similar principle applies to young couples ending a short marriage but who have children. The needs of the children will outweigh the fact that the marriage was short, not least because children are likely to diminish the earning capacity of the parent raising them (see *C v C (Financial Relief: Short Marriage)* [1997] 2 FLR 26).

In *Miller and McFarlane* (see **4.5.1.1**) the House of Lords said that the general approach in short marriages was to consider whether and to what extent there was a good reason to depart from equality. Lord Nichols referred to the 'instinctive feeling' that parties would generally have less call upon each other following the breakdown of a short marriage. Nevertheless the House of Lords was at pains to emphasise that the principles of 'needs, compensation and sharing' applied to short marriages as well as to long ones, and that each case would turn upon its own facts. On the unusual facts of *Miller*, the high standard of living that the parties had enjoyed and the fact that Mr Miller's wealth had increased dramatically during the marriage justified Mrs Miller receiving £5 million after less than three years of marriage.

It is the cohabitation during the marriage which is relevant in s 25(2)(d): the Court of Appeal in *Krystman v Krystman* [1973] 3 All ER 247 refused to order financial provision where the couple lived together for only two weeks of their 26-year marriage. As for cohabitation prior to marriage, the court is not required to take this into account under s 25(2)(d); however, it may be taken into account when the court considers 'all the circumstances of the case' under s 25(1) (*Kokosinski v Kokosinski* [1980] Fam 72). In the case of *Gojkovic v Gojkovic* [1990] 1 FLR 140, the wife received a substantial award based on her contributions to the family fortune made largely during their pre-marital cohabitation.

4.5.1.6   Disability

If a party suffers from a physical or mental disability, this may affect that party's resources as he may have a reduced (or no) earning capacity. It will also affect the sufferer's needs if, for example, expensive care, treatment or equipment is required. The court will also bear in mind the effect of any future deterioration in the party's condition. It has been held that damages awarded to compensate a party for personal injury are rightly to be regarded as a resource for that party under s 25(2)(a), notwithstanding that they were assessed to compensate that party for his loss, pain and suffering.

4.5.1.7 Contributions to the family

The court is required by s 25(2)(f) to consider the parties' past and anticipated future contributions to the welfare of the family, both materially and otherwise. Where the wife has contributed in non-financial terms to the marriage, it is not necessary for her to show the extensive contributions in kind of the sort required to establish a proprietary interest under a constructive trust (see **Chapter 16**). The court is not deciding the ownership of the family assets, but rather how each party's assets should be shared.

It has been recognised for some time that a wife who cares for the home and the family contributes as much to the family as the wife who goes out to work. Indeed in *Miller and McFarlane* (see **4.5.1.1**) Lord Nichols described as 'a principle of universal application' the fact that in assessing the parties' contributions there should be no bias in favour of the money-earner and against the home-maker. So, the party who has been primarily responsible for raising the children will have that contribution recognised. The court will bear in mind the impact of that role on the carer's career. It will also take into account the continuing contributions that the parent will make as the children grow up.

In the case of *Cowan v Cowan* [2001] 2 FLR 192, the Court of Appeal recognised that one party may have made an exceptional contribution in some way. In this situation, the Court found that fairness permitted, and sometimes required, recognition of the product of the skill or genius with which only one of the spouses might be endowed. This decision led to a number of cases in which the husband argued that his special entrepreneurial skill constituted a justification to depart from equality. In *Lambert v Lambert* [2002] EWCA Civ 1685, [2003] 1 FLR 139, however, the Court of Appeal made it clear that such an approach would be followed only in a truly exceptional case. Thorpe LJ commented:

> If all that is regarded is the scale of the breadwinner's success then discrimination is almost bound to follow since there is no equal opportunity for the homemaker to demonstrate the scale of her comparable success.

Nevertheless, it would seem that the possibility of a special contribution remains, as is shown by the case of *Sorrell v Sorrell* [2006] 1 FLR 497, where Mr Sorrell's 'exceptional and individual qualities' justified him receiving 60% of the assets.

Conversely, the court may also take into account any negative contribution made by a party: in the case of *E v E (Financial Provision)* [1990] 2 FLR 233, Mrs E, while having an adulterous affair, was said to have spent thousands of pounds on clothes and to have withdrawn from family life. The judge found that 'the wife's contribution to the welfare of the family was negative' and added: 'I do not find it necessary to consider conduct as a separate item. Such conduct as has been shown can properly be dealt with by considering the contribution the wife has made to the welfare of the family'. Whilst, then, it would be exceptional for adultery to be taken into account under s 25(2)(g) (see **4.5.1.8**), if affairs have resulted in a party failing to contribute to the family, this may be taken into account.

4.5.1.8 Conduct

Either party to the divorce may apply for financial provision: it is not a case of the 'guilty respondent' maintaining the 'innocent petitioner'. Whether, and to what extent, one party will be required to support the other will depend on all the factors appearing in s 25, of which conduct is but one.

Prior to 1984 the court took into account only such conduct as could be described as 'gross and obvious'. Since s 25(2)(g) was introduced (by the Matrimonial and Family Proceedings Act 1984, s 3), the court is required to consider conduct which it would be inequitable to disregard. That must include, but is not confined to, gross and obvious conduct (*Kyte v Kyte* [1987] 3 All ER 1041).

If substantial allegations of misconduct are made, the case may be transferred to the High Court (see *Practice Direction (Family Business: Transfer between High Court and County Court)* [1992] 3 All ER 151).

In practice, it will be unusual for a party's misconduct to be raised. Conduct may particularly be an issue, however, where it has a direct bearing on the parties' finances. Examples of cases where conduct was an issue include:

(a)   *Martin v Martin* [1976] 3 All ER 625: the husband frittered away joint assets in recklessly hopeless business ventures.

(b)   *K v K (Conduct)* [1990] 2 FLR 225: the husband had a serious drink problem which contributed to his refusal to obtain employment and his neglect of the house which ultimately forced its sale. Although the husband succeeded in obtaining a lump sum, his application for periodical payments was dismissed.

(c)   *H v H (Financial Relief: Attempted Murder as Conduct)* [2005] EWHC 2911: the husband subjected the wife to a vicious knife attack and was subsequently convicted of attempted murder. As a result of the attack the wife could no longer continue with her career as a police officer. The court considered it fair in all the circumstances that the wife should receive the greater share of the matrimonial assets, including the entire sale proceeds from the former matrimonial home. The husband's conduct had had the effect of placing the wife's needs as a much higher priority than the husband's in the court's consideration of s 25 of the MCA 1973, because the situation in which the wife found herself was clearly the husband's fault.

(d)   *Evans v Evans* [1989] 1 FLR 351: the court discharged a maintenance order made in favour of the wife after she was convicted (and imprisoned) for inciting others to murder the husband.

The fact that an applicant has committed adultery will not bar her from seeking financial provision. The adultery itself will not be relevant unless there are aggravating circumstances, as there were in *Bailey v Tolliday* [1983] 4 FLR 542 where the petitioner's father was the co-respondent.

Another possibility is that a party's misconduct may relate to the proceedings themselves, such as failure to make full and frank disclosure of means. In *Clark v Clark* [1999] 2 FLR 498, the court distinguished between marital misconduct, which may affect the quantification of orders made, as opposed to litigation misconduct, which generally should only be penalised in costs. Examples of cases involving litigation misconduct include the following:

(a)   *T v T (Interception of Documents)* [1994] 2 FLR 1083: the wife intercepted the husband's mail and broke into his office in an attempt to ascertain his true financial position. The court's approach was that, whilst this misconduct would not be brought into the reckoning of the substantive award, it was relevant in respect of costs.

(b)   *P v P (Financial Relief: Non-Disclosure)* [1994] 2 FLR 381: the court found the wife guilty of misconduct when she concealed a number of assets and the presence of a cohabitee. Again, although she was not penalised by a reduction in the overall provision, she was ordered to pay her own costs (estimated at £40,000).

In *Clark* (above), the wife had committed both marital and litigation misconduct. However, in that case, both types of misconduct were reflected by reducing the wife's award for a lump sum because the reality was that both the husband's costs (approximately £200,000) and the wife's costs (approximately £250,000) were effectively being funded from the husband's assets. This meant that there was no point in making any order for costs.

Whilst the majority of cases on s 25(2)(g) deal with misconduct by one party, it should be noted that the wording of the sub-section is not restricted to 'wrongdoing'. In *K v K (Ancillary Relief: Prenuptial Agreement)* [2003] 1 FLR 120 the court found that the fact that the parties had previously entered into a pre-nuptial agreement was conduct which it would be inequitable to disregard.

4.5.1.9 Potential financial loss

When dealing with applications ancillary to divorce or nullity (but not judicial separation), s 25(2)(h) requires the court to consider any potential benefits a party might lose as a result of the termination of the marriage. The loss of pension rights is an example. As a widow or widower the applicant may be entitled to the deceased spouse's pension: that right would be lost on the termination of the marriage. This can be a serious problem to, say, a financially dependent middle-aged wife of a long marriage. In such cases there may be an argument for giving that spouse a greater share of the other matrimonial assets to mitigate the problem, and perhaps also for preserving the wife's claim under the Inheritance (Provision for Family and Dependants) Act 1975 (I(PFD)A 1975).

Other contingent benefits which a party might lose include a share in life policies which are yet to mature. The lost opportunity to share in the other party's prospective inheritance will be taken into account only if it is sufficiently certain in time and amount (see **4.4.1**).

4.5.1.10 Human rights

Some legislative provisions, including s 25 of the MCA 1973, cannot be interpreted in accordance with the European Convention on Human Rights. Article 5 of the Seventh Protocol states that 'spouses shall enjoy equality of rights and responsibilities of a private law character between them, and in their relations with their children, as to marriage, and in the event of dissolution'. Yet, under s 25, the starting point in an application for ancillary relief is not necessarily equality between the spouses. Even the cases of *White* and *Miller and McFarlane* (see **4.5.1.1**) rejected such a presumption. In *White*, the House of Lords stressed that, often, having looked at all the circumstances, the 'yardstick of equality' would be departed from. In *Miller and McFarlane* the House of Lords recognised that, in many cases, achieving fairness could not go beyond addressing the parties' needs. Because of the difficulty in interpretation of s 25 and other provisions, Article 5 was specifically excluded from being incorporated into the HRA 1998.

4.5.2 Provision for children

The interests of the children of the family are borne in mind when any financial order is made under the MCA 1973. Section 25(1) requires the court 'to give first consideration to the welfare while a minor of any child of the family' when making any financial order on divorce. Therefore, when considering its powers to provide for the parties, any order made will reflect not only the needs of those parties but also the needs of the children.

The court has wide powers to make capital orders in favour of the children of the family. However, it is not usual for the court to make capital orders in favour of children: in *Lord Lilford v Glynn* [1979] 1 WLR 78, Orr LJ stated that

> a father, even the richest father, ought not to be regarded as under financial obligations or responsibilities to provide funds for the purpose of such settlements that are envisaged in this case on children who are under no disability and whose maintenance and education are secure.

In contrast, provision will be required for children's maintenance. It has already been noted (at **4.1**) that applications for children's maintenance will usually be made under the CSA 1991 to the Child Support Agency rather than to the court. This is considered in detail in **Chapter 7**. However, the court will continue to have limited jurisdiction to deal with maintenance orders for certain children, and in such cases the factors in s 25 must be taken into account.

When considering what orders should be made for children, the court is guided by s 25(3) in all cases. Section 25(4) lists further factors to be taken into account where the payer is not the natural parent of the child.

4.5.2.1 Children of the family

Section 25(3) directs the court to consider the following factors when making orders for children of the family:

(a)   the financial needs of the child;

(b)   the income, earning capacity (if any), property and other financial resources of the child;

(c)   any physical or mental disability of the child;

(d)   the manner in which he was being and in which the parties to the marriage expected him to be educated or trained;

(e)   the considerations mentioned in relation to the parties to the marriage in section 25(2)(a), (b), (c) and (e).

The factors are generally self-explanatory, but one or two points are worth noting. Clearly, the needs of the child will increase with age: the section does not refer to the child's future needs as these are best dealt with by further applications for increased maintenance as and when required.

Most young children do not have any income or earning capacity. However, maintenance may be sought for children who are receiving wages, grants or scholarships whilst in education or training, and such sums would be taken into account. In wealthier families, children may have trust income to be borne in mind.

The court will wish to ensure that adequate provision is made for children with a disability. It might, in particular, consider making secure PPOs to provide for a stable income. It might also be appropriate to make lump sum orders to meet capital expenditure on, for example, special equipment adapted for the child's handicap. The disability may also affect the duration of the order, as special circumstances could lead to the provision continuing well into adulthood.

Section 25(3)(e) requires the court to look at the parties' resources, needs, standard of living and any disability. This is because the parties' ability to provide for their children is directly related to and dependent upon their own circumstances.

4.5.2.2 Step-children

Section 25(4) requires the following additional factors to be considered where the child in question, although a child of the family, is not the natural child of the party against whom an order is being sought:

(a)   whether that party assumed any responsibility for the child's maintenance, and, if so, to the extent to which, and the basis upon which, that party assumed such responsibility and to the length of time for which that party discharged such responsibility;

(b)   whether in assuming and discharging such responsibility that party did so knowing that the child was not his or her own;

(c)   the liability of any other person to maintain the child.

The section recognises that a child may be a child of more than one family and, as a consequence, several people may be liable to maintain that child. For example, a husband may have treated his wife's child from a previous relationship as his own: in such a case both the husband and the father could be looked to for support. Clearly, the factors in s 25(4) will be highly relevant in determining the extent of this support. If the child's father is meeting the child's maintenance requirement under the CSA 1991 (see **Chapter 7**), this may relieve the step-father from paying maintenance.

Again it should be noted that the nature of the civil partnership family is such that it will more frequently be the case than with a married couple that these additional factors (mirrored in CPA 2004, Sch 5, Pt 5, para 22) will have to be considered.

4.6 The clean break

4.6.1 The principle

The object of the clean break is to settle once and for all the parties' financial responsibility towards each other and to end their financial interdependence to enable them to leave their past behind them and begin anew. The advantages of such an approach have long been recognised, but with the enactment of the Matrimonial and Family Proceedings Act 1984, which introduced s 25A into the MCA 1973, the concept of the clean break was given statutory backing. Since the 1984 Act the court has a duty to consider whether a clean break should be achieved.

Section 25A(1) states:

> Where on or after the grant of a decree of divorce or nullity of marriage the court decides to exercise its powers under sections 23(1)(a), (b) or (c), 24 or 24A above in favour of a party to the marriage, it shall be the duty of the court to consider whether it would be appropriate so to exercise those powers that the financial obligations of each party towards the other will be terminated as soon after the grant of the decree as the court considers just and reasonable.

The wording of the section only imposes a duty to consider the appropriateness of a clean break, it does not oblige the court to make a clean break wherever possible. In practice the judiciary view a clean break as the preferred outcome. For example, in *M v M (Ancillary Relief: Division of Assets Accrued Post Separation)* [2004] All ER (D) 83, Baron J commented: 'If it can be attained, it is better for there to be a clean break'. But the clean break is not to be imposed at all cost. In reality the court must weigh all the statutory factors in deciding whether a clean break is appropriate on the facts of the particular case; as Lord Nichols said in *Miller and McFarlane* (see **4.5.1.1**):

> ... if the claimant is owed compensation and capital assets are not available, it is difficult to see why the social desirability of a clean break should be sufficient reason for depriving the claimant of that compensation.

It will never be appropriate to have a clean break between a parent and child, as a party can never sever his responsibility towards a child of the family. It is possible, however, to have a clean break between the parties even where there are children involved. In cases where the court has jurisdiction to make orders for children, it might award less than it would otherwise do because the parent with whom the children are residing has agreed a clean break settlement. For example, the father might be using a significant amount of his income to pay for a loan which was raised in order to make a generous lump sum payment for the mother who is caring for the children. The father would clearly have less income available to support the children directly, but they will be benefiting indirectly from the lump sum payment. However, should the mother subsequently apply for a maintenance assessment under the CSA 1991, the father might then find himself being required to pay substantially more maintenance than he had bargained for. This is because when calculating the non-resident parent's liability to pay maintenance under the 1991 Act, generally no account is taken of any clean break made on divorce. However, if the clean break settlement was made before April 1993 (ie before the CSA 1991 came into force) then some allowance can be made (see **7.6.4.2**).

4.6.2   The practice

4.6.2.1   Income orders

So far as periodical payments are concerned, the most extreme form of clean break is an order dismissing the application coupled with a bar against the making of any further applications. Section 25A(3) empowers the court to make such an order:

> Where on or after the grant of a decree of divorce or nullity of marriage an application is made by a party to the marriage for a periodical payments order in his or her favour, then, if the court considers that no continuing obligation should be imposed on either party to make or secure periodical payments in favour of the other, the court may dismiss the application with a direction that the applicant shall not be entitled to make any further application in relation to the marriage for an order under section 23(1)(a) or (b) above.

The court may even take such a step without the consent of the applicant, but would generally do so only where compelling reasons exist. Less extreme than this immediate clean break is an order for 'term maintenance'. Such an order allows a party to receive maintenance for a limited period only in order to tide him over while he adapts to becoming financially self-sufficient. The clean break will be deferred to a future date. The term of the maintenance will vary from case to case: it may be for six months to enable the party to find a job, or for two or three years to allow for retraining. If there are children, it may be for a longer period until they are less dependent on the applicant. If the children are very young, the court is unlikely to consider term maintenance to be appropriate (see *Suter v Suter and Jones* [1987] 2 All ER 336).

It is also not usually considered appropriate to provide for the termination of periodical payments for a spouse in her late forties or fifties, unless she has substantial capital of her own and significant earning capacity (see *Flavell v Flavell* [1997] 1 FLR 353). The courts are much more likely to favour at least a nominal periodical payments order (eg 5p per year), thereby keeping the spouse's periodical payments claim 'alive' so that it can be varied, if necessary, in the future (see *SRJ v DWJ (Financial Provision)* [1999] 2 FLR 176).

The benefits of term maintenance have been given statutory support by s 25A(2), which states:

> Where the court decides in such a case to make a periodical payments or secured periodical payments order in favour of a party to the marriage, the court shall in particular consider whether it would be appropriate to require those payments to be made or secured only for such term as would in the opinion of the court be sufficient to enable the party in whose favour the order is made to adjust without undue hardship to the termination of his or her financial dependence on the other party.

The question arises as to what happens if events do not work out according to plan and the applicant fails to achieve the anticipated financial independence? The answer is that most applicants could apply under s 31 of the MCA 1973 to extend the maintenance for a further period. It is essential that any such application is made before the expiry of the term as the order itself ceases at that point. In deciding whether to grant such a request, however, the court would enquire into the reason for the applicant's failure to become self-sufficient. If, for example, the availability of work decreases and the court is satisfied that the applicant has made genuine efforts to seek employment, it is likely to deal with the application sympathetically.

The court is empowered under s 28(1A) to direct that the applicant will not be entitled to make any application to extend the term regardless of any change of circumstances. Whilst this has the advantage for the payer of certainty, in that he will eventually be rid of the obligation to maintain his ex-spouse, the inflexibility can lead to hardship to the recipient (see *Waterman v Waterman* [1989] 1 FLR 380).

An alternative approach, mentioned above, is to order substantive maintenance for a fixed period, after which it will drop to a nominal sum of, say, 5p per year, so keeping alive the recipient's option of applying for an increase. Such an order is not a clean break at all as it affords no certainty to the payer. However, substantive maintenance would be revived beyond the original term only if the circumstances justified it.

4.6.2.2   Capital orders

A clean break is commonly achieved by means of a lump sum payment in return for a dismissal of all other claims. One party may prefer to pay a relatively substantial lump sum rather than have the burden of even modest maintenance hanging over him for an indefinite period. This is possible, though, only if there are sufficient capital assets available. A party may need to borrow in order to raise the necessary capital.

Particular problems arise if the main asset involved is a business. Selling the business to realise capital may be 'killing the goose that lays the golden egg'.

Lump sums are discussed further at **9.7**. It may be that there is no clean break initially between the parties, but that one occurs later on; see **11.8.1**, which deals with the court's power to impose a clean break at a later stage, by making lump sum adjustment orders, on an application for variation or discharge of an existing periodical payment or secured periodical payments order.

There are only two ways of dealing with the matrimonial home to achieve an immediate clean break: by immediate sale, or by a transfer into one party's sole name. These and other orders for the matrimonial home are considered in detail in **Chapter 9**.

As part of a clean break package a provision is often included under s 15 of the Inheritance (Provision for Family and Dependants) Act 1975. This enables the court to direct that neither party may apply under s 2 of the 1975 Act for financial provision out of the other's estate.

4.7 Pensions on divorce

A pension is often a person's most valuable asset, or it will be when it comes to being paid, so it is not surprising that dividing it should be a major consideration in settling the financial aspects of divorce, particularly for older couples. Historically, the courts were reluctant to interfere in the operation of the pension scheme itself in order to redress the balance for one party to a marriage who had a lesser earning capacity than the other. The Pensions Act 1995 and the Welfare Reform and Pensions Act 1999 introduced amendments to MCA 1973 which made significant reforms in this area.

There are three possible ways of dealing with pension rights on divorce. These are:

(a)   follow the traditional approach by adjusting the other matrimonial assets to take account of pension rights (often described as 'off-setting');

(b)   seek an order which allows for all or part of any pension or lump sum arising at retirement to be 'earmarked' for the other spouse (known as 'pension attachment');

(c)   apply for the pension to be split so that the pension benefits are physically subdivided at the time of the divorce; the parties will then have two entirely separate pensions which they can contribute to in the future in the normal way (known as 'pension sharing').

4.7.1 The traditional approach – 'off-setting'

As originally enacted, the MCA 1973 referred, in a limited way, to pension rights. These provisions remain despite the subsequent amendments to the Act. Section 25(2)(a) says that when the courts consider the 'financial resources' of the parties this can include those which will be available 'in the foreseeable future'. However, this phrase is not defined and the courts have sometimes interpreted it as meaning not more than 10 years away (*Milne v Milne* (1981) 2 FLR 286 and *Hedges v Hedges* [1991] 1 FLR 196). This used to mean that pension rights which were payable after that time were often ignored completely, despite their potential value.

Although s 25(2)(h) says that the court must have regard to the value of any benefit which a party will lose the chance of acquiring as a result of the divorce, such as pension rights, the courts, in the past, did not have any powers to make orders specifically dealing with the parties' pension arrangements. Historically, the best that the courts could do in making appropriate settlements on divorce was to allocate to one spouse (normally the wife) a proportion of the matrimonial assets equivalent to the approximate value of the pension benefits lost. This meant that a trade-off was being made between the pension rights and other matrimonial assets. However, this is not always an entirely appropriate solution: there are problems of valuation, and there is the fact that the trade-off must be made immediately at the time of the divorce, yet the pension benefits themselves will be in the future and are contingent on certain events (eg retirement, death) and possibly may never materialise. In past years there was also the problem that the value of the matrimonial home (most couples' other main asset) might have fallen. This meant that there may not have been sufficient other matrimonial assets to trade off against pension benefits.

4.7.2 'Pension attachments'

Section 166 of the Pensions Act 1995 brought about important changes in relation to provision for pensions on divorce. Three new sections were inserted into the MCA 1973 namely ss 25B, 25C and 25D (see **Appendix 1(A)**). These sections allow the court to make pension attachment orders so that certain payments under a pension are to be paid not to the member of the pension scheme but to his former spouse.

4.7.2.1 Section 25B

This section says that, in relation to benefits under a pension scheme, the words 'in the foreseeable future' in s 25(2)(a) shall not apply. This means that the court can take into account any future pension benefits.

The section also gives the court the power, when making a financial provision order, to direct the trustees or managers of a pension scheme to pay some (or even all) of the pension to the spouse without the pension rights. If the pension is not yet payable (ie the member-spouse has not yet retired) the court may make a deferred order. Such orders will effectively be like deferred maintenance orders.

4.7.2.2 Section 25C

Most pension schemes include a lump sum benefit payable on retirement, or on the death of the member before retirement. This section gives the court the power to make a lump sum order which directs the trustees or managers of the pension scheme to pay the whole or part of that lump sum, when it becomes due, to the other spouse.

4.7.2.3 Section 25D

This section deals with supplementary provisions, such as valuations and what happens if the member-spouse transfers from one pension scheme to another.

4.7.2.4 Application of the court's powers under ss 25B–25D

The court can apply its powers under these sections only in relation to an application for financial provisions arising where the petition was filed with the court on or after 1 July 1996. Orders could be made from 1 July 1996, although orders relating to pension payments (as opposed to lump sums) could only be in relation to benefits falling due on or after 6 April 1997.

There have only been a few reported cases involving pension attachments (eg *T v T (Financial Relief: Pensions)* [1998] 1 FLR 1072, and *Burrow v Burrow* [1999] 1 FLR 508). In both these cases, the courts held that the provisions allowed under ss 25B–25D did not create a statutory right to a share in a spouse's pension fund. The court, in determining whether to make a pension attachment and the amount, if any, should exercise its discretion under the established s 25 criteria.

4.7.3 'Pension sharing'

Although the Pensions Act 1995 gave the courts more possibilities for redressing the harsh effects of loss of pension rights on divorce, there were still problems.

Pension attachments will usually be deferred until the member-spouse retires or dies. This means that the other spouse has no control over the money until that time and, for example, the member-spouse could decide to retire early or late. Also, such orders are contrary to the clean break principle. As a result of these (and other) problems, it seems that, as mentioned at **4.7.2.4**, very few pension attachments are being made in practice.

The Pensions Act 1995 stopped short of the proposals set out in the report *Pensions on Divorce* produced in 1993 by an independent working group appointed by the Pensions Management Institute in agreement with The Law Society. This report proposed that the courts should be able to split pension rights at the time of divorce. This could be done by directing that a transfer payment equal in value to a proportion of the member-spouse's pension rights should be made to a pension arrangement which could then provide retirement benefits for the other spouse. In this way, both parties would have immediate control over their own pension provisions.

Although the Government of the day resisted pension sharing in the Pensions Act 1995, it was defeated on this issue when the FLA 1996 was debated in the House of Lords. As a result, s 16 of the FLA 1996 provided, in principle, for pension sharing by the courts and was followed by the Welfare Reform and Pensions Act 1999 (WRPA 1999), in force from 1 December 2000.

4.7.3.1 When a pension sharing order can be made

Schedule 3 to the WRPA 1999 inserted s 24B into the MCA 1973, sub-section (1) of which states:

> On granting a decree of divorce or a decree of nullity of marriage or at any time thereafter (whether before or after the decree is made absolute) the court may, on an application made under this section, make one or more pension sharing orders in relation to the marriage.

This pension sharing provision applies only to petitions filed after 1 December 2000 as the legislation is not retrospective. Also, pension sharing is available on divorce (or nullity) but not on judicial separation.

Any pension sharing order made will not take effect until the divorce decree has been made absolute.

4.7.3.2 Types of pension which can be shared

A party can apply for a pension sharing order if her spouse is a member of an occupational pension scheme or personal pension scheme. Pension sharing also applies to most public service pensions and the State Earnings Related Pension Schemes (SERPS), but not to the basic State retirement pension.

4.7.3.3 The pension sharing order

The WRPA 1999 inserted s 21A into the MCA 1973:

> (1)   For the purposes of this Act, a pension sharing order is an order which—
>> (a)   provides that one party's—
>>> (i)   shareable rights under a specified pension arrangement, or
>>> (ii)   shareable State scheme rights
>>> be subject to pension sharing for the benefit of the other party, and
>> (b)   specifies the percentage value to be transferred.

The types of pension covered by this section have already been mentioned at **4.7.3.2**.

On the making of a pension sharing order, the transferor loses the percentage required to be transferred which reduces the value of his fund – 'the pension debit'. The transferee acquires the right to be credited with that amount – 'the pension credit'. The transferee thus gains an amount which will fund a quite separate pension of her own, which is not in any way contingent on the transferor taking his own pension.

Depending on the type of pension scheme involved, the transferee may have a choice as to whether to become a member of the transferor's pension scheme, but in her own right (known as an 'internal transfer'), or to transfer to a different pension scheme (an 'external transfer').

Pension rights will be valued using the method already in use for valuing the rights of 'early leavers' from occupational pension schemes, or of members of personal pension schemes who wish to transfer their accrued rights to another pension scheme. This is known as the Cash Equivalent Transfer Value.

The amount to be transferred must be expressed as a percentage of this value rather than in cash terms (WRPA 1999, s 29(2)). It is important to remember that an order may be made stipulating any percentage the court considers appropriate, not necessarily 50:50.

Any solicitor advising a client about pension sharing must be careful not to infringe the provisions of the Financial Services and Markets Act 2000. For advice on, for example, whether to opt for an internal or external transfer, the client needs to be referred to an independent financial adviser.

4.7.3.4   Pension sharing and the other options

There is no obligation on the court to make a pension sharing order, and 'offsetting' or pension attachment orders remain an alternative. The court must, as always in ancillary relief matters, consider each case on its facts by applying the principles and factors set out in s 25 of the MCA 1973 (see **4.5**).

One restriction on the options available to the court is that it is not possible to make both a pension sharing order and a pension attachment in relation to the same pension arrangement. Therefore, the court could not, for example, make a pension attachment in relation to the lump sum death benefit and share the member's other rights. Also, a pension sharing order may not be made in relation to a pension arrangement which is already subject to such an order in respect of that marriage (MCA 1973, s 24B(3) and (4)). However, the fact that a pension is already subject to a sharing order made in respect of a previous marriage would not prevent a further order being made as a result of a second divorce.

4.8   Ancillary relief in the future

Calls for a review of the law on ancillary relief have been growing louder in recent years. The legislation remains in substantially the same form as when originally enacted over 30 years ago. Ancillary relief has always been an area dominated by judicial discretion. Yet the flurry of litigation which followed *White* and more recently *Miller and McFarlane* has arguably only served to add to the law's uncertainty. In *Charman v Charman* [2007] EWCA Civ 503 the President of the Family Division commented:

Arguably . . . [the MCA] is . . . in need of modernisation in the light of social and other changes as well as in the light of experience.

Whether the calls for reform will be heeded by the Government is yet to be seen.

4.9   Financial provision during marriage

It may be that a spouse is in need of financial provision during a marriage and yet is not ready to make a decision regarding divorce or judicial separation. In such circumstances, a spouse may bring proceedings under s 27 of the MCA 1973 in a divorce county court (under CPA 2004, Sch 5, Pt 9 for civil partners), or under the Domestic Proceedings and Magistrates' Courts Act 1978 (DPMCA 1978) in the family proceedings court (see **Appendix 1(C)**).

4.9.1   Matrimonial Causes Act 1973, s 27

Section 27 of the MCA 1973 allows either party to a marriage to apply for financial provision on the ground that the respondent has failed to provide reasonable maintenance for the applicant, or has failed to provide or make a proper contribution towards the reasonable maintenance of any child of the family. The court can make orders for periodical payments (including secured provision) and lump sums. In contrast to the DPMCA 1978, there is no ceiling on the amount of any lump sum, although as with the 1978 Act there is no power to make property adjustment orders. In determining whether to make provision, the court will have regard to all the circumstances of the case, including many of the factors set out in s 25 (see **4.5.1**).

The duration of periodical payments orders made under s 27 is precisely the same as for ordinary periodical payments made on divorce (see **4.3.2**). The court also has power to make interim orders, and orders for periodical payments may be varied under s 31 of the MCA 1973 in the usual way (see **11.8**).

Applications under s 27 of the MCA 1973 have never been common. The need for such applications is now diminished since, where a married couple are separated and have natural children, the appropriate application for maintenance for the children will be to the Child Support Agency rather than under s 27 of the MCA 1973.

4.9.2   Financial provision in the family proceedings court

The DPMCA 1978 enables a party to a marriage to seek financial provision in the family proceedings court during the subsistence of the marriage. The court may make orders for periodical payments for a spouse as well as for a child of the family, and it may make lump sum orders. There are two main types of application under the DPMCA 1978: contested applications under s 2; and applications by consent under s 6.

4.9.2.1   Contested applications

In order to bring an application under s 2 of the DPMCA 1978, the applicant must establish one of the grounds in s 1, ie that the respondent has not sufficiently provided for the applicant or a child of the family, or the respondent's behaviour has been unreasonable, or the respondent has deserted the applicant. The court will have regard to the factors listed in s 3, which are broadly similar to s 25 of the MCA 1973.

Any lump sum order made on a contested application is limited to £1,000, although, unlike s 23 of the MCA 1973, there is no bar against making further applications.

4.9.2.2 Agreed applications

If the parties agree financial provision, either may apply for an order under s 6 of the DPMCA 1978 to endorse their agreement.

The court is also able to approve agreements to pay a lump sum of any amount.

4.9.2.3 Duration of periodical payments

Whether the order is made pursuant to s 2 or s 6, it may be backdated to the date of application. The order will cease on the death of either party, or on the remarriage of the recipient. It is unaffected by the termination of the marriage, although it will usually be discharged and replaced by any order made under s 23 of the MCA 1973 by the divorce county court. Periodical payments to a spouse for herself or for the benefit of a child will cease if the parties resume cohabitation for a continuous period of more than six months (MCA 1973, s 25(1)). Payments ordered to be payable direct to a child will be unaffected by cohabitation. The child's maintenance will terminate in the same circumstances as under s 29(3) of the MCA 1973 (see **4.3.2**).

Use of the DPMCA 1978 is less common following the enactment of the CSA 1991 (considered in detail in **Chapter 7**). If a couple separates, the parent with care may seek provision through the Child Support Agency unless the child does not qualify (eg a step-child). If a maintenance calculation could be made under the CSA 1991, it must be pursued through the Agency rather than the family proceedings court. However, the DPMCA 1978 may be invoked by children who are in higher education (and therefore no longer liable to be maintained under the CSA 1991) and for lump sum orders.

4.10 Chapter summary

(1) On divorce, a divorce county court (or the High Court) can make one or more of the following financial orders in favour of a spouse:

    (a) maintenance pending suit;

    (b) periodical payments;

    (c) secured periodical payments;

    (d) lump sum order;

    (e) property adjustment order;

    (f) order for sale;

    (g) pension sharing order.

(2) The court can also make any of these orders (except for maintenance pending suit and pension sharing orders) in favour of a child. However, in most cases, periodical payments for a child are now dealt with by the Child Support Agency, and it is unusual to obtain the other types of order, such as a lump sum order, for a child.

(3) Whenever the court considers making a financial order on divorce, it must consider:

    (a) the general principle in s 25(1), ie all the circumstances of the case, with first consideration given to the welfare of any child of the family under 18 years; and

    (b)   the factors in s 25(2):

        (i)   income, earning capacity and other resources;

        (ii)   needs and responsibilities;

        (iii) standard of living;

        (iv) age of the parties and duration of the marriage;

        (v)   disability;

        (vi) contributions to the family;

        (vii) conduct;

        (viii) potential financial loss.

The House of Lords in *White* and *Miller and McFarlane* has reaffirmed that no one s 25 factor is more important than the others. The objective for the court is to achieve fairness.

There are other factors for the court to refer to when considering making financial orders for a child or step-child (s 25(3) and (4)).

(4)   Under s 25A, the court always has a duty to consider whether a clean break should be achieved.

(5)   It is important to be aware of the significance of pensions on divorce and the ways in which the court can try to adjust the financial position of the parties on retirement.

(6)   A spouse who is not divorcing can still apply to the court for financial provision, either:

    (a)   to the divorce county court, under s 27 of the MCA 1973, for periodical payments and/or a lump sum order; or

    (b)   to the family proceedings court, under the DPMCA 1978, for periodical payments and/or a maximum £1,000 lump sum order.

Chapter 5

Tax on Marriage Breakdown

5.1 Introduction

This chapter deals with the effect of marriage breakdown on the tax position of the couple.

5.2 Tax on marriage breakdown

Where the assets owned by the divorcing couple are numerous and complicated, it may be wise to enlist the help of an accountant when considering tax planning. Nonetheless, the solicitor should be aware of the major tax effects of marriage breakdown and some basic tax planning points. For a reminder of the basic principles of income tax, capital gains tax and inheritance tax, see *Legal Foundations*.

5.2.1 Income tax

Changes to the income tax regime which came into effect in April 2000 effectively removed the scope for tax planning. There is now:

(a) no tax relief on maintenance payments, whether for a spouse or a child (maintenance is tax free in the hands of the recipient);

(b) no married couple's or single parent allowance;

(c) no tax relief on mortgage interest payments.

Consequently, how maintenance payments are arranged will no longer be influenced by fiscal considerations.

There are four ways in which maintenance may be paid:

(a) purely voluntary payment;

(b) under a written agreement;

(c) by court order (whether made by consent or after a contested hearing);

(d) in compliance with a maintenance assessment by the Child Support Agency.

Voluntary payments are normally only a short-term arrangement. As between a written agreement and a court order, it is a question of balancing the potential advantages of speed, lower costs and flexibility of an agreement against the better provisions for disclosure and enforcement with a court order (see **12.3.3** and **12.3.4** for a more detailed comparison).

5.2.2 Capital gains tax

Capital gains tax (CGT) is charged on the chargeable gains made by a person on the disposal of chargeable assets. On marriage breakdown, capital assets commonly have to be sold or divided between the spouses, and this may give rise to a chargeable gain. Ordinarily transfers of assets between spouses are deemed to have occurred at a consideration which gives rise to neither a gain nor a loss. However, the benefit of this rule is lost at the end of the tax year of separation. The impact of CGT cannot be ignored as it may alter the effect of any negotiated settlement or court order.

5.2.2.1 Capital gains tax and the home

The home is often the largest capital asset and any transfer of it, or of a share in it, could potentially give rise to CGT. However, liability may be avoided due to two important exemptions:

(a)   The private residence exemption: to qualify for full exemption, an individual must have occupied the home as his only or main residence throughout the period of his ownership. If he has occupied during part only of his ownership then the relief will be proportionately reduced, except that he is deemed to have occupied during the last three years of ownership whether or not this is in fact so (further details of this exemption can be found in *Property Law and Practice*).

(b)   Extra-statutory concession D6: this will apply where:

(i)   a husband and wife separate or divorce and one of them moves out of the home whilst the other continues to live there;

(ii)   under the subsequent financial settlement the non-occupying spouse transfers the home or an interest in it to the occupying spouse; and

(iii)   the non-occupying spouse has not elected to treat another property as his only or main residence.

If these conditions are fulfilled, the non-occupying spouse will be treated as having continued to occupy so that his gain will be exempt.

How do these exemptions work in practice?

Sale of the home to a third party

If the sale is within three years of the separation, any gain is exempt, being covered by the private residence exemption. If the sale is later, the proportion of the non-occupying spouse's gain not covered by the exemption may be taxable. When calculating the gain, an indexation allowance applies up to April 1998. For 1998/99 onwards, the gain is reduced by taper relief according to the length of ownership. The annual exemption, if available, can then be applied to reduce the gain. (The spouse who has continued to occupy will, of course, be covered by the private residence exemption.)

Transfer of the home between spouses

This will be necessary where the court orders an outright transfer, or deferred trust of land or deferred charge where this requires a transfer, ie disposal of some interest in the home. The transferor's gain may be exempted under the following rules:

(a)   where the transfer takes place in the tax year of separation, the rule relating to inter-spouse disposals; or

(b)   where the transfer takes place within three years of separation, the deemed occupation rule; or

(c)   extra-statutory concession D6 if later.

Where none of the above applies, probably because the transferor has made an election in respect of another home and the separation exceeds three years, the gain will be calculated in the same way as above. A proportion of the gain will thus be exempt due to the private residence exemption. Indexation and/or taper relief, together with the annual exemption, may help to reduce the remainder.

Future sale of home subject to a deferred trust of land or deferred charge

When the deferred trust of land or deferred charge is set up, one spouse may be required to transfer some, or all, of their interest in the home to the other. The CGT consequences of this have been dealt with above. However, when the house eventually comes to be sold, possibly many years into the future, a further CGT liability may arise.

The occupying spouse's gain will be exempt under the private residence exemption. The position of the non-occupying spouse will depend on whether the home was subject to a deferred trust of land, or a deferred charge:

(a)   *Deferred trust of land.* As the court order created a settlement, it would appear that the non-occupying spouse will avoid CGT liability completely because of rules exempting gains on property occupied by a beneficiary entitled to do so under a settlement (Taxation of Chargeable Gains Act 1992, s 225).

(b)   *Deferred charge.* Where the charge is expressed as a proportion of the proceeds, for example, one-third, the value of that share may have increased by the time the property is sold. In this situation, the non-occupier is likely to be liable to CGT, the redemption monies being a capital sum derived from an asset, ie the charge (Taxation of Chargeable Gains Act 1992, s 21). Indexation and/or taper relief, together with the annual exemption, may help to reduce the bill. However, if the deferred charge is for a fixed sum (rather than a proportion of the proceeds), there is no charge to CGT when the debt is paid (Taxation of Chargeable Gains Act 1992, s 251).

5.2.2.2   Other assets

Disposals giving rise to liability to CGT are most likely to arise, for example, on sale of an asset (say a valuable painting) to raise a lump sum, or on the transfer of property (say shares) between the parties.

Example

Jim and Kate bought a painting jointly seven years ago for £10,000. They separated two years ago. The ancillary relief order is made today, when the painting is worth £16,000. Under the order Jim must transfer his share in the painting to Kate. Jim has made a gain of £3,000 (£16,000 – £10,000 = £6,000, Jim's gain is half of this).

The gain on many disposals of matrimonial property may, however, be eliminated or reduced by an exemption or relief. The following should be considered:

(a)   wasting assets, for example, the family car or electrical items;

(b)   tangible moveable property disposed of for a consideration of less than £6,000;

(c)   the indexation allowance and/or taper relief;

(d)   the annual exemption;

(e)   the rule relating to inter-spouse transfers.

But these exemptions and reliefs will not eliminate CGT in every case. Consequently, the family solicitor must always have the impact of CGT in mind and ensure that settlements and orders are framed in a tax-efficient manner where possible. There may, for example, be merit in arranging a financial settlement so as to enable assets to be transferred between spouses before the tax year of separation expires. Similarly, the family solicitor may need to structure a financial settlement so as to stagger the disposal of assets across two tax years so that the transferor can take advantage of two annual exemptions.

5.2.3 Inheritance tax

Inheritance tax (IHT) is charged on the value transferred by a chargeable transfer. Transfers of assets or money between spouses on marriage breakdown have the potential to give rise to a charge to IHT as lifetime transfers. However, in reality there is rarely any liability to IHT on marriage breakdown. This is due to the following exemptions and reliefs.

5.2.3.1 The spouse exemption (Inheritance Tax Act 1984, s 18)

The spouse exemption exempts transfers between the parties before decree absolute, even if separated. However, this exemption will rarely apply since lump sum and property adjustment orders are not effective until decree absolute (see **4.4.1** and **4.4.2**).

5.2.3.2 Dispositions for family maintenance (Inheritance Tax Act 1984, s 11)

This relief provides that a disposition is not a transfer of value if made by one spouse for the maintenance of the other spouse or of a child of either spouse, and applies both before and after divorce. The term 'maintenance' is not defined in the Act but clearly covers periodical payments. There is, however, doubt as to whether it is wide enough to cover capital provision, such as lump sum or property adjustment orders. However, capital orders should be covered by the following relief.

5.2.3.3 Dispositions without donative intent (Inheritance Tax Act 1984, s 10)

This provides that a disposition is not a transfer of value if it was not intended to confer a gratuitous benefit and that either:

(a) it was made in a transaction at arm's length between unconnected persons; or

(b) it was such as might be expected to be made in such a transaction.

To avoid any doubt about the application of this exemption to transfers on marriage breakdown, the Senior Registrar of the Family Division, with the agreement of the then Revenue, issued the following statement:

> Transfers of money or property pursuant to an order of the court in consequence of a decree of divorce or nullity will, in general, be regarded as exempt from [IHT] as transactions at arm's length which are not intended to confer any gratuitous benefit. ((1975) 119 SJ 596)

5.2.4 Stamp duty land tax

Where property is transferred under a separation agreement or court order on divorce, the instrument effecting the conveyance is exempt from stamp duty land tax (Finance Act 1985, s 83 and Stamp Duty (Exempt Instruments) Regulations 1987 (SI 1987/516)).

5.3 Chapter summary

(1) The payment of maintenance, whether to a spouse or child, does not give rise to any income tax consequences.

(2) CGT may have to be paid when the matrimonial assets are divided on divorce.

(3) Where the asset is the home and it is transferred from one spouse to the other, CGT will not usually be payable. However, if the home is sold to a third party, some CGT may have to be paid by the non-occupying spouse.

Chapter 6

Welfare and Local Authority Housing

6.1 Introduction

When a married couple or civil partners separate and the main earner leaves the home, the other spouse may be left with little or no money. Although this may be only a temporary situation and it is possible to apply for maintenance (see **4.3.1** and **4.9**), it may be preferable for that spouse to apply for welfare benefits (for reasons explained at **4.3.1**). In addition, since it is more expensive to run two households than one, many people, particularly if they are lone parents, find themselves reliant on welfare benefits on a more permanent basis after marriage breakdown.

In terms of eligibility for welfare benefits, cohabiting couples (ie those who are 'living together as husband and wife' or 'living together as civil partners') are treated in the same way as married couples and so, for example, their income will be aggregated.

The matrimonial solicitor thus needs to have a working knowledge of the main benefits available and how they may be affected by any financial settlement which the couple later reach.

The following is an outline of the most important current benefits for the family client. Further detail on these and other benefits can be found in specialist publications, such as *Welfare Benefits and Tax Credits Handbook* (Child Poverty Action Group, 2007).

Where examples are given, for the sake of simplicity, notional figures are used for the amount of benefit payable.

6.2 Child benefit

Child benefit is payable irrespective of the claimant's income (ie it is not means-tested) and is non-taxable. It is a weekly sum payable in respect of each child or qualifying young person to the person responsible for maintaining that child or qualifying young person. A 'child' is defined as being someone under 16. A 'qualifying young person' is defined as being someone who is under 20 and still in full-time secondary education. A higher amount of benefit is paid for the eldest child.

6.3 Income support

Income support has now largely been replaced by the jobseeker's allowance. However, income support is still available for, amongst others, lone parents who are looking after a child or children under 16, and so will continue to be important where a marriage has broken down.

6.3.1 Eligibility

The claimant must:

(a)   have a right to reside and be habitually resident in Great Britain;

(b)   be at least 16;

(c)   not be in full-time work or full-time non-advanced education (most students will also be ineligible to claim). 'Full-time work' means working for at least 16 hours per week;

(d)   not have income which exceeds his family's 'applicable amount' (see 6.3.2);

(e)   not have capital exceeding £16,000. Some capital will be ignored, eg the value of the home;

(f)   usually attend work-focused interviews every six months.

6.3.2 Applicable amount

The maximum amount of benefit payable is called the applicable amount. The applicable amount will be made up of the following:

(a)   Personal allowance: the amount of this will depend upon the age of the claimant.

(b)   Various premiums, for example, for pensioners and those with disabilities.

(c)   Child maintenance premium, which allows all families on income support to keep up to £10 a week of any child maintenance paid.

(d)   Mortgage interest (rent is covered by housing benefit, see 6.6): interest at a standard rate will generally be paid on mortgages of up to £100,000 direct to the lender. Mortgage interest only is paid and not other housing costs, eg repayments of capital, insurance premiums payable on an endowment policy, or payments for the insurance of the building or contents.

Borrowers who take out a new mortgage after 1 October 1995 and subsequently claim income support will not have their mortgage payments included in their applicable amount for 39 weeks. Existing borrowers who start claiming income support will not be able to include their mortgage interest payments for eight weeks and will be able to include only half of their mortgage interest payments in their applicable amount for the following 18 weeks. A claimant who is a 'new borrower' may be treated as an 'existing borrower' where that claimant is a lone parent and claiming income support because her partner has deserted her.

6.3.3 Income

Any income the claimant may have will reduce the amount of benefit payable pound for pound. The claimant's income will include:

(a)   any earnings of the claimant net of tax, national insurance contributions and half of pension contributions. It is possible for a claimant to work for less than 16 hours per week and still claim income support. Earnings of dependent children, for example from a paper round, will not be included. There is an earnings disregard of £20. Thus, for example, if Sally is a lone parent who earns £50 per week net from a part-time cleaning job, only £30 will count as income for income support purposes;

(b)   any maintenance payments paid to the claimant, whether for his or her own benefit, or the benefit of a dependent child, for example, under a CSA maintenance calculation;

(c)   income from capital. If the claimant has capital of more than £16,000, she will be ineligible for income support (see 6.3.1). Any interest actually earned on capital of less than that amount will be ignored. However, capital of over £6,000 will be deemed to produce income at the rate of £1 per week for every £250 of capital over the £6,000 limit. So, for example, capital of £8,000 will be deemed to produce income of £8 per week (£8,000 – £6,000 = £2,000/250 = £8).

Note that child benefit and child tax credit are not included as income for income support purposes.

Any income will be deducted from the applicable amount to determine the amount of income support payable.

6.3.4 Passport benefits

Income support is a 'passport' to certain other benefits, ie where the claimant is claiming income support he will automatically be entitled to these other benefits as well. These passport benefits include:

(a)   free school meals;

(b)   exemption from NHS charges for prescriptions, dental treatment and eye-tests, and vouchers to help with the cost of glasses;

(c)   Healthy Start food vouchers and Healthy Start vitamins for expectant and nursing mothers and pre-school children. Healthy Start food vouchers can be exchanged for cows' milk, cows' milk formula, fruit or vegetables;

(d)   full housing and council tax benefits;

(e)   the opportunity to apply for interest-free loans from the social fund (see 6.9).

In addition, a claimant who is in receipt of maintenance may be able to make use of the diversion procedure (see 6.10.1).

These passport benefits can be quite valuable. Thus it may be worth making a claim for income support even where the amount of income support paid will be small in order to take advantage of them. It is also important to consider the passport benefits when negotiating maintenance payments. It is often unwise to accept an offer of maintenance which is just sufficient to take the client off income support, as the value of these benefits will be lost (see also 8.4).

6.3.5 Job grant

A lone parent who loses income support because she starts full-time work (or increases her working hours to at least 16 hours a week) will be entitled to a job grant of £250 if she has been claiming income support for at least 26 weeks and expects to be in full-time work for at least five weeks. In these circumstances, she will also be entitled to extended payments of housing benefit and council tax benefit at the rate she received them before obtaining the job (or increasing her hours) for up to four weeks.

6.4 Jobseeker's allowance

Jobseeker's allowance will be the appropriate benefit for the client to claim if he is not in full-time work and either has no children living with him, or lives with a new partner who is also not in full-time work.

6.4.1 Eligibility

Eligibility is similar to that for income support (see **6.3.1**), but there is also a requirement that the claimant signs on as available for and actively seeking work.

In addition, the claimant's partner (if any) must not work for more than 24 hours per week.

Any capital of a partner will be added to the claimant's own when assessing eligibility.

6.4.2 Applicable amount

This is the same as for income support (see **6.3.2**). However, the personal allowance will be higher where the claimant is part of a couple.

6.4.3 Income

This is similar to income support (see **6.3.3**). The income of any partner must be included. The earnings disregard is £5 if the claimant is single, or £10 if part of a couple.

6.4.4 Passport benefits

These are the same as for income support (see **6.3.4**).

6.5 Working tax credit and child tax credit

Note that although these credits are administered and generally paid by HM Revenue and Customs, they are not credits against tax and are payable whether or not the claimant has taxable income.

6.5.1 Working tax credit

6.5.1.1 Eligibility

The claimant must:

(a)   be present and ordinarily resident in Great Britain;

(b)   not be subject to immigration control;

(c)   work (and/or partner must work) 16 or more hours a week and be responsible for a child or children, or be disabled; *or*

(d)   work 30 or more hours a week and be over 25; *or*

(e)   work 16 or more hours a week and qualify for a disability element; *or*

(f)   work (and/or partner must work) 16 or more hours per week and qualify for a 50-plus element.

6.5.1.2 Amount

Working tax credit consists of a number of elements. The relevant ones for the family course are:

(a)   basic element: payable to all qualifying claimants;

(b)   couple and lone parent element: payable to qualifying claimants who are members of a couple, or who are lone parents;

(c)   30-hour element: payable to qualifying claimants who work 30 or more hours per week;

(d)   childcare costs: for one child 80% of the weekly cost of childcare up to £175; for two or more children 80% of the weekly cost of childcare up to £300.

6.5.2 Child tax credit

6.5.2.1 Eligibility

The claimant must:

(a)   be present and ordinarily resident in Great Britain;

(b)   have a child or children under 16, or under 20 and in full-time secondary education, for whom he is responsible;

(c)   not be subject to immigration control.

6.5.2.2 Amount

Child tax credit consists of a number of elements. The relevant ones for the family course are:

(a)   family element: payable to all qualifying claimants;

(b)   baby element: payable where there is a child under the age of one in the family;

(c)   child element: one child element is payable per child.

6.5.3 Income

For both child tax credit and working tax credit any gross income will usually be taken into account. Capital is ignored, although income from capital (save the first £300 pa) will be taken into account. The following are *not* taken into account as income: maintenance payments, child benefit, housing or council tax benefit, student loans.

Awards will be made at the beginning of the tax year based on income from the last tax year. Where a couple have split up, only the income of the claimant will be taken into account. Should the claimant's income change during the year an adjustment can be made, but the first £2,500 rise in income will be ignored. The claimant has a choice whether to advise HM Revenue and Customs immediately of any change in income, or whether to wait until the end of the tax year. However, if the Revenue is not informed immediately of any significant increase in income, this is likely to result in an overpayment which the Revenue will recoup in subsequent years.

6.5.4 Means testing

There are two lower income thresholds. These are currently:

(a)   £5,220 pa (£100.38 per week) for people claiming working tax credit, or working tax credit and child tax credit;

(b)   £14,495 pa (£278.75 per week) for people claiming child tax credit only (eg because they are not working, or working less than 16 hours a week).

If a person's gross income is over the threshold, his tax credits are reduced at the rate of 37p for every pound that his income exceeds the threshold. Working tax credit is reduced first then, once that has been reduced to nil, child tax credit is reduced.

There is also a higher income threshold of (at present) £50,000 for the family element of child tax credit. All families will receive the family element (£545 pa or £10.45 per week) unless their income exceeds £50,000. If it does exceed £50,000 then the family element is reduced by £1 for every £15 over the threshold.

Example

Bethan is a lone parent with two children under 16, Caspar and Milo. She works 35 hours per week and earns £600 per week (£31,200 pa). She pays £350 per week in childcare.

Bethan's maximum tax credit entitlements (*using notional figures*) are:

Child tax credit

Family element	£10.50
Element for Caspar	£34.00
Element for Milo	£34.00
Total	£78.50

Working tax credit

Basic element	£32.00
Lone parent element	£31.50
30 hour element	£13.00
Childcare element*	£240.00
Total	£316.50

*Bethan pays £350 per week childcare. However, only £300 of this is eligible. She is entitled to 80% of that, ie 80% x £300 = £240 pw.

However, as Bethan's income exceeds the £100.38 threshold, credit will taper. She earns £600. This exceeds the threshold by £600 – £100.38 = £499.62.

She will lose credit at the rate of 37p in the £, ie £499.62 × 37% = £184.86. Thus she will get £316.50 – 184.86 = £131.64 working tax credit.

As her working tax credit has not been tapered to nil, Bethan will retain the full amount of child tax credit.

6.5.5   Passport benefits

6.5.5.1   Exemption from NHS charges etc

Where a claimant has gross income of £15,050 or less and is claiming:

(a)   child tax credit alone; or

(b)   both child tax credit and working tax credit; or

(c)   working tax credit alone, but only if she gets a disability element;

she will be entitled to exemption from NHS charges for prescriptions, dental treatment and eye-tests, and to vouchers to help with the cost of glasses. An Exemption Certificate will automatically be sent to the claimant by the Prescription Pricing Authority if she fulfils these criteria.

6.5.5.2   Free school meals etc

Where a claimant has gross income of £14,495 or less and is claiming child tax credit alone (ie must not also be claiming working tax credit), she can claim free school meals for any of her children who are at a State school. In these circumstances she is also entitled to Healthy Start vouchers and Healthy Start vitamins for herself, if she is pregnant or nursing, and for her pre-school children.

6.6   Housing benefit

6.6.1   Eligibility

The claimant:

(a)   must have a right to reside in and be habitually resident in Great Britain;

(b)   must be liable to make payments of rent in respect of his home. Where a spouse is not technically liable to make such payments but is liable in practice, housing benefit will be available. For example, if the husband, who is the tenant of a council flat which is used as the family home, leaves home, the wife will be able to claim housing benefit;

(c)   need not be in receipt of income support, jobseeker's allowance or working tax credit;

(d)   must not have capital exceeding £16,000. Capital of over £6,000 will reduce the amount of housing benefit payable.

6.6.2   Amount

The method of assessing the amount of housing benefit to be paid to those who are not local authority tenants is quite complex. Factors to be taken into account include:

(a)   whether the amount of rent being paid is too high;

(b)   whether the accommodation is considered too large; and

(c)   the average rents in the area.

Where the claimant is on income support or jobseeker's allowance, the benefit will be a maximum of 100% of the rent payable, but may be less. For local authority tenants, the amount will generally be 100% of the rent payable (subject to any reductions mentioned below).

Housing benefit will be reduced by approximately 65 pence for each pound by which the claimant's income exceeds the income support level.

Income is calculated in much the same way as for income support (see **6.3.3**). However, there are some disregards, for example for maintenance received, child care bills and earnings. Child benefit, working tax credit and child tax credit count as income for housing benefit purposes.

The amount of benefit will be reduced if one or more non-dependants (who are not on income support or jobseeker's allowance) share the property.

Where the claimant is a council tenant, housing benefit will reduce the amount of rent payable so that no money will pass through his hands. Where the claimant is a private tenant, benefit will usually be paid direct to the landlord.

Changes are due to be made to the way the amount of housing benefit is calculated for renting in the private sector. Under the Welfare Reform Act 2007, a 'Local Housing Allowance' will be paid, regardless of how much rent is actually paid. The aims behind this change are to make the system fairer, so that the same amount will be paid to claimants in similar circumstances in the same area, and to allow for greater choice. Claimants could either increase their income by moving to a less attractive property (although the amount that the claimant receives will be capped), or decide to live more luxuriously, thus decreasing their income. The Government plans that this change, which is currently being piloted in 18 local authority areas, will be rolled out nationally in 2008.

The Welfare Reform Act 2007 also provides for a reduction in housing benefit where a person has been evicted from his home on the grounds of anti-social behaviour and refuses to undergo rehabilitation. The local authority must warn the claimant that such refusal will affect his housing benefit. The sanction is a 10% loss of benefit for four weeks, 20% for a further four weeks, and then a total removal for up to five years if the claimant does not co-operate. Lower rates will apply in cases of hardship. Normal payments would be reinstated at any time if the claimant agreed to undergo rehabilitation. There will be a right of appeal to the Tribunal Service. The Government's present intention is that these measures will be piloted for a period of two years starting in late 2007 or 2008.

6.7   Council tax benefit

6.7.1   Eligibility

The claimant:

(a)   must be liable to pay council tax. Couples (whether married or cohabiting) will be jointly responsible for their council tax bill. Each of them can claim council tax benefit;

(b)   need not be in receipt of any other benefits;

(c)   must not have capital exceeding £16,000. Capital over £6,000 will reduce the amount of any council tax benefit payable.

6.7.2   Amount

(a)   For claimants on income support (or whose income does not exceed the income support level), the amount is usually 100% of the council tax payable.

(b)   Council tax benefit will be reduced by approximately 20 pence for each pound by which the claimant's income exceeds the income support level.

(c)   Income is calculated in much the same way as for housing benefit.

(d)   Council tax benefit may also be reduced where there are one or more non-dependants (who are not on income support) living with the claimant.

Council tax benefit is given by a reduction in the council tax bill.

6.8   Discretionary housing payments

Discretionary housing payments can be paid by the local authority to anyone entitled to housing benefit or council tax benefit who appears to require additional financial assistance to meet their housing costs (which include council tax). They are paid by the local authority from a cash-limited fund.

6.9   The social fund

The social fund is a fund operated by the Department of Work and Pensions out of which loans and grants may be paid to those in need. The first part of the fund, which is known as the 'regulated social fund', makes payments which are mandatory where the claimant meets all the qualifying conditions. The second part of the fund is known as the 'discretionary social fund'.

6.9.1   The regulated social fund

There are four types of payment which are made from the regulated social fund:

(a)   Sure Start maternity grants to those on income support, jobseeker's allowance or child tax credit (provided this is paid at a rate which exceeds the family element). The maternity grant is paid at a flat rate.

(b)   Funeral grants paid to those in receipt of income support, job seeker's allowance, housing benefit or child tax credit (provided this is paid at a rate which exceeds the family element) who were the partner or close relative of the deceased and are therefore responsible for making arrangements for the funeral. There is a ceiling on the amount which can be claimed. Wherever possible, the Department of Work and Pensions will recover these costs from the deceased person's estate.

(c)   Cold weather payments to those on income support or jobseeker's allowance where this includes one of the pensioner or disability premiums, or the family includes a child under five years of age. Payments will be made automatically whenever the average temperature for seven days in a row is, or is forecast to be, freezing point or below.

(d)   Winter fuel payments to certain people aged 60 or over.

6.9.2   The discretionary social fund

Payments from the discretionary social fund may be by way of grant or loan. There are three types of payment which may be made:

(a)   Community care grants to those on income support or jobseeker's allowance. Such grants can be made in a number of situations, for example, to help elderly or disabled people to lead independent lives in the community when they leave hospital or residential care. Community care grants may also be made, for example, to ease exceptional pressures on families, and are subject to a wide discretion on the part of officers administering the fund. There is no maximum amount laid down for a community care grant, but claimants will have to use any savings they have in excess of £500 before a grant is payable.

(b)   Crisis loans to meet expenses which arise as the result of some disaster such as flood or fire. A crisis loan could, for example, cover living expenses for a short period (usually 14 days), or such items as essential household equipment. The loan is interest-free. The rate and period of repayment are based on the claimant's income and circumstances. To be eligible for a crisis loan, the claimant does not have to be in receipt of any other welfare benefit, but he must be without sufficient resources to meet the immediate short-term needs of himself and/or his family. The maximum amount of a crisis loan is £1,500.

(c)   Budgeting loans to those who have been on income support or jobseeker's allowance for at least 26 weeks to meet large, one-off expenses, for example, a replacement cooker or furniture. Claimants will be expected to use any savings they have in excess of £1,000 before a loan will be made. The social fund officer has a wide discretion as to the amount and purpose of these loans. However, there is a minimum of £100 and a maximum of £1,500. The loans are interest-free and repaid by deductions from benefit, the amount of the deduction depending on the claimant's individual circumstances.

6.10   Welfare benefits and marriage breakdown

6.10.1   Maintenance and income support/jobseeker's allowance

Any maintenance paid to the claimant (whether under a court order for herself, or as child maintenance assessed by the Child Support Agency) will count as income and will reduce income support or jobseeker's allowance paid pound for pound (save for the first £10 of child maintenance – see **6.3.2**). Thus, where the maintenance is not sufficient to take the claimant above the income support/ jobseeker's allowance level, she will receive her income partly from maintenance payments and partly from income support/jobseeker's allowance. If the payer is erratic in his payments, the claimant will be forced to apply for further income support/jobseeker's allowance to top up her income whenever payments are not made.

To avoid this problem and to ensure that the claimant receives a regular income, she can ask for her child support maintenance to be paid to the Child Support Agency. She will then receive the child support maintenance as part of her income support/jobseeker's allowance.

It may also be possible to assign the benefit of any maintenance order in her favour to the Department of Work and Pensions. The Department will then collect payments due under the order and pay the claimant her full benefit entitlement. The Department will also be responsible for enforcing any arrears. Before the Department accepts an assignment under this 'diversion procedure', any county court maintenance order must be registered in the family proceedings court. In addition, it will usually allow the diversion procedure to be used only where the payer has defaulted on past payments (practice differs from area to area, but usually the payer must have missed at least two monthly payments out of the last 12 payments).

If the maintenance eliminates the income support/jobseeker's allowance claim altogether, the claimant will also lose her passport benefits (see **6.3.4**).

6.10.2   Maintenance and working tax credit/ child tax credit

Any maintenance paid will not affect the amount of working tax credit or child tax credit received.

6.10.3   Maintenance and housing benefit/council tax benefit

Unless the claimant is on income support, any maintenance can reduce her entitlement to housing benefit and council tax benefit, or even eliminate it.

6.10.4   Lump sum payments

Where a lump sum payment brings the claimant's capital above the relevant capital limits, entitlement to the appropriate benefit will be eliminated.

Where a lump sum payment brings the claimant's capital to over £6,000 but under the relevant capital limits, the capital will be deemed to produce income (see **6.3.3**).

Special rules apply to lump sum payments where the claimant is on income support or jobseeker's allowance. These rules are meant to ensure that the claimant cannot avoid losing income support or jobseeker's allowance by accepting a lump sum payment rather than maintenance. Thus, when a lump sum payment is intended as a form of maintenance, it will be treated as income and may debar the claimant from income support or jobseeker's allowance for a period of time while the lump sum is used up. The formula applied when decapitalising lump sums is:

$$\frac{\text{Lump sum}}{\text{Weekly income support} + 2} = \begin{array}{l}\text{Number of weeks income support or} \\ \text{jobseeker's allowance is eliminated}\end{array}$$

Example

Willa receives £48 income support per week. She receives no maintenance from Den, her ex-husband, but one day Den offers her a lump sum of £500, which she accepts. Willa will be denied income support for:

$$\frac{500}{48 + 2} = 10 \text{ weeks}$$

During this time, Willa must live off the lump sum at the rate of £50 per week.

None of the above rules will apply where the lump sum payment represents the claimant's share in the home and it is used to buy another home within six months, when the payment will be ignored.

6.10.5 Property adjustment

The value of the claimant's home is generally ignored in assessing benefits.

6.11 Local authority housing

The family solicitor must be able to give immediate advice to a client who finds herself in a situation where she is, or might be, without a roof over her head. The two most common situations where this might occur are where the client has been subjected to domestic abuse (see **Chapter 15**), or when she cannot stay in the former matrimonial home for financial reasons (eg because there are large mortgage arrears and the home must be sold).

Local authorities are under certain duties to provide help (including, in some cases, accommodation) to people who are homeless or threatened with homelessness. These duties are set out in the Housing Act 1996, as amended by the Homelessness Act 2002. The duty owed will depend upon whether the person applying is homeless or threatened with homelessness, whether that homelessness is intentional and whether the applicant has a priority need.

6.11.1 Homelessness

A person is homeless if:

(a)   there is no reasonable accommodation which he and his family are entitled to occupy; or

(b)   he has such accommodation but he cannot secure entry.

A person may also be entitled to local authority help if he is 'threatened' with homelessness, which means that he is likely to become homeless in the next 28 days.

6.11.2 Intentional homelessness

A person is intentionally homeless if he deliberately does or fails to do anything in consequence of which he ceases to occupy accommodation which was available for occupation by him and his family and which it would have been reasonable for him to continue to occupy.

6.11.3 Priority need

The applicant will be treated as having a priority need if:

(a)   he has dependent children who are living with him or might reasonably be expected to live with him; or

(b)   his homelessness resulted from flood, fire or other disaster; or

(c)   he (or a member of his household) is vulnerable through old age, mental illness or handicap, physical disability or other special reasons; or

(d)   she (or a member of the household) is pregnant; or

(e)   he is aged 16 or 17, has not been in care and no duty to accommodate is owed to him under s 20 of the CA 1989; or

(f)   he is aged under 21 and was in care whilst aged 16–18, but has now left care; or

(g)   he is 'vulnerable' as a result of having been in care, having served in the armed forces, or having been in prison, custody or detention; or

(h)   he has ceased to occupy accommodation as a result of violence or threats of violence.

6.11.4 Local authority duties

The local authority has the following duties:

(a)   to rehouse a homeless person with a priority need who did not become homeless intentionally;

(b)   to provide temporary housing for a homeless person with a priority need who did become homeless intentionally. This accommodation must be provided for such period as the authority considers will give the homeless person a reasonable opportunity of finding his own accommodation. The authority is under a further duty to give advice and assistance to help him find such accommodation;

(c)   to advise and assist a homeless person without a priority need to help him find his own accommodation. In addition, if satisfied that he did not become homeless intentionally, the authority *may* secure that accommodation is available for his occupation.

6.11.5 Local connection provisions

Generally, the local authority to which the applicant applies will be the one under the duty mentioned at **6.11.4**. However, that local authority may not be under such a duty if the applicant has no local connection with its area. This is so that local authorities in, for example, seaside areas do not become overwhelmed with applications. In this case, the local authority can refer the applicant to a local authority with which he does have a local connection (provided that the applicant is not at risk of domestic abuse in that authority's area).

The applicant will have a local connection with the area in which he is normally resident, or where he is employed, or where he has family associations.

6.11.6 Local authority tenancies

A local authority tenancy is classed as a secure tenancy under the Housing Act 1985. This means that a council tenant has a great deal of security of tenure. In particular, he cannot be evicted without an order for possession from the court, and such an order is available only on specified grounds, for example, non-payment of rent. This security depends partly on the tenant (or one of them where the property is on a joint tenancy) remaining in occupation.

On divorce, the court can order the tenant spouse to transfer the tenancy to the other spouse, and when this is done security of tenure is not lost (see further **9.5**).

6.12 Chapter summary

(1) On marriage breakdown one or both of the parties may need to claim welfare benefits. The following may be available:

(a) child benefit;

(b) income support or jobseeker's allowance or working tax credit;

(c) child tax credit;

(d) housing benefit;

(e) council tax benefit;

(f) loans or grants from the social fund.

(2) Local authorities have duties towards homeless people. Where a person is homeless unintentionally and has a priority need (eg if she has a child with her) the local authority must generally rehouse her.

Chapter 7

Calculating Child Maintenance

7.1 Introduction

This chapter covers the Child Support Act 1991 (CSA 1991) which deals with maintenance for most children. In response to some of the criticisms raised against the Child Support Agency ('the Agency'), the CSA 1991 was amended by the Child Support Act 1995 and the Child Support, Pensions and Social Security Act 2000 (CSPSSA 2000). Throughout this book, any reference to the CSA 1991 includes the 1995 and 2000 Acts.

Chapter 4 dealt with the statutory criteria used by the court when considering applications for child maintenance under the MCA 1973 on marriage breakdown. These factors are of a general nature and do not assist the court in arriving at specific figures for maintenance. Accordingly, the orders for children's maintenance could vary enormously from one court to another.

However, the intention is that most applications for child maintenance are now made under the CSA 1991, where the approach is entirely different; this legislation introduced a precise method of assessing maintenance using a formula. The CSA 1991, as it was originally enacted, used a detailed and complex formula. This led to long delays in assessing liability and enforcement. The Act has now been amended by the CSPSSA 2000, and this chapter deals in detail with its provisions. The 2000 Act replaced the detailed formula with a calculation based on a simple percentage of the non-resident parent's net income. This will be discussed in detail at **7.6.2**. The CSPSSA 2000 came into effect on 3 March 2003 for new cases. Assessments made using the old formula will continue to be payable until a further date to be appointed.

Application for child maintenance must usually be made to the Child Support Agency, although in certain cases (see **7.4**) application may be made to the court. The Agency operates under the authority of the Secretary of State for Work and Pensions. This Agency has, in theory at least, ousted the jurisdiction of the courts in the vast majority of cases. The Child Support Agency, through its officers, is responsible for making maintenance calculations and, where necessary, collecting and enforcing the maintenance. It also provides information and advice. Fees were charged (to both parents) for the Agency's services (although, broadly, those on benefit were exempt from paying those fees). However, due to problems with the service that the Agency is providing, fees are currently suspended. These problems have proved to be ongoing, and the Government has announced its intention to scrap the Agency (see **7.7**).

7.2 Co-operation with the Agency

The driving force which led to the introduction of the CSA 1991 was the desire to reduce the huge sums of income support paid to lone parents. Very many lone parents received only modest or no maintenance at all from the non-resident parent, and consequently were forced to claim State benefits. In an effort to reduce this burden on the tax payer, s 6 provides that a claim for certain welfare benefits (including income support and jobseeker's allowance, but not working tax credit) is deemed to be an application for child support. This enables the Secretary of State to pursue the non-resident parent for maintenance, and the claimant is required to provide information to assist in that process.

The most important (and controversial) information is the naming of the non-resident parent. Many mothers might not wish to look to the non-resident father to maintain a child who may have had no relationship with him. Indeed, the non-resident parent may not even be aware that he has fathered the child. Despite such reluctance, the mother will be obliged to co-operate with the Agency or face the consequences. Unless a parent can show a legitimate reason for failing to co-operate, she will be penalised by reduction of her benefit. For three years, her benefit will be reduced by 40% of the adult personal allowance. If at any time during that period she decides to co-operate, her benefit will cease to be reduced and will recommence at the normal rate (CSA 1991, s 46 and Child Support (Maintenance Calculation Procedure) Regulations 2000 (SI 2001/157)).

It will be legitimate to request the Secretary of State not to pursue the application and to refuse to co-operate if there would be a risk of the parent with care or any child living with her suffering harm or undue distress as a result. Thus, if a parent is genuinely and reasonably afraid that co-operation might provoke a violent response from the non-resident parent, this would constitute good cause and her benefit would not be reduced. There is no requirement to substantiate that belief with hard evidence, although she would be required to be interviewed about her concern. Generally, if satisfied that the assertion is not implausible, the interviewing officer should waive the requirements to co-operate and allow the parent to continue to receive her full benefit entitlement. However, the case of *Secretary of State for Work and Pensions v Caroline Roach* [2006] EWCA Civ 1746 makes it clear that whether the parent or child will suffer undue distress is not a purely subjective test. The decision maker must make an objective judgement as to whether the foreseeable distress was unjustified in the context of the personal, subjective characteristics of the parent with care or child.

7.3 When does the CSA 1991 apply?

Section 11 of the CSA 1991 provides:

> For the purposes of this Act, each parent of a qualifying child is responsible for maintaining him.

This calls for a number of definitions to be considered.

Section 55(1) defines 'a child' as an unmarried person under 16, or a person under 19 receiving full-time education which is not advanced education.

Section 3(1) defines the 'qualifying child' as such if:

(a)   one of his parents is in relation to him a non-resident parent; or

(b)   both of his parents are, in relation to him, non-resident parents.

As the name suggests, a non-resident parent is one who is not living in the same household as the child (s 3(2)). The term 'parent' takes its usual meaning of being a person who is in law the mother or father of the child, ie the natural parent or adoptive parent of the child. It does not extend to a step-parent. Clearly, this includes unmarried as well as married parents, and it is immaterial whether or not the non-resident parent knows that the child is his. In cases of disputes over parentage, the Agency may make a maintenance calculation only in certain cases, for example, where the alleged father was married to the mother throughout the period of conception to birth, where the alleged father has been registered as the father of the child or where the alleged father has refused to take a scientific paternity test (CSA 1991, s 26). In other cases the Agency may not make a maintenance calculation until the court has determined parentage.

The CSA 1991 also refers to the person with care. Section 3(3) defines this person as one with whom the child lives and who usually provides the child's day-to-day care (this may not necessarily be the child's parent). It will generally be the person with care who will apply for the maintenance calculation, although the non-resident parent may choose to apply for a calculation against himself.

The child support officer has jurisdiction to make a maintenance calculation only if the qualifying child, the person with care and the non-resident parent are all habitually resident in the UK. This is subject to exceptions under s 44(2A) of the CSA 1991, relating to certain non-resident parents who are not habitually resident in the UK. These include civil servants and members of the armed forces working abroad, and employees of UK companies who are working abroad but whose employer calculates and arranges payment within the UK.

7.4 The jurisdiction of the court

By virtue of s 8 of the CSA 1991, the Agency, in theory, has almost exclusive jurisdiction to deal with child maintenance.

Section 8(3) states:

> Except as provided in subsection (3A), in any case where subsection (1) applies, no court shall exercise any power which it would otherwise have to make, vary or revise any maintenance order in relation to the child and non-resident parent concerned.

The cases covered by s 8(1) are those where a child support officer would have jurisdiction to make a maintenance calculation with respect to a qualifying child and his non-resident parent. In other words, if an application could be dealt with by the Agency, it must be pursued there. However, the court retains jurisdiction to deal with those cases in which the Agency has no jurisdiction. The court, therefore, continues to deal with maintenance for step-children who are children of the family, and for those natural children who are too old to be qualifying children, for example, those aged 19 or over who are in education or training. If either the child, or the non-resident parent or the person with care is not habitually resident in the UK, the Agency will have no jurisdiction, but the court would have jurisdiction. The court also retains jurisdiction to make capital orders on behalf of children, ie a lump sum or property adjustment order. The court has power to vary or revoke existing maintenance orders in all cases (CSA 1991, s 8(3A) and (4)).

In the limited cases where the court retains jurisdiction, it will have the widest discretion to determine the amount of a child's periodical payments. It will consider the factors listed in s 25(3) and (4) of the MCA 1973, giving first consideration to the child's welfare as directed in s 25(1) (discussed in **Chapter 4**).

In practice, the court is likely to take as the appropriate starting point for a child maintenance order the figure produced by a maintenance calculation under the CSA 1991 (*GW v RE* [2003] EWHC Fam 611). It will, therefore, be worthwhile calculating what a parent would be ordered to pay for a child were an application to the Agency possible. If the child is a step-child, regard must be had to the liability of the child's natural parents to maintain the child. Consequently, the step-parent may be ordered to pay an amount significantly less than a natural parent would be required to pay under the CSA 1991 formula, particularly if the parent with care could claim against the natural parent through the Agency.

In cases where a maintenance calculation has been (or is about to be) made, this must be taken into account in proceedings by the carer for maintenance for herself, as it will have a direct bearing on both parties' means (see **8.3**).

As well as dealing with those cases which cannot be dealt with by the Agency, the court retains jurisdiction to make maintenance orders for children in the three circumstances specified in s 8. These are discussed in **7.4.1** to **7.4.3** below.

[margin note: S.8 Circumstances]

7.4.1 Supplementary maintenance *(Wealthy families)*

Under s 8(6), the court will have jurisdiction if it is of the view that maintenance should be paid in addition to that assessed by the Agency. This will apply to wealthy families only as it is a prerequisite that the Agency has already made a calculation up to the maximum level and therefore that the non-resident parent has a net income of over £2,000 per week (see **7.6.2**).

There are unlikely to be many applications under this subsection as the courts will rarely be persuaded that further sums should be paid. The circumstances when a child might require further assistance, for example, because he needs school fees or because of a disability, are in any event separately provided for in s 8(7) and (8).

7.4.2 Educational expenses

Section 8(7) provides that the court may continue to exercise its jurisdiction if the child is in education and provision is required to meet some or all of the expenses connected with it.

Typically, applications under this section will be made to cover the cost of school fees which are not fully met from the maintenance calculation. They may also be made to cover the payment of school uniforms, sports equipment, books, etc.

7.4.3 Children with a disability

If a child has a disability, this is not taken into account by the Agency when making the maintenance calculation. Such children, however, will frequently have additional expenses to meet their needs. Section 8(8) enables the court to make an order to supplement the maintenance calculation to meet expenses attributable to that disability.

Section 8(9) defines a child as disabled if he is blind, deaf or dumb, or is substantially and permanently handicapped by illness, injury, mental disorder or congenital deformity, or such other disability as may be prescribed.

7.5 Maintenance agreements and consent orders

Section 8(3) restricts the jurisdiction of the court to determine maintenance for children. However, it is still open to parents who are not claiming the main welfare benefits to arrange maintenance for children without going to the Agency, and it seems that, in practice, many couples are making an effort to avoid the involvement of the Agency in the following ways.

7.5.1 Separation agreements

Separation agreements represent an alternative method of finalising family finances on the breakdown of the relationship. They are frequently used by those who are unable or do not wish to obtain a court order, and who have agreed their own arrangements and wish to put their agreements in writing. A separation agreement is not a court order but is enforceable in the same way as any other binding contract (see **12.3.4.1**).

Following the CSA 1991, parents may still make separation agreements, and s 9(2) specifically preserves this right for non-benefit cases. However, just as in the past such agreements could not oust the jurisdiction of the court to determine maintenance, neither can the jurisdiction of the Child Support Agency be ousted. Section 9(3) and (4) rule out any attempts to undermine the Agency's jurisdiction by prohibiting applications to it. As a result, any carer who enters into a separation agreement (even one which expressly purports to restrict the parties' rights to make any further claims) will, nevertheless, be able to apply to the Agency for a maintenance calculation. Indeed, as s 6 requires a parent who is receiving benefit to co-operate with the Secretary of State in taking action under the Act, a party to an agreement may find herself reluctantly obliged to renege on the agreement and co-operate with the Agency.

7.5.2 Consent orders

Some couples may want to do more than just put their agreement in writing; they may want their agreement embodied in a court order. If so, they can apply for a consent order.

Consent orders (ie court orders in terms agreed by the parties) have for some time been of widespread use and will continue to be important. Prior to the CSA 1991, couples were encouraged to consider the family finances as a package deal. A consent order would embody an overall agreement covering the home, maintenance of the parties and children. Frequently, a clean break would be agreed, whereby a parent would forgo maintenance entirely or accept only nominal maintenance for herself and the children in return for a capital settlement. On the whole, the opportunity for such a package deal approach is now closed because maintenance is determined without negotiation by the Agency. Clearly, it will be necessary for the solicitors to anticipate what the Agency's maintenance calculation will be, as it will inevitably have an influence on the issues remaining to be dealt with by the consent order.

In spite of the clear wording of s 8(3), which prohibits the court from making (varying or reviving) maintenance orders where the Agency would have jurisdiction, s 8(5) preserves the power of the court to make an order if:

(a)   a written agreement (whether or not enforceable) provides for the making or securing by a non-resident parent of the child of periodical payments to or for the benefit of the child; and

(b)   the maintenance order which the court makes is, in all material respects, in the same terms as that agreement.

This provision was implemented by the Child Maintenance (Written Agreements) Order 1993 (SI 1993/620). Therefore, a separation agreement may be converted into a court order in the same terms. All that is required is for there to be a written agreement (this can be evidenced in a separate agreement, or incorporated in the recitals to the consent order). As a result of s 8(5) and the Regulations, parents may continue to side-step the Agency and embody a clean break agreement in a consent order.

Where a consent order was made before 3 March 2003, no application can be made to the Agency under s 4 whilst that order is in force. If a consent order is made after 3 March 2003, no application can be made to the Agency under s 4 for one year (CSA 1991, s 4(10)). Thus consent orders made after 3 March 2003 will be binding as to child maintenance for only one year, after which the parent with care can apply for a maintenance calculation. The Family Law Committee of the Law Society recommended in its 2003 report, *Financial Provision on Divorce: Clarity and Fairness – Proposals for Reform*, that this provision be scrapped and that couples should still be able to agree consent orders in relation to child maintenance which will bind until the child(ren)'s majority. Unfortunately, the Child Maintenance Bill (see 7.7), as currently drafted, has not introduced this reform. Thus family law practitioners are having to use various devices to try to mitigate the effect of s 4(10) of the CSA 1991. One way is to enter a contract ancillary to the consent order whereby the parties agree to pay (or repay) any difference between the agreed maintenance order and a maintenance calculation subsequently made by the Child Support Agency. Another is to agree to an annual child periodical payments order (or 'Christmas order'). Such an order lasts for a day short of a year and is then replaced by an order in identical terms the following day. However, there is some criticism of such Christmas orders as contrary to public policy (see, for example, Nicholas Mostyn QC in *Child's Pay*, a computer package by Class Publishing). Lastly, '*Segal* orders' are global orders combining maintenance to both spouse and child. The amount to be paid is reduced by the amount of any subsequent maintenance calculation by the Child Support Agency. Such orders are possible only if there is a substantial element within them for the financial support of the parent with care. However, although it appears that some courts are prepared to endorse each of these mechanisms, there is no guarantee that they will be upheld by a higher court.

Irrespective of s 4(10) of the CSA 1991, if the order or agreement is revoked an application may be made to the Agency immediately. The decision whether or not to revoke an existing order rests with the court. It may not be prepared to revoke its original order, which would in effect block an early application to the Agency. In the case of *B v M (Child Support: Revocation of Order)* [1994] Fam Law 370, an order was made for the maintenance of three children in 1986. The mother wanted to apply under CSA 1991 for an assessment in respect of the two younger children, and applied for the original maintenance order to be revoked to enable her to do so. The father successfully appealed against the district judge's revocation. The court stated that the proper course would be to vary the original order, and that it was inappropriate to exercise its discretion to revoke the order purely because the mother wished to apply to the Agency. However, the court made it clear that each case must be considered on its merits.

Where a court order has been made, the court will retain its power to vary the order (CSA 1991, s 8(3A)).

7.6 Calculating the child maintenance

When an application is made to the Child Support Agency, a formula is applied in order to calculate the maintenance payable in respect of a child by the non-resident parent. It is applied to those required to make the application (by virtue of s 6) and those who choose to pursue a claim (under s 4) in the same way. The key elements of the formula are set out in Sch 1 to the Act (see **Appendix 1(F)**).

7.6.1   The formula before the CSPSSA 2000

The original formula was very complicated. It was based on the annually revised income support rates which were used to work out the notional expenses of caring for a child (the 'maintenance requirement'). This amount was apportioned between the parents according to their 'assessable income'. Once an initial maintenance assessment had been reached, checks were made to ensure that the payer was not reduced below his 'protected income' and would not be expected to pay more than 30% of his net income.

7.6.2   The new formula

This is very much simpler and is based solely on the non-resident parent's net earned income (ie income net of tax, national insurance and pension payments) and the number of children for whom that parent is responsible. The maintenance calculation is at one of four rates: the basic rate, the reduced rate, the flat rate or the nil rate.

7.6.2.1   The basic rate

This will be the usual rate. It provides that the non-resident parent should pay a proportion of his net income as follows:

Number of children	Proportion of net income
One	15%
Two	20%
Three or more	25%

Thus a non-resident parent with two children and a net weekly income of £500 will pay £100 per week. There is a cap on the amount of net income which will be taken into account, so that net weekly income of over £2,000 will be ignored.

If the non-resident parent has other children living with him, for whom either he or any partner he is living with receives child benefit, his net income is reduced by the following amount before the basic rate is applied:

Number of other children	Proportion net income is reduced
One	15%
Two	20%
Three or more	25%

Example

George is living with Linda and her two children, Doug (9) and Chloe (4). His ex-wife lives with their only child, Patricia (7). George has net income of £500. The maintenance calculation for Patricia will be:

£500 – £100 = £400

£400 × 15% = £60

7.6.2.2   The reduced rate

This will apply where the non-resident parent's net weekly income is more than £100 but less than £200. The amount payable increases in proportion to the amount by which the non-resident parent's income exceeds £100. The exact method of calculation is contained in the Child Support (Maintenance

Calculations and Special Cases) Regulations 2000 (SI 2001/155) (CS(MCSC) Regs 2000).

7.6.2.3   The flat rate

This will apply if the non-resident parent's net weekly income is £100 or less; he is in receipt of certain benefits, pensions or allowances (including income support, jobseeker's allowance and incapacity benefit), or his partner is in receipt of income support or income-based jobseeker's allowance. The flat rate is currently £5 per week (CS(MCSC) Regs 2000).

7.6.2.4   The nil rate

This applies where the non-resident parent has net income of below £5 or comes within a prescribed category (including full-time students in advanced education and prisoners).

7.6.3   Special cases

7.6.3.1   Apportionment

The position where a non-resident parent has more than one qualifying child and those children are looked after by more than one person with care is covered by Sch 1, para 6 to the CSA 1991. In such a case, the maintenance calculation is divided by the number of qualifying children and then shared between the parents with care in proportion to the number of qualifying children in each family.

Example

Jon has four qualifying children, one being cared for by Lisa and three by Anita. His net income is £800. The maintenance calculation is therefore 25% × £800 = £200. Lisa will receive £50 maintenance (one quarter) and Anita the remaining £150 (three quarters).

7.6.3.2   Shared care

Where both parents share care, the maintenance calculation will be reduced. The amount of this reduction will depend on the number of qualifying children and the amount of time they spend in the care of each parent (CSA 1991, Sch 1, para 7).

Shared care – basic and reduced rates

The amount of reduction for one child is:

No of nights per year	Fraction to subtract
52–103	one-seventh
104–155	two-sevenths
156–174	three-sevenths
175 or more	one half

Where the parent with care is looking after more than one qualifying child of the same non-resident parent the reduction will be the sum of the relevant fractions divided by the number of children. Put simply, this means that where the children stay the same number of nights each with the non-resident parent then, generally, the maintenance calculation will be reduced by one-seventh for each night of the week that they stay.

Example

Nick and Maria have three children. They all stay with Nick on Friday and Saturday night each week. The initial maintenance calculation is £210. This will be reduced by $\frac{2}{7}$ (ie $\frac{2}{7} + \frac{2}{7} + \frac{2}{7} \div 3$). $\frac{2}{7} \times £210 = £60$. So the final maintenance calculation will be £210 – £60 = £150.

However, note that there is a further reduction of a flat rate of £7 per child where that child is looked after by the non-resident parent for 175 nights or more. Care must also be taken in the calculation where the children stay for a different number of nights with the non-resident parent.

Example

Duncan and Nicola have two children, Jack and Georgia. Jack stays with Duncan for 180 nights a year, Georgia for 156. Duncan's maintenance calculation will be reduced by $\frac{13}{28}$ ($[\frac{7}{14} + \frac{6}{14}] \div 2$), and then by a further £7.

Shared care – flat rate

Where:

(a) child support maintenance would be payable at the flat rate because the non-resident parent is in receipt of prescribed benefits, pensions or allowances, or his partner is in receipt of prescribed benefits; and

(b) the non-resident parent cares for one or more qualifying children for at least 52 nights a year

then the maintenance calculation will be nil.

There is some criticism of the shared care provisions on the basis that they can encourage arguments about the amount of staying contact for the non-resident parent as this will affect the amount of child support he must pay. In *Re B (A Child)* [2006] EWCA Civ 1574 the court made it clear that when deciding the level of staying contact or whether a joint residence order was appropriate, any impact this would have on the amount of child support being paid should be ignored. The father argued that an increase in child support payable would impact on the welfare of the child, since it would reduce his disposable income and thus the child's enjoyment of contact. This argument was dismissed as being wrong in principle and impractical.

7.6.4 Variations

The application of a rigid formula may inevitably lead to harsh results in certain cases. For this reason, the CSA 1991 (as amended) allows for applications for variation. Any such application can be made either before a final maintenance calculation has been made (CSA 1991, s 28A), or after (CSA 1991, s 28G). However, variations will be allowed only in certain tightly defined circumstances as set out in Sch 4B to the CSA 1991 and the Child Support (Variations) Regulations 2000 (SI 2001/156) (see below). In addition, the Secretary of State must be of the opinion that, in all the circumstances of the case, it would be just and equitable to agree to a variation.

7.6.4.1 Special expenses

These are:

(a) costs incurred by the non-resident parent maintaining contact with a qualifying child;

(b)   costs attributable to a long-term illness or disability of another relevant child;

(c)   certain debts incurred before the parent became a non-resident parent (generally only if these debts were incurred for the benefit of both parents or the child);

(d)   the maintenance element of boarding school fees for the child in relation to whom the application for a maintenance calculation is made; and

(e)   mortgage payments on the home the non-resident parent and parent with care shared, provided the non-resident parent no longer has an interest in the property and the parent with care and child still live there.

These expenses must be of at least a 'threshold' amount to be taken into account (unless the expense relates to ground (b) when there is no threshold). Where the non-resident parent has a net weekly income of £200 or more these expenses must total in aggregate £15 or more a week. Where the non-resident parent has a net weekly income of less than £200 the expenses must in aggregate total £10 or more a week. If the Secretary of State considers any of these special expenses to be unreasonably high or to have been unreasonably incurred, he may substitute such lower amount as he considers reasonable (Child Support (Variations) Regulations 2000, reg 15).

Generally speaking, if allowable, these expenses will be deducted from the net weekly income of the non-resident parent before making the maintenance calculation (Child Support (Variations) Regulations 2000, reg 23). However, any reduction for boarding school fees are not to reduce the net weekly income by more than 50% (Child Support (Variations) Regulations 2000, reg 13).

7.6.4.2   Property or capital transfers

One of the main criticisms of the original formula was that it failed to take into account any capital transfers made by the non-resident parent to the parent with care. For example, one parent may have transferred the matrimonial home to the other parent, in return for which that parent agreed to forgo maintenance (entirely or in part) for herself and the children. A non-resident parent who, having entered into such a clean break agreement prior to the CSA 1991, subsequently faces a maintenance calculation, is likely to feel very aggrieved as this strikes at the very basis of the original settlement.

In response to these criticisms, the formula was revised in April 1995 to take such disposals broadly into account, and this has been kept (in a slightly amended form) by the CSPSSA 2000. However, this applies only to capital transfers made before the CSA 1991 came into force (ie before April 1993). On this basis, no further details of this variation will be considered here.

7.6.4.3   Additional cases

Non-resident parents may apply for a downwards variation of any maintenance calculation on the basis of special expenses, or property or capital transfers as set out above. However, Sch 4B, para 4 to the CSA 1991 and the Child Support (Variations) Regulations 2000, regs 18–20 allow for variations to be made in other cases which may result in an increase in the amount of child maintenance payable. These are:

(a)   The non-resident parent has assets, such as cash, shares or land but excluding, amongst other things, his home and business assets, with a net value exceeding £65,000. The value of these is calculated by applying the statutory rate of interest (currently 8% pa) and dividing by 52. This amount is then added to the non-resident parent's net income. For example, if the non-resident parent owned shares worth £80,000, these would be taken to produce income of (£80,000 × 8%) ÷ 52 = £123.08 per week.

(b)   The maintenance calculation is at the nil rate due to the non-resident parent coming within a prescribed category, or at the flat rate due to the non-resident parent being in receipt of a prescribed benefit, pension or allowance, but the Secretary of State is satisfied that the non-resident parent is in receipt of net income of over £100 which would otherwise be taken into account. This would cover, for example, the earnings of a non-resident parent who was a student. The whole of this income will be taken into account as net income.

(c)   The non-resident parent has the ability to control the amount of income he receives from a company or business, including earnings from employment or self-employment. The net weekly income so assessed must exceed £100. This would cover, for example, income received by way of dividends.

(d)   The Secretary of State is satisfied that the non-resident parent has unreasonably reduced the amount of his net income in order to reduce his liability to pay child support maintenance.

(e)   The non-resident parent's lifestyle is inconsistent with the amount of his declared income. In such a case a variation can be made on the basis that the non-resident parent is in fact in receipt of the amount of income required to support his lifestyle.

7.6.5   Default and interim maintenance decisions (CSA 1991, s 12)

In certain circumstances, it will not be possible to make a final maintenance calculation straightaway. If this is because there is insufficient information to complete the calculation, the Secretary of State may make a default maintenance decision. If it is because an application for variation is outstanding, the Secretary of State may make an interim maintenance decision.

7.6.5.1   Default maintenance decision

Where there is insufficient information to make a final maintenance calculation, maintenance can be calculated at the default rate. This is £30 per week if one qualifying child, £40 per week if two qualifying children and £50 per week if there are three or more qualifying children (Child Support (Maintenance Calculation Procedure) Regulations 2000 (SI 2001/157), reg 7). When the relevant information is provided, a new maintenance calculation will be made. If non-provision of information by the non-resident parent led to the making of the default maintenance decision, her maintenance liability for the period that the default rate was in place will be recalculated only if the full rate is higher than the default rate. The Government hopes that this will provide an incentive for non-resident parents to provide information quickly. It will also avoid the situation where overpayments need to be recovered from the parent with care.

7.6.5.2   Interim maintenance decision

Where there is an application for a variation outstanding, maintenance may be calculated as normal, ignoring the variation application. If the variation application is successful, this interim rate will be replaced with the new level of maintenance calculated taking into account the variation. The maintenance calculation at this new level will have retrospective effect.

7.6.6 Voluntary payments

A non-resident parent may wish to ensure that he is given credit for any payments of child support maintenance that he makes whilst a maintenance calculation is being made. Section 28J of the CSA 1991 provides that voluntary payments can be set off against any child support maintenance liability under a maintenance calculation, but, by s 28J(4), such a voluntary payment must be made to the Agency unless agreed otherwise.

Another possible device was discussed in *Dorney-Kingdom v Dorney-Kingdom* [2000] 2 FLR 855. The court stated that a provision in an order for spouse maintenance which incorporated some of the costs of caring for the children and which was reduced once the Agency had assessed child support was legitimate provided it included a substantial amount of spousal support. Such orders ('*Segal* orders') are useful since the ancillary relief proceedings are often heard before the child maintenance has been calculated and such an order will ensure that the parent with care has sufficient money to support the children in the interim.

7.7 Reform

To date, the Child Support Agency has not achieved its aim of saving the Government money. Neither has it managed to provide an efficient and effective system of child maintenance. Following an independent report by Sir David Henshaw published on 24 July 2006, the Government has introduced the Child Maintenance Bill into Parliament. Amongst other things the Bill proposes to:

(a)   scrap the Child Support Agency and replace it with the Child Maintenance and Enforcement Commission (C-MEC). C-MEC is expected to begin operation in 2008/2009 when it will begin to take on the caseload of the Child Support Agency. New cases will be accepted from 2010/2011;

(b)   repeal s 6 of the CSA 1991, meaning that those on benefit will no longer be forced to go through the Child Support Agency (or C-MEC);

(c)   increase the £10 per week child maintenance premium for those on income support to a 'significant' amount from 2010/2011;

(d)   use gross weekly income instead of net weekly income when calculating the amount of child maintenance to be paid. This will have the knock-on effect of reducing the percentages to be applied;

(e)   introduce a new (lower) percentage rate which will be used for earnings over a certain amount;

(f)   increase enforcement powers (see further **11.4**).

7.8 Chapter summary

(1)   The Child Support Agency will deal with maintenance for a child where the child is:

(a)   under 16;

(b)   under 19 and in full-time, non-advanced education.

(2)   The courts will deal with maintenance for a child in the following circumstances:

(a)   where the child is a step-child;

(b)   where the child is aged 16–19 and in advanced education or is aged over 19;

(c)   where either parent or the child is not habitually resident in the UK;

(d)   to provide top-up maintenance;

(e)   to cover education expenses;

(f)   to cover disability expenses; or

(g)   by making a consent order, if the parent with care is not on welfare benefits.

(3)   A simple formula is applied to calculate maintenance for a child under CSA 1991 based on a flat-rate percentage of the non-resident parent's net income.

(4)   Variations from the simple formula are possible in certain tightly defined cases.

Chapter 8

Maintenance for a Spouse

8.1 Introduction

The amount of maintenance to be paid by one spouse to the other will depend on numerous variables, and a case-by-case approach will be taken by the solicitor and the court. Figures cited in reported decisions are of little assistance as there are rarely two cases with identical facts. However, one variable will always be significant and that is the presence or otherwise of dependent children. If there are children to provide for, this will have a significant impact on each party's needs and resources. The maintenance being paid and received for children must be taken into account when calculating maintenance for a spouse. In many instances, there will be insufficient resources remaining for maintenance to be paid to a spouse after paying maintenance for children. It is especially so in low income families. In middle and higher income families, spouses may wish to pursue claims for their own provision in addition to maintenance for their children.

8.2 High income families

In high income families, the courts will be less concerned about meeting an applicant's basic needs than ensuring a fair apportionment of the family's wealth. In doing so, they will bear in mind the standard of living enjoyed prior to the breakdown of the marriage, as well as all the other relevant factors in the s 25 of the MCA 1973 (see **4.5.1**). Commonly, where significant capital is available, it will not be appropriate for there to be any maintenance payable between spouses. In such cases, a clean break will be favoured instead (see **4.6**).

A clean break will not always be appropriate in wealthy families as there may be insufficient liquid capital. Assets may be tied up in land or in a business. It will frequently be counter-productive to realise such assets, as their loss could have a disproportionately adverse effect on the income generated by the assets as a whole. In such cases, it would be more sensible and profitable for the assets to be retained and for a maintenance order to be made instead.

In certain cases there may be insufficient capital for an immediate clean break but a very large amount of income (perhaps, for example, a young person 'up and coming' in the City). In *Miller v Miller; McFarlane v McFarlane* [2006] UKHL 24, the House of Lords upheld an award of £250,000 per annum to Mrs McFarlane and extended its duration for her lifetime. The size of the award was partly to compensate her for the couple's joint decision that she should give up her successful career to care for the children. The House of Lords made it clear that it was in fact unlikely to be appropriate for maintenance to continue at this level indefinitely. However, their Lordships took the view that the onus should be on the husband to seek a variation once Mrs McFarlane had revived her earning capacity and he had reduced his outgoings, by which time a clean break might be possible.

8.3 Middle income families

The approach taken by the courts to the large group of people who are neither wealthy nor on or near subsistence level has varied over the years. The Court of Appeal suggested that a useful rule of thumb was to halve the payer spouse's income – half for him and half for the payee spouse and children (*Scheeres v Scheeres* [1999] 1 FLR 241), and this approach would appear to have been endorsed by the House of Lords in *White v White* [2000] 2 FLR 981. Such an approach may be used to establish a starting point from which the court can consider s 25, particularly in cases where no maintenance is payable under the CSA 1991. However, in cases where a maintenance calculation has been or is to be made by the Child Support Agency, the court is more likely to calculate whether the non-resident parent can afford to make any additional periodical payment to the parent with care of the children.

In order to decide what figure (if any) is appropriate for spouse maintenance, or to decide on whether a figure proposed by the other party is reasonable, the solicitor must make a calculation.

It is important to consider the reality behind a particular figure to ensure that the payer can afford to make any payment proposed and that the recipient can manage to live off her income (which will of course include the proposed maintenance). It is important to compare the size of their respective households and the extent of their liabilities. If maintenance is also being paid for children, this must also be borne in mind, as it represents an additional obligation for the payer and an additional resource for the parent to whom it is being paid.

The solicitor should calculate the parties' net income, taking into account any income tax, national insurance and pension contributions. The figure for any child support maintenance must be added to the recipient's income and correspondingly deducted as an expense from the payer's income. A budget will need to be drawn up for each household, which should be compared against the available income. Clearly, there is scope for argument about what represents a reasonable budget, and the solicitor will need to look at the figures carefully. However, care must be taken not to waste costs in a disproportionate manner.

Example

This simple example uses *notional figures* to establish whether maintenance should be paid to a wife in addition to child support. In reality, a budget is likely to include a number of other expenses, for example, holidays, etc.

Fergus and Rose have two children, aged 8 and 10. Fergus earns £25,000 annually (gross) and Rose earns £7,000 annually (gross). Fergus has been assessed to pay £70.00 per week by the Child Support Agency. Rose has remained in the family home with the children and Fergus is in rented accommodation.

Stage 1: Calculate each spouse's net income:

	Fergus	Rose
	£	£
Earnings	480.00	135.00
Less tax	96.00	14.00
National Insurance	36.00	12.00
	348.00	109.00
Child benefit	–	24.00
Child tax credit		65.00
	348.00	198.00

Stage 2: Take child maintenance of £70.00 into account:

	Fergus		Rose
	£		£
Net income	348.00	Net income	198.00
less	70.00	plus	70.00
	278.00		268.00

Stage 3: Deduct each spouse's budgeted expenses:

	Fergus			Rose
	£	£	£	£
Net income		278.00		268.00
Less expenses:				
Fuel	10.00		15.00	
Council tax	4.00		8.00	
Mortgage	–		135.00	
Rent	75.00		–	
Car tax and petrol	22.00		–	
TV licence	2.00		2.00	
Pension	30.00		5.00	
Bus fares	–		5.00	
Childcare	–		20.00	
Clothing	40.00		10.00	
Food	50.00		75.00	
Total		233.00		300.00
Balance available		45.00		– 32.00

Initially, it would appear that the books do not balance, even if Fergus pays over half of his available income. However, it can be seen that Fergus claims he needs £40 per week for clothes, whereas Rose is claiming she needs only £10 for herself and the two children. Thus it would be sensible to query Fergus's budgeted figure for clothing. Nonetheless, it can be seen that money is very tight. Perhaps the couple should consider whether Rose should stay in the family home given that the mortgage figure is relatively high.

8.4 Low income families

In the case of low income families a one-half starting point will rarely be appropriate. If the payer has low earnings and the recipient none, the payer could not afford to lose such a large proportion of his income and the recipient could not survive on it. In such cases, alternative means of calculating maintenance are used.

If there are clearly insufficient resources for both parties to be independent of welfare benefits, the court and practitioners take a pragmatic approach. Although generally a spouse cannot cast his or her responsibility to maintain the other and their children onto the State, common sense dictates that in low income cases the availability of welfare benefits must be taken into account. The calculation of maintenance in such cases will often be a relatively straightforward process, as it will be a matter of identifying how much the recipient needs to live on and how much the payer can spare. The court will never order a party to pay a sum which would place him below a notional subsistence level. This means the payer would be allowed to keep sufficient money to pay his housing costs, as well as the sum he would be entitled to were he to claim income support or jobseeker's allowance. The reason for this is plain: there would be little incentive for such a person to earn a living or to pay the maintenance if he would be worse off than if he were unemployed.

The court is even reluctant to make an order which would reduce the payer to this subsistence level. It is more common for the payer to be able to retain a percentage (say 15%) of his net earnings above his subsistence level.

If the recipient is receiving income support or jobseeker's allowance and will continue to do so when maintenance is paid, she will not be any better off as a result. This is because any maintenance she receives forms part of her income when calculating her benefit entitlement and reduces her entitlement pound for pound. Her income will, therefore, remain at the level of her applicable amount.

Example

Lucy is 45, unemployed and has no dependent children. Her applicable amount for jobseeker's allowance is £45. She has no income of her own and, therefore, receives £45 jobseeker's allowance. Her husband Bill is ordered to pay her £10 per week maintenance. Thereafter, she will receive only £35 jobseeker's allowance, but when this is added to her maintenance her income remains at £45 per week.

In such circumstances, clients may be unenthusiastic about claiming maintenance. However, if the client has any prospects of finding employment, even modest maintenance when combined with wages may, in time, assist her to become independent of State benefits altogether.

Careful calculation must be made in the case of low income families to ensure that the recipient is not worse off with maintenance than without it. This can arise if the maintenance raises the recipient's income to, or only slightly above, her applicable amount. If this occurs, she will lose her right to income support (or jobseeker's allowance), but more particularly to the passport benefits to which a claimant is automatically entitled. She will lose the right to free prescriptions and school meals for her children, and as a result would be worse off. She would also lose the right to full housing benefit and full council tax benefit, although she would be able to make a means-tested claim. It will often be appropriate to accept a reduced sum of maintenance to ensure that the recipient is still eligible for income support (or jobseeker's allowance), thereby enabling her to continue to qualify for these other benefits. This is discussed further in **Chapter 6**.

Where both parties are in receipt of income support or jobseeker's allowance, it will not usually be appropriate to apply for maintenance for a spouse. If a spouse is earning and receiving working tax credit, it may be possible (although uncommon) for very modest maintenance to be paid to the other spouse. The position is different, however, with children's maintenance. Even parents on income support or jobseeker's allowance may be expected to pay maintenance for their children under the CSA 1991 (see **Chapter 7**). In low income families in particular, if maintenance is payable for children, it is likely that the non-resident parent will have insufficient resources to pay maintenance for the parent with care as well. If, after paying the child maintenance, the payer's income is close to his subsistence level, no spouse maintenance will be paid.

8.5 Chapter summary

(1) In practice, it is not possible to isolate issues of maintenance from other issues, such as where the children are going to live and what is going to happen to the matrimonial home and other property.

(2) Maintenance for a spouse is dealt with by the courts under the MCA 1973. The court will consider what the Child Support Agency assessment will be for any relevant children and then decide whether any payment in addition for the spouse can be afforded and is appropriate, bearing in mind the s 25 factors. The court will consider the effect of any proposed order on both household's budgets.

Chapter 9

Dealing with the Capital Assets

9.1 Introduction

The matrimonial home is generally the most important property owned by the family. As well as providing a home for the parties and their children, it is an important capital asset. The court must decide whether it is appropriate to retain the property so that it will continue to provide a home, or whether to sell it and thereby realise the capital. The home also represents a liability, as it must be maintained and in most cases it will be subject to a mortgage. In deciding what should be done with the home, the court is required to have regard to the factors in s 25 of the MCA 1973, considered in **Chapter 4**. These factors assist the court in deciding which type of order to make and what size each party's respective share in the home should be. Although the court will take into account the financial contributions made by the parties to the purchase of the home, it is not fettered by proprietary interests, and such contributions will frequently be outweighed by other factors. The court has a wide discretion to determine how the property should be held and in what shares. It will take into account the parties' past and future non-financial contributions, as well as the other factors referred to in s 25, in an attempt to reach a fair outcome. The House of Lords has made it clear that there is no presumption that both spouses invariably have a right to be able to buy a new home from the assets available to the family. Instead, the court will exercise its discretion in each and every case, in the light of the relevant s 25 factors as applied to that case (*Piglowska v Piglowski* [1999] 2 FLR 763).

Although this chapter is confined to considering the matrimonial home, lump sum orders and pensions, it is important to bear in mind that the court will not look at the capital assets in isolation. It will decide upon a package of complementary orders dealing with income and capital. Any agreement will require careful drafting. In **Chapter 10**, consideration is given to drafting the various orders examined in this chapter.

The following property adjustment orders may be made and are considered below:

(a) Immediate sale.

(b) Outright transfer.

(c) Deferred trust of land.

(d) Deferred charge.

9.2 Selling the home

There is a variety of reasons why the court might exercise its powers under s 24A of the MCA 1973 to order the immediate sale of the matrimonial home and the division of the proceeds between the parties. Typically, an immediate sale of the house will be appropriate where the court is effecting an immediate clean break. Each party will be able to use his or her share of the equity towards purchasing separate homes. They will first redeem the existing mortgage from the proceeds of sale, which benefits the parties by releasing them from a significant debt which bound them together. For the sake of clarity, any order for sale should deal with the liabilities to be met out of the proceeds of sale such as the existing mortgage, estate agent's commission and solicitor's conveyancing fees. When calculating the value of the equity the costs of purchase and removal should also be borne in mind. For a publicly funded client the statutory charge will also be paid out of the proceeds of sale. However, it may be possible for the payment of the charge to be postponed by registering it against the assisted party's new home (see **2.9**).

Section 24A(2) (see **Appendix 1(A)**) provides that the order may contain such consequential or supplementary provisions as the court thinks fit. This, therefore, gives the court the widest discretion to make directions about the sale, for example, which party's solicitors should have the conduct of the sale, how the price is to be determined and what payments should be made out of the proceeds, etc.

There will not usually be sufficient equity for both parties to be able to purchase alternative homes outright. However, if the couple are both earning, they may be able to do so with the aid of a new mortgage. If one party has only low earnings (or low earning capacity), that party may receive a greater proportion of the equity to enable him to reaccommodate himself. A party may be willing to forgo some of his share of the equity in order to achieve a clean break. This may be regarded as the lesser of two evils if the only other viable alternative is for the other party to remain in the property for many years. If the parties are relatively young and without children, the house is likely to be sold even if the equity is very small, as there is a strong presumption in favour of a clean break in these circumstances. If there are young children the court will not readily order the sale of their home. The court must give first consideration to the welfare of minor children when determining what should happen to the matrimonial home, and will wish to be satisfied that they will be suitably accommodated. The court will also have regard to the disruption which a move might cause to the children and to the adverse effect this could have on their stability and security. If a move to a cheaper area would involve a change in the children's schooling, the court would be most hesitant to order this. However, children frequently adapt well to change and if the home (or the school) has been unhappy, a move might benefit them. If the house is larger than needed and has a substantial equity, it may be unduly harsh on the non-resident parent to deny him the opportunity to realise some of his capital. In such a case, the court may order sale and perhaps give a weighted share of the equity to the parent caring for the children, as she will require a larger property than the non-resident parent and will frequently have a smaller income.

An immediate sale may be ordered out of necessity if there are insufficient resources to retain and maintain the house. If the couple's finances were already stretched before the marriage breakdown, then plainly it would not be possible for one party to remain in the home and for the other party to accommodate himself as well. It may be that both parties will have to rent properties. Typically, the couple may have purchased the property relatively recently with the aid of a large mortgage, and consequently there may be little or (in times of falling house values) no equity.

If one party wishes to sell the home while the other wishes to remain in it, the former could transfer his interest in the home to the latter in return for a lump sum. Whether or not such a 'buy out' can be achieved depends upon whether the spouse who wishes to stay has the means to make the lump sum payment. He may have savings, or sufficient income to raise the sum by borrowing. Provided the equity is sufficient, the sum may be raised by increasing the mortgage. The spouse who wishes to sell may agree to a smaller lump sum rather than have the delay and inconvenience of sale on the open market.

9.3 Retaining the home

The matrimonial home may be retained for the occupation of one party and the children of the family. This occupation may be permanent in the case of an outright transfer, or in the medium to long term in the case of a deferred trust of land or deferred charge.

9.3.1 Outright transfer

Outright transfer is another method of achieving a clean break between the parties as it determines immediately and finally the ownership of the home. The court is unlikely to order an immediate outright transfer unless the transferee spouse has the means to pay the outgoings on the house, including the mortgage. It will also wish to ensure that the transferor spouse has suitable alternative accommodation. He need not necessarily own this accommodation: he may, for example, be provided with accommodation through his employment, or he may be living in his new partner's home.

If the transferor is giving up a significant amount of capital, the court will seek to compensate him for this loss. An order for the transfer of a property may be coupled with a lump sum payment from the transferee to the transferor (see the example of Shah at **10.13.13**). The extent to which the transferor spouse will be compensated depends on the value of the equity and on s 25 of the MCA 1973 factors in general. If the equity is small, the transferor may not receive anything in return. In a sluggish market, a party may be glad to be relieved of responsibility for the property.

Another means of compensating a transferor is by releasing him from paying maintenance to the transferee. However, a spouse cannot be compensated by being released from his obligations to pay maintenance for his children. This is because, in most cases, the transferor will be bound to pay maintenance for the children under the CSA 1991. When assessing the amount payable, the Child Support Agency will not generally take into account any disposals of capital made by the non-resident parent on divorce (see **7.6.4**). Similarly, any agreement by the transferee to forgo any claim under the CSA 1991 will be unenforceable (see **7.5**). Indeed, should the transferee find herself in need of welfare benefits, she will be obliged under s 6 of the CSA 1991 to pursue her ex-spouse for maintenance for the children. In the less common cases, where the court, rather than the Agency, has jurisdiction to make periodical payment orders for children, it will take into account all the circumstances of the case, including a sacrifice by the transferor of his interest in the matrimonial home. As a result, the court may take the view that the transferor should pay only modest maintenance for the children.

Faced with the prospect of forgoing capital in the matrimonial home and paying substantial income in the form of CSA 1991 maintenance, outright transfers of the matrimonial home are used less frequently than in the past. If the transferee spouse is unable to pay a lump sum to the transferor by way of compensation, the transferor may prefer to preserve his interest in the matrimonial home by means of a deferred charge or trust of land.

9.3.2 Deferred trust of land

The deferred trust of land is a compromise solution to the problem of the matrimonial home. Where the court is of the view that an immediate sale is inappropriate and an outright transfer too harsh on the transferring spouse, it can order the house to be held in the parties' joint names on trust of land. It will specify which spouse is to occupy the home pending sale. The sale of the property is postponed until the first of a number of specified triggering events occurs. The order will also settle how the net proceeds of sale are to be shared between the parties. The main advantage of the trust of land is that it allows a party and the children to remain in the home after the divorce, and it enables the non-occupying spouse to retain an interest in the home which may be realised at a later date.

There are several variations on the trust of land; the differences lie in the events which trigger sale. The main variations are known as the *'Mesher'* order (see *Mesher v Mesher and Hall* [1980] 1 All ER 126), the *'Martin'* order (see *Martin v Martin* [1978] Fam 12) and the *'Harvey'* order (see *Harvey v Harvey* [1982] 3 FLR 141), named after the cases in which they were considered.

9.3.2.1 *Mesher* order

Triggering events

Typically, the events which will trigger the sale in a *Mesher* order will be the first of the following to occur:

(a)   the occupying spouse dies, remarries or voluntarily leaves the property; or

(b)   the youngest child reaches a specified age (usually 17 or 18 years), or ceases full-time education (if this happens earlier/later).

For an example of a *Mesher* order, see Levy at **10.13.13**.

The advantage of this order is that it provides a secure home for the children of the family and offers medium-term security to the occupying spouse. In addition, each party will know fairly clearly when the sale will take place and can plan accordingly. The non-occupying spouse can be confident that the day will come when he will realise his capital and be released from making any contributions towards the outgoings on the former matrimonial home.

The court's attitude towards the sale of the home on the occupying spouse's remarriage varies. Given that the court's primary consideration is the welfare of the minor children, there is some force to the argument that the children's home should not be jeopardised by the remarriage of their parent. Their step-parent may have little or no resources of his own. On the other hand, the non-occupying spouse will feel aggrieved to watch another person living in his property with his ex-spouse and children. Consequently, most judges are prepared to order that the sale is triggered by the occupying spouse's remarriage. A more controversial trigger for sale is cohabitation by the occupying spouse with a new partner. Such orders require careful drafting, as cohabitation is by no means as clearly definable as marriage. Further, a cohabitee would be under no obligation to maintain his partner or her family. It is also arguable that such a trigger would be unduly restrictive on the occupying spouse's personal freedom.

If the occupying spouse gives up occupation of the home, this would trigger sale. The order may, however, provide for the occupying spouse to move to an alternative property without having to settle the non-occupying party's share. Care must be taken when drafting such a clause; the non-occupying spouse will wish to ensure that the substitute property will adequately protect his interest by being marketable and of sound construction, etc. The substitute property may also be cheaper or more expensive than the original property, which requires further consideration.

Reference to the youngest child may be drafted so that the sale is triggered on the child reaching the specified age whether or not he or she remains in education. Alternatively, it may be worded so that the sale is postponed while the child is in full-time secondary (or even higher) education on the basis that the adult child will still require a home.

Use

As we have seen, the *Mesher* order is a compromise solution; it does not resolve all the difficulties with the matrimonial home. Its main shortcoming is that it is only a medium-term solution. The widespread use of *Mesher* orders has been criticised for simply postponing the 'evil day' so as to avoid facing the harsh reality of the present (*Harvey v Harvey* [1982] 3 FLR 141). Sooner or later the occupying spouse will have to leave the home and then start from scratch to find new accommodation. A wife may have to take that step at a vulnerable time in her life when she has a diminishing earning capacity. The court cannot predict with any accuracy how much time the occupying spouse will need to reaccommodate herself, or what the housing and job market will be many years ahead. The court has no discretion to postpone the sale beyond the triggering events and it may not interfere with the apportionment once it has been settled in the original order. On the other hand, the very fact that the sale is postponed will enable the wife to look to the future and make efforts to become financially independent. Her position may be eased to a certain extent by giving her a greater share of the net proceeds of sale on the assumption that the non-resident parent will have been able to establish himself and secure accommodation in the years which have elapsed since divorce.

9.3.2.2   *Martin* order

The *Martin* order operates in a similar way to the *Mesher* order, save that the triggers for sale make no reference to the children of the family. The result is that the house need be sold only if the occupying spouse so chooses by leaving or remarrying, or, ultimately, when she dies. Thus, she has the right to remain in the home for life. The *Martin* order will be most appropriate where one spouse is in a significantly weaker financial position than the other. For example, a middle-aged wife may not have worked for many years having cared for the home and family, whereas the husband may be living with a new partner and have reasonable earnings. In such a case, the capital realised by the sale would be a bonus to the husband, whereas the wife would have to apply her money towards a new property. The court is likely to order that the house should be retained to be used as a home for the wife for life. However, it would not make such an order if the matrimonial home were manifestly surplus to her needs. In such a case, an order for sale and division of the proceeds would be more appropriate.

The obvious advantage of this variation on the trust of land is that it avoids the 'evil day' encountered with the *Mesher* order. Provided the occupying spouse remains in the home and unmarried, she will not be faced with the prospect of a forced sale. The disadvantages of this type of order are equally apparent: the non-occupying spouse has an indefinite wait to realise his capital. Indeed, he may predecease his wife, in which case only his estate would benefit. As the occupying spouse has a secure home for life with this type of order, she will not have the same need for capital when the house is sold. The non-occupying spouse may therefore acquire a greater share of the equity than is usually the case with a *Mesher* order. This may go some way to compensate him for the indefinite wait to realise his capital. The court would be unlikely to make a *Martin* order if the occupying spouse could not afford to pay the outgoings on the property, as this would be unduly harsh on the non-occupying spouse. If, exceptionally, the non-occupying spouse is required to pay maintenance to the occupying spouse, he could expect that fact to be reflected by an order giving him an even larger share of the equity upon sale.

9.3.2.3   *Harvey* order

In *Harvey v Harvey* [1982] 3 FLR 141, the court sought to mitigate the hardship which a *Martin* order causes to the non-occupying spouse. A *Harvey* order has triggers similar to the *Martin* order, but in addition it provides for the payment of an 'occupation rent' by the occupying spouse. The obligation to pay the 'rent' is itself triggered by the children growing up or the mortgage being paid off, whichever first occurs. Although the order attempts to do justice between the parties, it is not without its difficulties and is not commonly made. Consideration would have to be given as to how the 'rent' is to be assessed and paid. The rent is taxable in the hands of the recipient spouse.

9.3.3   Deferred charge

A deferred charge is a further method of retaining a home for a spouse and the children. Although similar to the trust of land, the property remains (or is transferred) into the sole name of the occupying spouse. The non-occupying spouse's interest in the home is represented by a charge over the property. This charge cannot be enforced until one of the triggering events discussed in **9.3.2.1** and **9.3.2.2** occurs (*Mesher* or *Martin* triggers). If the occupying spouse cannot pay the charge, at this point the property must be sold. The charge will usually be expressed as a proportion of the net proceeds of sale, thereby allowing the charge holder to benefit from any increase in the value of the property (as in the Brown example at **10.13.13**). Less commonly, the charge may be expressed as a fixed sum, but this has the obvious disadvantage of its value being eroded by the effects of inflation. The charge will be registered against the title and will take priority over any subsequent liabilities incurred by the owner.

In practical terms, there is very little difference between the deferred charge and the trust of land, although the former is less advantageous from a CGT point of view (see **5.2.2**). If the property is already in the parties' joint names, a trust of land will be the preferred method as it avoids interfering with the legal estate. On the other hand, if the property is already in the name of the occupying spouse, the deferred charge may be the preferred method.

9.4 The interests of third parties

9.4.1 Co-owners

If a party owns property with a third party the court may make an order only with respect to the spouse's share of the asset. It cannot interfere with the third party's interest. A third party who is not a legal owner but claims to be beneficially entitled to a property may intervene in proceedings for sale and make representations. So, for example, a parent of one of the parties who has been living in the matrimonial home, having contributed towards the deposit or mortgage, may apply to have the extent of his beneficial interest determined by the court. If the court decided that the property should be sold in such a case, it would probably direct that the parent should be offered the right of first refusal.

9.4.2 Lenders

9.4.2.1 Undue influence

Where both husband and wife are parties to a mortgage, they will both be bound by the mortgage. This is true unless one of them can argue that the mortgage should not be enforced against them because their consent to the mortgage was obtained by undue influence. For example, a wife may argue that the mortgage should be set aside as against the husband because she was induced to enter into the mortgage as a result of his undue influence. In *Royal Bank of Scotland v Etridge (No 2)* [2001] 4 All ER 449, the House of Lords reviewed the law on undue influence, and it is now the leading case in this area. The wife may either prove actual undue influence (ie overt act(s) of the husband actually putting unfair pressure on her or making misrepresentations), or raise a 'rebuttable evidential presumption' of undue influence.

This 'rebuttable evidential presumption' arises where the wife shows that her relationship with her husband is one of trust and confidence in such matters and that the transaction 'calls for explanation' (ie if it is explicable only on the basis of undue influence). This may rarely be the case since such transactions will generally be likely to benefit the family as a whole. Therefore, in the future it is likely to be difficult for wives to argue undue influence.

If there is such undue influence, the wife can have the mortgage set aside as against the lender (ie the lender will not be able to enforce the mortgage against her) only if the lender had actual or constructive notice of the risk of this. The lender will now be 'put on inquiry' (ie fixed with constructive notice) whenever the relationship between debtor and guarantor is non-commercial (eg spouses). However, this will not apply where the money is being advanced jointly, as opposed to the wife acting as guarantor, unless the lender is aware that the loan is being made for the husband's purposes.

Where the lender has notice, either actual or constructive, it must take reasonable steps to satisfy itself that the transaction was properly entered into. In order to do this, the lender must comply with the requirements now laid down in *Royal Bank of Scotland v Etridge* regarding explanations and warnings. The lender may either do this itself, or send the necessary information to the wife's solicitor and obtain confirmation from the solicitor that the transaction and its practical implications have been fully explained. If the lender fails to comply with the requirements it may not be able to enforce the mortgage against the wife, who will be entitled to take her share of the house free from the mortgage. As these requirements are quite stringent, it is likely that, in future, most lenders will rely on the wife's solicitor, rather than attempting to comply with them themselves.

As a result of the House of Lords decision in *Royal Bank of Scotland v Etridge,* in future it will be more difficult for wives to argue undue influence; lenders are less likely to be 'put on inquiry' where the money is advanced jointly. Even where they are, the insistence on confirmation from solicitors is likely to mean that most transactions have been properly entered into and are therefore enforceable.

9.4.2.2   Property adjustment orders on divorce

Leaving aside the cases of possible undue influence and returning to more usual circumstances, what is the position of a lender when a court is considering making a property adjustment order with respect to a matrimonial home on divorce?

If a property is ordered to be sold immediately, there will be no problem with the lender: on completion the mortgage (including any arrears which may have built up) must be paid. It may be necessary to obtain the lender's agreement to postpone any possession proceedings to allow a private sale if substantial arrears have built up. The lender may agree to extend the mortgage term, or perhaps to accept only capital payments in the short term. Only mortgage interest at a standard rate may be paid through income support (and full mortgage interest will not be immediately included in a claim, see **6.3.2**).

If the property is to continue in the parties' joint names under a trust of land, this should not cause any difficulties with the lender. The parties may agree between themselves how the mortgage is to be paid. The occupying spouse may undertake to indemnify the non-occupying spouse for his liability under the mortgage. However, as joint owners and joint borrowers, the lenders have the right to look to both spouses to make the repayments. The lender's rights are unaffected by the terms of the trust. However, if the court alters the legal estate by transferring the property into a party's sole name, the lender is entitled to object. Invariably, the lender will be asked to release the transferor spouse from his liability under the mortgage and thereby relinquish the right to pursue the transferor for payment of the debt. Before agreeing to do so, the lender will need to be satisfied that the transferee spouse will be able to meet the payments. If the lender is not confident that this will be the case, it may refuse to release the transferor. This condition may defeat the object of the transaction, ie of achieving a clean break. Full disclosure of the transferee's resources should be made to the lender in advance of any hearing or agreement to avoid such an objection.

9.5   The rented home

If the former matrimonial home is a rented property, the court will have to consider whether the tenancy can and should be transferred into the sole name of one party. Section 24 of the MCA 1973 allows the court to transfer 'property': most tenancies will be regarded as 'property' for this purpose. If the tenancy contains a prohibition against assignment, the court cannot order the transfer under this provision unless the landlord consents. As with lenders, the landlord should be contacted at an early stage in the proceedings.

Statutory tenancies which arose under the Rent Act 1977 on the termination of a protected tenancy do not amount to 'property' for the purposes of s 24 of the MCA 1973, and cannot therefore be transferred under this section. However, under Sch 7 to the FLA 1996, a statutory tenancy can be vested in the name of one spouse. Strictly speaking this is not a transfer of the tenancy and so may be ordered notwithstanding a prohibition in the tenancy against assignment. However, the landlord would be entitled to make representations before the court, and if his objections were reasonable they would be unlikely to be overridden. Protected, assured and secured tenancies may be transferred under s 24 of the MCA 1973. Protected, assured and secured tenancies may also be transferred under FLA 1996. There will, therefore, be a choice (in most cases) of whether to deal with the tenancy under the MCA 1973, or under the FLA 1996. Legal representation for ancillary relief will normally specify that orders may be made only under the MCA 1973, and as proceedings will already have been brought under that Act, it will normally be convenient to use this jurisdiction.

9.6 Protecting the capital assets

The matrimonial home is almost invariably the most important (and valuable) family asset. It is also true to say that the issue of what to do with the home is among the most contentious on marriage breakdown. It is a subject on which emotions frequently run high. One fear which a party may have is that the other party will seek to avoid his responsibilities by disposing of the property. Such a suspicion may be well founded. There is a variety of measures available to prevent a party from disposing of (or charging) the matrimonial home, or any other property, and to reverse any attempt by a party to do so.

Whether or not any action need be taken will depend upon how the property is held.

9.6.1 Property in joint names

If the parties hold the property in joint names, neither party can deal with it unilaterally. Any sale or mortgage will require the consent and signature of both parties; therefore, no steps need be taken to guard against this other than advising the client not to sign anything without legal advice (see also **9.4.2** and the possible problem of undue influence).

However, consideration should be given to the question of the parties' beneficial interests in the property. If the parties hold the property jointly in law and equity then their interests will automatically pass to the survivor on death. Given the breakdown of the relationship, the parties are likely to want their shares in the property to form part of their own estates. If this is the case, the joint tenancy must be severed to allow the parties to become beneficial tenants in common. This may be achieved by giving written notice of severance to the other party. The severance should be recorded on the title of the property, by a restriction on the proprietorship register (if the property is registered) or by a memorandum of severance on the conveyance to the parties (if the title is unregistered).

Even if this step is taken, if a party dies intestate prior to decree absolute, the spouse is liable to inherit by default through the rules on intestacy. Clearly, the client should be advised to make a will, or any existing will may need to be reviewed.

9.6.2 Property in a party's sole name

9.6.2.1 Matrimonial home rights: FLA 1996, s 30

If a spouse is not a legal owner of the property, she may feel in a vulnerable position. In such a case, the spouse should be advised of her matrimonial home rights with respect to the matrimonial home by virtue of s 30 of the FLA 1996 (see

Appendix 1(G)). These rights protect a non-owning spouse (husband or wife) against eviction from the matrimonial home without the leave of the court. A spouse will be non-owning for these purposes even if she owns an equitable interest. The rights exist in respect of only one property at a time and it must have been the matrimonial home at some stage.

The rights under s 30 of the FLA 1996 terminate on the death of the owning spouse or on the grant of a decree absolute, although the court has power under s 33(5) of the FLA 1996 to direct that the rights should continue beyond these events.

The matrimonial home rights should be registered so that they bind any subsequent buyers and lenders. As always, the rights will not take priority over any pre-existing interests, such as a prior mortgage.

In order to ascertain where the registration should be made, it may be necessary to carry out an Index Map Search at Land Registry. This will indicate whether or not the property is registered and, if it is, its title number. If it is registered, an agreed notice should be placed on the register (despite the fact that this is an 'agreed notice', it does not need the owning spouse's consent to be registered). If the title is unregistered, a Class F land charge should be registered against the name of the owning spouse. If a spouse fails to register the rights, she will be unable to assert her rights against any third party.

In practice, Land Registry automatically notifies the registered proprietor that an entry relating to the matrimonial home has been made. It will also hold any application made for a period of one week to give the applicant the opportunity to consider fully the effect of her application.

A non-owning spouse may also have concerns about the payment of the original mortgage. Whether or not a spouse has registered her rights, s 30(3) of the FLA 1996 obliges a lender to accept payments from a non-owning spouse. (A similar principle applies to payments of rent by a non-tenant spouse.) If possession proceedings are brought, the non-owning spouse must be notified (if she has registered her rights) and she may apply to be made a party to the proceedings. If the court is persuaded that the non-owning spouse is able to pay the mortgage and the arrears within a reasonable time, it will usually refuse an order for possession.

A non-owning spouse may also feel vulnerable if the owning spouse faces bankruptcy, because bankruptcy vests the owning spouse's property in his trustee in bankruptcy. Once registered, the matrimonial home rights are binding on the trustee and on the creditors. However, the trustee may apply to the court to terminate the rights. If the application to terminate is made more than a year after the bankruptcy, the court is bound to grant it unless the circumstances are exceptional. The client should be advised of this and warned that having no alternative accommodation for herself and her children will not amount to exceptional circumstances.

9.6.2.2 Pending land action

The limitations of the matrimonial home rights may leave a spouse with inadequate protection. For this reason the registration of a pending land action should be considered. This can be done once proceedings have commenced in relation to property. A request for a property adjustment order in the prayer of the petition or Form A suffices. The registration is not confined to the matrimonial home and it is effective beyond the termination of the marriage. If the property in question is registered land, a unilateral notice should be lodged in the proprietorship register. If the land is unregistered, registration is by way of a pending action against the name of the owning spouse. This prevents any new dealing with the property taking place without first being brought to the attention of the non-owning spouse.

9.6.2.3 Injunctions: MCA 1973, s 37

Preventing disposals

It is possible to seek an injunction from the court under s 37(2)(a) of the MCA 1973 (see **Appendix 1(A)**) to prevent a party from disposing of property. This can be done in relation to any type of property, but if the property is land in England or Wales it is usually easier to protect it by registering a matrimonial home right or pending land action (as explained at **9.6.2.1** and **9.6.2.2**).

If a client wishes to make use of s 37, he must first have made an application for financial relief under the MCA 1973 (eg for a lump sum or property adjustment order). An injunction may then be granted where the court is satisfied that the other party is about to make a disposition of property with the intention of defeating the claim for financial relief, or with the intention of frustrating or impeding its enforcement. The court has power to make whatever order it thinks fit to restrain the party from making the disposition. The applicant must have placed evidence before the court that the disposition is likely and the application is not simply being taken as a precautionary measure. There is a (rebuttable) presumption that the respondent to the injunction application intends to make the disposition in order to jeopardise the applicant's claim, if it would have that consequence.

> **Example**
> Mrs Edwards learns that her husband is about to transfer the funds in his savings account to his girlfriend's account. Mrs Edwards can apply for an injunction to freeze the savings account. A copy of the injunction should be served on the bank.

Setting aside

If the spouse does not learn of the disposition until after it has taken place, all is not lost. Section 37(2)(b) empowers the court to grant an injunction setting aside a reviewable disposition made with the intention of defeating a claim for ancillary relief, if financial provision or different financial provision would be made to the applicant as a result.

A disposition will be reviewable unless it was made to a bona fide purchaser without notice of the respondent's intention. If the disposition took place less than three years before the application, the malevolent intention will be presumed.

> **Example**
> Mr Philips gave his valuable yacht to his brother 18 months ago. Regardless of whether the brother was aware of Mr Philips' purpose, the disposition may be set aside as it was not made for valuable consideration.

Avoiding enforcement

If a reviewable disposition is made after financial proceedings have been determined, with the object of avoiding enforcement of an order for financial relief, it may be set aside under s 37(2)(c) of the MCA 1973.

Example

Mr Clark is ordered to pay a lump sum of £10,000 to his wife. In order to frustrate this, he transfers his entire investments to his mother. Mrs Clark can seek an injunction to reverse this disposition and enforce the lump sum by means of an order for sale against the investments.

Dispositions

A disposition includes any disposal of property except one contained in a will.

9.7 Lump sums

9.7.1 Lump sums generally

The power of the court to make lump sum orders is discussed at **4.4.1**. Lump sums have also been examined throughout this chapter in the context of a division of the net sale proceeds of the matrimonial home. The assessment of the amount of a lump sum remains to be considered here.

Generally, no lump sum would be awarded where the family assets are modest, otherwise than in relation to a division of the net proceeds of the matrimonial home. However, if following the breakdown of the marriage the applicant spouse has incurred debts due to the failure of the respondent to maintain her, the court may remedy the problem by ordering a lump sum. Careful thought should be given to the impact of any lump sum on the recipient's eligibility for welfare benefits (see **Chapter 6**).

The impact of the statutory charge could also seriously erode the net value of any lump sum awarded (see **2.9**).

9.7.2 Lump sums in 'big money' cases

If the family assets are substantial, the court will usually consider making a lump sum order in addition to making an order regarding the matrimonial home. The reason for this can be traced to s 25A of the MCA 1973, which requires the court to facilitate a clean break wherever appropriate. If the family assets are substantial, there will be ample opportunity to achieve a clean break by making a lump sum order and dismissing any claim for spousal periodical payments.

In determining how much the lump sum should be, the court will have regard to the s 25 factors and the cases of *White* and *Miller v Miller; McFarlane v McFarlane* (examined in detail in **Chapter 4**). Any contributions made by a spouse towards the family prosperity or to the welfare of the family generally will be particularly influential.

It seems likely that, as a result of the case of *White* and the 'yardstick of equality', lump sum awards in 'big money' cases will be more substantial. A difficulty that may arise is one of liquidity, as one spouse may not have sufficient available resources to pay the other such significant sums of money. This may mean that a clean break may be more difficult to achieve in certain cases. It is particularly problematic if the main asset is a business (or various businesses). In the past, the courts tended to be very reluctant to break up such a business in order to give the other spouse their due. However, the case of *N v N (Financial Provision: Sale of Company)* [2001] 2 FLR 69 suggests that this attitude may be changing. As Coleridge J graphically explained:

> There is no doubt that had this case been heard before the *White* decision last year the court would have strained to prevent a disruption of the husband's business and

professional activities except to the minimum extent necessary to meet the wife's needs.

However, I think that it must now be taken that those old taboos against selling the goose that lays the golden egg have largely been laid to rest; some would say not before time. Nowadays the goose may well have to go to market for sale, but if it is necessary to sell her it is essential that her condition be such that her egg laying abilities are damaged as little as possible in the process. Otherwise there is a danger that the full value of the goose will not be achieved and the underlying basis of any order will turn out to be flawed.

So, whilst the business may have to be sold, it is important to consider how and when and to give the husband every opportunity to raise funds to buy out the wife's share if at all possible as an alternative.

However, as was emphasised in *D v D and B Ltd* [2007] EWHC 278 (Fam), despite the desirability of achieving a clean break, there will be some cases, especially those involving private companies, where the commercial reality was that a fairer result would be achieved by not selling the business. Thus it will not always be practical or desirable to value and sell the business and then divide the proceeds. The courts have used a variety of different devices where it is either not practical or not desirable to sell the business. For example, in *F v F (Clean Break: Balance of Fairness)* [2003] 1 FLR 847, the court ordered substantial periodical payments to the wife instead of imposing a clean break. In *R v R (Lump Sum Repayments)* [2004] 1 FLR 928, the court made a 'frankly unusual order for a lump sum payment'. This order provided that the husband would pay an initial lump sum instalment of £30,000, followed by 240 further monthly instalments of the amount needed to repay the wife's mortgage liability under a mortgage of £225,000. The judge explained that the reason that these payments were to be made by lump sum rather than periodical payments was that 'it will endure beyond remarriage, ie will in that regard equate to conventional capital provision, and will bind the husband's estate in the unlikely event of his death within the 20-year period'. The lump sum order was secured by giving the wife a first charge over the husband's shares in the company. In *C v C (Variation of Post-Nuptial Settlement: Company Shares)* [2003] 2 FLR 493, the court varied a post-nuptial settlement to give the wife a shareholding in the company.

In cases where a lump sum is used to capitalise maintenance, the courts have in the past based awards on actual assessments of the capital sum required to produce a given income for the remainder of the wife's life (see *Duxbury v Duxbury* [1987] 1 FLR 7). Computer programs have been devised by accountants and lawyers which can calculate the lump sum which, if invested, will produce enough to meet the recipient's requirements for the rest of her life. The calculations are based on certain assumptions, such as to life expectancy and rates of inflation, etc. This complicated method is designed to produce an index-linked net income where both the capital and income are used with the result that the fund would be exhausted, in the main, on the recipient's death. This method cannot, however, protect a spouse against unforeseen future adversity: it may be appropriate to increase the lump sum to provide additional resources to cushion a spouse against such unfortunate eventualities. Whichever method of assessment is used, such calculations can only ever be a guide to the court. The court will keep sight of its wide discretion and its obligation to consider all relevant factors in s 25. In various recent cases, the court has stressed that '*Duxbury* is a tool and not a rule' (as observed by Thorpe LJ in *White v White* [1998] 2 FLR 310 in the Court of Appeal).

Indeed, it has been recognised for some time that *Duxbury* calculations result in the paradox that the longer the marriage, and hence the older the wife, the less the capital sum required for a *Duxbury*-type fund. The case of *White* brought about the demise of the reliance on 'reasonable requirements' and emphasised the importance of considering all the relevant s 25 factors, including contributions. Since, after a long marriage, a spouse will almost certainly have made substantial contributions, whether financial or not, to the welfare of the family, this will have to be reflected in the award made. It seems then that *Duxbury* calculations may have a more limited role to play in the future.

9.8 Pensions

In many cases the pensions of either or both of the spouses will be a most valuable asset, and in some cases, *the* most valuable. There are three possible ways of dealing with pension rights on divorce: off-setting; pension attachment; and pension sharing (see **4.7**). One potential problem to be resolved in deciding which option to choose is how to value the pension rights.

This problem arises since a pension is not realisable as a capital sum and, unless the pension is already in payment, represents money which may not become payable until far into the future. The starting point is the Cash Equivalent Transfer Value ('CETV'), but it would often be inappropriate simply to include this sum as if it were extra capital. This problem was raised in two cases: *Maskell v Maskell* [2001] EWCA Civ 858, [2001] 1 FLR 1138 and *Norris v Norris* [2002] EWHC 2996 (Fam), [2003] 1 FLR 142. In *Maskell,* the Court of Appeal took the view that the pension should be valued at the amount of capital which could be taken on retirement, the rest providing an income stream. This amounted to only 25% of the CETV. However, in different circumstances in *Norris,* the court held that it would not be unfair to include the full CETV as part of the assets. The case of *Martin-Dye v Martin-Dye* [2006] EWCA Civ 681 may provide a solution. In this case the Court of Appeal took the view that the best way to achieve fairness was to exclude the pensions from the capital assets altogether and instead make a pension sharing order in the same percentages as the capital had been divided. Thus, as the capital assets had been divided 57:43 in favour of the wife, there should also be an order sharing the pensions 57:43 in favour of the wife. This case involved a pension in payment, but could equally apply when the respondent has not retired. However, it would not necessarily be fair in all cases. Cases will inevitably turn on their own facts and, in a case where pension rights are substantial, expert advice should be sought as to their valuation.

9.9 Bankruptcy

9.9.1 Bankruptcy and the matrimonial home

When a spouse becomes bankrupt, his property will vest in the trustee in bankruptcy. The making of a bankruptcy order will sever any joint tenancy. Where the matrimonial home is in the sole name of the bankrupt spouse, the non-owning spouse's matrimonial home rights bind the trustee and creditors (see **9.6.2.1**). However, the trustee in bankruptcy can apply to the court for the sale of the matrimonial home to satisfy the creditors, whether the home is in the sole name of the bankrupt or in the joint names of the bankrupt and spouse. In deciding whether to order a sale the court must take into account the following factors:

(a)   the interests of the bankrupt's creditors;

(b)   the conduct of the spouse or former spouse, so far as contributing to the bankruptcy;

(c)   the needs and financial resources of the spouse or former spouse;

(d)   the needs of the children; and

(e)   all the circumstances of the case other than the needs of the bankrupt.

However, if the trustee applies more than one year after the bankruptcy, the court must assume that the interests of the creditors outweigh all other considerations unless the circumstances are exceptional. There is no definition of what amounts to 'exceptional' circumstances and cases coming within this are likely to be rare. An example is *Judd v Brown* [1998] 2 FLR 360, where the wife was suffering from cancer and needed to undergo a course of chemotherapy. However, the fact that the wife and children will be rendered homeless is unlikely to be regarded as exceptional circumstances (*Re Citro* [1991] 1 FLR 71). In *Donohoe v Ingram (Trustee in Bankruptcy of Kirkup)* [2006] EWHC 292, the court held that such an interpretation of 'exceptional circumstances' did not breach Article 8 of the European Convention of Human Rights. Thus, generally, the non-bankrupt spouse and any children will have a one-year 'breathing space' in which to find themselves alternative accommodation.

9.9.2   Bankruptcy and ancillary relief orders

If the court has made a property adjustment order in favour of the spouse of a bankrupt, it would seem that in theory the trustee will take subject to that spouse's interest provided that the property adjustment order has become effective (ie, decree absolute has been pronounced) at the date of presentation of the bankruptcy petition (*Mountney v Treharne* [2002] EWCA Civ 1174). However, in practice, the recent case of *Hill v Haines* [2007] EWHC 1012 (Ch) states that the trustee in bankruptcy is likely to be able to have the property adjustment order set aside under s 339 of the Insolvency Act 1986. This is on the basis that it is a transaction at an undervalue which will be set aside if it was made less than two years before the bankruptcy petition (or five years before the bankruptcy petition if the bankrupt was insolvent at the time of the order). Thus, where one spouse would appear to be bankrupt it may be better for the other spouse to establish a proprietary claim using normal trust principles (if this is possible) rather than relying on the court's ancillary relief powers under the MCA 1973. If the property adjustment order has not been made and become effective by the date of the presentation of the bankruptcy petition, any property adjustment order made will be void (*Treharne & Sand v Forrester* [2004] 1 FLR 1173).

In *Re Nunn (Bankruptcy: Divorce: Pension Rights)* [2004] 1 FLR 1123, the court held that a pension attachment order made in 1994 was not enforceable against the trustee in bankruptcy as the order did not give the wife an equitable interest in the proceeds of the pension lump sum. However, since May 2000 pension rights under an approved pension scheme are excluded from the bankruptcy estate, and they may be excluded where the scheme is unapproved (see Welfare Reform and Pensions Act 1999, ss 11 and 12).

Under the Insolvency (Amendment) Rules 2005 (SI 2005/527), where the bankruptcy order was made on or after 1 April 2005, lump sum orders and costs orders made in family proceedings are provable in bankruptcy. Thus, where a lump sum order has been made and the payer then becomes bankrupt, the recipient spouse will be in the same position as the bankrupt's other creditors. Arrears of periodical payments and child support maintenance arrears are not provable.

9.10 Chapter summary

(1)   Under ss 24 and 24A of the MCA 1973, the court may make the following orders with respect to the matrimonial home:

(a)   immediate sale (and division of the proceeds, if any);

(b)   outright transfer to one spouse;

(c)   home retained under a deferred trust of land (eg a *Mesher* order) or subject to a deferred charge.

When deciding what order to make, the court will consider the factors in s 25 of the MCA 1973. It must also take into account the interests of any third party, such as a lender.

(2)   If the matrimonial home is rented, the court has powers under the MCA 1973 and FLA 1996 to order the transfer of the tenancy to one spouse.

(3)   Several measures are available (eg an injunction under MCA 1973, s 37) to protect against one party disposing of property in order to thwart the other party's financial claim. In particular, a non-owning spouse's matrimonial home rights, under s 30 of the FLA 1996, should be registered to prevent the owning spouse selling the matrimonial home.

(4)   Lump sums are most commonly ordered either in the context of a division of the net sale proceeds of the home (or other property), or as a form of capitalised maintenance, particularly in cases of substantial assets.

(5)   Where one spouse becomes bankrupt, the non-bankrupt spouse and any children will generally have one year in which to find alternative accommodation.

Chapter 10
Ancillary Finance Procedure

10.1 Introduction

This chapter deals with how to obtain a court order in divorce proceedings providing for the distribution of the matrimonial assets. The order may follow a court hearing or agreement between the parties. Throughout this chapter, the spouse who is applying for the order is called the applicant and the other spouse is called the respondent (regardless of who was the petitioner and respondent in the divorce itself).

The drafting of an order to record any agreement between the parties or order of the court will then be considered. Lastly, the chapter briefly examines the procedure to be followed to obtain a maintenance calculation under the CSA 1991.

10.2 Public funding

Before funding is applied for, unless the client is exempt, the solicitor will first need to make a referral appointment for mediation (see FLA 1996, s 29 and **2.5**). If it transpires that mediation is unsuitable, then the solicitor can apply for funding in the usual way. At this stage, the appropriate application is likely to be for General Family Help (see **2.6**), although if it is clear that there is no reasonable prospect of settlement then the solicitor should apply for Legal Representation (see **2.7**).

10.3 Overview of the procedure

The main aims of the procedure (which is set out in FPR 1991, rr 2.51D–2.71 (as amended) – see **Appendix 1(F)**) are: to identify the important issues for the parties and encourage them to reach agreement; to reduce unnecessary cost and delay by imposing a strict timetable; to restrict disclosure of financial information and ensure the parties are aware, at each stage, exactly what costs are being incurred in proceeding with the case. The Rules introduce an 'overriding objective' into the proceedings (FPR 1991, r 2.51D). This is similar to that contained in Part 1 of the Civil Procedure Rules 1998 (CPR 1998) and provides that cases should be dealt with proportionately, and this will be achieved partly through active case management by the court.

The procedure falls into three phases, each of which ends with a court hearing:

Phase 1:   Filing of the application until the end of the First Appointment.

Phase 2:   End of the First Appointment until the end of the Financial Dispute Resolution (FDR) hearing.

Phase 3:   End of FDR until the Final Hearing.

In many cases, only the first two phases will be needed to achieve a final consent order.

10.4   Pre-application protocol

A pre-application protocol for ancillary relief applications (annexed to *Practice Direction (Ancillary Relief: Procedure)* [2000] 1 FLR 997) came into effect in June 2000. It outlines the steps the parties should take to seek and provide information both from and to each other prior to the commencement of any ancillary relief application. It states that pre-application disclosure is usually appropriate only where both parties agree to it and disclosure is not likely to be an issue. Where pre-application disclosure is appropriate it must be carried out in accordance with the overriding objective and be cost effective. In other cases, it is better to commence proceedings to take advantage of the court timetable and court-managed process. It also states that, wherever possible, valuations should be carried out by a single joint expert. It now forms part of the Law Society's Family Law Protocol (see 1.2.3).

10.5   The application

10.5.1   Making the application for ancillary relief

The method of application will depend upon whether the applicant is the petitioner or the respondent in the divorce.

The petitioner-applicant makes the formal application in the prayer to the petition. Therefore, the applicant can simply leave unamended the prayers relating to financial relief which appear in the petition.

The petitioner-applicant must follow up the formal application in the petition by filing a notice of intention to proceed in Form A (see **Appendix 3(C)**). A respondent-applicant merely has to file Form A.

Form A is a straightforward form in tick-box format. However, further information will need to be given if the application is in relation to land, for example, for a property adjustment order. In these cases, the FPR 1991 state that Form A should:

(a)   identify the land;

(b)   state whether the title is registered or not and, if registered, its title number; and

(c)   give particulars of any mortgage or interest in the land (FPR 1991, r 2.59).

Where the applicant is seeking an order for attachment or sharing of a pension (see 4.7), the terms of the order requested must be specified in the notice in Form A.

It is good practice to apply for all available types of financial order (see **Chapter 4**). This not only prevents the client falling into the remarriage trap (see **10.5.2**), but also allows for a change in circumstances or for a clean break to be effected (see **4.6**).

10.5.2   Potential danger areas

Generally, the application should be made at an early stage. There are several reasons for this:

(a)   If the petitioner-applicant omits to apply in the petition then he may apply later using Form A, but only if either the respondent has agreed to the terms of the proposed order or the petitioner obtains the leave of the court. Although leave will usually be given where the applicant has a seriously arguable case and a reasonable prospect of obtaining the relief sought, it will not be given if there has been an unjustifiable delay. Clearly, it is not worth taking the risk of leave being refused, and so the application should be submitted as soon as possible.

(b)   The remarriage trap: this is caused by s 28(3) of the MCA 1973, which states: 'If after the grant of a decree . . . either party remarries . . . that party shall not be entitled to apply . . . for a financial provision order in his or her favour, or for a property adjustment order . . .'. Thus the court cannot make an order in such circumstances, even by consent; see *E v E (Premature Remarriage)* (Family Division, 10 October 2006).

Example

Henry has petitioned for divorce. His wife Eileen is very pleased since she wishes to marry her new partner. The decree absolute is granted and Eileen remarries. Only at this stage does she consult her solicitor about obtaining a lump sum order. It is too late – she has fallen into the remarriage trap.

Note that if Eileen had applied for a lump sum order at any time before remarrying, that application could be heard after her remarriage, as s 28(3) of the MCA 1973 prevents only the *making* of an application after remarriage.

(c)   A lengthy delay in making or proceeding with the application may result in a less advantageous order being made if, for example, the delay has prejudiced the respondent.

(d)   The court has power to backdate a periodical payments order to the date of the application (provided it believes the respondent has the means to pay). Therefore, the earlier the application, the further it can be backdated.

It is particularly important to remember to apply where the applicant is the respondent in the divorce, as the solicitor must file Form A without the benefit of any reminders. In contrast, the petitioner's solicitor is reminded by the petition itself.

Although the application should be made as soon as possible, the court has no power to make the order before decree nisi (and if it purports to do so, any order it makes is void). Also, most orders will not take effect until decree absolute (see **4.2**).

10.6   Filing and service

10.6.1   Filing

The applicant needs to file at court:

(a)   Form A in duplicate;

(b)   General Family Help/Legal Representation certificate and notice of issue (if relevant);

(c)   application fee;

(d)   notice of acting where the client received Legal Help in the divorce and now has General Family Help/Legal Representation. This is because the client will have been acting in person in the divorce. Now a solicitor is acting, he will need to ensure that his firm appears on the court file.

Upon filing the Form A, the court will at once (on Form C) fix the date for the First Appointment between 12 and 16 weeks ahead. The timing of this First Appointment cannot be altered without leave from the court. Within this period, much, if not most, of the important financial information-gathering and appraisal of the case will take place.

10.6.2   Service

The court must serve on the respondent a copy of Forms A and C within four days of filing (FPR 1991, r 2.61A(4)).

The applicant must serve on the respondent:

(a)   notice of issue of General Family Help/Legal Representation (if relevant);

(b)   copy of notice of acting (Legal Help divorce case only).

The Form A must also be served on any lender or person responsible for a pension arrangement mentioned in the application (FPR 1991, rr 2.59(4) and 2.70(6)). Although the applicant is required to confirm to the court prior to the First Appointment (see **10.8.1**) that this step has been taken, if it is overlooked and the lender or person responsible for a pension arrangement is not served with a copy of the application, the hearing may have to be adjourned while the mistake is rectified, with a consequent costs penalty.

10.6.3   Pensions

Unless the party with pension rights has a valuation less than 12 months old at the date of the first appointment, he must, within seven days of receiving notification of the date of the first appointment, request one from the pension arrangement. The pension arrangement must provide a valuation within six weeks. When the party with pension rights receives the valuation, he must send it to the applicant within seven days of receipt. Where the Pension Protection Fund has become involved with the pension scheme (the Pension Protection Fund is a body which pays compensation to members of certain pension schemes when there are insufficient assets in the pension fund to pay members), the party with pension rights must also send to the applicant a copy of any notification received from the Pension Protection Fund.

10.7   Obtaining the evidence

10.7.1   Duty of disclosure

Each party is under a duty of full and frank disclosure. This duty is underlined in the Law Society's Family Law Protocol. Should they not give full disclosure, this may result in a reduced order (if the party is the applicant); a penalty in costs (see, eg, *P v P (Financial Relief: Non-Disclosure)* [1994] 2 FLR 381); the forfeiture of legal professional privilege protection (see *Kimber v Brookman Solicitors* [2004] 2 FLR 221); or the final order being set aside at a later date (see *Livesey (formerly Jenkins) v Jenkins* [1985] AC 424 and **11.7**). The bulk of the information needed should be contained in each party's Form E (see **10.7.2**).

10.7.2 The evidence

Both parties must complete and swear a statement of property and income (Form E) (see **Appendix 3(D)**). This form is quite lengthy and gives details of: the parties and any children; means (including pension); capital and income needs; standard of living; contributions made to the family; conduct (in exceptional cases only); and any other relevant circumstances. Thus, all the essential information required by s 25 of the MCA 1973 should be included in Form E. Each party should also set out any order sought in Form E.

Certain essential documents must be filed and served with Form E:

(a)   last three payslips and last P60;

(b)   bank/building society statements for the last 12 months for all accounts;

(c)   any property valuation obtained during the last six months;

(d)   most recent mortgage statement(s);

(e)   the last two years' accounts for any business and/or partnership, and any documentation relating to a valuation of these;

(f)   valuation of any pension;

(g)   surrender value quotations for any life insurance policies; and

(h)   the latest statement or dividend counterfoil for any investments.

Any necessary explanatory documents must also be annexed.

Various computer packages have been developed to help the solicitor complete Form E, for example *Quantum Slip* (Class Publishing). There are no affidavits (although in complex cases affidavits may be ordered). Both Form Es should be filed and simultaneously exchanged at least 35 days before the First Appointment. What if one party's solicitor is ready to exchange Form E but the other side is refusing to? In such a situation, the solicitor who is ready to exchange should send a copy of Form E to the court (but not to the other side) to prove compliance with the FPR 1991. Additionally, the solicitor could apply for a without notice order that the defaulting party should comply, although it is probably better to wait until the First Appointment to ask for such an order.

Both parties should then draft the following documents:

(a)   A concise statement of the issues. This will require the parties to focus on the real issues in the application.

(b)   A chronology.

(c)   A questionnaire of further information and documents requested from the other party. This must be drafted with reference to the issues raised in the statement of issues. In many cases it may be that Form E and the attachments leave no matters outstanding and, in these cases, the parties will file a statement that no further information and documents are required.

(d)   A notice in Form G stating whether that party will be in a position at the First Appointment to proceed on that occasion to an FDR appointment. This will be the case where both parties feel that they have all the disclosure they need, and it allows a form of 'fast tracking' in these cases.

These four documents must be filed and served by both parties at least 14 days before the First Appointment. In addition, immediately before the First Appointment, the solicitors for both parties must produce a written estimate of the costs incurred so far in Form H. Note that this is something separate from the statement of costs required by the CPR 1998 (see **10.10.2**). Thus, if the solicitor wishes to claim the costs of the First Appointment, he must complete and serve a statement of costs at least 24 hours before the hearing.

10.8 Court hearings

10.8.1 The First Appointment

The court will fix a date for this when the applicant files Form A (see **10.6.1**). The short timetable is to allow the court to monitor the application and its progress from an early stage, with a view to limiting the issues and saving costs. Both parties and all legal representatives must attend. At this appointment, the district judge will give directions and decide how the application should proceed from then on.

The directions will deal with:

(a)   the extent to which the questionnaires need to be answered;

(b)   documents to be produced;

(c)   valuations or other expert evidence (joint independent experts should be instructed where practicable). Part 35 of the CPR 1998 on experts applies to ancillary relief applications and, thus, where necessary, the court can direct evidence to be given by a single joint expert;

(d)   the production of other evidence, such as schedules of assets or, in some cases, affidavits.

Particular considerations which may arise at this stage include the following:

(a)   *Valuation of the home.* Directions will usually require that the parties agree a valuation, and if they are unable to agree, that they appoint a joint expert valuer. If they cannot agree on a valuer then the court will appoint one.

(b)   *Valuation of the family business.* There may be a family business which the client wants to be valued. The court will not generally order a sale of the family business, nor make an order which would mean in effect that the owner was forced to sell to comply with the order or where such an order would prejudice third party investors (see **9.7**). The court will also be anxious to ensure that the family assets are not needlessly wasted on expensive valuations of the business (*Evans v Evans* [1990] 1 FLR 319). Therefore, usually, an approximate valuation is all that is needed. However, since *White v White* [2000] 2 FLR 981, a more exact valuation may be required in big money cases. Again, the court is likely to restrict the use of experts by giving a direction for joint appointment or, in default, only allowing one per party.

(c)   *New partners.* One party may claim that the other party has a new partner who is working and who, therefore, is able to contribute to the outgoings, thus freeing more cash for the former family or reducing the new family's needs. Say, for example, that the wife had a new partner. The husband might want to know what that partner's assets were. Although the district judge is empowered to order the attendance of any person at any stage of the proceedings (FPR 1991, r 2.62(4)), in practice this power has been restrictively interpreted. Accordingly, the court will not order a non-party to attend for cross-examination unless he has filed an affidavit (*W v W* (1981) 11 Fam Law 247). In addition, it has been held that the court cannot order a non-party to file an affidavit (*Wynne v Wynne* [1980] 3 All ER 659). In such a situation, the correct procedure is to apply for a subpoena that the new partner attend the final hearing under RSC Ord 32, r 7. In deciding whether to grant such a subpoena, the court will take into account that any requirement for a third party to disclose financial information is potentially a breach of their rights of privacy under Article 8 of the European Convention on Human Rights. Thus ordering disclosure must be necessary and proportionate (*M v M (Third Party Subpoena: Financial Conduct)* [2006] 2 FLR 1253).

In such a situation, it may be possible to persuade the court to order the non-party to attend an 'inspection appointment'. Rule 2.62(7) of the FPR 1991 provides that any party may apply to the court for an order that any person attend an inspection appointment, bringing with him such documents as are specified in the order and the inspection of which appears to the court to be necessary for disposing fairly of the case. The case of *Frary v Frary* [1993] 2 FLR 696 makes it clear, however, that r 2.62(7) of the FPR 1991 does not change the law relating to who the court can order to disclose their assets, it simply allows the court to order disclosure at an earlier date, ie before the hearing.

(d)   *Pensions.* Where a pension sharing or pension attachment order is sought, the court is likely to direct the completion of all or part of a Pension Inquiry Form (Form P) within a set time limit before the FDR. If the First Appointment is likely to be treated as an FDR appointment (see below), Form P can be completed voluntarily prior to the First Appointment.

The district judge will then usually give a date for a Financial Dispute Resolution (FDR) appointment unless, exceptionally, he decides that this is not appropriate. In these exceptional cases (which are likely to be those which are very complicated), the district judge must give one of the following directions:

(a)   that a further directions appointment be fixed;

(b)   that an appointment be fixed for an interim order;

(c)   that the case be fixed for a final hearing; or

(d)   that the case be adjourned for mediation or negotiation, or (in exceptional cases) generally.

Alternatively, unless there are considerable assets involved or the assets require further investigation, the district judge will treat the First Appointment as an FDR appointment.

Both parties' representatives will produce their written costs estimates. The district judge must consider whether he should make a costs order at this stage, having regard to the general rule on costs and the extent to which the parties have adhered to the rules (see **10.10.2**). Thus if, for example, one party fails to provide the relevant documentation with Form E, and this wastes the opportunity of having an FDR, he is likely to have a costs order made against him.

10.8.2   From First Appointment to FDR

Both parties should comply with all directions made at the First Appointment before the FDR. Neither party can insist on any further disclosure without leave of the court.

The applicant must inform the court of all offers or proposals and responses made to him at least seven days before the FDR. This should give the lawyers sufficient time to consider any proposals and ensure that their clients are not surprised by them at the hearing. Although there is no statutory requirement, the court will expect the parties to make offers and proposals, to give them proper consideration and not to attempt to exclude their consideration at the FDR (*Practice Direction (Ancillary Relief: Procedure)* [2000] 1 FLR 997).

Immediately before the FDR, both parties must produce a second written costs estimate in Form H.

10.8.3 The FDR appointment

The aim of the FDR is to produce a settlement. Both parties and all legal representatives must attend. The FDR will be conducted by a district judge who will then have nothing more to do with the case. The district judge will attempt to help the parties towards settlement by exploring common ground. Any offer made so far can be referred to at the FDR, even 'without prejudice' offers. All discussions at the FDR will be completely privileged. Documents referring to prior offers must be returned to the party who filed them at their request and not kept on the court file.

Where a settlement is reached at the FDR, the district judge may make a consent order reflecting the agreement. The district judge may also adjourn the FDR to allow one or both parties time to consider their position. Where no agreement is reached, the judge may make further directions, including, where appropriate, setting a hearing date. In cases involving large sums of money, the district judge may make a direction that narrative affidavits be filed by the parties at this stage to give a broader presentation of the historical background of the application than that allowed for in Form E. These might cover, for example, the respective contributions of the parties, the genesis of current resources and the standard of living during the marriage (*W v W (Ancillary Relief: Practice)* [2000] Fam Law 473).

10.8.4 From FDR to hearing

Any directions made at the FDR should be complied with. Either party can apply for further directions, and the court may direct a further FDR.

Before the hearing, both parties must draft a statement of proposed orders, file this at court and serve it on the other party. The applicant must do this at least 14 days before the hearing, and the respondent within seven days of being served with the applicant's proposals. These statements are open and no privilege will attach to them. However, this rule has no effect on without prejudice offers and such offers may continue to be made at any time.

At least 14 days before the final hearing both parties must file and serve on the other party a statement of costs in Form H1. This requires full details of all costs incurred to date in the proceedings and an estimate of those to be incurred (including the estimated costs of implementation of the order).

The applicant's solicitor should ensure that the relevant bundle of documents is prepared and lodged with the court at least two working days before the hearing, in accordance with the President's Practice Direction: *Family Proceedings: Court Bundles (Universal Practice to be applied in all Courts other than the Family Proceedings Court)* [2006] 2 FLR 199.

10.8.5 The Final Hearing

The hearing is usually before a district judge, in chambers and in private. The district judge has power to refer the case to a judge if necessary (FPR 1991, r 2.65).

In theory, the hearing should follow the same course as ordinary civil proceedings. However, such hearings are often much more informal. Having read the papers, the district judge may open by letting the parties know what he has in mind and inviting them to discuss and negotiate around this for a while.

If this does not succeed, or if the district judge wishes the proceedings to follow a more formal course, then the applicant's solicitor (or counsel) will open. He will outline the case and then call his evidence. The evidence will often consist only of that of the applicant, but other witnesses, for example a new partner or valuer, may be called. The witnesses will then be cross-examined by the respondent's solicitor. He will then present his own client's case. Once all the evidence has been given, the district judge will make the order (or may reserve his judgment until a later date). A careful note should be taken of exactly what is said in case it should be necessary to appeal.

It is possible that the district judge will not feel able to make a final order at this time, for example, because it appears that the respondent is about to obtain (or lose) a job, or because the respondent has not turned up to the hearing. In such a situation, the district judge could make an interim order on such terms as he considers just.

Copies of any order made are sent to both parties by the court. In addition, where relevant, within seven days of the making of the order or of the decree absolute (whichever is the later) the court must send a copy of the decree nisi, a copy of the decree absolute and a copy of the pension sharing order and annex to the pension sharing arrangement.

10.9 Interim orders

Despite the fact that one of the aims of the procedure is to save time, it may still be many months before a final order is made. Thus, the Rules allow a party to apply at any stage of the proceedings for an order for maintenance pending suit (see **4.3.1**), interim periodical payments or an interim variation order. The application will be made by notice of application. If the application is made before filing Form E, it must be accompanied by a draft of the order requested, together with a short sworn statement explaining why the order is necessary and giving necessary information about means. On filing the notice of application, the court will give a hearing date which must be at least 14 days later. The applicant must then immediately serve the respondent with a copy of the notice of application (and accompanying documents where relevant). Where the respondent has not already filed Form E, he must file and serve a short sworn statement setting out his means at least seven days before the hearing.

10.10 Costs

10.10.1 Costs generally

The importance of costs in ancillary proceedings cannot be over-emphasised. It is essential that the question of costs is kept in sight and in proportion to the overall assets in dispute. In the case of *Re T (Divorce: Interim Maintenance: Discovery)* [1990] 1 FLR 1, the entire litigation costs were said to exceed £1.2m. The impact of costs on the family finances is so significant that, under r 2.61 of the FPR 1991, each party must produce to the court, at each court appointment, a written estimate of costs and, before the Final Hearing, a written statement of costs (see **10.8.4**). In addition, adherence to the overriding objective and active case management by the courts under the new ancillary relief procedure should help to ensure that costs are kept in proportion to the overall assets.

10.10.2 The costs rules

The costs rules are set out in r 2.71 of the FPR 1991 (see **Appendix 1(F)**). The general rule is that the court will not make a costs order in ancillary relief proceedings unless such an order is justified by the litigation conduct of one of the parties. Costs will normally be treated as a liability of the relevant party and be taken into account when making the substantive order. To enable the court to have an accurate picture of the costs incurred, each party must file a statement of costs in Form H1 at least 14 days before the final hearing (see **10.8.4**).

In deciding whether to make a costs order on the basis of a party's litigation conduct the court must take into account the following factors:

(a)   any failure to comply with the rules, any court order or any practice direction which the court considers relevant. Thus, for example, where a party does not make any proposals for settlement before the FDR and in consequence the FDR is adjourned, he is likely to be ordered to pay the costs of the wasted hearing;

(b)   any open offer to settle made by a party;

(c)   whether it was reasonable for a party to raise, pursue or contest a particular allegation or issue. Thus, for example, it is likely to be unreasonable to raise an allegation that the other party is cohabiting when it is clear he or she is not;

(d)   the manner in which a party has pursued or responded to the application or a particular allegation or issue. This would cover, for example, the situation where an allegation of non-disclosure of assets was pursued too far;

(e)   any other aspect of a party's conduct in relation to the proceedings which the court considers relevant. This is a general sweeping-up factor which could cover, for example, where one party instructed a sole expert after a joint expert report had been prepared;

(f)   the financial effect on the parties of any costs order.

A party who intends to seek a costs order at a hearing must give advance notice of that fact in open correspondence or in his skeleton arguments (*Practice Direction (Ancillary Relief: Costs)*, 20 February 2006). If a summary assessment of costs is likely, the claiming party must also file a statement of costs in CPR Form N260, as Form H1 is insufficiently detailed for such an assessment.

10.11 Negotiations

One of the key features of the ancillary relief procedure is the promotion and facilitation of settlements. Most cases do, in fact, settle by agreement, often during informal discussions following the FDR. However, negotiations are an on-going process and may well commence at a very early stage. This is generally to be encouraged as it will probably be quicker and will cost the parties less, so leaving more of the assets available to be divided between them. Further, it may help to lessen any ill-feeling caused by the breakdown of the marriage and, therefore, aid the parties' future relations, in particular with the children. In addition, the respondent is more likely to comply with an order which he has agreed to, thus avoiding the need for enforcement proceedings.

However, the client must beware of settling at any price. Any agreement represents a compromise, but the solicitor must ensure that negotiations are carried out with full knowledge of all material facts. Both parties are under a duty of full and frank disclosure (see **10.7.1**). Do not be afraid to ask the other party for the same level of disclosure as he would give if the matter was to proceed to a hearing.

In addition, the solicitor should be aware of the type of order which the court might be expected to make, thus ensuring that he does not allow his client to accept too little or offer too much. Take care to check that the client is not willing to accept a very low offer simply because he is in an emotionally vulnerable state following the breakdown of the marriage.

If a settlement is reached, heads of agreement should be drawn up and signed by the parties and their legal representatives to evidence the necessary consensus. However, as was made clear in *Xydhias v Xydhias* [1999] 1 FLR 683, although the court will usually uphold the agreement, it is not enforceable in its own right.

10.12 Consent orders

Once the parties have reached agreement, the applicant's solicitor should draw up a draft consent order and send it to the respondent's solicitor. To enable the court to investigate the parties' means, a statement of information must also be completed (Form M1 – see **Appendix 3(E)**). This statement must include:

(a)   the duration of the marriage, the age of each party and the ages of any minor children of the family;

(b)   an estimate of the approximate value of the capital resources and net income of each party and of any minor child of the family;

(c)   what arrangements are intended for the accommodation of the parties and any minor child of the family;

(d)   whether either party has remarried, or has any present intention to remarry or to cohabit with another person;

(e)   where the order includes a transfer of property, whether any lender has been served with notice of application and whether it has objected to the transfer;

(f)   where the order includes a term which imposes any requirement on the person responsible for a pension arrangement, whether he has been served with the notice of application and whether he has objected to the order;

(g)   any other specially significant matters.

However, if the application is only to vary a periodical payments order, or for an interim periodical payments order, the statement of information can be restricted to an estimate of the net income of the parties and any minor children (FPR 1991, r 2.61).

Often the applicant's solicitor will insert the applicant's details in the statement and then send it to the respondent's solicitor with the draft order. The respondent's solicitor will then complete the statement with the respondent's details, indorse his consent on the order and return both to the applicant's solicitor. However, the statement of information does not have to be on one document, so each party can complete its own.

The applicant's solicitor should then file the draft order plus two copies together with the statement of information. He must also file Form A if agreement was reached at such an early stage that this has not yet been done.

The district judge will then peruse the filed documents and, if satisfied, can make an order in the agreed terms. In the rare event that he is not satisfied, he can order the parties to attend a hearing.

If agreement is reached at a hearing, the district judge can dispense with the need for filing a statement of information.

The consent order is then drafted immediately by both parties' solicitors, and approved and made by the district judge.

10.13 Drafting ancillary financial and property orders

It is very important for a family solicitor to be able to draft orders which give effect to any financial agreement between husband and wife (or order of the court) in the way intended. It is equally important for the solicitor to be able to spot any errors in a draft order that is sent to him for his approval. At **10.13.13**, there are three specimen orders: Shah, Levy and Brown. These should be read carefully, as they will be referred to throughout **10.13** to illustrate a variety of drafting points.

10.13.1 Form of order

The order should be set out in three parts as follows:

(a)   Title of suit.

(b)   Preamble. This can deal with matters the court has no power to order, for example, mortgage payments, paying for outgoings on the house (but see **10.13.5.3** – deferred trusts of land). It:

  (i)   states whether the order is made by consent (as in Shah and Levy) or (in a contested case) after hearing representations from the parties (and their solicitors/counsel) (see Brown);

  (ii)   may indicate the basis on which the order is made, for example, on the basis that the applicant pays the mortgage instalments out of her maintenance payments (see Levy);

  (iii)   recites any undertakings given by either party, for example, to discharge outgoings on the property (see Brown).

(c)   Operative part of order. This is prefaced by the words 'It is ordered'. It must be couched in clear and unambiguous terms so that each party can see, for example, what he or she is required to do, by when and/or until when. It must also reflect what the court's powers under ss 22–24D of the MCA 1973 actually are. Even by consent, the court cannot order a party to do something which it has no power to do (eg order the husband to pay the premiums on an insurance policy).

Note that third parties cannot be ordered to do anything, for example, a building society cannot be ordered to grant or transfer a mortgage.

10.13.2 Undertakings

An undertaking given to the court would appear to take effect (for all practical purposes) as if it were an order (see, for example, Lord Brandon in *Livesey (formerly Jenkins) v Jenkins* [1985] FLR 813 at 829). It is contempt of court to fail to comply with an undertaking, and the obligation can be enforced like an order; for example, if it is to pay money, third party debt actions or other methods of enforcement can be used (see **11.2.2**). The court may accept undertakings to do things which it cannot itself expressly order. The terms of an undertaking will be set out in the preamble to the order. Common examples would include provisions for one party:

(a)   to make payments to a third party, for example, the husband to pay mortgage instalments to the building society direct in addition to, or instead of, periodical payments, or to pay debts;

(b)   to take out a life insurance policy for the benefit of the other;

(c)   to seek the release of the other party from mortgage or leasehold covenants, or to indemnify him/her in respect of them;

(d)   to guarantee a mortgage;

(e)   to purchase property.

10.13.3   Periodical payments

The order must indicate in relation to the payments:

(a)   by whom they are payable;

(b)   to whom they are payable;

(c)   period by reference to when calculated, eg £2,000 per annum;

(d)   period by reference to which payable, eg monthly in advance;

(e)   from what date or event payments are to commence; and

(f)   until what date or event they are to continue (remember the age limits for children (see **4.3.2**)).

Example

The Husband shall pay periodical payments to the Wife. Payments shall be at the rate of £5,000 per annum payable monthly in advance. Payments shall commence on 1 April 2008. They will end on the first to occur of:

(a)   the death of the Husband or the Wife; or

(b)   the Wife's remarriage; or

(c)   further order of the court.

Spouse and child provision (if any) should appear in separate clauses. In cases where maintenance for a child is not covered by the CSA 1991, child provision should clearly indicate whether the payer is to:

(a)   pay direct to the child; or

(b)   pay to a third party (usually the other parent) for the child's benefit.

Where (as is usual) the order provides for payment to continue until the child reaches 17 (or 18) or ceases full-time education, the words 'whichever is the later' should be added.

Note that, where the Child Support Agency makes a calculation, this will not appear in the operative part of the order.

10.13.4   Lump sums

Remember that an order may provide that payment be deferred until a later date or an event and/or be by instalments (see **4.4.1**). The order must indicate in respect of each sum:

(a)   by whom it is payable;

(b)   to whom it is payable;

(c)   by what date or contingency it is to be paid;

For example, 'on or before the 30th day of June 2008'.

10.13.5 Property adjustment orders (not requiring an immediate sale)

Remember that although such orders usually affect only the home, any property may be covered, such as furnishings, stocks and shares, other land, cars (see Shah). The following points primarily relate to land, including the home.

10.13.5.1 Preliminary considerations

The order must make sense from a conveyancing and property law point of view. The solicitor will need to ascertain the following:

(a)   Where is the legal estate now? Is it in joint names, or his or hers alone?

(b)   Where is the legal estate going? Is it to stay in joint names, or to be put into joint names for the purposes of a deferred trust of land? Or is it to be transferred into the sole name of one? This will be so for an outright transfer (with or without a lump sum in return), or a deferred charge.

(c)   What are the equities now, and what are they going to be? This is relevant in two main cases:

    (i)   where the house is in one spouse's sole name but the other spouse may have an equitable interest from contributions to purchase or improvement. If the owning spouse is to keep the home outright, perhaps paying the other a lump sum, the non-owner should agree she has no interest in the property in the preamble;

    (ii)   a *Mesher-* or *Martin*-type order creating a deferred trust of land, where the new equities will be set out in the order.

10.13.5.2 Outright transfers (with or without lump sums in return)

The legal estate and/or equitable interests must be ordered to be transferred to one party as appropriate (see, eg, Shah, clause 2) and a date or event for compliance must be inserted. This date/event must be after the decree absolute (see **4.2**).

10.13.5.3 Deferred trusts of land

The legal estate must be vested in trustees (usually but not necessarily the parties) and ordered to be transferred if need be, with a date for compliance if that is so. The terms of the trust must be set out, including:

(a)   a statement of who has the right to occupy until sale;

(b)   the determining (or 'triggering') event(s) for sale to take place, for example, the occupying spouse's remarriage;

(c)   the proportions of the sale proceeds to which the parties will be entitled on sale.

Other provisions may be included, for example, detailed provisions to enable the original property to be sold and another bought on the same trusts if the occupier wishes to move, or as to who should have responsibility for repairs.

Contrary to the usual position, where there is a deferred trust the wording of s 24(1)(b) of the MCA 1973: 'an order that a settlement of such property ... be made to the satisfaction of the court ...', is wide enough to allow the court actually to order a party to pay the mortgage or insurance on the property, for example, rather than having to deal with it by way of undertaking (see, eg, Levy, clause 2.3).

10.13.5.4 Deferred charge

If necessary, the legal estate must be ordered to be transferred into the sole name of the intended occupier with a date for compliance. She will then be ordered to execute a legal charge (within a specified time) to secure payment to the non-occupier of a sum representing a proportion of the value of the property as defined in the order, or a fixed sum (as agreed). (See Brown in **10.13.13**.)

The order will require the charge deed to specify the events which will make the statutory power of sale arise and become exercisable, and may provide for matters such as removal and repairs to be covered by covenants to be set out in the deed.

10.13.5.5   Transfer of tenancies

The court also has power to order the transfer of most types of tenancy (see **9.5**). The wording of an order to effect this is relatively straightforward, for example, 'The Husband do transfer his tenancy in Flat 2, The Broadway, Guildshire, to the Wife within one month of decree absolute'. Remember that the landlord should be contacted at an early stage so that his consent can be obtained.

10.13.5.6   Further points

The orders do not operate to vest or transfer legal estates, nor to create legal charges. Conveyancing documents will be required to do this.

10.13.6   Orders for sale

In some cases, property may need to be sold in order to realise and divide the cash value. Where the home is in the sole name of one party this will most commonly be achieved by ordering the property owner to pay a lump sum to the other party equivalent to the desired share. The owner may raise the sum either by borrowing against the property, or by selling it, at his option. The non-owner is unaffected either way so long as the cash is paid.

Where property is in joint names, the court has power under s 17 of the the Married Women's Property Act 1882 (MWPA 1882) to order simply that the trust of land be executed and the proceeds divided. On divorce, the court may exercise its powers under s 17 of the MWPA 1882 without a separate formal application. A similar power exists in relation to civil partnerships under s 66 of the Civil Partnership Act 2004.

10.13.7   Pensions

The order must state that there is to be a provision by way of pension attachment or pension sharing in accordance with an annex in Form P1 (pension sharing) or Form P2 (pension attachment).

10.13.8   Dismissals

Just as an application for a particular type of order may be granted by the making of an order, for example, for the payment of a lump sum, so an application may be dismissed. Any application by either party which is not granted by the making of an order should be dismissed. The dismissal may be of an individual application, or the order may provide for the dismissal of all outstanding applications (see, eg, Levy, clause 7).

However, an application can be dismissed only if it has been made. If the husband is the respondent in the divorce, he may not have made any applications. Some courts will require that he files Form A so that his applications can be dismissed. However, no fee will be required if Form A is marked 'for dismissal purposes only'.

10.13.9 Clean break orders

Remember that such orders involve either an immediate dismissal of all maintenance claims, or an order that maintenance should be paid for a finite term only (see **4.6.2**).

Where an application for periodical payments for a spouse is dismissed to effect a clean break, the order should go on (under MCA 1973, s 25A) to direct that she 'shall not be entitled to make a further application in relation to the marriage' for a secured or unsecured periodical payments order (as in Shah, clause 4).

Where the order is for term maintenance, to effect a clean break it should direct that the applicant 'shall not be entitled to apply for an order to extend this deadline' (see Levy, clause 4).

The order should normally state that neither party, on the death of the other, shall be entitled to apply for an order under the I(PFD)A 1975 (see Shah, clause 5).

10.13.10 'Liberty to apply'

The words 'Liberty to apply' are conventionally included in an order. They simply envisage that the parties may need to come back to the court to resolve any difficulties over the interpretation of the order in the light of circumstances which may occur on putting it into effect, for example, if when the house is sold there is a dispute over which/how many estate agents to use. They do not in any way affect the court's power to vary an order and the restrictions on that power (see **11.8**).

10.13.11 Costs

The costs of each ancillary matter is a separate matter distinct from the main suit and any other application. When considering the costs of the ancillary relief proceedings, remember that the general rule is that the court will not make a costs order unless it is appropriate to do so because of the litigation conduct of one of the parties. On an earlier hearing, there may already have been a summary assessment of costs. Alternatively, if the order was silent as to costs, no party is entitled to costs in relation to that order (CPR 1998, r 44.13).

Where the court orders one party to pay the costs of the other party, it may either make a summary assessment, or order a detailed assessment of the costs (for further details, see *Civil Litigation*).

Where the general rule applies, the order will say that there be 'no order as to costs'. Where it is an application for a consent order (see **10.12**), the parties should agree a figure for costs to be inserted in the order, or agree there should be no order as to costs, as otherwise it will be necessary for attendance at the hearing.

If the receiving party is publicly funded:

(a)   there must be a detailed assessment of costs, if not agreed (see, eg, Brown, clause 9); and

(b)   where property or cash 'recovered or preserved' is intended to provide a house, a statement to that effect must be included in the body of the order to enable the Legal Services Commission to exercise its discretion to postpone the enforcement of the statutory charge. The Lord Chancellor has prescribed the following clause:

And it is certified for the purpose of the Community Legal Service (Financial) Regulations 2000 [that the lump sum of £X has been ordered to be paid to enable the applicant/respondent to purchase a home for himself/herself (or his/her dependants)] [that the property (address) has been preserved for/recovered by the applicant/respondent for use as a home for himself/herself (or his/her dependants)].

See Brown, clause 1.

Lastly, remember to deal with the costs of implementing the order, for example, conveyancing costs.

10.13.12 Side-letters

In some cases, it may be useful to record in a side-letter the background to the order and the result that it is trying to achieve. This can aid the court if at a later date one of the parties seeks to vary the order (see **11.8.3**).

10.13.13 Specimen orders

There follow three specimen orders: Shah, Levy and Brown. These should be read carefully as they are referred to throughout **10.13** to illustrate a variety of drafting points.

SHAH v SHAH

[Order for transfer of property with lump sum back or sale in default.]

There follows an outline of the facts of the case which resulted in the order below (note that these facts are *not* part of the order):

Mr and Mrs Shah are both working and self-supporting. There are no children. The matrimonial home is owned in joint names and is subject to a mortgage to the Halnat Building Society. It has been agreed that Mrs Shah (respondent) will transfer to Mr Shah her half share in the property in return for £15,000, being approximately half the net equity. Mr Shah will finance this by a second mortgage. Should it not be possible for him to raise the money within three months of decree absolute the house will be sold and the proceeds divided as to £15,000 to Mrs Shah and the balance to Mr Shah. Each party is to pay their own costs.

IN THE HULLPOOL COUNTY COURT		2008 No ....
BETWEEN	RAJ SHAH	Husband Applicant
	AND	
	GITA SHAH	Wife Respondent

ORDER

UPON the Husband and Wife agreeing that the terms of this order are accepted in full and final satisfaction of all claims for income, capital and pension sharing orders which either may be entitled to bring against the other in relation to the marriage

UPON the Husband UNDERTAKING to the court to indemnify the Wife against any future liability under the mortgage dated ... in favour of the Halnat Building Society ('the Mortgage') secured on the property at 93 Brook Court Hullpool ('the Home') and to use his best endeavours to obtain her release from her covenants under the Mortgage and to pay for the costs of transfer of the Home as set out in clause 2

BY CONSENT IT IS ORDERED THAT:

1. The Husband shall within 3 months of decree absolute in this cause ('the Payment Date') pay or cause to be paid to the Wife the sum of £15,000 (the 'Lump Sum').

2. On payment of the Lump Sum on or before the Payment Date the Wife shall transfer to the Husband;
   (i)   all her legal estate and beneficial interest in the Home
   (ii) all fixtures and chattels now in the Home which belong to her alone and her interest in any such items which are jointly owned.

3. If the Lump Sum is not paid by the Payment Date then the Home shall be sold on the open market and the following consequential provisions shall apply:

3.1 the Home shall be sold for such price as may be agreed by the parties or in default of agreement determined by the court;

3.2 both parties shall have the conduct of the sale;

3.3 the Husband's solicitors shall have the conduct of the conveyancing work relating to the sale;

3.4   the Home shall be offered for sale by such estate agents as may be agreed by the parties or in default of such agreement nominated by the court.

3.5   The proceeds of sale of the Home shall be applied as follows:

    (i)   to discharge the Mortgage

    (ii)   in payment of the Husband's solicitors' conveyancing costs and disbursements in connection with the sale;

    (iii) in payment of the charges of the estate agents;

    (iv)   in payment to the Wife of the Lump Sum of £15,000 referred to in Clause 1 of this order;

    (v)   in payment of the balance to the Husband.

4.   Upon compliance with clauses (1)–(3) and the Husband's undertakings to the court, the Husband's and the Wife's claims for financial provision, property adjustment and pension sharing orders do stand dismissed and neither the Husband nor the Wife shall be entitled to make any further application in relation to their marriage for an order under s 23(1)(a) or (b) of the Matrimonial Causes Act 1973.

5.   Neither the Husband nor the Wife shall be entitled on the death of the other to apply for an order for provision out of the other's estate.

6.   There be liberty to apply as to the implementation and timing of the terms of this order.

7.   It is ordered that the Husband and Wife shall each bear their own costs of this application and the ancillary negotiations.

Dated the   day of   2008.

Signed ....   Signed ....
Husband   Wife

We request that the court make an order as set out above to which our clients respectively consent.

Signed ....   Signed ....
Solicitors for the Husband   Solicitors for the Wife

LEVY v LEVY

[*Mesher* order: periodical payments to wife (linked to payment of mortgage) and step-child; dismissal of prayer for lump sum and respondent's application.]

Background information (note that this is *not* part of the order): Michelle Levy has recently obtained a decree absolute against Michael Levy under s 1(2)(d) of the MCA 1973. The parties have agreed that the three children of the family, Anthony (7) (who is Mrs Levy's child by her first husband who is now dead), Robert (5) and Peter (3), will remain with Mrs Levy. Mr Levy will pay maintenance for all three children (for his natural children via the Child Support Agency). The parties are in their mid-thirties. Mr Levy is a partner in a firm of surveyors. Mrs Levy has not been in paid employment since the birth of their first child. The former matrimonial home is in joint names and subject to a mortgage. Mr Levy has agreed that Mrs Levy and the children will remain in the home while the children are being educated. Mr Levy now lives in a flat. A consent order has been negotiated. Neither is publicly funded. Mr Levy had agreed to pay Mrs Levy's costs, the sum has already been agreed.

IN THE HIGHBRIDGE COUNTY COURT   2008   No ....

BETWEEN   MICHELLE ANN LEVY   Wife Applicant

AND

MICHAEL JAMES LEVY   Husband Respondent

ORDER

UPON the Husband and Wife agreeing that the terms of this order are accepted in full and final satisfaction of all claims for income, capital and pension sharing orders which either may be entitled to bring against the other in relation to the marriage.

AND UPON the Husband and the Wife agreeing that the contents of the Property (described below) and their personal belongings are to be divided in accordance with the schedules attached to this order

This order is on the basis that:

(a)   a Child Support Act calculation has been made in relation to Robert Levy and Peter Levy in the sum of £   to be paid each month from the 1st April 2008 and that it will continue at approximately this level for the foreseeable future AND

(b)   the wife will use the periodical payments made to her by clause 4 of this order to discharge the mortgage with Barcloyds Bank on the Property (described below)

BY CONSENT IT IS ORDERED:

1.   With effect from the making of this order the property known as Twintrees, Hill Road, Highbridge ('the Property') shall be held by the Wife and Husband upon a trust of land for themselves as beneficial tenants in common.

2.   That the trust be subject to the following terms and conditions:

2.1   The Wife shall be entitled to occupy the Property to the exclusion of the Husband until sale

2.2   The Property shall not be sold without the prior written consent of both parties or further order until the first to happen of the following events ('the Determining Events'), namely:

2.2.1   the Wife remarries; or

2.2.2   the Wife dies or (subject to clause 2.6) voluntarily leaves the Property; or

2.2.3   all the children of the family reach the age of 18 or finish full-time undergraduate education if later.

2.3   The Wife shall with effect from the date of this order be solely responsible for all payments of capital and interest on the mortgage in favour of Barcloyds Bank

2.4   The Wife shall be responsible for all routine maintenance and decorative repairs to the Property

2.5   The cost of insuring the Property and of any structural repairs shall be shared equally between the Wife and the Husband provided that no works of structural repair shall be carried out to the Property save by agreement between the parties or by further order of the court

2.6   In the event of the Wife wishing to move to another house with the agreement of the Husband (such agreement not to be unreasonably withheld) during the subsistence of this trust:

(i)   the trustees shall, if requested by the Wife, sell the Property and re-invest the proceeds in the purchase of such other dwelling ('the Substitute Property') as she shall direct for her occupation

(ii)   the Wife shall pay the costs of and incidental to such sale and purchase

(iii)   the Substitute Property shall be held on the same trusts terms and conditions as the Property and the trustees shall have full power as if they were beneficial owners to execute such mortgage deed as may be necessary to enable the purchase to be completed

(iv)   if the purchase price excluding stamp duty land tax, Land Registry fees and conveyancing costs of the Substitute Property shall be less than the net proceeds of the Property the difference shall be divided as to 75% to the Wife and 25% to the Husband

2.7   On or before the Determining Event the Wife shall have the right to purchase the Husband's interest in the Property at an open market valuation to be agreed, or in default of agreement, to be determined by a valuer nominated by the court

2.8   If either the Husband or the Wife shall die during the currency of the trust, the power of appointing a substitute trustee shall be exercised by his or her personal representatives.

3.   That upon sale (except in accordance with clause 2.6), the proceeds shall be applied in redeeming the mortgage, and paying the costs of the sale. The balance remaining shall be divided in the proportion of 75% to the Wife and 25% to the Husband.

4.   The Husband shall pay periodical payments to the Wife.

Payments shall be at the rate of £X per annum payable monthly in advance.

Payments shall commence on   .

They will end on the first to occur of:

(a)   the death of either the Husband or the Wife; or

(b)   the Wife's remarriage; or

(c)   (subject to clause 2.6) the Wife voluntarily vacating the Property for a period in excess of 3 months in any 12 month period; or

(d)   all the children of the family reaching the age of 18 or finishing full-time undergraduate education if later; or

(e)   further order of the court

after which the Wife will not be entitled to make any further application in relation to the marriage for an order under the Matrimonial Causes Act 1973, s 23(1)(a) or (b) for periodical payments or secured periodical payments. Furthermore, pursuant to the Matrimonial Causes Act 1973, s 28(1A), the Wife may not apply for an order to extend this deadline.

5.   The Husband shall make periodical payments to the Wife for the benefit of Anthony Levy at the rate of £X per month.

(a)   Payments shall be made monthly in advance on the 1st of each month

(b)   They shall commence on 1st April 2008

(c)   They shall end on the later of the child

(i)   reaching the age of 18; or

(ii)   ceasing full-time secondary education unless the court makes an order for the payments to continue to a later date.

6.   From the date when the Child Support Agency ceases to have jurisdiction for Robert Levy and Peter Levy because they are no longer in full-time, non-advanced education as set out in the Child Support Act 1991, s 55, the Husband shall pay periodical payments to the Wife for the benefit of Robert Levy at the rate of £X per month and for the benefit of Peter Levy at the rate of £X per month.

Payments shall be made monthly in advance on the 1st day of each month.

They shall commence on the date on which the Child Support Agency ceases to have jurisdiction for the child.

They shall end on the later of the children respectively:

(a)   reaching the age of 18; or

(b)   (if later) ceasing full-time secondary education unless the court makes an order for the payments to continue to a later date.

7.   Save as aforesaid, the applications by the Wife and the Husband for financial provision, property adjustment and pension sharing orders do stand dismissed and the Husband shall not be entitled to make any further application in relation to their marriage under the Matrimonial Causes Act 1973, s 23(1)(a) or (b).

8.   Liberty to each party to apply as to the implementation and timing of the terms of the order.

9.   That the Husband shall pay the Wife's costs of this application in the sum of £   .

Dated the   day of   2008.

Signed ....   Signed ....
Wife   Husband

We request that the court make an order as set out above to which our clients respectively consent.

Signed ....   Signed ....
Solicitors for the Wife   Solicitors for the Husband

BROWN v BROWN

[Deferred charge on *Martin* contingencies; order for nominal maintenance.]

Background information (note that this is *not* part of the order): Eileen and Arthur Brown are in their fifties, and were married for 35 years. Mr Brown is an office manager and Mrs Brown is a typist. The children of the family are married and self-supporting. Mrs Brown has obtained a decree absolute based on Mr Brown's adultery with a woman with whom he now lives permanently. Mrs Brown continues to live at the former matrimonial home, a small three bedroomed terraced house which is in Mr Brown's sole name. The mortgage was paid off two years ago, and Mrs Brown can afford to pay the outgoings from her earnings. Mrs Brown has arthritis and has been advised that she will probably have to stop work in about three years' time. Mr Brown wants the house sold, and has offered Mrs Brown one-third of the net proceeds. Mrs Brown, who has registered an agreed notice under the Family Law Act 1996, has rejected the offer, saying this will be insufficient to rehouse her. She wishes to remain in the house. Mrs Brown obtains public funding and applies to the court. The district judge makes the following order.

IN THE LOKE COUNTY COURT   2008   No ....

BETWEEN   EILEEN AUDREY BROWN   Wife Applicant

AND

ARTHUR GEORGE BROWN   Husband Respondent

ORDER

UPON the basis that the Property (described below) be used as a home for the Wife AND UPON the Wife UNDERTAKING to the court to discharge all outgoings and expenses on the Property

AND UPON the Husband UNDERTAKING not to change employment and not to retire until the pension sharing provision in clause 6 of this order is implemented

IT IS ORDERED:

1.   That the Husband shall on or before the   day of   transfer all his legal and beneficial interest in the property at 34, Lower Lane, Loke ('the Property') into the name of the Wife AND it is hereby certified for the purpose of the Community Legal Service (Financial) Regulations 2000 that the Property has been preserved for the Wife for use as a home for herself.

2.   The Wife shall within one month of the transfer of the Property execute a legal charge ('the Charge') to secure the payment to the Husband of a sum equivalent to one half of the Net Value of the Property as defined in clause 3 below.

3.   The Net Value of the Property shall mean the open market value of the property with vacant possession between willing seller and purchaser at the date of redemption of the legal charge or, if the property is to be sold, on completion of the sale of the property the gross sale price including any consideration paid for fixtures and fittings. The open market value of the property as between willing seller and purchaser as at the date of redemption of the legal charge shall in default of agreement between the Wife and the Husband be determined by a chartered surveyor appointed on the application of either party by the President for the time being of the Royal

Institution of Chartered Surveyors who shall act as an expert and not as an arbitrator and whose costs shall be borne equally by the Wife and the Husband.

4.   The Charge shall not become exercisable until:-

(a)   the death or remarriage of the Wife; or

(b)   voluntary vacation of the Property by the Wife for a period in excess of 4 months in any 12 month period; or

(c)   sale of the Property by the Wife; or

(d)   upon such earlier date as a further order of the court may provide

whichever occurs first.

5.   The Husband shall pay periodical payments to the Wife.

Payments shall be at the rate of 5 pence per annum payable in advance.

Payments shall commence on the   day of   2008.

They will end on the first to occur of:

(a)   the death of either the Husband or the Wife; or

(b)   the Wife's remarriage; or

(c)   further order of the court.

6.   There is to be provision by way of pension sharing in favour of the Wife in respect of the Husband's rights under his pension arrangement with [   ] in accordance with the annex to this order.

7.   Save as aforesaid, the applications by the Wife and the Husband for financial provision, pension sharing and property adjustment orders do stand dismissed and the Husband shall not be entitled to make any further application in relation to their marriage under the Matrimonial Causes Act 1973, s 23(1)(a) or (b).

8.   That there be liberty to both parties to apply as to the implementation and timing of the terms of the order.

9.   The Husband shall pay the costs of implementation of this order. Detailed assessment of the Wife's costs.

Dated the   day of   2008.

Signed:

District Judge

10.14 Summary of court procedure

Ancillary finance procedure can effectively be illustrated by way of checklists. Two such checklists follow. One shows the contested procedure and the other the procedure to be followed where the parties have reached agreement.

10.14.1 Application to the court for financial relief

	Applicant (A)	*Court*	*Respondent (R)*
(1)	Files at court: — Form A — court fee — public funding certificate (where appropriate) — notice of issue of public funding (where appropriate) — notice of acting (Legal Help divorce cases only)		
		(2) Fixes First Appointment (FA) 12–16 weeks ahead (Form C)	
		(3) Serves on Respondent within 4 days: — Copy Forms A and C	
(4)	Serves on Respondent — notice of public funding, (where appropriate) — copy notice of acting (Legal Help divorce cases only) Serves on lender and person responsible for any pension arrangement copy Form A		(4) Requests information from pension arrangement. Serves information on Applicant within 7 days of receipt.

Applicant (A)		Court	Respondent (R)	
(5)	Completes, files and exchanges Form E at least 35 days before FA		(5)	Completes, files and exchanges Form E at least 35 days before FA
(6)	Drafts, files and serves:		(6)	Drafts, files and serves:
	(a) statement of issues;			(a) statement of issues;
	(b) chronology;			(b) chronology;
	(c) questionnaire and documents requested;			(c) questionnaire and documents requested;
	(d) notice in Form G			(d) notice in Form G
	at least 14 days before FA			at least 14 days before FA
(7)	Produces costs estimate immediately before FA in Form H		(7)	Produces costs estimate immediately before FA in Form H
(8)	Attends FA with client		(8)	Attends FA with client
		(9) Makes directions; usually fixes FDR		
(10)	Complies with directions		(10)	Complies with directions
(11)	Gives notice to court of all offers and responses 7 days before FDR			
(12)	Produces costs estimate immediately before FDR		(12)	Produces costs estimate immediately before FDR
(13)	Attends FDR with client		(13)	Attends FDR with client
		(14) May:		
		(a) make consent order;		
		(b) give directions;		
		(c) fix final hearing;		
		(d) adjourn		

	Applicant (A)	Court	Respondent (R)
(15)	Drafts, files and serves on R statements of open proposals 14 days before hearing		
			(16) Drafts, files and serves on A statement of open proposals 7 days after receipt of A's proposals
(17)	Produces costs statement (H1) immediately before hearing		(17) Produces costs statement (H1) immediately before hearing
(18)	Attends hearing with client		(18) Attends hearing with client
		(19) Makes order	

10.14.2 Consent orders

There are two possible procedures. Which is appropriate depends on how far (if at all) the application has progressed on a contested basis when the parties reach agreement. Whichever is used, Form A must be filed before an order can be made. This will either have taken place before the steps described below, or (if not) can be incorporated into para 3 (see note (ii) below).

10.14.2.1 Normal consent procedure (no court attendance)

	Applicant (A)	Court	Respondent (R)
(1)	Completes Statement of Information Prepares draft order and submits it to R for approval/ amendment		
			(2) Completes Statement of Information. Endorses consent on draft order. Returns both documents to A

Applicant (A)	*Court*	*Respondent (R)*
(3) Files at court:		
(a) Draft order, endorsed with R's (and A's) consent, plus		
(b) 2 copies;		
(c) Statement of Information		
	(4) If satisfied, makes order.	
	Sends copy to A and R.	
	If not satisfied, may require parties to attend	

Notes

(i) Where appropriate, public funding certificate, notice of issue of certificate and notice of acting should be filed and/or served.

(ii) If A has not yet filed Form A, the draft order can conveniently be incorporated into that application which will be endorsed with R's consent.

10.14.2.2 Where attendance at court

The normal contested procedure will be followed up to the date of the hearing.

Once agreement has been reached, provided the district judge has the prescribed information as to parties' resources etc, an order may be made despite the lack of a draft order and written statement of information.

10.15 Maintenance calculations

The parent with care applies for a maintenance calculation using a standard form available from the Child Support Agency. Alternatively, the form can be completed on-line at the Child Support Agency website (www.csa.gov.uk).

The Child Support Agency must then notify the non-resident parent as soon as reasonably practicable, requesting such information as it may require to make the maintenance calculation (Child Support (Maintenance Calculation Procedure) Regulations 2000 (SI 2001/157), reg 5). This is usually done by telephone, with the Child Support Agency filling in the information on a Maintenance Enquiry Form. This form is then sent to the non-resident parent for his signature. At this time, the Child Support Agency will also inform the non-resident parent of the effective date of the maintenance calculation. Provided that the non-resident parent returns the form within 28 days, this will be eight weeks after the Maintenance Enquiry Form was sent. If he does not do so, the effective date will be the date that the form was sent out.

If the non-resident parent does not respond, or responds without having given all the information required, the Agency has a number of powers under the Act to enable it to obtain the information. For example, the Child Support Agency may approach other bodies, such as the local authority or HM Revenue & Customs, for information. In addition, the Secretary of State may appoint inspectors with power to enter premises where the non-resident parent is or has been employed, or where he carries out his trade, profession, vocation or business, to acquire information (CSA 1991, s 15). Lastly, s 14A of the CSA 1991 makes it a criminal offence for the non-resident parent to fail to supply information, or to supply false information. If after using these powers the Agency still does not have the information, it has the power to make a default maintenance decision (see **7.6.5**).

Chapter 11
Enforcement, Appeals, Setting Aside and Variation

11.1 Introduction

Frequently, the respondent to an order for financial relief will fail to comply with some, or all, of the provisions of that order. It is essential, therefore, that the solicitor should be aware not only of the methods of enforcement which are available, but also which of those methods is most appropriate in the circumstances.

A client may wish to appeal against an order which he thinks is unfair. In certain situations an order may even be set aside. If the circumstances have changed since the order was made, the client may wish to have that order varied. This chapter deals with what action the solicitor can take on these occasions.

11.2 Financial orders in the county court

Financial orders in the county court comprise all orders apart from property adjustment orders (which are considered at **11.5**), but most commonly will be spouse periodical payments orders or lump sum orders. Enforcement of child maintenance calculations will be effected by the Child Support Agency (see **11.4**), but where a child maintenance order has been made by the court, enforcement will generally be through the court in the usual way. However, the Child Support Agency can collect and enforce 'top-up' child maintenance orders made by the court under s 8 of the CSA 1991.

Payments of money orders made by the county court are made direct between the parties. This can sometimes lead to problems since not only may the parties have to remain in direct contact (which could result in continued acrimony), but, as there is no independent record of payments, proof of payment (or non-payment) may be difficult. These problems can be mitigated by use of the Maintenance Enforcement Act 1991. This Act provides that, when granting or varying a periodical payments order, the High Court or county court can order:

(a) payment by standing order;

(b) the payer to open a bank account;

(c) attachment of the payer's earnings (see **11.2.2**).

11.2.1 Preliminary steps

When the order is first obtained the solicitor should tell his client to contact him immediately if the respondent defaults. This is particularly important in the case of periodical payments, because leave will be required to enforce arrears that are more than 12 months old. The court may refuse leave, remit the arrears and give the respondent a fresh start.

If the client was in receipt of public funding for the ancillary proceedings and the certificate has not been discharged, the solicitor will need to extend the certificate to cover enforcement proceedings. If the certificate has been discharged then the solicitor must apply for a new certificate.

The method of enforcement used will depend upon the decision as to which method would be most effective. This in turn will usually depend upon the assets the respondent owns. The applicant will already have this information where the respondent has defaulted shortly after the order was made. However, in other cases, the applicant can apply to the district judge for an order to have the respondent attend court for questioning. If the district judge agrees to the application, the respondent will be ordered to attend court and asked to bring relevant documents with him. He will then be thoroughly examined by a court officer (or exceptionally by a judge) as to his means.

11.2.2 Methods of enforcement

11.2.2.1 Attachment of earnings

Under an attachment of earnings order (made under the Attachment of Earnings Act 1971) the respondent's employer will deduct a specified sum from his earnings. This sum will represent the amount of the maintenance order plus, possibly, a proportion of the arrears. The order must also specify a minimum amount, known as the 'protected earnings rate', below which the respondent's wages cannot fall. This rate is generally the amount that the respondent would be entitled to if he was reliant on welfare benefits. The employer will forward the money deducted from the respondent's wages to the court.

An attachment of earnings order is probably the best method of enforcement for a periodical payments order. It can be applied for either when the order is first made, or later when the respondent defaults. However, the drawback of this method of enforcement is that the respondent must be in employment. It cannot be used if the respondent is self-employed or unemployed, and can be administratively difficult if the respondent frequently changes jobs.

11.2.2.2 Warrant of execution

A warrant of execution enables the county court bailiff to seize and sell assets belonging to the respondent sufficient to meet the outstanding amount. The solicitor applies to the court for a warrant, no hearing is needed. This method is most useful for unpaid lump sums, but could also be used for substantial arrears of maintenance.

11.2.2.3 Third party debt order

A third party debt order enables the applicant to receive payment direct from a third party who owes the respondent money, for example, a bank or building society. Third party debt order proceedings involve two stages. At first, an interim third party debt order (obtained without notice) will freeze the account. At the subsequent 'on notice' hearing the district judge can make a final third party debt order, which will require the bank or building society to pay the applicant the amount outstanding. This method is most useful for unpaid lump sums.

11.2.2.4 MCA 1973, s 24A

Under s 24A of the MCA 1973, the court can make an order for sale to enforce, for example, a lump sum or secured periodical payments order (see **4.4.3**). The s 24A order for sale can be made at the same time as the original order as a type of precaution. Thus, for example, an order could provide that the respondent is to pay the applicant a lump sum of £30,000 (representing her share in the home) and that, if that sum is not paid within three months of decree absolute, the home is to be sold and the £30,000 paid to the applicant out of the proceeds of sale. Alternatively, the order for sale can be made later, if the respondent defaults.

11.2.2.5 Charging order

The applicant can apply to charge land (and/or certain securities) which the respondent owns, or in which he has an interest, with the amount outstanding. However, the procedure involved is protracted. The applicant needs to apply for an interim charging order which can be made final at the subsequent hearing. This will give the applicant security for the debt, but a further hearing is needed to obtain an order for sale. At that further hearing, the court will have total discretion as to whether to order sale and it may decide not to, for example, if the charging order is over the respondent's home and the amount owed is relatively small. It is usually far better to use s 24A (see **11.2.2.4**).

11.2.2.6 Judgment summons

Under the Debtors Act 1869, the court has power to commit to prison a respondent who has not paid a periodical payments order or a lump sum order. This can be done provided:

(a)   the respondent has defaulted; and

(b)   the respondent has the means to pay but is neglecting or refusing to do so.

Until recently, the judgment summons procedure provided that the respondent must attend before the judge and be examined as to his means. However, in *Mubarak v Mubarak* [2001] 1 FLR 698 the Court of Appeal held that this procedure was in breach of the European Convention on Human Rights, Article 6 in particular, since it breached the respondent's right not to incriminate himself. As a result of *Mubarak,* it is now necessary for the applicant to produce evidence to show beyond reasonable doubt that the respondent has the means to pay. This may be very difficult for the applicant to do. The Family Proceedings (Amendment) Rules 2003 (SI 2003/184), have subsequently amended the relevant procedure (under FPR 1991, rr 7.4–7.6) to make it compliant with the HRA 1998. The judgment summons procedure was already rarely used, partly because public funding is not available in the county court. A consequence of *Mubarak v Mubarak* and the amendments to the procedure mean that it is likely to be used even more rarely in the future and only as a last resort.

11.3 Enforcement in the family proceedings court

Where orders for maintenance have been made in the family proceedings court, the respondent must usually make payments to the clerk to the justices (although under the Maintenance Enforcement Act 1991 the family proceedings court can direct payments to be made in other ways, for example, by standing order between the parties). The court clerk will then forward the payments to the applicant.

Thus, the court will have a complete record of all payments made and the parties need not be in contact with each other.

Before enforcement proceedings are commenced, and if the client is eligible, the solicitor should apply for public funding.

11.3.1   Methods of enforcement

If it becomes necessary to enforce the order, four methods are available:

(a)   An attachment of earnings order. This has already been considered (see **11.2.2.1**).

(b)   Committal to prison. This is very much a last resort. Three conditions must be fulfilled (Magistrates' Courts Act 1980, s 93(6)). These are:

  (i)   the court must inquire, in the respondent's presence, whether the default was due to his wilful refusal or culpable neglect, and impose imprisonment only if satisfied that either was the case; and

  (ii)   the court must be satisfied that an attachment of earnings order is either not possible or not appropriate; and

  (iii) the respondent must be present when committal is ordered.

  The arrears will not continue to accrue while the respondent is in prison (unless the court directs that they should), although imprisonment does not discharge the arrears. The respondent can obtain his release if he pays the whole amount due, or reduce the length of detention if he makes part-payment. Imprisonment lasts for a maximum of six weeks. The committal can be suspended on condition that the respondent pays the order in future together with gradual repayment of the arrears.

(c)   A warrant of distress. This is similar to a warrant of execution (see **11.2.2.2**). It is an order to the police to seize and sell goods belonging to the respondent, using the proceeds of sale to repay the arrears. It is not an appropriate method for enforcing maintenance and is rarely used.

(d)   The order can be registered in the High Court or county court so that the methods of enforcement available in that court can be used. However, the arrears will rarely be substantial enough to make this course of action appropriate.

As in the county court, the family proceedings court has power to remit all or part of the arrears and will generally not enforce arrears which are more than 12 months old.

11.3.2   Registration of county court maintenance orders

Once a periodical payments order has been made in the county court, it can be registered in the family proceedings court. To do this, the solicitor lodges a standard form in duplicate plus a copy of the maintenance order at the court which made the order. Some district judges will not agree to the order being registered unless there are arrears of maintenance.

Once the order has been registered, payments under the order will be made to the clerk to the justices, so there will be a full record of all payments. Another consequence of registration is that if the applicant is on welfare benefits and the respondent is a persistently poor payer, the applicant may be able to take advantage of the diversion procedure (see **6.10.1**).

Lastly, once the order has been registered, the family proceedings court has power to vary the order, thus possibly making subsequent variation quicker and cheaper than in the county court.

11.4 Collection and enforcement by the Child Support Agency

The Child Support Agency will collect maintenance calculations for applicants. Applicants who are not on benefit can request this service. For those on benefit it will be provided automatically.

In cases where the Agency collects payments, it will consult both parents to decide which method of payment should be used. The most common method is likely to be by standing order. The Agency has power to compel the absent parent to open a bank account for this purpose (CSA 1991, s 29(3)).

The Agency may instead serve a deduction from earnings order on the absent parent's employer (CSA 1991, s 30(2)) and can use this as a method of enforcement. This will work in the same way as an attachment of earnings order but there is no court involvement (see **11.2.2.1**).

Where one or more payments remain unpaid and a deduction from earnings order is inappropriate or has proved ineffective, the Agency can apply to the family proceedings court for a liability order (CSA 1991, s 33). Once a liability order has been obtained, the debt can be recovered by distress. If this proves ineffective, the Agency can apply to the county court for a third party debt order or charging order. In the last resort, the Agency can apply to the family proceedings court to have the absent parent committed for up to six weeks or disqualified from driving for up to two years (CSA 1991, ss 39, 39A and 40).

Where the non-resident parent is in arrears with payments of child support maintenance, the Secretary of State may charge a penalty of up to 25% of the unpaid maintenance (CSA 1991, s 41A). This penalty is payable in addition to the arrears, and will be paid into central funds rather than going to the parent with care.

In *R (on the application of Kehoe) v Secretary of State for Work and Pensions* [2005] UKHL 48, Mrs Kehoe sought a declaration that her inability personally to enforce arrears of child maintenance under a maintenance calculation by the Agency breached her rights of access to the court under Article 6 of the European Convention on Human Rights. The House of Lords held that Mrs Kehoe had no right under the CSA 1991 which she could exercise against Mr Kehoe entitling her to play any part in the assessment or enforcement process. Thus her 'civil rights' had not been engaged for the purposes of Article 6 and her claim failed.

One of the major criticisms of the Agency has been its failure to enforce payments rigorously (with the consequence that by July 2006 there was £3 billion of debt outstanding). In order to mitigate this the Government has decided to contract out debt recovery work (the Contracting Out (Functions Relating to Child Support) Order 2006 (SI 2006/1692)). Despite this, the debt owed continues to rise (to £3.5 billion in July 2007). In *Rowley v Secretary of State for Work and Pensions* [2007] EWCA Civ 598, Mrs Rowley and her three children brought proceedings against the Secretary of State on the basis that he was negligent in carrying out his functions under the Child Support Act 1991, with the consequence that maintenance totalling £53,000 due to them remained unpaid. The Court of Appeal held that it was not just to impose a common law duty of care on the Secretary of State as such a duty would be inconsistent with the statutory scheme.

The Government is continuing to try novel ways of getting non-resident parents to pay. In June 2007 the Child Support Agency published on its website the names of 40 fathers who were failing to support their children in an attempt to 'name and shame'. The Child Maintenance Bill proposes to give C-MEC power to take money directly from non-payers' bank accounts; to confiscate their passports; or to impose a curfew on them.

11.5 Property adjustment orders

If the respondent fails to execute the documents required to effect a property adjustment order, then the court has power to order the document to be executed by another person, usually the district judge, on his behalf (County Courts Act 1984, s 38). Should there be a problem with drafting the documents, the court can refer the matter to conveyancing counsel. In such a case, the court can direct that the granting of any decree be deferred until the documents have been executed.

11.6 Appeals

11.6.1 County court orders

If either party is dissatisfied with an order made by the district judge after a contested hearing, he or she can appeal against that order to a judge in chambers within 14 days of the district judge's order. On appeal, it seems that the judge can rehear the case only if inadequate findings of fact had been made by the district judge, or there had been a procedural irregularity. New evidence may be admitted only if it is in the interests of justice to do so, for example, where the evidence was not available at the original trial to the party seeking to use it and it would have formed an important factor in the result (Family Proceedings (Amendment) Rules 2003 (SI 2003/184), r 14, amending FPR 1991, r 8.1).

11.6.2 Orders in the family proceedings court

A right of appeal lies from the magistrates making the order to the High Court (DPMCA 1978, s 29). The appeal should usually be made within 14 days of the order.

11.6.3 Maintenance assessments

Either the non-resident parent or the person with care can ask for a review of the maintenance calculation within one month of the date of the decision. If still dissatisfied, he can usually appeal to the Social Security and Child Support Appeals Tribunal (SSCSAT) again within one month of the decision. A decision of that tribunal can be appealed on a point of law to a Child Support Commissioner. There is a further right of appeal on a point of law to the Court of Appeal.

11.6.4 Welfare benefits

Generally, most decisions relating to welfare benefits will be reviewed internally on request. An appeal on fact or law can then be made to the SSCSAT, provided that the appeal is lodged within one month from the decision. Further appeal on a point of law then lies, with leave of the tribunal chairperson, to a Social Security Commissioner.

11.7 Setting aside

One of the parties may attempt to have the order set aside. Generally, the court is reluctant to set aside orders for reasons of certainty – divorcing couples should be able to organise their future lives without fear of their divorce settlement being reopened. An application to set aside therefore can be made only on narrow grounds, the scope of which is not totally clear. These grounds include:

(a)   Non-disclosure of material evidence. In the case of *Livesey (formerly Jenkins) v Jenkins* [1985] AC 424 (see **10.7.1**) the House of Lords stated that each party owed to the other a duty of full and frank disclosure. Where this duty is breached the order may be set aside. It must be emphasised, however, that not every non-disclosure will justify setting an order aside. The non-disclosure must have resulted in the court granting an order substantially different from that which it would have granted had the true facts been known or the court will not agree to set the original order aside.

(b)   Fraud. For example, if one party deliberately misrepresents the size of his assets.

(c)   Events occurring after the order is made. The House of Lords in *Barder v Barder* [1988] AC 20 laid down four conditions which must be fulfilled before the order will be set aside:

   (i)   the subsequent events must have invalidated the basis upon which the order was made; and

   (ii)   these events must have occurred within a relatively short time of the original order; and

   (iii)   the application to set aside must be made promptly; and

   (iv)   the granting of the application must not prejudice the rights of a bona fide purchaser for value of any property in question.

   The facts of *Barder v Barder* provide a useful example of the extreme circumstances which are necessary for the court to set aside an order on this ground. As part of a consent order, Mr Barder agreed to transfer the home to his ex-wife within 28 days so that she could live in it with their children. Before he had done so, Mrs Barder killed both children and committed suicide. Under her will, all her property would go to her mother. The House of Lords agreed to set the order aside. In *Williams v Lindley* [2005] EWCA Civ 103, the Court of Appeal set aside a consent order where the wife became engaged to (and subsequently married) a wealthy man within one month of the making of the order. This event invalidated the basis of the original order which had been to provide the wife and children with a home.

   In *Heard v Heard* [1995] 1 FLR 970 the house was valued at £67,000 at the time of the hearing. The wife was awarded £16,000, with the balance of the equity going to the husband. The house was sold some six months later for only £33,000. The Court of Appeal held that the basis of the original order, under which the district judge had intended to allow the husband enough money to rehouse himself, had been invalidated. However, in other cases, a fall in value of the home was found insufficient to set aside an order (see, eg, *B v B (Financial Provision: Leave to Appeal)* [1994] 1 FLR 219).

A subsequent maintenance calculation by the Child Support Agency will not be sufficient grounds for setting aside a clean break order (see *Crozier v Crozier* [1994] 1 FLR 126).

There are two routes by which an order may be set aside:

(a)   an application for permission to appeal out of time made to the relevant appeal court; or

(b)   an application to set aside made to the court which originally made the order.

It is not entirely clear when each route is appropriate and in most cases either procedure may be used. However, it would seem that where the applicant is arguing fraud or non-disclosure, set aside is the appropriate method; and where supervening events are argued, leave to appeal out of time is to be preferred. In either case it is essential that the application is made promptly (see, eg, *Burns v Burns* [2004] EWCA Civ 1258, where Mrs Burns's claim failed due to undue delay).

11.8 Variation

11.8.1 Types of county court order which can be varied

It is possible to apply to the court to vary an order not only where that order was made after a contested hearing, but also where the order was made by consent. However, it will not be possible to vary an order which effected a clean break.

Orders which can be varied are set out in s 31(2) of the MCA 1973 (see **Appendix 1(A)**), and include orders for:

(a)   maintenance pending suit and interim maintenance;

(b)   periodical payments and secured periodical payments. Periodical payments orders are the type of order most commonly varied. Applications are made either by the recipient to increase the amount being paid, or by the payer to reduce or extinguish the payments. Several points should be noted:

(i)   Where the court makes an order for fixed-term maintenance, the term can usually be extended, provided that the application for an extension is made before the original order has expired (although the actual hearing may take place after expiry). However, this can be prevented by the court including a direction in the original order that no application for an extension may be made (see MCA 1973, s 28(1A) and **4.6**).

(ii)   The court may impose a 'deferred clean break'. To achieve this, the court has power when discharging a periodical payments order or varying it to last for a further limited time only, also to make a lump sum order, or one or more property adjustment orders or one or more pension sharing orders. It may also include a direction that no application for an extension of a limited-term periodical payments order can be made. Whether a deferred clean break is appropriate will depend on much the same factors as those taken into account when deciding whether a clean break is appropriate (see **4.6**). In particular, the payer should consider whether the recipient is likely to remarry in the near future. If publicly funded, the recipient should be reminded that a lump sum payment will attract immediate enforcement of the statutory charge, unless the money is to be used to purchase a home and the order includes the necessary clause to enable the Legal Services Commission to postpone the charge (see **2.9**). In *Pearce v Pearce* [2003] 2 FLR 1144, the Court of Appeal made it clear that when making such a deferred clean break the court was only entitled to capitalise the remaining periodical payments and could not reopen capital claims and further redistribute the capital assets. The court also stated that, in deciding what substitute order to make, a pension sharing order should be the first choice if it were available. This is because no capital would have to be raised or paid by the payer, and the recipient would continue to get regular income.

(iii) When varying a periodical payments order the court has power to remit any arrears due under the order (MCA 1973, s 31(2A)). This power could be used, for example, where the payer had become unemployed and arrears had built up before he had a chance to apply for a downward variation;

(c) payment of a lump sum by instalments. Generally, this power will only enable the court to vary the number and amount of the instalments so that the amount payable overall will remain the same. However, the Court of Appeal stated in *Westbury v Sampson* [2001] EWCA Civ 407, [2002] 1 FLR 166 that the power to vary included varying the overall sum. Nevertheless, the court made clear that, in order to achieve finality, this would be done only in exceptional cases where the anticipated circumstances had changed significantly, making it unjust to hold the payer to the original quantum agreed;

(d) payment of a lump sum ordered in relation to pensions under s 25B(4) or s 25C of the MCA 1973;

(e) the sale of property under s 24A of the MCA 1973. This could be used, for example, where the order for sale was made as a way of enforcing a lump sum order. If the payer could find some other means to pay, he could then apply to have the order for sale discharged.

11.8.2 Types of county court order which cannot be varied

Orders for capital provision usually cannot be varied. This is to avoid uncertainty and so that the parties can make plans for the future on the basis that the distribution of capital is permanent.

(a) Lump sum orders cannot be varied unless they are payable by instalments, or ordered in relation to a pension (see **11.8.1**).

(b) Transfer of property and settlement of property orders cannot be varied. So, for example, if the court orders a deferred trust of land on *Mesher* contingencies, the occupier will not be able successfully to apply to court at a later date to have the sale further postponed. However, it may sometimes be possible to obtain a sale at a date earlier than that set out in the original order by applying for an order for sale under s 24A of the MCA 1973. The court can make an order for sale either at the same time as making the original order, or at a later date (see **4.4.3**). It is totally in the court's discretion whether to make such an order, but it may do so if, for example, it is the spouse in occupation who is seeking the sale against the wishes of the non-occupying spouse. On the other hand, an application by the non-occupying spouse is likely to be rejected if the home is still needed for the children (see, eg, *Thompson v Thompson* [1986] Fam 38).

(c) Pension sharing orders cannot generally be varied. The only exception to this is when the variation takes place before the order comes into effect and before the decree absolute. Once the decree has been made absolute, or if the order is in effect, it cannot be varied.

Many orders contain a clause which gives the parties 'liberty to apply'. This does not allow the parties to return to court to vary the order. Instead, it gives the parties the opportunity to return to court if they experience trouble implementing the order, for example, due to conveyancing difficulties or misunderstanding of minor terms where property is settled (see *Practice Direction (Applications: Liberty to Apply)* [1980] 1 All ER 1008).

11.8.3 Factors to be considered on a variation

The factors to be considered on a variation are set out in s 31(7) of the MCA 1973 (see **Appendix 1(A)**), which requires the court to have regard to all circumstances of the case, giving first consideration to the welfare of any child of the family who is not yet 18. This subsection also states that 'all the circumstances of the case' includes any change in the matters which the court was required to consider when making the original order, ie any change in the s 25 factors. Where the party against whom the order was made has died, 'all the circumstances of the case' include the change in circumstances as a result of his death. This will generally be relevant only in the case of secured periodical payments orders. However, case law makes clear (see, eg, *Flavell v Flavell* [1997] Fam Law 237) that the court is not restricted to considering changes in the matters which were taken into account when making the original order, but can consider the case afresh. In *K v K (Periodical Payment: Cohabitation)* [2005] EWHC 2886 (Fam), the court held that one of the 'circumstances of the case' was the wife's cohabitation with another man. It was clear that the wife and her partner were likely to stay together and that they should strive towards financial independence from the husband. Thus the husband should be expected to support the wife for a shorter period than that agreed in the original consent order. In such a situation, however, the court is likely to order a tapering off of periodical payments to allow the recipient to adjust without undue hardship, rather than an immediate cessation of all payments.

The court must also consider on a variation application (even if it decides not to vary the amount of the order) whether the term of any payments ordered could be limited without causing undue hardship to the payee. In *Fleming v Fleming* [2004] 1 FLR 667, the Court of Appeal stated that there was an enhanced obligation on the court to do this when the order which was under consideration was for a limited term. In this situation the intention of both the parties and the court was that the payer's obligations would terminate on a specific date. In such circumstances the exercise of the court's power to extend the term would require some exceptional justification.

The court will need to take into account the 'package' made by the original order for financial relief. For example, perhaps the wife received less maintenance than she otherwise would have done in return for a greater share in the home. This must be taken into consideration on the variation application in order to maintain the balance achieved by the original order.

Lastly, remember that it is possible to record in a side-letter the reasons why a particular order has been made (see **10.13.12**). Any side-letter should be drawn to the court's attention on a later variation application and, although it will not bind the court, it is likely that the court will uphold its terms (see *N v N (Consent Order: Variation)* [1993] 2 FLR 868).

11.8.4 Procedure

The procedure to be followed is very similar to that used for the original order (see **Chapter 10**). Where appropriate, an application for public funding should be made. If both parties agree to the variation sought, then the normal consent procedure must be followed (see **10.12**).

11.8.5 Variation in the family proceedings court

Either party can apply to vary or revoke a periodical payments order made in a family proceedings court. Either party can also apply for a lump sum order, or further lump sum order. In deciding whether or not to grant the application, the court will have regard to any change in the circumstances since the original order was made (DPMCA 1978, s 20).

11.9 Chapter summary

(1) Financial orders can be enforced by the county court, or the family proceedings court.

(2) The order will usually be enforced in the court that made it; however, sometimes it can be advantageous to register an order obtained in the county court with the family proceedings court and then enforce it in the family proceedings court.

(3) The following methods of enforcement are available in the county court:

(a) attachment of earnings;

(b) warrant of execution;

(c) third party debt order proceedings;

(d) s 24A of the MCA 1973;

(e) charging order;

(f) judgment summons.

(4) The following methods of enforcement are available in the family proceedings court:

(a) attachment of earnings;

(b) committal to prison;

(c) warrant of distress.

(5) The Child Support Agency will enforce payments of child maintenance where a maintenance assessment has been made.

(6) The county court can execute documents to transfer property where the respondent fails to do so.

(7) It may be possible to appeal an order for ancillary relief, but this must be done without delay.

(8) In exceptional circumstances the court may set aside an order. This may happen if, for example, the respondent did not disclose the existence of certain of his assets and this led to a substantially different order being made.

(9) Orders for maintenance can be varied, as can instalments of a lump sum and lump sum orders made in relation to a pension.

(10) Other lump sum orders, pension sharing orders and property adjustment orders cannot be varied.

Chapter 12

Pre-marital Agreements and Separation Agreements

12.1 Introduction

This chapter looks at the ways in which married couples can achieve a binding agreement to cover maintenance and other matters without starting court proceedings. It looks at the validity of agreements entered into before marriage. It then examines how a spouse can enter into a maintenance or separation agreement as an alternative to starting divorce proceedings or obtaining an order under the DPMCA 1978.

12.2 Pre-marital agreements

12.2.1 General

An increasing number of cohabiting couples are entering into 'cohabitation agreements' governing the ownership of property and chattels (see **Chapter 16**). The general consensus is that, subject to general contractual principles, cohabitation agreements are binding.

What if a couple wish to enter a pre-marital agreement? At present, such agreements are not binding in English law on the basis of public policy (see *N v N (Jurisdiction: Prenuptial Agreement)* [1999] 2 FLR 745). At most, the court may take them into account as 'one of the circumstances of the case', or as 'conduct which it would be inequitable to disregard' under s 25 of the MCA 1973.

Traditionally, the courts have been reluctant to attach much weight to such agreements (*F v F (Ancillary Relief: Substantial Assets)* [1995] 2 FLR 45). However, in certain cases, the courts are beginning to be prepared to consider the terms of a pre-marital agreement as a significant factor (*M v M (Prenuptial Agreement)* [2002] 1 FLR 654). In *K v K (Ancillary Relief: Prenuptial Agreement)* [2003] 1 FLR 120, the court held the parties to the terms as to capital provision as set out in their pre-marital agreement. The judge outlined a series of questions that must be asked in order to decide how much weight to attach to a pre-marital agreement – questions such as, were the parties properly advised as to its terms; was either party under any pressure to sign it; and would an injustice be done by now holding the parties to its terms?

Despite the uncertainty, some couples do choose to use pre-marital agreements and there are precedents available to use (see 'Precedents for Separation Agreements and Pre-marital Agreements' (Resolution, 2005)). Such an agreement would assist in resolving matters if the breakdown was amicable.

A pre-marital agreement will need to comply with general contract principles. There will need to be offer and acceptance, intention to create legal relations, certainty and consideration. Unless the contract is by deed there could be a problem in establishing consideration. The agreement would also be set aside if a party could show that undue influence was exerted over him or her when the agreement was entered into.

The only type of agreement that the law will definitely give weight to is a reconciliation agreement, which can be entered into when spouses have already separated but have decided to cohabit again to give the marriage another chance. In an agreement made at this stage the parties will agree to resume cohabitation, but can also make provision for maintenance and property division should they separate in future.

12.2.2 Law of Property (Miscellaneous Provisions) Act 1989, s 2

Section 2 of the Law of Property (Miscellaneous Provisions) Act 1989 provides that all the terms of any contract for the disposition of any interest in land must be in writing and signed by all the parties. This means that any informal agreement between spouses relating to ownership of the home will not be enforceable unless it is properly recorded.

12.2.3 Reform

The Government announced in May 1998 in its consultation document 'Supporting Families' that it was considering introducing legislation to make pre-marital contracts binding. There are likely to be some significant exceptions to this, for example, where there is a child of the family, or where either or both of the parties failed to receive independent legal advice before entering the contract. In such situations it is likely that the court would retain full discretion over the making of financial orders. To date, however, these limited proposals have not been taken further.

In November 2004 Resolution published its recomendations for reform in this area – *A more certain future – Recognition of Pre-marital Agreements in England and Wales* – which propose amending s 25 so that any pre-marital agreement becomes binding unless to do so would cause significant injustice.

12.3 Separation agreements

12.3.1 General

If spouses separate, they can, as an alternative to divorce or other court proceedings, enter into an agreement which provides for maintenance, care of the children and division of any property (for precedents, see 'Precedents for Separation Agreements and Pre-marital Agreements' (Resolution, 2005)). These agreements are known as either separation agreements or maintenance agreements. The only distinction is that a separation agreement will always include a clause in which the parties agree to an immediate separation. If a married couple have decided to separate but are still living together at the time of the agreement, it is essential to use a separation agreement, as the inclusion of this clause agreeing to separate immediately will ensure that the agreement will not be void on grounds of public policy, as it will establish that the marriage had broken down before the agreement was made. If the parties have already separated, either type of agreement can be entered into depending on whether the parties agree to the separation. If one party has deserted the other, it is important that, if the parties have agreed on financial matters, a maintenance agreement is used. This will ensure that there is no suggestion that the other spouse is agreeing to the separation, which would end the desertion and the possibility of obtaining a divorce using Fact C (see **3.4.4**).

The rest of this chapter uses the term 'separation agreement' to include both types of agreement.

A separation agreement, like any other contract, must be formed in accordance with contract principles. A vital element is an intention to create legal relations. The agreement can be challenged by a party on the grounds of fraud, mistake, duress or undue influence. It is therefore important that both parties have independent legal advice before entering into this type of agreement.

12.3.2 Contents

The matters that typically are covered by a separation agreement are as follows.

12.3.2.1 Agreement to separate

The parties can state that they are going to live apart. Their agreement releases them from the duty married persons have to cohabit and effectively prevents either party being in desertion (but see **12.3.1** above for the use of maintenance agreements). The agreement is also evidence that the parties are treating the marriage as at an end, so that a period of separation can begin to run for the purposes of divorce on the grounds of two or five years' separation (Facts D or E: see **3.4.5** and **3.4.6**).

12.3.2.2 Periodical payments

The agreement can contain provision for the payment of maintenance to the parties and any children. In relation to children, any agreement to pay money will be binding. However, a separation agreement cannot oust the jurisdiction of the Child Support Agency under the CSA 1991, so either party can at any later time apply to the Agency to determine the amount of maintenance payable. Any agreement to pay maintenance to a spouse cannot prevent either party applying to the court for ancillary relief as part of divorce, nullity or judicial separation proceedings. However, were this to happen, the separation agreement would be one of the factors that the court would consider under s 25 of the MCA 1973 in the ancillary relief proceedings. Care must also be taken to draft maintenance provisions for spouse and child clearly, making provision for how long the maintenance is to last and what will happen if the parties resume cohabitation.

12.3.2.3 Property

If appropriate, an agreement about the home can be included. Often, as the parties may have only recently separated and not yet decided whether the separation will be long term, it is too soon to decide matters concerning the home and other property. However, the agreement could cover matters such as payment of the mortgage, outgoings and repairs in the short term.

12.3.2.4 Children

There is no need for any arrangements to be included relating to the children. Both parents still share parental responsibility and can make decisions jointly or alone relating to the children. However, if the parents wish, any agreement about where the children should live and how much contact is to be given to the parent with whom they do not live can be included. This would not prevent either parent from making an application under the CA 1989 at any later date.

12.3.3 Advantages of a separation agreement

The parties' decision to enter into a separation agreement will usually be based largely on a desire to avoid court proceedings, including applying to court for a consent order. They should also take into account the following factors.

12.3.3.1 Speed

A separation agreement can be entered into quickly; a contested court order may not be made for a considerable time. A separation agreement is, therefore, cheaper. It may also assist the parties by avoiding the confrontation and bitterness that is often caused by protracted court proceedings.

12.3.3.2 Flexibility

Anything can be agreed and included in a separation agreement. So, for example, a husband could agree to pay the outgoings and repairs on the home in which the wife and family remained living, or to pay off outstanding hire-purchase debts. Neither of these matters can be ordered by the divorce courts under the MCA 1973, even if the parties apply for a consent order.

12.3.4 Disadvantages of a separation agreement

12.3.4.1 Enforceability

A separation agreement is enforced in the same way as any other contract. The usual remedies for breach of contract must, therefore, be sought, ie damages to cover any loss from arrears of maintenance payments and the equitable remedies of specific performance or an injunction to force the other party to carry it out. This means that in comparison with a court order (see **Chapter 11**), a separation agreement is much more difficult to enforce.

12.3.4.2 Finality

A court order for a 'clean break' can prevent either party from applying to court again and achieves a once and for all settlement. A separation agreement can never be a guaranteed final solution. A party to a separation agreement can always apply at a later date, for example on divorce, for further provision from the court. However, on a later application the separation agreement will be taken into account under s 25 of the MCA 1973, and may be followed. In *Edgar v Edgar* [1980] 3 All ER 887, the court laid down the principle that formal agreements properly and fairly arrived at, with competent advice, should not be displaced unless there are good and substantial grounds for concluding that an injustice will be done by holding the parties to the terms of their agreement. In *G v G (Financial Provision: Separation Agreement)* [2000] 2 FLR 18, the court confirmed that an earlier separation agreement between the parties should be taken into account, either as part of 'all the circumstances of the case' (MCA 1973, s 25(1)) or as 'conduct which it would be inequitable to disregard' (MCA 1973, s 25(2)(g)). Such an agreement may be strongly persuasive in deciding what orders to make, but not conclusive, as all the s 25 factors must be considered. In deciding what weight to attach to an agreement, the court said that the most relevant questions to ask are:

(a)   how did the agreement come to be made?

(b)   did the parties themselves attach importance to it?

(c)   have the parties themselves acted upon it?

In the recent case of *A v B (Ancillary Relief: Property Division)* [2005] EWHC 314 (Fam), the court upheld a separation agreement giving the wife approximately

75% of the assets on the basis that at the time of making the agreement it was not unfair to the husband and at the time of the hearing the husband was able to meet his needs from his own resources, albeit that some adjustments to his living arrangements might be necessary.

12.3.4.3 Variation

A court order for periodical payments can always be varied by the court by an application by either party at a later date. All written separation agreements can also be varied by the court (see **12.3.5**). However, if the agreement is not in writing it can be varied only by agreement between the parties.

12.3.5 MCA 1973, ss 34–36

Despite the fact that separation agreements are made between the parties and do not involve the court, the MCA 1973 does contain provisions giving the court power to vary them.

The court will have jurisdiction if the agreement comes within the wide definition of 'maintenance agreement' under s 34(2) of the MCA 1973. This will include any written agreement containing financial arrangements, or any written agreement to separate which does not contain any financial arrangements (where no other document exists which does contain such arrangements).

12.3.5.1 The court's jurisdiction

Any provision in a maintenance agreement which restricts the right of either party to apply to court for financial provision is void. However, any other provision in the agreement will still be binding.

12.3.5.2 Variation

If the parties can agree a variation, the original separation agreement can be varied by them without application to the court. If they cannot agree, either party can apply to court and the court has jurisdiction to vary or to insert financial arrangements in a written maintenance agreement during the lives of the parties under s 35 of the MCA 1973. It will vary the agreement only if there has been a change in circumstances justifying this. The court can then make such order as it thinks just having regard to all the circumstances.

The court can also in certain circumstances vary a written maintenance agreement after the death of one of the parties (MCA 1973, s 36). The application should be made within six months of the grant of representation being taken out in respect of the estate, otherwise permission from the court is required (see FPR 1991, r 3.3).

12.4 Chapter summary

(1) Pre-marital agreements (ie agreements made *before* marriage dealing with what will happen on divorce) are not necessarily binding (although there are reform proposals to change this).

(2) Separation agreements (ie agreements made when a couple *actually* separate) *can* be binding contracts.

(3) A separation agreement can be made as an alternative to a court order.

(4) The advantages of a separation agreement are:

    (a)   speed;

    (b)   flexibility.

(5) The disadvantages of a separation agreement: are
     (a) difficult to enforce;
     (b) not final;
     (c) variation by court.

Chapter 13

Children

13.1 Introduction

The Children Act 1989 (CA 1989) has been described as 'the most comprehensive and far reaching reform of child law ... in living memory' (Lord Mackay, Hansard, House of Lords, 6 December 1988). The aim of the Act was to simplify the law relating to children, making it more consistent and more flexible, and to make the law more appropriate to the needs of children by making it more child-centred. The 1989 Act deals with both public and private law. Most of the existing legislation concerning children was repealed when the 1989 Act came into force on 14 October 1991.

Children are sometimes described as a solicitor's invisible clients in divorce proceedings. The client is the parent, not the child, but a solicitor must consider the effect of his client's actions on the child involved. A solicitor may often feel that the client would be helped by mediation in relation to decisions about the children, and should recommend that an appropriate agency is consulted (see **1.3.2**).

The CA 1989 enables a child to apply for an order himself. The requirements involved are considered in this chapter. Provisions dealing with financial orders for children are summarised at **13.10**.

The Resolution Code of Practice (see **Appendix 2**) sets out useful reminders of how to approach children matters and how to deal with the conflicts which can arise. Resolution (formerly the SFLA) has also produced a *Guide to Good Practice for Solicitors Acting for Children* (6th edn, 2002), which should be referred to when representing a child. This sets out general guidance, as well as dealing with particular problems, for example, interviewing and taking instructions from a child. It also provides very useful guidance to further reading.

The Criminal Justice and Court Services Act 2000 established the Children and Family Court Advisory and Support Service (Cafcass). Cafcass is a non-departmental body, accountable to the Lord Chancellor. In respect of family proceedings in which the welfare of children is in question, the Service has the principal function of safeguarding and promoting the welfare of the children, giving advice to any court about any application made to it in such proceedings, making provision for the children to be represented in such proceedings, and providing information, advice and other support for the children and their families. Cafcass 'case workers' now fulfil the roles of children and family reporters (in private law proceedings) and children's guardians (in public law proceedings).

13.2 Parental responsibility

13.2.1 What is parental responsibility?

The CA 1989 introduced the concept of parental responsibility, which was a deliberate shift away from the idea that parents have 'rights' over their child towards the idea that they have 'responsibilities' towards their child. Parental power to control a child is not for the benefit of the parents but for that of the child. The Act defines this term as 'all the rights, duties, powers, responsibilities and authority which by law a parent of a child has in relation to the child and his property' (CA 1989, s 3(1) – see **Appendix 1(E)**). In reality, it gives the parent responsibility for taking all the important decisions in the child's life, for example, education, religion and medical care. It also enables a parent to take day-to-day decisions, for example, in relation to nutrition, recreation and outings. The duties involved in parental responsibility will change from time to time with differing needs and circumstances, and vary with the age and maturity of the child. It is important to bear in mind that a child will gradually become mature enough to take decisions himself. The House of Lords, in *Gillick v West Norfolk and Wisbech Area Health Authority* [1986] AC 112, said that 'parental authority ceases in respect of any aspect of a child's upbringing about which the child himself is sufficiently mature to make decisions for himself'.

13.2.2 Who has parental responsibility?

Married parents have joint parental responsibility; if parents are not married, only the mother has parental responsibility. However, an unmarried father can acquire parental responsibility in any one of six ways:

(a)   by being registered as the father on the child's birth certificate with the consent of the mother (after 1 December 2003) (CA 1989, s 4(1)(a));

(b)   by entering into a 'parental responsibility agreement' with the mother (CA 1989, s 4(1)(b)): this must be on a prescribed printed form (see **Appendix 3(F)**);

(c)   by applying to the court for a parental responsibility order (CA 1989, s 4(1)(c)) (see **16.4.1** for the courts' approach on such applications);

(d)   by being appointed a guardian either by the mother or by the court, although in these cases he will assume parental responsibility only on the mother's death;

(e)   by obtaining a residence order from the court (see **13.3.1**);

(f)   by marrying the mother.

For further discussion of an unmarried father's position and the criteria on which the court will decide whether to grant parental responsibility, see **16.4.1**.

Various other people may also acquire parental responsibility towards the child. A local authority will acquire parental responsibility if a care order is made in relation to the child, or anyone who is granted a residence order in relation to the child, or even the court if the child is made a ward of court. Also anyone obtaining a new special guardianship order will acquire parental responsibility (see **14.13**). The recently inserted s 4A of the CA 1989 allows step-parents and civil partners to obtain parental responsibility agreements (with the consent of all parents with parental responsibility), or to apply to the court for a parental responsibility order.

13.2.3   How can you lose parental responsibility?

There is no limit to the number of people who can have parental responsibility at any one time, and no one will lose parental responsibility just because another person acquires it (CA 1989, s 2(5)). If, on divorce, a residence order is made in favour of a grandparent, this will mean that the child's mother, father and grandparent will all have parental responsibility. The parents 'lose' the responsibility of having the child living with either of them because of the residence order but retain all other responsibilities. If a care order is made, the local authority acquires parental responsibility but the parents still, in theory, retain parental responsibility. However, in practice the local authority is given the discretion to determine the extent to which a parent may meet his or her parental responsibility (CA 1989, s 33(3)).

Two situations in which parents will lose parental responsibility are:

(a)   the parent's death; and

(b)   the child's adoption. Section 12 of the Adoption Act 1976 provides that an adoption order will automatically extinguish the parental responsibility which any person had before the making of the order.

An unmarried father who has acquired parental responsibility by a parental responsibility order or parental responsibility agreement, or by registration on the birth certificate, can lose it if the court makes a further order ending it. (See *Re P (Terminating Parental Responsibility)* [1995] 1 FLR 1048, where an unmarried father who had acquired parental responsibility then lost it under a court order, having inflicted serious injury on the child.) Similarly, a step-parent or civil partner who acquires parental responsibility under s 4A of the 1989 Act (see **13.2.2** above) can have it removed by the court.

Anyone other than an unmarried father, who has acquired parental responsibility by being granted a residence order, will lose it automatically when the residence order terminates.

The acquisition and loss of parental responsibility in the case of unmarried fathers raises potential issues of discrimination under the HRA 1998. However, in *McMichael v UK* (1995) 20 EHRR 205, the European Court of Human Rights accepted that discrimination between married and unmarried fathers could be justified as identifying 'meritorious' fathers who might be accorded parental rights, thereby protecting the interests of the child and the mother.

13.2.4   Exercising parental responsibility

Even though several people may have parental responsibility for a child, in theory it is possible for each to act alone with no duty to consult anyone else (CA 1989, s 2(7)). However, in *Re C (Change of Surname)* [1998] 1 FLR 549, the court held that when there was joint parental responsibility, this did not confer the right unilaterally to change the child's surname, and suggested that good practice is to refer to the court all disputed issues regarding change of surname regardless of who has parental responsibility. Also, in *Re J (Child's Religious Upbringing and Circumcision)* [2000] 1 FLR 571, the court held that there is a small group of important decisions made on behalf of a child which, in the absence of agreement by all those with parental responsibility, ought not to be carried out or arranged by the one-parent carer, notwithstanding s 2(7). Instead, they should be referred to the court for the court's determination, on the facts of the case each time, by way of a specific issue order. As well as change of a child's surname, the court gave sterilisation and circumcision as examples of such decisions. In *Re H (Parental Responsibility)* [1998] 1 FLR 855, the court also said that a parent with parental responsibility would have the right to be consulted on schooling.

In *Re D (Contact and Parental Responsibility: Lesbian Mothers and Known Father)* [2006] EWHC 2 (Fam), the court made a parental responsibility order in favour of the father on the basis the father would not contact the child's school or any health care professional involved in her care without the consent of the child's mother or her female partner, who had a shared residence order in respect of the child.

Subject to these exceptions, one parent can determine questions such as medical treatment and religion without consulting the other. The only way to challenge a decision is to make an application to court, for example, for a specific issue order or a prohibited steps order. If a child is being adopted, or taken out of the UK, there are specific provisions requiring both parents' consent, or the consent of the court.

It is not possible to transfer or surrender parental responsibility (CA 1989, s 2(9)). However, parents can delegate responsibility for a child on a temporary basis, for example, to a school for a school trip, or to a nanny or childminder. Temporary carers do not acquire parental responsibility but 'may do what is reasonable in all the circumstances of the case for the purpose of safeguarding or promoting the child's welfare' (CA 1989, s 3(5)). This could cover emergency medical treatment for the child if needed when the parent is absent, for example during a school trip, or when the parent is at work during the day and a nanny is in charge.

13.3 Section 8 orders

Under s 8 of the CA 19898 (see **Appendix 1(E)**), four different types of orders can be made in relation to children:

(a)   residence orders;

(b)   contact orders;

(c)   prohibited steps orders;

(d)   specific issue orders.

Each of these orders will determine a particular matter relating to the child's upbringing. A s 8 order lasts until the child reaches the age of 16 (or 18, in exceptional circumstances) (CA 1989, s 91(10)).

13.3.1 Residence order

A residence order is an order settling the arrangements to be made as to the person with whom the child is to live.

Following a divorce, parents will share parental responsibility and, therefore, the making of a residence order will only decide where a child will live.

A residence order can be made in favour of non-parents and, if this is done, the non-parent will automatically have parental responsibility as well, but only for so long as the residence order is in force (CA 1989, s 12(2)). The parental responsibility acquired in this way also has two limitations as, first, no agreement or refusal to an adoption order or freeing for adoption can be given and, secondly, no guardian can be appointed by the non-parent.

A residence order can be made in favour of two or more persons who do not all live together. The order can specify the periods during which the child is to live in the different households involved (CA 1989, s 11(4)). This means that a court could order that a child lives alternate weeks with each parent, or lives during term-time with one parent and during the holidays with the other, or spends a fixed period (say, the summer holidays) with one parent. A residence order is therefore a flexible power which can be adapted to the needs of a particular family. Obviously, the court will make a shared residence order only if it feels that it is in the welfare of the child to do so. It is not the case that shared residence orders can be made only in exceptional circumstances (as was once thought): *Re D (Children) (Shared Residence Orders)* [2001] 1 FLR 495. In courts in some parts of the country, shared residence orders are becoming increasingly used.

In *Re G (Residence: Same Sex Partners)* [2005] EWCA Civ 462, the biological mother of two children conceived by artificial insemination by donor and her same-sex partner separated, leaving the children with the biological mother. The mother tried to marginalise the applicant's contact with the children. The applicant was granted a shared residence order as the only way to obtain parental responsibility and prevent such marginalisation.

The court is given wide powers to attach directions, conditions, and incidental and supplementary provisions to the residence order. These could, for example, direct where the child is to be educated, or impose a ban on removing the child from the country; or could direct that the non-resident parent be informed if the child requires medical treatment in circumstances where the parent with whom the child is living has religious objections to blood transfusions.

When a residence order has been made, two aspects of parental responsibility are automatically affected, as follows.

13.3.1.1   Change of surname

Where a residence order is in force, the order will provide that no person can cause the child to be known by a new surname without either:

(a)   the written consent of every person who has parental responsibility; or

(b)   the leave of the court (CA 1989, s 13(1)).

However, following *Re C* (see **13.2.4**), it seems that where there is joint parental responsibility, regardless of whether there is a residence order, the same conditions will apply.

If a mother wants to change her child's surname, perhaps following remarriage or reverting to a maiden surname herself, she will have to obtain the permission of the child's father; and if this is not given, she will have to apply to court. In *Re C* (see 13.2.4) it was suggested this would be good practice even if the father did not have parental responsibility. The court will base any decision on the welfare principle (see **13.4**). The court is generally reluctant to authorise a change of surname unless it is in the interests of the child to do so. Factors to weigh up include embarrassment to the child and parent of having different surnames, the child's wishes and the extent to which the child's original surname is important to maintain links with the parent and other relations with whom he does not live. In *W v A (Child: Surname)* [1981] 1 All ER 100, both parents had remarried. The mother wanted to emigrate to Australia with her second husband who was Australian, and take the two children (aged 12 and 14) from her first marriage with her. The mother wanted to change the children's surnames to the new husband's surname. The children, who were interviewed by the judge, also wanted to change their surname. The judge decided that the children should keep their natural father's name. He stressed that change of name was a serious issue and, in this case, it had not been shown that it was in the children's best interests to change their name. He did not place great weight on the children's wishes in this case as he felt that they had been influenced by their mother and were merely reflecting her view.

This case was followed in *Re F (Child: Surname)* [1993] 2 FLR 837, where it was stated that allowing a child to be known by a different surname is an important matter which is not to be undertaken lightly. In *Dawson v Wearmouth* [1999] 1 FLR 1167, the majority of the House of Lords considered that there had to be particular circumstances to justify a change of name; effectively, there is a presumption in favour of the status quo.

13.3.1.2   Leaving the UK

Where a residence order is in force, no person may remove the child from the UK without either:

(a)   the written consent of every person who has parental responsibility; or

(b)   leave of the court (CA 1989, s 13(1)).

The Act does allow the person in whose favour the residence order is made to take the child out of the UK for periods of less than one month without such consent.

Thus, the parent with whom the child lives can take the child abroad as many times as he or she likes, provided each individual trip does not last more than one month. The parent without the residence order needs to seek consent every time he or she wants to take the child abroad for whatever period. However, at the time that the residence order is granted, the court can add a direction authorising removal to avoid repeated applications to court. This would be sensible in a situation where the non-residential parent lives abroad, so that regular trips to stay with the parent will be permitted without consent being needed.

If no residence order is in force, either parent can (in theory) take the child abroad without any restriction or need for consent under the CA 1989. However, the parent proposing the trip could be prevented from going by the other parent obtaining a prohibited steps or specific issue order forbidding the child being taken abroad. Additionally, a criminal offence under the Child Abduction Act 1984 will be committed by the parent taking the child if permission of the other parent, or the court, is not obtained (see **13.9.1.3**).

If a parent needs to apply to court to seek permission to take the child abroad, the court will again base its decision on the welfare principle. It will, therefore, seldom be difficult to persuade the court that a holiday abroad is in the best interests of the child, unless, for example, it is a cover for an abduction. Where emigration is intended, in *Payne v Payne* [2001] EWCA Civ 166, [2001] 1 FLR 1052, the Court of Appeal stressed that there is no presumption in law in favour of the applicant parent wishing to move the child abroad. The welfare of the child is the paramount consideration, and the court must apply the principles and factors set out in s 1 of the CA 1989 (see **13.5**). The President of the Family Division also set out the following specific considerations which 'should be in the forefront of the mind of a judge' in these difficult cases:

(a)   the reasonable proposals of the parent with a residence order wishing to live abroad carry great weight;

(b) consequently, those proposals need to be scrutinised with care to ensure that there was a genuine motivation for the move;

(c) the effect on the applicant parent and any new family of the child of a refusal to grant leave had to be considered;

(d) the effect on the child of the potential denial of contact with the other parent and, in some cases, with their family was very important; and

(e) the opportunity for continuing contact between the child and the parent left behind might be very significant.

In *Re B (Removal from Jurisdiction); Re S (Removal from Jurisdiction)* [2003] EWCA Civ 1149, [2003] 2 FLR 1043, Thorpe LJ in the Court of Appeal extended the list in *Payne*, so that where the mother cares for a child within a new family, the impact of refusal on the new family and the stepfather or prospective stepfather must also be carefully evaluated.

Where there is concern over future contact arrangements, the court could impose conditions. For example, in *Re S (Removal from Jurisdiction)* [1999] 1 FLR 850, prior to authorising removal, the court required the resident parent to deposit a large sum of money pending authentication of the English contact order by the Chilean Supreme Court.

In *E v E* [2006] EWCA Civ 843, the Court of Appeal suggested that, in relocation cases within the jurisdiction where no formal leave was required, the *Payne* guidelines apply and the court has to decide if the relocation is in the best interests of the children. The judge's duty is to subject the relocating parent's proposals to rigorous scrutiny and to balance their benefits for the children, and the effect on the mother of refusing the application, against the effect on the children of the disruption of their relationship with their father.

13.3.2 Contact order

A contact order is an order requiring the person with whom the child lives, or is to live, to allow the child to visit or stay with the person named in the order, or for that person and the child otherwise to have contact with each other.

A contact order can authorise physical contact but can also cover contact by letter, e-mail or by telephone (or even by video). The amount of contact can either be specified in the order, to cover weekend visits or holidays, or the order could be for 'reasonable contact', in which case the arrangements can be made by the parents. The latter is obviously preferable as the parents can make and alter arrangements to suit the circumstances. A contact order can also be made preventing contact with someone (*Nottinghamshire County Council v P* [1993] 1 FLR 115). The alternative way to achieve this is by a prohibited steps order (see **13.3.3**).

Since the order can be made in favour of a parent or any other person, it could enable contact to be maintained with more distant relatives or other friends of the child.

A contact order can contain conditions and directions. These could be used to build up contact gradually between a young child and a parent who had not seen the child for a while, or to ensure supervised contact to protect the child. This could take place at a local Child Contact Centre. These centres have been set up across the country to provide an opportunity and setting for contact to take place in circumstances where arranging contact might otherwise be difficult. Only some centres can offer fully supervised contact, but most can provide 'supported' contact, whereby contact can take place in the centre or children can be handed from one parent to another.

The court's approach is that the child has a right to know both parents, and therefore the starting point is that a child should have contact with the non-resident parent (*Re D (A Minor) (Contact)* [1993] 1 FCR 9). However, the court will always consider all the circumstances and may decide that because of factors such as the parent's conduct, the emotional welfare and stability of the child, or even the attitude and behaviour of a step-parent, it is in the best interests of the child not to grant a contact order (*Re T (A Minor) (Parental Responsibility: Contact)* [1993] 2 FLR 450).

Although there is a presumption that a child should have contact with both parents (unless there are cogent reasons to the contrary), that is not necessarily the approach towards any other member of the family, such as a grandparent. In *Re A (Section 8 Order: Grandparent Application)* [1995] 2 FLR 153, the Court of Appeal stressed that just because the grandmother had succeeded in obtaining leave to apply for a contact order, that did not mean that there was a presumption that she should actually be granted a contact order; the court had to consider what was in the child's best interests (although see also the case of *Re W* [1997] 1 FLR 793).

In *Re O (A Minor) (Contact: Imposition of Conditions)* [1995] 2 FLR 124, the Court of Appeal confirmed that the court had a wide and comprehensive jurisdiction to make contact orders, including for indirect contact, such as the non-resident parent being sent school progress reports and any cards or letters sent by him being read to the child. The court rejected the mother's argument that it was wrong in principle to compel her to read the father's communications when she was unwilling and hostile to such contact, saying that would mean that the mother was being given a power of veto. She was subject to an enforceable duty to promote contact if the court considered that that promoted the child's welfare: that was a decision for the court, not for the mother.

However, a practical problem with contact orders is how to enforce them if the parent with day-to-day care is determined that contact will not occur. The court has power to enforce contact orders (FLA 1986, s 34). In practice, though, this is often ineffective in contact disputes. The court can penalise in costs the party who is breaching the contact order (*Re B (Contact Application: Costs)* [1995] Fam Law 650). Ultimately, contempt proceedings can be used, or at least threatened, when a parent with whom the child lives consistently and unreasonably refuses contact (*Re N (A Minor) (Access: Penal Notices)* [1992] 1 FLR 134 and *Re N (A Minor)* (1997) *The Times*, 11 October). However, these proceedings are often inappropriate and could cause the child added trauma, especially if the unfortunate result is the imprisonment of the parent with whom the child lives. Nevertheless, in *F v F (Contact: Committal)* [1998] 2 FLR 237, the Court of Appeal, concluding that the mother had sabotaged contact which was clearly in the interests of the children, confirmed a sentence of seven days' imprisonment, suspended for six months on condition that she complied with the contact order.

In *Re M (Intractable Contact Dispute: Interim Care Order)* [2003] EWHC 1024 (Fam), [2003] 2 FLR 636, Wall J directed the local authority to investigate the case under s 37 of the CA 1989 (see **13.3.6**) with a view to taking care proceedings when faced with a mother who repeatedly frustrated contact. This resulted in the children being removed from the care of their mother under an interim care order, followed by a residence order in favour of the father.

This and a series of other recent cases have highlighted the difficulties in enforcement of contact orders. In *Re D (Intractable Contact Dispute: Publicity)* [2004] EWHC 727, [2004] 1 FLR 1226, Munby J listed a catalogue of failings in the court system in dealing with problems in contact, and said it could no longer be assumed that our approach to enforcement of contact orders meets the standards required by Article 6 and Article 8 of the European Convention on Human Rights.

As a result of the concerns raised in these cases, the Children and Adoption Act 2006 was passed in June 2006 to give the courts more powers to enforce contact orders. When this Act is in force it will allow the courts to require parties involved in contact disputes to attend activities such as classes or meetings with a counsellor (activity directions and conditions). A court will also be able to ask a Cafcass officer to monitor compliance with any contact order, or with activity directions and conditions, and to report to the court. In cases where contact orders have been breached, the Act also introduces enforcement orders which impose unpaid work on the party in breach and makes financial compensation payable from one party to another (for example, where the cost of a holiday has been lost). Also the new Act will provide, where a contact order and a family assistance order are in force together (see **13.3.5**), for the officer to give advice and assistance to establish, improve and maintain contact.

A distinction must be made between cases where a parent is opposed to contact for no good reason, when the court will be very slow to conclude contact would harm the child, and those where there are genuine and rational reasons for opposing contact. A particular difficulty arises where, during the relationship, the resident parent has been subjected to violence by the other parent. In *Re H (Contact: Domestic Violence)* [1998] 2 FLR 42, the Court of Appeal stated that domestic violence was not, of itself, a bar to contact but one factor in a very complex equation. While the courts have re-emphasised the presumption in favour of contact, some cases have shown a willingness to hold that the presumption is rebutted on the facts. See, for example, *Re M (Contact: Violent Parent)* [1999] 2 FLR 321, where Wall J stated:

> Too often, notwithstanding that domestic violence had been found, the mother was none the less ordered to arrange for contact with the father, the courts neglecting the other side of the equation which was that such a father should first demonstrate by changing his behaviour, that he was a fit person to have contact and would not destabilise or upset the children.

See also *Re K (Contact: Mother's Anxiety)* [1999] Fam Law 527, where the court found that the mother had been so traumatised by the father's behaviour that direct contact would bring about a state of heightened anxiety and fear which would inevitably be conveyed to the boy, causing him significant emotional harm.

The issue came before the Court of Appeal in four cases, heard together, where, in each case, the father's application for direct contact was refused because of a background of domestic abuse between the parents (*Re L (Contact: Domestic Violence)* [2000] 2 FLR 334). The Court of Appeal eschewed any presumption either for or against direct contact in cases involving domestic abuse. The balancing exercise required to determine what was best for a child's welfare had to be carried out in the usual way. However, the court should particularly consider the following points:

(a)   the past and present conduct of both parties;

(b)   the effect of the violence on the child and the residential parent;

(c)   the motivation of the parent seeking contact; and

(d)   in cases of serious domestic violence, the ability of the offending parent to recognise his past conduct, be aware of the need to change and to make genuine efforts to do so .

The Court of Appeal also pointed out the need for family judges and magistrates to have a heightened awareness of the effects on children of being exposed to domestic abuse by one parent against the other.

The Children Act Sub-Committee of the Lord Chancellor's Advisory Board on Family Law issued guidelines in April 2002 for *Good Practice on Parental Contact in Cases Where There is Domestic Violence*. These are extensive but include steps to be taken, such as an initial fact-finding hearing to determine the issue of violence and the consideration of separate representation for the children. Where a welfare report is ordered, the court order should contain specific directions to the reporter to address the issue of domestic violence. On the making of a contact order where domestic violence has been proved, the guidelines state that the court should consider what directions should be attached, whether the contact should be supervised and whether the court should make a non-molestation order (see **15.2**).

In *Re H (Contact: Domestic Violence)* [2005] EWCA Civ 1404, the Court of Appeal set aside an order allowing contact as the judge had failed to follow the guidance in *Re L* (above) and the guidelines of the Children Act Sub-Committee (above).

13.3.3   Prohibited steps order

A prohibited steps order is an order that no step that could be taken by a parent in meeting his or her parental responsibilities for a child and which is of a kind specified in the order, shall be taken by any person without the consent of the court. This order deals with a specific problem which has arisen. However, it cannot overlap with a residence or contact order. Section 9(5) of the CA 1989 provides that the court cannot make a prohibited steps order or a specific issue order with a view to achieving a result that could be achieved by a residence or contact order. For example, the court could not grant an order prohibiting the child living with anyone other than the applicant as this would in effect be a residence order. It can be used to restrict anyone, not just a parent. So, it could be used to prevent a grandparent with whom the child lived from removing the child from the jurisdiction.

Another situation in which the overlap between the various s 8 orders must be considered is child abduction. If, in an abduction case, the result that is required is for the abducted child to be returned to live with the non-abducting parent, the correct order for this parent to seek is a residence order (with appropriate conditions and directions) and not a specific issue order ordering return of the child coupled with a prohibited steps order to prevent further removal (*Re W (A Minor) (Residence Order)* [1992] 2 FLR 332). If the required result is to obtain the return of the child to the UK and prevent further removal, but the child is to remain living with the abducting parent, then a prohibited steps order is the correct order to obtain (*Re D (A Minor) (Child: Removal from Jurisdiction)* [1992] 1 FLR 637).

If no residence order were in force, a prohibited steps order could be used to prohibit the removal of the child from the country, or to prevent a change of surname.

If it is desired to prevent someone having contact with the child, it is possible to make a contact order providing for no contact. Therefore, the person with whom a child lives could be prevented from allowing contact with an abusing parent or anyone else who the court considered was harming the child in any way. However, in *Re H (Prohibited Steps Order)* [1995] 1 FLR 638, where the mother's cohabitee had abused the children, the court decided that a 'negative' contact order preventing the mother from allowing contact would afford only partial protection. Instead, the court made a prohibited steps order against the cohabitee, even though he was not a party to the proceedings and had not been given notice.

An important restriction on a prohibited steps order is that it can relate only to matters which are included within parental responsibility. If an order is needed to restrict publicity, for example, the wider powers of wardship are needed as this is not one of the matters included within parental responsibility.

13.3.4 Specific issue order

A specific issue order is an order giving directions for the purpose of determining a specific question which has arisen or which may arise in connection with any aspect of parental responsibility for a child.

It does not give a parent a general power, it just makes a decision on one issue over which there is a disagreement which cannot be resolved. It could be used to decide which school a child should attend, whether a child should have a particular operation (including, for example, sterilisation or circumcision) or course of treatment or immunisation (such as the MMR vaccination), or the religion a child should adopt.

It can be used by non-parents, for example the local authority, or doctor or relation, to resolve issues involving the child, for example, over abortion or life-saving medical decisions. In *Re R (A Minor) (Blood Transfusion)* [1993] 2 FLR 757, a specific issue order was used to deal with a situation where a child needed a blood transfusion and his parents refused to give consent due to their religious beliefs.

Again, it cannot be used to achieve a 'back-door' residence or contact order, for example by ordering a child to attend a particular school thereby necessitating a change of residence (see **13.3.3**).

13.3.5 Family assistance order

A family assistance order is not a s 8 order at all, although it is closely connected. Section 16 of the CA 1989 allows the court in any family proceedings where it has power to make a s 8 order to make an order requiring, for example, a Cafcass officer or local authority officer to be made available to advise, assist and befriend any person named in the order. Until recently, it could be made only in exceptional circumstances and only if everyone named in the order, excluding the child, consented. Section 6 of the Children and Adoption Act 2006, which came into force on 1 October 2007, removes the requirement that the order be made only in exceptional circumstances and also provides, where a contact order is in force, that the officer give advice and assistance to establish, improve and maintain contact.

The aim of the family assistance order is to support the family in the immediate aftermath of a family breakdown and to help everyone to adjust to the changed circumstances. The order can only be made by the court of its own motion and is likely to be made in conjunction with one or more s 8 orders.

13.3.6 Special guardianship order

The new ss 14A to 14F of the CA 1989 provide for special guardianship orders, a new type of order. Those able to apply for the order are, amongst others, any guardian of the child, any holder of a residence order or anyone who has been the child's foster carer for one year. It is a private law order, but it is envisaged it will be useful in cases where the local authority is or has been involved. It provides permanence without the legal separation involved in adoption. For example, it can be used in the case of an older child in long-term foster care, or for a child being looked after permanently by a member of his extended family.

In *A Local Authority v YZ and Others* [2006] 2 FLR 41, on the local authority's application for care orders in respect of five children, the court made special guardianship orders in respect of the three eldest children. The two eldest had lived with an aunt and uncle for two years and the third child, aged five, had lived with another aunt and her partner for almost two years. The two youngest were made subject to care orders with a care plan for adoption.

The special guardianship order gives the holder parental responsibility, which he is entitled to exercise to the exclusion of any other person with parental responsibility. However, it does not extinguish the parents' parental responsibility. The local authority must provide special guardian support services, including counselling, advice and financial support.

Since their introduction, special guardianship orders are being increasingly used in practice.

13.3.7 Local authority investigation

If exceptional circumstances are revealed in family proceedings, for example on an application for a s 8 order serious neglect is discovered which makes it unlikely that either parent should look after the children, the court may not be prepared to grant either parent a s 8 order. The court does not have the power to make a care order relating to a child without an application from the local authority, and what it will have to do is to make an order under s 37 of the CA 1989 to direct the local authority to investigate the child's circumstances. It is then for the local authority to decide whether or not to bring care or supervision proceedings, depending on the outcome of its inquiries. The court can, when making a s 37 order, make an interim care order to protect a child pending the investigation (see **14.9.1**).

13.4 Welfare principle

Section 1(1) of CA 1989 states:

> When a court determines any question with respect to—
> (a)   the upbringing of a child; or
> (b)   the administration of the child's property or the application of any income arising from it,
> the child's welfare shall be the court's paramount consideration.

The welfare principle will determine any contested proceedings under s 8 of the CA 1989, and it will also extend to care proceedings (CA 1989, s 31) and related public law orders.

It is a concept that has been used for many years in cases concerning children, and is summarised by the words of Lord MacDermott in *J and Another v C and Others* [1969] 1 All ER 788:

> More than that the child's welfare is to be treated as the top item in a list of items relevant to the matter in question, [the words] connote a process whereby, when all the relevant facts, relationships, claims and wishes of parents, risks, choices and their circumstances are taken into account and weighed, the course to be followed will be

that which is most in the interest of the child's welfare as that term has now to be understood ... [It is] the paramount consideration because it rules upon or determines the course to be followed.

13.4.1 Human Rights Act 1998

Article 8 of the European Convention on Human Rights provides that 'everyone has the right to respect for his private and family life, his home and his correspondence'. Although the welfare of the child is paramount under CA 1989, under Article 8 the starting point is that each family member is on an equal footing.

There has been debate as to whether the welfare principle is incompatible with Article 8 and an individual's right to respect for family life. In other words, placing the child's welfare as paramount does not involve balancing the family rights of the other relevant individuals. In the past, the European Court has tended to adopt more of a straightforward balancing exercise and the idea of paramountcy has not been supported.

Any inconsistency between the approach of the English courts and the minimum standards required by the Convention needed to be reconciled. For example, in contact applications, it could be argued that the court must consider the right of the parent and other family members to contact, as opposed to this being the right of the child.

Similarly, where an application is made to remove a child from the jurisdiction, the welfare of the child is paramount. If this means that the resident parent is allowed to leave with the child, the other parent's right to family life has been infringed. On the other hand, if the resident parent's application is refused, this inhibits his right to a private life. Nevertheless, in *Payne v Payne* [2001] EWCA Civ 166, [2001] 1 FLR 1052, the Court of Appeal held that the Convention had not affected the longstanding underlying principles (focusing on the welfare of the child) to be applied when dealing with such applications .

The position was confirmed by the case of *Hoppe v Germany* [2003] 1 FLR 384, where the European Court of Human Rights finally made plain its acceptance of the primacy of the interests of the child where a balance was required to be struck between competing Convention rights.

13.5 Checklist of factors to be taken into account in applying welfare principle

Section 1(3) of CA 1989 (see **Appendix 1(E)**) directs the court to pay particular attention to seven factors when it is applying the welfare principle in contested s 8 proceedings and any proceedings for care and supervision orders.

The aim of the checklist is to promote a consistent approach by providing a framework to use when solicitors are preparing evidence and when courts are making decisions. It could sometimes be a very useful tool to use to explain to clients the approach that they should, and that the court certainly will, take in making a decision.

It provides a minimum that must be considered in every case. The Act gives no indication of the relative importance of the factors, so the court is left to assess the relative importance of each factor in the circumstances of each case. The checklist is not exhaustive and the court can also take any other relevant factors into account. For example, in *Re R (Residence Order: Finance)* [1995] 2 FLR 612 it was confirmed that a judge was entitled to look at the case in the round, which could include taking into account financial considerations, such as a possible assessment by the Child Support Agency.

13.5.1 The ascertainable wishes and feelings of the child concerned (considered in the light of his age and understanding)

This factor reflects the importance of allowing the child's wishes to be given a place in deciding what is in his or her welfare (see the *Gillick* case at **13.2.1**). Lord Justice Butler-Sloss (as she was then) in the Cleveland Report made the point that 'a child is a person, not an object of concern'.

There are a number of cases where, on the particular facts, the court not only considered but also followed the wishes of children. In *M v M (Transfer of Custody: Appeal)* [1987] 1 WLR 404, the trial judge said that it was wrong to order that a 12-year-old girl should live with her father instead of her mother without taking proper account of her adamant and strong opposition to this. In another case, the wishes of a 'sensible and mature' boy aged 14 years were the deciding factor in ordering that he should go to a local day school, enabling him to live with his father rather than go away to a boarding school. The boy was very anxious to build a relationship with his father with whom he had not lived for five years (see *Re P (A Minor) (Education: Child's Views)* [1992] 1 FLR 316). In *S v S (Child Abduction: Child's Views)* [1992] 2 FLR 492, the Court of Appeal said that there was no age below which a child was to be considered as not having attained sufficient maturity for his views to be taken automatically into account.

A child's wishes do not necessarily always take precedence and the court may sometimes feel that the children's wishes are not in their best interests (*Re DW (A Minor)* [1984] Fam Law 17).

However, in *Re S (Contact: Children's Views)* [2002] EWHC 540 (Fam), [2002] 1 FLR 1156, the court expressed the view that if young people (here a 14- and a 16-year-old) are to respect the law, the law has to respect them and their wishes, even to the extent of allowing them, as occasionally they may do, to make mistakes.

There are a number of ways in which the child's wishes and feelings can be made known. The court will place great importance on the welfare report prepared by the children and family reporter, which will consider the child's wishes as well as the maturity of the child and the extent to which the parents may have exerted influence over the child in forming any views. In some cases, a judge may interview a child privately during the case to form his own opinion. This is not common and will not be done in relation to children under eight years of age (see *B v B (Minors)* [1994] 2 FLR 489). Magistrates can also see a child in private, but this power must be exercised only in rare and exceptional cases, and should not be used if the child's wishes are adequately dealt with in the Cafcass report. Alternatively, the child may need separate legal representation. This may happen in difficult cases, with disputed facts, and where the child's views are perhaps not sufficiently dealt with in the welfare report (see *Re A (Contact: Separate Representation)* [2001] 1 FLR 715, CA and **13.8.3**). This situation may change as s 122 of the Adoption and Children Act 2002 states that rules may be made allowing s 8 proceedings to be specified under s 41 of the CA 1989, thus requiring appointment of a children's guardian or a solicitor (see **14.11.7** and **14.11.8**). No such rules have yet been made.

A wider issue involving a child's wishes is the extent to which a child can consent to or refuse medical treatment (see *Re W (A Minor) (Consent to Medical Treatment)*

[1993] 1 FLR 1). If a child is sufficiently mature, he can consent to treatment and only the court can override his consent. If such a child refuses consent to treatment then either the court or anyone with parental responsibility can give consent.

13.5.2 The child's physical, emotional and educational needs

This factor focuses on the child and will look at accommodation, medical needs and education, as well as how close the child is to brothers and sisters and others with whom he may lose touch if a particular order is made.

When the court has to decide between placing a child with a parent or another carer, there is a strong supposition that, other things being equal, it is in the interests of the child that it shall remain with its natural parents (*Re H (A Minor) (Custody: Interim Care and Control)* [1991] 2 FLR 109). In *In re G (Children)* [2006] UKHL 43, Baroness Hale identified three ways in which a person may be or may become the natural parent of a child: the genetic parent; the gestational parent; or the social and psychological parent. In most cases, the natural mother combines all three. This was a case which involved former lesbian partners. One of the partners (CG) had had two children by artificial insemination, which both partners raised. The court said that the fact that CG was the natural mother in every sense of the term, whilst raising no presumption in her favour, was undoubtedly an important and significant factor in determining what was best for the children.

The court will not equate welfare with material advantages and the fact that one parent can offer more is of little weight, particularly because the court could compensate for this when making financial orders.

The court will consider the circumstances very carefully before splitting brothers and sisters (*C v C (Minors: Custody)* [1988] 2 FLR 291). This will mean that it will be unusual to separate siblings, especially when they are close in age, although the larger the age gap, especially if linked with the fact that one child is at boarding school, could mean that children might be happier separated with generous contact during holidays.

13.5.3 The likely effect on the child of any change in circumstances

If the current arrangements for a child are working satisfactorily the court will be very unlikely to change them. This attitude, which is often referred to as maintaining the status quo, was explained in *Allington v Allington* [1985] FLR 586:

> It is generally accepted by those who are professionally concerned with children that particularly in the early years, continuity of care is a most important part of a child's sense of security and that disruption of established bonds is to be avoided whenever it is possible to do so.

A result of this attitude is that the person with whom the child is living is at a considerable advantage, and it may encourage them to increase this advantage by delaying the proceedings. This problem is tackled by the Act, where it provides that any delay is 'likely to prejudice the welfare of the child' (CA 1989, s 1(2)), and it further discourages delay by its imposition of a litigation timetable (CA 1989, s 11(1) and see **13.8.10**).

13.5.4 The child's age, sex, background and any characteristics of the child which the court considers relevant

Age may be important as very young babies tend to need to live with their mothers, whereas a 15-year-old child can generally cope with living with either parent. Also, age has a decisive influence on the importance a court will attach to a child's wishes, but there is no presumption of law that a child of any age should be with one parent or the other (*Re W (A Minor) (Residence Order)* [1992] 2 FLR 332).

The sex of the child can be taken into account. In *Re H (A Minor)* (1990) *The Times*, 20 June, the court agreed that a two-year-old girl should live with her father and stated that 'It may be natural for young children to be with their mothers but this is merely one consideration not a presumption'. Obviously, the needs of a teenager might best be met by living with a parent of the same sex. The factor also refers to the background of the child. This can cover race, culture and religion. The needs of a mixed-race child are of particular difficulty when deciding where a child should live. The court will look at how the child has been brought up and the influence of each culture, and make appropriate residence and contact arrangements (see *Re P (A Minor) (Adoption)* [1990] 1 FLR 96).

13.5.5   Any harm that the child has suffered or is at risk of suffering

This factor will cover any past or future harm to the child. Harm is a very broad term and will cover both physical and psychological injury.

The court will also consider the harm caused to a child by not seeing both parents. In the case of *Re S (Minors: Access)* [1990] 2 FLR 166, the court said that contact 'is the right of the child not of the parent ... The child has a right to know his other parent'.

13.5.6   How capable each of the child's parents and any other person in relation to whom the court considers the question relevant is of meeting the child's needs

This factor involves the court looking at the parents or other proposed carers to assess their ability to care for the child. The parents' conduct will be relevant to the extent that it may affect their suitability as a parent. Any criminal record, say, for violence or dishonesty, will be relevant.

In disputes between a natural parent and another, for example a grandparent, the courts tend to presume that, unless there is positive evidence to the contrary, it is in the child's interests to live with his natural parent. The question was not which household would provide the best home (*Re D (Care: Natural Parent Presumption)* [1999] 1 FLR 134).

Whether a parent works will influence the care of the child. A parent's lifestyle and sexual orientation may also be relevant. Issues of homosexuality and lesbianism can affect the child, especially if this causes problems, for example teasing or bullying, at school. However, the courts' attitudes to homosexual parenting are now very different to what they were several years ago and these issues are now likely to carry less weight.

A parent who suffers from a mental or physical illness which could mean sudden or long-term stays in hospital might also be less suitable as a full-time carer. Religion, too, may have an influence on a court's decision, especially if it may adversely affect a child's health, or have a harmful influence on the child's development. In *Re R (A Minor) (Residence: Religion)* [1993] 2 FLR 163, the court said that there was no rule of law or legal principle that it could never be right to force a child to abandon his religious beliefs. The court made a residence order that a child of nine years of age live with his father, even though the child had been brought up in a strict religious sect from which the father had been excluded.

The court took the religious issue into account but felt that it was in the child's best interests to be with his father.

If a parent is proposing to share care with someone else, that person's capabilities will also be considered. This means that new partners or spouses, relatives and friends may be relevant, as well as nannies and childminders.

13.5.7 The range of powers available to the court under this Act in the proceedings in question

This factor encourages the court to think laterally and consider every option open to it, including that of not making an order at all (see **13.6**).

The court has the power to make any order in favour of any person, irrespective of who has applied and for what. Thus, in the course of an application for a residence order by a parent, the court may decide that the child would be better off living with a grandparent. It can make this order even though the grandparents were not parties to the application. The deciding factor is the welfare of the child.

The court could also adjourn s 8 proceedings brought by a parent if it felt that a care or supervision order would be the best thing for the child (CA 1989, s 37(1)). This section enables the court to direct the local authority to investigate the circumstances of the child and, following this, the local authority could start care proceedings. The divorce courts do not have the power to make a care or supervision order themselves.

13.6 The 'no order' presumption

Section 1(5) of the CA 1989 states:

> Where a court is considering whether or not to make one or more orders under this Act with respect to a child, it shall not make the order or any of the orders unless it considers that doing so would be better for the child than making no order at all.

This means that there is a policy that the court will not intervene and make an order unless it can be shown that there is a positive need and benefit to the child in doing so.

On divorce, the court should not make an order automatically for the children as part of the 'divorce package'. If the parties agree on where a child is to live after the divorce and when the other parent should see him, no court will make an order.

The aim of this presumption is to try to reduce the bitterness felt by a parent who may feel that he has 'lost' if a court order is imposed ordering the child to live with the other parent, or allowing him contact only at defined times. The long-term damage to a child following divorce is greatly reduced if bitterness can be minimised, and the absence of unnecessary court intervention will help this. If parents are in dispute from the outset, or if agreed arrangements break down, the court can always be asked to make appropriate orders.

Other circumstances when the court will be likely to consider that an order is necessary include where there is a real danger that one parent may abduct the child and it is, therefore, an advantage to have in operation the restrictions on removal from the UK contained in a residence order, or, perhaps, where both parents agree that an order is preferable. Another situation where the court made an order despite the fact that all parties were in agreement was where parents agreed with the maternal grandmother that the child should live with her. The court said that there was a reason to grant a residence order to the grandmother as it would give her parental responsibility for the child and give her important rights, for example, it would enable her to give consent to medical treatment and authorise school trips. The granting of a residence order also gave the arrangement more stability, as the parents could not change their minds without going back to court (*B v B (A Minor) (Residence Order)* [1992] 2 FLR 327).

13.7 Avoiding delay

Section 1(2) of the CA 1989 states:

> In any proceedings in which any question with respect to the upbringing of a child arises, the court shall have regard to the general principle that any delay in determining the question is likely to prejudice the welfare of the child.

Delay can be particularly damaging in children cases, as a child's timescale is different from that of an adult. Six months is half a lifetime to a one-year-old child. The object is to avoid drift or delay for no reason, which can be very damaging to a child. Note, though, that sometimes delay can be positively beneficial, for example an adjournment to see how the child is settling down to new arrangements.

Inappropriate delay may also now be a breach of Article 6 of the European Convention on Human Rights (the right to a hearing within a reasonable time).

13.8 Procedure for s 8 orders

The procedure for making applications is governed by the FPR 1991 in the county court or High Court, and by the Family Proceedings Courts (Children Act 1989) Rules 1991 (SI 1991/1395) in the family proceedings court.

13.8.1 Public funding

Legal Representation is available for Children Act proceedings. If an application is made, both the means and merits tests must be satisfied (see **Chapter 2**). If a Legal Representation certificate has already been issued, for example for ancillary financial proceedings in a divorce, the Legal Representation certificate issued in these proceedings will need to be amended. In urgent cases, emergency Legal Representation can be used.

13.8.2 Jurisdiction

Applications for s 8 orders can be made within any family proceedings; in fact the court can make an order of its own motion in such proceedings. Family proceedings are defined in the Act and cover divorce, nullity or judicial separation, financial relief applications (MCA 1973 and DPMCA 1978) and domestic abuse applications under the FLA 1996. Alternatively, 'freestanding' applications can be made where no order other than under the CA 1989 is needed.

13.8.3 Is leave of the court needed?

13.8.3.1 Who can apply for a s 8 order?

The following can apply for *any* s 8 order without leave of the court:

(a)   a parent (which includes an unmarried father, whether or not he has parental responsibility); or

(b)   a guardian; or

(c) any person with a residence order in his or her favour (CA 1989, s 10(5): see **Appendix 1(E)**).

The following can apply for a residence or contact order *only* without leave:

(a) a step-parent or civil partner who has treated the child as a child of the family; or

(b) any person with whom the child has lived for at least three years out of the last five years (but the period must not have ended more than three months before the application is made); or

(c) any person who has obtained the consent of all those people whose legal position would be affected, ie anyone with parental responsibility, or anyone with a residence order or the local authority if the child is in care.

All other people not within the above require leave.

Therefore, for example, grandparents will require leave unless the child has been living with them for three years or they have the necessary consents. However, grandparents will normally readily be given leave if they can show that they have a genuine interest and commitment to the child (*Re A (Section 8 Order: Grandparent Application)* [1995] 2 FLR 153). An application for leave must be made in writing.

It is unlikely that the requirement for certain categories of parties to apply for leave violates Article 6(1) of the European Convention on Human Rights, as it is not a blanket denial of access to the court but rather a hurdle to overcome.

13.8.3.2 Application by the child

A child can apply on his own behalf for a s 8 order, but leave of the court is required (see FPR 1991, r 9.2A(2)). There have been several cases where teenage children have been granted leave to apply and have gone on to obtain s 8 orders (see *Re AD (A Minor) (Child's Wishes)* [1993] 1 FCR 573). Even if a child obtains a residence order allowing him to live apart from his parents, his parents will still retain parental responsibility. Orders have been sought to enable a child to live with grandparents or the parents of the child's boyfriend, and could also be used where a pregnant teenager did not want an abortion which her parents were forcing her to undergo.

The Resolution (formerly SFLA) *Guide to Good Practice for Solicitors Acting for Children* gives practical and very useful guidance for solicitors asked to act for children.

If a child wants to obtain a s 8 order, there are four hurdles to overcome:

(a) *To obtain a solicitor to act for him.* A minor can start proceedings without a next friend provided the court gives leave to proceed without a next friend *or* a solicitor considers that the child has sufficient understanding to give instructions. If the leave of the court is sought, it will base its decision on whether the child is mature enough to exercise a wise choice in his own interests in the circumstances that exist (*Re S (A Minor) (Independent Representation)* [1993] 3 All ER 36). In complex cases, the court is likely to recommend that a third party, such as an officer of Cafcass Legal (in a role formerly carried out by the Official Solicitor) or a children's guardian, acts for the child. This situation may change now that s 122 of the Adoption and Children Act 2002 is in force, as this states that rules of court may specify s 8 proceedings under s 41 of the CA 1989, thus requiring appointment of a children's guardian or a solicitor (see **14.11.7** and **14.11.8**). No such rules have yet been made.

If a child approaches a solicitor direct, that solicitor can take the decision whether to act for the child. The Resolution guidelines (Section F: Assessing Understanding) point out that initially it is the solicitor's duty to assess the child's understanding. (See *Re CT (A Minor) (Wardship: Representation)* [1993] 2 FLR 278.) The solicitor must also be sensitive to his duty of confidentiality to the child.

(b)   *To obtain public funding.* A child will usually need public funding and will have to convince the Legal Services Commission that his application has merit. The means test will usually not be a problem, as it is the child's resources that are relevant when assessing financial eligibility. Legal Help is also available to a child to cover the cost of the initial interview.

(c)   *To obtain the court's leave.* The child will need to obtain leave of the court to start s 8 proceedings (CA 1989, s 10(8)). Leave will be given only if the court is satisfied that the child has sufficient understanding to make the application. All applications for leave in these circumstances must be dealt with by the High Court (*Practice Direction (Children Act 1989: Applications by Children)* [1993] 1 FLR 668).

In *Re H (Residence Order: Child's Application For Leave)* [2000] 1 FLR 781, a 12-year-old boy was refused leave to apply for a residence order in the course of his parents' divorce proceedings. The boy wished to live with his father and was worried that the court would not attach enough weight to his wishes unless he made his own application. The court decided that, although he had sufficient understanding to instruct a solicitor independently, the boy did not have a separate argument to make that would not be made on the father's behalf. The judge also said that the boy must be assured that experienced judges would take full account of his wishes and are conscious that it is not usually a good idea to impose a result contrary to a child's wishes, even though those wishes are not decisive.

(d)   *To show that the merits of the case justify the order sought.* At the eventual hearing the court will consider the child's welfare and the statutory checklist (see **13.5**) when deciding whether to grant the order sought.

13.8.4   Which court?

If there are pending matrimonial proceedings, the application for a s 8 order must be made in the cause. Otherwise, the applicant has a free choice between the family proceedings court, a county court or the High Court. One of the changes brought about by the CA 1989 was to introduce this concurrent jurisdiction and to ensure that specially trained officials and judiciary are available at each level to deal with CA 1989 matters.

13.8.4.1   The family proceedings court

The family proceedings court can deal with private law applications for s 8 orders but it does not deal with divorce cases. In practice, as many s 8 applications will be linked to divorce proceedings they will be dealt with by the county court (see **13.8.4.2**). Most public law cases, for example for care or supervision orders, will start in the family proceedings court (see **14.11.2**).

The work is mainly dealt with by lay magistrates, who have had special training to deal with family cases and are therefore on a Family Panel.

13.8.4.2   County court

Any judge hearing family work in the county court must be nominated by the Lord Chancellor to hear family work and receive special training. There are various categories of judge who have been allocated particular areas of work. The detailed provisions are set out in *Practice Direction (Family Proceedings (Allocation to Judiciary) Directions 1999)* [1999] 2 FLR 799.

Not all county courts have jurisdiction to hear cases under CA 1989. There are four classes of county court, each with different types of jurisdiction:

(a)   *Non-divorce county courts.* These courts have no family jurisdiction and therefore no involvement with the CA 1989, except for domestic abuse orders. The work is carried out by non-nominated circuit judges and district judges.

(b)   *Divorce county courts.* These courts have jurisdiction to hear divorces and all uncontested private law CA 1989 cases. If any of these matters become contested they will be transferred to a family hearing centre. The work is carried out by non-nominated circuit judges and district judges.

(c)   *Family hearing centres.* These courts have jurisdiction to hear all private law CA 1989 cases, whether or not contested. The work is carried out by nominated circuit judges and (to a limited extent) district judges.

(d)   *Care centres.* These courts have jurisdiction to hear all private and public law (eg, care and supervision orders) CA 1989 cases, both contested and uncontested. The work is carried out by designated family judges, nominated care judges and nominated care district judges.

13.8.4.3 High Court

The High Court can hear all types of CA 1989 cases, as well as appeals in CA 1989 cases from the family proceedings court. In practice, it will generally deal with the more complex cases, which could either be started there or which are transferred from other courts.

13.8.4.4 Transfer of cases

Irrespective of where a case started, it can be transferred to another, more appropriate court. This is essentially governed by the general principle that any delay is likely to prejudice the child's welfare, but other factors will be considered, such as the complexity of the case and the need to consolidate it with proceedings which may have been started in another court (see Children (Allocation of Proceedings) Order 1991 (SI 1991/1677)). It is possible for cases to be transferred either vertically or horizontally. Thus, a difficult case could be transferred from the family proceedings court up to the county court, or, if a family proceedings court is too busy, it could transfer the case to another family proceedings court. If CA 1989 proceedings are commenced in a divorce county court ancillary to divorce, and the application is then opposed, the case will have to be transferred to a family hearing centre. In these circumstances, it is possible for the whole cause to be transferred rather than just the CA 1989 application. It is also possible for a case to be transferred down from the High Court to a county court.

13.8.5 The application

The applicant must file Form C1 (see **Appendix 3(G)**) (or Form C2 if there are already existing family proceedings), together with sufficient copies for service (and a fee). If the applicant alleges that the child has suffered or is at risk of suffering harm, he must also file a Form C1A (see **Appendix 3(H)**). The standard form enables the applicant to include the details of the order needed, any directions and the reasons for applying. Form C1 (and all other documents used in the proceedings) should be simply worded using non-inflammatory language.

Form C1 also refers parents to a Parenting Plan booklet, which offers guidance to parents on making arrangements for their children on relationsip breakdown.

On filing, the court fixes a date for a preliminary hearing or directions appointment (or, in some courts, a conciliation appointment).

The applicant must join as a party every person whom he believes to have parental responsibility for the child. This would not cover a step-parent or putative father. However, any person may apply to be joined, and the court has power to direct that anyone else be joined as a party. Therefore, all people with a genuine interest and active role in the child's upbringing can be involved in court proceedings.

In some cases the child may be made a party to the proceedings. Rule 9.5 of the FPR 1991 provides for the appointment of a Cafcass officer to be the guardian for a child party unless the child has sufficient understanding to participate in the proceedings without one. In *Re A (Contact: Separate Representation)* [2001] 1 FLR 715, the Court of Appeal granted permission for a 4-year-old child to be made a party and to have separate legal representation in a parental contact dispute case. There were concerns that otherwise the views of the child and her older step-brother would not be sufficiently heard.

The President's Direction, 5 April 2004, stated that a child will be made a party only in cases involving significant difficulty, and therefore only in a minority of cases, and set out guidance on the sort of circumstances in which this will be appropriate. The further President's Direction, 25 February 2005, stated that such appointment should be made only by a circuit judge, or in exceptional circumstances by a district judge, in an attempt to reduce the increasing number of appointments under r 9.5.

In 2006 the (then) Department for Constitutional Affairs carried out a consultation exercise, 'Separate Representation of Children' (2006), proposing restricting representation of children in private law proceedings to cases involving specific legal issues, such as where the child has to give evidence or has a legal submission to make that cannot be made by another party. At the time of writing, the Government is considering the responses and it is not known what action will be taken as a result.

13.8.6 Service

Copies of the application must be served on all parties at least 14 days before the hearing, together with a Notice of Proceedings (Form C6) showing the date for the directions appointment, and blank Acknowledgement (Form C7). The applicant must then file a Statement of Service (Form C9) at court, setting out how service was effected.

The FPR 1991 also provide that notice of the application must be given to a number of other interested people, so that they are given the chance to decide whether they want to be joined as a party. This will include anyone caring for the child, or anyone who is a party to other proceedings which affect the child.

13.8.7 Without notice applications

All s 8 orders can be made without notice. However, without notice interim orders should be made only in exceptional circumstances where it is necessary to protect the child. For example, a without notice application would be justified in a 'snatch' situation, where no order was made at the time of the divorce but a crisis arose when the parent failed to return the child to the other parent following a day's contact, or where an urgent medical problem arose and the parents were in dispute over a life-threatening decision. In *Re G (Minors) (Ex parte Interim Residence Order)* [1993] 1 FLR 910, the Court of Appeal granted an interim residence order to a father because of evidence that the mother was taking drugs and that the children needed to be removed from her care immediately.

When a without notice application is made, the full application should be filed either at the same time, or within 24 hours if the order is obtained by telephone. The application and order must be served on the respondent within 48 hours after the making of the without notice order.

13.8.8 Acknowledgement

Within 14 days of service the respondent must complete the Acknowledgement (Form C7), file it at court and serve a copy on the other party. If the applicant has filed Form C1A then the respondent may make comments on the form in response to the information given on Form C1A by the applicant.

13.8.9 The Private Law Programme

There are slight variations in detail between courts on the procedure on s 8 applications. In November 2004, the then President of the Family Division published the Private Law Programme, which provided guidance on best practice in procedure for the judiciary, courts and Cafcass. This Programme allows for local variations in procedure but seeks to promote dispute resolution at the first hearing, ie attendance of a Cafcass officer to facilitate early dispute resolution. It also seeks to promote early referrals to other resources which provide support and assistance, such as mediation. The Programme also requires effective court control, ie active case management, including early timetabling, monitoring and reviewing outcomes, and enforcing the court's orders.

13.8.10 First Appointment

The court will fix a First Directions Appointment when an application is issued. In many courts, and in accordance with the Private Law Programme, a Cafcass officer will be present to provide 'in court' conciliation and the hearing will be a Dispute Resolution Appointment. The parties will attend, and in some courts which have appropriate resources children over 9 years of age will also attend.

The task of the court at the First Appointment is to:

(a) investigate the issues;

(b) inquire into the possibility of settlement; and

(c) give directions in any case which has to proceed.

When giving directions, the court will normally consider the following issues.

13.8.10.1 A timetable for the proceedings

As a result of the 'no delay' principle, the court will want to ensure that the case proceeds as quickly as possible. By discussing the probable timing of the matter at the outset, problems and delays can be minimised.

13.8.10.2 Preparation of a welfare report by the children and family reporter

The court will often order a welfare report in contested s 8 proceedings. This will be prepared by the court's children and family reporter (who is an officer of Cafcass) and must be filed with the court at least 14 days before the hearing and made available to the parties. The reporter will have access to the court file and will interview the parties and the child, as well as anyone else who appears relevant, for example schoolteachers, the family doctor, grandparents. A written welfare report will be prepared, which will often include conclusions and recommendations as to which order should be made.

The Government's aim is, however, to reduce the number and length of Cafcass reports ordered by the courts, to free up Cafcass officers' time so that they can take on a more problem-solving role to facilitate agreement between parties.

Section 7 of the Children and Adoption Act 2006, which came into force on 1 October 2007, creates a new s 16A of the CA 1989, which requires a welfare officer to carry out a risk assessment and provide it to the court if, when carrying out his duties under Pt II of the CA 1989, he is given cause to suspect that a child is at risk of harm.

13.8.10.3   Submission of expert evidence

In some cases, expert evidence is required. The court must give its leave before any medical or psychiatric examination or other assessment of the child can take place. This is to protect the child from unnecessary and repeated assessment. The court tends to prefer to rely on the report prepared by the court's children and family reporter.

13.8.10.4   Exchange of witness statements

It is usual for the parties to file witness statements (see **13.8.11**). The court controls the time when evidence is submitted, as no document can be filed or served without the court's leave. This is to prevent the parties from filing destructive documents which could lead them to take entrenched positions.

13.8.10.5   Attendance of the child

As the child is not a party to the proceedings, a child can attend a hearing only by direction of the court. Practice is normally not to direct the child's attendance.

13.8.10.6   Next appointment

Unless the issues are resolved, at the end of every court appointment a date must be fixed for the next appointment. Normally, even if only provisionally, the court will also fix the date of the Final Hearing.

Usually a Final Directions Appointment will be timetabled to take place when any welfare report and all the evidence has been filed. This will consider what evidence can be agreed and what is in dispute, together with final arrangements for the hearing.

The parties cannot extend any time-limit ordered by the court by consent. This implements the 'no delay' philosophy and gives the court control of the litigation timetable.

13.8.11   Witness statements

All evidence must be filed at court in the form of written statements of the oral evidence which each party intends to use, together with copies of the documents which will be relied on. A witness statement must be signed and dated, and include a declaration that the maker of the statement believes it to be true and understands that it may be placed before the court (FPR 1991, r 4.17). This is similar to the Statement of Truth required by the CPR 1998 on witness statements in other types of civil proceedings.

These statements can be filed only when the court gives a direction to do this. Hearsay evidence may be included (as in other civil proceedings). So, for example, a children and family reporter in his report can include a remark made in a conversation he had with the child's schoolteacher that 'the child was always upset on the Mondays following a visit to his father'. The court can decide what weight to give to such evidence.

13.8.12 Judgment

The Final Hearing will be held in chambers before the appropriate judge. *Practice Direction (Children Cases: Time Estimates)* [1994] 1 WLR 16 says that when a hearing is expected to last one day or more, the parties must provide the court with a written time estimate. Judgment must be delivered as soon as possible after the Final Hearing. Orders must be in writing and a record of any finding of fact and the reasons for the decision will be kept on the file. A copy of the order must be served on each party and on any person with whom the child is living.

The fact that children cases are heard in private (and also that judgment is pronounced in private) was challenged as infringing the requirement to hold public hearings, contained in Article 6(1) of the European Convention on Human Rights. The challenge was unsuccessful. In *B v United Kingdom; P v United Kingdom* [2001] 2 FLR 261, the European Court of Human Rights pointed out that Article 6 is expressly stated to be subject to exceptions. In the court's view, s 8 cases, such as residence order applications, are prime examples of cases where the exclusion of the press and public may be justified in order to protect the privacy of the child and the parties and to avoid prejudicing the interests of justice. To enable the judge to gain as full and accurate a picture as possible of the advantages and disadvantages of the various residence and contact options open to the child, it was essential that the parents and other witnesses felt able to express themselves candidly on highly personal issues without fear of public curiosity or comment.

In response to concern over the privacy of CA 1989 proceedings, in July 2006 the Department for Constitutional Affairs published a consultation paper, 'Confidence and Confidentiality: Improving Transparency and Privacy in Family Courts', which includes proposals to allow the media to attend family proceedings. In June 2007 a further consultation was launched, 'Confidence and Confidentiality', which is due to close in October 2007.

It is general practice not to order costs in children cases, although it may be appropriate to do so if the parent goes beyond what is reasonable. This means unreasonableness in relation to the conduct of the litigation, rather than unreasonableness in relation to the child. In *Re G (Costs: Child Case)* [1999] 2 FLR 250, the court drew a distinction between 'hopeless' and 'unreasonable' applications. In that case, although the court considered the father's application for a residence order was hopeless, it was not in itself unreasonable. However, it is possible that the stage will be reached where the pursuit of a hopeless application becomes, in itself, unreasonable. In *Re T (A Child) (Order for Costs)* [2005] EWCA Civ 311 the court made an order for costs against a mother who, it found, was behaving unreasonably in obstructing contact.

13.8.13 Duration of s 8 orders

Section 8 orders will normally be expressed to cease to have effect when the child reaches 16 years of age (CA 1989, s 91(10)). In any event, they will end when the child reaches 18 years of age (CA 1989, s 91(11)).

The court has power in exceptional circumstances to make or extend an order beyond the child's 16th birthday (CA 1989, s 9(6)). When making a residence order in favour of a person who is not a parent or guardian, the court can order that it continue in force until the child reaches 18.

If a residence or contact order is made in favour of a parent, these orders will automatically end if the child's parents live together for a continuous period of more than six months (CA 1989, s 11(5) and (6)). The only difference between the two types of orders is that a residence order will automatically end in the circumstances only if both parents have parental responsibility.

13.9 Protection of children

This section deals with emergency situations concerning children. It covers the threatened abduction of the child, recovering a child already removed from the UK, general emergency protection of a child by a parent or other interested person and, lastly, an outline of how a local authority may protect children.

13.9.1 Abduction of children

If a child is not returned to the parent with whom he lives following an agreed visit to the other parent and abduction is suspected, a legal adviser needs to assess the situation quickly and obtain such protection as the law offers to try to ensure that the child is returned as soon as possible. A list of relevant considerations is set out at **13.9.1.1** to **13.9.1.7** below.

13.9.1.1 Has a s 8 order already been made?

If the parent with whom the child normally lives already has a residence order in his or her favour, this will contain a provision preventing the other parent removing the child from the UK without consent of the parent with the residence order or consent of the court (CA 1989, s 13(1) and see **13.3.1**). This provision can be enforced by the court by an order that the child be produced to the parent with the residence order (CA 1989, s 14; FLA 1986, s 34).

If there is no s 8 order in force, a without notice application for a residence order or prohibited steps order could be applied for and then enforced by the court.

A court has the power, in proceedings for or relating to an order under s 8, to order any person who may have information as to the child's whereabouts to disclose it to the court (FLA 1986, s 33). This could be used to force relations or friends of the abductor to disclose addresses or likely destinations.

13.9.1.2 Family Law Act 1986

If a child has been removed from the jurisdiction of the English courts to another part of the UK, for example to Scotland or Northern Ireland, this Act enables a s 8 order to be recognised and enforced by the local court. In order for this to be done, the s 8 order must first be registered with the appropriate court in the other part of the UK.

13.9.1.3 Child Abduction Act 1984

The Child Abduction Act 1984 (CAA 1984) (see **Appendix 1(D)**) contains criminal offences which will be committed if a child is removed without the appropriate consents, irrespective of whether any residence order is in force:

(a) It is an offence for a parent of a child, or any person with parental responsibility for a child, to take or send that child out of the UK without either the consent of all persons with parental responsibility, or the leave of the court (CAA 1984, s 1).

However, no offence is committed by a person in whose favour a residence order is in force who takes or sends the child out of the UK for a period of less than a month. There are also provisions in the Act, which apply where no residence order has been made, which provide a defence if the person who removes the child either reasonably believes that he has consent, or has taken all reasonable steps to obtain it.

If, following divorce, no s 8 order has been made, neither parent will be in contempt of court if they remove the child without the consent of the other under the CA 1989 as each has parental responsibility. However, neither can take the child out of the UK for any time whatsoever without committing a criminal offence under the CAA 1984, unless they obtain the appropriate consents.

(b) It is also an offence for any person, except a person with parental responsibility for a child, to take that child from any other person who has lawful control of the child without lawful authority or reasonable excuse (CAA 1984, s 2).

This will not affect married parents. However, a putative father who has not obtained parental responsibility will commit the s 2 offence, but has a defence if he can show that he had reasonable grounds for believing that he was the child's father. He will nevertheless be liable under s 1 (above) if he takes the child abroad, unless he has the mother's consent.

Difficult ethical problems can arise for a solicitor if a client informs him that he intends to abduct his child from the mother. There is a duty of confidentiality towards a client, but a solicitor cannot ignore the interests of the child and must decide which duty prevails. A solicitor in this situation should discuss the issue with the Solicitors Regulation Authority's Professional Ethics Department (see the Law Society's Family Law Protocol, para 3.4.10). It is important that a solicitor ensures that a client is made fully aware of the consequences of the crime he is proposing to commit and that the solicitor does not assist him to commit it.

13.9.1.4 'Port alert' procedure

The provisions in both the CA 1989 and the CAA 1984 may deter a potential abductor but do not contain any practical safeguards actually to prevent a determined abductor from removing the child. The 'port alert' procedure is designed physically to prevent a child from being taken abroad. The detail of this procedure is set out in *Practice Direction (Minor: Preventing Removal Abroad)* [1986] 1 WLR 475.

It is operated by the police on a 24-hour basis. If instituted, the police will liaise with immigration or security officials at ports and airports to try to find and stop the child from being taken abroad. The police have the power to arrest without warrant. There is no need for a s 8 order to have been obtained if the child is under 16, although if there is an order it should be produced to the police. The system is available for children over 16 only if, unusually, a s 8 order exists. The police will operate the port alert procedure only if they are satisfied that there is a real and imminent risk that a child will be taken out of the UK. 'Imminent' is taken to mean within 24 to 48 hours, and 'real' means that the system is not being used just as insurance.

Application should be made to a police station (preferably the applicant's local station) with full details of the grounds for applying, the child, the person likely to remove the child, the applicant, the likely destination, and the likely time of travel and port of embarcation. Any other helpful information should also be given, as well as recent photographs of the child and the abductor. If the police feel that the requirements are satisfied, they will put the child's name on a stop list which is circulated to all ports and airports. The child will remain on this list for four weeks, and will then be removed unless a further application is made.

13.9.1.5 Passports

Preventing issue of a passport

If the child does not have a passport already, it is possible for an interested party to give written notice to the Identity and Passport Service that a passport should not be issued to a child without the consent of the court, or of both parents or others (*Practice Direction (Minor: Preventing Removal Abroad)* [1986] 1 All ER 983). In *Hamilton Jones v David & Snape (A Firm)* [2003] EWHC 3147 (Ch), solicitors were found negligent in failing to re-register children with the passport agency or advising the mother to do so.

Surrender of passports

If the above provision is not applicable as the child already has a passport, an order can be obtained for the surrender of the relevant passport. This can be done only if there is in existence an order prohibiting or restricting the removal of the child from the UK. A without notice application for a residence order or a prohibited steps order may therefore need to be made. If a residence order or other s 8 order (eg a prohibited steps order) has been obtained, the court that made the order can order any person to surrender the child's passport, or any other passport which includes details of the child.

If a contact order has been made, it is possible to include a direction that the parent exercising contact must lodge his passport with his solicitor during contact visits. Care must be taken by a solicitor acting for the parent with contact in these circumstances, as if this involves giving an undertaking to the court, there will be a conflict of interest if the client subsequently requests the return of the passport in breach of any undertaking given. If the solicitor returns the passport to his client, this will be a matter of professional misconduct, as well as a contempt of court which could lead to a fine or imprisonment. If the client has given an undertaking to the court to lodge his passport with his solicitor, again the solicitor should not aid or abet his client to disobey a lawful court order (see rule 11.02 (and guidance) of the Solicitors' Code of Conduct 2007).

13.9.1.6 Recovering a child abducted abroad

If the child has been removed from the UK, the abductor will have committed a criminal offence under the CAA 1984, but this by itself will not bring about the return of the child. Provisions do exist to obtain an order from the country to which the child has been taken to return the child. The Child Abduction and Custody Act 1985 (CACA 1985) brought the provisions of the Hague Convention on International Child Abduction into force in this country. If a child is taken to a country which is a party to this Convention, it is possible to request the return of the child. This will usually be ordered if less than one year has elapsed since the removal. After this time the child will still be returned, unless settled in his new environment. The CACA 1985 also brought the provisions of the European Convention on Recognition and Enforcement of Custody Decisions into force. This should also mean that provided the country to which the child has been taken is a party to the Convention, an order can be obtained for the return of the child, although there are certain grounds on which the court in the country to which the child has been taken can decide that it is in the child's best interests to remain there.

Reference should be made to the CACA 1985 and specialist textbooks for the detail of this area.

International child abduction is a specialist area and solicitors should take specialist advice. Solicitors should discuss all such cases with the Department of Constitutional Affairs' Child Abduction Unit. A source of general advice and support for clients with problems in this area is an organisation called Reunite, the International Child Abduction Centre.

13.9.1.7   Practical advice

In considering the legal steps which can be taken in this area, the solicitor must remind the client of the practical steps that can be taken to prevent an abduction occurring. These could include notifying the child's school to ensure that the child will not be collected by the potential abductor, in serious cases refusing to allow unsupervised contact, ensuring that the child's passport is kept safe and ensuring that the telephone number of the local police station is kept to hand.

13.9.2   General protection of children

The protection a child needs may relate to a wide range of issues. It might concern a medical issue, an abortion, a proposed marriage, a change of name or religion, or protection from a violent parent. Those with parental responsibility may not be prepared to make a decision, or may have made a decision with which another interested party disagrees. In this situation, a s 8 order may be used by parents and others to obtain a court decision. In urgent cases, all s 8 orders can be obtained without notice.

The availability and flexibility of s 8 orders means that there is less need to resort to the High Court's wardship jurisdiction. However, there is no restriction on anyone (other than a local authority) making a child a ward of court. If this is done, parental responsibility will vest in the High Court. The High Court will also have the power to make any s 8 order, unless the child is also subject to a care order.

13.9.3   Protection of a child by the local authority

The CA 1989 introduced a new legal framework for care and supervision orders (see **Chapter 14**).

A care or supervision order can be applied for only by the local authority, or by the NSPCC. The effect of a care order will be to vest parental responsibility in the local authority, who will then take over responsibility for the child from his parents or other carers, including deciding where he lives. A supervision order gives someone, usually a social worker, the duty to oversee the child, who will generally remain living in his home.

The 1989 Act also introduced new orders for the emergency protection of children. These are:

(a)   emergency protection orders: these are usually obtained by the local authority to protect the child in an urgent case where, because of some neglect or abuse, it is essential to remove the child from his home immediately;

(b)   child assessment orders: these can be used by the local authority to ensure that an essential examination or other assessment of the child, for example a medical examination, can be undertaken in circumstances where the parents are unco-operative and where the local authority suspects some harm is occurring but does not have enough evidence to bring care proceedings.

13.10   Financial provision and property orders for children

The law relating to financial provision and property orders for children is complex and is scattered throughout a number of statutes. This section summarises and cross-refers the main provisions, as well as dealing with the financial provisions contained in the CA 1989.

The following jurisdictions are relevant:

(a)   maintenance under the CSA 1991;

(b)   maintenance and property orders in matrimonial proceedings under the MCA 1973;

(c)   maintenance and lump sums during marriage under the DPMCA 1978;

(d)   financial relief under the CA 1989.

13.10.1   Maintenance under the Child Support Act 1991

The maintenance of most children is currently dealt with by the Child Support Agency using the statutory formula. The CSA 1991 has ousted the court's jurisdiction to make maintenance orders in the majority of cases (see **Chapter 7**).

The Agency will have jurisdiction whether the parents are married or unmarried, but can make an order only if the parents are no longer living together. Orders can be made in favour of children under 16 years of age, and those under 19 years of age who are in full-time education. The Agency does not have jurisdiction to deal with step-children or children over 19 years still in full-time education, and in these cases application will have to be made to the courts to determine maintenance. Other situations where the courts can still be used include payment of school fees and, in wealthy families, when an amount exceeding the maximum figure payable by the Agency's calculation is sought, and also where the child lives abroad.

13.10.2   Maintenance and property orders in matrimonial proceedings

If a parent is involved in divorce, judicial separation or nullity proceedings, he could apply for a lump sum or property adjustment order for a child of the family as part of these proceedings (see **Chapter 4**). However, in practice, unless the family is wealthy, relatively few orders of this type are made in favour of children.

Apart from the situations mentioned above (see **13.10.1**), maintenance will generally be dealt with by the Child Support Agency.

13.10.3 Maintenance and lump sums during marriage

A married parent can apply during marriage for a maintenance order and a lump sum order of up to £1,000 for a child of the family from the other parent. This can be done using the DPMCA 1978 in the family proceedings court (see **4.9.2**), or s 27 of the MCA 1973 in the county court (see **4.9.1**). However, in most cases, maintenance will be dealt with by the Child Support Agency under the CSA 1991 as the courts will have no jurisdiction.

13.10.4 Financial relief under the Children Act 1989

Section 15 of and Sch 1 to the CA 1989 enable a parent (for these purposes, 'parent' includes an unmarried parent, a parent with whom the child does not reside (*Re S (Child: Financial Provision)* [2004] EWCA Civ 1685), a step-parent and a civil partner), guardian, anyone with a residence order in their favour or a child to apply for the following orders against one or both parents of a child:

(a)   periodical payments to the applicant for the benefit of the child, or to the child direct;

(b)   lump sum to the applicant for the benefit of the child, or to the child direct;

(c)   settlement of property for the benefit of the child;

(d)   transfer of property to the applicant for the benefit of the child or to the child direct.

Application can be made to the High Court or county court for any of the orders. An application to the family proceedings court can be made only for periodical payments and/or a lump sum up to £1,000.

If the child lives abroad with one parent and the other parent lives in the UK, the court can make orders for periodical payments only.

There is no limit to the amount of orders for periodical payments or lump sum orders, but the court can make only one order for either a settlement of property or a transfer of property for the child. In *Phillips v Peace* [2004] EWHC 3180 (Fam), where a settlement of property order had already been made for the child, the mother, who wanted capital to buy a larger home, was precluded from applying for a further settlement of property or property adjustment order. She therefore applied for a lump sum to fund the rehousing, on conditions including that it was to be repaid to the father when the child was older. The court stated that a lump sum was not intended to revert to the payer and that the proposals would produce an effect so close to a settlement that it would be tantamount to varying the settlement or ordering a second settlement, which it could not do.

The principles which the court must use in deciding whether to make an order are broadly similar to s 25 of the MCA 1973. This means that the child's welfare is not paramount when deciding financial provision (*K v K (Minors: Property Transfer)* [1992] 2 FLR 220). In very wealthy families, standard of living is to be considered as part of all the circumstances even though it is not included specifically in the checklist in Sch 1 (*F v G (Child: Financial Provision)* [2005] 1 FLR 261).

The provisions in the CA 1989 are rarely needed by married parents as they will normally apply only on marriage breakdown, when the MCA 1973 can be used for lump sums and property adjustment orders, and the CSA 1991 will be used for maintenance. However, the CA 1989 can be very important to an unmarried parent as it can be used to obtain property orders for the benefit of the child, which could secure the right for the child and the caring parent to occupy the home (*J v J (A Minor: Property Transfer)* [1993] 2 FLR 56). In *Re P (Child Financial Provision)* [2003] EWCA Civ 837, which involved a very wealthy father, the Court of Appeal gave guidance on how applications involving very wealthy parents should be dealt with. The Court said that the starting point should be to determine the home that needed to be provided, and then to decide the lump sum needed, usually to furnish the home and to provide a car. Then the court should determine what budget the carer required and, in assessing this, should recognise the responsibility and often the sacrifice of the carer. The Court of Appeal said that the budget should reflect the social and financial position of the carer and the absent parent.

The order must be for the benefit of the child: contrast *W v J (Child: Variation of Financial Provision)* [2003] EWHC 2657 (Fam), where the court held that the mother's request to vary periodical payments by £146,000 per annum to fund future litigation against the father over the children was not for the benefit of the child, with *Re S (Child: Financial Provision)* [2004] EWCA Civ 1685, where the court was asked to make financial orders in favour of a mother whose child had been wrongfully retained by the father in Sudan after a contact visit. The money was to be used by the mother to travel to the Sudan to have contact with the child and to enforce the child's return through the Sudanese courts. The Court of Appeal did not finally decide the matter, but indicated that the courts should give the term 'for the benefit of the child' a wide construction.

The court can make any s 8 order it considers necessary in the financial proceedings.

13.10.5   Summary of financial orders for children

13.10.5.1   Parties divorcing

(a)   CSA 1991 for maintenance;

(b)   MCA 1973 for lump sum/property adjustment order.

13.10.5.2   Parties staying married

(a)   CSA 1991 for maintenance;

(b)   DPMCA 1978 for £1,000 maximum lump sum;

(c)   MCA 1973, s 27 for lump sum;

(d)   CA 1989 for lump sum/property adjustment order.

13.10.5.3   Parties never married

(a)   CSA 1991 for maintenance;

(b)   CA 1989 for lump sum/property adjustment order.

13.11   Chapter summary

(1)   Issues concerning children are dealt with under the CA 1989.

(2)   Married parents have joint parental responsibility for their child. An unmarried mother has parental responsibility but an unmarried father does not, although he can acquire it in various ways.

(3)   The court can make s 8 orders. These are:

(a)   residence orders;

(b)   contact orders;

      (c)   prohibited steps orders; and

      (d)   specific issue orders.

(4)   When making any order, the court must consider:

      (a)   the welfare principle;

      (b)   the 'no order' presumption; and

      (c)   the principle of avoiding delay.

(5)   When applying the welfare principle, the court must pay attention to the factors in s 1(3):

      (a)   the ascertainable wishes and feelings of the child;

      (b)   the child's physical, emotional and educational needs;

      (c)   the likely effect on the child of any change in circumstances;

      (d)   the child's age, sex, background, etc;

      (e)   any harm the child has suffered/may suffer;

      (f)   the capability of the parents (and other relevant people) to care for the child; and

      (g)   the range of powers available to the court.

(6)   A checklist for the procedure for a contested s 8 application is set out below.

(7)   There are various procedures available to try to prevent the abduction of a child. The CAA 1984 is also relevant.

(8)   Financial provision for children can be obtained under several different jurisdictions, including the CA 1989.

CHECKLIST FOR THE PROCEDURE FOR A CONTESTED S 8 APPLICATION IN THE COUNTY COURT

OBTAIN LEGAL REPRESENTATION IF RELEVANT

OBTAIN LEAVE OF THE COURT IF NECESSARY

A FILES AT COURT:
(i)   Application (Form C1 or Form C2 (existing family proceedings) and Form C1A (if harm alleged) in duplicate
(ii)   Fee [Legal Representation (LR) Certificate]
[(iii) Notice of Acting (if necessary)]

A SERVES ON R:
(i)   Copy Application (and Form C1A if filed)
(ii)   Notice of Proceedings (Form C6)   → Date for 1st hearing.
(iii) Blank Acknowledgement (Form C7)
[(iv) Notice of Issue of LR Certificate]
[(v)   Copy Notice of Acting (if necessary)]
[Give at least 14 days' notice of first hearing]   → By post

A FILES AT COURT:
Statement of Service (Form C9)

R FILES AND SERVES:
Completed Acknowledgement [within 14 days] and Form C1A (if necessary)

ATTEND FIRST HEARING (directions hearing and/or Dispute Resolution Appointment):
Conciliation and directions
[Court fixes next hearing date]

PREPARE FOR HEARING
(i)   Witness statements filed and exchanged
(ii)   Welfare report filed at least 14 days before hearing
(iii) Written estimate of length of hearing if necessary

FINAL DIRECTIONS APPOINTMENT

ATTEND HEARING:
Before a judge in chambers

ORDER MADE:
Served on each party

Note: The procedure followed in the High Court or family proceedings court is broadly similar.

Chapter 14

Children: Public Law

14.1 Introduction

The CA 1989 introduced fundamental changes to child law, and this chapter considers those changes in relation to public law proceedings. The Act followed a number of reviews and reports, notably the *Cleveland Report*, which expressed concern that the local authority had acted too precipitately in removing children from their parents. Paradoxically, in other cases, the concern was that the authority had not acted promptly enough. One of the aims of the Act was to have a more balanced approach to the protection of children. Central to this is the concept of partnership: partnership between the local authority and parents, and co-operation between all the agencies relevant to the child's well-being. To this end, the Act is supplemented by guidance in a document called 'Working Together to Safeguard Children: A guide to inter-agency working to safeguard and promote the welfare of children' (TSO, 2006) (together with various regulations). Although 'Working Together to Safeguard Children' does not have the force of statute, the guidance must be complied with and can be departed from only if good reasons can be shown.

There is a Protocol for Judicial Case Management in Public Law Children Act Cases, which came into force on 1 November 2003. The main objective of this Protocol was to tackle delay in public law cases. Before this, an average case lasted about one year. Under the Protocol, cases should now be dealt with within 40 weeks. To achieve this, the Protocol sets out every step in the process to be taken by the court and every party involved, with relevant time limits. It also prescribes standard forms and checklists for the parties to use. At the time of writing, a revised Protocol for Judicial Case Management in Public Law Children Act Cases ('The Public Law Outline') is being consulted upon and piloted in 10 centres around the country, with a view to it being finalised by the end of 2007 for implementation in April 2008.

14.2   Local authority support for children and families (CA 1989, Pt III)

14.2.1   Introduction

The Act imposes responsibilities on local authorities to provide certain services, in particular for 'children in need' (see **14.2.3**). The local authority has to make an initial assessment as to whether a child is a 'child in need'. The local authority then has to decide how to discharge its responsibilities to that child, either by providing services directly or by facilitating their provision by, for example, voluntary organisations.

14.2.2   Prevention of harm

Every local authority must take reasonable steps through the provision of services to prevent children in its area suffering ill-treatment or neglect. There is also a related duty to take reasonable steps to reduce the need to bring care or supervision proceedings.

14.2.3   Children in need

14.2.3.1   Definition of a child 'in need'

A child is to be taken to be 'in need' if:

(a)   he is unlikely to achieve or maintain, or to have the opportunity of achieving or maintaining, a reasonable standard of health or development without the provision for him of services by a local authority; or

(b)   his health or development is likely to be significantly impaired, or further impaired, without the provision for him of such services; or

(c)   he is disabled (s 17(10)).

The definition therefore includes not just those children who are suffering, but also those who may be prejudiced in the future, if assistance is not provided for them.

'Development' is defined as physical, intellectual, emotional, social or behavioural development; 'health' as meaning physical or mental health; and 'disabled' as blind, deaf, dumb, suffering from mental disorder, or substantially and permanently handicapped by illness, injury or congenital deformity.

The definition of 'in need' is therefore very wide and reflects the Act's emphasis on local authorities taking preventative action through the provision of support services to families and commencing court proceedings only where absolutely necessary to protect the child.

The linking of 'need' to the provision of 'services' means that an authority could not identify a child as 'in need' and at the same time refuse to provide any service to meet that need. However, although the authority is obliged to provide some service to meet the child's needs, it has a discretion in deciding which service and at what level. In *R v London Borough of Barnet, ex p B* [1994] 1 FLR 592, the court held that the obligations placed on a local authority to provide services must be subject to the ability to do so within its own budget restraints.

14.2.3.2   Duty to children in need (s 17)

It is the duty of every local authority:

(a)   to safeguard and promote the welfare of children within its area who are in need; and

(b)   so far as is consistent with that duty, to promote the upbringing of such children by their families,

by providing a range and level of services appropriate to those children's needs.

Any service provided by the authority to the child can also be provided to the child's family or any member of the family, if it is provided with a view to safeguarding or promoting the child's welfare. 'Family' is widely defined to include any person with parental responsibility and any other person with whom the child is living.

A local authority could provide a range of services to help the parents cope with a child with disabilities, for example: a home help, day-care provision (whether for the disabled child or another child in the household) and a short-term placement for the child to relieve the carers.

In support of the general duty under s 17 to provide services, local authorities are given a number of specific duties, such as to provide day-care services for pre-school children in need and to provide family centres. The definition of a family centre in Sch 2, para 9 is a centre where family members may attend for, among other things, advice, guidance or counselling and may be provided with accommodation while receiving advice, guidance or counselling.

14.2.4   Provision of accommodation (s 20)

A local authority must provide accommodation for any child in need within its area if there is no person who has parental responsibility for him, he is lost or abandoned, or the person who has been caring for him is prevented (whether or not permanently and for whatever reason) from providing him with suitable accommodation or care.

14.2.4.1   Limits on providing accommodation

A local authority may not provide accommodation if anyone with parental responsibility, who is willing and able to provide accommodation, objects. This means that if both parents have parental responsibility and one places the child in accommodation, the other parent can remove him.

The right of a person with parental responsibility to object does not apply if a person or persons with a residence order in their favour agree to the child being accommodated.

Also, the right of a person with parental responsibility to remove a child in these circumstances does not apply where the child is aged 16 or over and the child agrees to being accommodated by the local authority (s 20(11)). This is a reflection of the principle of allowing the mature child more say in important decisions, such as where he or she should live.

14.2.4.2   Preventing removal from accommodation

The local authority should ensure that all those with parental responsibility are involved in the initial negotiations and agree on the provision of accommodation to avoid any subsequent problems. However, it is always open to a person with parental responsibility to remove the child at any time without notice.

If there is a risk that one parent may seek to remove the child, the authority may suggest that the other seeks a residence order (which may be granted without notice) to prevent the removal (a local authority cannot itself apply for a residence order (s 9(2)).

If that is not appropriate, or if both parents are seeking the child's return which the authority does not consider to be in the child's best interests, it could apply for an emergency protection order or interim care order.

14.2.5 Children 'looked after' by a local authority

Children who are in care (pursuant to a care order) or provided with accommodation (for a continuous period of more than 24 hours) are 'looked after' by the authority. This also includes children accommodated by a local authority under an emergency protection order, or in police protection (see **14.10**).

When an authority is 'looking after' a child, it is acting in a parental role. It is under a duty to safeguard and promote the child's welfare and to make use of services available for children (ie under Pt III).

It is central to the philosophy of the Act that an authority should seek to act in consultation (and, it is hoped, agreement) with all interested parties. Before making any decision with regard to the child it must find out, if reasonably practicable, the wishes and feelings of the child, parents and other relevant persons. Any decision should give due consideration to those wishes and to the child's religious persuasion, racial origin, and cultural and linguistic background.

Where the child is accommodated is of crucial importance. To foster the prospect of rehabilitation, the authority should first consider whether it is practicable for the child to live with a member of his family or other persons connected with him. If it is not practicable, consideration should be given to placing the child near to the family home.

14.2.6 Significance of the provision of services

As already seen, so far as it is consistent with the child's welfare, the local authority's duty under s 17 is to promote the upbringing of the child by his family through the provision of services. The authority should not initiate care proceedings unless there is clear evidence that the provision of services has failed to meet the child's needs, or is unlikely to be successful in meeting them.

In most cases, it is better to advise the parents to co-operate and throw the onus onto the local authority to show it has done everything reasonable to assist the child and his parents.

Accordingly, in appropriate circumstances, a local authority should be required to explain:

(a)   what steps it took to identify the child as being in need;

(b)   what its plans are if a care order is made; in particular, what services it would then provide which it could not provide without a court order;

(c)   what evidence there is that what the authority is seeking to achieve by means of a court order could not be more satisfactorily achieved by the provision of appropriate services, with the child remaining at home.

In *Re K (Supervision Orders)* [1999] 2 FLR 303, the court said it was wrong to make a supervision order where the duties imposed on the local authority (under Pt III) would sufficiently meet the child's needs.

14.2.7 Challenging the local authority

There is no provision in Pt III for compelling a local authority to provide services. Neither can a specific issue order be used for that purpose. The courts have said that a local authority's powers and duties under Pt III should not be subject to judicial scrutiny except by way of judicial review (*Re J (Specific Issue Order: Leave to Apply)* [1995] 1 FLR 669).

14.2.7.1 Complaints procedure (s 26)

Every local authority must establish a procedure for considering representations about the discharge of any of its functions under Pt III.

If dissatisfied with the local authority's response, the complainant can require that the matter is referred to a review panel which must then make a recommendation. Although the ultimate decision remains with the local authority, if it ignores the panel's findings, or fails to give satisfactory reasons for not implementing the recommendation, its actions may be subject to judicial review. In *Re T (Accommodation by Local Authority)* [1995] 1 FLR 159, the court quashed the refusal of the authority to ratify the recommendation of the panel on the basis that it had failed to take into account the correct considerations in deciding that the child's welfare would not be seriously prejudiced by not being accommodated.

14.2.7.2 Judicial review

Only in exceptional circumstances will the court consider an application for judicial review where the statutory right of appeal under the complaints procedure has not been exhausted (*R v London Borough of Brent, ex p S* [1994] 1 FLR 203). Even if the statutory procedures have been exhausted, judicial review is unlikely to be successful if there has been a genuine and fair consultation. In *R v London Borough of Barnet, ex p B* [1994] 1 FLR 592, the court said that it is essentially a matter for the local authority, not the court, to decide what consideration and what weight should be given to the circumstances of any given child. In *Re T (Judicial Review: Local Authority Decisions Concerning Child in Need)* [2003] EWHC 2515 (Admin), the court confirmed it could only direct the local authority to reconsider the services it should provide by quashing the local authority's decision and directing reconsideration, it could not direct the local authority to take a particular course.

In a recent case, *R (CD) v Isle of Anglesey County Council* [2005] 1 FLR 59, the court found that the local authority's care plan for a 15-year-old girl with cerebral palsy who was being accommodated under s 20 of CA 1989 was unlawful, as it failed to provide services appropriate to her needs and did not give due consideration to her wishes.

14.3 Preventing neglect or abuse

A central feature of the provisions for the protection of children is that this should be done in partnership with the family and in full consultation with other relevant agencies and professionals. Any assessment of the child should, wherever possible, be done following consultation and with the family's co-operation. The authority should seek to agree any protection plan for the child with the parents.

14.3.1 Court-directed investigation (s 37)

The court has no power to direct a local authority to commence proceedings for a care or supervision order. However, if in any 'family proceedings' where the court is considering the child's welfare, it appears to the court that it may be appropriate for a care or supervision order to be made, the court may direct the authority to investigate the child's circumstances. In deciding whether to make a direction under s 37 (see **Appendix 1(E)**), the child's welfare must be the court's paramount consideration.

'Family proceedings' include divorce, judicial separation, financial relief applications, domestic abuse applications under FLA 1996 and all Children Act proceedings other than emergency provisions (see **14.11.1**).

When undertaking the investigation, the local authority must consider whether it should apply for a care or supervision order, provide services or assistance for the child or his family, or whether to take any other action with respect to the child. If the authority decides not to apply for a care or supervision order it must inform the court within eight weeks (unless otherwise directed) of its reasons and other action, if any, it intends to take.

When directing an investigation, as an exception to the general rule, the court may make an interim care or supervision order without a formal application if satisfied as to the criteria in s 38 (see **14.9**). It would be usual in such circumstances for a children's guardian to be appointed for the child.

14.3.2 Local authority investigation (s 47)

When a child is subject to an emergency protection order, in police protection or where the authority suspects the child is suffering or likely to suffer significant harm, it must investigate the child's circumstances. (See **Appendix 1(E)**.)

The enquiries should involve a detailed assessment of the needs of the child and his family, and may lead to the provision of services under Pt III, including an offer of accommodation. Alternatively, the authority may decide it is necessary to commence proceedings for a care or supervision order (or an emergency protection order if the child's immediate protection is in issue).

As part of its investigation, the authority should normally see the child. If access is refused, or it is denied information as to the child's whereabouts, the authority *must* make an application to the court unless satisfied that his welfare can be safeguarded without such an order (s 47(6)).

14.3.3 Child protection conferences

Where, following an investigation, the local authority considers that there might be a risk of significant harm to the child, the local authority will consider convening a child protection conference.

This is a formal meeting attended by representatives from all the agencies concerned with the child's welfare, ie social services, police, health and education, and often the child's parents. Its purpose is to gather together and evaluate all the relevant information about the child and plan any immediate action which may be necessary to protect the child.

Parents should be encouraged to attend and may bring a solicitor or other person to support them. Certainly, in the case of *R v Cornwall County Council, ex p LH* [2000] 1 FLR 234, the court made it clear that it would be unlawful for a local authority to have a policy of a blanket refusal of attendance of solicitors.

The conference has to decide whether the child should be the subject of a child protection plan. It must do this if it decides that the child is at continuing risk of significant harm under the category of either physical, emotional or sexual abuse, or neglect. If the conference decides that a child protection plan is necessary, it must also formulate an outline child protection plan.

If a child becomes the subject of a child protection plan, this must be reviewed after three months and thereafter at no more than six-monthly intervals at child protection review conferences.

Even if the decision is that the child does not require a child protection plan, the conference may decide what further support and services may be offered to the family.

14.3.4 Recording that a child is the subject of a child protection plan

All local authorities should record that a child is the subject of a child protection plan. This record is known as the child protection register and makes agencies and professionals aware of children judged to be at risk of significant harm. This enables legitimate enquirers such as police and health professionals to obtain information about children they have concerns about.

The 2006 edition of 'Working Together to Safeguard Children' requires local authorities to record this information electronically on a nationally integrated register, but these provisions are not fully in force at the time of writing.

The act of registration itself provides no protection and must always be supported by a child protection plan.

14.4 Care and supervision orders (CA 1989, Pt IV)

A care order is an order placing the child in the care of a designated local authority.

A supervision order is an order putting the child under the supervision of a designated local authority, or of a probation officer.

14.4.1 Application

An application for a care order or supervision order can be made only by a local authority (or NSPCC). The court has no power to require a local authority to commence proceedings, nor can it make an order unless there has been an application (*Nottinghamshire County Council v P* [1993] 1 FLR 115).

14.4.2 Grounds for a care or supervision order (s 31)

A court may make a care order or supervision order in respect of a child under 17 only if it is satisfied that:

(a) the child concerned is suffering, or is likely to suffer, significant harm; and

(b) the harm or likelihood of harm is attributable to –

    (i) the care given to the child, or likely to be given to him if the order were not made, not being what it would be reasonable to expect a parent to give to him; or

    (ii) the child's being beyond parental control.

These conditions have become known as the 'threshold criteria', because they are not in themselves grounds for making a care or supervision order but the minimum circumstances which must be found before the court could be justified in making such an order.

Accordingly, in considering an application, the court must approach the matter in two distinct stages. First, it must establish whether the threshold criteria are satisfied and, secondly, if the criteria are satisfied, whether an order should be made and, if so, what type of order, bearing in mind the welfare principle (see

13.4). Note, however, that the court has power to make a s 8 order (eg a residence order) whether or not the threshold criteria are satisfied (see 13.3).

14.4.3 Interpreting the criteria

14.4.3.1 Significant harm

The central concept is whether there is harm which is significant. 'Harm' is defined as ill-treatment, or the impairment of health or development, including, for example, impairment suffered from seeing or hearing the ill-treatment of another. These terms are further defined:

(a) 'ill-treatment' includes sexual abuse and forms of ill-treatment which are not physical;

(b) 'health' means physical or mental health;

(c) 'development' covers physical, intellectual, emotional, social or behavioural development.

Where the question of whether the harm suffered by a child is significant turns on the child's health or development, it is necessary to compare his health or development with what could reasonably be expected of a similar child (s 31(10)). In *Re O (A Minor) (Care Order: Education: Procedure)* [1992] 2 FLR 7, it was held that, in relation to a truant child, the comparison should be made with a child attending school rather than one who was not. Where the child has learning difficulties or medical problems it would seem appropriate to compare with a child suffering similar difficulties.

The court must be satisfied that the child is suffering, or is likely to suffer harm.

14.4.3.2 'Is suffering'

In *Re M (A Minor) (Care Order: Threshold Conditions)* [1994] 2 FLR 577, the House of Lords held that the relevant date for ascertaining whether the child is suffering significant harm is either at the hearing of the application for a care or supervision order, or the date on which the local authority initiated 'protective arrangements' for the child, provided there has been no lapse in those arrangements before the hearing of the application. Protective arrangements could, for example, be an emergency protection order, an interim care order or being 'looked after' by the local authority. Accordingly, the court can find that the child is suffering significant harm at the date of the hearing, or alternatively, looking backwards, was so suffering when steps were taken to protect the child, provided these steps have continued in place until the hearing.

14.4.3.3 'Is likely to suffer'

This allows the court to consider whether a child is likely to suffer significant harm in the future, and would enable the court to protect a child where, for example, an acknowledged abuser returns to the household, or where another child has suffered in the same family.

In *Re H and R (Child Sexual Abuse: Standard of Proof)* [1996] 1 FLR 80, the court stated that in assessing the evidence, the standard of proof is the balance of probabilities. However, when assessing the probabilities, it should bear in mind that the more serious the allegation, the less likely it is that the event occurred and therefore the stronger the evidence needed before the court could conclude that the allegation was established. In other words, the inherent probability or improbability of the alleged act or event was itself a relevant factor when weighing the probabilities.

The court also held that 'likely to suffer' meant 'a real possibility, a possibility that cannot sensibly be ignored having regard to the nature and gravity of the feared harm in the particular case'.

The approach which should therefore be adopted is that, first, the local authority must prove the disputed facts on the balance of probabilities. Secondly, on the strength of such facts as are proved, the authority must ask: is there a real possibility that future significant harm will occur?

14.4.3.4   Causation of the harm

A finding of significant harm or its likelihood is not sufficient. There must be a link between that finding and either the standard of parental care, or the child being beyond parental control.

The standard of care against which parental care is judged is not what it would be reasonable to expect *this* parent to give, but what a hypothetical reasonable parent would give to meet the child's needs. Accordingly, the fact that the parents have their own particular problems (eg low intelligence, addiction, mental or physical disability) does not justify them in providing a lower standard of care.

Where the care of the child is shared between a number of individuals and the child has suffered serious harm through lack of proper care, there is no need to prove that it was due to a failure by one or more indentified individuals before the court can make a care order. See *Lancashire County Council v B* [2000] 1 FLR 583, where a baby had suffered non-accidental head injuries. The House of Lords held that the threshold criteria were met (and a care order was made) even though it was not possible to make a definitive finding of fact on whether the injuries were caused by the parents or the child minder. The court acknowledged that this might mean that innocent parents might face the possibility of losing their child, but held that the factor which outweighed all others was the prospect that any unidentified, and unidentifiable, carers might inflict further damage on the child.

In *CL v East Riding Yorkshire Council and Others* [2006] EWCA Civ 49, injuries were caused to a child whilst in the care of both parents, which could not be proved to be non-accidental. The Court of Appeal said that if non-accidental injury cannot be proved then the court should not use that injury as a basis for submitting that the threshold criteria are established in relation to that injury and that one or both of the parents are responsible. But the court is allowed to use the parents' behaviour in failing to ensure the child received immediate medical treatment and lying over how the injury occurred, as a basis for reaching the conclusion that a child is likely to suffer significant harm.

14.4.3.5   Concurrent applications

Where there has been an application for a care order, the court may be faced with a competing application for a residence order. Before considering the merits of making a residence order, the court should decide whether the criteria for a care order are satisfied, and therefore whether the full range of orders is available to the court (see **14.4.5** and *Re M* (at **14.4.3.2**)).

14.4.4   Welfare principle (s 1)

If the court is satisfied that the threshold criteria are met, it must then decide what order, if any, to make. In doing so, it must apply the principle contained in s 1 (that the welfare of the child is the paramount consideration and that delaying a decision is likely to prejudice the child: see **13.4**), consider the checklist (see **13.5**) and not make an order unless it considers that doing so would be better for the child than making no order at all (see **13.6**).

14.4.5   Orders available to the court

Even if the threshold criteria are satisfied and the court considers that it is in the child's interests to make an order, as applications under Pt IV are 'family proceedings' it is not merely a question of whether to make a care or supervision order.

Under s 1(3)(g), the court is required to have regard to the range of orders available to it. On hearing an application for a care or supervision order, the court may make, amongst others:

(a)   a care order *or* supervision order if the threshold criteria are satisfied;

(b)   a residence or other s 8 order, whether or not the criteria are satisfied, (however, a residence or contact order cannot be made in favour of a local authority);

(c)   a s 8 order in combination with a supervision order if the criteria are satisfied;

(d)   a family assistance order under s 16, with the agreement of all the persons (other than the child) named in the order, whether or not the criteria are satisfied.

14.4.6   Care plans

In the application for a care order, the authority should outline what plans it has if a care order is made.

Guidelines on the structure, content and format of care plans for use in court proceedings are set out in Local Authority Circular LAC (99) 29 (12 August 1999) 'Care Plans and Care Proceedings under the Children Act 1989'.

Examples of some of the typical matters to be covered in the care plan are:

(a)   the child's identified needs (including needs arising from race, culture, religion or language, special education or health needs) and how those needs might be met;

(b)   the aim of the plan and the time-scale;

(c)   the proposed placement (type and details) and a contingency plan if the placement breaks down;

(d)   other services to be provided to the child and/or the family;

(e)   arrangements for contact and reunification; and

(f)   the extent to which the wishes of the child, his or her parents and anyone else relevant have been obtained and acted upon, or the reasons why such wishes have been discounted.

Section 31A of the CA 1989 requires the local authority to prepare a care plan in every case in which it seeks a care order. The court will not be able to make a care order until it has considered such a 's 31A care plan'.

Any care plan is carefully scrutinised by the court. If it is not satisfied about material aspects of the care plan (eg where it is proposed to place the child with identified foster-parents, failure to give details as to the foster-parents and the proposed placement) it may refuse to make a care order, or adjourn and invite the local authority to reconsider its care plan (*Re S (Children) and W (A Child)* [2007] EWCA Civ 232). Alternatively, it seems that the court may choose to make an interim order instead, until satisfied about the details of the care plan (*Re W and B, Re W (Care Plan)* [2001] EWCA Civ 757, [2001] 2 FLR 582).

Before making a care order the court must also consider the authority's arrangements for contact and invite the parties to comment (s 34(11)).

14.4.7 Effect of a care order

The order remains in force until the child reaches 18, unless it is brought to an end earlier.

The local authority must receive the child into its care and provide accommodation and maintain the child for the duration of the order.

The care order gives the local authority parental responsibility jointly with any other holder. However, it is not an equal partnership. The authority has the power to determine the extent to which a parent may exercise parental responsibility, provided it is necessary to do so in the child's welfare. However, before making any decision, the authority should take into account the wishes and feelings of the child and parents.

While a care order is in force, as with a residence order, no person may change the child's surname without the written consent of every person with parental responsibility, or leave of the court. In addition, the child may not be removed from the UK without similar consent or leave. This does not prevent the authority arranging for the child's temporary removal for a period of less than one month.

Most other court orders are incompatible with a care order and, accordingly, the making of a care order automatically discharges any s 8 order (but not a s 4 parental responsibility order). Interestingly, however, the fact that the local authority has a care order in relation to a child does not mean that it can prevent the mother from entering into a parental responsibility agreement with the father (*Re X (Parental Responsibility Agreement: Children in Care)* [2000] 1 FLR 517).

On the making of a final care order, the court is effectively handing over responsibility for the child to the local authority. The court cannot impose any conditions on the local authority, nor seek to keep the implementation of the care plan by the local authority under review. This has meant that the local authority can either change the care plan, or simply fail to deliver aspects of the plan without being challenged. There was a significant, but ultimately unsuccessful, challenge to this position using Articles 6 and 8 of the European Convention on Human Rights in *Re S (Minors) (Care Order: Implementation of Care Plan); Re W (Minors) (Care Order: Adequacy of Care Plan)* [2002] UKHL 10, [2002] 1 FLR 815, where the local authority had promised support and therapy for the mother, leading to rehabilitation with the children. This support was not provided, mostly due to a funding crisis at the local authority. The House of Lords stressed the pressing need for the Government to consider whether some court supervision might improve the quality of child care provided by local authorities.

Following this, the Adoption and Children Act 2002 amended s 26 of the CA 1989 and, since 2004, local authorities are required to appoint an Independent Reviewing Officer (IRO) in connection with each child subject to a care order. The care plans for these children must be kept under review, and the IRO must monitor the local authority's performance, make sure the child's views are understood and taken into account, ensure that any matters of concern are brought to the attention of an appropriately senior member of the local authority and, in necessary cases, refer the matter to Cafcass, who will have the power to bring the case back to court for directions. So far, IROs have not made any significant use of this referral system.

14.5 Contact (s 34)

Regular contact with parents and other relatives can be important in enabling the child to adjust to his new environment, and is essential if there is to be a successful rehabilitation with the family.

Section 34 (see **Appendix 1(E)**) is a self-contained section and provides a completely different structure from private law proceedings. Any s 8 contact order is discharged upon the making of a care order.

14.5.1 Initial considerations

Before making a care order, including an interim order, the court must consider the local authority's arrangements for contact and invite the parties to comment.

As contact is so important for a child, the local authority should, if possible, place the child with a member of his family or, if that is not appropriate, in accommodation near to the child's home. The local authority may also give assistance in travel and other expenses incurred in visiting the child to any person to whom there is a duty to promote contact.

14.5.2 Local authority duties

There is a general duty to promote contact between a child 'looked after' and his parents, others with parental responsibility and relatives, friends and other persons connected with him, unless it is not reasonably practicable or consistent with the child's welfare.

By s 34(1), the authority is also under a *positive* duty to allow a child in care reasonable contact with his parents (including a father without parental responsibility) and any person with whom the child previously lived by virtue of a court order, for example a residence order. The courts have said that reasonable contact is not the same as contact at the discretion of the local authority. 'Reasonable' means contact which is agreed, or, in the absence of agreement, contact which the authority can demonstrate is objectively reasonable.

14.5.3 Application to the court

Any person mentioned in s 34(1), for example parents, can apply as of right to be allowed contact with the child. As there is a presumption of reasonable contact in this case, usually contact will be by agreement. It would be necessary for the parents to apply only if they were dissatisfied with the level of contact offered.

In *Re G (Domestic Violence: Direct Contact)* [2000] 2 FLR 865 the court stated that *Re L (Contact: Domestic Violence)* [2000] 2 FLR 334 (see **13.3.2**) applied equally in public law cases when parents were applying for contact with their child, and made an order allowing the local authority to terminate direct contact.

Any other person, for example grandparents, can apply with leave. On an application for leave the court should apply the criteria set out in s 10(9) (*Re M (Care: Contact: Grandmother's Application for Leave)* [1995] 2 FLR 86). In particular, it should consider the nature of the contact sought, the connection of the applicant to the child, the risk of harm to the child and the wishes of the local authority and the parents.

A child in care has a right to apply for contact under s 34 with any named person. However, where contact is sought in relation to another child then, unless the local authority is opposing contact, the application should be under s 8 (requiring leave) rather than s 34, and it is the respondent child's welfare which is paramount (*Re F (Contact: Child in Care)* [1995] 1 FLR 510).

14.5.4 Refusal of contact

Where an application for a contact order under s 34 is refused, no further application can be made by the applicant for six months, without leave. Furthermore, on disposing of *any* application for an order, the court may direct that no application for any specified order may be made by a person without leave (s 91(14)). Such a direction would be made only in exceptional circumstances (*F v Kent County Council and Others* [1993] 1 FLR 432). Although the most likely reason for granting a restriction is where the applicant has made repeated and unreasonable applications with no hope of success, the court could make such an order, in the absence of repeated applications, if the welfare of the child requires it. In *Re M (Section 91(14) Order)* [1999] 2 FLR 553, the court imposed a restriction because it considered that the children urgently needed to settle down and make a permanent home away from their mother, and that a premature application by her could disrupt them and hinder their permanent placement. Such a restriction is unlikely to infringe the Human Rights Act 1998, as it does not restrict access to the courts but just imposes a requirement for leave.

The local authority cannot refuse contact with persons to whom the presumption of reasonable contact applies. However, the authority can apply to the court for an order authorising it to refuse contact between the child and any person mentioned in s 34(1). In an emergency, the local authority can temporarily suspend contact without an order, for a period of not more than seven days.

Although the court can authorise the refusal of contact by a local authority, it cannot, on the other hand, use its jurisdiction under s 34 to prohibit the local authority from allowing parental contact which the local authority considers to be advantageous to a child's welfare (*Re W (Section 34(2) Orders)* [2000] 1 FLR 502).

A contact order may be varied or discharged on the application of the child, local authority or the person named in the order. If the order is discharged, the presumption of reasonable contact with persons mentioned in s 34(1) still applies.

14.6 Discharge of care orders (s 39)

A care order remains in force until the child reaches 18, unless it is brought to an end earlier. The order may be brought to an end by the making of a residence order (the only s 8 order which can be applied for), the substitution of a supervision order, or by the making of an adoption order or a discharge order.

The application for a discharge can be made by any person with parental responsibility, the child or the local authority. There is no requirement for a child to seek leave before making an application.

On hearing an application to discharge the care order, the court may substitute a supervision order. The court must apply the welfare principle in s 1, but there is no requirement to find that the threshold criteria are still satisfied.

Where there has been a previous application to discharge a care order (other than an interim order) or to substitute a supervision order, no further application can be made for six months without leave.

If the care order is discharged without any other order being made, care of the child reverts to those having parental responsibility. A pre-care residence order will not be revived, although on discharge the court has power to make any s 8 order.

There has been an increasing trend for children in the care of local authorities (either under care orders, or being accommodated by voluntary agreement) to leave care early (ie between the ages of 16 and 18) with very little support provided for them. Research carried out by the Department of Health showed that the future for these children is often bleak. As a result, the Government introduced the Children (Leaving Care) Act 2000. It amended ss 22–24 of the CA 1989 to provide that it is the duty of the local authority looking after children to advise, assist and befriend them with a view to promoting their welfare when it has ceased to look after them. Each child must have a 'pathway plan' to cover the period from 16 to independence (whether they remain in care until then or not) and to look beyond the age of 18 to 21. The plan will be reviewed at least every six months. The local authority must also arrange for each child to have a personal adviser (who does not necessarily have to be a social worker). With regard to education and training, the local authority has a power, but not a duty, to assist with the cost of this up to the age of 24 (CA 1989, s 24B).

14.7 Effect of a supervision order

Although the criteria are the same as for a care order (see **14.4.2**), the effect of a supervision order is very different. The order places the child under the supervision of a local authority, but the supervisor does not acquire parental responsibility.

The basic duties of the supervisor are to advise, assist and befriend the child, and to take steps to give effect to the order. Other powers of the supervisor depend on the order.

The order could include:

(a) a requirement for the child to live at a specified place, or participate in specified activities;

(b) with the consent of any 'responsible person' (any person with parental responsibility and any other person with whom the child lives), a requirement for that person to take all reasonable steps to ensure the child complies with any direction and also to comply with any directions to take part in specified activities. This has been used to require the responsible person to undergo treatment, for example in relation to sexual offences;

(c) a requirement that the child submits to specified medical or psychiatric examination or treatment. Where the child has sufficient understanding to make an informed decision, he may refuse to submit to the examination or assessment. However, it has been held that under its inherent jurisdiction, the High Court has power to override a child's refusal (*South Glamorgan County Council v W and B* [1993] 1 FLR 574).

The court decides on the broad structure of the supervision to take place, but the detailed implementation of any requirement in the order is left to the supervisor (ie the local authority). If the supervisor's directions are not complied with, the supervisor can only seek a variation or discharge of the order. The directions cannot be directly enforced either by the supervisor, or by the court.

A supervision order is normally made for up to one year, but it can be extended for a further period of up to three years from the date of the original order. An application to extend the supervision order is governed by the principles in s 1, but there is no need to consider whether the threshold criteria are satisfied.

14.8 Care or supervision order

The protection of the child is the decisive factor when the court is deciding whether to make a care or supervision order. The court must weigh the likelihood of future harm to the child against the potential harm of removing the child from his parents under a care order. Note, however, that a care order may still be justified where the local authority intends for the child to remain at home (*Re T (A Minor) (Care or Supervision Order)* [1994] 1 FLR 103).

With a care order, the authority acquires parental responsibility and has an obligation to safeguard the child's welfare. In an emergency it can remove the child without recourse to a court.

In contrast, a supervision order is made to help and assist the child; responsibility for safeguarding the child's welfare rests with his parents. In an emergency, the local authority would have to apply to the court to remove the child. However, a supervision order does give the court a degree of control over the upbringing of the child.

In recent cases, the courts have emphasised that, when deciding whether to make a care order or a supervision order, the order that represented the most proportionate response to the risks involved should be made. When the balance between the two orders is equal, the court should adopt the least interventionist approach (see *Re C and B (Care Order: Future Harm)* [2001] 1 FLR 611 and *Re C (Care Order or Supervision Order)* [2001] 2 FLR 466).

14.9 Interim orders (s 38)

14.9.1 The court's powers to make interim orders

Once care proceedings have been instituted, the court has the power to make:

(a)   an interim care order;

(b)   an interim supervision order;

(c)   a residence or other s 8 order for a limited period.

See **Appendix 1(E)**.

Where care or supervision proceedings are adjourned, or the court in any proceedings (eg divorce proceedings) gives a direction to a local authority under s 37 to investigate the child's circumstances (see **14.3.1**), the court may make an interim care or supervision order.

It may not make the order unless satisfied that there are reasonable grounds for believing that the threshold criteria (s 31: see **14.4.2**) are satisfied. At this stage, 'reasonable grounds' means that the court is likely to be relying to a large extent on the child's version of events, or on medical evidence that certain symptoms are consistent with abuse. The fact that belief suffices at the interim stage should be contrasted with the position at the Final Hearing, where the court must be satisfied by proof that the threshold criteria are met.

Alternatively, if the court makes a residence order pending the outcome of the care/supervision application, it must also make an interim supervision order (unless satisfied that the child's welfare will be satisfactorily safeguarded without it).

An interim order has the same effect as a final care or supervision order, except that the order can include directions as to the examination or assessment of the child and will be of limited duration.

It is common for a number of interim orders to be made pending a Final Hearing, although on each renewal the court must be satisfied that the criteria are still met.

In *Re G (Minors) (Interim Care Order)* [1993] 2 FLR 839, the court stated that an interim care order was an impartial step to preserve the status quo pending the Final Hearing and did not give a tactical advantage to the local authority.

It may be appropriate to delay making a final decision pending the outcome of an assessment of the child or a parent, or until the court is in possession of all material facts. The court must also be satisfied the local authority care plan is in the child's best interest. In *Re W and B, Re W (Care Plan)* [2001] EWCA Civ 757, [2001] 2 FLR 582, the Court of Appeal held that trial judges should have a wide discretion to make use of interim care orders where the proposed care plan seems uncertain or incomplete, or could be clarified after a relative brief adjournment. This may lead to an increased use of interim care orders on this ground than in the past.

When the court makes an interim care or supervision order, it may direct a medical, or psychiatric or other assessment of the child, under s 38(6) of CA 1989. In *Re G (Interim Care Order: Residential Assessment)* [2005] UKHL 68, the House of Lords held that, to come within s 38(6), the assessment must be of 'the child' and the main focus must be on the child. It may include an assessment of the child's relationship with his or her parents, the risk the parents may present to him or her, and ways in which those risks may be avoided or managed, all with a view to enabling the court to make decisions under the Act. Any services which are provided for the child and his family must be ancillary to that end; they must not be an end in themselves.

14.9.2　Exclusion requirements

If the court makes an interim care order, it may include an 'exclusion requirement', provided there is reasonable cause to believe that if a person is excluded from the house where the child lives, the child will no longer suffer, or be likely to suffer, significant harm (s 38A(2)).

Before including such a requirement, another person (whether or not a parent) living in the house with the child must be able to look after the child and consent to the requirement being made. The 'exclusion requirement' may require the person to leave the dwelling house, or not to enter the dwelling house. It can also require the person not to enter an area surrounding the house. A power of arrest can be attached to the exclusion requirement. The requirement will cease to have effect if the local authority removes the child to other accommodation for a continuous period of more than 24 hours.

14.9.3　Contact

The provisions regarding contact with a child in care (see **14.5**) apply equally on the making of an interim care order. However, as the issue is only being considered pending a Final Hearing, contact between a parent and child should be maintained unless there are exceptional circumstances.

14.10 Emergency protection and assessment (CA 1989, Pt V)

14.10.1 Emergency protection order (s 44)

An emergency protection order (EPO) is an order, initially limited to eight days, to protect a child in an emergency where he is otherwise likely to suffer significant harm (see **Appendix 1(E)**). Recent cases have emphasised that the draconian nature of an EPO removing a child from his parent requires exceptional circumstances and proof of imminent danger *X Council v B (Emergency Protection Orders)* [2004] EWHC 2015 (Fam).

14.10.2 Grounds

The court may make an EPO on the application of any person, if it is satisfied that there is reasonable cause to believe that the child is likely to suffer significant harm if he:

(a)   is not removed to accommodation provided by or on behalf of the applicant; or

(b)   does not remain in the place where he is being accommodated.

The application will usually be made by a local authority, but anyone (such as a police officer or a relative) can apply. If the local authority is not the applicant, it has power to take over the order.

A local authority can also apply for an order where it is making enquiries because, for example, it suspects the child may be suffering significant harm and believes access is required as a matter of urgency, which is being unreasonably refused.

If the court finds that either condition applies, before making an order it must consider the welfare principle (s 1(1): see **14.4.4**) and the no order presumption (s 1(5): see **13.6**), although there is no requirement to apply the checklist under s 1(3) (see **13.5**).

If the court makes an order under s 44, it may include an 'exclusion requirement' if there is reasonable cause to believe that if a person is excluded from the dwelling house in which the child lives, the child is unlikely to suffer significant harm (s 44A(2)). The exclusion requirements and conditions are the same as when made in conjunction with an interim care order (see **14.9.2**).

14.10.3 Application

The application must be made to a family proceedings court unless it arises out of a direction under s 37 to the local authority to investigate, when it should be made to the court which gave that direction. The application may not be transferred to a higher court and there is no appeal against the making or refusal of an order.

The application can be made on one day's notice. The application may also be made without notice with the consent of the justices' clerk and may be heard by a single justice. However, due consideration must be given to parents' rights under Articles 6 and 8 of the European Convention on Human Rights, and notice of the hearing should generally be given, unless it is genuinely an emergency or a case of great urgency. A copy of the application and order must be served on each party (every person with parental responsibility and the child) within 48 hours of the order.

In *X Council v B* (see **14.10.1**) the court gave detailed guidance on emergency protection orders generally and also on the use of without notice applications, stating that, save in wholly exceptional cases, parents must be given notice. The case also stated the need for courts hearing without notice applications to keep a note of the evidence received, of its reasons and any findings of fact. This guidance was endorsed in *Re X (Emergency Protection Orders)* [2006] EWHC 510 (Fam) which said it is the duty of an applicant in an emergency protection order to ensure that the guidance in *X Council v B* is brought to the court's attention, ie, following a without notice hearing, the parents should be given a copy of the clerk's notes, a copy of any material submitted to the court and a copy of the justices' reasons. *Re X (Emergency Protection Orders)* also stated that, on a without notice application, the court needed to determine whether or not the hearing should proceed on a without notice basis and to give reasons for that decision.

The court will normally appoint a children's guardian for the child (see **14.11.7**). The court may take account of any statement contained in any report made to the court, or any evidence given during the hearing which is relevant to the application.

14.10.4   Effect of the order

The order operates as a direction to any person who is in a position to do so to comply with any request to produce the child to the applicant, and authorises the removal or prevention of removal of the child from his present accommodation. The order may authorise the applicant to enter specified premises and search for the child. If the applicant is likely to be refused entry, the court can issue a warrant authorising the police to assist, using reasonable force if necessary.

The order also gives the applicant parental responsibility for the child, but this is limited to doing what is necessary to safeguard and promote the child's welfare.

The local authority should return the child to his parents as soon as it appears safe to do so, thus it should review the case regularly to ensure that the parents and child are separated for no longer than is necessary.

14.10.5   Contact

During the currency of the order, the applicant must, subject to any direction of the court, allow the child reasonable contact with his parents, any other person with parental responsibility, any person with whom he was living prior to the order and any person in whose favour there is an existing contact order.

The court can give such directions and impose such conditions as it considers appropriate in relation to contact. However, where the applicant is a local authority, the court will usually leave contact to be negotiated between the parties unless the issue is clearly disputed. In *X Council v B (Emergency Protection Orders)* (see **14.10.1**), Mumby J emphasised that arrangements for contact must be driven by the needs of the family, not stunted by lack of resources.

14.10.6   Examination or assessment

The court may give directions as to a medical, or psychiatric examination or other assessment of the child, or may alternatively direct that there be no such examination or assessment. However, in an emergency, where the examination is required for medical reasons, this could be undertaken without the need for a court order under the applicant's parental responsibility.

A child of sufficient understanding to make an informed decision may refuse to submit to an examination or assessment, but it has been held that the High Court may overrule the child and give consent under its inherent jurisdiction (*South Glamorgan County Council v W and B* [1993] 1 FLR 574).

14.10.7 Duration

An EPO order may be granted for up to eight days, although it should not be granted for any longer than is necessary to protect the child. The court can grant one extension for up to seven days on the application of the local authority, if it has reasonable cause to believe the child is likely to suffer significant harm if the order is not extended.

An application to discharge the order can be made on one day's notice, but cannot be heard before the expiry of 72 hours from the making of the order. The application can be made by the child, a parent, any other person with parental responsibility or any person with whom the child was living prior to the order, unless that person was present at the hearing. As an application to extend the duration must be on notice, no one can apply for a discharge once the order has been extended.

14.10.8 Police protection (s 46)

A child may be taken into 'police protection' for up to 72 hours if a constable has reasonable cause to believe that the child is likely to suffer significant harm if he does not remove the child to suitable accommodation, or take steps to prevent removal from his present accommodation (these are the same criteria on which the *court* must be satisfied to make an EPO: see **14.10.2**). This power could be used, for example, where a child has run away, been abandoned or is found in unsuitable home circumstances, or alternatively to prevent his removal from, say, a hospital. (See **Appendix 1(E)**.)

The police do not acquire parental responsibility but must do what is reasonable in the circumstances to safeguard or promote the child's welfare. They must inform the local authority who, if requested, must provide accommodation for the child. Following investigation, the police or local authority could, if appropriate, apply for an emergency protection order.

In *Langley v Liverpool City Council* [2005] EWCA Civ 1173 the Court of Appeal held that, where an EPO is in force, the police can remove a child under s 46 only if there are 'compelling reasons' to do so. If the police, knowing that an EPO was in force, removed a child under s 46 without compelling reasons, the police would be acting unlawfully and in breach of the family's rights under Article 8 of the European Convention on Human Rights.

14.10.9 Child assessment order (s 43)

This is an order for the assessment of the child's health or development, or of the way in which he has been treated. It is intended to deal with the situation where there is a suspicion that the child is suffering and there has been a denial of co-operation on the part of the child's carers. It is part of the 'planned responses' by a local authority rather than a device to provide emergency protection.

The grounds for the order are very specific. Essentially, the local authority must have reasonable cause to suspect the child is suffering, or is likely to suffer, significant harm. The court must be satisfied that an assessment is necessary to confirm or dismiss those suspicions and that the child's carers are unlikely to co-operate with such an assessment. Although the checklist in s 1(3) need not be applied, the court must have regard to the welfare principle (s 1(1)) and no order presumption (s 1(5)).

Under s 43(3), the court may make an EPO on an application for a child assessment order.

14.11　Procedure for care and supervision orders

The procedure for making applications in the family proceedings court is governed by the Family Proceedings Courts (Children Act 1989) Rules 1991 (SI 1991/1395) and in the county court or High Court by FPR 1991. It is also now governed by the Protocol for Judicial Case Management in Public Law Children Act Cases. This Protocol aims to cut down delay and sets out a 40-week guideline for the conclusion of most cases. A revised Protocol ('The Public Law Outline') is currently being consulted upon and piloted (see **14.1**).

14.11.1　Jurisdiction

Proceedings under Pt IV of the CA 1989 (care and supervision orders, contact orders) are classified as 'family proceedings', allowing the court to make any of the orders under the Act, including s 8 orders. Proceedings under Pt V (emergency protection orders, child assessment orders) are not included in the definition, but, by virtue of s 92(2), all Children Act proceedings in the family proceedings court are to be treated as 'family proceedings'.

14.11.2　Which court?

The jurisdiction of a particular tier of court to entertain an application is governed by the Children (Allocation of Proceedings) Order 1991 (SI 1991/1677).

An application for a care or supervision order (or for an emergency protection or child assessment order) must normally be made to a family proceedings court. However, the general rule is subject to two provisos. First, if the application arose in consequence of a direction under s 37 (eg during divorce proceedings) for the local authority to investigate, the application should be made to the court which gave the direction. Secondly, any application to extend, vary or discharge an order under the Act, or where the outcome of the proceedings may have that effect, should be made to the court which made the original order.

14.11.3　Transfer of cases

Irrespective of where a case started, it can be transferred to another, more appropriate court. It is possible for cases to be transferred either horizontally or vertically. The exception is an application for an emergency protection order, which cannot be transferred from the family proceedings court to a higher court (see **14.10.3**).

Transfers between the same tier of court are essentially governed by the general principle that the child's welfare is the paramount consideration and any delay is likely to prejudice his welfare. Accordingly, if, for example, a particular family proceedings court is too busy to deal with the application, or it is desirable to consolidate with other pending proceedings, the application could be transferred to another family proceedings court.

Applications commenced in the family proceedings court can be transferred to the county court under one or more of three heads:

(a)　exceptional complexity, importance or gravity;

(b)   the need to consolidate with other proceedings;

(c)   the urgency of the case.

A transfer under the first head would be justified because of complicated or conflicting evidence about the risks to the child's welfare, the large number of parties involved or because of a difficult point of law. The courts have also indicated that cases with a time estimate of three days for the hearing should be transferred to the county court. If the magistrates refuse to transfer, application can be made to the county court for a transfer order.

The county court can transfer a case to the High Court if 'appropriate' and 'in the interests of the child'.

14.11.4   Public funding

Legal Representation is available for public law proceedings under the Children Act, but is based on a special regime which depends on the nature of the proceedings and the status of the party.

14.11.4.1   Automatic Legal Representation for certain parties

Legal Representation must be granted, without regard to a means or merits test, to the child, the parents and any other person with parental responsibility in relation to proceedings for care, supervision, emergency protection or child assessment orders.

14.11.4.2   Other potential parties

Any other person who applies to be joined as a party to any of the above proceedings is subject to the usual means test. In addition, Legal Representation can be refused on the ground that representation is not necessary.

14.11.4.3   Other applications

Applications by anyone for s 34 contact orders, s 39 discharge orders or any s 8 order are subject to the usual means and merits test.

14.11.4.4   Related proceedings

In those cases where Legal Representation can be granted automatically, the certificate can cover proceedings relating to the application in question. A related matter is one where an order is sought at the same time as, and as an alternative to, the main proceedings. So, for example, applying for a s 8 residence order in the context of care or supervision proceedings would be covered by the Legal Representation certificate (although it should be formally amended).

Legal Representation is not available to a children's guardian, but Cafcass is responsible for paying for the services of the guardian.

14.11.5   The application

The application must be made on Form C1 (see **Appendix 3(G)**) (or C2 if made in existing proceedings), together with supplement C13 containing a summary of all the facts and matters relied on, in particular those necessary to satisfy the threshold criteria, with sufficient copies for service.

On filing, the court fixes a date for the First Hearing.

The applicant must join as a party the child and every person whom he believes to have parental responsibility. In public law proceedings, unlike private law proceedings, the child is automatically a party. This is because public law proceedings are based on the concept of significant harm attributable to the standard of parental care. This can create a conflict of interest between the child and his parents and between the child and the local authority, and therefore requires the child to be separately represented. In the case of parents, consideration should always be given as to whether separate representation is appropriate because of a potential conflict of interest.

In addition, any person who is not automatically a respondent may apply to be joined. A distinction is drawn between a putative father and other applicants. In the case of a putative father, his application should be granted unless there is some justifiable reason for not doing so (see *Re K (Care Proceedings: Notification of Father without Parental Responsibility)* [1999] 2 FLR 408). In the case of other applicants, the court will not join someone (other than a parent) where their interests and views are the same as an existing party. In *Re M (Minors) (Sexual Abuse: Evidence)* [1993] 1 FLR 822, the court held that, where the grandparents were offering a 'fall back' position to that of the mother, and were presenting the same case as her, there was no purpose in their separate representation and they should not have been made parties unless they had a separate point to advance.

14.11.6   Service

Under the Protocol, copies of the application must be served on all respondents within three days of issue, together with a Notice of Proceedings (C6) giving the date of the hearing. The applicant must file a Statement of Service (C9). As an additional step introduced by the Protocol, the local authority must also file and serve (by the third day) further documents, such as an Initial Social Work Statement. This sets out the reasons for the application, relevant facts relating to the child and his family within the knowledge of the social worker, and any initial proposals the local authority may have at this early stage.

Within the same time period, the applicant must also give notice of the proceedings (C6A) to anyone caring for the child, an unmarried father who does not have parental responsibility and anyone who is a party to other relevant proceedings, so that they can consider whether to apply to be joined as a party.

In relation to a child, service must be on the solicitor acting for the child, or, if none, on the children's guardian. The court has power to direct that a requirement as to service on anyone shall not apply, or shall be effected in such manner as the court directs.

14.11.7   Appointment of a children's guardian

On the day the application is issued, the court must appoint a children's guardian for the child, unless the court considers it is not necessary to safeguard the child's interests.

Children's guardians are usually experienced social workers who are contracted to Cafcass as officers of the service. They operate through regional offices around the country. According the Protocol, a guardian must be allocated by Cafcass within the following two days. Complying with this requirement has resource implications for Cafcass as, in the past, it has taken an average of 24 working days for Cafcass to be able to allocate a guardian.

It is important to appreciate that the guardian is 'for the child', rather than to 'represent' the child. Accordingly, the guardian's role is to put forward what he considers to be in the best interests of the child, even though that may not coincide with the child's views.

14.11.7.1 Duties of the guardian

The guardian must appoint and instruct a solicitor to represent the child (unless a solicitor has already been appointed), give the child appropriate advice, investigate the case and file a written report at least seven days before the Final Hearing.

In addition, the guardian must attend all directions appointments and hearings (unless excused) and advise the court, amongst other things, on:

(a)   whether the child is of sufficient understanding for any purpose;

(b)   the wishes of the child in respect of any relevant matter;

(c)   the appropriate timing of the proceedings;

(d)   the options available to the court in respect of the child;

(e)   any other appropriate matter.

14.11.8 Appointment of solicitor for the child

Where a children's guardian has been appointed, he should immediately appoint a solicitor to represent the child.

Alternatively, the court may appoint a solicitor in any of the following circumstances:

(a)   where no children's guardian has been appointed;

(b)   where the child has sufficient understanding to instruct a solicitor and wishes to do so;

(c)   where the court considers it in the child's best interests.

Additionally, the child could appoint a solicitor directly where he is of sufficient understanding.

14.11.8.1 Duties of the solicitor

Where a children's guardian has been appointed, the solicitor must follow the instructions given by the guardian. However, in some cases it becomes apparent that the views of the child do not coincide with what the guardian considers to be in his best interests. In circumstances where the child wishes to give instructions which conflict with those of the guardian and the solicitor considers that the child is able, having regard to his understanding, to give such instructions, the solicitor must follow the child's instructions. Where this happens, the guardian must notify the court and may seek leave to have separate legal representation.

14.11.9 The First Hearing

On the filing of the application, the court must fix a date for a preliminary hearing and appoint a children's guardian. According to the Protocol, this First Hearing should take place within six days of the issuing of the application. At the First Hearing, the following directions may be given:

(a)   appointment of a children's guardian or solicitor for the child, if this has not already happened;

(b)   joinder of other parties (such as an unmarried father who does not have parental responsibility);

(c)   transfer of the proceedings to another court;

(d)   fixing a timetable for the proceedings (eg, dates for the case management conference, pre-hearing review (if necessary) and Final Hearing);

(e)   attendance of the child (although this would be unusual);

(f)   submission of evidence, including expert reports.

The Protocol provides a standard directions form.

The court can make an interim care or supervision order if the conditions in s 38 are met, or a s 8 residence order together with a supervision order, or list the application for an urgent contested interim hearing.

14.11.9.1   Timetable for the proceedings

Having regard to the 'no delay' principle, the court is required to draw up a timetable for the proceedings and give appropriate directions to ensure it is adhered to.

The fact that there are criminal proceedings pending (eg in relation to a parent) is not usually a reason to adjourn the application because the inevitable delay would not be in the child's best interests. A person cannot refuse to give evidence on the grounds of self-incrimination, but any statement or admission made in the proceedings is not admissible in criminal cases (other than for perjury).

14.11.9.2   Attendance

The parties must attend any court appointments unless otherwise directed.

The court has power to direct that a child does not, or need not, attend. The general tendency is to allow the child's attendance only if satisfied that it would clearly be in his interests, and in practice the courts tend to assume that the child will not attend without the need to make a formal direction.

14.11.10   Evidence

14.11.10.1   Admissibility

As in private law children proceedings, the general rules as to the admissibility of evidence are relaxed.

Of particular relevance is that any statement contained in a children's guardian's report, and any evidence given in respect of matters referred to in it, is admissible. This provision is very wide in that 'any statement' is not restricted to one made by the guardian himself and could include a statement made by, for example, a home help or a school teacher. Further, the court may allow 'any evidence' from any witness to be admitted if it relates to a matter referred to in the report.

A children's guardian has the right to examine and take copies of records held by a local authority. However, the local authority may claim, for example in relation to social work records, that public interest requires that the evidence should be excluded. In that case, the guardian would have to apply to the court for a direction as to its admissibility.

14.11.10.2   Witness statements

Each party must file and serve on the other parties and on the children's guardian written statements of the oral evidence it intends to use, together with copies of any documents, including expert reports, which will be relied on, at or by such time as the court directs. Failure to do so means the evidence can be admitted only with leave.

14.11.10.3 Expert evidence

The court's leave is needed for any medical or psychiatric examination, or other assessment of the child for the purpose of preparing expert evidence. In addition, no document relating to the proceedings can be disclosed, without leave, other than to a party, a legal representative, the children's guardian or the Legal Services Commission.

An application for leave should be made as early as possible, the applicant having identified the expert and relevance to the issues in question. Leave will be granted only on condition of disclosure of both the letter of instruction and the subsequent report.

14.11.11 Disclosure

In children cases, there is a duty to give full and frank disclosure (*Practice Direction (Case Management)* [1995] 1 FLR 456).

Although privilege from disclosure applies to solicitor/client communications, it does not apply in children cases to reports and other documents prepared for the purpose of the proceedings. Accordingly, where a party obtains an expert report, with or without the court's leave, no privilege will attach to the report and it must be disclosed to the court and to the other parties (*Re L (Police Investigation: Privilege)* [1996] 1 FLR 731).

14.11.12 Case management conference

This step in the procedure was introduced by the Protocol. At the conference, all the parties meet to consider the documents and try to narrow down the issues in the case. The Protocol provides case management checklists and questionnaires to help the parties and the court conduct the case more effectively. The Protocol also requires all the advocates involved in the case to meet shortly before the case management conference to carry out a preliminary consideration of these checklists and questionnaires, and to draw up between themselves a schedule of issues in the case.

14.11.13 The Final Hearing

The children's guardian must file a written report at least seven days before the Final Hearing. The court will then serve a copy on every party.

Prior to the hearing there will be a pre-hearing review, if necessary, to determine the procedure to be adopted. This will seek to resolve what issues are still in dispute, the number of witnesses to be called and the length of the hearing.

Where all the parties are agreed that a care order should be made, the court's consideration may be limited to a perusal of the documentation and approval of the agreed order. On the other hand, where there are unresolved issues, for example as to physical or sexual abuse, the court may order a split hearing (*Re S (Care Proceedings: Split Hearing)* [1996] 2 FLR 773) – the first hearing to resolve these issues; the second, substantive hearing to concentrate on what is in the child's best interests.

14.11.14 Judgment

Judgment must be given as soon as practicable after the hearing. The court must state any findings of fact and the reasons for its decision.

The order must be in writing (on Form C32) and a copy served on each party and on any person with whom the child is living.

14.11.15 After a care order is made

Once a final care order has been made, the local authority has control over decisions relating to the child's welfare. The local authority should review its care plan on a regular basis and, before conducting such reviews, it should seek and take into account the wishes and views of the child and his parents.

The court has no future role in monitoring the local authority or the execution of its care plan unless some substantive issue comes before the court, such as an application for contact or discharge of the care order. This is a situation which has caused increasing judicial concern over the years, especially since the Human Rights Act 1998, and as a result the Adoption and Children Act 2002 has amended s 26 of the CA 1989 and required local authorities to appoint an Independent Reviewing Officer (IRO) in connection with each child subject to a care order. The care plan for these children must be kept under review, and the IRO must monitor the local authority's performance, make sure the child's views are understood and taken into account, ensure that any matters of concern are brought to the attention of an appropriately senior member of the local authority and, in necessary cases, refer the matter to Cafcass, who will have the power to bring the case back to court for directions. So far, IROs have not made use of this referral system.

14.12 Human rights implications

Taking a child into care clearly constitutes an interference with family life under Article 8 of the European Convention on Human Rights. The local authority, as a public body, must act in a way that is compatible with Convention rights. Taking a child into care will not breach Article 8 provided the interference is in accordance with the law, it pursues a legitimate aim (namely, the protection of children) and is necessary.

In the context of public law proceedings, the European Court of Human Rights has repeatedly emphasised that interference in the right to family life by taking a child into care should be regarded as a temporary measure to be discontinued as soon as circumstances permit (*Johansen v Norway* (1996) 23 EHRR 33).

The manner in which a child is taken into care may also be open to challenge. The European Court of Human Rights has emphasised that it is important to involve parents in the decision-making process leading to care proceedings. This would include being involved in child protection conferences. In addition, in *P, C and S v United Kingdom* [2002] 2 FLR 631, the European Court of Human Rights stated that it is essential that parents involved in care proceedings have effective and competent legal representation. If they do not, Article 6 and the procedural guarantees inherent in Article 8 of the Convention are breached.

14.12.1 The welfare principle

As mentioned in **Chapter 13**, there is a debate as to whether the welfare principle in s 1(1) of the CA 1989 is incompatible with Article 8 of the European Convention on Human Rights and an individual's right to respect for family life. In other words, placing the child's welfare as paramount does not involve balancing the family rights of the other relevant individuals. But the decisions of the European Court of Human Rights make it clear that the rights of the parent may have to defer to the interests of the child. In *Johansen v Norway* (see above), the court said that 'the parent cannot be entitled under Article 8 ... to have such measures taken as would harm the child's health and development'.

In the domestic case of *Dawson v Wearmouth* [1999] 1 FLR 1167 the court said:

> It is submitted that the father's rights under Article 8 are infringed. There is no basis for this submission. The present case is concerned with the welfare of the child, not with the rights of the father. There is nothing in the Convention which requires the courts of this country to act otherwise than in the interests of the child.

Also, in *KD (A Minor) (Access: Principles)* [1998] 2 FLR 139, there was an argument between the local authority and the parent as to contact. The mother relied on Article 8 of the Convention and submitted that contact was a parental right and not a child's right. Lord Oliver said it would not be inappropriate to describe a parent's claim to contact as a 'right' It was also a normal assumption that a child will benefit from continuing contact with his natural parents:

> But both the 'right'and the assumption will always be displaced if the interests of the child dictate otherwise.

These cases suggest that there is no conflict between s 1(1) and Article 8, because Article 8(2) contains the important qualification of the right to respect for family life that 'there shall be no interference except such as in accordance with the law and is necessary in a democratic society for the protection of health or morals or for the protection of the rights and freedoms of others' (ie the child involved).

14.12.2 Compensation for local authority failings

For policy reasons, domestic law has established that it would not be fair, just and reasonable to impose a duty of care on local authorities. This means that the local authority cannot be sued in negligence if it fails to take the appropriate steps needed to protect a child, such as starting care proceedings (see *X Minors v Bedfordshire CC* [1995] 2 FLR 276). However, in the case of *D v East Berkshire Community NHS Trust, MAK v Dewsbury Healthcare NHS Trust, RK v Oldham NHS Trust* [2003] EWCA Civ 1151, the Court of Appeal preferred a more narrow interpretation of the *Bedfordshire CC* case and stated that in certain circumstances the local authority may owe a duty of care to the child (but not to the parent). In *Lawrence v Pembrokeshire County Council* [2007] EWCA Civ 446, the Court of Appeal confirmed that there was no duty of care owed by investigating professionals to parents suspected of abusing their children.

In the *Bedfordshire CC* case the claim ultimately succeeded. Here, the social services department allowed over four years to go by before it took four siblings into care, despite overwhelming evidence of neglect and ill-treatment during that time. When the children were eventually placed in emergency foster care, the consultant psychiatrist who examined the children found that the older three were seriously psychologically disturbed and that it was the worst case of neglect and emotional abuse she had ever seen. The Official Solicitor, on behalf of the children, sued the local authority claiming damages for negligence for failing to take effective steps to protect the children's welfare. These proceedings were struck out by the House of Lords on the grounds of public policy, to prevent potentially heavy damages claims against local authorities. The Official Solicitor then took the case to the European Court of Human Rights (*Z and Others v UK* [2001] 2 FLR 612, ECtHR).

The Court held that there was a breach of Article 3 of the European Convention on Human Rights in that the local authority had failed to protect the children from inhuman and degrading treatment. Also, the consequence of the House of Lords striking out the action was that the children were left with no effective domestic remedy. This was a breach of Article 13. This meant that the European Court of Human Rights could invoke Article 41, so as to provide just satisfaction, and award damages in favour of the children.

In another case, *TP and KM v United Kingdom* [2001] 2 FLR 549, ECtHR, a local authority was criticised for removing children from the care of their mother on the basis of an allegation of sexual abuse by the mother's partner which was not properly investigated by the local authority and which turned out to be erroneous. Again, Convention Articles were relevant. There had clearly been a breach of Article 8, the right to family life, because the family had been torn apart by the local authority's failure to investigate properly and disclose its information promptly. As in the *Z v UK* case, the European Court of Human Rights held that, because the domestic courts had struck out the negligence claim, under Article 13 there had been a failure to provide an effective domestic remedy. Article 41 was, therefore, invoked to award damages to the family.

For causes of action arising after the implementation of the HRA 1998, it is now possible for claimants to pursue breaches of Convention rights in the domestic courts.

14.12.3 The care plan

One significant impact of the HRA 1998 in public law cases is how it has been used to highlight the courts' inability to maintain some judicial control over the implementation of a care plan by the local authority.

If the court makes a care order, it then has no further control over the care plan for the child and the local authority can change that plan at any time. If the parents are unhappy about the care plan, all they can do is apply to discharge the care order, or apply for contact if the arrangements are unreasonable.

This position has been criticised by many for some time as conflicting with the principle that the interests of the parent and of the child in the decision-making process should be given sufficient procedural protection. It has also been argued that the inability of the parents to question or call for any review of the care plan can lead to breaches of Articles 6 and 8 of the Convention and is incompatible with HRA 1998.

As a result, the Government has introduced an amendment to the Adoption and Children Act 2002 (s 118 amending CA 1989, s 26(2)). This provides for the local authority to appoint a reviewing officer (IRO) to monitor the local authority's review of any care plan and to refer the case to Cafcass if appropriate. It seems that Cafcass may then be able to take consequential court proceedings on behalf of the child. At the time of writing only one such case has been referred to Cafcass in England (see also **14.10.4** and **14.11.15**).

14.13 Special guardianship order

The new ss 14A to 14F of CA 1989 provide for special guardianship orders, a new type of order. Those able to apply for the order are, amongst others, any guardian of the child, any holder of a residence order or anyone who has been the child's foster carer for one year. It is a private law order, but it is envisaged that it will be useful in cases where the local authority is or has been involved. It provides permanence without the legal separation involved in adoption. For example, it can be used in the case of an older child in long-term foster care, or for a child being looked after permanently by a member of his extended family (see *A Local Authority v YZ and Others* [2006] 2 FLR 41 at **13.3.6**).

The special guardianship order gives the holder parental responsibility, which he is entitled to exercise to the exclusion of any other person with parental responsibility. However, it does not extinguish the parents' parental responsibility. The local authority must provide special guardian support services, including counselling, advice and financial support.

14.14 Chapter summary

(1)   There is a duty on local authorities to take reasonable steps through the provision of services to avoid the need for court proceedings.

(2)   A care or supervision order can be made only on application by a local authority (or NSPCC).

(3)   In contrast to private law proceedings, the child is always a party.

(4)   Before making a care or supervision order, the court must be satisfied both that the threshold criteria are met and that such an order is in the child's best interests.

(5)   Legal Representation for the main respondents is automatic.

(6)   There is a presumption of reasonable contact for parents.

(7)   In an emergency, anyone can apply for an emergency protection order.

(8)   Checklists detailing grounds for a care or supervision order and the procedure are set out below.

GROUNDS FOR A CARE OR SUPERVISION ORDER – CHECKLIST

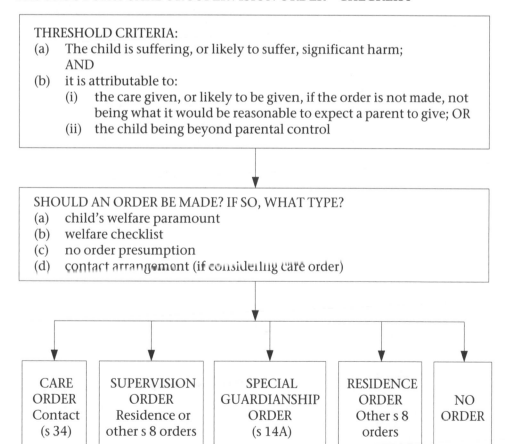

THRESHOLD CRITERIA:
(a)   The child is suffering, or likely to suffer, significant harm;
      AND
(b)   it is attributable to:
      (i)   the care given, or likely to be given, if the order is not made, not being what it would be reasonable to expect a parent to give; OR
      (ii) the child being beyond parental control

SHOULD AN ORDER BE MADE? IF SO, WHAT TYPE?
(a)   child's welfare paramount
(b)   welfare checklist
(c)   no order presumption
(d)   contact arrangement (if considering care order)

| CARE ORDER Contact (s 34) | SUPERVISION ORDER Residence or other s 8 orders | SPECIAL GUARDIANSHIP ORDER (s 14A) | RESIDENCE ORDER Other s 8 orders | NO ORDER |

PROCEDURAL CHECKLIST FOR A CARE ORDER

1.	Applicant	Local authority (or NSPCC)
2.	Which court?	Family proceedings court (unless s 37 direction or effect existing order)
3.	Application	Form C1 and C13
4.	Children's guardian	Appointed by the court. Guardian appoints solicitor for child
5.	Respondents	Every person with parental responsibility and the child
6.	Notice	Parent without parental responsibility Person with whom child living
7.	Legal Representation	As of right for child, parents and others with parental responsibility
8.	Service	Three days' notice
9.	First Hearing	Timetable/evidence/reports
10.	Interim order	Care/supervision orders if criteria satisfied or s 8 residence order with supervision order
11.	Case management conference	Case management directions
12.	Pre-hearing review	To narrow remaining issues
13.	Final Hearing	Findings of fact/reasons

Chapter 15

Domestic Abuse

15.1 Introduction

The term 'domestic abuse' is adopted by the Law Society's Family Law Protocol to cover cases involving personal violence, threats, intimidation and harassment. Particular sensitivity needs to be employed by the solicitor in such cases, as the client is likely to be distressed and may be reluctant to talk about the abuse.

This chapter is written on the basis that it is the wife or female partner who is seeking protection since this is the most common situation. However, men can be the victims of abuse too and are entitled to the same legal remedies. Any children who are with the victim can usually be protected at the same time as their carer. However, if protection is needed specifically for the children alone, this should generally be dealt with by using the procedures outlined in **Chapters 13** or **14**.

Although there is a variety of potential remedies available in situations of domestic abuse, the solicitor must be careful not to raise the client's expectations too high. A court order may give limited protection, but much will depend on the personality of the respondent. When the respondent is served with a court order, or arrested by the police (and later released), further violence may result. It is therefore crucial for the solicitor to adapt his advice to the particular circumstances of the applicant, taking into account the personalities of the parties, and to avoid giving the applicant a false sense of security.

The main emphasis here is on how to proceed in the civil courts, but the solicitor should be aware that court action is not the only possible remedy, and may not be the most appropriate one. For example, a solicitor's letter warning the perpetrator to desist from his behaviour or face court action may act as a deterrent. However, this would not be appropriate in cases of serious violence. In these cases the victim may consider going to the police. Police forces are now becoming more involved in cases of domestic violence and may have their own domestic violence unit.

Finally, if the client is in such fear that she does not want to return home, the solicitor should consider the possibility of finding a place for her in a women's refuge or in temporary local authority housing (see **6.11**).

Part IV of the FLA 1996 codified the law in this area, making the same remedies available in any level of court and extending protection to a wider group of people than before.

Another relevant statute in this area is the Protection from Harassment Act 1997 (PHA 1997). This Act will be considered briefly, later in the chapter.

The Domestic Violence, Crime and Victims Act 2004, which is at the time of writing not fully in force, is intended to strengthen the position of victims. It makes several significant changes to the FLA 1996, which will be highlighted in this chapter.

15.2 Protection under Pt IV of the Family Law Act 1996

The FLA 1996 is likely to provide the remedies which will be most frequently utilised by the family law practitioner. Its provisions are therefore dealt with in some detail.

15.2.1 Types of order available

The types of order available fall into two main categories:

(a) 'Non-molestation orders' for the protection of parties and any children. These can be applied for by a wide range of 'associated persons'.

(b) 'Occupation orders' which exclude the other party from occupation of the home. They can extend to excluding that party from a specified area around the home if necessary. Occupation orders can be applied for by spouses and cohabitants. Other 'associated persons' can apply only in specified circumstances.

15.2.2 Who can apply?

One of the most important changes brought about by FLA 1996 was the extension of the right to apply for non-molestation and (sometimes) occupation orders to a wide group of associated persons. Section 62 states that a person is associated with another if:

(a) they are or have been married to each other, or they are or have been civil partners of each other;

(b) they are cohabitants or former cohabitants (ie they are or have been living together as husband and wife) (this includes same-sex couples);

(c) they live or have lived in the same household, otherwise than by reason of one of them being the other's employee, tenant, lodger or boarder;

(d) they are relatives (this term includes immediate relations and other close relations such as grandparents, grandchildren, aunts, uncles, nieces, nephews, cousins, step-parents and step-children);

(e) they have agreed to marry one another (whether or not that agreement has been terminated – however, where the agreement has been terminated, any application must be made within three years of the termination date), or, since 1 July 2007, they have or have had an intimate personal relationship with each other which was of significant duration;

(f) in relation to a child, they are both parents or have, or have had, parental responsibility (where a child has been adopted or freed for adoption, two people will be associated if one is the natural parent and the other is the child or adoptive parent of the child);

(g) they are parties to the same family proceedings (other than proceedings under Pt IV of the FLA 1996 itself).

In addition, children (ie those under 18) can apply for non-molestation and/or occupation orders in their own right. However, if they are under 16 they will require leave of the court, which will be given only if the court is satisfied that the child has sufficient understanding to make the application (s 43).

15.2.3 Non-molestation orders (s 42)

The court can grant an order prohibiting the respondent from molesting the applicant or a child. The word 'molestation' covers not only violence and threats of violence, but also pestering. Thus, such an order could be granted against a respondent who sends abusive letters to his wife, or who persistently telephones his former partner in the middle of the night.

The court can grant a non-molestation order on the application of any associated person within any family proceedings, or the applicant may make a 'free standing' application under the FLA 1996. The court can also make such an order of its own motion in family proceedings. Since 1 July 2007, the court is required, when considering making an occupation order, also to consider making a non-molestation order.

15.2.3.1 Factors that the court must consider

Section 42(5) specifies that the court must have regard to all circumstances, including the need to secure the health, safety and well-being of the applicant and any child. Thus, provided the applicant can show a genuine need for protection, a non-molestation order will be granted.

15.2.3.2 Duration

Section 42(7) states that the order may be made for a specified period or until further order. Thus, such an order may be made for an indefinite period (*Re B-J (Power of Arrest)* [2000] 2 FLR 443).

15.2.4 Occupation orders (ss 33 and 35–38)

The provisions relating to occupation orders are quite detailed and complex. The status of the applicant (ie whether she has a right to occupy the home, or is a former spouse, cohabitant or former cohabitant) will determine:

(a)   whether the proposed applicant can apply for an order;

(b)   the provisions of any order granted;

(c)   the factors that the court will take into account in deciding whether to grant any order; and

(d)   the duration of any occupation order.

An application for an occupation order can be made in the course of other family proceedings, or the applicant can make a 'free standing' application under FLA 1996.

15.2.4.1 Applicant has an existing right to occupy the home (s 33)

An applicant will have a right to occupy the home for the purposes of this section if she is entitled to occupy by virtue of a beneficial estate, or interest, or contract or statutory entitlement (eg under s 30 of the FLA 1996). The home in question must be, have been or have been intended to be the home of the applicant and the person with whom she is associated (the respondent). Thus *any* associated person can apply under s 33 where she has an existing legal right to occupy the home.

Where the above conditions are satisfied, the applicant can apply for an occupation order which may:

(a)   require the respondent to permit the applicant to enter and remain in the home or part of the home;

(b)   regulate the occupation of the home by either or both parties;

(c)   prohibit, suspend or restrict the respondent's exercise of his right to occupy the home;

(d)   require the respondent to leave the home; or

(e)   exclude the respondent from a defined area in which the home is situated.

Where the applicant has a right of occupation under s 30 of the FLA 1996 and the respondent is the other spouse, the occupation order may further provide that those rights will not be brought to an end by the death of the other spouse or dissolution of the marriage. Unless such a provision is included in the order, it will cease to have effect on the death of either party or dissolution of the marriage.

Factors that the court must consider

Section 33(6) provides that in deciding whether to grant the order sought, the court must take into account all circumstances, including:

(a)   the respective housing needs and housing resources of the parties and any child;

(b)   the respective financial resources of the parties;

(c)   the likely effect of any order, or of any decision by the court not to make such an order, on the health, safety or well-being of the parties and any relevant child; and

(d)   the conduct of the parties in relation to each other and otherwise.

However, s 33(6) is subject to the 'balance of harm' test contained in s 33(7). This provides that if it appears to the court that the applicant or any child is likely to suffer significant harm attributable to the conduct of the respondent if an occupation order is not made, then the court *shall* make such an order unless it appears to the court that:

(a)   the respondent or any child is likely to suffer significant harm if the order is made; and

(b)   the harm likely to be suffered by the respondent or child is as great as or greater than the harm attributable to the conduct of the respondent which is likely to be suffered by the applicant or child if the order is not made.

The case of *Chalmers v Johns* [1999] 1 FLR 392 makes it clear that the applicant must show that she would suffer significant harm attributable to the respondent's conduct before the court applies the balance of harm test. Where such harm was not shown, the case would be determined on the basis of the factors in s 33(6) alone. Therefore, if the balance of harm test is made out in the applicant's favour, the court must make the order. If the test is not made out then the court has a discretion to make the order by applying the factors in s 33(6).

The case of *B v B (Occupation Order)* [1999] 1 FLR 715 illustrates the interrelationship of s 33(6) and s 33(7) and the balance of harm test. The wife moved out of the matrimonial home with the couple's two-year-old daughter due to the husband's violence. They were then temporarily rehoused by the local authority. The husband remained in the matrimonial home with his son (aged six) from a previous relationship. Should the wife be granted an occupation order under FLA 1996, s 33? The Court of Appeal held that she should not. Although the wife and child would suffer significant harm attributable to the husband's conduct if an order were not made, the harm which the husband's child would be likely to suffer if an order were made was greater. This was on the basis of the housing needs of both parties and children. Whereas the wife was entitled to be rehoused by the local authority as she was not intentionally homeless, the husband would not be so entitled since he would be considered to be intentionally homeless on account of his violence. If the husband were forced to move out, his son would also need to change schools.

Duration

An occupation order made under s 33 may be for a specified period, until the occurrence of a specified event or until further order. Thus, such an order can be for an indefinite period. In practice it is likely, at least initially, to be for a specified period, probably six months.

15.2.4.2 Applicant has no existing right to occupy the home and respondent has such a right (s 35 and s 36)

Applicant is former spouse (s 35)

An applicant under s 35 must be the former spouse of the respondent. The respondent must be entitled to occupy the home (by virtue of a beneficial estate, or interest, or contract or by statute). The home must be, or have been or have been intended to be, the matrimonial home.

Where these conditions are satisfied, the applicant can apply for an occupation order. Any order granted under s 35 *must* contain a provision (an 'occupation provision') stating:

(a) if the applicant is in occupation, that the applicant has a right not to be excluded from the home or part of it by the respondent for a specified period and prohibiting the respondent from excluding the applicant during that period;

(b) if the applicant is not in occupation, that the applicant be given a right to enter and occupy the home for a specified period and requiring the respondent to permit the exercise of that right.

In addition, the order *may* contain one or more provisions ('exclusion provisions'):

(a) regulating the occupation of the home by either party;

(b) prohibiting, suspending or restricting the respondent's right to occupy;

(c) requiring the respondent to leave the home or part of it;

(d) excluding the respondent from a defined area in which the home is situated.

Factors that the court must consider

Note that the factors are slightly different for occupation provisions and exclusion provisions.

In deciding whether to make an *occupation provision*, the court must take into account all circumstances, including:

(a) the respective housing needs and housing resources of the parties and any child;

(b) the respective financial resources of the parties;

(c) the likely effect of any order, or of any decision by the court not to make such an order, on the health, safety or well-being of the parties and any relevant child;

(d) the conduct of the parties in relation to each other and otherwise;

(e)   the length of time that has elapsed since the parties ceased to live together;

(f)   the length of time that has elapsed since the marriage ended; and

(g)   the existence of any pending proceedings between the parties under s 23A or s 24 of the MCA 1973 and Sch 1 to the CA 1989 (financial orders relating to children), or relating to the legal or beneficial ownership of the home (s 35(6)).

The factors the court must take into account when making an *exclusion provision* are the same as (a)–(e) above for an occupation provision. However, for an exclusion provision, the balance of harm test mentioned in **15.2.4.1** in relation to s 33 applies.

Duration

An occupation order made under s 35 must be made for a specified period not exceeding six months. The order can be extended any number of times, but any extension must be for a further specified period not exceeding six months. In addition, any order shall cease to have effect on the death of either party.

Applicant is cohabitant or former cohabitant (s 36)

An applicant under s 36 must be the cohabitant or former cohabitant of the respondent. Thus, other associated persons may not apply under this section. For example, a niece may not apply for an occupation order against her uncle under s 36. The respondent must be entitled to occupy the home (by virtue of a beneficial estate, or interest, or contract or by statute). The home must be, or have been or have been intended to be, the couple's home.

Where these conditions are satisfied, the applicant can apply for an occupation order. Any order granted *must* contain the same occupation provision as an order under s 35. In addition, it *may* contain any of the same exclusion provisions as an order under s 35.

Factors that the court must consider

In deciding whether to make an *occupation provision*, the relevant factors are in many ways similar to those under s 35. The court must take into account all circumstances, including:

(a)   the respective housing needs and housing resources of the parties and any child;

(b)   the respective financial resources of the parties;

(c)   the likely effect of any order, or of any decision by the court not to make such an order, on the health, safety or well-being of the parties and any relevant child;

(d)   the conduct of the parties in relation to each other and otherwise;

(e)   the nature of the parties' relationship, and in particular the level of commitment involved in it;

(f)   the length of time that they have lived together as husband and wife;

(g)   whether there are or have been any children who are children of both parties, or for whom both parties have or have had parental responsibility;

(h)   the length of time that has elapsed since the parties ceased to live together; and

(i)   the existence of any pending proceedings between the parties under Sch 1 to CA 1989 (financial orders relating to children), or relating to the legal or beneficial ownership of the home (s 36(6)).

In deciding whether to make an *exclusion provision*, the court must take into account all circumstances, including the factors (a)–(d) above in relation to an occupation provision. In addition, the court must consider the following balance of harm questions:

(a)   whether the applicant or any relevant child is likely to suffer significant harm attributable to the conduct of the respondent if the exclusion provision is not made; and

(b)   whether the harm likely to be suffered by the respondent or child if the provision is included is as great or greater than the harm attributable to the conduct of the respondent which is likely to be suffered by the applicant or child if the provision is not included.

This is similar to the balance of harm test in ss 33 and 35. However, there is no duty on the court to make an order where the greater harm to the applicant or child is established, it is just one question to be considered.

Once an order has been made and for so long as it is in force, s 36(13) provides that the applicant will be afforded the same protection as a spouse under s 30(3)–(6). This means that a mortgagee or landlord must accept payments towards the mortgage or rent made by the applicant.

Duration

An occupation order made under s 36 must be for a specified period not exceeding six months. The order can be extended only once, for a further specified period not exceeding six months. Thus the longest period for which a cohabitant or former cohabitant can obtain an occupation order is one year. In addition, any order shall cease to have effect on the death of either party.

15.2.4.3   Neither party has a right to occupy the home (ss 37 and 38)

These sections enable one spouse, a former spouse, cohabitant or former cohabitant to obtain an occupation order against the other in relation to a home in which they both live or lived together but which neither of them has a right to occupy. These sections could be used, for example, to give the applicant a licence to occupy a home which is owned by the respondent's parents. Section 37 applies to spouses or former spouses; s 38 to cohabitants or former cohabitants.

As with ss 33, 35 and 36, such an order may, amongst other things, exclude the respondent from the home or an area in which the home is situated.

Factors that the court must consider

In deciding whether to grant an order under this section, the court must take into account similar factors to those under s 33 (where a spouse or former spouse is applying) or s 36 (where a cohabitant or former cohabitant is applying).

Duration

Any order granted will last for a specified period not exceeding six months. Where the applicant is a spouse or former spouse, the order can be extended on one or more occasions, each time for a specified period not exceeding six months. Where the applicant is a cohabitant or former cohabitant, the order can be extended once only for a further specified period not exceeding six months.

15.2.4.4   Examples

The following examples illustrate the above provisions. You may also find the flowchart at **15.2.4.6** helpful.

(a)   Eric and Nicola are married. They live in a house left to Eric by his parents. Eric has begun drinking heavily recently and been very violent towards Nicola.

Nicola would apply under s 33. As she is married, she would have a right to occupy the matrimonial home under s 30 of the FLA 1996 as Eric owns it.

(b)   Lillian and John cohabit in John's flat which he bought years ago. John has told Lillian the relationship is over and that she must leave. She is unable to do so, as she is totally financially dependent on him and is not well at the moment. This has made John very angry and he has used violence against Lillian to try to make her leave.

Lillian would apply under s 36 as she is a cohabitant and she has no right to occupy the home, but John does.

(c)   Jenny and Agnes live in flat which is a tenancy in their joint names. Agnes, who is suffering from depression, has been using violence against Jenny, who is now frightened to return home.

Jenny will apply under s 33 as she is entitled to occupy the home by virtue of her tenancy.

(d)   Katie and Steve live in Steve's parents' holiday home as they cannot afford to live elsewhere. They are not married. Katie has recently become pregnant and Steve is furious as he does not want the baby; he has been violent towards Katie almost every day since he found out.

Katie will apply under s 38, as neither of them has a right to occupy the home and they are cohabitants.

15.2.4.5   Additional provisions in occupation orders made under s 33, s 35 or s 36 (s 40)

Section 40 enables the court, when making an occupation order under s 33, s 35 or s 36, to make an ancillary order dealing with such matters as the payment of the mortgage or other outgoings, and payment for repair and maintenance of the home. The court can also order the occupying party to pay the excluded party rent where the excluded party would (but for the occupation order) have a right to occupy the home. In addition, the court can grant either party use of the furniture or other contents of the home and order either party to take reasonable care of the furniture or other contents. In deciding whether to make such an ancillary order and in what terms, the court shall have regard to all circumstances of the case, including the financial needs, resources and obligations of the parties. Any ancillary order made will last for the same length of time as the occupation order itself.

There is, however, a problem of enforcement of any order for payments made under s 40. In *Nwogbe v Nwogbe* [2000] 2 FLR 744, the husband was ordered to pay rent, council tax and water rates but did not do so. The Court of Appeal held that it had no power to commit him. The payments did not fall within any of the exceptions to the Debtors Act 1869 (which abolished imprisonment for debt), neither did they come within the Attachment of Earnings Act 1971. Since payments were made to a third party, the wife did not become a judgment creditor and so none of the usual methods of enforcement were available to her. The court accepted that there was a clear lacuna in the law which would need to be filled by Parliament.

15.2.4.6 Flowchart

The flowchart set out below explains who can apply for occupation orders and the appropriate section of the FLA 1996 to use.

OCCUPATION ORDERS – WHO CAN APPLY?

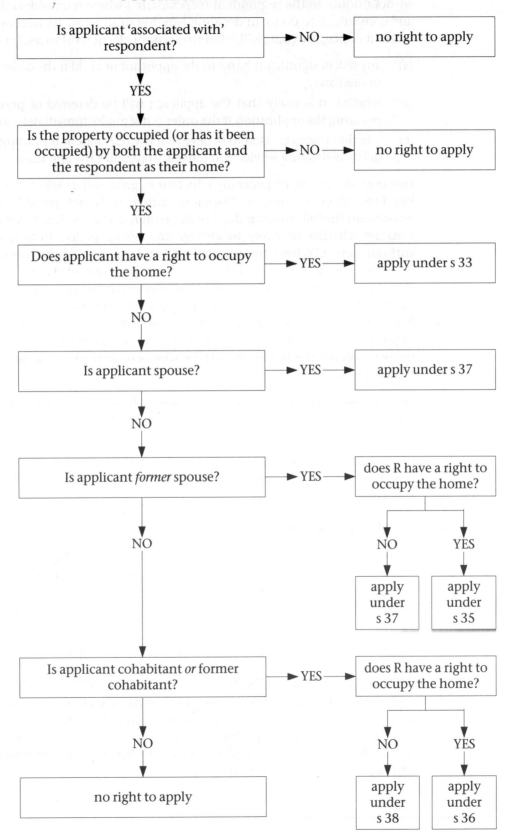

15.2.5 Emergency applications (s 45)

In urgent cases, it may be possible for the solicitor to protect an applicant or child on the same day that she comes to see him, or at least on the next day. Under s 45 of the FLA 1996, the court can make both non-molestation and occupation orders without notice to the respondent (or 'ex parte') where it considers that it is 'just and convenient' to do so. In deciding whether to allow an application to proceed without notice, the court will take into account all circumstances, including:

(a)   any risk of significant harm to the applicant or child if the order is not made immediately;

(b)   whether it is likely that the applicant will be deterred or prevented from pursuing the application if the order is not made immediately; and

(c)   whether there is reason to believe that the respondent is evading service and delay in effecting service will seriously prejudice the applicant or child.

However, the courts are generally reluctant to grant orders where the respondent has been given no notice. Therefore, where it is not possible to give the respondent the full two clear days' notice required, the applicant's solicitor should consider whether to apply to abridge the notice period instead of applying without notice. Where the respondent has been given some notice (however short), he may be able to attend court to give his version of events. This will mean that the court will be in a better position to assess the situation and may therefore be persuaded to grant more wide-ranging relief than where the respondent has been given no notice at all. However, if the respondent has not had an opportunity to instruct a solicitor then the court is likely to make an interim (rather than final) order to allow the respondent time to seek legal advice before the final hearing.

Occupation orders are more rarely granted without notice, especially where they would involve ousting the respondent from his home.

It must be stressed that any order obtained without notice will be temporary only (an interim order). During the few days that the interim order is in force, the solicitor must obtain a hearing date for the final hearing and give the respondent the required notice.

15.2.6 Undertakings (s 46)

In the past, the necessity for a full hearing was often avoided by the respondent offering to give an undertaking, ie a promise to the court on similar terms to the proposed order. This avoided a court order being made against the respondent. The applicant was often prepared to accept the undertaking since, as it was made voluntarily, it was more likely to be complied with.

Under s 46 of the FLA 1996, the court may still accept an undertaking in any case where it has power to make an occupation or non-molestation order. However, no power of arrest can be attached to an undertaking, and the court will not accept an undertaking in a case where it would otherwise attach a power of arrest to an occupation order. The court will not accept an undertaking on an application for a non-molestation order where the respondent has used or threatened violence or a non-molestation order is necessary so that any breach can be punishable under s 42A as a criminal offence (see **15.2.9.1**)).

15.2.7 Procedure

15.2.7.1 Which court?

One of the innovations of Pt IV of the FLA 1996 was to introduce a unified system of courts to deal with domestic abuse applications. This means that the applicant's solicitor generally has a free choice whether to make the application in the county court, or in the family proceedings court.

The family proceedings court has no power to deal with disputes between the applicant and the respondent over the applicant's right to occupy the home (FLA 1996, s 59). A family proceedings court can make an order in such a case only where it is unnecessary to determine the ownership dispute in order to do so. Thus, any proceedings involving such a dispute should sensibly be commenced in the county court. However, where such proceedings are commenced in the family proceedings court and the court decides that it cannot deal with the application, it has the power to transfer the application to a county court.

Applications in the county court can be made only in divorce county courts or family hearing centres. Where proceedings are already pending in a particular court (eg divorce proceedings), the application should generally be made in those proceedings. Any application to extend, vary or discharge an order should be made to the court which originally made the order.

Lastly, any application made by an applicant who is under 18 must be commenced in the High Court.

15.2.7.2 Transfer of cases

Irrespective of where a case started, it can be transferred to a more appropriate court. This will depend, amongst other things, upon whether the case raises a difficult point of law or a question of general public interest, and the need to consolidate it with proceedings which may have been started in another court (see Family Law Act 1996 (Part IV) (Allocation of Proceedings) Order 1997 (SI 1997/1896)).

Cases can be transferred either vertically or horizontally and between any level of court. Thus it would be possible, for example, for the High Court to transfer proceedings to a family proceedings court.

15.2.7.3 Public funding

Provided that the client is eligible, initial advice and assistance will be covered by Legal Help.

Once the decision has been taken to bring proceedings for a non-molestation order and/or an occupation order, Legal Representation should be applied for immediately. If there is an existing certificate for Legal Representation in force in matrimonial proceedings, the solicitor should apply to amend this rather than obtain a new certificate. Note that where the Legal Services Commission considers that it would be appropriate to write a warning letter to the respondent and/or to try to enlist the assistance of the police, it will not grant funding until these steps have been taken and proved ineffective. In addition, funding is likely to be refused unless the conduct complained of took place within the last two to three weeks, or if the conduct complained of is not likely to be repeated or is of a 'trivial nature'.

In most cases, it will also be necessary to apply for Emergency Legal Representation. Family solicitors can themselves grant Emergency Legal Representation under the terms of their contract. The solicitor will need to complete the appropriate section in Form CLSAPP3 and satisfy himself that the client is likely to be financially eligible. The solicitor must then submit an application to the regional office of the Legal Services Commission for both Emergency and Full Legal Representation within five working days of the grant of Emergency Legal Representation.

The procedure set out below assumes that the applicant is entitled to public funding. For a privately paying client, simply omit all steps relating to public funding and remember that a court fee must be paid.

15.2.7.4 Obtaining a non-molestation or an occupation order without notice (ex parte)

(a) Grant Emergency Legal Representation. Emergency cover should only be granted for without notice proceedings where the applicant or child is in imminent danger of significant harm (ie there is a real risk that it will occur before a substantive application can be processed and brought before the court).

(b) Telephone the court to make an appointment before the judge or magistrate if necessary. In the family proceedings court, the clerk or the court must give leave to make an application without notice.

(c) Telephone a process server so that he can be at court at the end of the hearing to collect the without notice order to serve it on the respondent. The order must be served personally, and it is not usually thought wise for the solicitor to do this.

(d) Draft the following:

(i) application in Form FL401 (see **Appendix 3(I)**);

(ii) statement in support. This must give details of the respondent's behaviour and both parties' housing needs and financial resources. It should also explain why the application is made without notice. The statement must be signed by the applicant and sworn to be true in the county court, or declared to be true in the family proceedings court (which may also give leave to allow oral evidence instead of a written statement);

(iii) notice of issue of Emergency Legal Representation;

(iv) where the application is ancillary to a divorce under Legal Help, a notice of acting (for the reasons mentioned at **10.6.1**).

(e) It is not essential to draft the order sought. Generally, however, the court would find it helpful to have a draft and so, if time permits, draft the without notice order(s) on Form FL404 (occupation order) or Form FL404a (non-molestation order).

(f) File at court notice of issue of Emergency Legal Representation, the application in duplicate and the statement in support in duplicate, and notice of acting (if appropriate). A fee must be paid.

(g) Attend the hearing before the judge, district judge or magistrate (in the family proceedings court an application without notice can be heard by a single magistrate, on-notice applications must be heard by a panel – see **15.2.7.5**). The magistrate, judge or district judge will read the statement in support and listen to the applicant's oral evidence. Hand any draft order to the magistrate, judge or district judge.

(h) Any occupation order made will be issued in Form FL404 and any non-molestation order in Form FL404a. Where a power of arrest is attached to any of the provisions of an occupation order, those provisions shall be set out in Form FL406. A record of the hearing will be made on Form FL405. On filing, the court fixes a date for the on notice hearing, which will be inserted in a notice of proceedings (Form FL402). The respondent must be given two clear days' notice of this date.

(i) Hand the process server the without notice order(s), sealed copy application, copy statement in support, notice of proceedings and notice of issue of Emergency Legal Representation. Ask the process server to serve these documents on the respondent personally and then to swear an affidavit of service.

(j) If the court has made an occupation order, serve a copy of the application and the order on any mortgagee or landlord, together with a notice in Form FL416 informing him that he has a right to make representations in writing or at any hearing. These documents should be served by first-class post.

(k) If the court has made a non-molestation order or attached a power of arrest to an occupation order (see **15.2.9**), take a copy of Form FL404a or Form FL406 to the police station nearest to where the applicant lives and a statement showing that the respondent has been served with the order or informed of its terms. The police will not be prepared to exercise any power of arrest unless they have notice of it. Many breaches of orders occur shortly after they are made, so it is important to give the police notice of the order or the power of arrest as soon as possible.

Remember that any hearing without notice must be followed by a hearing on notice so that the respondent has an opportunity to put his side of the story.

15.2.7.5   Obtaining a non-molestation or an occupation order on notice

If a without notice order has been obtained, many of these steps may already have been completed:

(a) Grant Emergency Legal Representation.

(b) Draft the following:

(i) application in Form FL401;

(ii) statement in support. It must give details of the respondent's behaviour and both parties' housing needs and financial resources. The statement must be signed by the applicant and sworn to be true in the county court, or declared to be true in the family proceedings court (which may also give leave to allow oral evidence instead of a written statement). Where a without notice order has been obtained, the statement will probably already have been drafted. The same statement is generally used for both without notice and on notice hearings. However, where further instances of violence have occurred, or the initial statement has been hurriedly drafted, a further statement should be drafted;

(iii) notice of issue of Legal Representation;

(iv) where the application is ancillary to a divorce under Legal Help, a notice of acting (for the reasons mentioned at **10.6.1**).

(c) File the application in duplicate, statement in duplicate, notice of issue of Legal Representation, notice of acting (where appropriate) and Emergency Legal Representation certificate (where appropriate). A fee must be paid.

(d) On filing, the court fixes a hearing date which will be inserted in a notice of proceedings (Form FL402). The respondent must be given two clear days' notice of this date. Hand to a process server sealed copy application, copy statement in support, notice of hearing, notice of issue of Emergency Legal

Representation and notice of acting (where appropriate). Ask him to serve these documents on the respondent personally and to swear an affidavit to confirm service.

(e)   If the FL401 includes an application for an occupation order, serve any mortgagee or landlord with a copy of the application and a notice in Form FL416 informing him that he has a right to make representations in writing or at the hearing. These documents should be served by first-class post.

(f)   Once the respondent (and mortgagee/landlord) has been served, file a statement confirming that this has been done in Form FL415.

(g)   Prepare the draft order(s) required on Form FL404 or Form FL404a. This is not essential, but the court will find it useful.

(h)   Attend the hearing before the judge or the district judge in chambers, or a panel of magistrates. In the family proceedings court, the hearing will take place before the domestic panel. This is a panel of magistrates who have received special training in family proceedings. The panel should consist of at least two magistrates, and should preferably include one man and one woman. The hearing will be in private. If the respondent fails to attend, service can be proved using the affidavit. The court can then make an order in the absence of the respondent.

Hand any order(s) drafted to the judge, district judge or magistrates. The judge, district judge or magistrates will read any statements filed by the parties and may hear oral evidence from the applicant and respondent. If either of the parties has witnesses (eg a neighbour or relative) they may then give evidence. Any occupation order made will be issued on Form FL404 and any non-molestation order on Form FL404a. Where a power of arrest is attached to any of the provisions of an occupation order, those provisions will be set out on Form FL406. A record of the hearing will be made on Form FL405. The court may direct a further hearing to hear representations from any mortgagee or landlord.

(i)   The respondent must be served personally with the order (even if he was present when it was made). Again, this is usually done by a process server who should swear an affidavit of service.

(j)   If the court has made a non-molestation order or attached a power of arrest to an occupation order (see 15.2.9), take a copy of Form FL404a or Form FL406 to the police station nearest to where the applicant lives.

15.2.8 Procedural checklist

A checklist of the appropriate procedure may be helpful. One is set out below.

ON NOTICE PROCEDURE CHECKLIST

OBTAIN LEGAL REPRESENTATION IF RELEVANT

FILE:
(i)   Application (Form FL 401) in duplicate
(ii)   Statement in support in duplicate
(iii) Legal Representation Certificate and Notice of Issue
(iv)   Fee
(v)   Notice of Acting (if client in divorce under Legal Help)

SERVE ON R:
(i)   Copy Application
(ii)   Copy Statement
[(iii) Notice of Issue of LR Certificate]
(iv)   Notice of Hearing (Form FL 402)
[(v)   Copy Notice of Acting]
[Give two clear days' notice]

SERVE ON MORTGAGEE/LANDLORD:
Notice in Form FL 416

FILE:
Statement of Service

ATTEND FIRST HEARING:
Present case
Produce draft order (if drafted)

SERVE order on R and mortgagee/landlord
LODGE copy at police station of Form FL404a or Form FL406

15.2.9 Enforcement

Since 1 July 2007 breach of a non-molestation order is a criminal offence (FLA 1996, s 42A). Before 1 July 2007 the basic method of enforcement where a respondent had breached a non-molestation order or an occupation order was committal for contempt of court. How the respondent came before the court depended generally on whether or not the order had a power of arrest attached to it. This position remains the same for breaches of an occupation order, but for non-molestation orders made after 1 July 2007 breach will be a criminal offence and dealt with differently.

15.2.9.1 Breach of a non-molestation order

Section 42A of the FLA 1996 makes breach of a non-molestation order a criminal offence punishable by up to five years' imprisonment on indictment and 12 months' imprisonment on conviction in the magistrates' court. Where a respondent breaches a non-molestation order, he will be arrested for the crime of breaching the order and can be charged and brought before a criminal court. The prosecution will be handled by the CPS and the solicitors for the complainant will not play any roll.

A respondent cannot, however, be punished for the same offence twice, so if he is convicted of an offence under s 42A he cannot be punished for contempt of court for the same conduct.

15.2.9.2 Breach of an occupation order

Power of arrest

Under s 47 of the FLA 1996, where the court makes an occupation order (or, before 1 July 2007, where it made a non-molestation order) and it appears to the court that the respondent has used or threatened violence against the applicant (ie any associated person) or a child, then it *shall* attach a power of arrest to one or more provisions of the order. The only exception to this is where the court is satisfied that the applicant or child will be adequately protected without such a power of arrest.

The court can attach a power of arrest to one or more provisions of the order. Any power of arrest will be drafted on Form FL406, which will set out which provisions the power of arrest will apply to.

A power of arrest can also be attached to one or more provisions of a without notice order, but only where it appears to the court that the respondent has used or threatened violence against the applicant or child and that there is a risk of significant harm to the applicant or child if the power of arrest is not attached immediately.

Any power of arrest granted will usually be expressed to last for the same period as the provisions of the order to which it is attached (although this will not always be the case). This period can be extended any number of times.

A police officer will have the power to arrest the respondent without warrant if he has reasonable cause to suspect the respondent of being in breach of any of the terms of the order set out in the power of arrest. Once arrested, the respondent must be brought before a judge, district judge or magistrate within 24 hours.

Warrant of arrest

Where the court has not attached a power of arrest, or the respondent's breach is not covered by the power of arrest, or an undertaking is breached, the applicant may apply for a warrant of arrest. The applicant will need to give evidence on oath to satisfy the judge, district judge or magistrate that there are reasonable grounds for believing that the respondent has breached the order. The judge, district judge or magistrate can then issue a warrant of arrest.

Penalty

The penalty available will depend upon whether the respondent is brought before a judge in the county court, or a magistrate in the family proceedings court. In the county court, the judge can commit the respondent for up to two years (and/or impose an unlimited fine). In the family proceedings court, the respondent can be fined up to £5,000 or committed for up to two months.

In both courts, immediate committal was a remedy of last resort and was unlikely to be ordered save in exceptional situations. General guidelines on committal were given by the Court of Appeal in *Hale v Tanner* [2000] 2 FLR 879. These include:

(a)   that imprisonment is not the automatic consequence of the breach of an order but there was no principle that imprisonment should not be imposed on a first breach;

(b)   that the court should bear in mind the context – there could be aggravating or mitigating factors;

(c)   that the length of committal had to bear some reasonable relationship to the maximum available;

(d)   that suspension was available in a much wider range of circumstances than in a criminal case and should usually be used initially where committal is contemplated to try to secure compliance with the order.

Since the Protection from Harassment Act 1997 (see **15.4** below), which provides greater sentencing powers, recent cases have seemed to indicate that courts are willing to impose longer custodial sentences for breaches of FLA 1996 orders than in the past. In *Lomas v Parle* [2003] EWCA Civ 1804, the Court of Appeal increased a sentence of imprisonment from four months to eight months, and said care must be taken that sentences for breach of FLA 1996 orders are not manifestly discrepant with those under the Protection from Harassment Act 1997. In *H v O (Contempt of Court: Sentencing)* [2004] EWCA Civ 1691, the Court of Appeal, whilst reducing a sentence of imprisonment from 12 months to nine months, stated that it felt that Parliament and society now demanded more deterrent punishment than in the past for domestic violence. In *Robinson v Murray* [2005] EWCA Civ 935, where the Court of Appeal upheld a sentence of eight months' imprisonment, it suggested if a case warranted a sentence near the top of the range, the appropriate course is to bring proceedings under the Protection from Harassment Act 1997 so that the greater powers of punishment are available to the court.

Finally, if the order had no power of arrest attached, the judge or magistrate may attach a power of arrest.

15.3   Human Rights Act 1998

Non-molestation or occupation orders may raise issues under Article 6 of the European Convention on Human Rights. Public funding is often denied to respondents to such orders, who may be advised to give undertakings on the basis of no admissions. Consideration may have to be given as to whether public funding should be provided, given that undertakings can be the first step in committal proceedings which may result in imprisonment or a fine. One of the Article 6 guarantees is that the proceedings are fair and that each party has 'equality of arms' with the other. Yet if a respondent is not represented on an application, can he be said to have 'equality of arms'?

Occupation orders may also raise issues under Article 8 (the right to respect for family life and home). Interference with this right must be necessary and proportionate. Courts must therefore give careful consideration to the duration and scope of such orders.

15.4 Protection from Harassment Act 1997

In the past, when an applicant did not come within the ambit of the relevant domestic abuse legislation, for example if she was the partner of the abuser but they had not cohabited, she would have to bring an action for an appropriate tort, for example, assault. However, until recently, there was no tort of harassment, so protection could be obtained only where the conduct complained of amounted to an established tort (see, eg, *Burris v Azadani* [1995] 4 All ER 802).

The Protection from Harassment Act (PHA) 1997 plugged this gap in the law. Section 3 of the PHA 1997 created a statutory tort where a person pursues a course of conduct which amounts to harassment of another and which he knows or ought to know amounts to harassment of the other. There is no definition of harassment, save that the PHA 1997 states that this includes 'alarming the person or causing them distress' (s 7). A 'course of conduct' must include conduct on at least two occasions.

Section 3 provides that where the statutory tort has been committed or is apprehended, the victim may claim damages and/or an injunction. Should the injunction be breached, then the victim may apply for a warrant of arrest in the same way as under the FLA 1996. Also, breach of the injunction may be a criminal offence, punishable by up to five years' imprisonment on conviction on indictment (s 3(6) and (9)).

The PHA 1997 also created two new criminal offences, criminal harassment and the more serious offence of putting someone in fear of violence (ss 2 and 4 respectively). In addition, s 5 gives the criminal courts power to make restraining orders prohibiting the perpetrator from engaging in further harassment. This power will be widened when the Domestic Violence, Crime and Victims Act 2004 is fully in force, to allow criminal courts to make restraining orders on conviction of any offence, not just an offence under the PHA 1997, and even to make such orders on acquittal of a defendant if they consider it necessary to protect a person from harassment by the defendant.

15.5 Chapter summary

(1)   In cases of domestic abuse, a solicitor will have to decide whether to take action in the civil courts, or whether other remedies, for example writing a warning letter, involving the police or removing the victim to a safe environment, may be more appropriate.

(2)   The FLA 1996 allows applicants to apply for two main types of relief:

(a)   non-molestation orders;

(b)   occupation orders.

(3) Non-molestation orders can be obtained by a wide range of 'associated persons'.

(4) Occupation orders can be applied for by a more limited range of people. Whether a person has a right to occupy the home, or is a former spouse, cohabitant or former cohabitant will determine whether they can apply at all and the relief they can obtain.

(5) In urgent cases, it may be possible to obtain orders under the FLA 1996 without notice.

(6) The respondent may give an undertaking instead of having an order made against him.

(7) A power of arrest must generally be attached to an occupation order unless the court is satisfied that the applicant will be adequately protected without it.

(8) Where a non-molestation order is breached it is a criminal offence.

(9) Where an occupation order is breached it can be enforced by applying for committal of the respondent for contempt of court.

(10) The PHA 1997 created a new statutory tort of harassment which may be used where the applicant does not fall within the provisions of the FLA 1996.

Chapter 16

The Cohabiting Family

16.1 Introduction

In this chapter the terms 'cohabiting family' and 'cohabiting couples' are used to refer to couples who live together without marrying (or entering into a civil partnership).

The number of couples who are living together has dramatically increased in recent years and over 40% of births are outside marriage. Family lawyers have traditionally been consulted by such couples when their relationship breaks down; but increasingly nowadays, they are being instructed by couples who want advice on setting up home together.

In July 2004 the (then) Department for Constitutional Affairs launched a public information campaign, 'Living Together'. This had the aim of making cohabiting couples more aware of their legal status and providing them with practical advice on how they can protect themselves and their families, as survey results have shown there is a common public misconception that cohabiting couples enjoy similar rights to married couples.

The financial orders available under the MCA 1973 do not apply to cohabiting couples, and to date English law has developed piecemeal to deal with the problems of such couples. For several years the Law Society and Resolution have been actively considering the question of a comprehensive reform of this area of the law and have set out detailed proposals.

The Civil Partnership Act 2004 arose as a result of pressure for reform in this area. However, this deals with the position of same-sex couples only. The Government's reason for not extending it to heterosexual couples was that they already have the option of marriage available to them.

During the passage of the Civil Partnership Act through Parliament, concerns were expressed about the lack of a coherent scheme of remedies to relieve the potential financial hardship of cohabiting couples on relationship breakdown. As a result of this the Law Commission was asked to review the law in this area and to suggest possible reforms. In July 2007 the Law Commission published its report, 'Cohabitation: The Financial Consequences of Relationship Breakdown', which proposes a scheme to provide remedies for eligible applicants (such as those with children or who have lived together for a specified time), so long as they had not agreed to disapply the scheme and only if the applicant has made qualifying contributions to the relationship giving rise to enduring consequences at the point of separation (such as giving up a career to care for the couple's children).

This chapter summarises the current legal position both during the time when the couple are living together, including advice on how to avoid problems in the first place, and when the relationship breaks down.

16.2 Setting up home together

16.2.1 Ownership of the home

16.2.1.1 Duty of the buyers' solicitor

When a solicitor acts for joint buyers, he has a duty to advise on the relative merits of owning as joint tenants and tenants in common, and may be sued in negligence if he fails to do this (see *Walker v Hall* [1984] FLR 126, *Taylor v Warners* (1988) 85(25) LSG 26).

It is also important to consider when advising joint buyers whether there is any conflict, or potential conflict, of interest between them, in which case a solicitor should not act for both of them.

16.2.1.2 Declaration as to beneficial interests

An effective way to clarify beneficial interests in a jointly-owned property is by using a declaration of trust. Section 53(1)(b) of the Law of Property Act 1925 requires that a declaration must be in writing signed by the buyers. This will generally be conclusive evidence as to the ownership (*Pettit v Pettit* [1970] AC 777). Since there is no equivalent to s 25 of the MCA 1973 (see **4.5**) for an unmarried couple, the arrangement cannot be undone by the court at a later stage. Therefore, the buyers must both understand the position and be in agreement as to their respective shares at the time of purchase.

The declaration can either be included in the purchase deed, or be contained in a separate deed. On balance, it is preferable to prepare a separate document, especially if the property is registered, because Land Registry will not return the transfer after registration.

A further advantage is that some other important matters can be dealt with in a separate document, for example division of outgoings such as repairs, insurance and the mortgage repayments; circumstances in which a sale may take place or be postponed; and, if necessary, provisions giving one party an option to buy the other's share.

16.2.2 Life insurance

It is important that couples living together make provision for life insurance to cover each of them against the financial consequences of the death of the other.

There is a legal requirement that provides that the person for whom the benefit of a life assurance policy is made must have an insurable interest in the life of the assured, otherwise the policy will be void and illegal (Life Assurance Act 1774, s 1). This interest must be of a financial nature. This can be a problem because, whilst marriage is recognised as giving the parties an insurable interest in each others' lives without the need to prove financial loss, cohabitation is not so recognised. It is therefore essential that where couples are living together, mutual financial support can be shown.

Most couples are concerned with life insurance in relation to an endowment or repayment mortgage upon their home. Clear advice must be given to them on the validity of the policy and the consequences if they split up. Insurance is also relevant in the guise of death benefit paid as part of an employment contract. Often the employee can nominate to whom the money should be paid by giving instructions to the trustees of the scheme.

16.2.3 Wills

The vast majority of people die intestate. This is not advisable, especially for a cohabiting couple (see **16.6.2**). When a couple decide to live together, they should discuss whether provisions should be made for the survivor if one of them should die. Wills that contain complementary provisions could then be made. A solicitor acting on a house purchase can explain the problems and encourage the buyers to make a will. A will might appoint a guardian for any children and deal with the division of assets.

16.2.4 Cohabitation agreements

A cohabiting couple can enter into an agreement setting out arrangements which will apply while they are living together, as well as establishing rights on the breakdown of the relationship. This is a developing area of the law and as yet there is no modern decision on the validity of such agreements. However, in *Sutton v Mischon De Reya and Gower & Co* [2003] EWHC 3166 (Ch), [2004] 1 FLR 837, the court gave the strongest indication yet that there was nothing contrary to public policy in a cohabitation agreement. It is clear that solicitors are increasingly being asked to advise on and draft agreements in this field. The Law Commission, in its report (see **16.1**), recommends legislation to make clear that cohabitation agreements are not contrary to public policy.

16.2.4.1 Validity of cohabitation agreements

In the absence of modern authority, cohabitation agreements are governed by general principles of the law of contract. The following issues could therefore be relevant.

Illegality on grounds of public policy

To avoid challenge on the ground of illegality on grounds of public policy an agreement must avoid any implication that cohabitation is part of the obligations of the agreement. It is, therefore, safer to enter into the agreement after, rather than before, the couple have started living together.

Undue influence

Undue influence may arise if the agreement is unduly favourable to one party and that party cannot show that it was entered into freely or following independent advice (see *Zamet and Others v Hyman and Another* [1961] 3 All ER 933).

A related issue for a solicitor is to bear in mind that it is likely to be impossible to act for both parties due to the potential conflict of interest. For example, one party may be contributing all the finance for a house purchase, which would mean that the other party, in agreeing to this in a cohabitation agreement, would give up any chance of obtaining a share if the relationship broke down. As a general principle, The Law Society's Family Law Protocol (Part V, para 2.2) says that solicitors should advise clients that they can only act for one party in drawing up such an agreement and that the other party should be separately represented.

Intention to create legal relations

In domestic circumstances there is a rebuttable presumption that the parties did not intend to enter into a contract. Where the couple have a written agreement, especially if they received separate legal advice upon it, it should not be difficult to rebut the presumption (see *Balfour v Balfour* [1919] 2 KB 571 and *Merritt v Merritt* [1970] 1 WLR 1121).

Certainty

Any arrangements proposed must be set out clearly, otherwise the agreement may fail through lack of certainty.

Consideration

Any potential problem arising from a failure of consideration can be avoided by making the agreement a deed.

16.2.4.2   Matters to be covered in a cohabitation agreement

The main issues which could usefully be covered in a cohabitation agreement are as follows:

(a)   ownership of real and personal property (see **16.2.1**);

(b)   finances, for example, how to divide bills and resolve ownership of joint accounts;

(c)   children, for example, their maintenance and surnames. Any agreement made in relation to children will be limited by the CA 1989 and the CSA 1991 and will be open to review by the court (see **16.4**);

(d)   other matters: here it is important not to include matters which are too trivial, or personal matters, for example housework or division of chores, because this could make it more likely that a court would hold that the parties did not intend to create legal relations.

16.2.4.3   Enforcement of cohabitation agreements

The general rules of contract will apply to the enforcement of cohabitation agreements. It might also be advisable to include an arbitration clause in the agreement for dealing with disputes between the parties. The Family Law Bar Association Conciliation Board's conciliation procedure is available to unmarried couples who have lived together.

16.3   Breaking up

When cohabiting couples split up, neither party has any right to claim maintenance from the other. Maintenance can nevertheless be claimed for children of the relationship (see **16.4.2**). Major disputes are therefore likely to centre around the ownership or occupation of their home. It is possible to bring the dispute before the court by seeking a declaration of ownership of the home under s 14 of the Trusts of Land and Appointment of Trustees Act 1996 (TLATA 1996) (see **Appendix 1(H)**).

If the couple were engaged within three years before the dispute, it might be possible to use s 17 of the Married Women's Property Act 1882. This Act enables property disputes to be determined summarily by the county court; generally it is used only by married couples. The Act confers no jurisdiction to vary property rights and so the court's powers are purely declaratory (*Mossop v Mossop* [1988] 2 All ER 20).

16.3.1   Ownership of the home

16.3.1.1   Jointly owned property

If the correct procedure was adopted when the property was purchased, the couple's intentions as to ownership should be clear from the purchase deed or declaration of trust. If the couple purchased as joint tenants, either could apply to the court for an order of sale under s 14 of the TLATA 1996 and the proceeds would then be divided equally. If the couple purchased as tenants in common, or if the joint tenancy was severed, only a declaration of trust made by them will be decisive (see **16.2.1.2**).

If they own as tenants in common and there is no declaration of trust, it will be presumed they own in equal shares unless the contrary can be proved (*Stack v Dowden* [2007] UKHL 17). In *Stack v Dowden*, the House of Lords said it would look at many factors as well as the financial contributions the parties made, such as how the parties conducted their finances and why the house was acquired, to determine whether they intended to own it in unequal shares.

It is open to one partner to buy out the other's interest. If this is done, the prior permission of any lender must be sought. In contrast to divorcing couples, any transfer will be liable to stamp duty land tax on the consideration paid plus the amount of any mortgage debt assumed (see Stamp Act 1891, s 57, Inland Revenue SP 27 April 1990, Finance Act 1985, s 83(1), and Stamp Duty (Exempt Instruments) Regulations 1987 (SI 1987/516) Category H).

16.3.1.2   Legal estate in one name only

If a property is in the sole legal ownership of one party, the presumption is that that party also owns all the beneficial interest. In this situation the other party will have to establish a claim in equity. This will involve establishing a resulting or constructive trust, or proprietary estoppel. The court cannot alter an unmarried partner's share to reflect MCA 1973, s 25 principles as it is able to do with a married couple.

If a claim is successful and a trust is established, the non-legal owner will be entitled to a share in the property equal to his beneficial interest as determined by the court in accordance with land law principles. If proprietary estoppel is established then one of the remedies available is to give the claimant an interest in the property.

Until recently, interests based on direct contributions, for example, to the purchase price of a property have been dealt with under resulting trusts; interests founded on wider equitable principles, for example on the basis that it is just and equitable, are clearly constructive trusts or proprietary estoppel.

Resulting trusts

Resulting trusts can be established only by a direct contribution to the purchase price by the partner who is not the legal owner. *Curley v Parkes* [2004] EWCA Civ 1515 suggested that the contribution must be made at the time of purchase and that subsequent payments, such as mortgage payments, would not suffice. However, a direct contribution to the purchase price will not establish a trust if given by way of gift or loan. The successful claimant will be awarded a share to reflect the initial contribution made (contrast this with the position under constructive trusts (below) where, in the absence of any express agreement as to the size of the share, the court will decide what shares the parties intended by looking at the their whole course of conduct in relation to the property). *Stack v Dowden* suggests that, in domestic cases of cohabitants, resulting trusts are no longer the appropriate approach, and that these cases should be decided under the principle of constructive trusts (see below).

Constructive trusts

In *Lloyds Bank plc v Rosset* [1990] 2 WLR 867, [1990] 1 All ER 1111, the House of Lords considered the law in this area in detail, and the case contains a clear analysis of the circumstances where equity will impose a trust on the legal owner.

For a constructive trust to arise the claimant must show there was a common intention to share ownership and that the claimant acted in reliance on this to his detriment.

The common intention can be established by an express agreement. In *H v M (Property: Beneficial Interest)* [1992] 1 FLR 229, the parties lived together for 11 years, had two children, but never married. The assets included two bungalows in Essex and a property in Spain, all in the legal ownership of the man. The woman claimed a beneficial interest in the property. The court looked very closely at exactly what had been said by the parties as to how any assets would be divided. The man had said to the woman, 'Don't worry about the future because when we are married it will be half yours anyway and I'll always look after you and the boy'. The man also made an excuse that the property was in his name alone for 'tax reasons'. As on the facts there was an express common intention (his statements to her), the woman had to show only that she had acted on this to her detriment. The court accepted that her detrimental action was the execution of a mortgage deed by her 'as occupier' postponing any rights she might have to the lender, thus prejudicing her domestic security. On this basis, the court awarded her an equal share in the English property, but dismissed her claim for a share of the Spanish house as no similar conversation had taken place.

The court will generally find a trust from discussions in the course of which the legal owner gives an excuse why legal ownership is not to be shared. In *Eves v Eves* [1975] 1 WLR 1338, a man told the woman that the property was only in his name as she was under 21 years of age. Subsequently, she worked on various structural alterations to it. She was held to be entitled to a 25% share (see also *Grant v Edwards* [1986] Ch 638).

If there is no evidence of an express agreement, a common intention to share the property can be inferred from the parties' conduct. Conduct such as payment of mortgage instalments and financial contributions to improvements to the property can be used to infer the common intention to share the property.

Contributions by labour may also count. In *Cooke v Head* [1972] 1 WLR 518, the woman non-legal owner made a small contribution to the mortgage payments as well as contributions by manual labour in helping to build a bungalow on land owned by the man. She was entitled to a one-third share for their 'joint efforts'. However, in the *Lloyds Bank* case (above) it was pointed out that a common intention by the parties to renovate a house as a joint venture did not throw any light on their intentions with respect to the beneficial ownership of the property. The work done by the wife in supervising and helping with work and decorating was not enough on its own in this case to justify the inference of a common intention to share.

Generally, contributions to household expenses other than the mortgage are much less likely to establish a trust. In *Burns v Burns* [1984] Ch 317, an unmarried couple with two children occupied for 17 years a house bought in the man's name. The woman made no contribution towards deposit or mortgage repayments, but fully performed the tasks expected of a wife and mother and, when able to return to work, was content to meet the household expenses out of her earnings. At no time did the man depend on her financial help. In that case, it was held that the necessary common intention could not be inferred from her natural concern with the well-being of the household. More recently, however, in *Le Foe v Le Foe and Woolwich plc; Woolwich plc v Le Foe and Le Foe* [2001] 2 FLR 970, the court decided that it was entitled to infer that the parties commonly intended that the wife should have a beneficial interest as a result of her indirect contributions to the mortgage.

However, in addition there must be detrimental reliance. The court appears to take a wide view of this, as illustrated above in *H v M*. Nevertheless, in *Midland Bank v Dobson and Dobson* [1986] 1 FLR 171, the performance by the woman of normal household duties and the purchase by her of household items were 'quite consistent with the man's absolute ownership of the house'. Unless followed by conduct of a sacrificial nature, the expression of intention was at best an unenforceable declaration of trust lacking the written evidence required by Law of Property Act 1925, s 53(1)(b).

In *Stack v Dowden*, the House of Lords said that when determining the size of a claimant's share, where there had been no express agreement, the court had to determine what the parties' intentions had been, actual or inferred, with respect to the property in the light of their whole course of conduct in relation to it.

Proprietary estoppel

The doctrine of estoppel has been used to give rights of ownership: see *Pascoe v Turner* [1979] 1 WLR 431 (although remedies also include granting a licence to occupy (see **16.3.2**) or payment of money to the claimant). Three elements are required:

(a) an assurance of an interest in the property;

(b) reliance on that assurance;

(c) detriment suffered as a result.

Proprietary estoppel is wider and more flexible than a constructive trust, which requires common intention to be shown rather than just an assurance.

16.3.2 Occupation of home

If a non-legal owner does not have any beneficial interest in the property under the principles discussed above, he or she will have no right to remain there and may be excluded by the owner at any time on giving reasonable notice. However, in these circumstances the following ways of protecting the non-legal owner must be considered:

(a) contractual licence;

(b) licence by estoppel;

(c) FLA 1996, Pt IV;

(d) CA 1989, s 15 and Sch 1.

16.3.2.1 Contractual licence

It is necessary to establish the existence of a contract creating a licence. This means that a party will have to show that there was an intention to create legal relations, offer and acceptance, and consideration.

In *Tanner v Tanner* [1975] 3 All ER 776, a woman gave up a rent-controlled flat to occupy a house bought by the man, in which she brought up their children. The court found a licence for her to occupy the property did exist which would last until the children grew up.

Each case must depend on the particular circumstances and often the necessary elements for a contract will not be established (see *Coombes v Smith* [1986] 1 WLR 808).

16.3.2.2 Licence by estoppel

If there is insufficient evidence to establish a contract, the doctrine of estoppel has sometimes been invoked to give rise to rights of occupation rather than ownership.

Three elements are required:

(a)   assurance of the right to occupy;

(b)   reliance on that assurance;

(c)   detriment suffered as a result.

In *Greasley v Cooke* [1980] 3 All ER 710, the woman was engaged initially as a maid, but subsequently cohabited with the son of the family for 30 years. The woman looked after the children and was led to believe she could remain in the property for as long as she wished. The court held that an equity had been raised that could only be satisfied by allowing her to remain in the house for as long as she wished (see also *Maharaj v Chand* [1986] AC 898).

16.3.2.3 Family Law Act 1996

Provided the man and woman are cohabitants or former cohabitants, an unmarried partner may obtain an order under the FLA 1996 either to protect her and any children living with her from further violence from her partner, or, in certain circumstances, an order to remove her partner from the home (see **Chapter 15**).

Even if the FLA 1996 is used, it will provide only short-term protection as the order will give no long-term right to remain in the home.

Reference should be made to the Housing Act 1996 (see **6.10**) to establish whether the local authority has any duty to provide alternative housing.

16.3.2.4 Children Act 1989, s 15 and Sch 1

An unmarried parent could apply on behalf of a child for financial orders from the other parent (see **13.10.4**). The orders that can be obtained include a property adjustment order or a settlement. It would be possible for a child to be granted a transfer of property order (which will include a tenancy), or a *Mesher* order to provide the child with a home until he is no longer dependent. The non-owning partner looking after the child would, therefore, be able to occupy the property as he would be looking after the child (see *J v J (A Minor: Property Transfer)* [1993] 2 FLR 56).

16.3.3   Sale of the property

If the property is jointly owned, or if it is established that a trust of land does exist by virtue of a resulting or constructive trust, one partner can apply to the court for an order to deal with any dispute. The most likely dispute is that one partner will want to sell the house and the other will wish to remain living there. The application will now be made under the TLATA 1996 (see **Appendix 1(H)**).

Sections 14 and 15 of the TLATA 1996 give the court wide powers to deal with any disputes concerning land subject to a trust. Section 14 gives the court power to make an order that reflects the underlying nature and purpose of the trust. Section 15 sets out the matters to which the court must have regard in determining any application for an order under s 14. They include:

(a)   the intention of the person or persons who created the trust;

(b)   the purpose for which the property subject to the trust is held;

(c)   the welfare of any minor who occupies, or might reasonably be expected to occupy any trust property as his home; and

(d)   the interests of any secured creditor (eg a mortgagee) of any beneficiary.

If the court finds that the home is still needed as a family home it will delay a sale. This could be until the children grow up. Even where there are no children, the court could postpone the sale of the house for a specified period, for example to give the occupier time to buy out the non-occupier, or until the occupier finds alternative accommodation. This will only be a postponement for a few months at the most.

The effect of the TLATA 1996 is to combine the old legal provisions in the Law of Property Act 1925, s 30 and the existing case law under that section (*Re Ever's Trust* [1980] 1 WLR 1327; *Bernard v Josephs* [1983] 4 FLR 178) to ensure that the court has broad and flexible powers.

If the client is publicly funded, the statutory charge will apply to proceedings under s 14 of the TLATA 1996 (see **2.9**). However, the Legal Services Commission has power, at its discretion, to postpone enforcement of the statutory charge in any case where the home is recovered or preserved under s 14 proceedings, or the proceedings result in the payment of a lump sum to the applicant which is to be used to purchase a home.

16.3.4   Tenancies

The FLA 1996 has altered the position of cohabitants in relation to certain tenancies. The basic position before the Act (which will still be the position if the FLA 1996 does not apply) is that if a tenancy is in the name of one partner, the other has no protection and will be a bare licensee who can be evicted on 'reasonable notice'. An occupation order may give protection under the FLA 1996 for a limited period (see **Chapter 15**). If the couple are joint tenants, both will be entitled to occupy the property. If one gives up occupation, the other's continued occupation ensures the continuance of the tenancy.

Sch 7 to the FLA 1996 introduced for the first time the right, in some circumstances, for a cohabitant to obtain a tenancy transfer order in relation to certain tenancies. The right to apply for a transfer order will apply irrespective of whether the tenancy is held jointly by the couple or by one of them alone, and will only be available on separation where the tenancy was of a dwelling house the couple occupied together as husband and wife. The court's powers are available only in relation to tenancies specified in the Act, including protected and statutory tenancies within the Rent Act 1977, some agricultural tenancies, a secure tenancy (Housing Act 1985, s 79) and an assured tenancy (Housing Act 1988, Pt VII).

When deciding whether to make a tenancy transfer order the court must have regard to all the circumstances of the case, including the circumstances in which the tenancy was granted or in which either party became the tenant, similar factors to those relevant when granting occupation orders (see **Chapter 15**) and the suitability of the parties as tenants. Schedule 7 contains detailed provisions specifying the transfer orders that can be made, and also gives the court a discretion to award compensation to the transferor. Orders under Sch 7 take effect without the need for any further document transferring the tenancy. The power to transfer tenancies could, therefore, be used as an alternative to an occupation order.

16.4   Children

There is an increasing number of children born each year to parents who are not married to each other. This makes no difference to the day-to-day care of the child while they are cohabiting, but there are legal differences which will alter the legal position if the parents separate. This section looks at the differences in the legal position where a child's parents are not married.

16.4.1   Parental responsibility

Where the parents of a child are not married at the time of the child's birth, the mother will have sole parental responsibility for the child (CA 1989, s 2(2)(a) (see **Appendix 1(E)**)). The father will not have parental responsibility unless he acquires it in accordance with the provisions of the Act. Strictly, only the mother will have the right to sign a form of consent to an operation, decide where the child should be educated, or appoint a guardian for the child if the father does not have parental responsibility.

Not having parental responsibility does not cut the father off completely, because the Act allows even a father without parental responsibility to apply for any s 8 order without leave as he will come within the definition of 'parent' for the purposes of the Act. So, if he is unhappy about any aspect of the child's upbringing, he could apply for a specific issue order to determine the dispute with the mother. He could also apply for a residence order, so the child could live with him. If his child is in care, he can apply for contact with the child (CA 1989, s 34). However, in any event he may still prefer formally to share parental responsibility. This could be reassuring for him if, for example, the child's mother has religious objections to blood transfusions, and parental responsibility will give him more rights if the child is taken into care or put up for adoption.

The ways in which an unmarried father can acquire parental responsibility for his child are examined in **16.4.1.1** to **16.4.1.6** below.

16.4.1.1   Registration as the child's father

If the father is registered on the child's birth certificate as the father then he acquires parental responsibility. This must be done with the consent of the mother.

16.4.1.2   Parental responsibility order

If the father wants to share parental responsibility with the mother and she is not willing to agree to this, the father can apply to court for a parental responsibility order. Such an order will give him joint parental responsibility with the mother and place him in virtually the same position legally as if he were married. Since the parents may not be living with each other when this order is made, he may wish to apply at the same time for a contact order (*Re H (A Minor) (Parental Responsibility)* [1993] 1 FLR 484).

If there is a dispute about paternity, s 20(1) of the Family Law Reform Act 1969 can be used to obtain a court direction that there be blood tests. The court has a discretion to give such a direction (*Re F (A Minor) (Blood Tests)* [1993] 1 FLR 598).

In deciding whether to grant the parental responsibility order, the court will use the welfare principle (but not, specifically, the statutory checklist). The court will also have regard to the non-intervention principle, although it will generally be necessary to intervene when this order is sought as the parents will be in dispute. In *Re H (Minors) (Local Authority: Parental Rights) (No 3)* [1991] 2 WLR 763, the court looked at which factors would be important in this situation and concluded that it was important to look at the father's degree of commitment to the child, the state of the father's current relationship with the child and his reasons for making the application. The court will not automatically refuse an order just because at the present time there is no likelihood of the order resulting in the father being able to exercise any of his responsibilities. A committed father could be granted the order if it would ultimately be in the welfare of the child to make it (*Re C (Minors) (Parental Rights)* [1992] 1 FLR 1). In *Re A (Minors) (Parental Responsibility)* [1993] Fam Law 464, the father, who had lived with the mother, was present at the child's birth and whose name was entered on the birth certificate (this case predated the changes to the CA 1989 which would mean this automatically gave him parental responsibility), was granted a parental responsibility order (despite the mother's resistance and the fact that he had not seen the child for one year) as he had shown considerable commitment.

A series of more recent cases has shown that the court is willing to make a parental responsibility order to give a father a recognised legal status, and objections, such as a mother's hostility to a father's involvement in the child's life, or that the court refuses to grant the father a contact order, do not necessarily prevent the parental responsibility order being made (*Re G (A Minor) (Parental Responsibility Order)* [1994] 1 FLR 504) (and see *Re D (Contact and Parental Responsibility: Lesbian Mothers and Known Father)* [2006] EWHC 2 (Fam), where unusually the court made a parental responsibility order in favour of the father on the basis the father would not contact the child's school or any health care professional involved in her care without the consent of the child's mother or her female partner, who had a shared residence order in respect of the child).

However, the court may still refuse a parental responsibility order where the father has shown a high degree of commitment if it is clear that the father may abuse his parental responsibility. Thus in *Re P (Parental Responsibility)* [1998] 2 FLR 96, the Court of Appeal refused to grant a parental responsibility order where the father had been very critical of the mother's care and made it clear that he would use his parental responsibility order as an excuse to monitor the arrangements for the child's care. In another case, *M v M (Parental Responsibility)* [1999] 2 FLR 737, the court declined to make a parental responsibility order where the unmarried father had been involved in an accident, resulting in serious, permanent brain injuries. Although there had been a significant degree of commitment and attachment to the child, the father was incapable of exercising parental responsibility (and, in fact, required something akin to parental responsibility to be exercised by others over him).

A parental responsibility order, once made, will end automatically on the following events:

(a)   the majority of the child;

(b)   the marriage of the father to the mother during the minority of the child. The marriage will give the father parental responsibility for his child;

(c)   a court order discharging the parental responsibility order. An application to discharge the original order can be made by anyone who has parental responsibility for the child, for example the mother, or by the child himself provided the court is satisfied that the child has sufficient understanding to make the application.

The application for a parental responsibility order can be made in the family proceedings court, High Court or county court. There is a standard application form which sets out details of the child and the applicant, including his reasons for applying. Figures available show that, in a typical year, about 5,500 parental responsibility orders are made, the majority in the family proceedings court.

16.4.1.3   Residence order

If a father obtains a residence order in his favour, the court must at the same time grant him a separate parental responsibility order. If the residence order is subsequently changed, the parental responsibility order will not automatically end. This is in contrast to anyone else who loses a residence order, for example a grandparent, who will also lose parental responsibility.

16.4.1.4   Parental responsibility agreement

Many unmarried parents will be living together and will be happy to acknowledge their shared responsibility for their children. In this case, they are able to enter into an agreement which will give the father joint parental responsibility with the mother. It will put them into the same position as if a parental responsibility order had been made.

Regulations provide that the agreement must be in a prescribed form, signatures of the parents must be witnessed by a JP, a justices' clerk or a county court officer (not by a solicitor), and the agreement must be recorded by sending it together with two copies to the Principal Registry of the Family Division. No fee is payable. The Registry will seal the copies and send one to the mother and one to the father. Agreements are open to public inspection (Parental Responsibility Agreement Regulations 1991 (SI 1991/1478)).

Even though a parental responsibility agreement was entered into with the agreement of the parents, it cannot be ended by agreement. It will end only when the child reaches 18 years of age, unless a court order has been obtained either on the application of anyone with parental responsibility or on the application of the child (with leave).

Figures available show that, in a typical year, only about 3,700 agreements are registered, which represents a tiny proportion of children born outside marriage. It appears that either lack of information about these agreements, or the formalities involved or the reluctance of mothers to sign them is discouraging parents from entering into parental responsibility agreements. These agreements are likely to be even less common now that parental responsibility can be obtained by registration on the birth certificate (see **16.4.1.1**).

16.4.1.5   Guardianship (CA 1989, s 5)

A mother with sole parental responsibility could appoint the father as a guardian in her will. On her death, the father would then acquire parental responsibility because he was guardian, even if he had never obtained it during the mother's lifetime. If the mother had not appointed a guardian on her death, the court has the power to appoint a guardian and it could decide to appoint the father. Alternatively, in these circumstances the father could apply to the court to be appointed guardian (CA 1989, s 5(1)(a): see **Appendix 1(E)**).

If a mother with sole parental responsibility has appointed someone other than the child's father as guardian, this appointment will take effect on her death and give the guardian sole parental responsibility, which the father could challenge only by applying for a residence order and/or a parental responsibility order (CA 1989).

If the father has acquired parental responsibility during the mother's lifetime, any appointment by her of a guardian will be postponed while the surviving parent has parental responsibility. The only way a mother in this situation could ensure that the appointment of a guardian had immediate effect would be for her to seek a residence order in her own favour. In this case, on her death, the guardian and the father would share parental responsibility. This could be of great importance to a mother who is no longer cohabiting with the father of her child and who is anxious to safeguard a child after her death by making, for example, her mother a joint guardian with the father.

16.4.1.6   Marriage

If the child's parents marry, this will automatically give the father joint parental responsibility with the mother for any of his children.

16.4.1.7   Human Rights Act 1998

The fact that some unmarried fathers (currently) have to apply for parental responsibility, unlike all mothers and married fathers, has not been found to violate their rights under the HRA 1998. In the Scottish case of *McMichael v UK* (1995) 20 EHRR 205, the child of unmarried parents was placed in care and then freed for adoption. The parents were denied access to essential documents and the mother brought a successful complaint under Article 6 of the European Convention on Human Rights. The father complained that, as an unmarried father without parental rights, he was discriminated against as he had no right to the legal custody of his son or to participate in the care proceedings. The European Court of Human Rights held that the relevant legislation, which distinguished between married and unmarried fathers, had the legitimate aim of providing a mechanism for identifying meritorious fathers. The conditions imposed on natural fathers for obtaining recognition of their parental rights were proportionate to that aim.

What is of perhaps greater concern is the fact that the court can remove parental responsibility from unmarried fathers but not from mothers or married fathers. In *Smallwood v UK* (1999) 2 EHRLR 221, a father whose contact order had been revoked then lost parental responsibility after the court considered that he would use it to disrupt the children. The father's application to the Commission was declared inadmissible on the basis that differences in treatment between married and unmarried men had an objective and reasonable justification. The Commission also said it was compatible with the Convention to have a system whereby the rights of unmarried fathers concerning care or custody over their children were more limited than those of the mother.

Removal of parental responsibility is clearly a serious interference with a father's right to family life under Article 8. Yet, on the basis of Convention cases, it seems likely that applications under the HRA 1998 may similarly fail on the basis that interference with this particular Convention right is justifiable and necessary.

In addition, there are other areas of potential disadvantage to unmarried fathers without parental responsibility where they may be able to argue a breach of Article 8 and Article 14 (the right not to be discriminated against in the delivery of Convention rights). For example, a child may not be removed from the jurisdiction without either the consent of everyone with parental responsibility or the leave of the court, which means that an unmarried father without parental responsibility has no right to object.

16.4.2   Financial provision and property orders

The ways of applying for maintenance and property orders for the benefit of children of unmarried parents are much more limited than those available for children of married parents (see **Chapter 13**). The two methods available are, first, to apply for maintenance using the CSA 1991 (this Act applies to all absent parents irrespective of their marital status) and, secondly, to apply under the CA 1989.

The CA 1989 expressly provides that a father's obligation to maintain his children does not depend on his having parental responsibility. The financial provisions contained in s 15 of and Sch 1 to the CA 1989 apply to both married and unmarried parents. The most useful provisions for an unmarried parent are those enabling lump sum orders and property transfer and settlement orders (see **13.10.4** and **16.3.2.4**).

16.5   Bankruptcy

A bankrupt's property vests in the trustee in bankruptcy. A partner remaining in the home may be a joint owner or have a beneficial interest. The trustee in bankruptcy can apply for an order for sale of the home and is likely to be successful. If the application for sale is made more than one year after the bankruptcy, the court must assume that the interests of the creditors outweigh all other considerations unless the circumstances of the case are exceptional (see **9.9.1**).

16.6   Death

16.6.1   Ownership rights

If the home was jointly owned as beneficial joint tenants, on the death of one party the survivor will become the sole owner. If the home was jointly owned as beneficial tenants in common, the deceased's share will pass in accordance with his will, or under the intestacy rules. In both cases there are inheritance tax problems because, as the parties were not married, the spouse exemption does not apply.

The sole legal owner of the home may die without leaving it by will to the other partner. If the survivor wishes to obtain a share, he will have to establish, either that he had a beneficial interest in the property, or successfully bring a claim under the I(PFD)A 1975 (see **16.6.3**). If the survivor is not successful, he will be a bare licensee. The licence can be terminated by the deceased's personal representatives on giving notice to the surviving partner.

If the survivor was the sole legal owner, there could still be complications if the deceased had a beneficial interest in the property which has passed by his will or intestacy to someone other than the survivor.

16.6.2 Intestacy

The intestacy rules do not make any provision for an unmarried partner. However, any children of the couple will have rights on their parents' intestacy. It is, therefore, essential that an unmarried couple make wills.

16.6.3 Family provision

If the survivor can establish that, before the deceased's death, he was being maintained by the deceased, he is likely to be able to bring a claim under the I(PFD)A 1975 (see **Appendix 1(B)**). Periodical payments, lump sum and transfer or settlement of property orders can be made by the court.

A change to the I(PFD)A 1975 introduced by the Law Reform (Succession) Act 1995 extended the circumstances in which a claim can be made. It is possible for an unmarried cohabitee to claim financial provision out of the deceased partner's estate if he or she lived with the deceased as husband and wife throughout a period of two years prior to the death, irrespective of whether he or she was financially dependent upon the deceased. The Civil Partnership Act 2004 has extended this provision to include same-sex partners. In addition to the common guidelines (I(PFD)A 1975, s 3) there are special guidelines for the court to consider in an application by an unmarried partner. The court must have regard to the age of the applicant, the length of the cohabitation with the deceased and the contributions made by the applicant to the welfare of the family of the deceased, including contributions made by looking after the home or caring for the family.

Despite these changes, an unmarried partner is still not treated as generously as a surviving spouse. First, the court can award an unmarried partner only such financial provision as it would be reasonable to receive for maintenance. A surviving spouse can be awarded such financial provision as it would be reasonable to receive whether or not the provision is required for maintenance. Secondly, on an application by a spouse, the court will have regard to the provision that would have been awarded had the marriage ended with a divorce rather than with death. There is no similar provision for unmarried partners.

16.7 Chapter summary

(1) When couples decide to cohabit the following issues should be clarified:

    (a) how any property (especially the home) is owned as between the couple;

    (b) life insurance cover;

    (c) wills.

The couple should be advised to enter into a cohabitation agreement.

(2) When a cohabiting couple split up:

    (a) neither party can claim maintenance from the other;

    (b) maintenance for any children of the relationship can usually be claimed from the Child Support Agency;

(c)   ownership of the home will be determined by land law principles and an order for sale may be obtained;

(d)   occupation of the home may be obtained by establishing a contractual licence, or by obtaining a property order in favour of a child under the CA 1989 or, temporarily, by obtaining an occupation order under the FLA 1996;

(e)   transfer of tenancy orders can be made in some circumstances under the FLA 1996;

(f)   as regards children of an unmarried couple:

    (i)   mother has sole parental responsibility,

    (ii)   father can obtain parental responsibility by:

        –   registration on the child's birth certificate;

        –   court order;

        –   residence order;

        –   parental responsibility agreement;

        –   guardianship;

        –   marriage to mother;

(g)   if partner is bankrupt, sale of home can be delayed only if there are dependent children, and then only for 12 months;

(h)   if a cohabiting partner dies intestate there is no provision under the intestacy rules for the other partner to obtain any part of the estate. Any children of the couple will have a claim;

(i)   the I(PFD)A 1975 may be available to a cohabiting partner.

(3)   There are various proposals for reform of the law relating to cohabiting couples.

APPENDICES

Appendix 1 – Legislation

(A)   Matrimonial Causes Act 1973

1   Divorce on breakdown of marriage

(1)   Subject to section 3 below, a petition for divorce may be presented to the court by either party to a marriage on the ground that the marriage has broken down irretrievably.

(2)   The court hearing a petition for divorce shall not hold the marriage to have broken down irretrievably unless the petitioner satisfies the court of one or more of the following facts, that is to say—

(a)   that the respondent has committed adultery and the petitioner finds it intolerable to live with the respondent;

(b)   that the respondent has behaved in such a way that the petitioner cannot reasonably be expected to live with the respondent;

(c)   that the respondent has deserted the petitioner for a continuous period of at least two years immediately preceding the presentation of the petition;

(d)   that the parties of the marriage have lived apart for a continuous period of at least two years immediately preceding the presentation of the petition (hereafter in this Act referred to as 'two years' separation') and the respondent consents to a decree being granted;

(e)   that the parties to the marriage have lived apart for a continuous period of at least five years immediately preceding the presentation of the petition (hereafter in this Act referred to as 'five years' separation').

(3)   On a petition for divorce it shall be the duty of the court to inquire, so far as it reasonably can, into the facts alleged by the petitioner and into any facts alleged by the respondent.

(4)   If the court is satisfied on the evidence of any such fact as is mentioned in subsection (2) above, then, unless it is satisfied on all the evidence that the marriage has not broken down irretrievably, it shall, subject to section 5 below, grant a decree of divorce.

(5)   Every decree of divorce shall in the first instance be a decree nisi and shall not be made absolute before the expiration of six months from its grant unless the High Court by general order from time to time fixes a shorter period, or unless in any particular case the court in which the proceedings are for the time being pending from time to time by special order fixes a shorter period than the period otherwise applicable for the time being by virtue of this subsection.

2   Supplemental provisions as to facts raising presumption of breakdown

(1)   One party to a marriage shall not be entitled to rely for the purposes of section 1(2)(a) above on adultery committed by the other if, after it became known to him that the other had committed that adultery, the parties have lived with each other for a period exceeding, or periods together exceeding, six months.

(2)   Where the parties to a marriage have lived with each other after it became known to one party that the other had committed adultery, but subsection (1) above does not apply, in any proceedings for divorce in which the petitioner relies on that adultery the fact that the parties have lived with each other after that time shall be disregarded in determining for the purposes of section 1(2)(a) above whether the petitioner finds it intolerable to live with the respondent.

(3)   Where in any proceedings for divorce the petitioner alleges that the respondent has behaved in such a way that the petitioner cannot reasonably be expected to live with him, but the parties to the marriage have lived with each other for a period or periods after the date of the occurrence of the final incident relied on by the petitioner and held by the court to support his allegation, that fact shall be disregarded in

determining for the purposes of section 1(2)(b) above whether the petitioner cannot reasonably be expected to live with the respondent if the length of that period or of those periods together was six months or less.

(4)   For the purposes of section 1(2)(c) above the court may treat a period of desertion as having continued at a time when the deserting party was incapable of continuing the necessary intention if the evidence before the court is such that, had that party not been so incapable, the court would have inferred that his desertion continued at that time.

(5)   In considering for the purposes of section 1(2) above whether the period for which the respondent has deserted the petitioner or the period for which the parties to a marriage have lived apart has been continuous, no account shall be taken of any one period (not exceeding six months) or of any two or more periods (not exceeding six months in all) during which the parties resumed living with each other, but no period during which the parties lived with each other shall count as part of the period of desertion or of the period for which the parties to the marriage lived apart, as the case may be.

(6)   For the purposes of section 1(2)(d) and (e) above and this section a husband and wife shall be treated as living apart unless they are living with each other in the same household, and references in this section to the parties to a marriage living with each other shall be construed as references to their living with each other in the same household.

(7)   Provision shall be made by rules of court for the purpose of ensuring that where in pursuance of section 1(2)(d) above the petitioner alleges that the respondent consents to a decree being granted the respondent has been given such information as will enable him to understand the consequences to him of his consenting to a decree being granted and the steps which he must take to indicate that he consents to the grant of a decree.

3   Bar on petitions for divorce within one year of marriage

(1)   No petition for divorce shall be presented to the court before the expiration of the period of one year from the date of the marriage.

(2)   Nothing in this section shall prohibit the presentation of a petition based on matters which occurred before the expiration of that period.

5   Refusal of decree in five year separation cases on grounds of grave hardship to respondent

(1)   The respondent to a petition for divorce in which the petitioner alleges five years' separation may oppose the grant of a decree on the ground that the dissolution of the marriage will result in grave financial or other hardship to him and that it would in all the circumstances be wrong to dissolve the marriage.

(2)   Where the grant of a decree is opposed by virtue of this section, then—

(a)   if the court finds that the petitioner is entitled to rely in support of his petition on the fact of five years' separation and makes no such finding as to any other fact mentioned in section 1(2) above, and

(b)   if apart from this section the court would grant a decree on the petition,

the court shall consider all the circumstances, including the conduct of the parties to the marriage and the interests of those parties and of any children or other persons concerned, and if of opinion that the dissolution of the marriage will result in grave financial or other hardship to the respondent and that it would in all the circumstances be wrong to dissolve the marriage it shall dismiss the petition.

(3)   For the purposes of this section hardship shall include the loss of the chance of acquiring any benefit which the respondent might acquire if the marriage were not dissolved.

6   Attempts at reconciliation of parties to marriage

(1)   Provision shall be made by rules of court for requiring the solicitor acting for a petitioner for divorce to certify whether he has discussed with the petitioner the possibility of a reconciliation and given him the names and addresses of persons qualified to help effect a reconciliation between parties to a marriage who have become estranged.

(2)   If at any stage of proceedings for divorce it appears to the court that there is a reasonable possibility of a reconciliation between the parties to the marriage, the court may adjourn the proceedings for such period as it thinks fit to enable attempts to be made to effect such a reconciliation.

    The power conferred by the foregoing provision is additional to any other power of the court to adjourn proceedings.

10   Proceedings after decree nisi: special protection for respondent in separation cases

(1)   Where in any case the court has granted a decree of divorce on the basis of a finding that the petitioner was entitled to rely in support of his petition on the fact of two years' separation coupled with the respondent's consent to a decree being granted and has made no such finding as to any other fact mentioned in section 1(2) above, the court may, on an application made by the respondent at any time before the decree is made absolute, rescind the decree if it is satisfied that the petitioner misled the respondent (whether intentionally or unintentionally) about any matter which the respondent took into account in deciding to give his consent.

(2)   The following provisions of this section apply where—

    (a)   the respondent to a petition for divorce in which the petitioner alleged two years' or five years' separation coupled, in the former case, with the respondent's consent to a decree being granted, has applied to the court for consideration under subsection (3) below of his financial position after the divorce; and

    (b)   the court has granted a decree on the petition on the basis of a finding that the petitioner was entitled to rely in support of his petition on the fact of two years' or five years' separation (as the case may be) and has made no such finding as to any other fact mentioned in section 1(2) above.

(3)   The court hearing an application by the respondent under subsection (2) above shall consider all the circumstances, including the age, health, conduct, earning capacity, financial resources and financial obligations of each of the parties, and the financial position of the respondent as, having regard to the divorce, it is likely to be after the death of the petitioner should the petitioner die first; and, subject to subsection (4) below, the court shall not make the decree absolute unless it is satisfied

    (a)   that the petitioner should not be required to make any financial provision for the respondent, or

    (b)   that the financial provision made by the petitioner for the respondent is reasonable and fair or the best that can be made in the circumstances.

(4)   The court may if it thinks fit make the decree absolute notwithstanding the requirements of subsection (3) above if—

    (a)   it appears that there are circumstances making it desirable that the decree should be made absolute without delay, and

    (b)   the court has obtained a satisfactory undertaking from the petitioner that he will make such financial provision for the respondent as the court may approve.

10A   Proceedings after decree nisi: religious marriage

(1)   This section applies if a decree of divorce has been granted but not made absolute and the parties to the marriage concerned -

    (a)   were married in accordance with—

        (i)   the usages of the Jews, or

(ii)   any other prescribed religious usages; and

(b)   must co-operate if the marriage is to be dissolved in accordance with those usages.

(2)   On the application of either party, the court may order that a decree of divorce is not to be made absolute until a declaration made by both parties that they have taken such steps as are required to dissolve the marriage in accordance with those usages is produced to the court.

(3)   An order under subsection (2)—

(a)   may be made only if the court is satisfied that in all the circumstances of the case it is just and reasonable to do so; and

(b)   may be revoked at any time.

(4)   A declaration of a kind mentioned in subsection (2)—

(a)   must be in a specified form;

(b)   must, in specified cases, be accompanied by such documents as may be specified; and

(c)   must, in specified cases, satisfy such other requirements as may be specified.

(5)   The validity of a decree of divorce made by reference to such a declaration is not to be affected by any inaccuracy in that declaration.

(6)   'Prescribed' means prescribed in an order made by the Lord Chancellor after consulting the Lord Chief Justice and such an order—

(a)   must be made by statutory instrument;

(b)   shall be subject to annulment in pursuance of a resolution of either House of Parliament.

(7)   'Specified' means specified in rules of court.

(8)   The Lord Chief Justice may nominate a judicial office holder (as defined in section 109(4) of the Constitutional Reform Act 2005) to exercise his functions under this section.

17   Judicial separation

(1)   A petition for judicial separation may be presented to the court by either party to a marriage on the ground that any such fact as is mentioned in section 1(2) above exists, and the provisions of section 2 above shall apply accordingly for the purposes of a petition for judicial separation alleging any such fact, as they apply in relation to a petition for divorce alleging that fact.

(2)   On a petition for judicial separation it shall be the duty of the court to inquire, so far as it reasonably can, into the facts alleged by the petitioner and into any facts alleged by the respondent, but the court shall not be concerned to consider whether the marriage has broken down irretrievably, and if it is satisfied on the evidence of any such fact as is mentioned in section 1(2) above it shall, subject to section 41 below, grant a decree of judicial separation.

(3)   Sections 6 and 7 above shall apply for the purpose of encouraging the reconciliation of parties to proceedings for judicial separation and of enabling the parties to a marriage to refer to the court for its opinion an agreement or arrangement relevant to actual or contemplated proceedings for judicial separation, as they apply in relation to proceedings for divorce.

18   Effects of judicial separation

(1)   Where the court grants a decree of judicial separation it shall no longer be obligatory for the petitioner to cohabit with the respondent.

(2)   If while a decree of judicial separation is in force and the separation is continuing either of the parties to the marriage dies intestate as respects all or any of his or her real or personal property, the property as respects which he or she died intestate shall devolve as if the other party to the marriage had then been dead.

(3)   (Not reproduced)

22   Maintenance pending suit

On a petition for divorce, nullity of marriage or judicial separation, the court may make an order for maintenance pending suit, that is to say, an order requiring either party to the marriage to make to the other such periodical payments for his or her maintenance and for such term, being a term beginning not earlier than the date of the presentation of the petition and ending with the date of the determination of the suit, as the court thinks reasonable.

23   Financial provision orders in connection with divorce proceedings etc

(1)   On granting a decree of divorce, a decree of nullity of marriage or a decree of judicial separation or at any time thereafter (whether, in the case of a decree of divorce or of nullity of marriage, before or after the decree is made absolute), the court may make any one or more of the following orders, that is to say—

   (a)   an order that either party to the marriage shall make to the other such periodical payments, for such term, as may be specified in the order;

   (b)   an order that either party to the marriage shall secure to the other to the satisfaction of the court such periodical payments, for such term, as may be so specified;

   (c)   an order that either party to the marriage shall pay to the other such lump sum or sums as may be so specified;

   (d)   an order that a party to the marriage shall make to such person as may be specified in the order for the benefit of a child of the family, or to such a child, such periodical payments, for such term, as may be so specified;

   (e)   an order that a party to the marriage shall secure to such person as may be so specified for the benefit of such a child, or to such a child, to the satisfaction of the court, such periodical payments, for such term, as may be so specified;

   (f)   an order that a party to the marriage shall pay to such person as may be so specified for the benefit of such a child, or to such a child, such lump sum as may be so specified;

subject, however, in the case of an order under paragraph (d), (e) or (f) above, to the restrictions imposed by section 29(1) and (3) below on the making of financial provision orders in favour of children who have attained the age of eighteen.

(2)   The court may also, subject to those restrictions, make any one or more of the orders mentioned in subsection (1)(d), (e) and (f) above—

   (a)   in any proceedings for divorce, nullity of marriage or judicial separation, before granting a decree; and

   (b)   where any such proceedings are dismissed after the beginning of the trial, either forthwith or within a reasonable period after the dismissal.

(3)   Without prejudice to the generality of subsection (1)(c) or (f) above—

   (a)   an order under this section that a party to a marriage shall pay a lump sum to the other party may be made for the purpose of enabling that other party to meet any liabilities or expenses reasonably incurred by him or her in maintaining himself or herself or any child of the family before making an application for an order under this section in his or her favour;

   (b)   an order under this section for the payment of a lump sum to or for the benefit of a child of the family may be made for the purpose of enabling any liabilities or expenses reasonably incurred by or for the benefit of that child before the making of an application for an order under this section in his favour to be met; and

   (c)   an order under this section for the payment of a lump sum may provide for the payment of that sum by instalments of such amount as may be specified in the order and may require the payment of the instalments to be secured to the satisfaction of the court.

(4)   The power of the court under subsection (1) or (2)(a) above to make an order in favour of a child of the family shall be exercisable from time to time; and where the court

makes an order in favour of a child under subsection (2)(b) above, it may from time to time, subject to the restrictions mentioned in subsection (1) above, make a further order in his favour of any of the kinds mentioned in subsection (1)(d), (e) or (f) above.

(5)   Without prejudice to the power to give a direction under section 30 below for the settlement of an instrument by conveyancing counsel, where an order is made under subsection (1)(a), (b) or (c) above on or after granting a decree of divorce or nullity of marriage, neither the order nor any settlement made in pursuance of the order shall take effect unless the decree has been made absolute.

(6)   Where the court—

(a)   makes an order under this section for the payment of a lump sum; and

(b)   directs—

(i)   that payment of that sum or any part of it shall be deferred; or

(ii)   that the sum or any part of it shall be paid by instalments,

the court may order that the amount deferred or the instalments shall carry interest at such rate as may be specified by the order from such date, not earlier than the date of the order, as may be so specified, until the date when payment of it is due.

24   Property adjustment orders in connection with divorce proceedings etc

(1)   On granting a decree of divorce, a decree of nullity of marriage or a decree of judicial separation or at any time thereafter (whether, in the case of a decree of divorce or of nullity of marriage, before or after the decree is made absolute), the court may make any one or more of the following orders, that is to say—

(a)   an order that a party to the marriage shall transfer to the other party, to any child of the family or to such person as may be specified in the order for the benefit of such a child such property as may be so specified, being property to which the first-mentioned party is entitled, either in possession or reversion;

(b)   an order that a settlement of such property as may be so specified, being property to which a party to the marriage is so entitled, be made to the satisfaction of the court for the benefit of the other party to the marriage and of the children of the family or either or any of them;

(c)   an order varying for the benefit of the parties to the marriage and of the children of the family or either or any of them any ante-nuptial or post-nuptial settlement (including such a settlement made by will or codicil) made on the parties to the marriage, other than one in the form of a pension arrangement (within the meaning of section 25D below);

(d)   an order extinguishing or reducing the interest of either of the parties to the marriage under any such settlement, other than one in the form of a pension arrangement (within the meaning of section 25D below);

subject, however, in the case of an order under paragraph (a) above, to the restrictions imposed by section 29(1) and (3) below on the making of orders for a transfer of property in favour of children who have attained the age of eighteen.

(2)   The court may make an order under subsection (1)(c) above notwithstanding that there are no children of the family.

(3)   Without prejudice to the power to give a direction under section 30 below for the settlement of an instrument by conveyancing counsel, where an order is made under this section on or after granting a decree of divorce or nullity of marriage, neither the order nor any settlement made in pursuance of the order shall take effect unless the decree has been made absolute.

24A   Orders for sale of property

(1)   Where the court makes under section 23 or 24 of this Act a secured periodical payments order, an order for the payment of a lump sum or a property adjustment order, then, on making that order or at any time thereafter, the court may make a further order for the sale of such property as may be specified in the order, being

property in which or in the proceeds of sale of which either or both of the parties to the marriage has or have a beneficial interest, either in possession or reversion.

(2) Any order made under subsection (1) above may contain such consequential or supplementary provisions as the court thinks fit and, without prejudice to the generality of the foregoing provision, may include—

   (a) provision requiring the making of a payment out of the proceeds of sale of the property to which the order relates, and

   (b) provision requiring any such property to be offered for sale to a person, or class of persons, specified in the order.

(3) Where an order is made under subsection (1) above on or after the grant of a decree of divorce or nullity of marriage, the order shall not take effect unless the decree has been made absolute.

(4) Where an order is made under subsection (1) above, the court may direct that the order, or such provision thereof as the court may specify, shall not take effect until the occurrence of an event specified by the court or the expiration of a period so specified.

(5) Where an order under subsection (1) above contains a provision requiring the proceeds of sale of the property to which the order relates to be used to secure periodical payments to a party to the marriage, the order shall cease to have effect on the death or re-marriage of, or formation of a civil partnership by, that person.

(6) Where a party to a marriage has a beneficial interest in any property, or in the proceeds of sale thereof, and some other person who is not a party to the marriage also has a beneficial interest in that property or in the proceeds of sale thereof, then, before deciding whether to make an order under this section in relation to that property, it shall be the duty of the court to give that other person an opportunity to make representations with respect to the order; and any representations made by that other person shall be included among the circumstances to which the court is required to have regard under section 25(1) below.

24B   Pension sharing orders in connection with divorce proceedings etc

(1) On granting a decree of divorce or a decree of nullity of marriage or at any time thereafter (whether before or after the decree is made absolute), the court may, on an application made under this section, make one or more pension sharing orders in relation to the marriage.

(2) A pension sharing order under this section is not to take effect unless the decree on or after which it is made has been made absolute.

(3) A pension sharing order under this section may not be made in relation to a pension arrangement which—

   (a) is the subject of a pension sharing order in relation to the marriage, or

   (b) has been the subject of pension sharing between the parties to the marriage.

(4) A pension sharing order under this section may not be made in relation to shareable state scheme rights if—

   (a) such rights are the subject of a pension sharing order in relation to the marriage, or

   (b) such rights have been the subject of pension sharing between the parties to the marriage.

(5) A pension sharing order under this section may not be made in relation to the rights of a person under a pension arrangement if there is in force a requirement imposed by virtue of section 25B or 25C below which relates to benefits or future benefits to which he is entitled under the pension arrangement.

24C   Pension sharing orders: duty to stay

(1) No pension sharing order may be made so as to take effect before the end of such period after the making of the order as may be prescribed by regulations made by the Lord Chancellor.

(2)   The power to make regulations under this section shall be exercisable by statutory instrument which shall be subject to annulment in pursuance of a resolution of either House of Parliament.

24D   Pension sharing orders: apportionment of charges

If a pension sharing order relates to rights under a pension arrangement, the court may include in the order provision about the apportionment between the parties of any charge under section 41 of the Welfare Reform and Pensions Act 1999 (charges in respect of pension sharing costs), or under corresponding Northern Ireland legislation.

25   Matters to which court is to have regard in deciding how to exercise its powers under ss 23, 24 and 24A

(1)   It shall be the duty of the court in deciding whether to exercise its powers under section 23, 24, 24A or 24B above and, if so, in what manner, to have regard to all the circumstances of the case, first consideration being given to the welfare while a minor of any child of the family who has not attained the age of eighteen.

(2)   As regards the exercise of the powers of the court under section 23(1)(a), (b) or (c), 24, 24A or 24B above in relation to a party to the marriage, the court shall in particular have regard to the following matters—

(a)   the income, earning capacity, property and other financial resources which each of the parties to the marriage has or is likely to have in the foreseeable future, including in the case of earning capacity any increase in that capacity which it would in the opinion of the court be reasonable to expect a party to the marriage to take steps to acquire;

(b)   the financial needs, obligations and responsibilities which each of the parties to the marriage has or is likely to have in the foreseeable future;

(c)   the standard of living enjoyed by the family before the breakdown of the marriage;

(d)   the age of each party to the marriage and the duration of the marriage;

(e)   any physical or mental disability of either of the parties to the marriage;

(f)   the contributions which each of the parties has made or is likely in the foreseeable future to make to the welfare of the family, including any contribution by looking after the home or caring for the family;

(g)   the conduct of each of the parties, if that conduct is such that it would in the opinion of the court be inequitable to disregard it;

(h)   in the case of proceedings for divorce or nullity of marriage, the value to each of the parties to the marriage of any benefit … which, by reason of the dissolution or annulment of the marriage, that party will lose the chance of acquiring.

(3)   As regards the exercise of the powers of the court under section 23(1)(d), (e) or (f), (2) or (4), 24 or 24A above in relation to a child of the family, the court shall in particular have regard to the following matters—

(a)   the financial needs of the child;

(b)   the income, earning capacity (if any), property and other financial resources of the child;

(c)   any physical or mental disability of the child;

(d)   the manner in which he was being and in which the parties to the marriage expected him to be educated or trained;

(e)   the considerations mentioned in relation to the parties to the marriage in paragraphs (a), (b), (c) and (e) of subsection (2) above.

(4)   As regards the exercise of the powers of the court under section 23(1)(d), (e) or (f), (2) or (4), 24 or 24A above against a party to a marriage in favour of a child of the family who is not the child of that party, the court shall also have regard—

(a)   to whether that party assumed any responsibility for the child's maintenance, and, if so, to the extent to which, and the basis upon which, that party assumed such responsibility and to the length of time for which that party discharged such responsibility;

(b)   to whether in assuming and discharging such responsibility that party did so knowing that the child was not his or her own;

(c)   to the liability of any other person to maintain the child.

25A   Exercise of court's powers in favour of party to marriage on decree of divorce or nullity of marriage

(1)   Where on or after the grant of a decree of divorce or nullity of marriage the court decides to exercise its powers under section 23(1)(a), (b) or (c), 24, 24A or 24B above in favour of a party to the marriage, it shall be the duty of the court to consider whether it would be appropriate so to exercise those powers that the financial obligations of each party towards the other will be terminated as soon after the grant of the decree as the court considers just and reasonable.

(2)   Where the court decides in such a case to make a periodical payments or secured periodical payments order in favour of a party to the marriage, the court shall in particular consider whether it would be appropriate to require those payments to be made or secured only for such term as would in the opinion of the court be sufficient to enable the party in whose favour the order is made to adjust without undue hardship to the termination of his or her financial dependence on the other party.

(3)   Where on or after the grant of a decree of divorce or nullity of marriage an application is made by a party to the marriage for a periodical payments or secured periodical payments order in his or her favour, then, if the court considers that no continuing obligation should be imposed on either party to make or secure periodical payments in favour of the other, the court may dismiss the application with a direction that the applicant shall not be entitled to make any future application in relation to that marriage for an order under section 23(1)(a) or (b) above.

25B   Pensions

(1)   The matters to which the court is to have regard under section 25(2) above include—

(a)   in the case of paragraph (a), any benefits under a pension arrangement which a party to the marriage has or is likely to have, and

(b)   in the case of paragraph (h), any benefits under a pension arrangement which, by reason of the dissolution or annulment of the marriage, a party to the marriage will lose the chance of acquiring,

and, accordingly, in relation to benefits under a pension arrangement, section 25(2)(a) above shall have effect as if 'in the foreseeable future' were omitted.

(2)   ...

(3)   The following provisions apply where, having regard to any benefits under a pension arrangement, the court determines to make an order under section 23 above.

(4)   To the extent to which the order is made having regard to any benefits under a pension arrangement, the order may require the person responsible for the pension arrangement in question, if at any time any payment in respect of any benefits under the arrangement becomes due to the party with pension rights, to make a payment for the benefit of the other party.

(5)   The order must express the amount of any payment required to be made by virtue of subsection (4) above as a percentage of the payment which becomes due to the party with pension rights.

(6)   Any such payment by the person responsible for the arrangement—

(a)   shall discharge so much of his liability to the party with pension rights as corresponds to the amount of the payment, and

(b)   shall be treated for all purposes as a payment made by the party with pension rights in or towards the discharge of his liability under the order.

(7)   Where the party with pension rights has a right of commutation under the arrangement, the order may require him to exercise it to any extent; and this section

applies to any payment due in consequence of commutation in pursuance of the order as it applies to other payments in respect of benefits under the arrangement.

(7A) The power conferred by subsection (7) above may not be exercised for the purpose of commuting a benefit payable to the party with pension rights to a benefit payable to the other party.

(7B) The power conferred by subsection (4) or (7) above may not be exercised in relation to a pension arrangement which—

(a) is the subject of a pension sharing order in relation to the marriage, or

(b) has been the subject of pension sharing between the parties to the marriage.

(7C) In subsection (1) above, references to benefits under a pension arrangement include any benefits by way of pension, whether under a pension arrangement or not.

25C   Pensions: lump sums

(1) The power of the court under section 23 above to order a party to a marriage to pay a lump sum to the other party includes, where the benefits which the party with pension rights has or is likely to have under a pension arrangement include any lump sum payable in respect of his death, power to make any of the following provision by the order.

(2) The court may—

(a) if the person responsible for the pension arrangement in question has power to determine the person to whom the sum, or any part of it, is to be paid, require him to pay the whole or part of that sum, when it becomes due, to the other party,

(b) if the party with pension rights has power to nominate the person to whom the sum, or any part of it, is to be paid, require the party with pension rights to nominate the other party in respect of the whole or part of that sum,

(c) in any other case, require the person responsible for the pension arrangement in question to pay the whole or part of that sum, when it becomes due, for the benefit of the other party instead of to the person to whom, apart from the order, it would be paid.

(3) Any payment by the person responsible for the arrangement under an order made under section 23 above by virtue of this section shall discharge so much of his liability in respect of the party with pension rights as corresponds to the amount of the payment.

(4) The powers conferred by this section may not be exercised in relation to a pension arrangement which—

(a) is the subject of a pension sharing order in relation to the marriage, or

(b) has been the subject of pension sharing between the parties to the marriage.

27   Financial provision orders etc in case of neglect by party to marriage to maintain other party or child of the family

(1) Either party to a marriage may apply to the court for an order under this section on the ground that the other party to the marriage (in this section referred to as the respondent)—

(a) has failed to provide reasonable maintenance for the applicant, or

(b) has failed to provide, or to make a proper contribution towards, reasonable maintenance for any child of the family.

(2) The court shall not entertain an application under this section unless—

(a) the applicant or the respondent is domiciled in England and Wales on the date of the application; or

(b) the applicant has been habitually resident there throughout the period of one year ending with that date; or

(c) the respondent is resident there on that date.

(3) Where an application under this section is made on the ground mentioned in subsection (1)(a) above then, in deciding—

(a)   whether the respondent has failed to provide reasonable maintenance for the applicant, and

(b)   what order, if any, to make under this section in favour of the applicant,

the court shall have regard to all the circumstances of the case including the matters mentioned in section 25(2) above, and where an application is also made under this section in respect of a child of the family who has not attained the age of eighteen, first consideration shall be given to the welfare of the child while a minor.

(3A)   Where an application under this section is made on the ground mentioned in subsection (1)(b) above then, in deciding—

(a)   whether the respondent has failed to provide, or to make a proper contribution towards, reasonable maintenance for the child of the family to whom the application relates, and

(b)   what order, if any, to make under this section in favour of the child,

the court shall have regard to all the circumstances of the case including the matters mentioned in section 25(3)(a) to (e) above, and where the child of the family to whom the application relates is not the child of the respondent, including also the matters mentioned in section 25(4) above.

(3B)   In relation to an application under this section on the ground mentioned in subsection (1)(a) above, section 25(2)(c) above shall have effect as if for the reference therein to the breakdown of the marriage there were substituted a reference to the failure to provide reasonable maintenance for the applicant, and in relation to an application under this section on the ground mentioned in subsection (1)(b) above, section 25(2)(c) above (as it applies by virtue of section 25(3)(e) above) shall have effect as if for the reference therein to the breakdown of the marriage there were substituted a reference to the failure to provide, or to make a proper contribution towards, reasonable maintenance for the child of the family to whom the application relates.

(4)   ...

(5)   Where on an application under this section it appears to the court that the applicant or any child of the family to whom the application relates is in immediate need of financial assistance, but it is not yet possible to determine what order, if any, should be made on the application, the court may make an interim order for maintenance, that is to say, an order requiring the respondent to make to the applicant until the determination of the application such periodical payments as the court thinks reasonable.

(6)   Where on an application under this section the applicant satisfies the court of any ground mentioned in subsection (1) above, the court may make any one or more of the following orders, that is to say—

(a)   an order that the respondent shall make to the applicant such periodical payments, for such term, as may be specified in the order;

(b)   an order that the respondent shall secure to the applicant, to the satisfaction of the court, such periodical payments, for such term, as may be so specified;

(c)   an order that the respondent shall pay to the applicant such lump sum as may be so specified;

(d)   an order that the respondent shall make to such person as may be specified in the order for the benefit of the child to whom the application relates, or to that child, such periodical payments, for such term, as may be so specified;

(e)   an order that the respondent shall secure to such person as may be so specified for the benefit of that child, or to that child, to the satisfaction of the court, such periodical payments, for such term, as may be so specified;

(f)   an order that the respondent shall pay to such person as may be so specified for the benefit of that child, or to that child, such lump sum as may be so specified;

subject, however, in the case of an order under paragraph (d), (e) or (f) above, to the restrictions imposed by section 29(1) and (3) below on the making of financial provision orders in favour of children who have attained the age of eighteen.

(6A)   An application for the variation under section 31 of this Act of a periodical payments order or secured periodical payments order made under this section in favour of a child may, if the child has attained the age of sixteen, be made by the child himself.

(6B)   Where a periodical payments order made in favour of a child under this section ceases to have effect on the date on which the child attains the age of sixteen or at any time after that date but before or on the date on which he attains the age of eighteen, then, if, on an application made to the court for an order under this subsection, it appears to the court that—

(a)   the child is, will be or (if an order were made under this subsection) would be receiving instruction at an educational establishment or undergoing training for a trade, profession or vocation, whether or not he also is, will be or would be in gainful employment; or

(b)   there are special circumstances which justify the making of an order under this subsection,

the court shall have power by order to revive the first-mentioned order from such date as the court may specify, not being earlier than the date of the making of the application, and to exercise its powers under section 31 of this Act in relation to any order so revived.

(7)   Without prejudice to the generality of subsection (6)(c) or (f) above, an order under this section for the payment of a lump sum—

(a)   may be made for the purpose of enabling any liabilities or expenses reasonably incurred in maintaining the applicant or any child of the family to whom the application relates before the making of the application to be met;

(b)   may provide for the payment of that sum by instalments of such amount as may be specified in the order and may require the payment of the instalments to be secured to the satisfaction of the court.

(8)   ...

28   Duration of continuing financial provision orders in favour of party to marriage, and effect of remarriage or formation of civil partnership

(1)   Subject in the case of an order made on or after the grant of a decree of a divorce or nullity of marriage to the provisions of sections 25A(2) above and 31(7) below, the term to be specified in a periodical payments or secured periodical payments order in favour of a party to a marriage shall be such term as the court thinks fit, except that the term shall not begin before or extend beyond the following limits, that is to say—

(a)   in the case of a periodical payments order, the term shall begin not earlier than the date of the making of an application for the order, and shall be so defined as not to extend beyond the death of either of the parties to the marriage or, where the order is made on or after the grant of a decree of divorce or nullity of marriage, the remarriage of, or formation of a civil partnership by, the party in whose favour the order is made; and

(b)   in the case of a secured periodical payments order, the term shall begin not earlier than the date of the making of an application for the order, and shall be so defined as not to extend beyond the death or, where the order is made on or after the grant of such a decree, the remarriage of the party, or formation of a civil partnership by, in whose favour the order is made.

(1A)   Where a periodical payments or secured periodical payments order in favour of a party to a marriage is made on or after the grant of a decree of divorce or nullity of marriage, the court may direct that that party shall not be entitled to apply under section 31 below for the extension of the term specified in the order.

(2)   Where a periodical payments or secured periodical payments order in favour of a party to a marriage is made otherwise than on or after the grant of a decree of divorce or nullity of marriage, and the marriage in question is subsequently dissolved or annulled but the order continues in force, the order shall, notwithstanding anything in it, cease to have effect on the remarriage of, or formation of the civil partnership

by, that party, except in relation to any arrears due under it on the date of the remarriage or formation of the civil partnership.

(3)   If after the grant of a decree dissolving or annulling a marriage either party to that marriage remarries whether at any time before or after the commencement of this Act or forms a civil partnership, that party shall not be entitled to apply, by reference to the grant of that decree, for a financial provision order in his or her favour, or for a property adjustment order, against the other party to that marriage.

29 Duration of continuing financial provision orders in favour of children, and age limit on making certain orders in their favour

(1)   Subject to subsection (3) below, no financial provision order and no order for a transfer of property under section 24(1)(a) above shall be made in favour of a child who has attained the age of eighteen.

(2)   The term to be specified in a periodical payments or secured periodical payments order in favour of a child may begin with the date of the making of an application for the order in question or any later date or a date ascertained in accordance with subsection (5) or (6) below but—

(a)   shall not in the first instance extend beyond the date of the birthday of the child next following his attaining the upper limit of the compulsory school age (construed in accordance with section 8 of the Education Act 1996) unless the court considers that in the circumstances of the case the welfare of the child requires that it should extend to a later date; and

(b)   shall not in any event, subject to subsection (3) below, extend beyond the date of the child's eighteenth birthday.

(3)   Subsection (1) above, and paragraph (b) of subsection (2), shall not apply in the case of a child, if it appears to the court that—

(a)   the child is, or will be, or if an order were made without complying with either or both of those provisions would be, receiving instruction at an educational establishment or undergoing training for a trade, profession or vocation, whether or not he is also, or will also be, in gainful employment; or

(b)   there are special circumstances which justify the making of an order without complying with either or both of those provisions.

(4)   Any periodical payments order in favour of a child shall, notwithstanding anything in the order, cease to have effect on the death of the person liable to make payments under the order, except in relation to any arrears due under the order on the date of the death.

(5)   Where—

(a)   a maintenance calculation ('the current calculation') is in force with respect to a child; and

(b)   an application is made under Part II of this Act for a periodical payments or secured periodical payments order in favour of that child—

(i)   in accordance with section 8 of the Child Support Act 1991, and

(ii)   before the end of the period of 6 months beginning with the making of the current calculation,

the term to be specified in any such order made on that application may be expressed to begin on, or at any time after, the earliest permitted date.

(6)   For the purposes of subsection (5) above, 'the earliest permitted date' is whichever is the later of—

(a)   the date 6 months before the application is made; or

(b)   the date on which the current calculation took effect or, where successive maintenance calculations have been continuously in force with respect to a child, on which the first of those calculations took effect.

(7)   Where—

(a)   a maintenance calculation ceases to have effect ... by or under any provision of the Child Support Act 1991; and

(b)   an application is made, before the end of the period of 6 months beginning with the relevant date, for a periodical payments or secured periodical payments order in favour of a child with respect to whom that maintenance calculation was in force immediately before it ceased to have effect,

the term to be specified in any such order made on that application may begin with the date on which that maintenance calculation ceased to have effect, ... or any later date.

(8)   In subsection (7)(b) above—

(a)   where the maintenance calculation ceased to have effect, the relevant date is the date on which it so ceased

(b)   ...

30   Direction for settlement of instrument for securing payments or effecting property adjustment

Where the court decides to make a financial provision order requiring any payments to be secured or a property adjustment order—

(a)   it may direct that the matter be referred to one of the conveyancing counsel of the court for him to settle a proper instrument to be executed by all necessary parties; and

(b)   where the order is to be made in proceedings for divorce, nullity of marriage or judicial separation it may, if it thinks fit, defer the grant of the decree in question until the instrument has been duly executed.

31   Variation, discharge etc of certain orders for financial relief

(1)   Where the court has made an order to which this section applies, then, subject to the provisions of this section and of section 28(1A) above, the court shall have power to vary or discharge the order or to suspend any provision thereof temporarily and to revive the operation of any provision so suspended.

(2)   This section applies to the following orders, that is to say—

(a)   any order for maintenance pending suit and any interim order for maintenance;

(b)   any periodical payments order;

(c)   any secured periodical payments order;

(d)   any order made by virtue of section 23(3)(c) or 27(7)(b) above (provision for payment of a lump sum by instalments);

(dd)   any deferred order made by virtue of section 23(1)(c) (lump sums) which includes provision made by virtue of—

(i)   section 25B(4), or

(ii)   section 25C,

(provision in respect of pension rights);

(e)   any order for a settlement of property under section 24(1)(b) or for a variation of settlement under section 24(1)(c) or (d) above, being an order made on or after the grant of a decree of judicial separation;

(f)   any order made under section 24A(1) above for the sale of property.

(g)   a pension sharing order under section 24B above which is made at a time before the decree has been made absolute.

(2A)   Where the court has made an order referred to in subsection (2)(a), (b) or (c) above, then, subject to the provisions of this section, the court shall have power to remit the payment of any arrears due under the order or of any part thereof.

(2B)   Where the court has made an order referred to in subsection (2)(dd)(ii) above, this section shall cease to apply to the order on the death of either of the parties to the marriage.

(3)   The powers exercisable by the court under this section in relation to an order shall be exercisable also in relation to any instrument executed in pursuance of the order.

(4) The court shall not exercise the powers conferred by this section in relation to an order for a settlement under section 24(1)(b) or for a variation of settlement under section 24(1)(c) or (d) above except on an application made in proceedings—

    (a) for the rescission of the decree of judicial separation by reference to which the order was made, or

    (b) for the dissolution of the marriage in question.

(4A) In relation to an order which falls within paragraph (g) of subsection (2) above ('the subsection (2) order')—

    (a) the powers conferred by this section may be exercised—

        (i) only on an application made before the subsection (2) order has or, but for paragraph (b) below, would have taken effect; and

        (ii) only if, at the time when the application is made, the decree has not been made absolute; and

    (b) an application made in accordance with paragraph (a) above prevents the subsection (2) order from taking effect before the application has been dealt with.

(4B) No variation of a pension sharing order shall be made so as to take effect before the decree is made absolute.

(4C) The variation of a pension sharing order prevents the order taking effect before the end of such period after the making of the variation as may be prescribed by regulations made by the Lord Chancellor.

(5) Subject to subsections (7A) to (7G) below and without prejudice to any power exercisable by virtue of subsection (2)(d), (dd), (e) or (g) above or otherwise than by virtue of this section, no property adjustment order or pension sharing order shall be made on an application for the variation of a periodical payments or secured periodical payments order made (whether in favour of a party to a marriage or in favour of a child of the family) under section 23 above, and no order for the payment of a lump sum shall be made on an application for the variation of a periodical payments or secured periodical payments order in favour of a party to a marriage (whether made under section 23 or under section 27 above).

(6) Where the person liable to make payments under a secured periodical payments order has died, an application under this section relating to that order (and to any order made under section 24A(1) above which requires the proceeds of sale of property to be used for securing those payments) may be made by the person entitled to payments under the periodical payments order or by the personal representatives of the deceased person, but no such application shall, except with the permission of the court, be made after the end of the period of six months from the date on which representation in regard to the estate of that person is first taken out.

(7) In exercising the powers conferred by this section the court shall have regard to all the circumstances of the case, first consideration being given to the welfare while a minor of any child of the family who has not attained the age of eighteen, and the circumstances of the case shall include any change in any of the matters to which the court was required to have regard when making the order to which the application relates, and—

    (a) in the case of a periodical payments or secured periodical payments order made on or after the grant of a decree of divorce or nullity of marriage, the court shall consider whether in all the circumstances and after having regard to any such change it would be appropriate to vary the order so that payments under the order are required to be made or secured only for such further period as will in the opinion of the court be sufficient (in the light of any proposed exercise by the court, where the marriage has been dissolved, of its powers under subsection (7B) below) to enable the party in whose favour the order was made to adjust without undue hardship to the termination of those payments;

    (b) in a case where the party against whom the order was made has died, the circumstances of the case shall also include the changed circumstances resulting from his or her death.

(7A) Subsection (7B) below applies where, after the dissolution of a marriage, the court—

(a) discharges a periodical payments order or secured periodical payments order made in favour of a party to the marriage; or

(b) varies such an order so that payments under the order are required to be made or secured only for such further period as is determined by the court.

(7B) The court has power, in addition to any power it has apart from this subsection, to make supplemental provision consisting of any of—

(a) an order for the payment of a lump sum in favour of a party to the marriage;

(b) one or more property adjustment orders in favour of a party to the marriage;

(ba) one or more pension sharing orders;

(c) a direction that the party in whose favour the original order discharged or varied was made is not entitled to make any further application for—

(i) a periodical payments or secured periodical payments order, or

(ii) an extension of the period to which the original order is limited by any variation made by the court.

(7C) An order for the payment of a lump sum made under subsection (7B) above may—

(a) provide for the payment of that sum by instalments of such amount as may be specified in the order; and

(b) require the payment of the instalments to be secured to the satisfaction of the court.

(7D) Section 23(6) above applies where the court makes an order for the payment of a lump sum under subsection (7B) above as it applies where the court makes such an order under section 23 above.

(7E) If under subsection (7B) above the court makes more than one property adjustment order in favour of the same party to the marriage, each of those orders must fall within a different paragraph of section 21(2) above.

(7F) Sections 24A and 30 above apply where the court makes a property adjustment order under subsection (7B) above as they apply where it makes such an order under section 24 above.

(7G) Subsections (3) to (5) of section 24B above apply in relation to a pension sharing order under subsection (7B) above as they apply in relation to a pension sharing order under that section.

(8) The personal representatives of a deceased person against whom a secured periodical payments order was made shall not be liable for having distributed any part of the estate of the deceased after the expiration of the period of six months referred to in subsection (6) above on the ground that they ought to have taken into account the possibility that the court might permit an application under this section to be made after that period by the person entitled to payments under the order; but this subsection shall not prejudice any power to recover any part of the estate so distributed arising by virtue of the making of an order in pursuance of this section.

(9) In considering for the purposes of subsection (6) above the question when representation was first taken out, a grant limited to settled land or to trust property shall be left out of account and a grant limited to real estate or to personal estate shall be left out of account unless a grant limited to the remainder of the estate has previously been made or is made at the same time.

(10) Where the court, in exercise of its powers under this section, decides to vary or discharge a periodical payments or secured periodical payments order, then, subject to section 28(1) and (2) above, the court shall have power to direct that the variation or discharge shall not take effect until the expiration of such period as may be specified in the order.

(11) Where—

(a) a periodical payments or secured periodical payments order in favour of more than one child ('the order') is in force;

(b) the order requires payments specified in it to be made to or for the benefit of more than one child without apportioning those payments between them;

(c)   a maintenance calculation ('the calculation') is made with respect to one or more, but not all, of the children with respect to whom those payments are to be made; and

(d)   an application is made, before the end of the period of 6 months beginning with the date on which the calculation was made, for the variation or discharge of the order,

the court may, in exercise of its powers under this section to vary or discharge the order, direct that the variation or discharge shall take effect from the date on which the calculation took effect or any later date.

(12)   Where—

(a)   an order ('the child order') of a kind prescribed for the purposes of section 10(1) of the Child Support Act 1991 is affected by a maintenance calculation;

(b)   on the date on which the child order became so affected there was in force a periodical payments or secured periodical payments order ('the spousal order') in favour of a party to a marriage having the care of the child in whose favour the child order was made; and

(c)   an application is made, before the end of the period of 6 months beginning with the date on which the maintenance calculation was made, for the spousal order to be varied or discharged,

the court may, in exercise of its powers under this section to vary or discharge the spousal order, direct that the variation or discharge shall take effect from the date on which the child order became so affected or any later date.

(13)   For the purposes of subsection (12) above, an order is affected if it ceases to have effect or is modified by or under section 10 of the Child Support Act 1991.

(14)   Subsections (11) and (12) above are without prejudice to any other power of the court to direct that the variation of discharge of an order under this section shall take effect from a date earlier than that on which the order for variation or discharge was made.

(15)   The power to make regulations under subsection (4C) above shall be exercisable by statutory instrument which shall be subject to annulment in pursuance of a resolution of either House of Parliament.

37   Avoidance of transactions intended to prevent or reduce financial relief

(1)   For the purposes of this section 'financial relief' means relief under any of the provisions of sections 22, 23, 24, 24B, 27, 31 (except subsection (6)) and 35 above, and any reference in this section to defeating a person's claim for financial relief is a reference to preventing financial relief from being granted to that person, or to that person for the benefit of a child of the family, or reducing the amount of any financial relief which might be so granted, or frustrating or impeding the enforcement of any order which might be or has been made at his instance under any of those provisions.

(2)   Where proceedings for financial relief are brought by one person against another, the court may, on the application of the first-mentioned person—

(a)   if it is satisfied that the other party to the proceedings is, with the intention of defeating the claim for financial relief, about to make any disposition or to transfer out of the jurisdiction or otherwise deal with any property, make such order as it thinks fit for restraining the other party from so doing or otherwise for protecting the claim;

(b)   if it is satisfied that the other party has, with that intention, made a reviewable disposition and that if the disposition were set aside financial relief or different financial relief would be granted to the applicant, make an order setting aside the disposition;

(c)   if it is satisfied, in a case where an order has been obtained under any of the provisions mentioned in subsection (1) above by the applicant against the other party, that the other party has, with that intention, made a reviewable disposition, make an order setting aside the disposition;

and an application for the purposes of paragraph (b) above shall be made in the proceedings for the financial relief in question.

(3)   Where the court makes an order under subsection (2)(b) or (c) above setting aside a disposition it shall give such consequential directions as it thinks fit for giving effect to the order (including directions requiring the making of any payments or the disposal of any property).

(4)   Any disposition made by the other party to the proceedings for financial relief in question (whether before or after the commencement of those proceedings) is a reviewable disposition for the purposes of subsection (2)(b) and (c) above unless it was made for valuable consideration (other than marriage) to a person who, at the time of the disposition, acted in relation to it in good faith and without notice of any intention on the part of the other party to defeat the applicant's claim for financial relief.

(5)   Where an application is made under this section with respect to a disposition which took place less than three years before the date of the application or with respect to a disposition or other dealing with property which is about to take place and the court is satisfied—

(a)   in a case falling within subsection (2)(a) or (b) above, that the disposition or other dealing would (apart from this section) have the consequence, or

(b)   in a case falling within subsection (2)(c) above, that the disposition has had the consequence,

of defeating the applicant's claim for financial relief, it shall be presumed, unless the contrary is shown, that the person who disposed of or is about to dispose of or deal with the property did so or, as the case may be, is about to do so, with the intention of defeating the applicant's claim for financial relief.

(6)   In this section 'disposition' does not include any provision contained in a will or codicil but, with that exception, includes any conveyance, assurance or gift of property of any description, whether made by an instrument or otherwise.

(7)   This section does not apply to a disposition made before 1st January 1968.

41   Restrictions on decrees for dissolution, annulment or separation affecting children

(1)   In any proceedings for a decree of divorce or nullity of marriage, or a decree of judicial separation, the court shall consider—

(a)   whether there are any children of the family to whom this section applies; and

(b)   where there are any such children, whether (in the light of the arrangements which have been, or are proposed to be, made for their upbringing and welfare) it should exercise any of its powers under the Children Act 1989 with respect to any of them.

(2)   Where, in any case to which this section applies, it appears to the court that—

(a)   the circumstances of the case require it, or are likely to require it, to exercise any of its powers under the Act of 1989 with respect to any such child;

(b)   it is not in a position to exercise that power or (as the case may be) those powers without giving further consideration to the case; and

(c)   there are exceptional circumstances which make it desirable in the interests of the child that the court should give a direction under this section,

it may direct that the decree of divorce or nullity is not to be made absolute, or that the decree of judicial separation is not to be granted, until the court orders otherwise.

(3)   This section applies to—

(a)   any child of the family who has not reached the age of sixteen at the date when the court considers the case in accordance with the requirements of this section; and

(b)   any child of the family who has reached that age at that date and in relation to whom the court directs that this section shall apply.

(B) Inheritance (Provision for Family and Dependants) Act 1975

1 Application for financial provision from deceased's estate

(1) Where after the commencement of this Act a person dies domiciled in England and Wales and is survived by any of the following persons—

    (a) the spouse or civil partner of the deceased;

    (b) a former spouse or former civil partner of the deceased, but not one who has formed a subsequent marriage or civil partnership;

    (ba) any person (not being a person included in paragraph (a) or (b) above) to whom subsection (1A) or (1B) below applies;

    (c) a child of the deceased;

    (d) any person (not being a child of the deceased) who, in the case of any marriage or civil partnership to which the deceased was at any time a party, was treated by the deceased as a child of the family in relation to that marriage or civil partnership;

    (e) any person (not being a person included in the foregoing paragraphs of this subsection) who immediately before the death of the deceased was being maintained, either wholly or partly, by the deceased;

that person may apply to the court for an order under section 2 of this Act on the ground that the disposition of the deceased's estate affected by his will or the law relating to intestacy, or the combination of his will and that law, is not such as to make reasonable financial provision for the applicant.

(1A) This subsection applies to a person if the deceased died on or after 1st January 1996 and, during the whole of the period of two years ending immediately before the date when the deceased died, the person was living—

    (a) in the same household as the deceased, and

    (b) as the husband or wife of the deceased.

(1B) This subsection applies to a person if for the whole of the period of two years ending immediately before the date when the deceased died the person was living—

    (a) in the same household as the deceased, and

    (b) as the civil partner of the deceased.

(2) In this Act 'reasonable financial provision'—

    (a) in the case of an application made by virtue of subsection (1)(a) above by the husband or wife of the deceased (except where the marriage with the deceased was the subject of a decree of judicial separation and at the date of death the decree was in force and the separation was continuing), means such financial provision as it would be reasonable in all the circumstances of the case for a husband or wife to receive, whether or not that provision is required for his or her maintenance;

    (aa) in the case of an application made by virtue of subsection (1)(a) above by the civil partner of the deceased (except where, at the date of death, a separation order under Chapter 2 of Part 2 of the Civil Partnership Act 2004 was in force in relation to the civil partnership and the separation was continuing), means such financial provision as would be reasonable in all the circumstances of the case for a civil partner to receive, whether or not that provision is required for his or her maintenance;

    (b) in the case of any other application made by virtue of subsection (1) above, means such financial provision as it would be reasonable in all the circumstances of the case for the applicant to receive for his maintenance.

(3) For the purposes of subsection (1)(e) above, a person shall be treated as being maintained by the deceased, either wholly or partly, as the case may be, if the deceased, otherwise than for full valuable consideration, was making a substantial contribution in money or money's worth towards the reasonable needs of that person.

2   Powers of court to make orders

(1)   Subject to the provisions of this Act, where an application is made for an order under this section, the court may, if it is satisfied that the disposition of the deceased's estate effected by his will or the law relating to intestacy, or the combination of his will and that law, is not such as to make reasonable financial provision for the applicant, make any one or more of the following orders—

    (a)   an order for the making to the applicant out of the net estate of the deceased of such periodical payments and for such term as may be specified in the order;

    (b)   an order for the payment to the applicant out of that estate of a lump sum of such amount as may be so specified;

    (c)   an order for the transfer to the applicant of such property comprised in that estate as may be so specified;

    (d)   an order for the settlement for the benefit of the applicant of such property comprised in that estate as may be so specified;

    (e)   an order for the acquisition out of property comprised in that estate of such property as may be so specified and for the transfer of the property so acquired to the applicant or for the settlement thereof for his benefit;

    (f)   an order varying any ante-nuptial or post-nuptial settlement (including such a settlement made by will) made on the parties to a marriage to which the deceased was one of the parties, the variation being for the benefit of the surviving party to that marriage, or any child of that marriage, or any person who was treated by the deceased as a child of the family in relation to that marriage;

    (g)   an order varying any settlement made—

        (i)   during the subsistence of a civil partnership formed by the deceased, or

        (ii)   in anticipation of the formation of a civil partnership by the deceased, on the civil partners (including such a settlement made by will), the variation being for the benefit of the surviving civil partner, or any person who was treated by the deceased as a child of the family in relation to the civil partnership.

(2)–(4)   (not reproduced)

15   Restriction imposed in divorce proceedings etc on application under this Act

(1)   On the grant of a decree of divorce, a decree of nullity of marriage or a decree of judicial separation or at any time thereafter the court, if it considers it just to do so, may, on the application of either party to the marriage, order that the other party to the marriage shall not on the death of the applicant be entitled to apply for an order under section 2 of this Act.

In this subsection 'the court' means the High Court or, where a county court has jurisdiction by virtue of Part V of the Matrimonial and Family Proceedings Act 1984, a county court.

(2)   In the case of a decree of divorce or nullity of marriage an order may be made under subsection (1) above before or after the decree is made absolute, but if it is made before the decree is made absolute it shall not take effect unless the decree is made absolute.

(3)   Where an order made under subsection (1) above on the grant of a decree of divorce or nullity of marriage has come into force with respect to a party to a marriage, then, on the death of the other party to that marriage, the court shall not entertain any application for an order under section 2 of this Act made by the first-mentioned party.

(4)   Where an order made under subsection (1) above on the grant of a decree of judicial separation has come into force with respect to any party to a marriage, then, if the other party to that marriage dies while the decree is in force and the separation is continuing, the court shall not entertain any application for an order under section 2 of this Act made by the first-mentioned party.

15ZA.   Restriction imposed in proceedings for the dissolution etc. of a civil partnership on application under this Act

(1)   On making a dissolution order, nullity order, separation order or presumption of death order under Chapter 2 of Part 2 of the Civil Partnership Act 2004, or at any time after making such an order, the court if it considers it just to do so, may, on the application of either of the civil partners, order that the other civil partner shall not on the death of the applicant be entitled to apply for an order under section 2 of this Act.

(2)   In subsection (1) above 'the court' means the High Court, or where a county court has jurisdiction by virtue of Part 5 of the Matrimonial and Family Proceedings Act 1984, a county court.

(3)   In the case of a dissolution order, nullity order or presumption of death order ('the main order') an order may be made under subsection (1) above before (as well as after) the main order is made final, but if made before the main order is made final it shall not take effect unless the main order is made final.

(4)   Where an order under subsection (1) above made in connection with a dissolution order, nullity order or presumption of death order has come into force with respect to a civil partner, then, on the death of the other civil partner, the court shall not entertain any application for an order under section 2 of the Act made by the surviving civil partner.

(5)   Where an order under subsection (1) above made in connection with a separation order has come into force with respect to a civil partner, then, if the other civil partner dies while the separation order is in force and the separation is continuing, the court shall not entertain any application for an order under section 2 of this Act made by the surviving civil partner.

(C)   Domestic Proceedings and Magistrates' Courts Act 1978

1   Grounds of application for financial provision

Either party to a marriage may apply to a magistrates' court for an order under section 2 of this Act on the ground that the other party to the marriage ...—

(a)   has failed to provide reasonable maintenance for the applicant; or

(b)   has failed to provide, or to make a proper contribution towards, reasonable maintenance for any child of the family; or

(c)   has behaved in such a way that the applicant cannot reasonably be expected to live with the respondent; or

(d)   has deserted the applicant.

2   Powers of court to make orders for financial provision

(1)   Where on an application for an order under this section the applicant satisfies the court of any ground mentioned in section 1 of this Act, the court may, subject to the provisions of this Part of this Act, make any one or more of the following orders, that is to say—

   (a)   an order that the respondent shall make to the applicant such periodical payments, and for such term, as may be specified in the order;

   (b)   an order that the respondent shall pay to the applicant such lump sum as may be so specified;

   (c)   an order that the respondent shall make to the applicant for the benefit of a child of the family to whom the application relates, or to such a child, such periodical payments, and for such term, as may be so specified;

   (d)   an order that the respondent shall pay to the applicant for the benefit of a child of the family to whom the application relates, or to such a child, such lump sum as may be so specified.

(2)   Without prejudice to the generality of subsection (1)(b) or (d) above, an order under this section for the payment of a lump sum may be made for the purpose of enabling any liability or expenses reasonably incurred in maintaining the applicant, or any child of the family to whom the application relates, before the making of the order to be met.

(3)   The amount of any lump sum required to be paid by an order under this section shall not exceed £1,000 or such larger amount as the Lord Chancellor may from time to time by order fix for the purposes of this subsection.

   ...

(4)   An order made by the Lord Chancellor under this section—

   (a)   shall be made only after consultation with the Lord Chief Justice;

   (b)   shall be made by statutory instrument and be subject to annulment in pursuance of a resolution of either House of Parliament.

(5)   The Lord Chief Justice may nominate a judicial office holder (as defined in section 109(4) of the Constitutional Reform Act 2005) to exercise his functions under this section.

3   Matters to which court is to have regard in exercising its powers under s 2

(1)   Where an application is made for an order under section 2 of this Act, it shall be the duty of the court, in deciding whether to exercise its powers under that section and, if so, in what manner, to have regard to all the circumstances of the case, first consideration being given to the welfare while a minor of any child of the family who has not attained the age of eighteen.

(2)   As regards the exercise of its powers under subsection (1)(a) or (b) of section 2, the court shall in particular have regard to the following matters—

   (a)   the income, earning capacity, property and other financial resources which each of the parties to the marriage has or is likely to have in the foreseeable future, including in the case of earning capacity any increase in that capacity which it would in the opinion of the court be reasonable to expect a party to the marriage to take steps to acquire;

(b)   the financial needs, obligations and responsibilities which each of the parties to the marriage has or is likely to have in the foreseeable future;

(c)   the standard of living enjoyed by the parties to the marriage before the occurrence of the conduct which is alleged as the ground of the application;

(d)   the age of each party to the marriage and the duration of the marriage;

(e)   any physical or mental disability of either of the parties to the marriage;

(f)   the contributions which each of the parties has made or is likely in the foreseeable future to make to the welfare of the family, including any contribution by looking after the home or caring for the family;

(g)   the conduct of each of the parties, if that conduct is such that it would in the opinion of the court be inequitable to disregard it.

(3)   As regards the exercise of its power under subsection (1)(c) or (d) of section 2, the court shall in particular have regard to the following matters—

(a)   the financial needs of the child;

(b)   the income, earning capacity (if any), property and other financial resources of the child;

(c)   any physical or mental disability of the child;

(d)   the standard of living enjoyed by the family before the occurrence of the conduct which is alleged as the ground of the application;

(e)   the manner in which the child was being and in which the parties to the marriage expected him to be educated or trained;

(f)   the matters mentioned in relation to the parties to the marriage in paragraphs (a) and (b) of subsection (2) above.

(4)   As regards the exercise of its power under section 2 in favour of a child of the family who is not the child of the respondent, the court shall also have regard—

(a)   to whether the respondent has assumed any responsibility for the child's maintenance and, if he did, to the extent to which, and the basis on which, he assumed that responsibility and to the length of time during which he discharged that responsibility;

(b)   to whether in assuming and discharging that responsibility the respondent did so knowing that the child was not his own child;

(c)   to the liability of any other person to maintain the child.

(D) Child Abduction Act 1984

1 Offence of abduction of child by parent, etc

(1) Subject to subsections (5) and (8) below, a person connected with a child under the age of sixteen commits an offence if he takes or sends the child out of the United Kingdom without the appropriate consent.

(2) A person is connected with a child for the purposes of this section if—

    (a) he is a parent of the child; or

    (b) in the case of a child whose parents were not married to each other at the time of his birth, there are reasonable grounds for believing that he is the father of the child; or

    (c) he is a guardian of the child; or

    (ca) he is a special guardian of the child; or

    (d) he is a person in whose favour a residence order is in force with respect to the child; or

    (e) he has custody of the child.

(3) In this section 'the appropriate consent', in relation to a child, means—

    (a) the consent of each of the following—

        (i) the child's mother;

        (ii) the child's father, if he has parental responsibility for him;

        (iii) any guardian of the child;

        (iiia) any special guardian of the child;

        (iv) any person in whose favour a residence order is in force with respect to the child;

        (v) any person who has custody of the child; or

    (b) the leave of the court granted under or by virtue of any provision of Part II of the Children Act 1989; or

    (c) if any person has custody of the child, the leave of the court which awarded custody to him.

(4) A person does not commit an offence under this section by taking or sending a child out of the United Kingdom without obtaining the appropriate consent if—

    (a) he is a person in whose favour there is a residence order in force with respect to the child, and he takes or sends him out of the United Kingdom for a period of less than one month; or

    (b) he is a special guardian of the child and he takes or sends the child out of the United Kingdom for a period of less than three months.

(4A) Subsection (4) above does not apply if the person taking or sending the child out of the United Kingdom does so in breach of an order under Part II of the Children Act 1989.

(5) A person does not commit an offence under this section by doing anything without the consent of another person whose consent is required under the foregoing provisions if—

    (a) he does it in the belief that the other person—

        (i) has consented; or

        (ii) would consent if he was aware of all the relevant circumstances; or

    (b) he has taken all reasonable steps to communicate with the other person but has been unable to communicate with him; or

    (c) the other person has unreasonably refused to consent, ...

(5A) Subsection (5)(c) above does not apply if—

    (a) the person who refused to consent is a person—

        (i) in whose favour there is a residence order in force with respect to the child; ...

        (ia) who is a special guardian of the child; or

        (ii) who has custody of the child; or

(b)   the person taking or sending the child out of the United Kingdom is, by so acting, in breach of an order made by a court in the United Kingdom.

(6)   Where, in proceedings for an offence under this section, there is sufficient evidence to raise an issue as to the application of subsection (5) above, it shall be for the prosecution to prove that that subsection does not apply.

(7)   For the purposes of this section—

(a)   'guardian of a child', 'special guardian', 'residence order' and 'parental responsibility' have the same meaning as in the Children Act 1989; and

(b)   a person shall be treated as having custody of a child if there is in force an order of a court in the United Kingdom awarding him (whether solely or jointly with another person) custody, legal custody or care and control of the child.

(8)   This section shall have effect subject to the provisions of the Schedule to this Act in relation to a child who is in the care of a local authority detained in a place of safety, remanded to a local authority accommodation or the subject of proceedings or an order relating to adoption.

2   Offence of abduction of child by other persons

(1)   Subject to subsection (3) below, a person, other than one mentioned in subsection (2) below, commits an offence if, without lawful authority or reasonable excuse, he takes or detains a child under the age of sixteen—

(a)   so as to remove him from the lawful control of any person having lawful control of the child; or

(b)   so as to keep him out of the lawful control of any person entitled to lawful control of the child.

(2)   The persons are—

(a)   where the father and mother of the child in question were married to each other at the time of his birth, the child's father and mother;

(b)   where the father and mother of the child in question were not married to each other at the time of his birth, the child's mother; and

(c)   any other person mentioned in section 1(2)(c) to (e) above.

(3)   In proceedings against any person for an offence under this section, it shall be a defence for that person to prove—

(a)   where the father and mother of the child in question were not married to each other at the time of his birth—

(i)   that he is the child's father; or

(ii)   that, at the time of the alleged offence, he believed, on reasonable grounds, that he was the child's father; or

(b)   that, at the time of the alleged offence, he believed that the child had attained the age of sixteen.

3   Construction of references to taking, sending and detaining

For the purposes of this Part of this Act—

(a)   a person shall be regarded as taking a child if he causes or induces the child to accompany him or any other person or causes the child to be taken;

(b)   a person shall be regarded as sending a child if he causes the child to be sent; ...

(c)   a person shall be regarded as detaining a child if he causes the child to be detained or induces the child to remain with him or any other person; and

(d)   references to a child's parents and to a child whose parents were (or were not) married to each other at the time of his birth shall be construed in accordance with section 1 of the Family Law Reform Act 1987 (which extends their meaning).

(E) Children Act 1989

1 Welfare of the child

(1)   When a court determines any question with respect to—

(a)   the upbringing of a child; or

(b)   the administration of a child's property or the application of any income arising from it,

the child's welfare shall be the court's paramount consideration.

(2)   In any proceedings in which any question with respect to the upbringing of a child arises, the court shall have regard to the general principle that any delay in determining the question is likely to prejudice the welfare of the child.

(3)   In the circumstances mentioned in subsection (4), a court shall have regard in particular to—

(a)   the ascertainable wishes and feelings of the child concerned (considered in the light of his age and understanding);

(b)   his physical, emotional and educational needs;

(c)   the likely effect on him of any change in his circumstances;

(d)   his age, sex, background and any characteristics of his which the court considers relevant;

(e)   any harm which he has suffered or is at risk of suffering;

(f)   how capable each of his parents, and any other person in relation to whom the court considers the question to be relevant, is of meeting his needs;

(g)   the range of powers available to the court under this Act in the proceedings in question.

(4)   The circumstances are that—

(a)   the court is considering whether to make, vary or discharge a section 8 order, and the making, variation or discharge of the order is opposed by any party to the proceedings; or

(b)   the court is considering whether to make, vary or discharge a special guardianship order or an order under Part IV.

(5)   Where a court is considering whether or not to make one or more orders under this Act with respect to a child, it shall not make the order or any of the orders unless it considers that doing so would be better for the child than making no order at all.

2 Parental responsibility for children

(1)   Where a child's father and mother were married to each other at the time of his birth, they shall each have parental responsibility for the child.

(2)   Where a child's father and mother were not married to each other at the time of his birth—

(a)   the mother shall have parental responsibility for the child;

(b)   the father shall have parental responsibility for the child if he has acquired it (and has not ceased to have it) in accordance with the provisions of this Act.

(3)   References in this Act to a child whose father and mother were, or (as the case may be) were not, married to each other at the time of his birth must be read with section 1 of the Family Law Reform Act 1987 (which extends their meaning).

(4)   The rule of law that a father is the natural guardian of his legitimate child is abolished.

(5)   More than one person may have parental responsibility for the same child at the same time.

(6)   A person who has parental responsibility for a child at any time shall not cease to have that responsibility solely because some other person subsequently acquires parental responsibility for the child.

(7)   Where more than one person has parental responsibility for a child, each of them may act alone and without the other (or others) in meeting that responsibility; but

nothing in this Part shall be taken to affect the operation of any enactment which requires the consent of more than one person in a matter affecting the child.

(8)   The fact that a person has parental responsibility for a child shall not entitle him to act in any way which would be incompatible with any order made with respect to the child under this Act.

(9)   A person who has parental responsibility for a child may not surrender or transfer any part of that responsibility to another but may arrange for some or all of it to be met by one or more persons acting on his behalf.

(10) The person with whom any such arrangement is made may himself be a person who already has parental responsibility for the child concerned.

(11) The making of any such arrangement shall not affect any liability of the person making it which may arise from any failure to meet any part of his parental responsibility for the child concerned.

3   Meaning of 'parental responsibility'

(1)   In this Act 'parental responsibility' means all the rights, duties, powers, responsibilities and authority which by law a parent of a child has in relation to the child and his property.

(2)   It also includes the rights, powers and duties which a guardian of the child's estate (appointed, before the commencement of section 5, to act generally) would have had in relation to the child and his property.

(3)   The rights referred to in subsection (2) include, in particular, the right of the guardian to receive or recover in his own name, for the benefit of the child, property of whatever description and wherever situated which the child is entitled to receive or recover.

(4)   The fact that a person has, or does not have, parental responsibility for a child shall not affect—

(a)   any obligation which he may have in relation to the child (such as a statutory duty to maintain the child); or

(b)   any rights which, in the event of the child's death, he (or any other person) may have in relation to the child's property.

(5)   A person who—

(a)   does not have parental responsibility for a particular child; but

(b)   has care of the child,

may (subject to the provisions of this Act) do what is reasonable in all the circumstances of the case for the purpose of safeguarding or promoting the child's welfare.

4   Acquisition of parental responsibility by father

(1)   Where a child's father and mother were not married to each other at the time of his birth, the father shall acquire parental responsibility for the child if—

(a)   he becomes registered as the child's father under any of the enactments specified in subsection (1A);

(b)   he and the child's mother make an agreement (a 'parental responsibility agreement') providing for him to have parental responsibility for the child; or

(c)   the court, on his application, orders that he shall have parental responsibility for the child.

(1A) The enactments referred to in subsection (1)(a) are—

(a)   paragraphs (a), (b) and (c) of section 10(1) and of section 10A(1) of the Births and Deaths Registration Act 1953;

(b)   paragraphs (a), (b)(i) and (c) of section 18(1), and sections 18(2)(b) and 20(1)(a) of the Registration of Births, Deaths and Marriages (Scotland) Act 1965; and

(c)   sub-paragraphs (a), (b) and (c) of Article 14(3) of the Births and Deaths Registration (Northern Ireland) Order 1976.

(1B) The Secretary of State may by order amend subsection (1A) so as to add further enactments to the list in that subsection.

(2)   No parental responsibility agreement shall have effect for the purposes of this Act unless—

(a)   it is made in the form prescribed by regulations made by the Lord Chancellor; and

(b)   where regulations are made by the Lord Chancellor prescribing the manner in which such agreements must be recorded, it is recorded in the prescribed manner.

(2A)   A person who has acquired parental responsibility under subsection (1) shall cease to have that responsibility only if the court so orders.

(3)   The court may make an order under subsection (2A) on the application—

(a)   of any person who has parental responsibility for the child; or

(b)   with the leave of the court, of the child himself,

subject, in the case of parental responsibility acquired under subsection (1)(c), to section 12(4).

(4)   The court may only grant leave under subsection (3)(b) if it is satisfied that the child has sufficient understanding to make the proposed application.

4A. Acquisition of parental responsibility by step-parent

(1)   Where a child's parent ('parent A') who has parental responsibility for the child is married to, or a civil partner of, a person who is not the child's parent ('the step-parent')—

(a)   parent A, or if the other parent of the child also has parental responsibility for the child, both parents may by agreement with the step-parent provide for the step-parent to have parental responsibility for the child; or

(b)   the court may, on the application of the step-parent, order that the step-parent shall have parental responsibility for the child.

(2)   An agreement under subsection (1)(a) is also a 'parental responsibility agreement', and section 4(2) applies in relation to such agreements as it applies in relation to parental responsibility agreements under section 4.

(3)   A parental responsibility agreement under subsection (1)(a), or an order under subsection (1)(b), may only be brought to an end by an order of the court made on the application—

(a)   of any person has parental responsibility for the child; or

(b)   with the leave of the court, of the child himself.

(4)   The court may only grant leave under subsection (3)(b) if it is satisfied that the child has sufficient understanding to make the proposed application.

5 Appointment of guardians

(1)   Where an application with respect to a child is made to the court by any individual, the court may by order appoint that individual to be the child's guardian if—

(a)   the child has no parent with parental responsibility for him; or

(b)   a residence order has been made with respect to the child in favour of a parent, guardian or special guardian of his who has died while the order was in force; or

(c)   paragraph (b) does not apply, and the child's only or last surviving special guardian dies.

(2)   The power conferred by subsection (1) may also be exercised in any family proceedings if the court considers that the order should be made even though no application has been made for it.

(3)   A parent who has parental responsibility for his child may appoint another individual to be the child's guardian in the event of his death.

(4)   A guardian of a child may appoint another individual to take his place as the child's guardian in the event of his death; and a special guardian of a child may appoint another individual to be the child's guardian in the event of his death.

(5)   An appointment under subsection (3) or (4) shall not have effect unless it is made in writing, is dated and is signed by the person making the appointment or—

    (a)   in the case of an appointment made by a will which is not signed by the testator, is signed at the direction of the testator in accordance with the requirements of section 9 of the Wills Act 1837; or

    (b)   in any other case, is signed at the direction of the person making the appointment, in his presence and in the presence of two witnesses who each attest the signature.

(6)   A person appointed as a child's guardian under this section shall have parental responsibility for the child concerned.

(7)   Where—

    (a)   on the death of any person making an appointment under subsection (3) or (4), the child concerned has no parent with parental responsibility for him; or

    (b)   immediately before the death of any person making such an appointment, a residence order in his favour was in force with respect to the child, or he was the child's only (or last surviving) special guardian

the appointment shall take effect on the death of that person.

(8)   Where, on the death of any person making an appointment under subsection (3) or (4)—

    (a)   the child concerned has a parent with parental responsibility for him; and

    (b)   subsection (7)(b) does not apply,

the appointment shall take effect when the child no longer has a parent who has parental responsibility for him.

(9)   Subsections (1) and (7) do not apply if the residence order referred to in paragraph (b) of those subsections was also made in favour of a surviving parent of the child.

(10)   Nothing in this section shall be taken to prevent an appointment under subsection (3) or (4) being made by two or more persons acting jointly.

(11)   Subject to any provision made by rules of court, no court shall exercise the High Court's inherent jurisdiction to appoint a guardian of the estate of any child.

(12)   Where the rules of court are made under subsection (11) they may prescribe the circumstances in which, and conditions subject to which, an appointment of such a guardian may be made.

(13)   A guardian of a child may only be appointed in accordance with the provisions of this section.

7   Welfare reports

(1)   A court considering any question with respect to a child under this Act may—

    (a)   ask an officer of the Service or a Welsh family proceedings officer; or

    (b)   ask a local authority to arrange for—

        (i)   an officer of the authority; or

        (ii)   such other person (other than an officer of the Service or a Welsh family proceedings officer) as the authority considers appropriate,

to report to the court on such matters relating to the welfare of that child as are required to be dealt with in the report.

(2)   The Lord Chancellor may, after consulting the Lord Chief Justice, make regulations specifying matters which, unless the court orders otherwise, must be dealt with in any report under this section.

(3)   The report may be made in writing, or orally, as the court requires.

(4)   Regardless of any enactment or rule of law which would otherwise prevent it from doing so, the court may take account of—

    (a)   any statement contained in the report; and

    (b)   any evidence given in respect of the matters referred to in the report,

in so far as the statement or evidence is, in the opinion of the court, relevant to the question which it is considering.

(5)   It shall be the duty of the authority or officer of the Service or a Welsh family proceedings officer to comply with any request for a report under this section.

(6)   The Lord Chief Justice may nominate a judicial office holder (as defined in section 109(4) of the Constitutional Reform Act 2005) to exercise his functions under subsection (2).

8   Residence, contact and other orders with respect to children

(1)   In this Act—

'a contact order' means an order requiring the person with whom a child lives, or is to live, to allow the child to visit or stay with the person named in the order, or for that person and the child otherwise to have contact with each other;

'a prohibited steps order' means an order that no step which could be taken by a parent in meeting his parental responsibility for a child, and which is of a kind specified in the order, shall be taken by any person without the consent of the court;

'a residence order' means an order settling the arrangements to be made as to the person with whom a child is to live; and

'a specific issue order' means an order giving directions for the purpose of determining a specific question which has arisen, or which may arise, in connection with any aspect of parental responsibility for a child.

(2)   In this Act 'a section 8 order' means any of the orders mentioned in subsection (1) and any order varying or discharging such an order.

(3)   For the purposes of this Act 'family proceedings' means any proceedings—

(a)   under the inherent jurisdiction of the High Court in relation to children; and

(b)   under the enactments mentioned in subsection (4),

but does not include proceedings on an application for leave under section 100(3).

(4)   The enactments are—

(a)   Parts I, II and IV of this Act;

(b)   the Matrimonial Causes Act 1973;

(ba)   Schedule 5 to the Civil Partnership Act 2004;

(c)   ...

(d)   the Adoption and Children Act 2002;

(e)   the Domestic Proceedings and Magistrates' Courts Act 1978;

(ea)   Schedule 6 to the Civil Partnership Act 2004;

(f)   ...

(g)   Part III of the Matrimonial and Family Proceedings Act 1984;

(h)   the Family Law Act 1996;

(i)   sections 11 and 12 of the Crime and Disorder Act 1998.

9   Restrictions on making section 8 orders

(1)   No court shall make any section 8 order, other than a residence order, with respect to a child who is in the care of a local authority.

(2)   No application may be made by a local authority for a residence order or contact order and no court shall make such an order in favour of a local authority.

(3)   A person who is, or was at any time within the last six months, a local authority foster parent of a child may not apply for leave to apply for a section 8 order with respect to the child unless—

(a)   he has the consent of the authority;

(b)   he is relative of the child; or

(c)   the child has lived with him for at least one year preceding the application.

(4)   . . .

(5)   No court shall exercise its powers to make a specific issue order or prohibited steps order—

(a)   with a view to achieving a result which could be achieved by making a residence or contact order; or

(b)   in any way which is denied to the High Court (by section 100(2)) in the exercise of its inherent jurisdiction with respect to children.

(6) Subject to section 12(5) no court shall make any section 8 order which is to have effect for a period which will end after the child has reached the age of sixteen unless it is satisfied that the circumstances of the case are exceptional.

(7) No court shall make any section 8 order, other than one varying or discharging such an order, with respect to a child who has reached the age of sixteen unless it is satisfied that the circumstances of the case are exceptional.

10　Power of court to make section 8 orders

(1) In any family proceedings in which a question arises with respect to the welfare of any child, the court may make a section 8 order with respect to the child if—

 (a) an application for the order has been made by a person who—

  (i) is entitled to apply for a section 8 order with respect to the child; or

  (ii) has obtained the leave of the court to make the application; or

 (b) the court considers that the order should be made even though no such application has been made.

(2) The court may also make a section 8 order with respect to any child on the application of a person who—

 (a) is entitled to apply for a section 8 order with respect to the child; or

 (b) has obtained the leave of the court to make the application.

(3) This section is subject to the restrictions imposed by section 9.

(4) The following persons are entitled to apply to the court for any section 8 order with respect to a child—

 (a) any parent, guardian or special guardian of the child;

 (aa) any person who by virtue of section 4A has parental responsibility for the child;

 (b) any person in whose favour a residence order is in force with respect to the child.

(5) The following persons are entitled to apply for a residence or contact order with respect to a child—

 (a) any party to a marriage (whether or not subsisting) in relation to whom the child is a child of the family;

 (aa) any civil partner in a civil partnership (whether or not subsisting) in relation to whom the child is a child of the family;

 (b) any person with whom the child has lived for a period of at least three years;

 (c) any person who—

  (i) in any case where a residence order is in force with respect to the child, has the consent of each of the persons in whose favour the order was made;

  (ii) in any case where the child is in the care of a local authority, has the consent of that authority; or

  (iii) in any other case, has the consent of each of those (if any) who have parental responsibility for the child.

(5A) A local authority foster parent is entitled to apply for a residence order with respect to a child if the child has lived with him for a period of at least one year immediately preceding the application.

(6) A person who would not otherwise be entitled (under the previous provisions of this section) to apply for the variation or discharge of a section 8 order shall be entitled to do so if—

 (a) the order was made on his application; or

 (b) in the case of a contact order, he is named in the order.

(7) Any person who falls within a category of person prescribed by rules of court is entitled to apply for any such section 8 order as may be prescribed in relation to that category of person.

(7A)   If a special guardianship order is in force with respect to a child, an application for a residence order may only be made with respect to him, if apart from this subsection the leave of the court is not required, with such leave.

(8)   Where the person applying for leave to make an application for a section 8 order is the child concerned, the court may only grant leave if it is satisfied that he has sufficient understanding to make the proposed application for the section 8 order.

(9)   Where the person applying for leave to make an application for a section 8 order is not the child concerned, the court shall, in deciding whether or not to grant leave, have particular regard to—

   (a)   the nature of the proposed application for the section 8 order;

   (b)   the applicant's connection with the child;

   (c)   any risk there might be of that proposed application disrupting the child's life to such an extent that he would be harmed by it; and

   (d)   where the child is being looked after by a local authority—

      (i)   the authority's plans for the child's future; and

      (ii)   the wishes and feelings of the child's parents.

(10)   The period of three years mentioned in subsection (5)(b) need not be continuous but must not have begun more than five years before, or ended more than three months before, the making of the application.

11   General principles and supplementary provisions

(1)   In proceedings in which any question of making a section 8 order, or any other question with respect to such an order, arises, the court shall (in the light of any rules made by virtue of subsection (2))—

   (a)   draw up a timetable with a view to determining the question without delay; and

   (b)   give such directions as it considers appropriate for the purpose of ensuring, so far as is reasonably practicable, that that timetable is adhered to.

(2)   Rules of court may—

   (a)   specify periods within which specified steps must be taken in relation to proceedings in which such questions arise; and

   (b)   make other provision with respect to such proceedings for the purpose of ensuring, so far as is reasonably practicable, that such questions are determined without delay.

(3)   Where a court has power to make a section 8 order, it may do so at any time during the course of the proceedings in question even though it is not in a position to dispose finally of those proceedings.

(4)   Where a residence order is made in favour of two or more persons who do not themselves all live together, the order may specify the periods during which the child is to live in the different households concerned.

(5)   Where—

   (a)   a residence order has been made with respect to a child; and

   (b)   as a result of the order the child lives, or is to live, with one of two parents who each have parental responsibility for him,

   the residence order shall cease to have effect if the parents live together for a continuous period of more than six months.

(6)   A contact order which requires the parent with whom a child lives to allow the child to visit, or otherwise have contact with, his other parent shall cease to have effect if the parents live together for a continuous period of more than six months.

(7)   A section 8 order may—

   (a)   contain directions about how it is to be carried into effect;

   (b)   impose conditions which must be complied with by any person—

      (i)   in whose favour the order is made;

      (ii)   who is a parent of the child concerned;

      (iii)   who is not a parent of his but who has parental responsibility for him; or

     (iv)   with whom the child is living,

and to whom the conditions are expressed to apply;

  (c)   be made to have effect for a specified period, or contain provisions which are to have effect for a specified period;

  (d)   make such incidental, supplemental or consequential provision as the court thinks fit.

12 Residence orders and parental responsibility

(1) Where the court makes a residence order in favour of the father of a child it shall, if the father would not otherwise have parental responsibility for the child, also make an order under section 4 giving him that responsibility.

(2) Where the court makes a residence order in favour of any person who is not the parent or guardian of the child concerned that person shall have parental responsibility for the child while the residence order remains in force.

(3) Where a person has parental responsibility for a child as a result of subsection (2), he shall not have the right—

  (a)   ...

  (b)   to agree, or refuse to agree, to the making of an adoption order, or an order under section 84 of the Adoption and Children Act 2002, with respect to the child; or

  (c)   to appoint a guardian for the child.

(4) Where subsection (1) requires the court to make an order under section 4 in respect of the father of a child, the court shall not bring that order to an end at any time while the residence order concerned remains in force.

(5) The power of a court to make a residence order in favour of any person who is not the parent or guardian of the child concerned includes power to direct, at the request of that person, that the order continue in force until the child reaches the age of eighteen (unless the order is brought to an end earlier); and any power to vary a residence order is exercisable accordingly.

(6) Where a residence order includes such a direction, an application to vary or discharge the order may only be made, if apart from this subsection the leave of the court is not required, with such leave.

13 Change of child's name or removal from jurisdiction

(1) Where a residence order is in force with respect to a child, no person may—

  (a)   cause the child to be known by a new surname; or

  (b)   remove him from the United Kingdom;

without either the written consent of every person who has parental responsibility for the child or the leave of the court.

(2) Subsection (1)(b) does not prevent the removal of a child, for a period of less than one month, by the person in whose favour the residence order is made.

(3) In making a residence order with respect to a child the court may grant the leave required by subsection (1)(b), either generally or for specified purposes.

14A Special guardianship orders

(1) A 'special guardianship order' is an order appointing one or more individuals to be a child's 'special guardian' (or special guardians).

(2) A special guardian—

  (a)   must be aged eighteen or over; and

  (b)   must not be a parent of the child in question,

and subsections (3) to (6) are to be read in that light.

(3) The court may make a special guardianship order with respect to any child on the application of an individual who—

  (a)   is entitled to make such an application with respect to the child; or

  (b)   has obtained the leave of the court to make the application, or on the joint application of more than one such individual.

(4)   Section 9(3) applies in relation to an application for leave to apply for a special guardianship order as it applies in relation to an application for leave to apply for a section 8 order.

(5)   The individuals who are entitled to apply for a special guardianship order with respect to a child are—

(a)   any guardian of the child;

(b)   any individual in whose favour a residence order is in force with respect to the child;

(c)   any individual listed in subsection (5)(b) or (c) of section 10 (as read with subsection (10) of that section);

(d)   a local authority foster parent with whom the child has lived for a period of at least one year immediately preceding the application.

(6)   The court may also make a special guardianship order with respect to a child in any family proceedings in which a question arises with respect to the welfare of the child if—

(a)   an application for the order has been made by an individual who falls within subsection (3)(a) or (b) (or more than one such individual jointly); or

(b)   the court considers that a special guardianship order should be made even though no such application has been made.

(7)   No individual may make an application under subsection (3) or (6)(a) unless, before the beginning of the period of three months ending with the date of the application, he has given written notice of his intention to make the application—

(a)   if the child in question is being looked after by a local authority, to that local authority, or

(b)   otherwise, to the local authority in whose area the individual is ordinarily resident.

(8)   On receipt of such a notice, the local authority must investigate the matter and prepare a report for the court dealing with—

(a)   the suitability of the applicant to be a special guardian;

(b)   such matters (if any) as may be prescribed by the Secretary of State; and

(c)   any other matter which the local authority consider to be relevant.

(9)   The court may itself ask a local authority to conduct such an investigation and prepare such a report, and the local authority must do so.

(10)   The local authority may make such arrangements as they see fit for any person to act on their behalf in connection with conducting an investigation or preparing a report referred to in subsection (8) or (9).

(11)   The court may not make a special guardianship order unless it has received a report dealing with the matters referred to in subsection (8).

(12)   Subsections (8) and (9) of section 10 apply in relation to special guardianship orders as they apply in relation to section 8 orders.

(13)   This section is subject to section 29(5) and (6) of the Adoption and Children Act 2002.

14B   Special guardianship orders: making

(1)   Before making a special guardianship order, the court must consider whether, if the order were made—

(a)   a contact order should also be made with respect to the child, and

(b)   any section 8 order in force with respect to the child should be varied or discharged.

(2)   On making a special guardianship order, the court may also—

(a)   give leave for the child to be known by a new surname;

(b)   grant the leave required by section 14C(3)(b), either generally or for specified purposes.

14C Special guardianship orders: effect

(1) The effect of a special guardianship order is that while the order remains in force—

    (a) a special guardian appointed by the order has parental responsibility for the child in respect of whom it is made; and

    (b) subject to any other order in force with respect to the child under this Act, a special guardian is entitled to exercise parental responsibility to the exclusion of any other person with parental responsibility for the child (apart from another special guardian).

(2) Subsection (1) does not affect—

    (a) the operation of any enactment or rule of law which requires the consent of more than one person with parental responsibility in a matter affecting the child; or

    (b) any rights which a parent of the child has in relation to the child's adoption or placement for adoption.

(3) While a special guardianship order is in force with respect to a child, no person may—

    (a) cause the child to be known by a new surname; or

    (b) remove him from the United Kingdom,

without either the written consent of every person who has parental responsibility for the child or the leave of the court.

(4) Subsection (3)(b) does not prevent the removal of a child, for a period of less than three months, by a special guardian of his.

(5) If the child with respect to whom a special guardianship order is in force dies, his special guardian must take reasonable steps to give notice of that fact to—

    (a) each parent of the child with parental responsibility; and

    (b) each guardian of the child,

but if the child has more than one special guardian, and one of them has taken such steps in relation to a particular parent or guardian, any other special guardian need not do so as respects that parent or guardian.

(6) This section is subject to section 29(7) of the Adoption and Children Act 2002.

14D Special guardianship orders: variation and discharge

(1) The court may vary or discharge a special guardianship order on the application of—

    (a) the special guardian (or any of them, if there are more than one);

    (b) any parent or guardian of the child concerned;

    (c) any individual in whose favour a residence order is in force with respect to the child;

    (d) any individual not falling within any of paragraphs (a) to (c) who has, or immediately before the making of the special guardianship order had, parental responsibility for the child;

    (e) the child himself; or

    (f) a local authority designated in a care order with respect to the child.

(2) In any family proceedings in which a question arises with respect to the welfare of a child with respect to whom a special guardianship order is in force, the court may also vary or discharge the special guardianship order if it considers that the order should be varied or discharged, even though no application has been made under subsection (1).

(3) The following must obtain the leave of the court before making an application under subsection (1)—

    (a) the child;

    (b) any parent or guardian of his;

    (c) any step-parent of his who has acquired, and has not lost, parental responsibility for him by virtue of section 4A;

(d)   any individual falling within subsection (1)(d) who immediately before the making of the special guardianship order had, but no longer has, parental responsibility for him.

(4)   Where the person applying for leave to make an application under subsection (1) is the child, the court may only grant leave if it is satisfied that he has sufficient understanding to make the proposed application under subsection (1).

(5)   The court may not grant leave to a person falling within subsection (3)(b)(c) or (d) unless it is satisfied that there has been a significant change in circumstances since the making of the special guardianship order.

15   Orders for financial relief with respect to children

(1)   Schedule 1 (which consists primarily of the re-enactment, with consequential amendments and minor modifications, of provisions of section 6 of the Family Law Reform Act 1969, the Guardianship of Minors Acts 1971 and 1973, the Children Act 1975 and of sections 15 and 16 of the Family Law Reform Act 1987) makes provision in relation to financial relief for children.

(2)   The powers of a magistrates' court under section 60 of the Magistrates' Courts Act 1980 to revoke, revive or vary an order for the periodical payment of money and the power of a clerk of a magistrates' court to vary such an order shall not apply in relation to an order made under Schedule 1.

16   Family assistance orders

(1)   Where, in any family proceedings, the court has power to make an order under this Part with respect to any child, it may (whether or not it makes such an order) make an order requiring—
(a)   an officer of the Service or a Welsh family proceedings officer to be made available; or
(b)   a local authority to make an officer of the authority available,
to advise, assist and (where appropriate) befriend any person named in the order.

(2)   The persons who may be named in an order under this section ('a family assistance order') are—
(a)   any parent, guardian or special guardian of the child;
(b)   any person with whom the child is living or in whose favour a contact order is in force with respect to the child;
(c)   the child himself.

(3)   No court may make a family assistance order unless—
(a)   it is satisfied that the circumstances of the case are exceptional; and
(b)   it has obtained the consent of every person to be named in the order other than the child.

(4)   A family assistance order may direct—
(a)   the person named in the order; or
(b)   such of the persons named in the order as may be specified in the order,
to take such steps as may be so specified with a view to enabling the officer concerned to be kept informed of the address of any person named in the order and to be allowed to visit any such person.

(5)   Unless it specifies a shorter period, a family assistance order shall have effect for a period of six months beginning with the day on which it is made.

(6)   Where—
(a)   a family assistance order is in force with respect to a child; and
(b)   a section 8 order is also in force with respect to the child,
the officer concerned may refer to the court the question whether the section 8 order should be varied or discharged.

(7)   A family assistance order shall not be made so as to require a local authority to make an officer of theirs available unless—
(a)   the authority agree; or

(b)   the child concerned lives or will live within their area.

(8), (9) ...

17   Provision of services for children in need, their families and others

(1)   It shall be the general duty of every local authority (in addition to the other duties imposed on them by this Part)—

(a)   to safeguard and promote the welfare of children within their area who are in need; and

(b)   so far as is consistent with that duty, to promote the upbringing of such children by their families,

by providing a range and level of services appropriate to those children's needs.

(2)   For the purpose principally of facilitating the discharge of their general duty under this section, every local authority shall have the specific duties and powers set out in Part I of Schedule 2.

(3)   Any service provided by an authority in the exercise of functions conferred on them by this section may be provided for the family of a particular child in need or for any member of his family, if it is provided with a view to safeguarding or promoting the child's welfare.

(4)   The Secretary of State may by order amend any provision of Part I of Schedule 2 or add any further duty or power to those for the time being mentioned there.

(4A)   Before determining what (if any) services to provide for a particular child in need in the exercise of functions conferred on them by this section, a local authority shall, so far as is reasonably practicable and consistent with the child's welfare—

(a)   ascertain the child's wishes and feelings regarding the provision of those services; and

(b)   give due consideration (having regard to his age and understanding) to such wishes and feelings of the child as they have been able to ascertain.

(5)   Every local authority—

(a)   shall facilitate the provision by others (including in particular voluntary organisations) of services which the authority have power to provide by virtue of this section, or section 18, 20, 23, 23B to 23D, 24A or 24B; and

(b)   may make such arrangements as they see fit for any person to act on their behalf in the provision of any such service.

(6)   The services provided by a local authority in the exercise of functions conferred on them by this section may include providing accommodation and giving assistance in kind or, in exceptional circumstances, in cash.

(7)   Assistance may be unconditional or subject to conditions as to the repayment of the assistance or of its value (in whole or in part).

(8)   Before giving any assistance or imposing any conditions, a local authority shall have regard to the means of the child concerned and of each of his parents.

(9)   No person shall be liable to make any repayment of assistance or of its value at any time when he is in receipt of income support under Part VII of the Social Security Contributions and Benefits Act 1992, of any element of child tax credit other than the family element, of working tax credit or of an income-based jobseeker's allowance.

(10)   For the purposes of this Part a child shall be taken to be in need if—

(a)   he is unlikely to achieve or maintain, or to have the opportunity of achieving or maintaining, a reasonable standard of health or development without the provision for him of services by a local authority under this Part;

(b)   his health or development is likely to be significantly impaired, or further impaired, without the provision for him of such services; or

(c)   he is disabled,

and 'family,' in relation to such a child, includes any person who has parental responsibility for the child and any other person with whom he has been living.

(11)   For the purposes of this Part, a child is disabled if he is blind, deaf or dumb or suffers from mental disorder of any kind or is substantially and permanently handicapped

by illness, injury or congenital deformity or such other disability as may be prescribed; and in this Part—

'development' means physical, intellectual, emotional, social or behavioural development; and

'health' means physical or mental health.

(12)   The Treasury may by regulations prescribe circumstances in which a person is to be treated for the purposes of this Part (or for such of those purposes as are prescribed) as in receipt of any element of child tax credit other than the family element or of working tax credit.

20   Provision of accommodation for children: general

(1)   Every local authority shall provide accommodation for any child in need within their area who appears to them to require accommodation as a result of—

   (a)   there being no person who has parental responsibility for him;

   (b)   his being lost or having been abandoned; or

   (c)   the person who has been caring for him being prevented (whether or not permanently, and for whatever reason) from providing him with suitable accommodation or care.

(2)   Where a local authority provide accommodation under subsection (1) for a child who is ordinarily resident in the area of another local authority, that other local authority may take over the provision of accommodation for the child within—

   (a)   three months of being notified in writing that the child is being provided with accommodation; or

   (b)   such other longer period as may be prescribed.

(3)   Every local authority shall provide accommodation for any child in need within their area who has reached the age of sixteen and whose welfare the authority consider is likely to be seriously prejudiced if they do not provide him with accommodation.

(4)   A local authority may provide accommodation for any child within their area (even though a person who has parental responsibility for him is able to provide him with accommodation) if they consider that to do so would safeguard or promote the child's welfare.

(5)   A local authority may provide accommodation for any person who has reached the age of sixteen but is under twenty-one in any community home which takes children who have reached the age of sixteen if they consider that to do so would safeguard or promote his welfare.

(6)   Before providing accommodation under this section, a local authority shall, so far as is reasonably practicable and consistent with the child's welfare—

   (a)   ascertain the child's wishes and feelings regarding the provision of accommodation; and

   (b)   give due consideration (having regard to his age and understanding) to such wishes and feelings of the child as they have been able to ascertain.

(7)   A local authority may not provide accommodation under this section for any child if any person who—

   (a)   has parental responsibility for him; and

   (b)   is willing and able to—

      (i)   provide accommodation for him; or

      (ii)   arrange for accommodation to be provided for him,

   objects.

(8)   Any person who has parental responsibility for a child may at any time remove the child from accommodation provided by or on behalf of the local authority under this section.

(9)   Subsections (7) and (8) do not apply while any person—

   (a)   in whose favour a residence order is in force with respect to the child; ...

   (aa)   who is a special guardian of the child; or

(b)   who has care of the child by virtue of an order made in the exercise of the High Court's inherent jurisdiction with respect to children,

agrees to the child being looked after in accommodation provided by or on behalf of the local authority.

(10)   Where there is more than one such person as is mentioned in subsection (9), all of them must agree.

(11)   Subsections (7) and (8) do not apply where a child who has reached the age of sixteen agrees to being provided with accommodation under this section.

22   General duty of local authority in relation to children looked after by them

(1)   In this Act, any reference to a child who is looked after by a local authority is a reference to a child who is—

(a)   in their care; or

(b)   provided with accommodation by the authority in the exercise of any functions (in particular those under this Act) which are social services functions within the meaning of the Local Authority Social Services Act 1970, apart from functions under sections 17, 23B and 24B.

(2)   In subsection (1) 'accommodation' means accommodation which is provided for a continuous period of more than 24 hours.

(3)   It shall be the duty of a local authority looking after any child—

(a)   to safeguard and promote his welfare; and

(b)   to make such use of services available for children cared for by their own parents as appears to the authority reasonable in his case.

(3A)   The duty of a local authority under subsection (3)(a) to safeguard and promote the welfare of a child looked after by them includes in particular a duty to promote the child's educational achievement.

(4)   Before making any decision with respect to a child whom they are looking after, or proposing to look after, a local authority shall, so far as is reasonably practicable, ascertain the wishes and feelings of—

(a)   the child;

(b)   his parents;

(c)   any person who is not a parent of his but who has parental responsibility for him; and

(d)   any other person whose wishes and feelings the authority consider to be relevant,

regarding the matter to be decided.

(5)   In making any such decision a local authority shall give due consideration—

(a)   having regard to his age and understanding, to such wishes and feelings of the child as they have been able to ascertain;

(b)   to such wishes and feelings of any person mentioned in subsection (4)(b) to (d) as they have been able to ascertain; and

(c)   to the child's religious persuasion, racial origin and cultural and linguistic background.

(6)   If it appears to a local authority that it is necessary, for the purposes of protecting members of the public from serious injury, to exercise their powers with respect to a child whom they are looking after in a manner which may not be consistent with their duties under this section, they may do so.

(7)   If the Secretary of State considers it necessary, for the purpose of protecting members of the public from serious injury, to give directions to a local authority with respect to the exercise of their powers with respect to a child whom they are looking after, he may give such directions to the authority.

(8)   Where any such directions are given to an authority they shall comply with them even though doing so is inconsistent with their duties under this section.

23 Provision of accommodation and maintenance by local authority for children whom they are looking after

(1)   It shall be the duty of any local authority looking after a child—

    (a)   when he is in their care, to provide accommodation for him; and

    (b)   to maintain him in other respects apart from providing accommodation for him.

(2)   A local authority shall provide accommodation and maintenance for any child whom they are looking after by—

    (a)   placing him (subject to subsection (5) and any regulations made by the Secretary of State) with—

        (i)   a family;

        (ii)   a relative of his; or

        (iii) any other suitable person,

        on such terms as to payment by the authority and otherwise as the authority may determine (subject to section 49 of the Children Act 2004);

    (aa) maintaining him in an appropriate children's home; or

    (f)   making such other arrangements as—

        (i)   seem appropriate to them; and

        (ii)   comply with any regulations made by the Secretary of State.

(2A) Where under subsection (2)(aa) a local authority maintains a child in a home provided, equipped and maintained by the Secretary of State under section 82(5), it shall do so on such terms as the Secretary of State may from time to time determine.

(3)   Any person with whom a child has been placed under subsection (2)(a) is referred to in this Act as a local authority foster parent unless he falls within subsection (4).

(4)   A person falls within this subsection if he is—

    (a)   a parent of the child;

    (b)   a person who is not a parent of the child but who has parental responsibility for him; or

    (c)   where the child is in care and there was a residence order in force with respect to him immediately before the care order was made, a person in whose favour the residence order was made.

(5)   Where a child is in the care of a local authority, the authority may only allow him to live with a person who falls within subsection (4) in accordance with regulations made by the Secretary of State.

(5A) For the purposes of subsection (5) a child shall be regarded as living with a person if he stays with that person for a continuous period of more than 24 hours.

(6)   Subject to any regulations made by the Secretary of State for the purposes of this subsection, any local authority looking after a child shall make arrangements to enable him to live with—

    (a)   a person falling within subsection (4); or

    (b)   a relative, friend or other person connected with him,

unless that would not be reasonably practicable or consistent with his welfare.

(7)   Where a local authority provide accommodation for a child whom they are looking after, they shall, subject to the provisions of this Part and so far as is reasonably practicable and consistent with his welfare, secure that—

    (a)   the accommodation is near his home; and

    (b)   where the authority are also providing accommodation for a sibling of his, they are accommodated together.

(8)   Where a local authority provide accommodation for a child whom they are looking after and who is disabled, they shall, so far as is reasonably practicable, secure that the accommodation is not unsuitable to his particular needs.

(9)   Part II of Schedule 2 shall have effect for the purposes of making further provision as to children looked after by local authorities and in particular as to the regulations that may be made under subsections (2)(a) and (f) and (5).

(10) In this Act—

'appropriate children's home' means a children's home in respect of which a person is registered under Part II of the Care Standards Act 2000; and

'children's home' has the same meaning as in that Act.

26 Review of cases and inquiries into representations

(1) The Secretary of State may make regulations requiring the case of each child who is being looked after by a local authority to be reviewed in accordance with the provisions of the regulations.

(2) The regulations may, in particular, make provision—

    (a) as to the manner in which each case is to be reviewed;

    (b) as to the considerations to which the local authority are to have regard in reviewing each case;

    (c) as to the time when each case is first to be reviewed and the frequency of subsequent reviews;

    (d) requiring the authority, before conducting any review, to seek the views of—

        (i) the child;

        (ii) his parents;

        (iii) any person who is not a parent of his but who has parental responsibility for him; and

        (iv) any other person whose views the authority consider to be relevant,

    including, in particular, the views of those persons in relation to any particular matter which is to be considered in the course of the review;

    (e) requiring the authority ..., in the case of a child who is in their care—

        (i) to keep the section 31A plan for the child under review and, if they are of the opinion that some change is required, to revise the plan, or make a new plan, accordingly,

        (ii) to consider whether an application should be made to discharge the care order;

    (f) requiring the authority ..., in the case of a child in accommodation provided by the authority—

        (i) if there is no plan for the future care of the child, to prepare one,

        (ii) if there is such a plan for the child, to keep it under review and, if they are of the opinion that some change is required, to revise the plan or make a new plan, accordingly,

        (iii) to consider whether the accommodation accords with the requirements of this Part;

    (g) requiring the authority to inform the child, so far as is reasonably practicable, of any steps he may take under this Act;

    (h) requiring the authority to make arrangements, including arrangements with such other bodies providing services as it considers appropriate, to implement any decision which they propose to make in the course, or as a result, of the review;

    (i) requiring the authority to notify details of the result of the review and of any decision taken by them in consequence of the review to—

        (i) the child;

        (ii) his parents;

        (iii) any person who is not a parent of his but who has parental responsibility for him; and

        (iv) any other person whom they consider ought to be notified;

    (j) requiring the authority to monitor the arranangements which they have made with a view to ensuring that they comply with the regulations;

    (k) for the authority to appoint a person in respect of each case to carry out in the prescribed manner the functions mentioned in subsection (2A) and any prescribed function.

(2A) The functions referred to in subsection (2)(k) are—

      (a)   participating in the review of the case in question,

      (b)   monitoring the performance of the authority's functions in respect of the review,

      (c)   referring the case to an officer of the Children and Family Court Advisory and Support Service or a Welsh family proceedings officer, if the person appointed under subsection (2)(k) considers it appropriate to do so.

(2B)   A person appointed under subsection (2)(k) must be a person of a prescribed description.

(2C)   In relation to children whose cases are referred to officers under subsection (2A)(c), the Lord Chancellor may by regulations—

      (a)   extend any functions of the officers in respect of family proceedings (within the meaning of section 12 of the Criminal Justice and Court Services Act 2000) to other proceedings,

      (b)   require any functions of the officers to be performed in the manner prescribed by the regulations.

(2D)   The power to make regulations in subsection (2C) is exercisable in relation to functions of Welsh family proceedings officers only with the consent of the National Assembly for Wales.

(3)   Every local authority shall establish a procedure for considering any representations (including any complaint) made to them by—

      (a)   any child who is being looked after by them or who is not being looked after by them but is in need;

      (b)   a parent of his;

      (c)   any person who is not a parent of his but who has parental responsibility for him;

      (d)   any local authority foster parent;

      (e)   such other person as the authority consider has a sufficient interest in the child's welfare to warrant his representations being considered by them,

about the discharge by the authority of any of their qualifying functions in relation to the child.

(3A)   The following are qualifying functions for the purposes of subsection (3)—

      (a)   functions under this Part,

      (b)   such functions under Part 4 or 5 as are specified by the Secretary of State in regulations.

(3B)   The duty under subsection (3) extends to representations (including complaints) made to the authority by—

      (a)   any person mentioned in section 3(1) of the Adoption and Children Act 2002 (persons for whose needs provision is made by the Adoption Service) and any other person to whom arrangements for the provision of adoption support services (within the meaning of that Act) extend,

      (b)   such other person as the authority consider has sufficient interest in a child who is or may be adopted to warrant his representations being considered by them,

about the discharge by the authority of such functions under the Adoption and Children Act 2002 as are specified by the Secretary of State in regulations.

(3C)   The duty under subsection (3) extends to any representations (including complaints) which are made to the authority by—

      (a)   a child with respect to whom a special guardianship order is in force,

      (b)   a special guardian or a parent of such a child,

      (c)   any other person the authority consider has a sufficient interest in the welfare of such a child to warrant his representations being considered by them, or

      (d)   any person who has applied for an assessment under section 14F(3) or (4),

about the discharge by the authority of such functions under section 14F as may be specified by the Secretary of State in regulations.

(4)   The procedure shall ensure that at least one person who is not a member or officer of the authority takes part in—

    (a)   the consideration; and

    (b)   any discussions which are held by the authority about the action (if any) to be taken in relation to the child in the light of the consideration,

but this subsection is subject to subsection (5A).

(4A)   Regulations may be made by the Secretary of State imposing time limits on the making of representations under this section.

(5)   In carrying out any consideration of representations under this section a local authority shall comply with any regulations made by the Secretary of State for the purpose of regulating the procedure to be followed.

(5A)   Regulations under subsection (5) may provide that subsection (4) does not apply in relation to any consideration or discussion which takes place as part of a procedure for which provision is made by the regulations for the purpose of resolving informally the matters raised in the representations.

(6)   The Secretary of State may make regulations requiring local authorities to monitor the arrangements that they have made with a view to ensuring that they comply with any regulations made for the purposes of subsection (5).

(7)   Where any representation has been considered under the procedure established by a local authority under this section, the authority shall—

    (a)   have due regard to the findings of those considering the representation; and

    (b)   take such steps as are reasonably practicable to notify (in writing)—

        (i)   the person making the representation;

        (ii)   the child (if the authority consider that he has sufficient understanding); and

        (iii)   such other persons (if any) as appear to the authority to be likely to be affected,

of the authority's decision in the matter and their reasons for taking that decision and of any action which they have taken, or propose to take.

(8)   Every local authority shall give such publicity to their procedure for considering representations under this section as they consider appropriate.

31   Care and supervision orders

(1)   On the application of any local authority or authorised person, the court may make an order—

    (a)   placing the child with respect to whom the application is made in the care of a designated local authority; or

    (b)   putting him under the supervision of a designated local authority. ...

(2)   A court may only make a care order or supervision order if it is satisfied—

    (a)   that the child concerned is suffering, or is likely to suffer, significant harm; and

    (b)   that the harm, or likelihood of harm, is attributable to—

        (i)   the care given to the child, or likely to be given to him if the order were not made, not being what it would be reasonable to expect a parent to give to him; or

        (ii)   the child's being beyond parental control.

(3)   No care order or supervision order may be made with respect to a child who has reached the age of seventeen (or sixteen, in the case of a child who is married).

(3A)   No care order made by made with respect to a child until the court has considered a section 31A care plan.

(4)   An application under this section may be made on its own or in any other family proceedings.

(5)   The court may—

    (a)   on an application for a care order, make a supervision order;

    (b)   on an application for a supervision order, make a care order.

(6)   Where an authorised person proposes to make an application under this section he shall—

(a)   if it is reasonably practicable to do so; and

(b)   before making the application,

consult the local authority appearing to him to be the authority in whose area the child concerned is ordinarily resident.

(7)   An application made by an authorised person shall not be entertained by the court if, at the time when it is made, the child concerned is—

(a)   the subject of an earlier application for a care order, or supervision order, which has not been disposed of; or

(b)   subject to—

(i)   a care order or supervision order;

(ii)   an order under section 63(1) of the Powers of Criminal Courts (Sentencing) Act 2000; or

(iii)   (applies to Scotland only)

(8)   The local authority designated in a care order must be—

(a)   the authority within whose area the child is ordinarily resident; or

(b)   where the child does not reside in the area of a local authority, the authority within whose area any circumstances arose in consequence of which the order is being made.

(9)   In this section—

'authorised person' means—

(a)   the National Society for the Prevention of Cruelty to Children and any of its officers; and

(b)   any person authorised by order of the Secretary of State to bring proceedings under this section and any officer of a body which is so authorised;

'harm' means ill-treatment or the impairment of health or development including, for example, impairment suffered from seeing or hearing the ill-treatment of another;

'development' means physical, intellectual, emotional, social or behavioural development;

'health' means physical or mental health; and

'ill-treatment' includes sexual abuse and forms of ill-treatment which are not physical.

(10)   Where the question of whether harm suffered by a child is significant turns on the child's health or development, his health or development shall be compared with that which could reasonably be expected of a similar child.

(11)   In this Act—

'a care order' means (subject to section 105(1)) an order under subsection (1)(a) and (except where express provision to the contrary is made) includes an interim care order made under section 38; and

'a supervision order' means an order under subsection (1)(b) and (except where express provision to the contrary is made) includes an interim supervision order made under section 38.

31A   Care orders: care plans

(1)   Where an application is made on which a care order might be made with respect to a child, the appropriate local authority must, within such time as the court may direct, prepare a plan ('a care plan') for the future care of the child.

(2)   While the application is pending, the authority must keep any care plan prepared by them under review and, if they are of the opinion some change is required, revise the plan, or make a new plan, accordingly.

(3)   A care plan must give any prescribed information and do so in the prescribed manner.

(4)   For the purposes of this section, the appropriate local authority, in relation to a child in respect of whom a care order might be made, is the local authority proposed to be designated in the order.

(5)   In section 31(3A) and this section, references to a care order do not include an interim care order.

(6)   A plan prepared, or treated as prepared, under this section is referred to in this Act as a 'section 31A care plan'.

33   Effect of care order

(1)   Where a care order is made with respect to a child it shall be the duty of the local authority designated by the order to receive the child into their care and to keep him in their care while the order remains in force.

(2)   Where—

(a)   a care order has been made with respect to a child on the application of an authorised person; but

(b)   the local authority designated by the order was not informed that that person proposed to make the application,

the child may be kept in the care of that person until received into the care of the authority.

(3)   While a care order is in force with respect to a child, the local authority designated by the order shall—

(a)   have parental responsibility for the child; and

(b)   have the power (subject to the following provisions of this section) to determine the extent to which—

(i)   a parent, guardian or special guardian of the child; or

(ii)   a person who by virtue of section 4A has parental responsibility for the child,

may meet his parental responsibility for him.

(4)   The authority may not exercise the power in subsection (3)(b) unless they are satisfied that it is necessary to do so in order to safeguard or promote the child's welfare.

(5)   Nothing in subsection (3)(b) shall prevent a person mentioned in that provision who has care of the child from doing what is reasonable in all the circumstances of the case for the purpose of safeguarding or promoting his welfare.

(6)   While a care order is in force with respect to a child, the local authority designated by the order shall not—

(a)   cause the child to be brought up in any religious persuasion other than that in which he would have been brought up if the order had not been made; or

(b)   have the right—

(i)   . . .

(ii)   to agree or refuse to agree to the making of an adoption order, or an order under section 84 of the Adoption and Children Act 2002, with respect to the child; or

(iii)   to appoint a guardian for the child.

(7)   While a care order is in force with respect to a child, no person may—

(a)   cause the child to be known by a new surname; or

(b)   remove him from the United Kingdom,

without either the written consent of every person who has parental responsibility for the child or the leave of the court.

(8)   Subsection (7)(b) does not—

(a)   prevent the removal of such a child, for a period of less than one month, by the authority in whose care he is; or

(b)   apply to arrangements for such a child to live outside England and Wales (which are governed by paragraph 19 of Schedule 2).

(9)   The power in subsection (3)(b) is subject (in addition to being subject to the provisions of this section) to any right, duty, power, responsibility or authority which a person mentioned in that provision has in relation to the child and his property by virtue of any other enactment.

34   Parental contact etc with children in care

(1)   Where a child is in the care of a local authority, the authority shall (subject to the provisions of this section) allow the child reasonable contact with—

(a)   his parents;

(b)   any guardian or special guardian of his;

(ba)   any person who by virtue of section 4A has parental responsibility for him;

(c)   where there was a residence order in force with respect to the child immediately before the care order was made, the person in whose favour the order was made; and

(d)   where, immediately before the care order was made, a person had care of the child by virtue of an order made in the exercise of the High Court's inherent jurisdiction with respect to children, that person.

(2)   On an application made by the authority or the child, the court may make such order as it considers appropriate with respect to the contact which is to be allowed between the child and any named person.

(3)   On an application made by—

(a)   any person mentioned in paragraphs (a) to (d) of subsection (1); or

(b)   any person who has obtained the leave of the court to make the application,

the court may make such order as it considers appropriate with respect to the contact which is to be allowed between the child and that person.

(4)   On an application made by the authority or the child, the court may make an order authorising the authority to refuse to allow contact between the child and any person who is mentioned in paragraphs (a) to (d) of subsection (1) and named in the order.

(5)   When making a care order with respect to a child, or in any family proceedings in connection with a child who is in the care of a local authority, the court may make an order under this section, even though no application for such an order has been made with respect to the child, if it considers that the order should be made.

(6)   An authority may refuse to allow the contact that would otherwise be required by virtue of subsection (1) or an order under this section if—

(a)   they are satisfied that it is necessary to do so in order to safeguard or promote the child's welfare; and

(b)   the refusal—

(i)   is decided upon as a matter of urgency; and

(ii)   does not last for more than seven days.

(7)   An order under this section may impose such conditions as the court considers appropriate.

(8)   The Secretary of State may by regulations make provision as to—

(a)   the steps to be taken by a local authority who have exercised their powers under subsection (6);

(b)   the circumstances in which, and conditions subject to which, the terms of any order under this section may be departed from by agreement between the local authority and the person in relation to whom the order is made;

(c)   notification by a local authority of any variation or suspension of arrangements made (otherwise than under an order under this section) with a view to affording any person contact with a child to whom this section applies.

(9)   The court may vary or discharge any order made under this section on the application of the authority, the child concerned or the person named in the order.

(10)   An order under this section may be made either at the same time as the care order itself or later.

(11)   Before making a care order with respect to any child the court shall—

    (a)   consider the arrangements which the authority have made, or propose to make, for affording any person contact with a child to whom this section applies; and

    (b)   invite the parties to the proceedings to comment on those arrangements.

35 Supervision orders

(1)   While a supervision order is in force it shall be the duty of the supervisor—

    (a)   to advise, assist and befriend the supervised child;

    (b)   to take such steps as are reasonably necessary to give effect to the order; and

    (c)   where—

        (i)   the order is not wholly complied with; or

        (ii)   the supervisor considers that the order may no longer be necessary,

        to consider whether or not to apply to the court for its variation or discharge.

(2)   Parts I and II of Schedule 3 make further provision with respect to supervision orders.

37 Powers of court in certain family proceedings

(1)   Where, in any family proceedings in which a question arises with respect to the welfare of any child, it appears to the court that it may be appropriate for a care or supervision order to be made with respect to him, the court may direct the appropriate authority to undertake an investigation of the child's circumstances.

(2)   Where the court gives a direction under this section the local authority concerned shall, when undertaking the investigation, consider whether they should—

    (a)   apply for a care order or for a supervision order with respect to the child;

    (b)   provide services or assistance for the child or his family; or

    (c)   take any other action with respect to the child.

(3)   Where a local authority undertake an investigation under this section, and decide not to apply for a care order or supervision order with respect to the child concerned, they shall inform the court of—

    (a)   their reasons for so deciding;

    (b)   any service or assistance which they have provided, or intend to provide, for the child and his family; and

    (c)   any other action which they have taken, or propose to take, with respect to the child.

(4)   The information shall be given to the court before the end of the period of eight weeks beginning with the date of the direction, unless the court otherwise directs.

(5)   The local authority named in a direction under subsection (1) must be—

    (a)   the authority in whose area the child is ordinarily resident; or

    (b)   where the child is not ordinarily resident in the area of a local authority, the authority within whose area any circumstances arose in consequence of which the direction is being given.

(6)   If, on the conclusion of any investigation or review under this section, the authority decide not to apply for a care order or supervision order with respect to the child—

    (a)   they shall consider whether it would be appropriate to review the case at a later date; and

    (b)   if they decide that it would be, they shall determine the date on which that review is to begin.

38 Interim orders

(1)   Where—

    (a)   in any proceedings on an application for a care order or supervision order, the proceedings are adjourned; or

    (b)   the court gives a direction under section 37(1),

    the court may make an interim care order or an interim supervision order with respect to the child concerned.

(2)   A court shall not make an interim care order or interim supervision order under this section unless it is satisfied that there are reasonable grounds for believing that the circumstances with respect to the child are as mentioned in section 31(2).

(3)   Where, in any proceedings on an application for a care order or supervision order, a court makes a residence order with respect to the child concerned, it shall also make an interim supervision order with respect to him unless satisfied that his welfare will be satisfactorily safeguarded without an interim order being made.

(4)   An interim order made under or by virtue of this section shall have effect for such period as may be specified in the order, but shall in any event cease to have effect on whichever of the following events first occurs—

(a)   the expiry of the period of eight weeks beginning with the date on which the order is made;

(b)   if the order is the second or subsequent such order made with respect to the same child in the same proceedings, the expiry of the relevant period;

(c)   in a case which falls within subsection (1)(a), the disposal of the application;

(d)   in a case which falls within subsection (1)(b), the disposal of an application for a care order or supervision order made by the authority with respect to the child;

(e)   in a case which falls within subsection (1)(b) and in which—

(i)   the court has given a direction under section 37(4), but

(ii)   no application for a care order or supervision order has been made with respect to the child,

the expiry of the period fixed by that direction.

(5)   In subsection (4)(b) 'the relevant period' means—

(a)   the period of four weeks beginning with the date on which the order in question is made; or

(b)   the period of eight weeks beginning with the date on which the first order was made if that period ends later than the period mentioned in paragraph (a).

(6)   Where the court makes an interim care order, or interim supervision order, it may give such directions (if any) as it considers appropriate with regard to the medical or psychiatric examination or other assessment of the child; but if the child is of sufficient understanding to make an informed decision he may refuse to submit to the examination or other assessment.

(7)   A direction under subsection (6) may be to the effect that there is to be—

(a)   no such examination or assessment; or

(b)   no such examination or assessment unless the court directs otherwise.

(8)   A direction under subsection (6) may be—

(a)   given when the interim order is made or at any time while it is in force; and

(b)   varied at any time on the application of any person falling within any class of person prescribed by rules of court for the purposes of this subsection.

(9)   Paragraphs 4 and 5 of Schedule 3 shall not apply in relation to an interim supervision order.

(10)   Where a court makes an order under or by virtue of this section it shall, in determining the period for which the order is to be in force, consider whether any party who was, or might have been, opposed to the making of the order was in a position to argue his case against the order in full.

38A   Power to include exclusion requirement in interim care order

(1)   Where—

(a)   on being satisfied that there are reasonable grounds for believing that the circumstances with respect to a child are as mentioned in section 31(2)(a) and (b)(i), the court makes an interim care order with respect to a child, and

(b)   the conditions mentioned in subsection (2) are satisfied,

the court may include an exclusion requirement in the interim care order.

(2)   The conditions are—

    (a)   that there is reasonable cause to believe that, if a person ('the relevant person') is excluded from a dwelling-house in which the child lives, the child will cease to suffer, or cease to be likely to suffer, significant harm, and

    (b)   that another person living in the dwelling-house (whether a parent of the child or some other person)—

        (i)   is able and willing to give to the child the care which it would be reasonable to expect a parent to give him, and

        (ii)   consents to the inclusion of the exclusion requirement.

(3)   For the purposes of this section an exclusion requirement is any one or more of the following—

    (a)   a provision requiring the relevant person to leave a dwelling-house in which he is living with the child,

    (b)   a provision prohibiting the relevant person from entering a dwelling-house in which the child lives, and

    (c)   a provision excluding the relevant person from a defined area in which a dwelling-house in which the child lives is situated.

(4)   The court may provide that the exclusion requirement is to have effect for a shorter period than the other provisions of the interim care order.

(5)   Where the court makes an interim care order containing an exclusion requirement, the court may attach a power of arrest to the exclusion requirement.

(6)   Where the court attaches a power of arrest to an exclusion requirement of an interim care order, it may provide that the power of arrest is to have effect for a shorter period than the exclusion requirement.

(7)   Any period specified for the purposes of subsection (4) or (6) may be extended by the court (on one or more occasions) on an application to vary or discharge the interim care order.

(8)   Where a power of arrest is attached to an exclusion requirement of an interim care order by virtue of subsection (5), a constable may arrest without warrant any person whom he has reasonable cause to believe to be in breach of the requirement.

(9)   Sections 47(7), (11) and (12) and 48 of, and Schedule 5 to, the Family Law Act 1996 shall have effect in relation to a person arrested under subsection (8) of this section as they have effect in relation to a person arrested under section 47(6) of that Act.

(10)   If, while an interim care order containing an exclusion requirement is in force, the local authority have removed the child from the dwelling-house from which the relevant person is excluded to other accommodation for a continuous period of more than 24 hours, the interim care order shall cease to have effect in so far as it imposes the exclusion requirement.

38B   Undertakings relating to interim care orders

(1)   In any case where the court has power to include an exclusion requirement in an interim care order, the court may accept an undertaking from the relevant person.

(2)   No power of arrest may be attached to any undertaking given under subsection (1).

(3)   An undertaking given to a court under subsection (1)—

    (a)   shall be enforceable as if it were an order of the court, and

    (b)   shall cease to have effect if, while it is in force, the local authority have removed the child from the dwelling-house from which the relevant person is excluded to other accommodation for a continuous period of more than 24 hours.

(4)   This section has effect without prejudice to the powers of the High Court and county court apart from this section.

(5)   In this section 'exclusion requirement' and 'relevant person' have the same meaning as in section 38A.

39   Discharge and variation etc of care orders and supervision orders

(1)   A care order may be discharged by the court on the application of—

    (a)   any person who has parental responsibility for the child;

    (b)   the child himself; or

(c)   the local authority designated by the order.

(2)   A supervision order may be varied or discharged by the court on the application of—

    (a)   any person who has parental responsibility for the child;

    (b)   the child himself; or

    (c)   the supervisor.

(3)   On the application of a person who is not entitled to apply for the order to be discharged, but who is a person with whom the child is living, a supervision order may be varied by the court in so far as it imposes a requirement which affects that person.

(3A)   On the application of a person who is not entitled to apply for the order to be discharged, but who is a person to whom an exclusion requirement contained in the order applies, an interim care order may be varied or discharged by the court in so far as it imposes the exclusion requirement.

(3B)   Where a power of arrest has been attached to an exclusion requirement of an interim care order, the court may, on the application of any person entitled to apply for the discharge of the order so far as it imposes the exclusion requirement, vary or discharge the order in so far as it confers a power of arrest (whether or not any application has been made to vary or discharge any other provision of the order).

(4)   Where a care order is in force with respect to a child the court may, on the application of any person entitled to apply for the order to be discharged, substitute a supervision order for the care order.

(5)   When a court is considering whether to substitute one order for another under subsection (4) any provision of this Act which would otherwise require section 31(2) to be satisfied at the time when the proposed order is substituted or made shall be disregarded.

44   Orders for emergency protection of children

(1)   Where any person ('the applicant') applies to the court for an order to be made under this section with respect to a child, the court may make the order if, but only if, it is satisfied that—

    (a)   there is reasonable cause to believe that the child is likely to suffer significant harm if—

        (i)   he is not removed to accommodation provided by or on behalf of the applicant; or

        (ii)   he does not remain in the place in which he is then being accommodated;

    (b)   in the case of an application made by a local authority—

        (i)   enquiries are being made with respect to the child under section 47(1)(b); and

        (ii)   those enquiries are being frustrated by access to the child being unreasonably refused to a person authorised to seek access and that the applicant has reasonable cause to believe that access to the child is required as a matter of urgency; or

    (c)   in the case of an application made by an authorised person—

        (i)   the applicant has reasonable cause to suspect that a child is suffering, or is likely to suffer, significant harm;

        (ii)   the applicant is making enquiries with respect to the child's welfare; and

        (iii) those enquiries are being frustrated by access to the child being unreasonably refused to a person authorised to seek access and the applicant has reasonable cause to believe that access to the child is required as a matter of urgency.

(2)   In this section—

    (a)   'authorised person' means a person who is an authorised person for the purposes of section 31; and

    (b)   'a person authorised to seek access' means—

> > > (i)   in the case of an application by a local authority, an officer of the local authority or a person authorised by the authority to act on their behalf in connection with the enquiries; or
> >
> > > (ii)   in the case of an application by an authorised person, that person.

(3)   Any person—

> (a)   seeking access to a child in connection with enquiries of a kind mentioned in subsection (1); and
>
> (b)   purporting to be a person authorised to do so,

shall, on being asked to do so, produce some duly authenticated document as evidence that he is such a person.

(4)   While an order under this section ('an emergency protection order') is in force it—

> (a)   operates as a direction to any person who is in a position to do so to comply with any request to produce the child to the applicant;
>
> (b)   authorises—
>
> > (i)   the removal of the child at any time to accommodation provided by or on behalf of the applicant and his being kept there; or
> >
> > (ii)   the prevention of the child's removal from any hospital, or other place, in which he was being accommodated immediately before the making of the order; and
>
> (c)   gives the applicant parental responsibility for the child.

(5)   Where an emergency protection order is in force with respect to a child, the applicant—

> (a)   shall only exercise the power given by virtue of subsection (4)(b) in order to safeguard the welfare of the child;
>
> (b)   shall take, and shall only take, such action in meeting his parental responsibility for the child as is reasonably required to safeguard or promote the welfare of the child (having regard in particular to the duration of the order); and
>
> (c)   shall comply with the requirements of any regulations made by the Secretary of State for the purposes of this subsection.

(6)   Where the court makes an emergency protection order, it may give such directions (if any) as it considers appropriate with respect to—

> (a)   the contact which is, or is not, to be allowed between the child and any named person;
>
> (b)   the medical or psychiatric examination or other assessment of the child.

(7)   Where any direction is given under subsection (6)(b), the child may, if he is of sufficient understanding to make an informed decision, refuse to submit to the examination or other assessment.

(8)   A direction under subsection (6)(a) may impose conditions and one under subsection (6)(b) may be to the effect that there is to be—

> (a)   no such examination or assessment; or
>
> (b)   no such examination or assessment unless the court directs otherwise.

(9)   A direction under subsection (6) may be—

> (a)   given when the emergency protection order is made or at any time while it is in force; and
>
> (b)   varied at any time on the application of any person falling within any class of person prescribed by rules of court for the purposes of this subsection.

(10)   Where an emergency protection order is in force with respect to a child and—

> (a)   the applicant has exercised the power given by subsection (4)(b)(i) but it appears to him that it is safe for the child to be returned; or
>
> (b)   the applicant has exercised the power given by subsection (4)(b)(ii) but it appears to him that it is safe for the child to be allowed to be removed from the place in question,

he shall return the child or (as the case may be) allow him to be removed.

(11)   Where he is required by subsection (10) to return the child the applicant shall—

    (a)   return him to the care of the person from whose care he was removed; or

    (b)   if that is not reasonably practicable, return him to the care of—

        (i)   a parent of his;

        (ii)   any person who is not a parent of his but who has parental responsibility for him; or

        (iii)   such other person as the applicant (with the agreement of the court) considers appropriate.

(12)   Where the applicant has been required by subsection (10) to return the child, or to allow him to be removed, he may again exercise his powers with respect to the child (at any time while the emergency protection order remains in force) if it appears to him that a change in the circumstances of the case makes it necessary for him to do so.

(13)   Where an emergency protection order has been made with respect to a child, the applicant shall, subject to any direction given under subsection (6), allow the child reasonable contact with—

    (a)   his parents;

    (b)   any person who is not a parent of his but who has parental responsibility for him;

    (c)   any person with whom he was living immediately before the making of the order;

    (d)   any person in whose favour a contact order is in force with respect to him;

    (e)   any person who is allowed to have contact with the child by virtue of an order under section 34; and

    (f)   any person acting on behalf of any of those persons.

(14)   Wherever it is reasonably practicable to do so, an emergency protection order shall name the child; and where it does not name him it shall describe him as clearly as possible.

(15)   A person shall be guilty of an offence if he intentionally obstructs any person exercising the power under subsection (4)(b) to remove, or prevent the removal of, a child.

(16)   A person guilty of an offence under subsection (15) shall be liable on summary conviction to a fine not exceeding level 3 on the standard scale.

46   Removal and accommodation of children by police in cases of emergency

(1)   Where a constable has reasonable cause to believe that a child would otherwise be likely to suffer significant harm, he may—

    (a)   remove the child to suitable accommodation and keep him there; or

    (b)   take such steps as are reasonable to ensure that the child's removal from any hospital, or other place, in which he is then being accommodated is prevented.

(2)   For the purposes of this Act, a child with respect to whom a constable has exercised his powers under this section is referred to as having been taken into police protection.

(3)   As soon as is reasonably practicable after taking a child into police protection, the constable concerned shall—

    (a)   inform the local authority within whose area the child was found of the steps that have been, and are proposed to be, taken with respect to the child under this section and the reasons for taking them;

    (b)   give details to the authority within whose area the child is ordinarily resident ('the appropriate authority') of the place at which the child is being accommodated;

    (c)   inform the child (if he appears capable of understanding)—

        (i)   of the steps that have been taken with respect to him under this section and of the reasons for taking them; and

        (ii)   of the further steps that may be taken with respect to him under this section;

    (d)   take such steps as are reasonably practicable to discover the wishes and feelings of the child;

    (e)   secure that the case is inquired into by an officer designated for the purposes of this section by the chief officer of the police area concerned; and

    (f)   where the child was taken into police protection by being removed to accommodation which is not provided—

        (i)   by or on behalf of a local authority; or

        (ii)   as a refuge, in compliance with the requirements of section 51,

    secure that he is moved to accommodation which is so provided.

(4)   As soon as is reasonably practicable after taking a child into police protection, the constable concerned shall take such steps as are reasonably practicable to inform—

    (a)   the child's parents;

    (b)   every person who is not a parent of his but who has parental responsibility for him; and

    (c)   any other person with whom the child was living immediately before being taken into police protection,

of the steps that he has taken under this section with respect to the child, the reasons for taking them and the further steps that may be taken with respect to him under this section.

(5)   On completing any inquiry under subsection (3)(e), the officer conducting it shall release the child from police protection unless he considers that there is still reasonable cause for believing that the child would be likely to suffer significant harm if released.

(6)   No child may be kept in police protection for more than 72 hours.

(7)   While a child is being kept in police protection, the designated officer may apply on behalf of the appropriate authority for an emergency protection order to be made under section 44 with respect to the child.

(8)   An application may be made under subsection (7) whether or not the authority know of it or agree to its being made.

(9)   While a child is being kept in police protection—

    (a)   neither the constable concerned nor the designated officer shall have parental responsibility for him; but

    (b)   the designated officer shall do what is reasonable in all the circumstances of the case for the purpose of safeguarding or promoting the child's welfare (having regard in particular to the length of the period during which the child will be so protected).

(10)   Where a child has been taken into police protection, the designated officer shall allow—

    (a)   the child's parents;

    (b)   any person who is not a parent of the child but who has parental responsibility for him;

    (c)   any person with whom the child was living immediately before he was taken into police protection;

    (d)   any person in whose favour a contact order is in force with respect to the child;

    (e)   any person who is allowed to have contact with the child by virtue of an order under section 34; and

    (f)   any person acting on behalf of any of those persons,

to have such contact (if any) with the child as, in the opinion of the designated officer, is both reasonable and in the child's best interests.

(11)   Where a child who has been taken into police protection is in accommodation provided by, or on behalf of, the appropriate authority, subsection (10) shall have effect as if it referred to the authority rather than to the designated officer.

47 Local authority's duty to investigate

(1)   Where a local authority—

    (a)   are informed that a child who lives, or is found, in their area—

        (i)   is the subject of an emergency protection order; or

        (ii)   is in police protection; or

        (iii)   has contravened a ban imposed by a curfew notice within the meaning of Chapter I of Part I of the Crime and Disorder Act 1998; or

    (b)   have reasonable cause to suspect that a child who lives, or is found, in their area is suffering, or is likely to suffer, significant harm,

the authority shall make, or cause to be made, such enquiries as they consider necessary to enable them to decide whether they should take any action to safeguard or promote the child's welfare.

In the case of a child falling within paragraph (a)(iii) above, the enquiries shall be commenced as soon as practicable and, in any event, within 48 hours of the authority receiving the information.

(2)   Where a local authority have obtained an emergency protection order with respect to a child, they shall make, or cause to be made, such enquiries as they consider necessary to enable them to decide what action they should take to safeguard or promote the child's welfare.

(3)   The enquiries shall, in particular, be directed towards establishing—

    (a)   whether the authority should make any application to the court, or exercise any of their other powers under this Act or section 11 of the Crime and Disorder Act 1998 (child safety orders), with respect to the child;

    (b)   whether, in the case of a child—

        (i)   with respect to whom an emergency protection order has been made; and

        (ii)   who is not in accommodation provided by or on behalf of the authority,

        it would be in the child's best interests (while an emergency protection order remains in force) for him to be in such accommodation; and

    (c)   whether, in the case of a child who has been taken into police protection, it would be in the child's best interests for the authority to ask for an application to be made under section 46(7).

(4)   Where enquiries are being made under subsection (1) with respect to a child, the local authority concerned shall (with a view to enabling them to determine what action, if any, to take with respect to him) take such steps as are reasonably practicable—

    (a)   to obtain access to him; or

    (b)   to ensure that access to him is obtained, on their behalf, by a person authorised by them for the purpose,

unless they are satisfied that they already have sufficient information with respect to him.

(5)   Where, as a result of any such enquiries, it appears to the authority that there are matters connected with the child's education which should be investigated, they shall consult the relevant local education authority.

(5A)   For the purposes of making a determination under this section as to the action to be taken with respect to a child, a local authority shall, so far as is reasonably practicable and consistent with the child's welfare—

    (a)   ascertain the child's wishes and feelings regarding the action to be taken with respect to him; and

    (b)   give due consideration (having regard to his age and understanding) to such wishes and feelings of the child as they have been able to ascertain.

(6)   Where, in the course of enquiries made under this section—

    (a)   any officer of the local authority concerned; or

    (b)   any person authorised by the authority to act on their behalf in connection with those enquiries—

> (i)   is refused access to the child concerned; or
>
> (ii)   is denied information as to his whereabouts,

the authority shall apply for an emergency protection order, a child assessment order, a care order or a supervision order with respect to the child unless they are satisfied that his welfare can be satisfactorily safeguarded without their doing so.

(7)   If, on the conclusion of any enquiries or review made under this section, the authority decide not to apply for an emergency protection order, a care order, a child assessment order or a supervision order they shall—

    (a)   consider whether it would be appropriate to review the case at a later date; and

    (b)   if they decide that it would be, determine the date on which that review is to begin.

(8)   Where, as a result of complying with this section, a local authority conclude that they should take action to safeguard or promote the child's welfare they shall take that action (so far as it is both within their power and reasonably practicable for them to do so).

(9)   Where a local authority are conducting enquiries under this section, it shall be the duty of any person mentioned in subsection (11) to assist them with those enquiries (in particular by providing relevant information and advice) if called upon by the authority to do so.

(10)   Subsection (9) does not oblige any person to assist a local authority where doing so would be unreasonable in all the circumstances of the case.

(11)   The persons are—

    (a)   any local authority;

    (b)   any local education authority;

    (c)   any local housing authority;

    (d)   any Local Health Board, Special Health Authority, Primary Care Trust, National Health Service trust or NHS Foundation trust; and

    (e)   any person authorised by the Secretary of State for the purposes of this section.

(12)   Where a local authority are making enquiries under this section with respect to a child who appears to them to be ordinarily resident within the area of another authority, they shall consult that other authority, who may undertake the necessary enquiries in their place.

SCHEDULE 2

LOCAL AUTHORITY SUPPORT FOR CHILDREN AND FAMILIES

Sections 17, 23, 29

PART I

PROVISION OF SERVICES FOR FAMILIES

Identification of children in need and provision of information

1.— (1)   Every local authority shall take reasonable steps to identify the extent to which there are children in need within their area.

    (2)   Every local authority shall—

      (a)   publish information—

        (i)   about services provided by them under sections 17, 18, 20, 23B to 23D, 24A and 24B; and

        (ii)   where they consider it appropriate, about the provision by others (including, in particular, voluntary organisations) of services which the authority have power to provide under those sections; and

      (b)   take such steps as are reasonably practicable to ensure that those who might benefit from the services receive the information relevant to them.

Children's services plans

1A.— (1)   Every local authority shall, on or before 31st March 1997—

      (a)   review their provision of services under sections 17, 20, 21, 23 and 24; and

      (b)   having regard to that review and to their most recent review under section 19, prepare and publish a plan for the provision of services under Part III.

(2)   Every local authority—

      (a)   shall, from time to time review the plan prepared by them under sub-paragraph (1)(b) (as modified or last substituted under this sub-paragraph), and

      (b)   may, having regard to that review and to their most recent review under section 19, prepare and publish—

          (i)   modifications (or, as the case may be, further modifications) to the plan reviewed; or

          (ii)   a plan in substitution for that plan.

(3)   In carrying out any review under this paragraph and in preparing any plan or modifications to a plan, a local authority shall consult—

      (a)   every Local Health Board, Health Authority or Primary Care Trust the whole or any part of whose area lies within the area of the local authority;

      (b)   every National Health Service trust which manages a hospital, establishment or facility (within the meaning of the National Health Service and Community Care Act 1990) in the authority's area;

      (ba)   every NHS foundation trust which manages a hospital (within the meaning of the Health and Social Care (Community Health and Standards) Act 2003) in the authority's area;

      (c)   if the local authority is not itself a local education authority, every local education authority the whole or any part of whose area lies within the area of the local authority;

      (d)   any organisation which represents schools in the authority's area which are grant-maintained schools or grant-maintained special schools (within the meaning of the Education Act 1993);

      (e)   the governing body of every such school in the authority's area which is not so represented;

      (f)   such voluntary organisations as appear to the local authority—

          (i)   to represent the interests of persons who use or are likely to use services provided by the local authority under Part III; or

          (ii)   to provide services in the area of the local authority which, were they to be provided by the local authority, might be categorised as services provided under that Part;

      (g)   the chief constable of the police force for the area;

      (h)   the probation committee for the area;

      (i)   such other persons as appear to the local authority to be appropriate; and

      (j)   such other persons as the Secretary of State may direct.

(4)   Every local authority shall, within 28 days of receiving a written request from the Secretary of State, submit to him a copy of—

      (a)   the plan prepared by them under sub-paragraph (1); or

      (b)   where that plan has been modified or substituted, the plan as modified or last substituted.

Maintenance of a register of disabled children

2.— (1)   Every local authority shall open and maintain a register of disabled children within their area.

     (2)   The register may be kept by means of a computer.

Assessment of children's needs

3.   Where it appears to a local authority that a child within their area is in need, the authority may assess his needs for the purposes of this Act at the same time as any assessment of his needs is made under—

(a)   the Chronically Sick and Disabled Persons Act 1970;

(b)   Part IV of the Education Act 1996;

(c)   the Disabled Persons (Services, Consultation and Representation) Act 1986; or

(d)   any other enactment.

Prevention of neglect and abuse

4.—   (1)   Every local authority shall take reasonable steps, through the provision of services under Part III of this Act, to prevent children within their area suffering ill-treatment or neglect.

(2)   Where a local authority believe that a child who is at any time within their area—

(a)   is likely to suffer harm; but

(b)   lives or proposes to live in the area of another local authority they shall inform that other local authority.

(3)   When informing that other local authority they shall specify—

(a)   the harm that they believe he is likely to suffer; and

(b)   (if they can) where the child lives or proposes to live.

Provision of accommodation in order to protect child

5.—   (1)   Where—

(a)   it appears to a local authority that a child who is living on particular premises is suffering, or is likely to suffer, ill treatment at the hands of another person who is living on those premises; and

(b)   that other person proposes to move from the premises,

the authority may assist that other person to obtain alternative accommodation.

(2)   Assistance given under this paragraph may be in cash.

(3)   Subsections (7) to (9) of section 17 shall apply in relation to assistance given under this paragraph as they apply in relation to assistance given under that section.

Provision for disabled children

6.   Every local authority shall provide services designed—

(a)   to minimise the effect on disabled children within their area of their disabilities; and

(b)   to give such children the opportunity to lead lives which are as normal as possible.

Provision to reduce need for care proceedings etc

7.   Every local authority shall take reasonable steps designed—

(a)   to reduce the need to bring—

(i)   proceedings for care or supervision orders with respect to children within their area;

(ii)   criminal proceedings against such children;

(iii)   any family or other proceedings with respect to such children which might lead to them being placed in the authority's care; or

(iv)   proceedings under the inherent jurisdiction of the High Court with respect to children;

(b)   to encourage children within their area not to commit criminal offences; and

(c)   to avoid the need for children within their area to be placed in secure accommodation.

Provision for children living with their families

8.   Every local authority shall make such provision as they consider appropriate for the following services to be available with respect to children in need within their area while they are living with their families—

(a)   advice, guidance and counselling;

(b)   occupational, social, cultural, or recreational activities;

(c)   home help (which may include laundry facilities);

(d)   facilities for, or assistance with, travelling to and from home for the purpose of taking advantage of any other service provided under this Act or of any similar service;

(e)   assistance to enable the child concerned and his family to have a holiday.

Family centres

9.—   (1)   Every local authority shall provide such family centres as they consider appropriate in relation to children within their area.

(2)   'Family centre' means a centre at which any of the persons mentioned in sub-paragraph (3) may—

(a)   attend for occupational, social, cultural or recreational activities;

(b)   attend for advice, guidance or counselling; or

(c)   be provided with accommodation while he is receiving advice, guidance or counselling.

(3)   The persons are—

(a)   a child;

(b)   his parents;

(c)   any person who is not a parent of his but who has parental responsibility for him;

(d)   any other person who is looking after him.

Maintenance of the family home

10.   Every local authority shall take such steps as are reasonably practicable, where any child within their area who is in need and whom they are not looking after is living apart from his family—

(a)   to enable him to live with his family; or

(b)   to promote contact between him and his family,

if, in their opinion, it is necessary to do so in order to safeguard or promote his welfare.

Duty to consider racial groups to which children in need belong

11.   Every local authority shall, in making any arrangements—

(a)   for the provision of day care within their area; or

(b)   designed to encourage persons to act as local authority foster parents, have regard to the different racial groups to which children within their area who are in need belong.

PART II
CHILDREN LOOKED AFTER BY LOCAL AUTHORITIES

Regulations as to placing of children with local authority foster parents

12.   Regulations under section 23(2)(a) may, in particular, make provision—

(a)   with regard to the welfare of children placed with local authority foster parents;

(b)   as to the arrangements to be made by local authorities in connection with the health and education of such children;

(c)   as to the records to be kept by local authorities;

(d)   for securing that a child is not placed with a local authority foster parent unless that person is for the time being approved as a local authority foster parent by such local authority as may be prescribed;

(e)   for securing that where possible the local authority foster parent with whom a child is to be placed is—

    (i)   of the same religious persuasion as the child; or

    (ii)   gives an undertaking that the child will be brought up in that religious persuasion;

(f)   for securing that children placed with local authority foster parents, and the premises in which they are accommodated, will be supervised and inspected by a local authority and that the children will be removed from those premises if their welfare appears to require it;

(g)   as to the circumstances in which local authorities may make arrangements for duties imposed on them by the regulations to be discharged, on their behalf.

Regulations as to arrangements under section 23(2)(f)

13.   Regulations under section 23(2)(f) may, in particular, make provisions as to—

(a)   the persons to be notified of any proposed arrangements;

(b)   the opportunities such persons are to have to make representations in relation to the arrangements proposed;

(c)   the persons to be notified of any proposed changes in arrangements;

(d)   the records to be kept by local authorities;

(e)   the supervision by local authorities of any arrangements made.

Regulations as to conditions under which child in care is allowed to live with parent, etc

14.   Regulations under section 23(5) may, in particular, impose requirements on a local authority as to—

(a)   the making of any decision by a local authority to allow a child to live with any person falling within section 23(4) (including requirements as to those who must be consulted before the decision is made, and those who must be notified when it has been made);

(b)   the supervision or medical examination of the child concerned;

(c)   the removal of the child, in such circumstances as may be prescribed, from the care of the person with whom he has been allowed to live;

(d)   the records to be kept by local authorities.

Promotion and maintenance of contact between child and family

15.— (1)   Where a child is being looked after by a local authority, the authority shall, unless it is not reasonably practicable or consistent with his welfare, endeavour to promote contact between the child and—

(a)   his parents;

(b)   any person who is not a parent of his but who has parental responsibility for him; and

(c)   any relative, friend or other person connected with him.

(2)   Where a child is being looked after by a local authority—

(a)   the authority shall take such steps as are reasonably practicable to secure that—

    (i)   his parents; and

    (ii)   any person who is not a parent of his but who has parental responsibility for him,

    are kept informed of where he is being accommodated; and

(b)   every such person shall secure that the authority are kept informed of his or her address.

(3)   Where a local authority ('the receiving authority') take over the provision of accommodation for a child from another local authority ('the transferring authority') under section 20(2)—

(a)   the receiving authority shall (where reasonably practicable) inform—

    (i)   the child's parents; and

    (ii)   any person who is not a parent of his but who has parental responsibility for him;

(b)   sub-paragraph (2)(a) shall apply to the transferring authority, as well as the receiving authority, until at least one such person has been informed of the change; and

(c)   sub-paragraph (2)(b) shall not require any person to inform the receiving authority of his address until he has been so informed.

(4)   Nothing in this paragraph requires a local authority to inform any person of the whereabouts of a child if—

(a)   the child is in the care of the authority; and

(b)   the authority has reasonable cause to believe that informing the person would prejudice the child's welfare.

(5)   Any person who fails (without reasonable excuse) to comply with sub-paragraph (2)(b) shall be guilty of an offence and liable on summary conviction to a fine not exceeding level 2 on the standard scale.

(6)   It shall be a defence in any proceedings under sub-paragraph (5) to prove that the defendant was residing at the same address as another person who was the child's parent or had parental responsibility for the child and had reasonable cause to believe that the other person had informed the appropriate authority that both of them were residing at that address.

Visits to or by children: expenses

16.— (1)   This paragraph applies where—

(a)   a child is being looked after by a local authority; and

(b)   the conditions mentioned in sub-paragraph (3) are satisfied.

(2)   The authority may—

(a)   make payments to—

    (i)   a parent of the child;

    (ii)   any person who is not a parent of his but who has parental responsibility for him; or

    (iii) any relative, friend or other person connected with him,

in respect of travelling, subsistence or other expenses incurred by that person in visiting the child; or

(b)   make payments to the child, or to any person on his behalf, in respect of travelling, subsistence or other expenses incurred by or on behalf of the child in his visiting—

    (i)   a parent of his;

    (ii)   any person who is not a parent of his but who has parental responsibility for him; or

    (iii) any relative, friend or other person connected with him.

(3)   The conditions are that—

(a)   it appears to the authority that the visit in question could not otherwise be made without undue financial hardship; and

(b)   the circumstances warrant the making of the payments.

Appointment of visitor for child who is not being visited

17.— (1)   Where it appears to a local authority in relation to any child that they are looking after that—

(a)   communication between the child and—

    (i)   a parent of his, or

    (ii)   any person who is not a parent of his but who has parental responsibility for him,

has been infrequent; or

(b)   he has not visited or been visited by (or lived with) any such person during the preceding twelve months,

and that it would be in the child's best interests for an independent person to be appointed to be his visitor for the purposes of this paragraph, they shall appoint such a visitor.

(2)   A person so appointed shall—

    (a)   have the duty of visiting, advising and befriending the child; and

    (b)   be entitled to recover from the authority who appointed him any reasonable expenses incurred by him for the purposes of his functions under this paragraph.

(3)   A person's appointment as a visitor in pursuance of this paragraph shall be determined if—

    (a)   he gives notice in writing to the authority who appointed him that he resigns the appointment; or

    (b)   the authority give him notice in writing that they have terminated it.

(4)   The determination of such an appointment shall not prejudice any duty under this paragraph to make a further appointment.

(5)   Where a local authority propose to appoint a visitor for a child under this paragraph, the appointment shall not be made if—

    (a)   the child objects to it; and

    (b)   the authority are satisfied that he has sufficient understanding to make an informed decision.

(6)   Where a visitor has been appointed for a child under this paragraph, the local authority shall determine the appointment if—

    (a)   the child objects to its continuing; and

    (b)   the authority are satisfied that he has sufficient understanding to make an informed decision.

(7)   The Secretary of State may make regulations as to the circumstances in which a person appointed as a visitor under this paragraph is to be regarded as independent of the local authority appointing him.

Power to guarantee apprenticeship deeds etc

18.— (1)   While a child is being looked after by a local authority, or is a person qualifying for advice and assistance, the authority may undertake any obligation by way of guarantee under any deed of apprenticeship or articles of clerkship which he enters into.

(2)   Where a local authority have undertaken any such obligation under any deed or articles they may at any time (whether or not they are still looking after the person concerned) undertake the like obligation under any supplemental deed or articles.

Arrangements to assist children to live abroad

19.— (1)   A local authority may only arrange for, or assist in arranging for, any child in their care to live outside England and Wales with the approval of the court.

(2)   A local authority may, with the approval of every person who has parental responsibility for the child arrange for, or assist in arranging for, any other child looked after by them to live outside England and Wales.

(3)   The court shall not give its approval under sub-paragraph (1) unless it is satisfied that—

    (a)   living outside England and Wales would be in the child's best interests;

    (b)   suitable arrangements have been, or will be, made for his reception and welfare in the country in which he will live;

    (c)   the child has consented to living in that country; and

    (d)   every person who has parental responsibility for the child has consented to his living in that country.

    (4)   Where the court is satisfied that the child does not have sufficient understanding to give or withhold his consent, it may disregard sub-paragraph (3)(c) and give its approval if the child is to live in the country concerned with a parent, guardian, special guardian, or other suitable person.

    (5)   Where a person whose consent is required by sub-paragraph (3)(d) fails to give his consent, the court may disregard that provision and give its approval if it is satisfied that that person—

        (a)   cannot be found;

        (b)   is incapable of consenting; or

        (c)   is withholding his consent unreasonably.

    (6)   Section 85 of the Adoption and Children Act 2002 (which imposes restrictions on taking children out of the United Kingdom) shall not apply in the case of any child who is to live outside England and Wales with the approval of the court given under this paragraph.

    (7)   Where a court decides to give its approval under this paragraph it may order that its decision is not to have effect during the appeal period.

    (8)   In sub-paragraph (7) 'the appeal period' means—

        (a)   where an appeal is made against the decision, the period between the making of the decision and the determination of the appeal; and

        (b)   otherwise, the period during which an appeal may be made against the decision.

    (9)   This paragraph does not apply to a local authority placing a child for adoption with prospective adopters.

Preparation for ceasing to be looked after

19A.   It is the duty of the local authority looking after a child to advise, assist and befriend him with a view to promoting his welfare when they have ceased to look after him.

19B.—(1)   A local authority shall have the following additional functions in relation to an eligible child whom they are looking after.

    (2)   In sub-paragraph (1) 'eligible child' means, subject to sub-paragraph (3), a child who—

        (a)   is aged sixteen or seventeen; and

        (b)   has been looked after by a local authority for a prescribed period, or periods amounting in all to a prescribed period, which began after he reached a prescribed age and ended after he reached the age of sixteen.

    (3)   The Secretary of State may prescribe—

        (a)   additional categories of eligible children; and

        (b)   categories of children who are not to be eligible children despite falling within sub-paragraph (2).

    (4)   For each eligible child, the local authority shall carry out an assessment of his needs with a view to determining what advice, assistance and support it would be appropriate for them to provide him under this Act—

        (a)   while they are still looking after him; and

        (b)   after they cease to look after him,

and shall then prepare a pathway plan for him.

    (5)   The local authority shall keep the pathway plan under regular review.

    (6)   Any such review may be carried out at the same time as a review of the child's case carried out by virtue of section 26.

    (7)   The Secretary of State may by regulations make provision as to assessments for the purposes of sub-paragraph (4).

    (8)   The regulations may in particular provide for the matters set out in section 23B(6).

Personal advisers

19C.   A local authority shall arrange for each child whom they are looking after who is an eligible child for the purposes of paragraph 19B to have a personal adviser.

Death of children being looked after by local authorities

20.— (1) If a child who is being looked after by a local authority dies, the authority—

    (a) shall notify the Secretary of State and (in the case of a local authority in England) Her Majesty's Chief Inspector of Education, Children's Services and Skills;

    (b) shall, so far as is reasonably practicable, notify the child's parents and every person who is not a parent of his but who has parental responsibility for him;

    (c) may, with the consent (so far as it is reasonably practicable to obtain it) of every person who has parental responsibility for the child, arrange for the child's body to be buried or cremated; and

    (d) may, if the conditions mentioned in sub-paragraph (2) are satisfied, make payments to any person who has parental responsibility for the child, or any relative, friend or other person connected with the child, in respect of travelling, subsistence or other expenses incurred by that person in attending the child's funeral.

  (2) The conditions are that—

    (a) it appears to the authority that the person concerned could not otherwise attend the child's funeral without undue financial hardship; and

    (b) that the circumstances warrant the making of the payments.

  (3) Sub-paragraph (1) does not authorise cremation where it does not accord with the practice of the child's religious persuasion.

  (4) Where a local authority have exercised their power under sub-paragraph (1)(c) with respect to a child who was under sixteen when he died, they may recover from any parent of the child any expenses incurred by them.

  (5) Any sums so recoverable shall, without prejudice to any other method of recovery, be recoverable summarily as a civil debt.

  (6) Nothing in this paragraph affects any enactment regulating or authorising the burial, cremation or anatomical examination of the body of a deceased person.

PART III

CONTRIBUTIONS TOWARDS MAINTENANCE OF CHILDREN LOOKED AFTER BY LOCAL AUTHORITIES

Liability to contribute

21.— (1) Where a local authority are looking after a child (other than in the cases mentioned in sub-paragraph (7)) they shall consider whether they should recover contributions towards the child's maintenance from any person liable to contribute ('a contributor').

  (2) An authority may only recover contributions from a contributor if they consider it reasonable to do so.

  (3) The persons liable to contribute are—

    (a) where the child is under sixteen, each of his parents;

    (b) where he has reached the age of sixteen, the child himself.

  (4) A parent is not liable to contribute during any period when he is in receipt of income support under Part VII of the Social Security Contributions and Benefits Act 1992, of any element of child tax credit other than the family element, of working tax credit or of an income-based jobseeker's allowance.

  (5) A person is not liable to contribute towards the maintenance of a child in the care of a local authority in respect of any period during which the child is allowed by the authority (under section 23(5)) to live with a parent of his.

  (6) A contributor is not obliged to make any contribution towards a child's maintenance except as agreed or determined in accordance with this Part of this Schedule.

  (7) The cases are where the child is looked after by a local authority under—

(a)   section 21;

(b)   an interim care order;

(c)   section 92 of the Powers of Criminal Courts (Sentencing) Act 2000.

Agreed contributions

22.— (1)   Contributions towards a child's maintenance may only be recovered if the local authority have served a notice ('a contribution notice') on the contributor specifying—

(a)   the weekly sum which they consider that he should contribute; and

(b)   arrangements for payment.

(2)   The contribution notice must be in writing and dated.

(3)   Arrangements for payment shall, in particular, include—

(a)   the date on which liability to contribute begins (which must not be earlier than the date of the notice);

(b)   the date on which liability under the notice will end (if the child has not before that date ceased to be looked after by the authority); and

(c)   the date on which the first payment is to be made.

(4)   The authority may specify in a contribution notice a weekly sum which is a standard contribution determined by them for all children looked after by them.

(5)   The authority may not specify in a contribution notice a weekly sum greater than that which they consider—

(a)   they would normally be prepared to pay if they had placed a similar child with local authority foster parents; and

(b)   it is reasonably practicable for the contributor to pay (having regard to his means).

(6)   An authority may at any time withdraw a contribution notice (without prejudice to their power to serve another).

(7)   Where the authority and the contributor agree—

(a)   the sum which the contributor is to contribute; and

(b)   arrangements for payment,

(whether as specified in the contribution notice or otherwise) and the contributor notifies the authority in writing that he so agrees, the authority may recover summarily as a civil debt any contribution which is overdue and unpaid.

(8)   A contributor may, by serving a notice in writing on the authority, withdraw his agreement in relation to any period of liability falling after the date of service of the notice.

(9)   Sub-paragraph (7) is without prejudice to any other method of recovery.

Contribution orders

23.— (1)   Where a contributor has been served with a contribution notice and has—

(a)   failed to reach any agreement with the local authority as mentioned in paragraph 22(7) within the period of one month beginning with the day on which the contribution notice was served; or

(b)   served a notice under paragraph 22(8) withdrawing his agreement,

the authority may apply to the court for an order under this paragraph.

(2)   On such an application the court may make an order ('a contribution order') requiring the contributor to contribute a weekly sum towards the child's maintenance in accordance with arrangements for payment specified by the court.

(3)   A contribution order—

(a)   shall not specify a weekly sum greater than that specified in the contribution notice; and

(b)   shall be made with due regard to the contributor's means.

(4)   A contribution order shall not—

(a)   take effect before the date specified in the contribution notice; or

(b)   have effect while the contributor is not liable to contribute (by virtue of paragraph 21); or

(c)   remain in force after the child has ceased to be looked after by the authority who obtained the order.

(5)   An authority may not apply to the court under sub-paragraph (1) in relation to a contribution notice which they have withdrawn.

(6)   Where—

(a)   a contribution order is in force;

(b)   the authority serve another contribution notice; and

(c)   the contributor and the authority reach an agreement under paragraph 22(7) in respect of that other contribution notice,

the effect of the agreement shall be to discharge the order from the date on which it is agreed that the agreement shall take effect.

(7)   Where an agreement is reached under sub-paragraph (6) the authority shall notify the court—

(a)   of the agreement; and

(b)   of the date on which it took effect.

(8)   A contribution order may be varied or revoked on the application of the contributor or the authority.

(9)   In proceedings for the variation of a contribution order, the authority shall specify—

(a)   the weekly sum which, having regard to paragraph 22, they propose that the contributor should contribute under the order as varied; and

(b)   the proposed arrangements for payment.

(10)   Where a contribution order is varied, the order—

(a)   shall not specify a weekly sum greater than that specified by the authority in the proceedings for variation; and

(b)   shall be made with due regard to the contributor's means.

(11)   An appeal shall lie in accordance with rules of court from any order made under this paragraph.

Enforcement of contribution orders etc

24.— (1)   A contribution order made by a magistrates' court shall be enforceable as a magistrates' court maintenance order (within the meaning of section 150(1) of the Magistrates' Courts Act 1980).

(2)   Where a contributor has agreed, or has been ordered, to make contributions to a local authority, any other local authority within whose area the contributor is for the time being living may—

(a)   at the request of the local authority who served the contributions notice; and

(b)   subject to agreement as to any sum to be deducted in respect of services rendered,

collect from the contributor any contributions due on behalf of the authority who served the notice.

(3)   In sub-paragraph (2) the reference to any other local authority includes a reference to—

(a)   a local authority within the meaning of section 1(2) of the Social Work (Scotland) Act 1968; and

(b)   a Health and Social Services Board established under Article 16 of the Health and Personal Social Services (Northern Ireland) Order 1972.

(4)   The power to collect sums under sub-paragraph (2) includes the power to—

(a)   receive and give a discharge for any contributions due; and

(b)   (if necessary) enforce payment of any contributions,

even though those contributions may have fallen due at a time when the contributor was living elsewhere.

(5)   Any contribution collected under sub-paragraph (2) shall be paid (subject to any agreed deduction) to the local authority who served the contribution notice.

(6)   In any proceedings under this paragraph, a document which purports to be—

(a)   a copy of an order made by a court under or by virtue of paragraph 23; and

(b)   certified as a true copy by the designated officer for the court,

shall be evidence of the order.

(7)   In any proceedings under this paragraph, a certificate which—

(a)   purports to be signed by the clerk or some other duly authorised officer of the local authority who obtained the contribution order; and

(b)   states that any sum due to the authority under the order is overdue and unpaid,

shall be evidence that the sum is overdue and unpaid.

Regulations

25.   The Secretary of State may make regulations—

(a)   as to the considerations which a local authority must take into account in deciding—

(i)   whether it is reasonable to recover contributions; and

(ii)   what the arrangements for payment should be;

(b)   as to the procedures they must follow in reaching agreements with—

(i)   contributors (under paragraphs 22 and 23); and

(ii)   any other local authority (under paragraph 23).

(F)　Child Support Act 1991

1　The duty to maintain

(1)　For the purposes of this Act, each parent of a qualifying child is responsible for maintaining him.

(2)　For the purposes of this Act, a non-resident parent shall be taken to have met his responsibility to maintain any qualifying child of his by making periodical payments of maintenance with respect to the child of such amount, and at such intervals, as may be determined in accordance with the provisions of this Act.

(3)　Where a maintenance calculation made under this Act requires the making of periodical payments, it shall be the duty of the non-resident parent with respect to whom the calculation was made to make those payments.

2　Welfare of children: the general principle

Where, in any case which falls to be dealt with under this Act, the Secretary of State ... is considering the exercise of any discretionary power conferred by this Act, he shall have regard to the welfare of any child likely to be affected by his decision.

3　Meaning of certain terms used in this Act

(1)　A child is a 'qualifying child' if—

    (a)　one of his parents is, in relation to him, a non-resident parent; or

    (b)　both of his parents are, in relation to him, non-resident parents.

(2)　The parent of any child is a 'non-resident parent', in relation to him, if—

    (a)　that parent is not living in the same household with the child; and

    (b)　the child has his home with a person who is, in relation to him, a person with care.

(3)　A person is a 'person with care', in relation to any child, if he is a person—

    (a)　with whom the child has his home;

    (b)　who usually provides a day to day care for the child (whether exclusively or in conjunction with any other person); and

    (c)　who does not fall within a prescribed category of person.

(4)　The Secretary of State shall not, under subsection (3)(c), prescribe as a category—

    (a)　parents;

    (b)　guardians;

    (c)　persons in whose favour residence orders under section 8 of the Children Act 1989 are in force;

    (d)　(not reproduced)

(5)　For the purposes of this Act there may be more than one person with care in relation to the same qualifying child.

(6)　Periodical payments which are required to be paid in accordance with a maintenance calculation are referred to in this Act as 'child support maintenance'.

(7)　Expressions are defined in this section only for the purposes of this Act.

4　Child support maintenance

(1)　A person who is, in relation to any qualifying child or any qualifying children, either the person with care or the non-resident parent may apply to the Secretary of State for a maintenance calculation to be made under this Act with respect to that child, or any of those children.

(2)　Where a maintenance calculation has been made in response to an application under this section the Secretary of State may, if the person with care or non-resident parent with respect to whom the calculation was made applies to him under this subsection, arrange for—

    (a)　the collection of the child support maintenance payable in accordance with the calculation;

(b)   the enforcement of the obligation to pay child support maintenance in accordance with the calculation.

(3)   Where an application under subsection (2) for the enforcement of the obligation mentioned in subsection (2)(a) authorises the Secretary of State to take steps to enforce that obligation whenever he considers it necessary to do so, the Secretary of State may act accordingly.

(4)   A person who applies to the Secretary of State under this section shall, so far as that person reasonably can, comply with such regulations as may be made by the Secretary of State with a view to the Secretary of State ... being provided with the information which is required to enable—

(a)   the non-resident parent to be identified or traced (where that is necessary);

(b)   the amount of child support maintenance payable by the non-resident parent to be calculated; and

(c)   that amount to be recovered from the non-resident parent.

(5)   Any person who has applied to the Secretary of State under this section may at any time request him to cease acting under this section.

(6)   It shall be the duty of the Secretary of State to comply with any request made under subsection (5) (but subject to any regulations made under subsection (8)).

(7)   The obligation to provide information which is imposed by subsection (4)—

(a)   shall not apply in such circumstances as may be prescribed; and

(b)   may, in such circumstances as may be prescribed, be waived by the Secretary of State.

(8)   The Secretary of State may by regulations make such incidental, supplemental or transitional provision as he thinks appropriate with respect to cases in which he is requested to cease to act under this under this section.

(9)   No application may be made under this section if there is in force with respect to the person with care and non-resident parent in question a maintenance calculation made in response to an application treated as made under section 6.

(10) No application may be made at any time under this section with respect to a qualifying child or any qualifying children if—

(a)   there is in force a written maintenance agreement made before 5 April 1993, or a maintenance order made before a prescribed date, in respect of that child or those children and the person who is, at that time, the non-resident parent; or

(aa) a maintenance order made on or after the date prescribed for the purposes of paragraph (a) is in force in respect of them, but has been so for less than the period of one year beginning with the date on which it was made; or

(b)   benefit is being paid to, or in respect of, a parent with care of that child or those children.

(11) In subsection (10) 'benefit' means any benefit which is mentioned in, or prescribed by regulations under, section 6(1).

5   Child support maintenance: supplemental provisions

(1)   Where—

(a)   there is more than one person with care of a qualifying child; and

(b)   one or more, but not all, of them have parental responsibility for ... the child;

no application may be made for a maintenance calculation with respect to the child by any of those persons who do not have parental responsibility for ... the child.

(2)   Where more than one application for a maintenance calculation is made with respect to the child concerned, only one of them may be proceeded with.

(3)   The Secretary of State may by regulation make provision as to which of two or more applications for a maintenance calculation with respect to the same child is to be proceeded with.

6 Applications by those claiming or receiving benefit

(1) This section applies where income support, an income-based jobseeker's allowance or any other benefit of a prescribed kind is claimed by or in respect of, or paid to or in respect of, the parent of a qualifying child who is also a person with care of the child.

(2) In this section, that person is referred to as 'the parent'.

(3) The Secretary of State may—

    (a) treat the parent as having applied for a maintenance calculation with respect to the qualifying child and all other children of the non-resident parent in relation to whom the parent is also a person with care; and

    (b) take action under this Act to recover from the non-resident parent, on the parent's behalf, the child support maintenance so determined.

(4) Before doing what is mentioned in subsection (3), the Secretary of State must notify the parent in writing of the effect of subsections (3) and (5) and section 46.

(5) The Secretary of State may not act under subsection (3) if the parent asks him not to (a request which need not be in writing).

(6) Subsection (1) has effect regardless of whether any of the benefits mentioned there is payable with respect to any qualifying child.

(7) Unless she has made a request under subsection (5), the parent shall, so far as she reasonably can, comply with such regulations as may be made by the Secretary of State with a view to the Secretary of State's being provided with the information which is required to enable—

    (a) the non-resident parent to be identified or traced;

    (b) the amount of child support maintenance payable by him to be calculated; and

    (c) that amount to be recovered from him.

(8) The obligation to provide information which is imposed by subsection (7)—

    (a) does not apply in such circumstances as may be prescribed; and

    (b) may, in such circumstances as may be prescribed, be waived by the Secretary of State.

(9) If the parent ceases to fall within subsection (1), she may ask the Secretary of State to cease acting under this section, but until then he may continue to do so.

(10) The Secretary of State must comply with any request under subsection (9) (but subject to any regulations made under subsection (11)).

(11) The Secretary of State may by regulations make such incidental or transitional provision as he thinks appropriate with respect to cases in which he is asked under subsection (9) to cease to act under this section.

(12) The fact that a maintenance calculation is in force with respect to a person with care does not prevent the making of a new maintenance calculation with respect to her as a result of the Secretary of State's acting under subsection (3).

8 Role of the courts with respect to maintenance for children

(1) This subsection applies in any case where the Secretary of State would have jurisdiction to make a maintenance calculation with respect to a qualifying child and a non-resident parent of his on an application duly made (or treated as made) by a person entitled to apply for such a calculation with respect to that child.

(2) Subsection (1) applies even though the circumstances of the case are such that the Secretary of State would not make a calculation if it were applied for.

(3) Except as provided in subsection (3A), in any case where subsection (1) applies, no court shall exercise any power which it would otherwise have to make, vary or revive any maintenance order in relation to the child and non-resident parent concerned.

(3A) Unless a maintenance calculation has been made with respect to the child concerned, subsection (3) does not prevent a court from varying a maintenance order in relation to that child and the non-resident parent concerned—

    (a) if the maintenance order was made on or after the date prescribed for the purposes of section 4(10)(a) or 7(10)(a); or

(b)   where the order was made before then, in any case in which section 4(10) or 7(10) prevents the making of an application for a maintenance calculation with respect to or by that child.

(4)   Subsection (3) does not prevent a court from revoking a maintenance order.

(5)   The Lord Chancellor . . . may by order provide that, in such circumstances as may be specified by the order, this section shall not prevent a court from exercising any power which it has to make a maintenance order in relation to a child if—

(a)   a written agreement (whether or not enforceable) provides for the making, or securing, by a non-resident parent of the child of periodical payments to or for the benefit of the child; and

(b)   the maintenance order which the court makes is, in all material respects, in the same terms as that agreement.

(5A)   The Lord Chancellor may make an order under subsection (5) only with the concurrence of the Lord Chief Justice.

(6)   This section shall not prevent a court from exercising any power which it has to make a maintenance order in relation to a child if—

(a)   a maintenance calculation is in force with respect to the child;

(b)   the non-resident parent's net weekly income exceeds the figure referred to in paragraph 10(3) of Schedule 1 (as it has effect from time to time pursuant to regulations made under paragraph 10A(1)(b)); and

(c)   the court is satisfied that the circumstances of the case make it appropriate for the non-resident parent to make or secure the making of periodical payments under a maintenance order in addition to the child support maintenance payable by him in accordance with the maintenance calculation.

(7)   This section shall not prevent a court from exercising any power which it has to make a maintenance order in relation to a child if—

(a)   the child is, will be or (if the order were to be made) would be receiving instruction at an educational establishment or undergoing training for a trade, profession or vocation (whether or not while in gainful employment); and

(b)   the order is made solely for the purposes of requiring the person making or securing the making of periodical payments fixed by the order to meet some or all of the expenses incurred in connection with the provision of the instruction or training.

(8)   This section shall not prevent a court from exercising any power which it has to make a maintenance order in relation to a child if—

(a)   a disability living allowance is paid to or in respect of him; or

(b)   no such allowance is paid but he is disabled,

and the order is made solely for the purpose of requiring the person making or securing the making of periodical payments fixed by the order to meet some or all of any expenses attributable to the child's disability.

(9)   For the purposes of subsection (8), a child is disabled if he is blind, deaf or dumb or is substantially and permanently handicapped by illness, injury, mental disorder or congenital deformity or such other disability as may be prescribed.

(10)   This section shall not prevent a court from exercising any power which it has to make a maintenance order in relation to a child if the order is made against a person with care of the child.

(11)   In this Act 'maintenance order', in relation to any child, means an order which requires the making or securing of periodical payments to or for the benefit of the child and which is made under—

(a)   Part II of the Matrimonial Causes Act 1973;

(b)   the Domestic Proceedings and Magistrates' Courts Act 1978;

(c)   Part III of the Matrimonial and Family Proceedings Act 1984;

. . .

(e)   Schedule 1 to the Children Act 1989; ...

(ea)   Schedule 5, 6 or 7 of the Civil Partnership Act 2004; or

(f)   any other prescribed enactment,

and includes any order varying or reviving such an order.

(12)   The Lord Chief Justice may nominate a judicial office holder (as defined in section 109(4) of the Constitutional Reform Act 2005) to exercise his functions under this section.

9   Agreements about maintenance

(1)   In this section 'maintenance agreement' means any agreement for the making, or for securing the making, of periodical payments by way of maintenance, or in Scotland aliment, to or for the benefit of any child.

(2)   Nothing in this Act shall be taken to prevent any person from entering into a maintenance agreement.

(3)   Subject to section 4(10)(a) and section 7(10), the existence of a maintenance agreement shall not prevent any party to the agreement, or any other person, from applying for a maintenance calculation with respect to any child to or for whose benefit periodical payments are to be made or secured under the agreement.

(4)   Where any agreement contains a provision which purports to restrict the right of any person to apply for a maintenance calculation, that provision shall be void.

(5)   Where section 8 would prevent any court from making a maintenance order in relation to a child and a non-resident parent of his, no court shall exercise any power that it has to vary any agreement so as—

(a)   to insert a provision requiring that non-resident parent to make or secure the making of periodical payments by way of maintenance, or in Scotland aliment, to or for the benefit of that child; or

(b)   to increase the amount payable under such a provision.

(6)   In any case in which section 4(10) or 7(10) prevents the making of an application for a maintenance calculation, and—

(a)   no parent has been treated under section 6(3) as having applied for a maintenance calculation with respect to the child; or

(b)   a parent has been so treated but no maintenance calculation has been made,

subsection (5) shall have effect with the omission of paragraph (b).

10   Relationship between maintenance calculations and certain court orders and related matters

(1)   Where an order of a kind prescribed for the purposes of this subsection is in force with respect to any qualifying child with respect to whom a maintenance calculation is made, the order—

(a)   shall, so far as it relates to the making or securing of periodical payments, cease to have effect to such extent as may be determined in accordance with regulations made by the Secretary of State; or

(b)   where the regulations so provide, shall, so far as it so relates, have effect subject to such modifications as may be so determined.

(2)   Where an agreement of a kind prescribed for the purposes of this subsection is in force with respect to any qualifying child with respect to whom a maintenance calculation is made, the agreement—

(a)   shall, so far as it relates to the making or securing of periodical payments, be unenforceable to such extent as may be determined in accordance with regulations made by the Secretary of State; or

(b)   where the regulations so provide, shall, so far as it so relates, have effect subject to such modifications as may be so determined.

(3)   Any regulations under this section may, in particular, make such provision with respect to—

(a)   any case where any person with respect to whom an order or agreement of a kind prescribed for the purposes of subsection (1) or (2) has effect applies to the prescribed court, before the end of the prescribed period, for the order or agreement to be varied in the light of the maintenance calculation and of the provisions of this Act;

(b)   the recovery of any arrears under the order or agreement which fell due before the coming into force of the maintenance calculation,

as the Secretary of State considers appropriate and may provide that, in prescribed circumstances, an application to any court which is made with respect to an order of a prescribed kind relating to the making or securing of periodical payments to or for the benefit of a child shall be treated by the court as an application for the order to be revoked.

(4)   The Secretary of State may by regulations make provision for—

(a)   notification to be given by the Secretary of State concerned to the prescribed person in any case where he considers that the making of a maintenance calculation has affected, or is likely to affect, any order of a kind prescribed for the purposes of this subsection;

(b)   notification to be given by the prescribed person to the Secretary of State in any case where a court makes an order which it considers has affected, or is likely to affect, a maintenance calculation.

(5)   Rules may be made under section 144 of the Magistrates' Courts Act 1980 (rules of procedure) requiring any person who, in prescribed circumstances, makes an application to a magistrates' court for a maintenance order to furnish the court with a statement in a prescribed form, and signed by an officer of the Secretary of State, as to whether or not, at the time when the statement is made, there is a maintenance calculation in force with respect to that person or the child concerned.

In this subsection—

'maintenance order' means an order of a prescribed kind for the making or securing of periodical payments to or for the benefit of a child; and

'prescribed' means prescribed by the rules.

11   Maintenance calculations

(1)   An application for a maintenance calculation made to the Secretary of State shall be dealt with by him in accordance with the provision made by or under this Act.

(2)   The Secretary of State shall (unless he decides not to make a maintenance calculation in response to the application, or makes a decision under section 12) determine the application by making a decision under this section about whether any child support maintenance is payable and, if so, how much.

(3)   Where—

(a)   a parent is treated under section 6(3) as having applied for a maintenance calculation; but

(b)   the Secretary of State becomes aware before determining the application that the parent has ceased to fall within section 6(1),

he shall, subject to subsection (4), cease to treat that parent as having applied for a maintenance calculation.

(4)   If it appears to the Secretary of State that subsection (10) of section 4 would not have prevented the parent with care concerned from making an application for a maintenance calculation under that section he shall—

(a)   notify her of the effect of this subsection; and

(b)   if, before the end of the period of one month beginning with the day on which notice was sent to her, she asks him to do so, treat her as having applied not under section 6 but under section 4.

(5)   Where subsection (3) applies but subsection (4) does not, the Secretary of State shall notify—

(a)   the parent with care concerned; and

(b)   the non-resident parent (or alleged non-resident parent), where it appears to him that that person is aware that the parent with care has been treated as having applied for a maintenance calculation.

(6)   The amount of child support maintenance to be fixed by a maintenance calculation shall be determined in accordance with Part I of Schedule 1 unless an application for a variation has been made and agreed.

(7)   If the Secretary of State has agreed to a variation, the amount of child support maintenance to be fixed shall be determined on the basis he determines under section 28F(4).

(8)   Part II of Schedule 1 makes further provision with respect to maintenance calculations.

44   Jurisdiction

(1)   The Secretary of State shall have jurisdiction to make a maintenance calculation with respect to a person who is—

    (a)   a person with care;

    (b)   a non-resident parent; or

    (c)   a qualifying child,

only if that person is habitually resident in the United Kingdom, except in the case of a non-resident parent who falls within subsection (2A).

(2)   Where the person with care is not an individual, subsection (1) shall have effect as if paragraph (a) were omitted.

(2A)   A non-resident parent falls within this subsection if he is not habitually resident in the United Kingdom, but is—

    (a)   employed in the civil service of the Crown, including Her Majesty's Diplomatic Service and Her Majesty's Overseas Civil Service;

    (b)   a member of the naval, military or air forces of the Crown, including any person employed by an ssociation established for the purposes of Part XI of the Reserves Forces Act 1996;

    (c)   employed by a company of a prescribed description registered under the Companies Act 1985 in England and Wales or in Scotland, or under the Companies (Northern Ireland) Order 1986; or

    (d)   employed by a body of a prescribed description.

(3)   (not reproduced)

Schedule 1
Maintenance Calculations

Part I
Calculation of Weekly Amount of Child Support Maintenance

1   General rule

(1)   The weekly rate of child support maintenance is the basic rate unless a reduced rate, a flat rate or the nil rate applies.

(2)   Unless the nil rate applies, the amount payable weekly to a person with care is—

    (a)   the applicable rate, if paragraph 6 does not apply; or

    (b)   if paragraph 6 does apply, that rate as apportioned between the persons with care in accordance with paragraph 6,

as adjusted, in either case, by applying the rules about shared care in paragraph 7 or 8.

2   Basic rate

(1)   The basic rate is the following percentage of the non-resident parent's net weekly income—

15% where he has one qualifying child;

20% where he has two qualifying children;

25% where he has three or more qualifying children.

(2)   If the non-resident parent also has one or more relevant other children, the appropriate percentage referred to in sub-paragraph (1) is to be applied instead to his net weekly income less—

15% where he has one relevant other child;

20% where he has two relevant other children;

25% where he has three or more relevant other children.

3   Reduced rate

(1)   A reduced rate is payable if—

    (a)   neither a flat rate nor the nil rate applies; and

    (b)   the non-resident parent's net weekly income is less than £200 but more than £100.

(2)   The reduced rate payable shall be prescribed in, or determined in accordance with, regulations.

(3)   The regulations may not prescribe, or result in, a rate of less than £5.

4   Flat rate

(1)   Except in a case falling within sub-paragraph (2), a flat rate of £5 is payable if the nil rate does not apply and—

    (a)   the non-resident parent's net weekly income is £100 or less; or

    (b)   he receives any benefit, pension or allowance prescribed for the purposes of this paragraph of this sub-paragraph; or

    (c)   he or his partner (if any) receives any benefit prescribed for the purposes of this paragraph of this sub-paragraph.

(2)   A flat rate of a prescribed amount is payable if the nil rate does not apply and—

    (a)   the non-resident parent has a partner who is also a non-resident parent;

    (b)   the partner is a person with respect to whom a maintenance calculation is in force; and

    (c)   the non-resident parent or his partner receives any benefit prescribed under sub-paragraph (1)(c).

(3)   The benefits, pensions and allowances which may be prescribed for the purposes of sub-paragraph (1)(b) include ones paid to the non-resident parent under the law of a place outside the United Kingdom.

5   Nil rate

The rate payable is nil if the non-resident parent—

    (a)   is of a prescribed description; or

    (b)   has a net weekly income of below £5.

6   Apportionment

(1)   If the non-resident parent has more than one qualifying child and in relation to them there is more than one person with care, the amount of child support maintenance payable is (subject to paragraph 7 or 8) to be determined by apportioning the rate between the persons with care.

(2)   The rate of maintenance liability is to be divided by the number of qualifying children, and shared among the persons with care according to the number of qualifying children in relation to whom each is a person with care.

7   Shared care—basic and reduced rate

(1)   This paragraph applies only if the rate of child support maintenance payable is the basic rate or a reduced rate.

(2)   If the care of a qualifying child is shared between the non-resident parent and the person with care, so that the non-resident parent from time to time has care of the child overnight, the amount of child support maintenance which he would otherwise have been liable to pay the person with care, as calculated in accordance with the preceding paragraphs of this Part of this Schedule, is to be decreased in accordance with this paragraph.

(3) First, there is to be a decrease according to the number of such nights which the Secretary of State determines there to have been, or expects there to be, or both during a prescribed twelve-month period.

(4) The amount of that decrease for one child is set out in the following Table—

Number of nights	Fraction to subtract
52 to 103	One-seventh
104 to 155	Two-sevenths
156 to 174	Three-sevenths
175 or more	One-half

(5) If the person with care is caring for more than one qualifying child of the non-resident parent, the applicable decrease is the sum of the appropriate fractions in the Table divided by the number of such qualifying children.

(6) If the applicable fraction is one-half in relation to any qualifying child in the care of the person with care, the total amount payable to the person with care is then to be further decreased by £7 for each such child.

(7) If the application of the preceding provisions of this paragraph would decrease the weekly amount of child support maintenance (or the aggregate of all such amounts) payable by the non-resident parent to the person with care (or all of them) to less than £5, he is instead liable to pay child support maintenance at the rate of £5 a week, apportioned (if appropriate) in accordance with paragraph 6.

8   Shared care—flat rate

(1) This paragraph applies only if—

    (a) the rate of child support maintenance payable is a flat rate; and

    (b) that rate applies because the non-resident parent falls within paragraph 4(1)(b) or (c) or 4(2).

(2) If the care of a qualifying child is shared as mentioned in paragraph 7(2) for at least 52 nights during a prescribed 12-month period, the amount of child support maintenance payable by the non-resident parent to the person with care of that child is nil.

9   Regulations about shared care

The Secretary of State may by regulations provide—

(a) for which nights are to count for the purposes of shared care under paragraphs 7 and 8, or for how it is to be determined whether a night counts;

(b) for what counts, or does not count, as 'care' for those purposes; and

(c) for paragraph 7(3) or 8(2) to have effect, in prescribed circumstances, as if the period mentioned there were other than 12 months, and in such circumstances for the Table in paragraph 7(4) (or that Table as modified pursuant to regulations made under paragraph 10A(2)(a)), or the period mentioned in paragraph 8(2), to have effect with prescribed adjustments.

10   Net weekly income

(1) For the purposes of this Schedule, net weekly income is to be determined in such manner as is provided for in regulations.

(2) The regulations may, in particular, provide for the Secretary of State to estimate any income or make an assumption as to any fact where, in his view, the information at his disposal is unreliable, insufficient, or relates to an atypical period in the life of the non-resident parent.

(3) Any amount of net weekly income (calculated as above) over £2,000 is to be ignored for the purposes of this Schedule.

10A   Regulations about rates, figures, etc

(1)   The Secretary of State may by regulations provide that—

    (a)   paragraph 2 is to have effect as if different percentages were substituted for those set out there;

    (b)   paragraph 3(1) or (3), 4(1), 5, 7(7) or 10(3) is to have effect as if different amounts were substituted for those set out there.

(2)   The Secretary of State may by regulations provide that—

    (a)   the Table in paragraph 7(4) is to have effect as if different numbers of nights were set out in the first column and different fractions were substituted for those set out in the second column;

    (b)   paragraph 7(6) is to have effect as if a different amount were substituted for that mentioned there, or as if the amount were an aggregate amount and not an amount for each qualifying child, or both.

10B   Regulations about income

The Secretary of State may by regulations provide that, in such circumstances and to such extent as may be prescribed—

(a)   where the Secretary of State is satisfied that a person has intentionally deprived himself of a source of income with a view to reducing the amount of his net weekly income, his net weekly income shall be taken to include income from that source of an amount estimated by the Secretary of State;

(b)   a person is to be treated as possessing income which he does not possess;

(c)   income which a person does possess is to be disregarded.

10C   References to various terms

(1)   References in this Part of this Schedule to 'qualifying children' are to those qualifying children with respect to whom the maintenance calculation falls to be made.

(2)   References in this Part of this Schedule to 'relevant other children' are to—

    (a)   children other than qualifying children in respect of whom the non-resident parent or his partner receives child benefit under Part IX of the Social Security Contributions and Benefits Act 1992; and

    (b)   such other description of children as may be prescribed.

(3)   In this Part of this Schedule, a person 'receives' a benefit, pension, or allowance for any week if it is paid or due to be paid to him in respect of that week.

(4)   In this Part of this Schedule, a person's 'partner' is—

    (a)   if they are a couple, the other member of that couple;

    (b)   if the person is a husband or wife by virtue of a marriage entered into under a law which permits polygamy, another party to the marriage who is of the opposite sex and is a member of the same household.

(5)   In sub-paragraph (4)(a), 'couple' means—

    (a)   a man and a woman who are married to each other and are members of the same household,

    (b)   a man and a woman who are not married to each other but are living together as husband and wife,

    (c)   two people of the same sex who are civil partners of each other and are members of the same household, or

    (d)   two people of the same sex who are not civil partners of each other but are living together as if they were civil partners.

(6)   For the purposes of this paragraph, two people of the same sex are to be regarded as living together as if they were civil partners if, but only if, they would be regarded as living together as husband and wife were they instead two people of the opposite sex.

Part II
General Provisions about Maintenance Calculations

11 Effective date of calculation

(1)   A maintenance calculation shall take effect on such date as may be determined in accordance with regulations made by the Secretary of State.

(2)   That date may be earlier than the date on which the calculation is made.

12 Form of calculation

Every maintenance calculation shall be made in such form and contain such information as the Secretary of State may direct.

13 (not reproduced)

14 Consolidated applications and calculations

(1)   The Secretary of State may by regulations provide—

    (a)   for two or more applications for maintenance calculations to be treated, in prescribed circumstances, as a single application; and

    (b)   for the replacement, in prescribed circumstances, of a maintenance calculation made on the application of one person by a later maintenance calculation made on the application of that or any other person.

(2)   In sub-paragraph (1), the references (however expressed) to applications for maintenance calculations include references to applications treated as made.

15 Separate calculations for different periods

Where the Secretary of State is satisfied that the circumstances of a case require different amounts of child support maintenance to be calculated in respect of different periods, he may make separate maintenance calculations each expressed to have effect in relation to a different specified period.

16 Termination of calculations

(1)   A maintenance calculation shall cease to have effect—

    (a)   on the death of the non-resident parent, or of the person with care, with respect to whom it was made;

    (b)   on there no longer being any qualifying child with respect to whom it would have effect;

    (c)   on the non-resident parent with respect to whom it was made ceasing to be a parent of—

        (i)   the qualifying child with respect to whom it was made; or

        (ii)   where it was made with respect to more than one qualifying child, all of the qualifying children with respect to whom it was made;

    (d), (e) (not reproduced)

(2)–(9) (not reproduced)

(10)   A person with care with respect to whom a maintenance calculation is in force shall provide the Secretary of State with such information, in such circumstances, as may be prescribed, with a view to assisting the Secretary of State ... in determining whether the calculation has ceased to have effect ...

(11)   The Secretary of State may by regulations make such supplemental, incidental or transitional provision as he thinks necessary or expedient in consequence of the provisions of this paragraph.

(G)   Family Law Act 1996

30   Rights concerning home where one spouse or civil partner has no estate, etc.

(1)   This section applies if—

    (a)   one spouse or civil partner ('A') is entitled to occupy a dwelling-house by virtue of—

        (i)   a beneficial estate or interest or contract; or

        (ii)   any enactment giving A the right to remain in occupation; and

    (b)   the other spouse or civil partner ('B') is not so entitled.

(2)   Subject to the provisions of this Part, B has the following rights ('home rights')—

    (a)   if in occupation, a right not to be evicted or excluded from the dwelling-house or any part of it by A except with the leave of the court given by an order under section 33;

    (b)   if not in occupation, a right with the leave of the court so given to enter into and occupy the dwelling-house.

(3)   If B is entitled under this section to occupy a dwelling-house or any part of a dwelling-house, any payment or tender made or other thing done by B in or towards satisfaction of any liability of A in respect of rent, mortgage payments or other outgoings affecting the dwelling-house is, whether or not it is made or done in pursuance of an order under section 40, as good as if made or done by A.

(4)   B's occupation by virtue of this section—

    (a)   is to be treated, for the purposes of the Rent (Agriculture) Act 1976 and the Rent Act 1977 (other than Part V and sections 103 to 106 of that Act), as occupation by A as A's residence, and

    (b)   if B occupies the dwelling-house as B's only or principal home, is to be treated, for the purposes of the Housing Act 1985, Part I of the Housing Act 1988 and Chapter I of Part V of the Housing Act 1996, as occupation by A as A's only or principal home.

(5)   If B—

    (a)   is entitled under this section to occupy a dwelling-house or any part of a dwelling-house, and

    (b)   makes any payment in or towards satisfaction of any liability of A in respect of mortgage payments affecting the dwelling-house,

the person to whom the payment is made may treat it as having been made by A, but the fact that that person has treated any such payment as having been so made does not affect any claim of B against A to an interest in the dwelling-house by virtue of the payment.

(6)   If B is entitled under this section to occupy a dwelling-house or part of a dwelling-house by reason of an interest of A under a trust, all the provisions of subsections (3) to (5) apply in relation to the trustees as they apply in relation to A.

(7)   This section does not apply to a dwelling-house which—

    (a)   in the case of spouses, has at no time been, and which was at the time intended by them to be, a matrimonial home of theirs, and

    (b)   in the case of civil partners, has at no time been, and was at no time intended to be, a civil partnership home of theirs.

(8)   B's home rights continue—

    (a)   only so long as the marriage or civil partnership subsists, except to the extent that an order under section 33(5) otherwise provides; and

    (b)   only so long as A is entitled as mentioned in subsection (1) to occupy the dwelling-house, except where provision is made by section 31 for those rights to be a charge on an estate or interest in the dwelling-house.

(9)   It is hereby declared that a person—

    (a)   who has an equitable interest in a dwelling-house or in its proceeds of sale, but

(b)   is not a person in whom there is vested (whether solely or as joint tenant) a legal estate in fee simple or a legal term of years absolute in the dwelling-house,

is to be treated, only for the purpose of determining whether he has home rights, as not being entitled to occupy the dwelling-house by virtue of that interest.

33 Occupation orders where applicant has estate or interest etc or has home rights

(1)   If—

    (a)   a person ('the person entitled')—

        (i)   is entitled to occupy a dwelling-house by virtue of a beneficial estate or interest or contract or by virtue of any enactment giving him the right to remain in occupation, or

        (ii)   has home rights in relation to a dwelling-house, and

    (b)   the dwelling-house—

        (i)   is or at any time has been the home of the person entitled and of another person with whom he is associated, or

        (ii)   was at any time intended by the person entitled and any such other person to be their home,

the person entitled may apply to the court for an order containing any of the provisions specified in subsections (3), (4) and (5).

(2)   If an agreement to marry is terminated, no application under this section may be made by virtue of section 62(3)(e) by reference to that agreement after the end of the period of three years beginning with the date on which it is terminated.

(2A)   If a civil partnership agreement (as defined by section 73 of the Civil Partnership Act 2004) is terminated, no application under this section may be made by virtue of section 62(3)(eza) by reference to that agreement after the period of three years beginning with the day on which it is terminated.

(3)   An order under this section may—

    (a)   enforce the applicant's entitlement to remain in occupation as against the other person ('the respondent');

    (b)   require the respondent to permit the applicant to enter and remain in the dwelling-house or part of the dwelling-house;

    (c)   regulate the occupation of the dwelling-house by either or both parties;

    (d)   if the respondent is entitled as mentioned in subsection (1)(a)(i), prohibit, suspend or restrict the exercise by him of his right to occupy the dwelling-house;

    (e)   if the respondent has home rights in relation to the dwelling-house and the applicant is the other spouse or civil partner, restrict or terminate those rights;

    (f)   require the respondent to leave the dwelling-house or part of the dwelling-house; or

    (g)   exclude the respondent from a defined area in which the dwelling-house is included.

(4)   An order under this section may declare that the applicant is entitled as mentioned in subsection (1)(a)(i) or has home rights.

(5)   If the applicant has home rights and the respondent is the other spouse or civil partner, an order under this section made during the marriage or civil partnership may provide that those rights are not brought to an end by—

    (a)   the death of the other spouse or civil partner; or

    (b)   the termination (otherwise than by death) of the marriage or civil partnership.

(6)   In deciding whether to exercise its powers under subsection (3) and (if so) in what manner, the court shall have regard to all the circumstances including—

    (a)   the housing needs and housing resources of each of the parties and of any relevant child,

    (b)   the financial resources of the parties;

(c)   the likely effect of any order, or of any decision by the court not to exercise its powers under subsection (3), on the health, safety or well-being of the parties and of any relevant child; and

(d)   the conduct of the parties in relation to each other and otherwise.

(7)   If it appears to the court that the applicant or any relevant child is likely to suffer significant harm attributable to conduct of the respondent if an order under this section containing one or more of the provisions mentioned in subsection (3) is not made, the court shall make the order unless it appears to the court that—

(a)   the respondent or any relevant child is likely to suffer significant harm if the order is made; and

(b)   the harm likely to be suffered by the respondent or child in that event is as great as, or greater than, the harm attributable to conduct of the respondent which is likely to be suffered by the applicant or child if the order is not made.

(8)   The court may exercise its powers under subsection (5) in any case where it considers that in all the circumstances it is just and reasonable to do so.

(9)   An order under this section—

(a)   may not be made after the death of either of the parties mentioned in subsection (1); and

(b)   except in the case of an order made by virtue of subsection (5)(a), ceases to have effect on the death of either party.

(10)   An order under this section may, in so far as it has continuing effect, be made for a specified period, until the occurrence of a specified event or until further order.

34   Effect of order under s 33 where rights are charge on dwelling-house

(1)   If B's home rights are a charge on the estate or interest of A or of trustees for A—

(a)   an order under section 33 against A has, except so far as a contrary intention appears, the same effect against persons deriving title under A or under the trustees and affected by the charge, and

(b)   sections 33(1), (3), (4) and (10) and 30(3) to (6) apply in relation to any person deriving title under A or under the trustees and affected by the charge as they apply in relation to A.

(2)   The court may make an order under section 33 by virtue of subsection (1)(b) if it considers that in all the circumstances it is just and reasonable to do so.

35   One former spouse or former civil partner with no existing right to occupy

(1)   This section applies if—

(a)   one former spouse or former civil partner is entitled to occupy a dwelling-house by virtue of a beneficial estate or interest or contract, or by virtue of any enactment giving him the right to remain in occupation;

(b)   the other former spouse or former civil partner is not so entitled; and

(c)   the dwelling-house—

(i)   in the case of former spouses, was at any time their matrimonial home or was at any time intended by them to be their matrimonial home, or

(ii)   in the case of former civil partners, was at any time their civil partnership home or was at any time intended by them to be their civil partnership home.

(2)   The former spouse or former civil partner not so entitled may apply to the court for an order under this section against the other former spouse or former civil partner ('the respondent').

(3)   If the applicant is in occupation, an order under this section must contain provision—

(a)   giving the applicant the right not to be evicted or excluded from the dwelling-house or any part of it by the respondent for the period specified in the order; and

(b) prohibiting the respondent from evicting or excluding the applicant during that period.

(4) If the applicant is not in occupation, an order under this section must contain provision—

(a) giving the applicant the right to enter into and occupy the dwelling-house for the period specified in the order; and

(b) requiring the respondent to permit the exercise of that right.

(5) An order under this section may also—

(a) regulate the occupation of the dwelling-house by either or both of the parties;

(b) prohibit, suspend or restrict the exercise by the respondent of his right to occupy the dwelling-house;

(c) require the respondent to leave the dwelling-house or part of the dwelling-house; or

(d) exclude the respondent from a defined area in which the dwelling-house is included.

(6) In deciding whether to make an order under this section containing provision of the kind mentioned in subsection (3) or (4) and (if so) in what manner, the court shall have regard to all the circumstances including—

(a) the housing needs and housing resources of each of the parties and of any relevant child;

(b) the financial resources of each of the parties;

(c) the likely effect of any order, or of any decision by the court not to exercise its powers under subsection (3) or (4), on the health, safety or well-being of the parties and of any relevant child;

(d) the conduct of the parties in relation to each other and otherwise;

(e) the length of time that has elapsed since the parties ceased to live together;

(f) the length of time that has elapsed since the marriage or civil partnership was dissolved or annulled; and

(g) the existence of any pending proceedings between the parties—

(i) for an order under section 23A or 24 of the Matrimonial Causes Act 1973 (property adjustment orders in connection with divorce proceedings etc);

(ia) for a property adjustment order under Part 2 of Schedule 5 to the Civil Partnership Act 2004;

(ii) for an order under paragraph 1(2)(d) or (e) of Schedule 1 to the Children Act 1989 (orders for financial relief against parents); or

(iii) relating to the legal or beneficial ownership of the dwelling-house.

(7) In deciding whether to exercise its power to include one or more of the provisions referred to in subsection (5) ('a subsection (5) provision') and (if so) in what manner, the court shall have regard to all the circumstances including the matters mentioned in subsection (6)(a) to (e).

(8) If the court decides to make an order under this section and it appears to it that, if the order does not include a subsection (5) provision, the applicant or any relevant child is likely to suffer significant harm attributable to conduct of the respondent, the court shall include the subsection (5) provision in the order unless it appears to the court that—

(a) the respondent or any relevant child is likely to suffer significant harm if the provision is included in the order; and

(b) the harm likely to be suffered by the respondent or child in that event is as great as or greater than the harm attributable to conduct of the respondent which is likely to be suffered by the applicant or child if the provision is not included.

(9) An order under this section—

(a) may not be made after the death of either of the former spouses or former civil partners; and

(b)   ceases to have effect on the death of either of them.

(10)   An order under this section must be limited so as to have effect for a specified period not exceeding six months, but may be extended on one or more occasions for a further specified period not exceeding six months.

(11)   A former spouse or former civil partner who has an equitable interest in the dwelling-house or in the proceeds of sale of the dwelling-house but in whom there is not vested (whether solely or as joint tenant) a legal estate in fee simple or a legal term of years absolute in the dwelling-house is to be treated (but only for the purpose of determining whether he is eligible to apply under this section) as not being entitled to occupy the dwelling-house by virtue of that interest.

(12)   Subsection (11) does not prejudice any right of such a former spouse or former civil partner to apply for an order under section 33.

(13)   So long as an order under this section remains in force, subsections (3) to (6) of section 30 apply in relation to the applicant—

(a)   as if he were B (the person entitled to occupy the dwelling-house by virtue of that section); and

(b)   as if the respondent were A (the person entitled as mentioned in subsection (1)(a) of that section).

36   One cohabitant or former cohabitant with no existing right to occupy

(1)   This section applies if—

(a)   one cohabitant or former cohabitant is entitled to occupy a dwelling-house by virtue of a beneficial estate or interest or contract or by virtue of any enactment giving him the right to remain in occupation;

(b)   the other cohabitant or former cohabitant is not so entitled; and

(c)   that dwelling-house is the home in which they cohabit or a home in which they at any time cohabited or intended to cohabit.

(2)   The cohabitant or former cohabitant not so entitled may apply to the court for an order under this section against the other cohabitant or former cohabitant ('the respondent').

(3)   If the applicant is in occupation, an order under this section must contain provision—

(a)   giving the applicant the right not to be evicted or excluded from the dwelling-house or any part of it by the respondent for the period specified in the order, and

(b)   prohibiting the respondent from evicting or excluding the applicant during that period.

(4)   If the applicant is not in occupation, an order under this section must contain provision—

(a)   giving the applicant the right to enter into and occupy the dwelling-house for the period specified in the order; and

(b)   requiring the respondent to permit the exercise of that right.

(5)   An order under this section may also—

(a)   regulate the occupation of the dwelling-house by either or both of the parties;

(b)   prohibit, suspend or restrict the exercise by the respondent of his right to occupy the dwelling-house;

(c)   require the respondent to leave the dwelling-house or part of the dwelling-house; or

(d)   exclude the respondent from a defined area in which the dwelling-house is included.

(6)   In deciding whether to make an order under this section containing provision of the kind mentioned in subsection (3) or (4) and (if so) in what manner, the court shall have regard to all the circumstances including—

(a)   the housing needs and housing resources of each of the parties and of any relevant child;

(b)   the financial resources of each of the parties;

(c)   the likely effect of any order, or of any decision by the court not to exercise its powers under subsection (3) or (4), on the health, safety or well-being of the parties and of any relevant child;

(d)   the conduct of the parties in relation to each other and otherwise;

(e)   the nature of the parties' relationship and in particular the level of commitment involved in it;

(f)   the length of time during which they have cohabited;

(g)   whether there are or have been any children who are children of both parties or for whom both parties have or have had parental responsibility;

(h)   the length of time that has elapsed since the parties ceased to live together; and

(i)   the existence of any pending proceedings between the parties—

    (i)   for an order under paragraph 1(2)(d) or (e) of Schedule 1 to the Children Act 1989 (orders for financial relief against parents), or

    (ii)   relating to the legal or beneficial ownership of the dwelling-house.

(7)   In deciding whether to exercise its powers to include one or more of the provisions referred to in subsection (5) ('a subsection (5) provision') and (if so) in what manner, the court shall have regard to all the circumstances including—

(a)   the matters mentioned in subsection (6)(a) to (d); and

(b)   the questions mentioned in subsection (8).

(8)   The questions are—

(a)   whether the applicant or any relevant child is likely to suffer significant harm attributable to conduct of the respondent if the subsection (5) provision is not included in the order; and

(b)   whether the harm likely to be suffered by the respondent or child if the provision is included is as great as or greater than the harm attributable to conduct of the respondent which is likely to be suffered by the applicant or child if the provision is not included.

(9)   An order under this section—

(a)   may not be made after the death of either of the parties; and

(b)   ceases to have effect on the death of either of them.

(10)   An order under this section must be limited so as to have effect for a specified period not exceeding six months, but may be extended on one occasion for a further specified period not exceeding six months.

(11)   A person who has an equitable interest in the dwelling-house or in the proceeds of sale of the dwelling-house but in whom there is not vested (whether solely or as joint tenant) a legal estate in fee simple or a legal term of years absolute in the dwelling-house is to be treated (but only for the purpose of determining whether he is eligible to apply under this section) as not being entitled to occupy the dwelling-house by virtue of that interest.

(12)   Subsection (11) does not prejudice any right of such a person to apply for an order under section 33.

(13)   So long as the order remains in force, subsections (3) to (6) of section 30 apply in relation to the applicant—

(a)   as if he were B (the person entitled to occupy the dwelling-house by virtue of that section); and

(b)   as if the respondent were A (the person entitled as mentioned in subsection (1)(a) of that section).

37   Neither spouse or civil partner entitled to occupy

(1)   This section applies if—

(a)   one spouse or former spouse and the other spouse or former spouse occupy a dwelling-house which is or was the matrimonial home; but

(b)   neither of them is entitled to remain in occupation—

    (i)   by virtue of a beneficial estate or interest or contract; or

    (ii)   by virtue of any enactment giving him the right to remain in occupation.

(1A)   This section applies if—

(a)   the civil partner or former civil partner and the other civil partner or former civil partner occupy a dwelling-house which is or was the civil partnership home; but

(b)   neither of them is entitled to remain in occupation—

(i)   by virtue of a beneficial estate or contract; or

(ii)   by virtue of any enactment giving him the right to remain in occupation.

(2)   Either of the parties may apply to the court for an order against the other under this section.

(3)   An order under this section may—

(a)   require the respondent to permit the applicant to enter and remain in the dwelling-house or part of the dwelling-house;

(b)   regulate the occupation of the dwelling-house by either or both of the parties;

(c)   require the respondent to leave the dwelling-house or part of the dwelling-house; or

(d)   exclude the respondent from a defined area in which the dwelling-house is included.

(4)   Subsections (6) and (7) of section 33 apply to the exercise by the court of its powers under this section as they apply to the exercise by the court of its powers under subsection (3) of that section.

(5)   An order under this section must be limited so as to have effect for a specified period not exceeding six months, but may be extended on one or more occasions for a further specified period not exceeding six months.

38   Neither cohabitant or former cohabitant entitled to occupy

(1)   This section applies if—

(a)   one cohabitant or former cohabitant and the other cohabitant or former cohabitant occupy a dwelling-house which is the home in which they cohabit or cohabited; but

(b)   neither of them is entitled to remain in occupation—

(i)   by virtue of a beneficial estate or interest or contract; or

(ii)   by virtue of any enactment giving him the right to remain in occupation.

(2)   Either of the parties may apply to the court for an order against the other under this section.

(3)   An order under this section may—

(a)   require the respondent to permit the applicant to enter and remain in the dwelling-house or part of the dwelling-house;

(b)   regulate the occupation of the dwelling-house by either or both of the parties;

(c)   require the respondent to leave the dwelling-house or part of the dwelling-house; or

(d)   exclude the respondent from a defined area in which the dwelling-house is included.

(4)   In deciding whether to exercise its powers to include one or more of the provisions referred to in subsection (3) ('a subsection (3) provision') and (if so) in what manner, the court shall have regard to all the circumstances including—

(a)   the housing needs and housing resources of each of the parties and of any relevant child;

(b)   the financial resources of each of the parties;

(c)   the likely effect of any order, or of any decision by the court not to exercise its powers under subsection (3), on the health, safety or well-being of the parties and of any relevant child;

(d)   the conduct of the parties in relation to each other and otherwise; and

(e)   the questions mentioned in subsection (5).

(5)   The questions are—

(a)   whether the applicant or any relevant child is likely to suffer significant harm attributable to conduct of the respondent if the subsection (3) provision is not included in the order; and

(b)   whether the harm likely to be suffered by the respondent or child if the provision is included is as great as or greater than the harm attributable to conduct of the respondent which is likely to be suffered by the applicant or child if the provision is not included.

(6)   An order under this section shall be limited so as to have effect for a specified period not exceeding six months, but may be extended on one occasion for a further specified period not exceeding six months.

39   Supplementary provisions

(1)   In this Part an 'occupation order' means an order under section 33, 35, 36, 37 or 38.

(2)   An application for an occupation order may be made in other family proceedings or without any other family proceedings being instituted.

(3)   If—

(a)   an application for an occupation order is made under section 33, 35, 36, 37 or 38, and

(b)   the court considers that it has no power to make the order under the section concerned, but that it has power to make an order under one of the other sections,

the court may make an order under that other section.

(4)   The fact that a person has applied for an occupation order under sections 35 to 38, or that an occupation order has been made, does not affect the right of any person to claim a legal or equitable interest in any property in any subsequent proceedings (including subsequent proceedings under this Part).

40   Additional provisions that may be included in certain occupation orders

(1)   The court may on, or at any time after, making an occupation order under section 33, 35 or 36—

(a)   impose on either party obligations as to—

(i)   the repair and maintenance of the dwelling-house; or

(ii)   the discharge of rent, mortgage payments or other outgoings affecting the dwelling-house;

(b)   order a party occupying the dwelling-house or any part of it (including a party who is entitled to do so by virtue of a beneficial estate or interest or contract or by virtue of any enactment giving him the right to remain in occupation) to make periodical payments to the other party in respect of the accommodation, if the other party would (but for the order) be entitled to occupy the dwelling-house by virtue of a beneficial estate or interest or contract or by virtue of any such enactment;

(c)   grant either party possession or use of furniture or other contents of the dwelling-house;

(d)   order either party to take reasonable care of any furniture or other contents of the dwelling-house;

(e)   order either party to take reasonable steps to keep the dwelling-house and any furniture or other contents secure.

(2)   In deciding whether and, if so, how to exercise its powers under this section, the court shall have regard to all the circumstances of the case including—

(a)   the financial needs and financial resources of the parties; and

(b)   the financial obligations which they have, or are likely to have in the foreseeable future, including financial obligations to each other and to any relevant child.

(3)   An order under this section ceases to have effect when the occupation order to which it relates ceases to have effect.

42   Non-molestation orders

(1)   In this Part a 'non-molestation order' means an order containing either or both of the following provisions—

(a)   provision prohibiting a person ('the respondent') from molesting another person who is associated with the respondent;

(b)   provision prohibiting the respondent from molesting a relevant child.

(2)   The court may make a non-molestation order—

(a)   if an application for the order has been made (whether in other family proceedings or without any other family proceedings being instituted) by a person who is associated with the respondent; or

(b)   if in any family proceedings to which the respondent is a party the court considers that the order should be made for the benefit of any other party to the proceedings or any relevant child even though no such application has been made.

(3)   In subsection (2) 'family proceedings' includes proceedings in which the court has made an emergency protection order under section 44 of the Children Act 1989 which includes an exclusion requirement (as defined in section 44A(3) of that Act).

(4)   Where an agreement to marry is terminated, no application under subsection (2)(a) may be made by virtue of section 62(3)(e) by reference to that agreement after the end of the period of three years beginning with the day on which it is terminated.

(4A)   A court considering whether to make an occupation order shall also consider whether to exercise the power conferred by subsection (2)(b).

(4B)   In this Part 'the applicant', in relation to a non-molestation order, includes (where the context permits) the person for whose benefit such an order would be or is made in exercise of the power conferred by subsection (2)(b).

(5)   In deciding whether to exercise its powers under this section and, if so, in what manner, the court shall have regard to all the circumstances including the need to secure the health, safety and well-being—

(a)   of the applicant . . .; and

(b)   of any relevant child.

(6)   A non-molestation order may be expressed so as to refer to molestation in general, to particular acts of molestation, or to both.

(7)   A non-molestation order may be made for a specified period or until further order.

(8)   A non-molestation order which is made in other family proceedings ceases to have effect if those proceedings are withdrawn or dismissed.

45   Ex parte orders

(1)   The court may, in any case where it considers that it is just and convenient to do so, make an occupation order or a non-molestation order even though the respondent has not been given such notice of the proceedings as would otherwise be required by rules of court.

(2)   In determining whether to exercise its powers under subsection (1), the court shall have regard to all the circumstances including—

(a)   any risk of significant harm to the applicant or a relevant child, attributable to conduct of the respondent, if the order is not made immediately;

(b)   whether it is likely that the applicant will be deterred or prevented from pursuing the application if an order is not made immediately; and

(c)   whether there is reason to believe that the respondent is aware of the proceedings but is deliberately evading service and that the applicant or a relevant child will be seriously prejudiced by the delay involved—

(i)   where the court is a magistrates' court, in effecting service of proceedings; or

(ii)   in any other case, in effecting substituted service.

(3)   If the court makes an order by virtue of subsection (1) it must afford the respondent an opportunity to make representations relating to the order as soon as just and convenient at a full hearing.

(4)   If, at a full hearing, the court makes an occupation order ('the full order'), then—

    (a)   for the purposes of calculating the maximum period for which the full order may be made to have effect, the relevant section is to apply as if the period for which the full order will have effect began on the date on which the initial order first had effect; and

    (b)   the provisions of section 36(10) or 38(6) as to the extension of orders are to apply as if the full order and the initial order were a single order.

(5)   In this section—

'full hearing' means a hearing of which notice has been given to all the parties in accordance with rules of court;

'initial order' means an occupation order made by virtue of subsection (1); and

'relevant section' means section 33(10), 35(10), 36(10), 37(5) or 38(6).

46 Undertakings

(1)   In any case where the court has power to make an occupation order or non-molestation order, the court may accept an undertaking from any party to the proceedings.

(2)   No power of arrest may be attached to any undertaking given under subsection (1).

(3)   The court shall not accept an undertaking under subsection (1) instead of making an occupation order in any case where apart from this section a power of arrest would be attached to the order.

(3A)   The court shall not accept an undertaking under subsection (1) instead of making a non-molestation order in any case where it appears to the court that—

    (a)   the respondent has used or threatened violence against the applicant or a relevant child; and

    (b)   for the protection of the applicant or child it is necessary to make a non-molestation order so that any breach may be punishable under section 42A.

(4)   An undertaking given to a court under subsection (1) is enforceable as if the court had made an occupation order or a non-molestation order in terms corresponding to those of the undertaking.

(5)   This section has effect without prejudice to the powers of the High Court and the county court apart from this section.

47 Arrest for breach of order

(1)   . . .

(2)   If—

    (a)   the court makes an occupation order; and

    (b)   it appears to the court that the respondent has used or threatened violence against the applicant or a relevant child,

it shall attach a power of arrest to one or more provisions of the order unless the court is satisfied that in all the circumstances of the case the applicant or child will be adequately protected without such a power of arrest.

(3)   Subsection (2) does not apply in any case where the occupation order is made by virtue of section 45(1), but in such a case the court may attach a power of arrest to one or more provisions of the order if it appears to it—

    (a)   that the respondent has used or threatened violence against the applicant or a relevant child; and

    (b)   that there is a risk of significant harm to the applicant or child, attributable to conduct of the respondent, if the power of arrest is not attached to those provisions immediately.

(4)   If, by virtue of subsection (3), the court attaches a power of arrest to any provisions of an occupation order, it may provide that the power of arrest is to have effect for a shorter period than the other provisions of the order.

(5)   Any period specified for the purposes of subsection (4) may be extended by the court (on one or more occasions) on an application to vary or discharge the occupation order.

(6)   If, by virtue of subsection (2) or (3), a power of arrest is attached to certain provisions of an order, a constable may arrest without warrant a person whom he has reasonable cause for suspecting to be in breach of any such provision.

(7)   If a power of arrest is attached under subsection (2) or (3) to certain provisions of the order and the respondent is arrested under subsection (6)—

(a)   he must be brought before the relevant judicial authority within the period of 24 hours beginning at the time of his arrest; and

(b)   if the matter is not then disposed of forthwith, the relevant judicial authority before whom he is brought may remand him.

In reckoning for the purposes of this subsection any period of 24 hours, no account is to be taken of Christmas Day, Good Friday or any Sunday.

(8)   If the court—

(a)   has made a non-molestation order, or

(b)   has made an occupation order but has not attached a power of arrest under subsection (2) or (3) to any provision of the order, or has attached that power only to certain provisions of the order,

then, if at any time the applicant considers that the respondent has failed to comply with the order, he may apply to the relevant judicial authority for the issue of a warrant for the arrest of the respondent.

(9)   The relevant judicial authority shall not issue a warrant on an application under subsection (8) unless—

(a)   the application is substantiated on oath; and

(b)   the relevant judicial authority has reasonable grounds for believing that the respondent has failed to comply with the order.

(10)   If a person is brought before a court by virtue of a warrant issued under subsection (9) and the court does not dispose of the matter forthwith, the court may remand him.

(11)   Schedule 5 (which makes provision corresponding to that applying in magistrates' courts in civil cases under sections 128 and 129 of the Magistrates' Courts Act 1980) has effect in relation to the powers of the High Court and a county court to remand a person by virtue of this section.

(12)   If a person remanded under this section is granted bail (whether in the High Court or a county court under Schedule 5 or in a magistrates' court under section 128 or 129 of the Magistrates' Courts Act 1980), he may be required by the relevant judicial authority to comply, before release on bail or later, with such requirements as appear to that authority to be necessary to secure that he does not interfere with witnesses or otherwise obstruct the course of justice.

62   Meaning of 'cohabitants', 'relevant child' and 'associated persons'

(1)   For the purposes of this Part—

(a)   'cohabitants' are two persons who are neither married to each other nor civil partners of each other but are living together as husband and wife or as if they were civil partners; and

(b)   'cohabit' and 'former cohabitants' are to be read accordingly, but the latter expression does not include cohabitants who have subsequently married each other or become civil partners of each other.

(2)   In this Part, 'relevant child', in relation to any proceedings under this Part, means—

(a)   any child who is living with or might reasonably be expected to live with either party to the proceedings;

(b)   any child in relation to whom an order under the Adoption Act 1976, the Adoption and Children Act 2002 or the Children Act 1989 is in question in the proceedings; and

(c)   any other child whose interests the court considers relevant.

(3)   For the purposes of this Part, a person is associated with another person if—

(a) they are or have been married to each other;

(aa) they are or have been civil partners of each other;

(b) they are cohabitants or former cohabitants;

(c) they live or have lived in the same household, otherwise than merely by reason of one of them being the other's employee, tenant, lodger or boarder;

(d) they are relatives;

(e) they have agreed to marry one another (whether or not that agreement has been terminated);

(eza) they have entered into a civil partnership agreement (as defined by section 73 of the Civil Partnership Act 2004) (whether or not that agreement has been terminated);

(ea) they have or have had an intimate personal relationship with each other which is or was of significant duration;

(f) in relation to any child, they are both persons falling within subsection (4); or

(g) they are parties to the same family proceedings (other than proceedings under this Part).

(4) A person falls within this subsection in relation to a child if—

(a) he is a parent of the child; or

(b) he has or has had parental responsibility for the child.

(5) If a child has been adopted or falls within subsection (7), two persons are also associated with each other for the purpose of this Part if—

(a) one is a natural parent of the child or a parent of such a natural parent; and

(b) the other is the child or any person—

(i) who has become a parent of the child by virtue of an adoption order or has applied for an adoption order, or

(ii) with whom the child has at any time been placed for adoption.

(6) A body corporate and another person are not, by virtue of subsection (3)(f) or (g), to be regarded for the purposes of this Part as associated with each other.

(7) A child falls within this section if—

(a) an adoption agency, within the meaning of section 2 of the Adoption and Children Act 2002, has power to place him for adoption under section 19 of that Act (placing children with parental consent) or he has become the subject of an order under section 21 of that Act (placement orders); or

(b) he is freed for adoption by virtue of an order made—

(i) in England and Wales, under section 18 of the Adoption Act 1976,

(ii) in Scotland, under section 18 of the Adoption (Scotland) Act 1978, or

(iii) in Northern Ireland, under Article 17(1) or 18(1) of the Adoption (Northern Ireland) Order 1987.

(H)   Trusts of Land and Appointment of Trustees Act 1996

14   Applications for order

(1)   Any person who is a trustee of land or has an interest in property subject to a trust of land may make an application to the court for an order under this section.

(2)   On an application for an order under this section the court may make any such order—

(a)   relating to the exercise by the trustees of any of their functions (including an order relieving them of any obligation to obtain the consent of, or to consult, any person in connection with the exercise of any of their functions), or

(b)   declaring the nature or extent of a person's interest in property subject to the trust,

as the court thinks fit.

(3)   The court may not under this section make any order as to the appointment or removal of trustees.

(4)   The powers conferred on the court by this section are exercisable on an application whether it is made before or after the commencement of this Act.

15   Matters relevant in determining applications

(1)   The matters to which the court is to have regard in determining an application for an order under section 14 include—

(a)   the intentions of the person or persons (if any) who created the trust,

(b)   the purposes for which the property subject to the trust is held,

(c)   the welfare of any minor who occupies or might reasonably be expected to occupy any land subject to the trust as his home, and

(d)   the interests of any secured creditor of any beneficiary.

(2)   In the case of an application relating to the exercise in relation to any land of the powers conferred on the trustees by section 13, the matters to which the court is to have regard also include the circumstances and wishes of each of the beneficiaries who is (or apart from any previous exercise by the trustees of those powers would be) entitled to occupy the land under section 12.

(3)   In the case of any other application, other than one relating to the exercise of the power mentioned in section 6(2), the matters to which the court is to have regard also include the circumstances and wishes of any beneficiaries of full age and entitled to an interest in possession in property subject to the trust or (in case of dispute) of the majority (according to the value of their combined interests).

(4)   This section does not apply to an application if section 335A of the Insolvency Act 1986 (which is inserted by Schedule 3 and relates to applications by a trustee of a bankrupt) applies to it.

(I) Family Proceedings Rules 1991

2.51B Application of ancillary relief rules

(1) The procedures set out in rules 2.51D to 2.71 ('the ancillary relief rules') apply to—

   (a) any ancillary relief application;

   (b) any application under section 10(2) of the Act of 1973; and

   (c) any application under section 48(2) of the Act of 2004.

(2) In the ancillary relief rules, unless the context otherwise requires:

   'applicant' means the party applying for ancillary relief;

   'respondent' means the respondent to the application for ancillary relief;

   'FDR appointment' means a Financial Dispute Resolution appointment in accordance with rule 2.61E.

2.51C Application under section 6 of the Gender Recognition Act 2004

(1) This rule applies to an application made under section 6(1) of the Gender Recognition Act 2004 in respect of a full gender recognition certificate issued by a court under section 5(1) or 5A(1) of that Act.

(2) The application must be made to the court which issued the certificate, unless otherwise directed.

(3) Where the applicant is—

   (a) the person to whom the certificate was issued, the Secretary of State must be a respondent;

   (b) the Secretary of State, the person to whom the certificate was issued must be a respondent.

(4) Where the court issues a corrected gender recognition certificate under section 6(4) of the Gender Recognition Act 2004, the proper officer must send a copy of the corrected certificate to the Secretary of State.

2.51D The overriding objective

(1) The ancillary relief rules are a procedural code with the overriding objective of enabling the court to deal with cases justly.

(2) Dealing with a case justly includes, so far as is practicable—

   (a) ensuring that the parties are on an equal footing;

   (b) saving expense;

   (c) dealing with the case in ways which are proportionate—

      (i) to the amount of money involved;

      (ii) to the importance of the case;

      (iii) to the complexity of the issues; and

      (iv) to the financial position of each party;

   (d) ensuring that it is dealt with expeditiously and fairly; and

   (e) allotting to it an appropriate share of the court's resources, while taking into account the need to allot resources to other cases.

(3) The court must seek to give effect to the overriding objective when it—

   (a) exercises any power given to it by the ancillary relief rules; or

   (b) interprets any rule.

(4) The parties are required to help the court to further the overriding objective.

(5) The court must further the overriding objective by actively managing cases.

(6) Active case management includes—

   (a) encouraging the parties to co-operate with each other in the conduct of the proceedings;

   (b) encouraging the parties to settle their disputes through mediation, where appropriate;

   (c) identifying the issues at an early date;

   (d) regulating the extent of disclosure of documents and expert evidence so that they are proportionate to the issues in question;

(e)   helping the parties to settle the whole or part of the case;

(f)   fixing timetables or otherwise controlling the progress of the case;

(g)   making use of technology; and

(h)   giving directions to ensure that the trial of a case proceeds quickly and efficiently.

2.52   Right to be heard on ancillary questions

A respondent may be heard on any question of ancillary relief without filing an answer and whether or not he has returned to the court office an acknowledgement of service stating his wish to be heard on that question.

2.53   Application by petitioner or respondent for ancillary relief

(1)   Any application by a petitioner, or by a respondent who files an answer claiming relief, for—

(a)   an order for maintenance pending suit,

(aa)   an order for maintenance pending outcome of proceedings,

(b)   a financial provision order,

(c)   a property adjustment order,

(d)   a pension sharing order

shall be made in the petition or answer, as the case may be.

(2)   Notwithstanding anything in paragraph (1), an application for ancillary relief which should have been made in the petition or answer may be made subsequently—

(a)   by leave of the court, either by notice in Form A or at the trial, or

(b)   where the parties are agreed upon the terms of the proposed order, without leave by notice in Form A.

(3)   An application by a petitioner or respondent for ancillary relief, not being an application which is required to be made in the petition or answer, shall be made by notice in Form A.

2.59   Evidence on application for property adjustment or avoidance of disposition order

(1)   ...

(2)   Where an application for a property adjustment order or an avoidance of disposition order relates to land, the notice in Form A shall identify the land and—

(a)   state whether the title to the land is registered or unregistered and, if registered, the Land Registry title number; and

(b)   give particulars, so far as known to the applicant, of any mortgage of the land or any interest therein.

(3)   Copies of Form A and of Form E completed by the applicant, shall be served on the following persons as well as on the respondent to the application, that is to say—

(a)   in the case of an application for an order for a variation of settlement ..., the trustees of the settlement and the settlor if living;

(b)   in the case of an application for an avoidance of disposition order, the person in whose favour the disposition is alleged to have been made;

and such other persons, if any, as the district judge may direct.

(4)   In the case of an application to which paragraph (2) refers, a copy of Form A, shall be served on any mortgagee of whom particulars are given pursuant to that paragraph; any person so served may apply to the court in writing, within 14 days after service, for a copy of the applicant's Form E.

(5)   Any person who—

(a)   is served with copies of Forms A and E pursuant to paragraph (3), or

(b)   receives a copy of Form E following an application made in accordance with paragraph (4),

may, within 14 days after service or receipt, as the case may be, file a statement in answer.

(6)   A statement filed under paragraph (5) shall be sworn to be true.

2.60   Service of statement in answer

(1)   Where a form or other document filed with the court contains an allegation of adultery or of an improper association with a named person ('the named person'), the court may direct that the party who filed the relevant form or document serve a copy of all or part of that form or document on the named person, together with Form F.

(2)   If the court makes a direction under paragraph (1), the named person may file a statement in answer to the allegations.

(3)   A statement under paragraph (2) shall be sworn to be true.

(4)   Rule 2.37(3) shall apply to a person served under paragraph (1) as it applies to a co-respondent.

2.61   Information on application for consent order for financial relief

(1)   Subject to paragraphs (2) and (3), there shall be lodged with every application for a consent order under any of sections 23, 24 or 24A of the Act of 1973, or Parts 1, 2 and 3 of Schedule 5 to the Act of 2004, two copies of a draft of the order in the terms sought, one of which shall be indorsed with a statement signed by the respondent to the application signifying his agreement, and a statement of information (which may be made in more than one document) which shall include—

(a)   the duration of the marriage or civil partnership, as the case may be, the age of each party and of any minor or dependent child of the family;

(b)   an estimate in summary form of the approximate amount or value of the capital resources and net income of each party and of any minor child of the family;

(c)   what arrangements are intended for the accommodation of each of the parties and any minor child of the family;

(d)   whether either party has subsequently married or formed a civil partnership or has any present intention to do so or to cohabit with another person;

(dd)   where the order includes provision to be made under section ... 25B or 25C of the Act of 1973 or under paragraphs ... 25 or 26 of Schedule 5 to the Act of 2004, a statement confirming that the person responsible for the pension arrangement in question has been served with the documents required by rule 2.70(11) and that no objection to such an order has been made by that person within 21 days from such service;

(e)   where the terms of the order provide for a transfer of property, a statement confirming that any mortgagee of that property has been served with notice of the application and that no objection to such a transfer has been made by the mortgagee within 14 days from such service; and

(f)   any other especially significant matters.

(2)   Where an application is made for a consent order varying an order for periodical payments paragraph (1) shall be sufficiently complied with if the statement of information required to be lodged with the application includes only the information in respect of net income mentioned in paragraph (1)(b) (and, where appropriate, a statement under paragraph (1)(dd)), and an application for a consent order for interim periodical payments pending the determination of an application for ancillary relief may be made in like manner.

(3)   Where all or any of the parties attend the hearing of an application for financial relief the court may dispense with the lodging of a statement of information in accordance with paragraph (1) and give directions for the information which would otherwise be required to be given in such a statement to be given in such a manner as it sees fit.

2.61A   Application for ancillary relief

(1)   A notice of intention to proceed with an application for ancillary relief made in the petition or answer or an application for ancillary relief must be made by notice in Form A.

(2)   The notice must be filed:

    (a)   if the case is pending in a designated county court, in that court; or

    (b)   if the case is pending in the High Court, in the registry in which it is proceeding.

(3)   Where the applicant requests an order for ancillary relief that includes provision to be made by virtue of section 24B, 25B or 25C of the Act of 1973 or under paragraphs 15, 25 or 26 of Schedule 5 to the Act of 2004 the terms of the order requested must be specified in the notice in Form A.

(4)   Upon the filing of Form A the court must:

    (a)   fix a first appointment not less than 12 weeks and not more than 16 weeks after the date of the filing of the notice and give notice of that date;

    (b)   serve a copy on the respondent within 4 days of the date of the filing of the notice.

(5)   The date fixed under paragraph (4) for the first appointment, or for any subsequent appointment, must not be cancelled except with the court's permission and, if cancelled, the court must immediately fix a new date.

2.61B   Procedure before the first appointment

(1)   Both parties must, at the same time, exchange with each other, and each file with the court, a statement in Form E, which—

    (a)   is signed by the party who made the statement;

    (b)   is sworn to be true, and

    (c)   contains the information and has attached to it the documents required by that Form.

(2)   Form E must be exchanged and filed not less than 35 days before the date of the first appointment.

(3)   Form E must have attached to it:

    (a)   any documents required by Form E; ...

    (b)   any other documents necessary to explain or clarify any of the information contained in Form E; ...

    (c)   any documents furnished to the party producing the form by a person responsible for a pension arrangement, either following a request under rule 2.70(2) or as part of a 'relevant valuation' as defined in rule 2.70(4); and

    (d)   any notification or other document referred to in paragraphs (2), (4) or (5) of rule 2.70A which has been received by the party producing the form.

(4)   Form E must have no documents attached to it other than the documents referred to in paragraph (3).

(5)   Where a party was unavoidably prevented from sending any document required by Form E, that party must at the earliest opportunity:

    (a)   serve copies of that document on the other party, and

    (b)   file a copy of that document with the court, together with a statement explaining the failure to send it with Form E.

(6)   No disclosure or inspection of documents may be requested or given between the filing of the application for ancillary relief and the first appointment, except—

    (a)   copies sent with Form E, or in accordance with paragraph (5); or

    (b)   in accordance with paragraph (7).

(7)   At least 14 days before the hearing of the first appointment, each party must file with the court and serve on the other party—

    (a)   a concise statement of the issues between the parties;

    (b)   a chronology;

(c)   a questionnaire setting out by reference to the concise statement of issues any further information and documents requested from the other party or a statement that no information and documents are required;

(d)   a notice in Form G stating whether that party will be in a position at the first appointment to proceed on that occasion to a FDR appointment.

(8)   ...

(9)   At least 14 days before the hearing of the first appointment, the applicant must file with the court and serve on the respondent, confirmation of the names of all persons served in accordance with rule 2.59(3) and (4), and that there are no other persons who must be served in accordance with those paragraphs.

2.61C   Expert evidence

CPR rules 35.1 to 35.14 relating to expert evidence (with appropriate modifications), except CPR rules 35.5(2) and 35.8(4)(b), apply to all ancillary relief proceedings.

2.61D   The first appointment

(1)   The first appointment must be conducted with the objective of defining the issues and saving costs.

(2)   At the first appointment the district judge—

(a)   must determine—

(i)   the extent to which any questions seeking information under rule 2.61B must be answered, and

(ii)   what documents requested under rule 2.61B must be produced,

and give directions for the production of such further documents as may be necessary;

(b)   must give directions about—

(i)   the valuation of assets (including, where appropriate, the joint instruction of joint experts);

(ii)   obtaining and exchanging expert evidence, if required; and

(iii)   evidence to be adduced by each party and, where appropriate, about further chronologies or schedules to be filed by each party;

(c)   must, unless he decides that a referral is not appropriate in the circumstances, direct that the case be referred to a FDR appointment;

(d)   must, where he decides that a referral to a FDR appointment is not appropriate, direct one or more of the following:

(i)   that a further directions appointment be fixed;

(ii)   that an appointment be fixed for the making of an interim order;

(iii)   that the case be fixed for final hearing and, where that direction is given, the district judge must determine the judicial level at which the case should be heard; ...

(iv)   that the case be adjourned for out-of-court mediation or private negotiation or, in exceptional circumstances, generally;

(e)   in considering whether to make a costs order under rule 2.71(4), must have particular regard to the extent to which each party has complied with the requirement to send documents with Form E; and

(f)   may—

(i)   make an interim order where an application for it has been made in accordance with rule 2.69F returnable at the first appointment;

(ii)   having regard to the contents of Form G filed by the parties, treat the appointment (or part of it) as a FDR appointment to which rule 2.61E applies;

(iii)   in a matrimonial cause, in a case where an order for ancillary relief is requested that includes provision to be made under section 24B, 25B or 25C of the Act 1973, direct any party with pension rights to file and serve

> > a Pension Inquiry Form (Form P), completed in full or in part as the court may direct;
> >
> > (iv)   in a civil partnership cause, in a case where an order for ancillary relief is requested that includes provision to be made under paragraphs 15, 25 or 26 of Schedule 5 to the Act of 2004, direct any civil partner with pension rights to file and serve a Pension Inquiry Form (Form P), completed in full or in part as the court may direct.

(3)   After the first appointment, a party is not entitled to production of any further documents except in accordance with directions given under paragraph (2)(a) above or with the permission of the court.

(4)   At any stage:

    (a)   a party may apply for further directions or a FDR appointment;

    (b)   the court may give further directions or direct that the parties attend a FDR appointment.

(5)   Both parties must personally attend the first appointment unless the court orders otherwise.

2.61E   The FDR appointment

(1)   The FDR appointment must be treated as a meeting held for the purposes of discussion and negotiation and paragraphs (2) to (9) apply.

(2)   The district judge or judge hearing the FDR appointment must have no further involvement with the application, other than to conduct any further FDR appointment or to make a consent order or a further directions order.

(3)   Not later than 7 days before the FDR appointment, the applicant must file with the court details of all offers and proposals, and responses to them.

(4)   Paragraph (3) includes any offers, proposals or responses made wholly or partly without prejudice, but paragraph (3) does not make any material admissible as evidence if, but for that paragraph, it would not be admissible.

(5)   At the conclusion of the FDR appointment, any documents filed under paragraph (3), and any filed documents referring to them, must, at the request of the party who filed them, be returned to him and not retained on the court file.

(6)   Parties attending the FDR appointment must use their best endeavours to reach agreement on the matters in issue between them.

(7)   The FDR appointment may be adjourned from time to time.

(8)   At the conclusion of the FDR appointment, the court may make an appropriate consent order, but otherwise must give directions for the future course of the proceedings, including, where appropriate, the filing of evidence and fixing a final hearing date.

(9)   Both parties must personally attend the FDR appointment unless the court orders otherwise.

2.61F   Costs

(1)   Subject to paragraph (2), at every hearing or appointment each party must produce to the court an estimate in Form H of the costs incurred by him up to the date of that hearing or appointment.

(2)   Not less than 14 days before the date fixed for the final hearing of an application for ancillary relief, each party must (unless the court directs otherwise) file with the court and serve on each other party a statement in Form H1 giving full particulars of all costs in respect of the proceedings which he has incurred or expects to incur, to enable the court to take account of the parties' liabilities for costs when deciding what order (if any) to make for ancillary relief.

2.62   Investigation by district judge of application for ancillary relief

(1)   ...

(2)   An application for an avoidance of disposition order shall, if practicable, be heard at the same time as any related application for financial relief.

(3)   ...

(4)   At the hearing of an application for ancillary relief the district judge shall, subject to rules 2.64, 2.65 and 10.10 investigate the allegations made in support of and in answer to the application, and may take evidence orally and may at any stage of the proceedings, whether before or during the hearing, order the attendance of any person for the purpose of being examined or cross-examined and order the disclosure and inspection of any document or require further statements.

(4A)   A statement filed under paragraph (4) shall be sworn to be true.

(5), (6) ...

(7)   Any party may apply to the court for an order that any person do attend an appointment (an 'inspection appointment') before the court and produce any documents to be specified or described in the order, the inspection of which appears to the court to be necessary for disposing fairly of the application for ancillary relief or for saving costs.

(8)   No person shall be compelled by an order under paragraph (7) to produce any document at an inspection appointment which he could not be compelled to produce at the hearing of the application for ancillary relief.

(9)   The court shall permit any person attending an inspection appointment pursuant to an order under paragraph (7) above to be represented at the appointment.

2.64   Order on application for ancillary relief

(1)   Subject to rule 2.65 the district judge shall, after completing his investigation under rule 2.62, make such order as he thinks just.

(2)   Pending the final determination of the application, and subject to rule 2.69F, the district judge may make an interim order upon such terms as he thinks just.

(3)   RSC Order 31, rule 1 (power to order sale of land) shall apply to applications for ancillary relief as it applies to causes and matters in the Chancery Division.

2.65   Reference of application to judge

The district judge may at any time refer an application for ancillary relief or any question arising thereon, to a judge for his decision.

2.68   Application for order under section 37(2)(a) of Act of 1973 or paragraph 74(2) of Schedule 5 to Act of 2004

(1)   An application under section 37(2)(a) of the Act of 1973 or paragraph 74(2) of Schedule 5 to the Act of 2004 for an order restraining any person from attempting to defeat a claim for financial provision or otherwise for protecting the claim may be made to the district judge.

(2)   Rules 2.65 and 2.66 shall apply, with the necessary modifications, to the application as if it were an application for ancillary relief.

2.69E   Open proposals

(1)   Not less than 14 days before the date fixed for the final hearing of an application for ancillary relief, the applicant must (unless the court directs otherwise) file with the court and serve on the respondent an open statement which sets out concise details, including the amounts involved, of the orders which he proposes to ask the court to make.

(2)   Not more than 7 days after service of a statement under paragraph (1), the respondent must file with the court and serve on the applicant an open statement which sets out concise details, including the amounts involved, of the orders which he proposes to ask the court to make.

2.69F   Application for interim orders

(1)   A party may apply at any stage of the proceedings for an order for maintenance pending suit or outcome of proceedings, as the case may be, interim periodical payments or an interim variation order.

(2)   An application for such an order must be made by notice of application and the date fixed for the hearing of the application must be not less than 14 days after the date the notice of application is issued.

(3)   The applicant shall forthwith serve the respondent with a copy of the notice of application.

(4)   Where an application is made before a party has filed Form E, that party must file with the application and serve on the other party, a draft of the order requested and a short sworn statement explaining why the order is necessary and giving the necessary information about his means.

(5)   Not less than 7 days before the date fixed for the hearing, the respondent must file with the court and serve on the other party, a short sworn statement about his means, unless he has already filed Form E.

(6)   A party may apply for any other form of interim order at any stage of the proceedings with or without notice.

(7)   Where an application referred to in paragraph (6) is made with notice, the provisions of paragraphs (1) to (5) apply to it.

(8)   Where an application referred to in paragraph (6) is made without notice, the provisions of paragraph (1) apply to it.

2.70   Pensions

(1)   This rule applies where an application for ancillary relief has been made, or notice of intention to proceed with the application has been given, in Form A, or an application has been made in Form B, and the applicant or respondent has or is likely to have any benefits under a pension arrangement.

(2)   When the court fixes a first appointment as required by rule 2.61A(4)(a),

(a)   in a matrimonial cause, the party with pension rights, and

(b)   in a civil partnership cause, the civil partner with pension rights,

shall within seven days after receiving notification of the date of that appointment, request the person responsible for each pension arrangement under which he has or is likely to have benefits to furnish the information referred to in regulation 2(2) of the Pensions on Divorce etc (Provision of Information) Regulations 2000.

(3)   Within seven days of receiving information under paragraph (2) the party with pension rights or civil partner with pension rights, as the case may be, shall send a copy of it to the other party or civil partner, together with the name and address of the person responsible for each pension arrangement.

(4)   A request under paragraph (2) above need not be made where the party with pension rights or the civil partner with pension rights is in possession of, or has requested, a relevant valuation of the pension rights or benefits accrued under the pension arrangement in question.

(5)   In this rule, a relevant valuation means a valuation of pension rights or benefits as at a date not more than twelve months earlier than the date fixed for the first appointment which has been furnished or requested for the purposes of any of the following provisions:—

(a)   the Pensions on Divorce etc (Provision of Information) Regulations 2000;

(b)   regulation 5 of and Schedule 2 to the Occupational Pension Schemes (Disclosure of Information) Regulations 1996 and regulation 11 of and Schedule 1 to the Occupational Pension Schemes (Transfer Value) Regulations 1996;

(c)   section 93A or 94(1)(a) or (aa) of the Pension Schemes Act 1993;

(d)   section 94(1)(b) of the Pension Schemes Act 1993 or paragraph 2(a) (or, where applicable, 2(b)) of Schedule 2 to the Personal Pension Schemes (Disclosure of Information) Regulations 1987.

(6)   Upon making or giving notice of intention to proceed with an application for ancillary relief which includes a request for a pensiion sharing order, or upon adding a request for such an order to an existing application for ancillary relief, the applicant

shall send to the person responsible for the pension arrangement concerned a copy of Form A.

(7)   Upon making or giving notice of intention to proceed with an application for ancillary relief which includes an application for a pension attachment order, or upon adding a request for such an order to an existing application for ancillary relief, the applicant shall send to the person responsible for the pension arrangement concerned—

(a)   a copy of Form A;

(b)   an address to which any notice which the person responsible is required to serve on the applicant under the Divorce etc (Pensions) Regulations 2000 or the Dissolution etc (Pensions) Regulations 2005, as the case may be, is to be sent;

(c)   an address to which any payment which the person responsible is required to make to the applicant is to be sent; and

(d)   where the address in sub-paragraph (c) is that of a bank, a building society or the Department of National Savings, sufficient details to enable payment to be made into the account of the applicant.

(8)   A person responsible for a pension arrangement on whom a copy of a notice under paragraph (7) is served may, within 21 days after service, require the party or civil partner with the pension rights, as the case may be, to provide him with a copy of section 2.13 of his Form E; and that party or civil partner must then provide that person with the copy of that section of the statement within the time limited for filing it by rule 2.61B(2), or 21 days after being required to do so, whichever is the later.

(9)   A person responsible for a pension arrangement who receives a copy of section 2.13 of Form E as required pursuant to paragraph (8) may within 21 days after receipt send to the court, the applicant and the respondent a statement in answer.

(10)   A person responsible for a pension arrangement who files a statement in answer pursuant to paragraph (9) shall be entitled to be represented at the first appointment, and the court must within 4 days of the date of filing of the statement in answer give the person notice of the date of the first appointment.

(11)   Where the parties have agreed on the terms of an order and the agreement includes a pension attachment order, then unless service has already been effected under paragraph (7), they shall serve on the person responsible for the pension arrangement concerned—

(a)   the notice of application for a consent order under rule 2.61(1);

(b)   a draft of the proposed order under rule 2.61(1), complying with paragraph (13) below; and

(c)   the particulars set out in sub-paragraphs (b), (c) and (d) of paragraph (7) above.

(12)   No consent order under paragraph (11) shall be made unless either—

(a)   the person responsible has not made any objection within 21 days after the service on him of such notice; or

(b)   the court has considered any such objection

and for the purpose of considering any objection the court may make such direction as it sees fit for the person responsible to attend before it or to furnish written details of his objection.

(13)   An order for ancillary relief, whether by consent or not, which includes a pension sharing order or a pension attachment order, shall—

(a)   in the body of the order, state that there is to be provision by way of pension sharing or pension attachment in accordance with the annex or annexes to the order; and

(b)   be accompanied by an annex in Form P1 (Pension Sharing annex) or Form P2 (Pension Attachment annex) as the case may require; and if provision is made in relation to more than one pension arrangement there shall be one annex for each pension arrangement.

(14), (15)   . . .

(16)   A court which makes, varies or discharges a pension sharing order or a pension attachment order, shall send, or direct one of the parties to send, to the person responsible for the pension arrangement concerned—

(a)   a copy of—

(i)   in a matrimonial cause, the decree of divorce, nullity of marriage or judicial separation; or

(ii)   in a civil partnership cause, the conditional order of dissolution, nullity of civil partnership or the order of separation;

(b)   in the case of—

(i)   divorce or nullity of marriage, a copy of the certificate under rule 2.51 that the decree has been made absolute; or

(ii)   dissolution or nullity of civil partnership, a copy of the order making the conditional order final under rule 2.51A; and

(c)   a copy of that order, or as the case may be of the order varying or discharging that order, including any annex to that order relating to that pension arrangement but no other annex to that order.

(17)   The documents referred to in paragraph (16) shall be sent—

(a)   in a matrimonial cause, within 7 days after—

(i)   the making of the relevant pension sharing or pension attachment order; or

(ii)   the decree absolute of divorce or nullity or decree of judicial separation, whichever is the later; and

(b)   in a civil partnership cause, within 7 days after—

(i)   the making of the relevant pension sharing or pension attachment order; or

(ii)   the final order of dissolution or nullity or order of separation, whichever is the later.

(18)   In this rule—

(a)   in a matrimonial cause all words and phrases defined in sections 25D(3) and (4) of the Act of 1973 have the meanings assigned by those subsections;

(ab)   in a civil partnership cause, all words and phrases defined in paragraphs 16(4) to (5) and 29 of Schedule 5 to the Act of 2004 have the meanings assigned by those paragraphs;

(b)   all words and phrases defined in section 46 of the Welfare Reform and Pensions Act 1999 have the meanings assigned by that section;

(c)   'pension sharing order' means—

(i)   in a matrimonial cause, an order making provision under section 24B of the Act of 1973; and

(ii)   in a civil partnership cause, an order making provision under paragraph 15 of Schedule 5 to the Act of 2004; and

(d)   'pension attachment order' means—

(i)   in a matrimonial cause, an order making provision under section 25B or 25C of the Act of 1973; and

(ii)   in a civil partnership cause, an order making provision under paragraph 25 and paragraph 26 of Schedule 5 to the Act of 2004.

2.71   Costs orders

(1)   CPR rule 44.3(1) to (5) shall not apply to ancillary relief proceedings.

(2)   CPR rule 44.3(6) to (9) apply to an order made under this rule as they apply to an order made under CPR rule 44.3.

(3)   In this rule 'costs' has the same meaning as in CPR rule 43.2(1)(a) and includes the costs payable by a client to his solicitor.

(4)   (a)   The general rule in ancillary relief proceedings is that the court will not make an order requiring one party to pay the costs of another party; but

(b)   the court may make such an order at any stage of the proceedings where it considers it appropriate to do so because of the conduct of a party in relation to the proceedings (whether before or during them).

(5)   In deciding what order (if any) to make under paragraph (4)(b), the court must have regard to—

(a)   any failure by a party to comply with these Rules, any order of the court or any practice direction which the court considers relevant;

(b)   any open offer to settle made by a party;

(c)   whether it was reasonable for a party to raise, pursue or contest a particular allegation or issue;

(d)   the manner in which a party has pursued or responded to the application or a particular allegation or issue;

(e)   any other aspect of a party's conduct in relation to the proceedings which the court considers relevant; and

(f)   the financial effect on the parties of any costs order.

(6)   No offer to settle which is not an open offer to settle shall be admissible at any stage of the proceedings, except as provided by rule 2.61E.

Appendix 2 – Code of Practice for Resolution Members

Membership of Resolution commits family lawyers to resolving disputes in a non-confrontational way.

We believe that family law disputes should be dealt with in a constructive way designed to preserve people's dignity and to encourage agreements.

Members of Resolution are required to:

- Conduct matters in a constructive and non-confrontational way
- Avoid use of inflammatory language both written and spoken
- Retain professional objectivity and respect for everyone involved
- Take into account the long term consequences of actions and communications as well as the short term implications
- Encourage clients to put the best interests of the children first
- Emphasise to clients the importance of being open and honest in all dealings
- Make clients aware of the benefits of behaving in a civilised way
- Keep financial and children issues separate
- Ensure that consideration is given to balancing the benefits of any steps against the likely costs – financial or emotional
- Inform clients of the options eg counselling, family therapy, round table negotiations, mediation, collaborative law and court proceedings
- Abide by the Resolution Guides to Good Practice

This Code should be read in conjunction with the Law Society's Family Law Protocol.

All solicitors are subject to the Solicitors Practice Rules

Reproduced with kind permission of Resolution.

Appendix 3 – Court Forms

(A) Divorce petition

Before completing this form, read carefully the attached **Notes for Guidance**.

In the   **County Court***
                                                                  *Delete as
                                                                  appropriate
In the Principal Registry*   **No.**

Introduction

This petition is issued by   ("the Petitioner")

The other party to the marriage is   ("the Respondent").

---

(1)   On the   day of   [19   ] [20   ]

                                                        was lawfully married to

                                          at

(1a)   Since the date of the marriage the name of the petitioner has not changed [has changed]

(1b)   The petitioner believes that since the date of the marriage the name of the respondent has not changed [has changed]

(2)   The petitioner and respondent last lived together as husband and wife at

(3)   The court has jurisdiction under Article 3(1) of the Council Regulation on the following ground(s):

(4)   The petitioner is by occupation a   and resides at

        The respondent is by occupation a   and resides at

(5)   There are no children of the family now living *except*

(6)   No other child, now living, has been born to the petitioner/respondent during the marriage (so far as is known to the petitioner) *except*

(7)   There are or have been no other proceedings in any court in England and Wales or elsewhere with reference to the marriage (or to any child of the family) or between the petitioner and respondent with reference to any property of either or both of them *except*

(8)   There are or have been no proceedings in the Child Support Agency with reference to the maintenance of any child of the family *except*

(9)   There are no proceedings continuing in any country outside England or Wales which are in respect of the marriage or are capable of affecting its validity or subsistence *except*

(10)   (This paragraph should be completed only if the petition is based on five years' separation.)
        No agreement or arrangement has been made or is proposed to be made between the parties for the support of the petitioner/respondent (and any child of the family) *except*

(11)   The said marriage has broken down irretrievably.

(12)

(13)   **Particulars**

Prayer

The petitioner therefore prays

(1)   **The suit**

That the said marriage be dissolved

(2)   **Costs**

That the   may be ordered to pay the costs of this suit

(3)   **Ancillary relief**

That the petitioner may be granted the following ancillary relief:

(a)   an order for maintenance pending suit

a periodical payments order

a secured provision order

a lump sum order

a property adjustment order

an order under section 24B, 25B or 25C of the Act of 1973 (Pension Sharing/Attachment Order)

(b)   **For the children**

a periodical payments order

a secured provision order

a lump sum order

a property adjustment order

Signed

The names and addresses of the persons to be served with the petition are:

Respondent:

Co-Respondent (adultery case only):

The Petitioner's address for service is:

Dated this   day of   20

Address all communications for the court to: The Court Manager, County Court,

The Court   }
office at   }

is open from 10 a.m. to 4 p.m. (4.30 p.m. at the Principal Registry of the Family Division) on Mondays to Fridays.

In the

County Court*

*Delete as
appropriate

No.

In the Principal Registry*

Between

Petitioner

and

Respondent

Divorce Petition

Full name and address of the petitioner or
of solicitors if they are acting for the petitioner.

(B) Form M4 (Statement of arrangements relating to the children)

Statement of Arrangements for Children

In the		County Court
Petitioner		
Respondent		
	No. of matter *(always quote this)*	

┌─ **To the Petitioner** ───────────────────────────────────┐

You must complete this form
If you or the respondent have any children   •   under 16
                                         or •   over 16 but under 18 if they are at school or college or are
                                                  training for a trade, profession or vocation.

Please use black ink.
Please complete Parts I, II and III.

Before you issue a petition for divorce or dissolution try to reach agreement with your spouse/civil partner over the proposals for the children's future. There is space for him/her to sign at the end of this form if agreement is reached.

If your spouse/civil partner does not agree with the proposals he/she will have an opportunity at a later stage to state why he/she does not agree and will be able to make his/her own proposals.

You should take or send the completed form, signed by you (and, if agreement is reached, by your spouse/civil partner) together with a copy to the court when you issue your petition.

Please refer to the explanatory notes issued regarding completion of the prayer of the petition if you are asking the court to make any order regarding the children.

The Court will only make an order if it considers that an order will be better for the child(ren) than no order.

If you wish to apply for any of the orders which may be available to you under Part I or II of the Children Act 1989 you are advised to see a solicitor.

You should obtain legal advice from a solicitor or, alternatively, from an advice agency. Addresses of solicitors and advice agencies can be obtained from the Yellow Pages and the Solicitors Regional Directory which can be found at Citizens Advice Bureaux, Law Centres and any local library.

└───┘

┌─ **To the Respondent** ───────────────────────────────────┐

The petitioner has completed Part I, II and III of this form
which will be sent to the Court at the same time that the petition for divorce or dissolution is filed.

Please read all parts of the form carefully.

If you agree with the arrangements and proposals for the children you should sign Part IV of the form.
Please use black ink. You should return the form to the petitioner, or his/her solicitor.

If you do not agree with all or some of the arrangements of proposals you will be given the opportunity of saying so when the petition for divorce or dissolution is served on you.

└───┘

Part 1 - Details of the children

Please read the instructions for boxes 1, 2 and 3 before you complete this section

1. **Children of both parties** *(Give details only of any children born to you and the Respondent or adopted by you both)*

	Forenames	Surname	Date of birth
(i)			
(ii)			
(iii)			
(iv)			
(v)			

2. **Other children of the family** *(Give details of any other children treated by both of you as children of the family: for example your own or the Respondent's)*

	Forenames	Surname	Date of birth	Relationship to Yourself	Respondent
(i)					
(ii)					
(iii)					
(iv)					
(v)					

3. **Other children who are not children of the family** *(Give details of any children born to you or the Respondent that have not been treated as children of the family or adopted by you both)*

	Forenames	Surname	Date of birth
(i)			
(ii)			
(iii)			
(iv)			
(v)			

Part II - Arrangements for the children of the family
This part of the form must be completed. Give details for each child if arrangements are different.
(if necessary, continue on another sheet and attach it to this form)

4.	**Home details**	*(please tick the appropriate boxes)*
(a)	The addresses at which the children now live	
(b)	Give details of the number of living rooms, bedrooms, etc. at the addresses in (a)	
(c)	Is the house rented or owned and by whom?	
	Is the rent or any mortgage being regularly paid?	☐ No ☐ Yes
(d)	Give the names of all other persons living with the children including your spouse/civil partner if he/she lives there. State their relationship to the children.	
(e)	Will there be any change in these arrangements?	☐ No ☐ Yes *(please give details)*

3

5.	**Education and training details**	*(please tick the appropriate boxes)*

(a) Give the names of the school, college or place of training attended by each child.	
(b) Do the children have any special educational needs?	☐ No ☐ Yes *(please give details)*
(c) Is the school, college or place of training, fee-paying?	☐ No ☐ Yes *(please give details of how much the fees are per term / year)*
Are fees being regularly paid?	☐ No ☐ Yes *(please give details)*
(d) Will there be any change in these arrangements?	☐ No ☐ Yes *(please give details)*

6.	**Childcare details**	*(please tick the appropriate boxes)*

(a) Which parent looks after the children from day to day? If responsibility is shared, please give details	
(b) Does that parent go out to work?	☐ No ☐ Yes *(please give details of his/her hour of work)*
(c) Does someone look after the children when the parent is not there?	☐ No ☐ Yes *(please give details)*
(d) Who looks after the children during school holidays?	
(e) Will there be any change in these arrangements?	☐ No ☐ Yes *(please give details)*

7.	**Maintenance**	*(please tick the appropriate boxes)*

(a) Does your spouse/civil partner pay towards the upkeep of the children? If there is another source of maintenance, please specify.	☐ No ☐ Yes *(please give details of how much)*
(b) Is the payment made under a court order?	☐ No ☐ Yes *(please give details, including the name of the court and the case number)*
(c) Is the payment following an assessment by the Child Support Agency?	☐ No ☐ Yes *(please give details of how much)*
(d) Has maintenance for the children been agreed?	☐ No ☐ Yes
(e) If not, will you be applying for: • a child maintenance order from the court	☐ No ☐ Yes
• child support maintenance through the Child Support Agency?	☐ No ☐ Yes

5

8.	**Details for contact with the children** *(please tick the appropriate boxes)*
(a) Do the children see your spouse/civil partner?	☐ No ☐ Yes *(please give details of how often and where)*
(b) Do the children ever stay with your spouse/civil partner?	☐ No ☐ Yes *(please give details of how much)*
(c) Will there be any change to these arrangements? Please give details of the proposed arrangements for contact and residence.	☐ No ☐ Yes *(please give details of how much)*

| 9. | **Details of health** *(please tick the appropriate boxes)* | | | | | |

| (a) Are the children generally in good health? | ☐ No | ☐ Yes | *(please give details of any serious disability or chronic illness)* |

| (b) Do the children have any special health needs? | ☐ No | ☐ Yes | *(please give details of the care needed and how it is to be provided)* |

| 10. | **Details of Care and other court proceedings** *(please tick the appropriate boxes)* | | | | | |

| (a) Are the children in the care of a local authority, or under the supervision of a social worker or probation officer? | ☐ No | ☐ Yes | *(please give details including any court proceedings)* |

| (b) Are any of the children on the Child Protection Register? | ☐ No | ☐ Yes | *(please give details of the local authority and the date of registration)* |

| (c) Are there or have there been any proceedings in any court involving the children, for example adoption, custody/residence, access/contact, wardship, care, supervision or maintenance?

(You need not include any Child Support Agency proceedings here) | ☐ No | ☐ Yes | *(please give details and send a copy of any order to the court)* |

Part III   To the Petitioner

Conciliation

If you and your spouse/civil partner do not agree about arrangements for the child(ren), would you agree to discuss the matter with a Conciliator and your spouse/civil partner?

☐ No   ☐ Yes

Declaration

I declare that the information I have given is correct and complete to the best of my knowledge.

Signed .... (Petitioner)

Date: ....

Part IV   To the Respondent

I agree with the arrangements and proposals contained in Part I and II of this form.

Signed .... (Respondent)

Date: ....

(C)   Form A (Application for ancillary relief)

Notice of [intention to proceed with] an Application for Ancillary Relief

In the	
	*[County Court] *[Principal Registry of the Family Division]

Case No. *Always quote this*	
Applicant's Solicitor's reference	
Respondent's Solicitor's reference	

(*delete as appropriate)

Respondents (Solicitor(s)) name and address

Postcode

Between   (petitioner)

and   (respondent)

Take Notice that

the Applicant intends;   *****to apply** to the Court for

*delete as appropriate   *****to proceed** with the application in the [petition][answer] for

                                  *****to apply to vary**:

☐ an order for maintenance pending suit or outcome of proceedings   ☐ a periodical payments order
☐ a secured provision order   ☐ a lump sum order
☐ a property adjustment order *(please provide address)*   ☐ a pension sharing order or a
                                                                            pension attachment order

If an application is made for any periodical payments or secured periodical payments for children:

*   and there is a written agreement made before 5 April 1993 about maintenance for the benefit of children,
    tick this box ☐
*   and there is a written agreement made on or after 5 April 1993 about maintenance for the benefit of children,
    tick this box ☐
*   but there is no agreement, tick any of the boxes below to show if you are applying for payment:
    *   ☐   for a stepchild or stepchildren
    *   ☐   in addition to child support maintenance already paid under a Child Support Agency assessment
    *   ☐   to meet expenses arising from a child's disability
    *   ☐   to meet expenses incurred by a child in being educated or training for work
    *   ☐   when either the child **or** the person with care of the child **or** the absent parent of the child
            is not habitually resident in the United Kingdom
    *   ☐   Other *(please state)*

Signed: Dated:

_____[Applicant/Solicitor for the Applicant]_____

The court office at

is open between 10 am and 4 pm (4.30pm at the Principal Registry of the Family Division) Monday to Friday. When corresponding with the court, please address forms or letters to the Court Manager and quote the case number. If you do not do so, your correspondence may be returned.

Form A Notice of [Intention to proceed with] an Application for Ancillary Relief (12.05)   HMCS

(D) Form E (Statement of property and income)

FINANCIAL STATEMENT OF	In the

In the

*[High/County Court]
*[Principal Registry of the Family Division]

Case No. *Always quote this*	
Petitioner's Solicitor's reference	
Respondent's Solicitor's reference	

*Husband/*Wife/*Civil partner

(*delete as apprpriate)

Between

	and	

Who is the *husband/*wife/*civil partner
*Petitioner/*Respondent in the
*divorce/*dissolution suit

Applicant in this matter

Who is the *husband/*wife/*civil partner
*Petitioner/*Respondent in the
*divorce/*dissolution suit

Respondent in this matter

Please fill in this form fully and accurately. Where any box is not applicable, write 'N/A'.

You have a duty to the court to give a full, frank and clear disclosure of all your financial and other relevant circumstances.

A failure to give full and accurate disclosure may result in any order the court makes being set aside.

If you are found to have been deliberately untruthful, criminal proceedings for perjury may be taken against you.

You must attach documents to the form where they are specifically sought and you may attach other documents where it is necessary to explain or clarify any of the information that you give.

Essential documents that must accompany this statement are detailed in the form.

If there is not enough room on the form for any particular piece of information, you may continue on an attached sheet of paper.

> If you are in doubt about how to complete any part of this form you should seek legal advice.
>
> This Statement must be sworn before a solicitor, a commissioner for oaths or an Officer of the Court or, if abroad, a notary or duly authorised official, before it is filed with the Court or sent to the other party (see last page).

This statement is filed by

Name and address of solicitor

Form E Financial Statement (12.05)   HMCS

1 General Information

1.1 Full name

1.2 Date of birth

Date	Month	Year

1.3 Date of the marriage/ civil partnership

Date	Month	Year

1.4 Occupation

1.5 Date of the separation

Date	Month	Year	Tick here if not applicable
			☐

1.6 Date of the

Petition			Decree nisi/Decree of judicial separation Conditional order/ Separation order			Decree absolute/ Final order (if applicable)		
Date	Month	Year	Date	Month	Year	Date	Month	Year

1.7 If you have subsequently married or formed a civil partnership, or will do so, state the date

Date	Month	Year

1.8 Are you co-habiting?   Yes ☐   No ☐

1.9 Do you intend to co-habit within the next six months?   Yes ☐   No ☐

1.10 Details of any children of the family

Full names	Date of birth			With whom does the child live?
	Date	Month	Year	

1.11 Details of the state of health of yourself and the children if you think this should be taken into account

Yourself	Children

2

1.12 Details of the present and proposed future educational arrangements for the children.

Present arrangements	Future arrangements

1.13 Details of any child support maintenance calculation or any maintenance order or agreement made in respect of any children of the family. If no calculation, order or agreement has been made, give an estimate of the liability of the non-resident parent in respect of the children of the family under the Child Support Act 1991.

1.14 If this application is to vary an order, attach a copy of the order and give details of the part that is to be varied and the changes sought. You may need to continue on a separate sheet.

1.15 Details of any other court cases between you and your spouse/civil partner, whether in relation to money, property, children or anything else.

Case No	Court

1.16 Your present residence and the occupants of it and on what terms you occupy it (e.g. tenant, owner-occupier).

Address	Occupants	Terms of occupation

2   Financial Details   *Part 1 Real Property and Personal Assets*

2.1 Complete this section in respect of the family home (the last family home occupied by you and your spouse/civil partner) if it remains unsold.

Documentation required for attachment to this section:

a)   A copy of any valuation of the property obtained within the last six months. If you cannot provide this document, please give your own realistic estimate of the current market value

b)   A recent mortgage statement confirming the sum outstanding on **each** mortgage

Property name and address	
Land Registry title number	
Mortgage company name(s) and address(es) and account number(s)	
Type of mortgage	
Details of who owns the property and the extent of your legal and beneficial interest in it (i.e. state if it is owned by you solely or jointly owned with your spouse/civil partner or with others)	
If you consider that the legal ownership as recorded at the Land Registry does not reflect the true position, state why	
Current market value of the property	
Balance outstanding on any mortgage(s)	
If a sale at this stage would result in penalties payable under the mortgage, state amount	
Estimate the costs of sale of the property	
Total equity in the property (i.e. market value less outstanding mortgage(s), penalties if any and the costs of sale)	

TOTAL value of your interest in the family home:
Total A   £

2.2 Details of your interest in any other property, land or buildings. Complete one page for each property you have an interest in.

Documentation required for attachment to this section:

a) A copy of any valuation of the property obtained within the last six months. If you cannot provide this document, please give your own realistic estimate of the current market value

b) A recent mortgage statement confirming the sum outstanding on **each** mortgage

Property name and address	
Land Registry title number	
Mortgage company name(s) and address(es) and account number(s)	
Type of mortgage	
Details of who owns the property and the extent of your legal and beneficial interest in it (i.e. state if it is owned by you solely or jointly owned with your spouse/civil partner or with others)	
If you consider that the legal ownership as recorded at the Land Registry does not reflect the true position, state why	
Current market value of the property	
Balance outstanding on any mortgage(s)	
If a sale at this stage would result in penalties payable under the mortgage, state amount	
Estimate the costs of sale of the property	
Total equity in the property (i.e. market value less outstanding mortgage(s), penalties if any and the costs of sale)	
Total value of your interest in this property	

TOTAL value of your interest in ALL other property:
Total B £

2.3 **Details of all personal bank, building society and National Savings Accounts that you hold or have held at any time in the last twelve months and which are or were either in your own name or in which you have or have had any interest. This applies whether any such account is in credit or in debit. For joint accounts give your interest and the name of the other account holder. If the account is overdrawn, show a minus figure.**

Documentation required for attachment to this section:

For each account listed, all statements covering the last 12 months.

Name of bank or building society, including branch name	Type of account *(e.g. current)*	Account number	Name of other account holder *(if applicable)*	Balance at the date of this statement	Total current value of your interest

TOTAL value of your interest in ALL accounts: (C1)	£ 0.00

2.4 **Details of all investments, including shares, PEPs, ISAs, TESSAs, National Savings Investments (other than already shown above), bonds, stocks, unit trusts, investment trusts, gilts and other quoted securities that you hold or have an interest in. (Do not include dividend income as this will be dealt with separately later on.)**

Documentation required for attachment to this section:

Latest statement or dividend counterfoil relating to each investment.

Name	Type of Investment	Size of Holding	Current value	Name of any other account holder *(if applicable)*	Total current value of your interest

TOTAL value of your interest in ALL holdings: (C2)	£ 0.00

2.5 **Details of all life insurance policies including endowment policies that you hold or have an interest in. Include those that do not have a surrender value. Complete one page for each policy.**

Documentation required for attachment to this section:
A surrender valuation of each policy that has a surrender value.

Name of company			
Policy type			
Policy number			
If policy is assigned, state in whose favour and amount of charge			
Name of any other owner and the extent of your interest in the policy			
Maturity date *(if applicable)*	Date	Month	Year
Current surrender value *(if applicable)*			
If policy includes life insurance, the amount of the insurance and the name of the person whose life is insured			
Total current surrender value of your interest in this policy			

TOTAL value of your interest in ALL policies: (C3) £

2.6 **Details of all monies that are OWED TO YOU. Do not include sums owed in director's or partnership accounts which should be included at section 2.11.**

Brief description of money owed and by whom	Balance outstanding	Total current value of your interest

TOTAL value of your interest in ALL debts owed to you: (C4) £   0.00

2.7 Details of all cash sums held in excess of £500. You must state where it is held and the currency it is held in.

Where held	Amount	Currency	Total current value of your interest
TOTAL value of your interest in ALL cash sums: (C5)			£ 0.00

2.8 Details of personal belongings individually worth more than £500.

INCLUDE:
- Cars (gross value)
- Collections, pictures and jewellery
- Furniture and house contents

Brief description of item	Total current value of your interest
TOTAL value of your interest in ALL personal belongings: (C6)	£
Add together all the figures in boxes C1 to C6 to give the TOTAL current value of your interest in personal assets: TOTAL C	£ 0.00

2   Financial Details   *Part 2   Capital: Liabilities and Capital Gains Tax*

2.9   Details of any liabilities you have.

EXCLUDE liabilities already shown such as:
- **Mortgages**
- **Any overdrawn bank, building society or National Savings accounts**

INCLUDE:
- **Money owed on credit cards and store cards**
- **Bank loans**
- **Hire purchase agreements**

List all credit and store cards held including those with a nil or positive balance. Where the liability is not solely your own, give the name(s) of the other account holder(s) and the amount of your share of the liability.

Liability	Name(s) of other account holder(s) *(if applicable)*	Total liability	Total current value of your interest in the liability
TOTAL value of your interest in ALL liabilities: (D1)			£

2.10   If any Capital Gains Tax would be payable on the disposal now of any of your real property or personal assets, give your estimate of the tax liability.

Asset	Total Capital Gains Tax liability
TOTAL value of ALL your potential Capital Gains Tax liabilities: (D2)	£
Add together D1 and D2 to give the TOTAL value of your liabilities: TOTAL D	£ 0.00

2   Financial Details   *Part 3 Capital: Business assets and directorships*

2.11 Details of all your business interests. Complete one page for each business you have an interest in.

Documentation required for attachment to this section:
a)   Copies of the business accounts for the last two financial years
b)   Any documentation, if available at this stage, upon which you have based your estimate of the current value of your interest in this business, for example a letter from an accountant or a formal valuation. It is not essential to obtain a formal valuation at this stage

Name of the business	
Briefly describe the nature of the business	
Are you *(Please delete all those that are not applicable)*	a) Sole trader b) Partner in a partnership with others c) Shareholder in a limited company
If you are a partner or a shareholder, state the extent of your interest in the business **(i.e. partnership share or the extent of your shareholding compared to the overall shares issued)**	
State when your next set of accounts will be available	
If any of the figures in the last accounts are not an accurate reflection of the current position, state why. **For example, if there has been a material change since the last accounts, or if the valuations of the assets are not a true reflection of their value (e.g. because property or other assets have not been re-valued in recent years or because they are shown at a book value)**	
Total amount of any sums owed to you by the business by way of a director's loan account, partnership capital or current accounts or the like. Identify where these appear in the business accounts	
Your estimate of the current value of your business interest. Explain briefly the basis upon which you have reached that figure	
Your estimate of any Capital Gains Tax that would be payable if you were to dispose of your business now	
Net value of your interest in this business after any Capital Gains Tax liability	

TOTAL value of ALL your interests in business assets: TOTAL E | £ |

2.12 List any directorships you hold or have held in the last 12 months (other than those already disclosed in Section 2.11).

2   Financial Details   *Part 4 Capital: Pensions*

2.13 Give details of all your pension rights. Complete a separate page for each pension.

EXCLUDE:
- **Basic State Pension**

INCLUDE (complete a separate page for each one):
- **Additional State Pension (SERPS and State Second Pension (S2P))**
- **Free Standing Additional Voluntary Contribution Schemes (FSAVC) separate from the scheme of your employer**
- **Membership of ALL pension plans or schemes**

Documentation required for attachment to this section:

a) A recent statement showing the cash equivalent transfer value (CETV) provided by the trustees or managers of each pension arrangement (or, in the case of the additional state pension, a valuation of these rights)

b) If any valuation is not available, give the estimated date when it will be available and attach a copy of your letter to the pension company or administrators from whom the information was sought and/or state the date on which an application for a valuation of a State Earnings Related Pension Scheme was submitted to the Department of Work and Pensions

Name and address of pension arrangement	
Your National Insurance Number	
Number of pension arrangement or reference number	
Type of scheme e.g. occupational or personal, final salary, money purchase, additional state pension or other (if other, please give details)	
Date the CETV was calculated	
Is the pension in payment or drawdown or deferment? *(Please answer Yes or No)*	
State the cash equivalent transfer value (CETV) quotation, or in the additional state pension, the valuation of those rights **If the arrangement is an occupational pension arrangement that is paying reduced CETVs, please quote what the CETV would have been if not reduced. If this is not possible, please indicate if the CETV quoted is a reduced CETV**	

TOTAL value of ALL your pension assets: TOTAL F   £

2   Financial Details   *Part 5   Capital: Other assets*

2.14 Give details of any other assets not listed in Parts 1 to 4 above.

INCLUDE (the following list is not exhaustive):
- **Any personal or business assets not yet disclosed**
- **Unrealisable assets**
- **Share option schemes, stating the estimated net sale proceeds of the shares if the options were capable of exercise now, and whether Capital Gains Tax or income tax would be payable**
- **Business expansion schemes**
- **Futures**
- **Commodities**
- **Trust interests (including interests under a discretionary trust), stating your estimate of the value of the interest and when it is likely to become realisable. If you say it will never be realisable, or has no value, give your reasons**
- **Any asset that is likely to be received in the foreseeable future**
- **Any asset held on your behalf by a third party**
- **Any asset not disclosed elsewhere on this form even if held outside England and Wales**

You are reminded of your obligation to disclose all your financial assets and interests of ANY nature.

Type of asset	Value	Total NET value of your interest

TOTAL value of ALL your other assets: TOTAL G	£	

13

2   Financial Details   *Part 6   Income: Earned income from employment*

2.15 Details of earned income from employment. Complete one page for each employment.

Documentation required for attachment to this section:

a)   P60 for the last financial year (you should have received this from your employer shortly after the last 5th April)

b)   Your last three payslips

c)   Your last Form P11D if you have been issued with one

Name and address of your employer	
Job title and brief details of the type of work you do	
Hours worked per week in this employment	
How long have you been with this employer?	
Explain the basis of your income i.e. state whether it is based on an annual salary or an hourly rate of pay and whether it includes commissions or bonuses	
Gross income for the last financial year as shown on your P60	
Net income for the last financial year i.e. gross income less income tax and national insurance	
Average net income for the last three months i.e. total income less income tax and national insurance divided by three	
Briefly explain any other entries on the attached payslips other than basic income, income tax and national insurance	
If the payslips attached for the last three months are not an accurate reflection of your normal income briefly explain why	
Details and value of any bonuses or other occasional payments that you receive from this employment not otherwise already shown, including the basis upon which they are paid	
Details and value of any benefits in kind, perks or other remuneration received from this employer in the last year (e.g. provision of a car, payment of travel, accommodation, meal expenses, etc.)	
Your estimate of your net income from this employment for the next 12 months. If this differs significantly from your current income explain why in box 4.1.2	

Estimated TOTAL of ALL net earned income from employment for the next 12 months: TOTAL H   £

14

2   Financial Details   *Part 7   Income: Income from self-employment or partnership*

2.16 You will have already given details of your business and provided the last two years accounts at section 2.11. Complete this section giving details of your income from your business. Complete one page for each business.

Documentation required for attachment to this section:

a)   A copy of your last tax assessment or, if that is not available, a letter from your accountant confirming your tax liability

b)   If net income from the last financial year and estimated net income for the next 12 months is significantly different, a copy of management accounts for the period since your last account

Name of the business	
Date to which your last accounts were completed	
Your share of gross business profit from the last completed accounts	
Income tax and national insurance payable on your share of gross business profit above	
Net income for that year (using the two figures directly above, gross business profit less income tax and national insurance payable)	
Details and value of any benefits in kind, perks or other remuneration received from this business in the last year **e.g. provision of a car, payment of travel, accommodation, meal expenses, etc.**	
Amount of any regular monthly or other drawings that you take from this business	
If the estimated figure directly below is different from the net income as at the end date of the last completed accounts, briefly explain the reason(s)	
Your estimate of your net annual income for the next 12 months	

Estimated **TOTAL** of **ALL** net income from self-employment or partnership for the next 12 months: **TOTAL I**	£

2   Financial Details   *Part 8 Income: Income from investments*
e.g. dividends, interest or rental income

2.17 Details of income received in the last financial year (the year ended last 5th April), and your estimate of your income for the current financial year. Indicate whether the income was paid gross or net of income tax. You are not required to calculate any tax payable that may arise.

Nature of income and the asset from which it derived	Paid gross or net	Income received in the last financial year	Estimated income for the next 12 months

Estimated TOTAL investment income for the next 12 months: TOTAL J | £

16

2   Financial Details   *Part 9 Income: Income from state benefits (including state pension and child benefit)*

2.18 Details of all state benefits that you are currently receiving.

Name of benefit	Amount paid	Frequency of payment	Estimated income for the next 12 months

Estimated TOTAL benefit income for the next 12 months: TOTAL K £

17

2   Financial Details   *Part 10 Income: Any other income*

2.19 Details of any other income not disclosed above.

INCLUDE:
- Any source from which income has been received during the last 12 months (even if it has now ceased)
- Any source from which income is likely to be received during the next 12 months

You are reminded of your obligation to give full disclosure of your financial circumstances.

Nature of income	Paid gross or net	Income received in the last financial year	Estimated income for the next 12 months

Estimated TOTAL other income for the next 12 months: TOTAL L £

2   Financial Details *Summaries*

2.20 Summary of your capital (Parts 1 to 5).

Description	Reference of the section on this statement	Value
Current value of your interest in the family home	A	
Current value of your interest in all other property	B	
Current value of your interest in personal assets	C	
Current value of your liabilities	D	
Current value of your interest in business assets	E	
Current value of your pension assets	F	
Current value of all your other assets	G	

TOTAL value of your assets (Totals A to G less D): £   0.00

2.21 Summary of your estimated income for the next 12 months (Parts 6 to 10).

Description	Reference of the section on this statement	Value
Estimated net total of income from employment	H	
Estimated net total of income from self-employment or partnership	I	
Estimated net total of investment income	J	
Estimated state benefit receipts	K	
Estimated net total of all other income	L	

Estimated TOTAL income for the next 12 months (Totals H to L): £   0.00

19

3   Financial Requirements   *Part 1 Income needs*

3.1   Income needs for yourself and for any children living with you or provided for by you. ALL figures should be annual, monthly or weekly (state which). You *must not* use a combination of these periods. State your current income needs and, if these are likely to change in the near future, explain the anticipated change and give an estimate of the future cost.

The income needs below are: *(delete those not applicable)*	Weekly	Monthly	Annual
I anticipate my income needs are going to change because			

3.1.1 Income needs for yourself.

INCLUDE:
- All income needs for yourself
- Income needs for any children living with you or provided for by you only if these form part of your total income needs (e.g. housing, fuel, car expenses, holidays, etc)

Item	Current cost	Estimated future cost
SUB-TOTAL your income needs:	£	

3.1.2 Income needs for children living with you or provided for by you.

INCLUDE:
- Only those income needs that are different to those of your household shown above

Item	Current cost	Estimated future cost
SUB-TOTAL children's income needs:	£	
TOTAL of ALL income needs:	£	0.00

3   Financial Requirements   *Part 2   Capital needs*

3.2   Set out below the reasonable future capital needs for yourself and for any children living with you or provided for by you.

3.2.1 Capital needs for yourself.

INCLUDE:
- **All capital needs for yourself**
- **Capital needs for any children living with you or provided for by you only if these form part of your total capital needs (e.g. housing, car, etc.)**

Item	Cost
SUB-TOTAL your capital needs:	£

3.2.2 Capital needs for children living with you or provided for by you.

INCLUDE:
- **Only those capital needs that are different to those of your household shown above**

Item	Cost
SUB-TOTAL your children's capital needs:	£
TOTAL of ALL capital needs:	£ 0.00

4   Other Information

4.1 Details of any significant changes in your assets or income.

At both sections 4.1.1 and 4.1.2, INCLUDE:
- ALL assets held both within and outside England and Wales
- The disposal of any asset

4.1.1 Significant changes in assets or income during the LAST 12 months.

4.1.2 Significant changes in assets or income likely to occur during the NEXT 12 months.

4.2 Brief details of the standard of living enjoyed by you and your spouse/civil partner during the marriage/ civil partnership.

4.3 Are there any particular contributions to the family property and assets or outgoings, or to family life, or the welfare of the family that have been made by you, your partner or anyone else that you think should be taken into account? If there are any such items, briefly describe the contribution and state the amount, when it was made and by whom.

INCLUDE:
- Contributions already made
- Contributions that will be made in the foreseeable future

4.4 Bad behaviour or conduct by the other party will only be taken into account in very exceptional circumstances when deciding how assets should be shared after divorce/dissolution. If you feel it should be taken into account in your case, identify the nature of the behaviour or conduct below.

4.5 Give details of any other circumstances that you consider could significantly affect the extent of the financial provision to be made by or for you or any child of the family.

INCLUDE (the following list is not exhaustive):
- Earning capacity
- Disability
- Inheritance prospects
- Redundancy
- Retirement
- Any plans to marry, form a civil partnership or cohabit
- Any contingent liabilities

4.6 **If you have subsequently married or formed a civil partnership (or intend to) or are living with another person (or intend to), give brief details, so far as they are known to you, of his or her income, assets and liabilities.**

Annual Income		Assets and Liabilities	
Nature of income	Value (if known, state whether gross or net))	Item	Value (if known)
	Total income: £		**Total assets/liabilities:** £

24

5   Order Sought

5.1   **If you are able at this stage, specify what kind of orders you are asking the court to make.**
Even if you cannot be specific at this stage, if you are able to do so, indicate:

a)   If the family home is still owned, whether you are asking for it to be transferred to yourself or your spouse/civil partner or whether you are saying it should be sold

b)   Whether you consider this is a case for continuing spousal maintenance/maintenance for your civil partner or whether you see the case as being appropriate for a "clean break". *(A 'clean break' means a settlement or order which provides amongst other things, that neither you nor your spouse/civil partner will have any further claim against the income or capital of the other party. A 'clean break' does not terminate the responsibility of a parent to a child.)*

c)   Whether you are seeking a pension sharing or pension attachment order

d)   If you are seeking a transfer or settlement of any property or assets, identify the property or assets in question

5.2   **If you are seeking a variation of an ante-nuptial or post-nuptial settlement or a relevant settlement made during, or in anticipation of, a civil partnership, identify the settlement, by whom it was made, its trustees and beneficiaries and state why you allege it is a settlement which the court can vary.**

5.3   **If you are seeking an avoidance of disposition order, or if you have already applied for such an order, identify the property to which the disposition relates and the person or body in whose favour the disposition is alleged to have been made.**

25

Sworn confirmation of the information

I   _____   *(the above-named Applicant/Respondent)*

         _____   MAKE OATH and confirm that the information
of   given above is a full, frank, clear and accurate
         _____   disclosure of my financial and other relevant
                                     circumstances.

Sworn by the above named

)
at   )
)
)
this   day of   20   )   ....

                          Before me, ...

                                     A solicitor, commissioner for oaths,
                                     an Officer of the Court appointed by the
                                     Judge to take affidavits, a notary or duly
                                     authorised official.

Address all communications to the Court Manager of the Court and quote the case number.
If you do not quote this number, your correspondence may be returned.

26

SCHEDULE OF DOCUMENTS TO ACCOMPANY FORM E

The following list shows the documents you must attach to your Form E if applicable. You may attach other documents where it is necessary to explain or clarify any of the information that you give in the Form E.

Form E paragraph	Document	Please tick		
		Attached	Not applicable	To follow
1.14	**Application to vary an order:** if applicable, attach a copy of the relevant order.			
2.1	**Matrimonial home valuation:** a copy of any valuation relating to the matrimonial home that has been obtained in the last six months.			
2.1	**Matrimonial home mortgage(s):** a recent mortgage statement in respect of each mortgage on the matrimonial home confirming the amount outstanding.			
2.2	**Any other property:** a copy of any valuation relating to each other property disclosed that has been obtained in the last six months.			
2.2	**Any other property:** a recent mortgage statement in respect of each mortgage on each other property disclosed confirming the amount outstanding.			
2.3	**Personal bank, building society and National Savings accounts:** copies of statements for the last 12 months for each account that has been held in the last twelve months, either in your own name or in which you have or have had any interest.			
2.4	**Other investments:** the latest statement or dividend counterfoil relating to each investment as disclosed in paragraph 2.4.			
2.5	**Life insurance (including endowment) policies:** a surrender valuation for each policy that has a surrender value as disclosed under paragraph 2.5.			
2.11	**Business interests:** a copy of the business accounts for the last two financial years for each business interest disclosed.			
2.11	**Business interests:** any documentation that is available to confirm the estimate of the current value of the business, for example, a letter from an accountant or formal valuation if that has been obtained.			
2.13	**Pension rights:** a recent statement showing the cash equivalent transfer value (CETV) provided by the trustees or managers of each pension arrangement that you have disclosed (or, in the case of the additional state pension, a valuation of these rights). If not yet available, attach a copy of the letter sent to the pension company or administrators requesting the information.			
2.15	**Employment income:** your P60 for the last financial year in respect of each employment that you have.			
2.15	**Employment income:** your last three payslips in respect of each employment that you have.			
2.15	**Employment income:** your last form P11D if you have been issued with one.			
2.16	**Self-employment or partnership income:** a copy of your last tax assessment or if that is not available, a letter from your accountant confirming your tax liability.			
2.16	**Self-employment or partnership income:** if net income from the last financial year and the estimated income for the next twelve months is significantly different, a copy of the management accounts for the period since your last accounts.			
State relevant Form E paragraph	Description of other documents attached:			

Case no.

In the

*[High/County Court]
*[Principal Registry of the Family Division]

In the marriage/Civil Partnership between

who is the husband/wife/civil partner

and

who is the husband/wife/civil partner

_____

Financial Statement on behalf of

who is the husband/wife/civil partner
and the Petitioner/Respondent in the
divorce/dissolution suit

_____

This statement is filed by

who are solicitors for the husband/wife/civil partner

Form E Financial Statement (12.05)   HMCS

(E) Form M1 (Statement of information)

In the

[County Court]*

[Principal Registry of the Family Division]*

*Delete as appropriate or amend if the proceedings are pending in the High Court

No. of matter

| Between | _____ | Petitioner | *Solicitor's ref* _____ |
| and | _____ | Respondent | *Solicitor's ref* _____ |

Statement of information for a consent order

Duration of Marriage or Civil Partnership

In the case of a marriage: Give the date of your marriage and the date of the decree absolute (if pronounced).
In the case of a civil partnership: Give the date of the formation of the civil partnership and the date of the final order (if made).

Ages of parties

Give the age of any minor (i.e. under the age of 18) or dependant child(ren) of the family.

Petitioner _____   Respondent _____

Child(ren) _____ _____ _____ _____ _____ _____

Summary of means

Give, as at the date this statement is signed overleaf:

(1) the approximate amount or value of **capital resources**. If there is a property give its net equity and details of the proposed distribution of the equity.

(2) the **net income** of the petitioner and respondent and, where relevant, of minor or dependant child(ren) of the family.

(3) the value of any benefits under a **pension arrangement** which you have, or are likely to have, including the most recent valuation (if any) provided by the pension scheme.

Note: if the application is only made for an order for interim periodical payments, or for variation of an order for periodical payments, you only need to give details of 'net income'.

	(1) **Capital Resources** *(less any unpaid mortgage or charge)*	(2) **Net Income**	(3) **Pension**
Petitioner			
Respondent			
Children			

Where the parties and the children will live

Give details of the arrangements which are intended for the accommodation of each of the parties and any minor or dependant child(ren) of the family.

Future plans

Please tick a box and, if appropriate, give the date of the marriage or formation of the civil partnership, if you know it.

	No intention to marry, form a civil partnership, or cohabit at present	Has remarried or formed a civil partnership	Intends to marry or form a civil partnership	Intends to cohabit with another person
Petitioner	☐	☐ Date of marriage or formation of civil partnership:	☐ Date of marriage or formation of civil partnership:	☐
Respondent	☐	☐ Date of marriage or formation of civil partnership:	☐ Date of marriage or formation of civil partnership:	☐

D81 Statement of information for a consent order (Family Proceedings Rules) (12.05)   HMCS

Notice to Mortgagee

These questions are to be answered by the applicant where the terms of the order provide for a transfer of property.

Has every mortgagee (if any) of the property been served with notice of the application?   Yes ☐   No ☐

Has any objection to a transfer of property been made by any mortgagee, within **14** days from the date when the notice of the application was served?   Yes ☐   No ☐

Notice to Pension Arrangement

These questions are to be answered by the applicant where the terms of an order include provision for a pension attachment order.

Has every person responsible for any pension arrangement been served with notice of the application and notice under Rule 2.70(7)(a) to (d) of the Family Proceedings Rules 1991?   Yes ☐   No ☐

Has any objection to an order under –
(i) section 23 of the Matrimonial Causes Act 1973 which includes provision by virtue of section 25B and section 25C of that Act; or
(ii) Part 1 of Schedule 5 to the Civil Partnership Act 2004 which includes provision by virtue of paragraphs 25 and 26 of Schedule 5 to that Act
– (as the case may be) been made by a Trustee or Manager within **21** days from the date when the notice of the application was served?   Yes ☐   No ☐

Pension Sharing on Divorce or Dissolution

These questions are to be answered by the applicant where the terms of the order include provision for a pension sharing order.

Has the Pension Arrangement furnished the information required by Regulation 4 of the Pensions on Divorce etc. (Provisions of Information) Regulations 2000?   Yes ☐   No ☐

Does it appear from that information that there is power to make an order including provision under section 24B of the Matrimonial Causes Act 1973 or under paragraph 15 of Schedule 5 to the Civil Partnership Act 2004 (Pension Sharing)?   Yes ☐   No ☐

Other information

Give details of any other especially significant matters.

Signed

[Solicitor for] Petitioner

Date

[Solicitor for] Respondent

Date

(F) Parental responsibility agreement (1)

Parental Responsibility Agreement
Section 4(1)(b) Children Act 1989

Keep this form in a safe place
*Date recorded at the Principal Registry
of the Family Division:*

**Read the notes on the other side
before you make this agreement.**

This is a Parental Responsibility Agreement regarding

the Child   *Full Name* _____

_____	_____	_____
Boy or Girl	*Date of birth*	*Date of 18th birthday*

Between

the Mother   *Name* _____

                        Address

and   the Father   *Name* _____

                        Address

We declare that   we are the mother and father of the above child and we agree that the child's father shall have
parental responsibility for the child (in addition to the mother having parental responsibility).

_____	_____
Signed **(Mother)**	Signed **(Father)**
_____	_____
Date	Date

**Certificate
of witness**

The following evidence of identity was produced by the person signing above:	The following evidence of identity was produced by the person signing above:
_____	_____
Signed in the presence of: *Name of Witness*	Signed in the presence of: *Name of Witness*
_____	_____
Address	*Address*
_____	_____
Signature of Witness	*Signature of Witness*
[A Justice of the Peace] [Justices' Clerk] [An assistant to a justices' clerk] [An officer of the court authorised by the judge to administer oaths]	[A Justice of the Peace] [Justices' Clerk] [An assistant to a justices' clerk] [An Officer of the Court authorised by the judge to administer oaths]

Notes about the Parental Responsibility Agreement

Read these notes before you make the agreement.

About the Parental Responsibility Agreement

The making of this agreement will affect the legal position of the mother and the father. You should both seek legal advice before you make the Agreement. You can obtain the name and address of a solicitor from the Children Panel (020 7242 1222)

or from   • your local family proceedings court, or county court

            • a Citizens Advice Bureau

            • a Law Centre

            • a local library.

You may be eligible for public funding.

When you fill in the Agreement

Please use black ink (the Agreement will be copied). Put the name of one child only. If the father is to have parental responsibility for more than one child, fill in a separate form for each child. **Do not sign the Agreement.**

When you have filled in the Agreement

Take it to a local family proceedings court, or county court, or the Principal Registry of the Family Division (the address is below).

A justice of the peace, a justices' clerk, an assistant to a justices' clerk, or a court official who is authorised by the judge to administer oaths, will witness your signature and he or she will sign the certificate of the witness. **A solicitor cannot witness your signature.**

To the mother: When you make the declaration you will have to prove that you are the child's mother so take to the court the child's full birth certificate.

            You will also need evidence of your identity showing a photograph and signature (for example, a photocard, official pass or passport). **Please note that the child's birth certificate cannot be accepted as sufficient proof of your identity.**

To the father: You will need evidence of your identity showing a photograph and signature (for example, a photocard, official pass or passport).

When the Certificate has been signed and witnessed

Make 2 copies of the Agreement form. You do not need to copy these notes.

Take, or send, this form and the copies to **The Principal Registry of the Family Division, First Avenue House, 42-49 High Holborn, London, WC1V 6NP.**

The Registry will record the Agreement and keep this form. The copies will be stamped and sent back to each parent at the address on the Agreement. The Agreement will not take effect until it has been received and recorded at the Principal Registry of the Family Division.

Ending the Agreement

Once a parental responsibility agreement has been made it can only end

            • by an order of the court made on the application of any person who has parental responsibility for the child

            • by an order of the court made on the application of the child with permission of the court

            • When the child reaches the age of 18.

C(PRA1) (Notes) (12.05)

(G) Parental responsibility agreement (2)

Step-Parent Parental Responsibility Agreement
Section 4A(1)(a) Children Act 1989

Keep this form in a safe place
Date recorded at the Principal Registry of the Family Division:

Read the notes on the other side before you make this agreement.

This is a Step-Parent Parental Responsibility Agreement regarding

the Child	Full Name _____

Boy or Girl	Date of birth	Date of 18th birthday

Between
Parent A

Name

Address

and
*the other parent
(with parental
responsibility)

Name

Address

and
the step-parent

Name

Address

We declare that we are the parents and step-parent of the above child and we agree that the above mentioned step-parent shall have parental responsibility for the child (in addition to those already having parental responsibility).

Signed (Parent A)	*Signed (Other Parent)	Signed (Step-Parent)
Date	Date	Date

Certificate of witness

The following evidence of identity was produced by the person signing above:	The following evidence of identity was produced by the person signing above:	The following evidence of identity was produced by the person signing above:
Signed in the presence of: Name of Witness	Signed in the presence of: Name of Witness	Signed in the presence of: Name of Witness
Address	Address	Address
Signature of Witness	Signature of Witness	Signature of Witness
[A Justice of the Peace] [Justices' Clerk] [An assistant to a justices' clerk] [An Officer of the Court authorised by the judge to administer oaths]	[A Justice of the Peace] [Justices' Clerk] [An assistant to a justices' clerk] [An Officer of the Court authorised by the judge to administer oaths]	[A Justice of the Peace] [Justices' Clerk] [An assistant to a justices' clerk] [An Officer of the Court authorised by the judge to administer oaths]

*If there is only one parent with parental responsibility, please delete this section.

C(PRA2) (12.05)

HMCS

Notes about the Step-Parent Parental Responsibility Form

Read these notes before you make the Agreement

About the Step-Parent Parental Responsibility Agreement

The making of this agreement will affect the legal position of the parent(s) and the step-parent. You should seek legal advice before you make the Agreement. You can obtain the name and address of a solicitor from the Children Panel (020 7242 1222) or from:

- your local family proceedings court, or county court,
- a Citizens Advice Bureau,
- a Law Centre,
- a local library.

You may be eligible for public funding.

When you fill in the Agreement

Please use black ink (the Agreement will be copied). Put the name of one child only. If the step-parent is to have parental responsibility for more than one child, fill in a separate form for each child. **Do not sign the Agreement.**

When you have filled in the Agreement

Take it to a local family proceedings court, or county court, or the Principal Registry of the Family Division (the address is below).

A justice of the peace, a justices' clerk, an assistant to a justices' clerk, or a court official who is authorised by the judge to administer oaths, will witness your signature and he or she will sign the certificate of the witness. **A solicitor cannot witness your signature.**

To Parent A and the Other Parent with parental responsibility:

When you make the declaration you will have to prove that you have parental responsibility for the child. You should therefore take with you to the court one of the following documents:

- the child's full birth certificate and a marriage certificate to show that the parents were married to each other at the time of birth or subsequently,
- a court order granting parental responsibility,
- a registered Parental Responsibility Agreement Form between the child's mother and father,
- if the birth was registered after the 1 December 2003, the child's full birth certificate showing that the parents jointly registered the child's birth.

C(PRA2) (Notes) (12.05)

You will also require evidence of your (both parents') identity showing a photograph and signature (for example, a photocard, official pass or passport) **(Please note that the child's birth certificate cannot be accepted as sufficient proof of your identity.)**

To the step-parent: When you make the declaration you will have to prove that you are married to, or the civil partner of, a parent of the child so take to the court your marriage certificate or certificate of civil partnership.

You will also need evidence of your identity showing a photograph and signature (for example, a photocard, official pass or passport).

When the Certificate has been signed and witnessed

Make sufficient copies of the Agreement Form for each person who has signed the form. You do not need to copy these notes.

Take, or send, the original form and the copies to: **The Principal Registry of the Family Division, First Avenue House, 42-49 High Holborn, London, WC1V 6NP.**

The Registry will record the Agreement and retain the original form. The copies will be stamped with the seal of the court and sent back to every person with parental responsibility who has signed the Agreement Form and to the step-parent. The Agreement will not take effect until it has been received and recorded at the Principal Registry of the Family Division.

Ending the Agreement

Once a step-parent parental responsibility agreement has been made it can only end:

- by an order of the court made on the application of any person who has parental responsibility for the child,
- by an order of the court made on the application of the child with permission of the court,
- when the child reaches the age of 18.

Application for an order

Children Act 1989

Form C1

The court	To be completed by the court
	Date issued
	Case number
The full name(s) of the child(ren)	Child(ren)'s number(s)

Important Note

You should only answer question 7 if you are asking the court to make one of the following orders:
a Contact Order, a Residence Order, a Prohibited Steps Order, a Specific Issue Order or a Parental Responsibility Order.

---

1 About you (the person completing this form known as 'the applicant')

State:
- *your title, full name, address, telephone number, date of birth and relationship to each child above*
- *your solicitor's name, address, reference, telephone, FAX and DX numbers.*

2 The child(ren) and the order(s) you are applying for

For each child state:
- *the full name, date of birth and sex*
- *the type of order(s) you are applying for (for example, residence order, contact order, supervision order).*

3   Other cases which concern the child(ren)

If there have ever been, or there are pending, any court cases which concern:
- *a child whose name you have put in paragraph 2*
- *a full, half or step brother or sister of a child whose name you have put in paragraph 2*
- *a person in this case who is or has been, involved in caring for a child whose name you have put in paragraph 2*

attach a copy of the relevant order and give:
- *the name of the court*
- *the name and contact address (if known) of the children's guardian, if appointed*
- *the name and contact address (if known) of the children and family reporter, if appointed*
- *the name and contact address (if known) of the welfare officer, if appointed*
- *the name and contact address (if known) of the solicitor appointed for the child(ren).*

4   The respondent(s)

Appendix 3 Family Proceedings Rules 1991; Schedule 2 Family Proceedings Courts (Children Act 1989) Rules 1991

For each respondent state:
- *the title, full name and address*
- *the date of birth (if known) or the age*
- *the relationship to each child.*

C1

5 Others to whom notice is to be given

Appendix 3 Family Proceedings Rules 1991; Schedule 2 Family Proceedings Courts (Children Act 1989) Rules 1991

For each person state:
- *the title, full name and address*
- *the date of birth (if known) or the age*
- *the relationship to each child.*

6 The care of the child(ren)

For each child in paragraph 2 state:
- *the child's current address and how long the child has lived there*
- *whether it is the child's usual address and who cares for the child there*
- *the child's relationship to the other children (if any).*

7 Domestic abuse, violence or harm

Do you believe that the child(ren) named above have suffered or are at risk of suffering any harm from any of the following:
- *any form of domestic abuse*
- *violence within the household*
- *child abduction*
- *other conduct or behaviour*

by any person who is or has been involved in caring for the child(ren) or lives with, or has contact with, the child(ren)?

Please tick the box which applies   Yes ☐   No ☐

If you tick the Yes box, you must *also fill in Supplemental Information Form (form C1A).* You can obtain a copy of this from a court office if one has not been enclosed with the papers served on you.

C1

3

8 Social Services

For each child in paragraph 2 state:
- *whether the child is known to the Social Services. If so, give the name of the social worker and the address of the Social Services department.*
- *whether the child is, or has been, on the Child Protection Register. If so, give details of registration.*

9 The education and health of the child(ren)

For each child state:
- *the name of the school, college or place of training which the child attends*
- *whether the child is in good health. Give details of any serious disabilities or ill health.*
- *whether the child has any special needs.*

10 The parents of the child(ren)

For each child state:
- *the full name of the child's parents*
- *whether the parents are, or have been, married to each other or civil partners of each other*
- *whether the parents live together. If so, where.*
- *whether, to your knowledge, either of the parents have been involved in a court case concerning a child. If so, give the date and the name of the court.*

C1

4

11 The family of the child(ren) (other children)

*For any other child not already mentioned in the family (for example, a brother or half sister)
state:*
- *the full name and address*
- *the date of birth (if known) or age*
- *the relationship of the child to you.*

12 Other adults

State:
- *the full name of any other adults (for example, lodgers) who live at the same address as any child named in paragraph 2*
- *whether they live there all the time*
- *whether, to your knowledge, the adult has been involved in a court case concerning a child. If so, give the date and the name of the court.*

13 Your reason(s) for applying and any plans for the child(ren)

State briefly your reasons for applying and what you want the court to order.
- ***Do not** give a full statement if you are applying for an order under Section 8 of Children Act 1989. You may be asked to provide a full statement later.*
- ***Do not** complete this section if this form is accompanied by a supplementary form.*

C1

14 Attending the court

State:
- *whether you will need an interpreter at court. If so, please indicate what language interpreter you will use. If you require an interpreter you must notify the court immediately so that one can be arranged.*
- *whether you have a disability for which you require special assistance or special facilities. If so, please say what your needs are. The court staff will get in touch with you about your requirements.*

15 Parenting Information – Arrangements after Separation

	Yes	No
Have you received a Parenting Plan booklet? *(If No, you may obtain a copy from a court office, a citizen's advice bureau or other family advice service.)*	☐	☐
Have you agreed to a Parenting Plan? *(If Yes, please include a copy of the Plan when you send your application to the court)*	☐	☐
If you did agree a Parenting Plan, has the Plan broken down?	☐	☐

If Yes, please explain briefly why the Plan broke down –

Signed   Date
(Applicant)

C1

(I) Form C1A (Supplemental information)

Supplemental Information Form	Form C1A

Children Act 1989

The court	To be completed by the court
	Date issued
	Case number
The full name(s) of the child(ren)	Child(ren)'s number(s)

Important Note
Please read the C1A Notes for Guidance before completing this form.

Section 1   About you (the person completing this form)

1   **Personal details**

Full Name (including any title):

Date of Birth:

*Do not state your
address if you
have asked the
court to withhold
your address*

Address*:

Day time telephone number:

Your relationship to each child named above:

2   **Your solicitor's details**

Name:

Address:

Reference:

Telephone Number:

Fax Number:

DX Number:

Section 2   Respondent's comments on allegations made by the Applicant

About this section:

- **Go straight to Section 3 (Further information) if:**
  - (a) you are the **Applicant**; or
  - (b) you are the **Respondent** and the Applicant has not filed form C1A Supplemental Information Form with his or her application.

- This section of the form should only be completed **by the Respondent** where the Applicant has served a completed form C1A with his or her application for an order.

- **You do not have to complete this section unless you wish to comment on any of the information given by the Applicant in his or her form C1A.** This section should not be used to comment on any other information given by the Applicant in his or her application.

- **Please comment in summary form only.** You will have an opportunity to make a more detailed statement later in the proceedings.

Comments on allegations made by the Applicant:

CIA

Section 3   Further Information

1   **Involvement with outside authorities and organisations**

If as a result of any incidence of domestic abuse, other harm or risk of harm to you or the child(ren) there is, has been or there is pending any known involvement with the police, social services, mental health services or other support services in respect of:

- *any child(ren)whose name(s) is/are given at the top of this form*
- *a full, half or step brother or sister of a child(ren) whose name(s) is/are given at the top of this form, or*
- *a person who is or has been involved in caring for the child(ren) or is having or has had contact with the child(ren) whose name(s) is/are given at the top of this form*

please provide details and identify:

- *which agency or service has been involved*
- *the name of the person who has been the main contact in that agency or service*
- *the date or dates of any involvement*
- *whether there is any current or continuing involvement*
- *whether or not you have any documents, reports or correspondence relating to the agency or service's involvement.*

C1A

2   **Incidents of abuse, violence or harm**

For each alleged incidence of violence, domestic abuse or harm, please provide in summary form the following information:

Note: You shall have an opportunity later in the proceedings to provide a more substantial statement

- *the date(s) on which the incident occurred*
- *the nature and seriousness of the alleged abuse, violence or harm*
- *by whom and against whom it was directed*
- *how frequently the alleged abuse, harm or violence occurred and the date(s) of the most recent occurrence(s)*
- *whether any hospital or medical treatment has been sought by the child(ren) whose name(s) is/are given at the top of this form, the applicant or other person in respect of any injuries sustained, and*
- *whether you consider there is a likelihood of further harm, abuse or violence occurring.*

3   **Involvement of the child(ren)**

If the child(ren) whose name(s) is/are given at the top of this form have seen or heard any of the alleged incident(s) of abuse within the household or been aware of any alleged abuse and its impact on the family, please give details and in particular state how you believe the child(ren) have been affected by this experience:

CIA

4

4   **Witnesses**
Has anyone else seen, heard or had reported to them any alleged incidence of violence, domestic abuse or harm? If Yes, would that person be able to provide supporting evidence?

---

5   **Medical treatment or other assessment of the child(ren)**
If any child(ren) whose name(s) is/are given at the top of this form have been referred for treatment or psychiatric or psychological assessment, by any medical or health service relating to his/her emotional, social or behavioural development (or where any such treatment or referral is pending), please state:
* *when and to whom such a referral was made*
* *details of any treatment or assessment recommended*
* *whether there is any continuing involvement with the relevant service in relation to the referral, and*
* *whether you are aware of or have in your possession any reports or other correspondence in relation to any treatment or assessment recommended.*

---

6   **Abduction**
If you feel the child(ren) whose name(s) is/are given at the top of this form are at real risk of being abducted please give the following information:
* *your reason for believing that the child(ren) may be abducted*
* *whether the child(ren) have previously been the subject of a threatened abduction, an attempted abduction or have been abducted*
* *whether the police or any other organisation has been involved in any alleged previous incident identified above, and*
* *whether each child has their own passport and who has that passport at the moment?*

CIA

7   **Steps or orders required to protect you and the children**
        Please indicate what steps or orders you believe the court should take or make in order to protect the safety of the child(ren) whose name(s) is/are given at the top of this form and/or yourself.

8   **Attending the Court**
        Please also indicate whether the court needs to make any special arrangements for you to attend court (e.g. providing you with a separate waiting room from the respondent or other security provision). Do you consider the court should give consideration to any special measures for you or any witnesses to give evidence at the hearing (e.g. use of video link equipment where available)? If Yes, please explain why.

Signed   Date
(Applicant/Respondent)

C1A

6

(J)   Form FL401 (Family Law Act application)

Application for:

a non-molestation order

an occupation order

Family Law Act 1996 (Part IV)

The court

To be completed by the court
Date issued
Case number

Please read the accompanying notes as you complete this form.

1   About you (the applicant)

State your title (Mr, Mrs etc), full name, address, telephone number and date of birth (if under 18):

State your solicitor's name, address, reference, telephone, FAX and DX numbers:

2   About the respondent

State the respondent's name, address and date of birth (if known):

3   The Order(s) for which you are applying

This application is for:

☐   a non-molestation order

☐   an occupation order

☐   Tick this box if you wish the court to hear your application without notice being given to the respondent. The reasons relied on for an application being heard without notice must be stated in the statement in support.

4   Your relationship to the respondent (the person to be served with this application)

Your relationship to the respondent is:

(Please tick only one of the following)

1 ☐ Married

2 ☐ Civil Partners

3 ☐ Were married

4 ☐ Former civil partners

5 ☐ Cohabiting

6 ☐ Were cohabiting

7 ☐ Both of you live or have lived in the same household

8 ☐ Relative
State how related:

9 ☐ Agreed to marry.
Give the date the agreement was made.
If the agreement has ended, state when.

10 ☐ Agreed to form a civil partnership.
Give the date the agreement was made.
If the agreement has ended, state when.

11 ☐ Both of you are parents of, or have parental responsibility for, a child

12 ☐ One of you is a parent of a child and the other has parental responsibility for that child

13 ☐ One of you is the natural parent or
grandparent of a child adopted, placed or freed
for adoption, and the other is:

    (i)   the adoptive parent

  or (ii) a person who has applied for an
          adoption order for the child

  or (iii) a person with whom the child has
          been placed for adoption

  or (iv) the child who has been adopted,
          placed or freed for adoption.

State whether (i), (ii), (iii) or (iv):

14 ☐ Both of you are the parties to the same family
proceedings (see also Section 11 below).

5 Application for a non-molestation order

If you wish to apply for a non-molestation order,
state briefly in this section the order you want.

Give full details in support of your application in
your supporting evidence.

6 Application for an occupation order

*If you do not wish to apply for an occupation order,
please go to section 9 of this form.*

(A) State the address of the dwelling-house to which
your application relates:

(B) State whether it is occupied by you or the respondent
now or in the past, or whether it was intended to be
occupied by you or the respondent:

(C) State whether you are entitled to occupy the
dwelling-house: ☐ Yes   ☐ No

If yes, explain why:

(D) State whether the respondent is entitled to occupy
the dwelling-house: ☐ Yes   ☐ No

If yes, explain why:

**On the basis of your answers to (C) and (D) above,
tick one of the boxes 1 to 6 below to show the category
into which you fit**

1 ☐ a spouse or civil partner who has home rights
in the dwelling-house, or a person who is
entitled to occupy it by virtue of a beneficial
estate or interest or contract or by virtue of
any enactment giving him or her the right to
remain in occupation.

If you tick box 1, state whether there is a
dispute or pending proceedings between you
and the respondent about your right to occupy
the dwelling-house.

2 ☐ a former spouse or former civil partner with no
existing right to occupy, where the respondent
spouse or civil partner is so entitled.

3 ☐ a cohabitant or former cohabitant with no
existing right to occupy, where the respondent
cohabitant or former cohabitant is so entitled.

4 ☐ a spouse or former spouse who is not entitled
to occupy, where the respondent spouse or
former spouse is also not entitled.

5 ☐ a civil partner or former civil partner who is not
entitled to occupy, where the respondent civil
partner or former civil partner is also not entitled.

6 ☐ a cohabitant or former cohabitant who is
not entitled to occupy, where the respondent
cohabitant or former cohabitant is also not
entitled.

Home Rights

If you do have home rights please:

State whether the title to the land is registered or unregistered (if known):

If registered, state the Land Registry title number (if known):

If you wish to apply for an occupation order, state briefly here the order you want. Give full details in support of your application in your supporting evidence:

7   Application for additional order(s) about the dwelling-house

If you want to apply for any of the orders listed in the notes to this section, state what order you would like the court to make:

8   Mortgage and rent

Is the dwelling-house subject to a mortgage?

☐ Yes   ☐ No

If yes, please provide the name and address of the mortgagee:

Is the dwelling-house rented?

☐ Yes   ☐ No

If yes, please provide the name and address of the landlord:

9   At the court

Will you need an interpreter at court?

☐ Yes   ☐ No

If yes, specify the language:

If you require an interpreter, you must notify the
court immediately so that one can be arranged.

If you have a disability for which you require special
assistance or special facilities, please state what your
needs are. The court staff will get in touch with you
about your requirements.

10   Other information

State the name and date of birth of any child living
with or staying with, or likely to live with or stay
with, you or the respondent:

State the name of any other person living in the same
household as you and the respondent, and say why
they live there:

11   Other Proceedings and Orders

If there are any other current family proceedings or
orders in force involving you and the respondent,
state the type of proceedings or orders, the court and
the case number. This includes any application for
an occupation order or non-molestation order against
you by the respondent.

This application is to be served upon the respondent

Signed: Date:

6

Application for non-molestation order or occupation order
Notes for guidance

Section 1

If you do not wish your address to be made known to the respondent, leave the space on the form blank and complete Confidential Address Form C8. The court can give you this form.

If you are under 18, someone over 18 must help you make this application. That person, who might be one of your parents, is called a 'next friend'.

If you are under 16, you need permission to make this application. You must apply to the High Court for permission, using this form. If the High Court gives you permission to make this application, it will then either hear the application itself or transfer it to a county court.

Section 3

An urgent order made by the court before the notice of the application is served on the respondent is called an ex-parte order. In deciding whether to make an ex-parte order the court will consider all the circumstances of the case, including:

- any risk of significant harm to the applicant or a relevant child, attributable to conduct of the respondent, if the order is not made immediately

- whether it is likely that the applicant will be deterred or prevented from pursuing the application if an order is not made immediately

- whether there is reason to believe that the respondent is aware of the proceedings but is deliberately evading service and that the applicant or a relevant child will be seriously prejudiced by the delay involved.

If the court makes an ex-parte order, it must give the respondent an opportunity to make representations about the order as soon as just and convenient at a full hearing.

'Harm' in relation to a person who has reached the age of 18 means ill-treatment or the impairment of health, and in relation to a child means ill-treatment or the impairment of health and development.

'Ill-treatment' includes forms of ill-treatment which are not physical and, in relation to a child, includes sexual abuse. The court will require evidence of any harm which you allege in support of your application.

Section 4

For you to be able to apply for an order you must be related to the respondent in one of the ways listed in this section of the form. If you are not related in one of these ways you should seek legal advice.

Cohabitants are two persons who, although not married to each other, nor civil partners of each other, are living together as husband and wife or civil partners. People who have cohabited, but have then married or formed a civil partnership will not fall within this category but will fall within the category of married people or people who are civil partners of each other.

Those who live or have lived in the same household do not include people who share the same household because one of them is the other's employee, tenant, lodger or boarder.

You will only be able to apply as a relative of the respondent if you are:
(A) the father, mother, stepfather, stepmother, son, daughter, stepson, stepdaughter, grandmother, grandfather, grandson, granddaughter of the respondent or of the respondent's spouse, former spouse, civil partner or former civil partner.

(B) the brother, sister, uncle, aunt, niece, nephew or first cousin (whether of the full blood or of the half blood or by marriage or by civil partnership) of the respondent or of the respondent's spouse, former spouse, civil partner or former civil partner.

This includes, in relation to a person who is living or has lived with another person as husband and wife or as civil partners, any person who would fall within (A) or (B) if the parties were married to, or civil partners of, each other (for example, your cohabitee's father or brother).

Agreements to marry: You will fall within this category only if you make this application within three years of the termination of the agreement. The court will require the following evidence of the agreement:

   evidence in writing

or   the gift of an engagement ring in contemplation of marriage

or   evidence that a ceremony has been entered into in the presence of one or more other persons assembled for the purpose of witnessing it.

Agreements to form a civil partnership: You will fall within this category only if you make this application within three years of the termination of the agreement. The court will require the following evidence of the agreement:

   evidence in writing

or   a gift from one party to the agreement to the other as a token of the agreement

or   evidence that a ceremony has been entered into in the presence of one or more other persons assembled for the purpose of witnessing it.

Section 4 continued

Parents and parental responsibility:
You will fall within this category if

both you and the respondent are either the parents of the child or have parental responsibility for that child

or if one of you is the parent and the other has parental responsibility.

Under the Children Act 1989, parental responsibility is held automatically by a child's mother, and by the child's father if he and the mother were married to each other at the time of the child's birth or have married subsequently. Where, a child's father and mother are not married to each other at the time of the child's birth, the father may also acquire parental responsibility for that child, if he registers the birth after 1st December 2003, in accordance with section 4(1)(a) of the Children Act 1989. Where neither of these circumstances apply, the father, in accordance with the provisions of the Children Act 1989, can acquire parental responsibility.

From 30 December 2005, where a person who is not the child's parent ("the step-parent") is married to, or a civil partner of, a parent who has parental responsibility for that child, he or she may also acquire parental responsibility for the child in accordance with the provisions of the Children Act 1989.

Section 5

A non-molestation order can forbid the respondent from molesting you or a relevant child. Molestation can include, for example, violence, threats, pestering and other forms of harassment. The court can forbid particular acts of the respondent, molestation in general, or both.

Section 6

If you wish to apply for an occupation order but you are uncertain about your answer to any question in this part of the application form, you should seek legal advice.

(A) A dwelling-house includes any building or part of a building which is occupied as a dwelling; any caravan, houseboat or structure which is occupied as a dwelling; and any yard, garden, garage or outhouse belonging to it and occupied with it.

(C) & (D) The following questions give examples to help you to decide if you or the respondent, or both of you, are entitled to occupy the dwelling-house:

(a) Are you the sole legal owner of the dwelling-house?

(b) Are you and the respondent joint legal owners of the dwelling-house?

(c) Is the respondent the sole legal owner of the dwelling-house?

(d) Do you rent the dwelling-house as a sole tenant?

(e) Do you and the respondent rent the dwelling-house as joint tenants?

(f) Does the respondent rent the dwelling-house as a sole tenant?

If you answer

- **Yes** to (a), (b), (d) or (e) you are likely to be entitled to occupy the dwelling-house

- **Yes** to (c) or (f) you may not be entitled (unless, for example, you are a spouse or civil partner and have home rights – see notes under 'Home Rights' below)

- **Yes** to (b), (c), (e) or (f), the respondent is likely to be entitled to occupy the dwelling-house

- **Yes** to (a) or (d) the respondent may not be entitled (unless, for example, he or she is a spouse or civil partner and has home rights).

Box 1 For example, if you are sole owner, joint owner or if you rent the property. If you are not a spouse, former spouse, civil partner, former civil partner, cohabitant or former cohabitant of the respondent, you will only be able to apply for an occupation order if you fall within this category.

If you answer yes to this question, it will not be possible for a magistrates' court to deal with the application, unless the court decides that it is unnecessary for it to decide this question in order to deal with the application or make the order. If the court decides that it cannot deal with the application, it will transfer the application to a county court.

Box 2 For example, if the respondent is or was married to you, or if you and the respondent are or were civil partners, and he or she is sole owner or rents the property.

Box 3 For example, if the respondent is or was cohabiting with you and is sole owner or rents the property.

Home Rights
Where one spouse or civil partner "**(A)**" is entitled to occupy the dwelling-house by virtue of a beneficial estate or interest or contract or by virtue of any enactment giving him or her the right to remain in occupation, and the other spouse or civil partner "**(B)**" is not so entitled, then **B** (who is not entitled) has home rights.

The rights are

(a) if **B** is in occupation, not to be evicted or excluded from the dwelling-house except with the leave of the court; and

(b) if **B** is not in occupation, the right, with the leave of the court, to enter into and occupy the dwelling-house.

Note: Home Rights do not exist if the dwelling-house has never been, and was never intended to be, the matrimonial or civil partnership home of the two spouses or civil partners. If the marriage or civil partnership has come to an end, home rights will also have ceased, unless a court order has been made during the marriage or civil partnership for the rights to continue after the end of that relationship.

Section 6 (continued)

Occupation Orders

The possible orders are:

If you have ticked box 1 above, an order under section 33 of the Act may:

- enforce the applicant's entitlement to remain in occupation as against the respondent

- require the respondent to permit the applicant to enter and remain in the dwelling-house or part of it

- regulate the occupation of the dwelling-house by either or both parties

- if the respondent is also entitled to occupy, the order may prohibit, suspend or restrict the exercise by him, of that right

- restrict or terminate any home rights of the respondent

- require the respondent to leave the dwelling-house or part of it

- exclude the respondent from a defined area around the dwelling-house

- declare that the applicant is entitled to occupy the dwelling-house or has home rights in it

- provide that the home rights of the applicant are not brought to an end by the death of the other spouse or civil partner or termination of the marriage or civil partnership.

If you have ticked box 2 or box 3 above, an order under section 35 or 36 of the Act may:

- give the applicant the right not to be evicted or excluded from the dwelling-house or any part of it by the respondent for a specified period

- prohibit the respondent from evicting or excluding the applicant during that period

- give the applicant the right to enter and occupy the dwelling-house for a specified period

- require the respondent to permit the exercise of that right

- regulate the occupation of the dwelling-house by either or both of the parties

- prohibit, suspend or restrict the exercise by the respondent of his right to occupy

- require the respondent to leave the dwelling-house or part of it

- exclude the respondent from a defined area around the dwelling-house.

If you have ticked box 4 or box 5 above, an order under section 37 or 38 of the Act may:

- require the respondent to permit the applicant to enter and remain in the dwelling-house or part of it

- regulate the occupation of the dwelling-house by either or both of the parties

- require the respondent to leave the dwelling-house or part of it

- exclude the respondent from a defined area around the dwelling-house.

You should provide any evidence which you have on the following matters in your evidence in support of this application. If necessary, further statements may be submitted after the application has been issued.

If you have ticked box 1, box 4 or box 5 above, the court will need any available evidence of the following:

- the housing needs and resources of you, the respondent and any relevant child

- the financial needs of you and the respondent

- the likely effect of any order, or any decision not to make an order, on the health, safety and well-being of you, the respondent and any relevant child

- the conduct of you and the respondent in relation to each other and otherwise.

If you have ticked box 2 above, the court will need any available evidence of:

- the housing needs and resources of you, the respondent and any relevant child

- the financial resources of you and the respondent

- the likely effect of any order, or of any decision not to make an order on the health, safety and well-being of you, the respondent and any relevant child

- the conduct of you and the respondent in relation to each other and otherwise

- the length of time that has elapsed since you and the respondent ceased to live together

- where you and the respondent were married, the length of time that has elapsed since the marriage was dissolved or annulled

- where you and the respondent were civil partners, the length of time that has elapsed since the dissolution or annulment of the civil partnership

Section 6 (continued)

- the existence of any pending proceedings between you and the respondent:

   under section 23A of the Matrimonial Causes Act 1973 (property adjustment orders in connection with divorce proceedings etc.)

   or   under Part 2 of Schedule 5 to the Civil Partnership Act 2004 (property adjustment on or after dissolution, nullity or separation)

   or   under Schedule 1 para 1(2)(d) or (e) of the Children Act 1989 (orders for financial relief against parents)

   or   relating to the legal or beneficial ownership of the dwelling-house.

If you have ticked box 3 above, the court will need any available evidence of:

- the housing needs and resources of you, the respondent and any relevant child

- the financial resources of you and the respondent

- the likely effect of any order, or of any decision not to make an order, on the health, safety and well-being of you, the respondent and any relevant child

- the conduct of you and the respondent in relation to each other and otherwise

- the nature of your and the respondent's relationship

- the length of time during which you have lived together as husband and wife or civil partners

- whether you and the respondent have had any children, or have both had parental responsibility for any children

- the length of time that has elapsed since you and the respondent ceased to live together

- the existence of any pending proceedings between you and the respondent under Schedule 1 para 1(2)(d) or (e) of the Children Act 1989 or relating to the legal or beneficial ownership of the dwelling-house.

Section 7

Under section 40 of the Act the court may make the following additional orders when making an occupation order:

- impose on either party obligations as to the repair and maintenance of the dwelling-house

- impose on either party obligations as to the payment of rent, mortgage or other outgoings affecting it

- order a party occupying the dwelling-house to make periodical payments to the other party in respect of the accommodation, if the other party would (but for the order) be entitled to occupy it

- grant either party possession or use of furniture or other contents

- order either party to take reasonable care of any furniture or other contents

- order either party to take reasonable steps to keep the dwelling-house and any furniture or other contents secure.

Section 8

If the dwelling-house is rented or subject to a mortgage, the landlord or mortgagee must be served with notice of the proceedings in Form FL416. He or she will then be able to make representations to the court regarding the rent or mortgage.

Section 10

A person living in the same household may, for example, be a member of the family or a tenant or employee of you or the respondent.

Index